READING GOD'S WORD
Daily and Sunday Mass Readings
Church Year A 2023

Creative Communications for the Parish
1564 Fencorp Drive
Fenton, MO 63026
www.creativecommunications.com

READING GOD'S WORD
Daily and Sunday Mass Readings
Church Year A 2023

© *2022 Creative Communications for the Parish,*
a division of Bayard, Inc.

Published with the authority of the Committee on Divine Worship,
United States Conference of Catholic Bishops.

ISBN Number: 978-1-68279-431-9

Cover Design: Jamie Wyatt
Cover Art: Adobe Stock/jorisvo

INTRODUCTION

What began primarily as an aid to lectors preparing for Mass has now become a regular part of the daily prayer of Catholics who know the value of praying with Scripture. *Reading God's Word* helps us to follow the daily worship of the Church in a simple and convenient form.

Reading God's Word has the exact passages for daily Mass for an entire year, and they are available whenever you want them. More than simply convenient, *Reading God's Word* offers a way to respond to God's invitation to share his life. As the world Synod of Bishops on the "Word of God in the Life and Mission of the Church" noted in October 2008, Scripture represents God's desire to speak directly to us. When we take up the texts in *Reading God's Word*, we enter into a relationship with God in a profound way, and these living words begin to take root in our lives and bear fruit.

True, some of the words are so familiar as to be commonplace after years of hearing them proclaimed at Mass. At the same time, new circumstances in our lives as well as the action of grace can give new meaning to a text that we have heard since childhood. When we hear or read these words intently, we discover that as St. Paul has taught us (Romans 15:4), everything written in Scripture is written as instruction for our benefit.

May *Reading God's Word* richly benefit you all during the coming year.

LITURGICAL CELEBRATIONS

2022

First Sunday of Advent .... Nov. 27
Immaculate Conception *(holyday of obligation)* .... Thu., Dec. 8
Christmas .... Sun., Dec. 25
The Holy Family of Jesus, Mary and Joseph .... Fri., Dec. 30

2023

Solemnity of Mary, the Holy Mother of God;
    The Octave Day of the Nativity of the Lord: .... Sun., Jan. 1
Epiphany .... Sun., Jan. 8
The Baptism of the Lord .... Mon., Jan. 9
The Presentation of the Lord .... Thu., Feb. 2
Ash Wednesday .... Feb. 22
St. Joseph, Spouse of the Blessed Virgin Mary .... Mon., Mar. 20
The Annunciation of the Lord .... Sat., Mar. 25
Palm Sunday of the Passion of the Lord .... Apr. 2
Holy Thursday .... Apr. 6
Good Friday .... Apr. 7
Holy Saturday .... Apr. 8
Easter Sunday of the Resurrection of the Lord .... Apr. 9
Ascension *(holyday of obligation)* .... Thu., May 18 or Sun., May 21
Pentecost Sunday .... May 28
The Most Holy Trinity .... Sun., June 4
The Most Holy Body and Blood of Christ .... Sun., June 11
The Most Sacred Heart of Jesus .... Fri., June 16
The Nativity of St. John the Baptist .... Sat., June 24
St. Peter and St. Paul .... Thu., June 29
The Transfiguration of the Lord .... Sun., Aug. 6
The Assumption of the Blessed Virgin Mary
    (holyday of obligation) .... Tue., Aug. 15
The Exaltation of the Holy Cross .... Thu., Sept. 14
All Saints *(holyday of obligation)* .... Wed., Nov. 1
The Commemoration of All the Faithful Departed (All Souls' Day) .. Thu., Nov. 2
The Dedication of the Lateran Basilica .... Thu., Nov. 9
Our Lord Jesus Christ, King of the Universe .... Sun., Nov. 26
First Sunday of Advent .... Dec. 3

NOTICE FOR LECTORS

If this book is used to prepare for reading at Mass, please note that the "announcement" formula is: *"A reading from the Book of ...,"* *"A reading from the Letter of ...,"* or *"A reading from the holy Gospel according to ..."* We have placed ✝ before the citation as a reminder of the announcement.

At the end of the readings, the lector or presider is to say, *"The word of the Lord."* We have placed ✚ at the end of texts as a reminder of that concluding declaration.

Also, herein the Responsorial Verse of each day's Psalm is printed only once in full, with an **R.** indicating where repetition is called for. The **R.** at the end of the Gospel Verse indicates that the response is one "Alleluia" or the acclamation used during Lent. ■

SUNDAY, NOVEMBER 27, 2022
FIRST SUNDAY OF ADVENT

† *Isaiah 2:1-5*
The Lord will gather all nations into the eternal peace of the Kingdom of God.

This is what Isaiah, son of Amoz,
  saw concerning Judah and Jerusalem.
  In days to come,
the mountain of the LORD's house
  shall be established as the highest mountain
  and raised above the hills.
All nations shall stream toward it;
  many peoples shall come and say:
"Come, let us climb the LORD's mountain,
  to the house of the God of Jacob,
that he may instruct us in his ways,
  and we may walk in his paths."
For from Zion shall go forth instruction,
  and the word of the LORD from Jerusalem.
He shall judge between the nations,
  and impose terms on many peoples.
They shall beat their swords into plowshares
  and their spears into pruning hooks;
one nation shall not raise the sword against another,
  nor shall they train for war again.
O house of Jacob, come,
  let us walk in the light of the LORD! ✛

  Psalm 122:1-2, 3-4b, 4cd-5, 6-7, 8-9
R. (see 1) **Let us go rejoicing to the house of the Lord.**
I rejoiced because they said to me,
  "We will go up to the house of the LORD."
And now we have set foot
  within your gates, O Jerusalem. **R.**
Jerusalem, built as a city
  with compact unity.
To it the tribes go up,
  the tribes of the LORD. **R.**
According to the decree for Israel,
  to give thanks to the name of the LORD.
In it are set up judgment seats,
  seats for the house of David. **R.**
Pray for the peace of Jerusalem!
  May those who love you prosper!
May peace be within your walls,

prosperity in your buildings. **R.**
Because of my brothers and friends
   I will say, "Peace be within you!"
Because of the house of the LORD, our God,
   I will pray for your good. **R.**

† Romans 13:11-14

Our salvation is nearer.

Brothers and sisters:
You know the time;
   it is the hour now for you to awake from sleep.
For our salvation is nearer now than when we first believed;
   the night is advanced, the day is at hand.
Let us then throw off the works of darkness
   and put on the armor of light;
   let us conduct ourselves properly as in the day,
   not in orgies and drunkenness,
   not in promiscuity and lust,
   not in rivalry and jealousy.
But put on the Lord Jesus Christ,
   and make no provision for the desires of the flesh. ✝

   See Psalm 85:8
R. Alleluia, alleluia.
Show us, Lord, your love;
and grant us your salvation. **R.**

† Matthew 24:37-44

Stay awake, that you may be prepared!

Jesus said to his disciples:
"As it was in the days of Noah,
   so it will be at the coming of the Son of Man.
In those days before the flood,
   they were eating and drinking,
   marrying and giving in marriage,
   up to the day that Noah entered the ark.
They did not know until the flood came and carried them all away.
So will it be also at the coming of the Son of Man.
Two men will be out in the field;
   one will be taken, and one will be left.
Two women will be grinding at the mill;
   one will be taken, and one will be left.
Therefore, stay awake!
For you do not know on which day your Lord will come.
Be sure of this: if the master of the house

had known the hour of night when the thief was coming,
he would have stayed awake
and not let his house be broken into.
So too, you also must be prepared,
for at an hour you do not expect,
the Son of Man will come." ✦

MONDAY, NOVEMBER 28
ADVENT WEEKDAY

† *Isaiah 4:2-6*
There will be splendor for the survivors.

On that day,
The branch of the LORD will be luster and glory,
and the fruit of the earth will be honor and splendor
for the survivors of Israel.
He who remains in Zion
and he who is left in Jerusalem
Will be called holy:
every one marked down for life in Jerusalem.
When the LORD washes away
the filth of the daughters of Zion,
And purges Jerusalem's blood from her midst
with a blast of searing judgment,
Then will the LORD create,
over the whole site of Mount Zion
and over her place of assembly,
A smoking cloud by day
and a light of flaming fire by night.
For over all, the LORD's glory will be shelter and protection:
shade from the parching heat of day,
refuge and cover from storm and rain. ✦

Psalm 122:1-2, 3-4b, 4cd-5, 6-7, 8-9
R. Let us go rejoicing to the house of the Lord.
I rejoiced because they said to me,
"We will go up to the house of the LORD."
And now we have set foot
within your gates, O Jerusalem. **R.**
Jerusalem, built as a city
with compact unity.
To it the tribes go up,
the tribes of the LORD. **R.**
According to the decree for Israel,
to give thanks to the name of the LORD.

In it are set up judgment seats,
   seats for the house of David. **R.**
Pray for the peace of Jerusalem!
   May those who love you prosper!
May peace be within your walls,
   prosperity in your buildings. **R.**
Because of my relatives and friends
   I will say, "Peace be within you!"
Because of the house of the LORD, our God,
   I will pray for your good. **R.**

See Psalm 80:4
R. Alleluia, alleluia.
Come and save us, LORD our God;
let your face shine upon us, that we may be saved. **R.**

† *Matthew 8:5-11*
Many will come from the east and the west into the Kingdom of heaven.

When Jesus entered Capernaum,
   a centurion approached him and appealed to him, saying,
   "Lord, my servant is lying at home paralyzed, suffering dreadfully."
He said to him, "I will come and cure him."
The centurion said in reply,
   "Lord, I am not worthy to have you enter under my roof;
   only say the word and my servant will be healed.
For I too am a man subject to authority,
   with soldiers subject to me.
And I say to one, 'Go,' and he goes;
   and to another, 'Come here,' and he comes;
   and to my slave, 'Do this,' and he does it."
When Jesus heard this, he was amazed and said to those following
     him,
   "Amen, I say to you, in no one in Israel have I found such faith.
I say to you, many will come from the east and the west,
   and will recline with Abraham, Isaac, and Jacob
   at the banquet in the Kingdom of heaven." ✛

TUESDAY, NOVEMBER 29
ADVENT WEEKDAY

† *Isaiah 11:1-10*
The Spirit of the LORD God shall rest upon him.

On that day,
A shoot shall sprout from the stump of Jesse,
   and from his roots a bud shall blossom.
The Spirit of the LORD shall rest upon him:

a Spirit of wisdom and of understanding,
A Spirit of counsel and of strength,
   a Spirit of knowledge and of fear of the LORD,
   and his delight shall be the fear of the LORD.
Not by appearance shall he judge,
   nor by hearsay shall he decide,
But he shall judge the poor with justice,
   and decide aright for the land's afflicted.
He shall strike the ruthless with the rod of his mouth,
   and with the breath of his lips he shall slay the wicked.
Justice shall be the band around his waist,
   and faithfulness a belt upon his hips.

Then the wolf shall be a guest of the lamb,
   and the leopard shall lie down with the kid;
The calf and the young lion shall browse together,
   with a little child to guide them.
The cow and the bear shall be neighbors,
   together their young shall rest;
   the lion shall eat hay like the ox.
The baby shall play by the cobra's den,
   and the child lay his hand on the adder's lair.
There shall be no harm or ruin on all my holy mountain;
   for the earth shall be filled with knowledge of the LORD,
   as water covers the sea.

   On that day,
The root of Jesse,
   set up as a signal for the nations,
The Gentiles shall seek out,
   for his dwelling shall be glorious. ✚

   Psalm 72:1-2, 7-8, 12-13, 17
R. (see 7) **Justice shall flourish in his time, and fullness of
   peace for ever.**
O God, with your judgment endow the king,
   and with your justice, the king's son;
He shall govern your people with justice
   and your afflicted ones with judgment. **R.**
Justice shall flower in his days,
   and profound peace, till the moon be no more.
May he rule from sea to sea,
   and from the River to the ends of the earth. **R.**
He shall rescue the poor when he cries out,
   and the afflicted when he has no one to help him.

He shall have pity for the lowly and the poor;
    the lives of the poor he shall save. **R.**
May his name be blessed forever;
    as long as the sun his name shall remain.
In him shall all the tribes of the earth be blessed;
    all the nations shall proclaim his happiness. **R.**

R. Alleluia, alleluia.
Behold, our Lord shall come with power;
he will enlighten the eyes of his servants. **R.**

† *Luke 10:21-24*
Jesus rejoices in the Holy Spirit.

Jesus rejoiced in the Holy Spirit and said,
    "I give you praise, Father, Lord of heaven and earth,
    for although you have hidden these things
    from the wise and the learned
    you have revealed them to the childlike.
Yes, Father, such has been your gracious will.
All things have been handed over to me by my Father.
No one knows who the Son is except the Father,
    and who the Father is except the Son
    and anyone to whom the Son wishes to reveal him."

Turning to the disciples in private he said,
    "Blessed are the eyes that see what you see.
For I say to you,
    many prophets and kings desired to see what you see,
    but did not see it,
    and to hear what you hear, but did not hear it." ✝

WEDNESDAY, NOVEMBER 30
St. Andrew

† *Romans 10:9-18*
Thus faith comes from what is heard,
and what is heard comes through the word of Christ.

Brothers and sisters:
If you confess with your mouth that Jesus is Lord
    and believe in your heart that God raised him from the dead,
    you will be saved.
For one believes with the heart and so is justified,
    and one confesses with the mouth and so is saved.
The Scripture says,
    No one who believes in him will be put to shame.
There is no distinction between Jew and Greek;

the same Lord is Lord of all,
  enriching all who call upon him.
For everyone who calls on the name of the Lord will be saved.

But how can they call on him in whom they have not believed?
And how can they believe in him of whom they have not heard?
And how can they hear without someone to preach?
And how can people preach unless they are sent?
As it is written,
  How beautiful are the feet of those who bring the good news!
But not everyone has heeded the good news;
  for Isaiah says, *Lord, who has believed what was heard from us?*
Thus faith comes from what is heard,
  and what is heard comes through the word of Christ.
But I ask, did they not hear?
Certainly they did; for

> *Their voice has gone forth to all the earth,*
>   *and their words to the ends of the world.* ✛

Psalm 19:8, 9, 10, 11

**R. (10) The judgments of the Lord are true, and all of them
  are just.**
or
(John 6:63) **Your words, Lord, are Spirit and life.**
The law of the LORD is perfect,
  refreshing the soul;
The decree of the LORD is trustworthy,
  giving wisdom to the simple. **R.**
The precepts of the LORD are right,
  rejoicing the heart;
The command of the LORD is clear,
  enlightening the eye. **R.**
The fear of the LORD is pure,
  enduring forever;
The ordinances of the LORD are true,
  all of them just. **R.**
They are more precious than gold,
  than a heap of purest gold;
Sweeter also than syrup
  or honey from the comb. **R.**

Matthew 4:19
R. Alleluia, alleluia.
Come after me, says the Lord,
and I will make you fishers of men. **R.**

† *Matthew 4:18-22*
Immediately they left their nets and followed him.

As Jesus was walking by the Sea of Galilee, he saw two brothers,
  Simon who is called Peter, and his brother Andrew,
  casting a net into the sea; they were fishermen.
He said to them,
  "Come after me, and I will make you fishers of men."
At once they left their nets and followed him.
He walked along from there and saw two other brothers,
  James, the son of Zebedee, and his brother John.
They were in a boat, with their father Zebedee, mending their nets.
He called them, and immediately they left their boat and their father
  and followed him. ✛

THURSDAY, DECEMBER 1
ADVENT WEEKDAY

† *Isaiah 26:1-6*
Let in a nation that is just, one that keeps faith.

On that day they will sing this song in the land of Judah:

"A strong city have we;
  he sets up walls and ramparts to protect us.
Open up the gates
  to let in a nation that is just,
  one that keeps faith.
A nation of firm purpose you keep in peace;
  in peace, for its trust in you."

Trust in the LORD forever!
  For the LORD is an eternal Rock.
He humbles those in high places,
  and the lofty city he brings down;
He tumbles it to the ground,
  levels it with the dust.
It is trampled underfoot by the needy,
  by the footsteps of the poor. ✛

Psalm 118:1 and 8-9, 19-21, 25-27a

R. (26a) **Blessed is he who comes in the name of the Lord.**
  (or **Alleluia.***)*
Give thanks to the LORD, for he is good,
  for his mercy endures forever.
It is better to take refuge in the LORD
  than to trust in man.
It is better to take refuge in the LORD

than to trust in princes. **R.**

Open to me the gates of justice;
   I will enter them and give thanks to the LORD.
This gate is the LORD's;
   the just shall enter it.
I will give thanks to you, for you have answered me
   and have been my savior. **R.**
O LORD, grant salvation!
   O LORD, grant prosperity!
Blessed is he who comes in the name of the LORD;
   we bless you from the house of the LORD.
   The LORD is God, and he has given us light. **R.**

   Isaiah 55:6
R. Alleluia, alleluia.
Seek the LORD while he may be found;
call him while he is near. **R.**

† *Matthew 7:21, 24-27*
Whoever does the will of my Father will enter the Kingdom of heaven.

Jesus said to his disciples:
"Not everyone who says to me, 'Lord, Lord,'
   will enter the Kingdom of heaven,
   but only the one who does the will of my Father in heaven.

"Everyone who listens to these words of mine and acts on them
   will be like a wise man who built his house on rock.
The rain fell, the floods came,
   and the winds blew and buffeted the house.
But it did not collapse; it had been set solidly on rock.
And everyone who listens to these words of mine
   but does not act on them
   will be like a fool who built his house on sand.
The rain fell, the floods came,
   and the winds blew and buffeted the house.
And it collapsed and was completely ruined." ✦

FRIDAY, DECEMBER 2
ADVENT WEEKDAY

† *Isaiah 29:17-24*
On that day, the eyes of the blind shall see.

Thus says the Lord GOD:
But a very little while,
   and Lebanon shall be changed into an orchard,
   and the orchard be regarded as a forest!

On that day the deaf shall hear
   the words of a book;
And out of gloom and darkness,
   the eyes of the blind shall see.
The lowly will ever find joy in the LORD,
   and the poor rejoice in the Holy One of Israel.
For the tyrant will be no more
   and the arrogant will have gone;
All who are alert to do evil will be cut off,
   those whose mere word condemns a man,
Who ensnare his defender at the gate,
   and leave the just man with an empty claim.
Therefore thus says the LORD,
   the God of the house of Jacob,
   who redeemed Abraham:
Now Jacob shall have nothing to be ashamed of,
   nor shall his face grow pale.
When his children see
   the work of my hands in his midst,
They shall keep my name holy;
   they shall reverence the Holy One of Jacob,
   and be in awe of the God of Israel.
Those who err in spirit shall acquire understanding,
   and those who find fault shall receive instruction. ✢

Psalm 27:1, 4, 13-14

R. (1a) The Lord is my light and my salvation.
The LORD is my light and my salvation;
   whom should I fear?
The LORD is my life's refuge;
   of whom should I be afraid? **R.**
One thing I ask of the LORD;
   this I seek:
To dwell in the house of the LORD
   all the days of my life,
That I may gaze on the loveliness of the LORD
   and contemplate his temple. **R.**
I believe that I shall see the bounty of the LORD
   in the land of the living.
Wait for the LORD with courage;
   be stouthearted, and wait for the LORD. **R.**

R. Alleluia, alleluia.
Behold, our Lord shall come with power;
he will enlighten the eyes of his servants. **R.**

† *Matthew 9:27-31*
Believing in Jesus, two who were blind are cured.

As Jesus passed by, two blind men followed him, crying out,
   "Son of David, have pity on us!"
When he entered the house,
   the blind men approached him and Jesus said to them,
   "Do you believe that I can do this?"
"Yes, Lord," they said to him.
Then he touched their eyes and said,
   "Let it be done for you according to your faith."
And their eyes were opened.
Jesus warned them sternly,
   "See that no one knows about this."
But they went out and spread word of him through all that land. ✝

SATURDAY, DECEMBER 3
St. Francis Xavier

† *Isaiah 30:19-21, 23-26*
The Merciful One will show you mercy when you cry out.

Thus says the Lord God,
   the Holy One of Israel:
O people of Zion, who dwell in Jerusalem,
   no more will you weep;
He will be gracious to you when you cry out,
   as soon as he hears he will answer you.
The Lord will give you the bread you need
   and the water for which you thirst.
No longer will your Teacher hide himself,
   but with your own eyes you shall see your Teacher,
While from behind, a voice shall sound in your ears:
   "This is the way; walk in it,"
   when you would turn to the right or to the left.

He will give rain for the seed
   that you sow in the ground,
And the wheat that the soil produces
   will be rich and abundant.
On that day your flock will be given pasture
   and the lamb will graze in spacious meadows;
The oxen and the asses that till the ground
   will eat silage tossed to them
   with shovel and pitchfork.
Upon every high mountain and lofty hill
   there will be streams of running water.

On the day of the great slaughter,
  when the towers fall,
The light of the moon will be like that of the sun
  and the light of the sun will be seven times greater
  like the light of seven days.
On the day the LORD binds up the wounds of his people,
  he will heal the bruises left by his blows. ✛

Psalm 147:1-2, 3-4, 5-6
R. (see Isaiah 30:18d) **Blessed are all who wait for the Lord.**
Praise the LORD, for he is good;
  sing praise to our God, for he is gracious;
  it is fitting to praise him.
The LORD rebuilds Jerusalem;
  the dispersed of Israel he gathers. **R.**
He heals the brokenhearted
  and binds up their wounds.
He tells the number of the stars;
  he calls each by name. **R.**
Great is our LORD and mighty in power:
  to his wisdom there is no limit.
The LORD sustains the lowly;
  the wicked he casts to the ground. **R.**

Isaiah 33:22
R. Alleluia, alleluia.
The LORD is our Judge, our Lawgiver, our King;
he it is who will save us. **R.**

† *Matthew 9:35—10:1, 5a, 6-8*
At the sight of the crowds, Jesus' heart was moved with pity for them.

Jesus went around to all the towns and villages,
  teaching in their synagogues,
  proclaiming the Gospel of the Kingdom,
  and curing every disease and illness.
At the sight of the crowds, his heart was moved with pity for them
  because they were troubled and abandoned,
  like sheep without a shepherd.
Then he said to his disciples,
  "The harvest is abundant but the laborers are few;
  so ask the master of the harvest
  to send out laborers for his harvest."

Then he summoned his Twelve disciples
  and gave them authority over unclean spirits to drive them out
  and to cure every disease and every illness.

Jesus sent out these Twelve after instructing them thus,
"Go to the lost sheep of the house of Israel.
As you go, make this proclamation: 'The Kingdom of heaven is at
hand.'
Cure the sick, raise the dead,
cleanse lepers, drive out demons.
Without cost you have received; without cost you are to give." ✟

SUNDAY, DECEMBER 4
SECOND SUNDAY OF ADVENT

† *Isaiah 11:1-10*
He shall judge the poor with justice.

On that day, a shoot shall sprout from the stump of Jesse,
and from his roots a bud shall blossom.
The spirit of the LORD shall rest upon him:
a spirit of wisdom and of understanding,
a spirit of counsel and of strength,
a spirit of knowledge and of fear of the LORD,
and his delight shall be the fear of the LORD.
Not by appearance shall he judge,
nor by hearsay shall he decide,
but he shall judge the poor with justice,
and decide aright for the land's afflicted.
He shall strike the ruthless with the rod of his mouth,
and with the breath of his lips he shall slay the wicked.
Justice shall be the band around his waist,
and faithfulness a belt upon his hips.
Then the wolf shall be a guest of the lamb,
and the leopard shall lie down with the kid;
the calf and the young lion shall browse together,
with a little child to guide them.
The cow and the bear shall be neighbors,
together their young shall rest;
the lion shall eat hay like the ox.
The baby shall play by the cobra's den,
and the child lay his hand on the adder's lair.
There shall be no harm or ruin on all my holy mountain;
for the earth shall be filled with knowledge of the LORD,
as water covers the sea.
On that day, the root of Jesse,
set up as a signal for the nations,
the Gentiles shall seek out,
for his dwelling shall be glorious. ✟

Psalm 72:1-2, 7-8, 12-13, 17

R. (see 7) **Justice shall flourish in his time, and fullness of
   peace for ever.**

O God, with your judgment endow the king,
   and with your justice, the king's son;
he shall govern your people with justice
   and your afflicted ones with judgment. **R.**

Justice shall flower in his days,
   and profound peace, till the moon be no more.
May he rule from sea to sea,
   and from the River to the ends of the earth. **R.**

For he shall rescue the poor when he cries out,
   and the afflicted when he has no one to help him.
He shall have pity for the lowly and the poor;
   the lives of the poor he shall save. **R.**

May his name be blessed forever;
   as long as the sun his name shall remain.
In him shall all the tribes of the earth be blessed;
   all the nations shall proclaim his happiness. **R.**

† *Romans 15:4-9*
Christ saves everyone.

Brothers and sisters:
Whatever was written previously was written for our instruction,
   that by endurance and by the encouragement of the Scriptures
   we might have hope.
May the God of endurance and encouragement
   grant you to think in harmony with one another,
   in keeping with Christ Jesus,
   that with one accord you may with one voice
   glorify the God and Father of our Lord Jesus Christ.

Welcome one another, then, as Christ welcomed you,
   for the glory of God.
For I say that Christ became a minister of the circumcised
   to show God's truthfulness,
   to confirm the promises to the patriarchs,
   but so that the Gentiles might glorify God for his mercy.
As it is written:
   *Therefore, I will praise you among the Gentiles
      and sing praises to your name.* ✛

Luke 3:4, 6

R. Alleluia, alleluia.

Prepare the way of the Lord, make straight his paths:
all flesh shall see the salvation of God. **R.**

† *Matthew 3:1-12*

Repent, for the kingdom of heaven is at hand!

John the Baptist appeared, preaching in the desert of Judea
and saying, "Repent, for the kingdom of heaven is at hand!"
It was of him that the prophet Isaiah had spoken when he said:
A voice of one crying out in the desert,
Prepare the way of the Lord,
make straight his paths.
John wore clothing made of camel's hair
and had a leather belt around his waist.
His food was locusts and wild honey.
At that time Jerusalem, all Judea,
and the whole region around the Jordan
were going out to him
and were being baptized by him in the Jordan River
as they acknowledged their sins.

When he saw many of the Pharisees and Sadducees
coming to his baptism, he said to them, "You brood of vipers!
Who warned you to flee from the coming wrath?
Produce good fruit as evidence of your repentance.
And do not presume to say to yourselves,
'We have Abraham as our father.'
For I tell you,
God can raise up children to Abraham from these stones.
Even now the ax lies at the root of the trees.
Therefore every tree that does not bear good fruit
will be cut down and thrown into the fire.
I am baptizing you with water, for repentance,
but the one who is coming after me is mightier than I.
I am not worthy to carry his sandals.
He will baptize you with the Holy Spirit and fire.
His winnowing fan is in his hand.
He will clear his threshing floor
and gather his wheat into his barn,
but the chaff he will burn with unquenchable fire." ✛

MONDAY, DECEMBER 5
ADVENT WEEKDAY

† *Isaiah 35:1-10*
God himself will come and save you.

The desert and the parched land will exult;
  the steppe will rejoice and bloom.
They will bloom with abundant flowers,
  and rejoice with joyful song.
The glory of Lebanon will be given to them,
  the splendor of Carmel and Sharon;
They will see the glory of the LORD,
  the splendor of our God.
Strengthen the hands that are feeble,
  make firm the knees that are weak,
Say to those whose hearts are frightened:
  Be strong, fear not!
Here is your God,
  he comes with vindication;
With divine recompense
  he comes to save you.
Then will the eyes of the blind be opened,
  the ears of the deaf be cleared;
Then will the lame leap like a stag,
  then the tongue of the mute will sing.

Streams will burst forth in the desert,
  and rivers in the steppe.
The burning sands will become pools,
  and the thirsty ground, springs of water;
The abode where jackals lurk
  will be a marsh for the reed and papyrus.
A highway will be there,
  called the holy way;
No one unclean may pass over it,
  nor fools go astray on it.
No lion will be there,
  nor beast of prey go up to be met upon it.
It is for those with a journey to make,
  and on it the redeemed will walk.
Those whom the LORD has ransomed will return
  and enter Zion singing,
  crowned with everlasting joy;
They will meet with joy and gladness,
  sorrow and mourning will flee. ✛

Psalm 85:9ab and 10, 11-12, 13-14

R. (Isaiah 35:4f) **Our God will come to save us!**

I will hear what God proclaims;
  the LORD—for he proclaims peace to his people.
Near indeed is his salvation to those who fear him,
  glory dwelling in our land. **R.**
Kindness and truth shall meet;
  justice and peace shall kiss.
Truth shall spring out of the earth,
  and justice shall look down from heaven. **R.**
The LORD himself will give his benefits;
  our land shall yield its increase.
Justice shall walk before him,
  and salvation, along the way of his steps. **R.**

R. Alleluia, alleluia.

Behold the king will come, the Lord of the earth,
and he himself will lift the yoke of our captivity. **R.**

✝ *Luke 5:17-26*
We have seen incredible things today.

One day as Jesus was teaching,
  Pharisees and teachers of the law,
  who had come from every village of Galilee and Judea and
    Jerusalem,
  were sitting there,
  and the power of the Lord was with him for healing.
And some men brought on a stretcher a man who was paralyzed;
  they were trying to bring him in and set him in his presence.
But not finding a way to bring him in because of the crowd,
  they went up on the roof
  and lowered him on the stretcher through the tiles
  into the middle in front of Jesus.
When Jesus saw their faith, he said,
  "As for you, your sins are forgiven."

Then the scribes and Pharisees began to ask themselves,
  "Who is this who speaks blasphemies?
Who but God alone can forgive sins?"
Jesus knew their thoughts and said to them in reply,
  "What are you thinking in your hearts?
Which is easier, to say, 'Your sins are forgiven,'
  or to say, 'Rise and walk'?
But that you may know
  that the Son of Man has authority on earth to forgive sins"—

he said to the one who was paralyzed,
"I say to you, rise, pick up your stretcher, and go home."

He stood up immediately before them,
   picked up what he had been lying on,
   and went home, glorifying God.
Then astonishment seized them all and they glorified God,
   and, struck with awe, they said,
   "We have seen incredible things today." ✛

TUESDAY, DECEMBER 6
ADVENT WEEKDAY, ST. NICHOLAS

✝ Isaiah 40:1-11
God consoles his people.

Comfort, give comfort to my people,
   says your God.
Speak tenderly to Jerusalem, and proclaim to her
      that her service is at an end,
      her guilt is expiated;
Indeed, she has received from the hand of the LORD
      double for all her sins.

   A voice cries out:
In the desert prepare the way of the LORD!
   Make straight in the wasteland a highway for our God!
Every valley shall be filled in,
      every mountain and hill shall be made low;
The rugged land shall be made a plain,
      the rough country, a broad valley.
Then the glory of the LORD shall be revealed,
      and all people shall see it together;
      for the mouth of the LORD has spoken.

A voice says, "Cry out!"
   I answer, "What shall I cry out?"
"All flesh is grass,
      and all their glory like the flower of the field.
The grass withers, the flower wilts,
      when the breath of the LORD blows upon it.
      So then, the people is the grass.
Though the grass withers and the flower wilts,
      the word of our God stands forever."

Go up onto a high mountain,
   Zion, herald of glad tidings;

Cry out at the top of your voice,
    Jerusalem, herald of good news!
Fear not to cry out
    and say to the cities of Judah:
    Here is your God!
Here comes with power
    the Lord GOD,
    who rules by his strong arm;
Here is his reward with him,
    his recompense before him.
Like a shepherd he feeds his flock;
    in his arms he gathers the lambs,
Carrying them in his bosom,
    and leading the ewes with care. ✚

Psalm 96:1-2, 3, 10ac, 11-12, 13

R. (see Isaiah 40:10ab) **The Lord our God comes with power.**
Sing to the LORD a new song;
    sing to the LORD, all you lands.
Sing to the LORD; bless his name;
    announce his salvation, day after day. **R.**
Tell his glory among the nations;
    among all peoples, his wondrous deeds.
Say among the nations: The LORD is king;
    he governs the peoples with equity. **R.**
Let the heavens be glad and the earth rejoice;
    let the sea and what fills it resound;
    let the plains be joyful and all that is in them!
Then let all the trees of the forest rejoice. **R.**
They shall exult before the LORD, for he comes;
    for he comes to rule the earth.
He shall rule the world with justice
    and the peoples with his constancy. **R.**

R. Alleluia, alleluia.
The day of the Lord is near:
Behold, he comes to save us. **R.**

† *Matthew 18:12-14*
God does not will that the little ones be lost.

Jesus said to his disciples:
"What is your opinion?
If a man has a hundred sheep and one of them goes astray,
    will he not leave the ninety-nine in the hills
    and go in search of the stray?

And if he finds it, amen, I say to you, he rejoices more over it
    than over the ninety-nine that did not stray.
In just the same way, it is not the will of your heavenly Father
    that one of these little ones be lost." ✛

WEDNESDAY, DECEMBER 7
St. Ambrose

✝ *Isaiah 40:25-31*
The Lord God is almighty and gives strength to the fainting.

To whom can you liken me as an equal?
    says the Holy One.
Lift up your eyes on high
    and see who has created these things:
He leads out their army and numbers them,
    calling them all by name.
By his great might and the strength of his power
    not one of them is missing!
Why, O Jacob, do you say,
    and declare, O Israel,
"My way is hidden from the Lord,
    and my right is disregarded by my God"?

Do you not know
    or have you not heard?
The Lord is the eternal God,
    creator of the ends of the earth.
He does not faint nor grow weary,
    and his knowledge is beyond scrutiny.
He gives strength to the fainting;
    for the weak he makes vigor abound.
Though young men faint and grow weary,
    and youths stagger and fall,
They that hope in the Lord will renew their strength,
    they will soar as with eagles' wings;
They will run and not grow weary,
    walk and not grow faint. ✛

Psalm 103:1-2, 3-4, 8 and 10

R. (1) O bless the Lord, my soul!
Bless the Lord, O my soul;
    and all my being, bless his holy name.
Bless the Lord, O my soul,
    and forget not all his benefits. **R.**
He pardons all your iniquities,
    he heals all your ills.

He redeems your life from destruction,
 he crowns you with kindness and compassion. **R.**
Merciful and gracious is the LORD,
 slow to anger and abounding in kindness.
Not according to our sins does he deal with us,
 nor does he requite us according to our crimes. **R.**

R. Alleluia, alleluia.
Behold, the Lord comes to save his people;
blessed are those prepared to meet him. **R.**

✝ Matthew 11:28-30
Come to me, all you who labor.

Jesus said to the crowds:
"Come to me, all you who labor and are burdened,
 and I will give you rest.
Take my yoke upon you and learn from me,
 for I am meek and humble of heart;
 and you will find rest for yourselves.
For my yoke is easy, and my burden light." ✝

THURSDAY, DECEMBER 8
THE IMMACULATE CONCEPTION OF THE BLESSED VIRGIN MARY, PATRONAL FEASTDAY OF THE UNITED STATES OF AMERICA

✝ Genesis 3:9-15, 20
I will put enmity between your offspring and hers.

After the man, Adam, had eaten of the tree,
 the LORD God called to the man and asked him, "Where are you?"
He answered, "I heard you in the garden;
 but I was afraid, because I was naked,
 so I hid myself."
Then he asked, "Who told you that you were naked?
You have eaten, then,
 from the tree of which I had forbidden you to eat!"
The man replied, "The woman whom you put here with me—
 she gave me fruit from the tree, and so I ate it."
The LORD God then asked the woman,
 "Why did you do such a thing?"
The woman answered, "The serpent tricked me into it, so I ate it."

Then the LORD God said to the serpent:
 "Because you have done this, you shall be banned
  from all the animals
  and from all the wild creatures;
 on your belly shall you crawl,

and dirt shall you eat
all the days of your life.
I will put enmity between you and the woman,
and between your offspring and hers;
he will strike at your head,
while you strike at his heel."

The man called his wife Eve,
because she became the mother of all the living. ✛

Psalm 98:1bcde, 2-3ab, 3cd-4

R. (1) **Sing to the Lord a new song, for he has done marvelous deeds.**

Sing to the LORD a new song,
for he has done wondrous deeds;
His right hand has won victory for him,
his holy arm. **R.**
The LORD has made his salvation known:
in the sight of the nations he has revealed his justice.
He has remembered his kindness and his faithfulness
toward the house of Israel. **R.**
All the ends of the earth have seen
the salvation by our God.
Sing joyfully to the LORD, all you lands;
break into song; sing praise. **R.**

✝ Ephesians 1:3-6, 11-12
He chose us in Christ before the foundation of the world.

Brothers and sisters:
Blessed be the God and Father of our Lord Jesus Christ,
who has blessed us in Christ
with every spiritual blessing in the heavens,
as he chose us in him, before the foundation of the world,
to be holy and without blemish before him.
In love he destined us for adoption to himself through Jesus Christ,
in accord with the favor of his will,
for the praise of the glory of his grace
that he granted us in the beloved.

In him we were also chosen,
destined in accord with the purpose of the One
who accomplishes all things according to the intention of his will,
so that we might exist for the praise of his glory,
we who first hoped in Christ. ✛

See Luke 1:28

R. Alleluia, alleluia.

Hail, Mary, full of grace, the Lord is with you;
blessed are you among women. **R.**

† *Luke 1:26-38*

Hail, full of grace! The Lord is with you.

The angel Gabriel was sent from God
to a town of Galilee called Nazareth,
to a virgin betrothed to a man named Joseph,
of the house of David,
and the virgin's name was Mary.
And coming to her, he said,
"Hail, full of grace! The Lord is with you."
But she was greatly troubled at what was said
and pondered what sort of greeting this might be.
Then the angel said to her,
"Do not be afraid, Mary,
for you have found favor with God.
Behold, you will conceive in your womb and bear a son,
and you shall name him Jesus.
He will be great and will be called Son of the Most High,
and the Lord God will give him the throne of David his father,
and he will rule over the house of Jacob forever,
and of his Kingdom there will be no end."
But Mary said to the angel,
"How can this be,
since I have no relations with a man?"
And the angel said to her in reply,
"The Holy Spirit will come upon you,
and the power of the Most High will overshadow you.
Therefore the child to be born
will be called holy, the Son of God.
And behold, Elizabeth, your relative,
has also conceived a son in her old age,
and this is the sixth month for her who was called barren;
for nothing will be impossible for God."
Mary said, "Behold, I am the handmaid of the Lord.
May it be done to me according to your word."
Then the angel departed from her. ✛

FRIDAY, DECEMBER 9
ADVENT WEEKDAY, ST. JUAN DIEGO CUAUHTLATOATZIN

† Isaiah 48:17-19
If only you would hearken to my commandments.

Thus says the LORD, your redeemer,
the Holy One of Israel:
I, the LORD, your God,
teach you what is for your good,
and lead you on the way you should go.
If you would hearken to my commandments,
your prosperity would be like a river,
and your vindication like the waves of the sea;
Your descendants would be like the sand,
and those born of your stock like its grains,
Their name never cut off
or blotted out from my presence. ✛

Psalm 1:1-2, 3, 4 and 6
R. (see John 8:12) **Those who follow you, Lord, will have the light of life.**
Blessed the man who follows not
the counsel of the wicked
Nor walks in the way of sinners,
nor sits in the company of the insolent,
But delights in the law of the LORD
and meditates on his law day and night. **R.**
He is like a tree
planted near running water,
That yields its fruit in due season,
and whose leaves never fade.
Whatever he does, prospers. **R.**
Not so the wicked, not so;
they are like chaff which the wind drives away.
For the LORD watches over the way of the just,
but the way of the wicked vanishes. **R.**

R. Alleluia, alleluia.
The Lord will come; go out to meet him!
He is the prince of peace. **R.**

† Matthew 11:16-19
They listened to neither John nor to the Son of Man.

Jesus said to the crowds:
"To what shall I compare this generation?
It is like children who sit in marketplaces and call to one another,

'We played the flute for you, but you did not dance,
we sang a dirge but you did not mourn.'
For John came neither eating nor drinking, and they said,
'He is possessed by a demon.'
The Son of Man came eating and drinking and they said,
'Look, he is a glutton and a drunkard,
a friend of tax collectors and sinners.'
But wisdom is vindicated by her works." ✝

SATURDAY, DECEMBER 10
Advent Weekday, Our Lady of Loreto

† *Sirach 48:1-4, 9-11*
Elijah was enveloped in a whirlwind.

In those days,
like a fire there appeared the prophet Elijah
whose words were as a flaming furnace.
Their staff of bread he shattered,
in his zeal he reduced them to straits;
By the LORD's word he shut up the heavens
and three times brought down fire.
How awesome are you, Elijah, in your wondrous deeds!
Whose glory is equal to yours?
You were taken aloft in a whirlwind of fire,
in a chariot with fiery horses.
You were destined, it is written, in time to come
to put an end to wrath before the day of the LORD,
To turn back the hearts of fathers toward their sons,
and to re-establish the tribes of Jacob.
Blessed is he who shall have seen you
and who falls asleep in your friendship. ✝

Psalm 80:2ac and 3b, 15-16, 18-19
R. (4) **Lord, make us turn to you; let us see your face and we
shall be saved.**
O shepherd of Israel, hearken,
From your throne upon the cherubim, shine forth.
Rouse your power. **R.**
Once again, O LORD of hosts,
look down from heaven, and see;
Take care of this vine,
and protect what your right hand has planted,
the son of man whom you yourself made strong. **R.**
May your help be with the man of your right hand,
with the son of man whom you yourself made strong.

Then we will no more withdraw from you;
    give us new life, and we will call upon your name. **R.**

Luke 3:4, 6
R. Alleluia, alleluia.
Prepare the way of the Lord, make straight his paths:
All flesh shall see the salvation of God. **R.**

† *Matthew 17:9a, 10-13*
Elijah has already come, and they did not recognize him.

As they were coming down from the mountain,
    the disciples asked Jesus,
    "Why do the scribes say that Elijah must come first?"
He said in reply, "Elijah will indeed come and restore all things;
    but I tell you that Elijah has already come,
    and they did not recognize him but did to him whatever they
        pleased.
So also will the Son of Man suffer at their hands."
Then the disciples understood
    that he was speaking to them of John the Baptist. ✠

SUNDAY, DECEMBER 11
THIRD SUNDAY OF ADVENT

† *Isaiah 35:1-6a, 10*
God himself will come to save us.

The desert and the parched land will exult;
    the steppe will rejoice and bloom.
They will bloom with abundant flowers,
    and rejoice with joyful song.
The glory of Lebanon will be given to them,
    the splendor of Carmel and Sharon;
they will see the glory of the LORD,
    the splendor of our God.
Strengthen the hands that are feeble,
    make firm the knees that are weak,
say to those whose hearts are frightened:
    Be strong, fear not!
Here is your God,
    he comes with vindication;
with divine recompense
    he comes to save you.
Then will the eyes of the blind be opened,
    the ears of the deaf be cleared;
then will the lame leap like a stag,
    then the tongue of the mute will sing.

Those whom the LORD has ransomed will return
   and enter Zion singing,
   crowned with everlasting joy;
they will meet with joy and gladness,
   sorrow and mourning will flee. ✛

Psalm 146:6c-7, 8-9a, 9b-10
R. (see Isaiah 35:4) **Lord, come and save us.** *(or* **Alleluia.***)*
The LORD God keeps faith forever,
   secures justice for the oppressed,
   gives food to the hungry.
The LORD sets captives free. **R.**
The LORD gives sight to the blind;
   the LORD raises up those who were bowed down.
The LORD loves the just;
   the LORD protects strangers. **R.**
The fatherless and the widow he sustains,
   but the way of the wicked he thwarts.
The LORD shall reign forever;
   your God, O Zion, through all generations. **R.**

† *James 5:7-10*
Make your hearts firm, because the coming of the Lord is at hand.

Be patient, brothers and sisters,
   until the coming of the Lord.
See how the farmer waits for the precious fruit of the earth,
   being patient with it
   until it receives the early and the late rains.
You too must be patient.
Make your hearts firm,
   because the coming of the Lord is at hand.
Do not complain, brothers and sisters, about one another,
   that you may not be judged.
Behold, the Judge is standing before the gates.
Take as an example of hardship and patience, brothers and sisters,
   the prophets who spoke in the name of the Lord. ✛

Isaiah 61:1 (cited in Luke 4:18)
R. Alleluia, alleluia.
The Spirit of the Lord is upon me,
because he has anointed me
to bring glad tidings to the poor. **R.**

† *Matthew 11:2-11*
Are you the one who is to come or should we look for another?

When John the Baptist heard in prison of the works of the Christ,

he sent his disciples to Jesus with this question,
"Are you the one who is to come,
or should we look for another?"
Jesus said to them in reply,
"Go and tell John what you hear and see:
the blind regain their sight,
the lame walk,
lepers are cleansed,
the deaf hear,
the dead are raised,
and the poor have the good news proclaimed to them.
And blessed is the one who takes no offense at me."

As they were going off,
Jesus began to speak to the crowds about John,
"What did you go out to the desert to see?
A reed swayed by the wind?
Then what did you go out to see?
Someone dressed in fine clothing?
Those who wear fine clothing are in royal palaces.
Then why did you go out? To see a prophet?
Yes, I tell you, and more than a prophet.
This is the one about whom it is written:
Behold, I am sending my messenger ahead of you;
he will prepare your way before you.
Amen, I say to you,
among those born of women
there has been none greater than John the Baptist;
yet the least in the kingdom of heaven is greater than he."✝

MONDAY, DECEMBER 12
OUR LADY OF GUADALUPE

✝*Zechariah 2:14-17 (or Revelation 11:19a; 12:1-6a, 10ab)*
Also permitted: Any readings from the *Lectionary for Mass* (volume IV),
the Common of the Blessed Virgin Mary, numbers 707-712.

Rejoice, O daughter Zion! See, I am coming.

Sing and rejoice, O daughter Zion!
See, I am coming to dwell among you, says the LORD.
Many nations shall join themselves to the LORD on that day,
and they shall be his people,
and he will dwell among you,
and you shall know that the LORD of hosts has sent me to you.
The Lord will possess Judah as his portion in the holy land,
and he will again choose Jerusalem.

Silence, all mankind, in the presence of the LORD!
    For he stirs forth from his holy dwelling. ✛

Judith 13:18bcde, 19
R. (15:9d) **You are the highest honor of our race.**
Blessed are you, daughter, by the Most High God,
    above all the women on earth;
    and blessed be the LORD God,
    the creator of heaven and earth. **R.**
Your deed of hope will never be forgotten
    by those who tell of the might of God. **R.**

R. Alleluia, alleluia.
Blessed are you, holy Virgin Mary, deserving of all praise;
from you rose the sun of justice, Christ our God. **R.**

*† **Luke 1:26-38** (or Luke 1:39-47)*
Behold, you will conceive in your womb and bear a son.

The angel Gabriel was sent from God
    to a town of Galilee called Nazareth,
    to a virgin betrothed to a man named Joseph,
    of the house of David,
    and the virgin's name was Mary.
And coming to her, he said,
    "Hail, full of grace! The Lord is with you."
But she was greatly troubled at what was said
    and pondered what sort of greeting this might be.
Then the angel said to her,
    "Do not be afraid, Mary,
    for you have found favor with God.
Behold, you will conceive in your womb and bear a son,
    and you shall name him Jesus.
He will be great and will be called Son of the Most High,
    and the Lord God will give him the throne of David his father,
    and he will rule over the house of Jacob forever,
    and of his Kingdom there will be no end."
But Mary said to the angel,
    "How can this be,
    since I have no relations with a man?"
And the angel said to her in reply,
    "The Holy Spirit will come upon you,
    and the power of the Most High will overshadow you.
Therefore the child to be born
    will be called holy, the Son of God.
And behold, Elizabeth, your relative,

has also conceived a son in her old age,
and this is the sixth month for her who was called barren;
for nothing will be impossible for God."
Mary said, "Behold, I am the handmaid of the Lord.
May it be done to me according to your word."
Then the angel departed from her. ✛

TUESDAY, DECEMBER 13
St. Lucy

† *Zephaniah 3:1-2, 9-13*
Messianic salvation is promised to all of the poor.

Thus says the LORD:
Woe to the city, rebellious and polluted,
   to the tyrannical city!
She hears no voice,
   accepts no correction;
In the LORD she has not trusted,
   to her God she has not drawn near.

For then I will change and purify
   the lips of the peoples,
That they all may call upon the name of the LORD,
   to serve him with one accord;
From beyond the rivers of Ethiopia
   and as far as the recesses of the North,
   they shall bring me offerings.

   On that day
You need not be ashamed
   of all your deeds,
   your rebellious actions against me;
For then will I remove from your midst
   the proud braggarts,
And you shall no longer exalt yourself
   on my holy mountain.
But I will leave as a remnant in your midst
   a people humble and lowly,
Who shall take refuge in the name of the LORD:
   the remnant of Israel.
They shall do no wrong
   and speak no lies;
Nor shall there be found in their mouths
   a deceitful tongue;
They shall pasture and couch their flocks
   with none to disturb them. ✛

Psalm 34:2-3, 6-7, 17-18, 19, 23

R. (7a) **The Lord hears the cry of the poor.**

I will bless the LORD at all times;
  his praise shall be ever in my mouth.
Let my soul glory in the LORD;
  the lowly will hear me and be glad. **R.**

Look to him that you may be radiant with joy,
  and your faces may not blush with shame.
When the poor one called out, the LORD heard,
  and from all his distress he saved him. **R.**

The LORD confronts the evildoers,
  to destroy remembrance of them from the earth.
When the just cry out, the LORD hears them,
  and from all their distress he rescues them. **R.**

The LORD is close to the brokenhearted;
  and those who are crushed in spirit he saves.
The LORD redeems the lives of his servants;
  no one incurs guilt who takes refuge in him. **R.**

R. Alleluia, alleluia.

Come, O Lord, do not delay;
forgive the sins of your people. **R.**

† *Matthew 21:28-32*

John came and sinners believed in him.

Jesus said to the chief priests and the elders of the people:
"What is your opinion?
A man had two sons.
He came to the first and said,
  'Son, go out and work in the vineyard today.'
The son said in reply, 'I will not,'
  but afterwards he changed his mind and went.
The man came to the other son and gave the same order.
He said in reply, 'Yes, sir,' but did not go.
Which of the two did his father's will?"
They answered, "The first."
Jesus said to them, "Amen, I say to you,
  tax collectors and prostitutes
  are entering the Kingdom of God before you.
When John came to you in the way of righteousness,
  you did not believe him;
  but tax collectors and prostitutes did.
Yet even when you saw that,
  you did not later change your minds and believe him." ✜

WEDNESDAY, DECEMBER 14
St. John of the Cross

† *Isaiah 45:6c-8, 18, 21c-25*
Let the clouds rain down.

I am the LORD, there is no other;
  I form the light, and create the darkness,
I make well-being and create woe;
  I, the LORD, do all these things.
Let justice descend, O heavens, like dew from above,
  like gentle rain let the skies drop it down.
Let the earth open and salvation bud forth;
  let justice also spring up!
  I, the LORD, have created this.

  For thus says the LORD,
The creator of the heavens,
  who is God,
The designer and maker of the earth
  who established it,
Not creating it to be a waste,
  but designing it be lived in:
I am the LORD, and there is no other.

Who announced this from the beginning
  and foretold it from of old?
Was it not I, the LORD,
  besides whom there is no other God?
  There is no just and saving God but me.

Turn to me and be safe,
  all you ends of the earth,
  for I am God; there is no other!
By myself I swear,
  uttering my just decree
  and my unalterable word:
To me every knee shall bend;
  by me every tongue shall swear,
Saying, "Only in the LORD
  are just deeds and power.
Before him in shame shall come
  all who vent their anger against him.
In the LORD shall be the vindication and the glory
  of all the descendants of Israel." ✝

Psalm 85:9ab and 10, 11-12, 13-14

R. (Isaiah 45:8) **Let the clouds rain down the Just One, and the earth bring forth a Savior.**

I will hear what God proclaims;
 the LORD—for he proclaims peace to his people.
Near indeed is his salvation to those who fear him,
 glory dwelling in our land. **R.**

Kindness and truth shall meet;
 justice and peace shall kiss.
Truth shall spring out of the earth,
 and justice shall look down from heaven. **R.**

The LORD himself will give his benefits;
 our land shall yield its increase.
Justice shall walk before him,
 and salvation, along the way of his steps. **R.**

See Isaiah 40:9-10

R. Alleluia, alleluia.

Raise your voice and tell the Good News:
Behold, the Lord GOD comes with power. **R.**

✝ *Luke 7:18b-23*

Go back and tell John what you have seen and heard.

At that time,
John summoned two of his disciples and sent them to the Lord to ask,
 "Are you the one who is to come, or should we look for another?"
When the men came to the Lord, they said,
 "John the Baptist has sent us to you to ask,
 'Are you the one who is to come, or should we look for another?'"
At that time Jesus cured many of their diseases, sufferings, and evil
  spirits;
 he also granted sight to many who were blind.
And Jesus said to them in reply,
 "Go and tell John what you have seen and heard:
 the blind regain their sight,
 the lame walk,
 lepers are cleansed,
 the deaf hear, the dead are raised,
 the poor have the good news proclaimed to them.
And blessed is the one who takes no offense at me." ✛

THURSDAY, DECEMBER 15
ADVENT WEEKDAY

† *Isaiah 54:1-10*
Like a forsaken wife, the LORD has called you back.

Raise a glad cry, you barren one who did not bear,
    break forth in jubilant song, you who were not in labor,
For more numerous are the children of the deserted wife
        than the children of her who has a husband,
        says the LORD.
Enlarge the space for your tent,
        spread out your tent cloths unsparingly;
        lengthen your ropes and make firm your stakes.
For you shall spread abroad to the right and to the left;
        your descendants shall dispossess the nations
        and shall people the desolate cities.

Fear not, you shall not be put to shame;
        you need not blush, for you shall not be disgraced.
The shame of your youth you shall forget,
        the reproach of your widowhood no longer remember.
For he who has become your husband is your Maker;
        his name is the LORD of hosts;
Your redeemer is the Holy One of Israel,
        called God of all the earth.
The LORD calls you back,
        like a wife forsaken and grieved in spirit,
A wife married in youth and then cast off,
        says your God.
For a brief moment I abandoned you,
        but with great tenderness I will take you back.
In an outburst of wrath, for a moment
        I hid my face from you;
But with enduring love I take pity on you,
        says the LORD, your redeemer.

This is for me like the days of Noah,
        when I swore that the waters of Noah
        should never again deluge the earth;
So I have sworn not to be angry with you,
        or to rebuke you.
Though the mountains leave their place
        and the hills be shaken,
My love shall never leave you
        nor my covenant of peace be shaken,
        says the LORD, who has mercy on you. ✛

Psalm 30:2 and 4, 5-6, 11-12a and 13b

R. (2a) **I will praise you, Lord, for you have rescued me.**

I will extol you, O LORD, for you drew me clear
    and did not let my enemies rejoice over me.
O LORD, you brought me up from the nether world;
    you preserved me from among those going down into the pit. **R.**
Sing praise to the LORD, you his faithful ones,
    and give thanks to his holy name.
For his anger lasts but a moment;
    a lifetime, his good will.
At nightfall, weeping enters in,
    but with the dawn, rejoicing. **R.**
"Hear, O LORD, and have pity on me;
    O LORD, be my helper."
You changed my mourning into dancing;
    O LORD, my God, forever will I give you thanks. **R.**

Luke 3:4, 6

R. Alleluia, alleluia.

Prepare the way of the Lord, make straight his paths:
All flesh shall see the salvation of God. **R.**

† *Luke 7:24-30*

John is the messenger who prepares the way of the Lord.

When the messengers of John the Baptist had left,
    Jesus began to speak to the crowds about John.
"What did you go out to the desert to see—a reed swayed by the
    wind?
Then what did you go out to see?
Someone dressed in fine garments?
Those who dress luxuriously and live sumptuously
    are found in royal palaces.
Then what did you go out to see?
A prophet? Yes, I tell you, and more than a prophet.
This is the one about whom Scripture says:

Behold, I am sending my messenger ahead of you,
he will prepare your way before you.

I tell you,
    among those born of women, no one is greater than John;
    yet the least in the Kingdom of God is greater than he."
(All the people who listened, including the tax collectors,
    who were baptized with the baptism of John,
    acknowledged the righteousness of God;
    but the Pharisees and scholars of the law,

who were not baptized by him,
rejected the plan of God for themselves.) ✛

FRIDAY, DECEMBER 16
ADVENT WEEKDAY

† Isaiah 56:1-3a, 6-8
My house shall be called a house of prayer for all peoples.

Thus says the LORD:
Observe what is right, do what is just;
   for my salvation is about to come,
   my justice, about to be revealed.
Blessed is the man who does this,
   the son of man who holds to it;
Who keeps the sabbath free from profanation,
   and his hand from any evildoing.
Let not the foreigner say,
   when he would join himself to the LORD,
   "The LORD will surely exclude me from his people."

The foreigners who join themselves to the LORD,
   ministering to him,
Loving the name of the LORD,
   and becoming his servants—
All who keep the sabbath free from profanation
   and hold to my covenant,
Them I will bring to my holy mountain
   and make joyful in my house of prayer;
Their burnt offerings and sacrifices
   will be acceptable on my altar,
For my house shall be called
   a house of prayer for all peoples.
Thus says the Lord GOD,
   who gathers the dispersed of Israel:
Others will I gather to him
   besides those already gathered. ✛

Psalm 67:2-3, 5, 7-8
R. (4) O God, let all the nations praise you!
May God have pity on us and bless us;
   may he let his face shine upon us.
So may your way be known upon earth;
   among all nations, your salvation. **R.**
May the nations be glad and exult
   because you rule the peoples in equity;
   the nations on the earth you guide. **R.**

The earth has yielded its fruits;
  God, our God, has blessed us.
May God bless us,
  and may all the ends of the earth fear him! **R.**

R. Alleluia, alleluia.
Come, Lord, bring us your peace
that we may rejoice before you with a perfect heart. **R.**

† *John 5:33-36*
John was a burning and shining lamp.

Jesus said to the Jews:
"You sent emissaries to John, and he testified to the truth.
I do not accept testimony from a human being,
  but I say this so that you may be saved.
John was a burning and shining lamp,
  and for a while you were content to rejoice in his light.
But I have testimony greater than John's.
The works that the Father gave me to accomplish,
  these works that I perform testify on my behalf
  that the Father has sent me." ✛

SATURDAY, DECEMBER 17
ADVENT WEEKDAY

† *Genesis 49:2, 8-10*
The scepter shall not depart from Judah.

Jacob called his sons and said to them:
  "Assemble and listen, sons of Jacob,
    listen to Israel, your father.

"You, Judah, shall your brothers praise
    —your hand on the neck of your enemies;
    the sons of your father shall bow down to you.
Judah, like a lion's whelp,
    you have grown up on prey, my son.
He crouches like a lion recumbent,
    the king of beasts—who would dare rouse him?
The scepter shall never depart from Judah,
    or the mace from between his legs,
While tribute is brought to him,
    and he receives the people's homage." ✛

Psalm 72:1-2, 3-4ab, 7-8, 17
R. (see 7) **Justice shall flourish in his time, and fullness of peace for ever.**

O God, with your judgment endow the king,
and with your justice, the king's son;
He shall govern your people with justice
and your afflicted ones with judgment. **R.**
The mountains shall yield peace for the people,
and the hills justice.
He shall defend the afflicted among the people,
save the children of the poor. **R.**
Justice shall flower in his days,
and profound peace, till the moon be no more.
May he rule from sea to sea,
and from the River to the ends of the earth. **R.**
May his name be blessed forever;
as long as the sun his name shall remain.
In him shall all the tribes of the earth be blessed;
all the nations shall proclaim his happiness. **R.**

R. Alleluia, alleluia.
O Wisdom of our God Most High,
guiding creation with power and love:
come to teach us the path of knowledge! **R.**

† *Matthew 1:1-17*
The genealogy of Jesus Christ, son of David.

The book of the genealogy of Jesus Christ,
the son of David, the son of Abraham.

Abraham became the father of Isaac,
Isaac the father of Jacob,
Jacob the father of Judah and his brothers.
Judah became the father of Perez and Zerah,
whose mother was Tamar.
Perez became the father of Hezron,
Hezron the father of Ram,
Ram the father of Amminadab.
Amminadab became the father of Nahshon,
Nahshon the father of Salmon,
Salmon the father of Boaz,
whose mother was Rahab.
Boaz became the father of Obed,
whose mother was Ruth.
Obed became the father of Jesse,
Jesse the father of David the king.

David became the father of Solomon,
whose mother had been the wife of Uriah.

Solomon became the father of Rehoboam,
　Rehoboam the father of Abijah,
　Abijah the father of Asaph.
Asaph became the father of Jehoshaphat,
　Jehoshaphat the father of Joram,
　Joram the father of Uzziah.
Uzziah became the father of Jotham,
　Jotham the father of Ahaz,
　Ahaz the father of Hezekiah.
Hezekiah became the father of Manasseh,
　Manasseh the father of Amos,
　Amos the father of Josiah.
Josiah became the father of Jechoniah and his brothers
　at the time of the Babylonian exile.

After the Babylonian exile,
　Jechoniah became the father of Shealtiel,
　Shealtiel the father of Zerubbabel,
　Zerubbabel the father of Abiud.
Abiud became the father of Eliakim,
　Eliakim the father of Azor,
　Azor the father of Zadok.
Zadok became the father of Achim,
　Achim the father of Eliud,
　Eliud the father of Eleazar.
Eleazar became the father of Matthan,
　Matthan the father of Jacob,
　Jacob the father of Joseph, the husband of Mary.
Of her was born Jesus who is called the Christ.

Thus the total number of generations
　from Abraham to David
　is fourteen generations;
　from David to the Babylonian exile, fourteen generations;
　from the Babylonian exile to the Christ,
　fourteen generations. ✙

SUNDAY, DECEMBER 18
FOURTH SUNDAY OF ADVENT

† Isaiah 7:10-14
Behold, the virgin shall conceive.

The LORD spoke to Ahaz, saying:
　Ask for a sign from the LORD, your God;
　let it be deep as the netherworld, or high as the sky!

But Ahaz answered,
"I will not ask! I will not tempt the LORD!"
Then Isaiah said:
Listen, O house of David!
Is it not enough for you to weary people,
must you also weary my God?
Therefore the Lord himself will give you this sign:
the virgin shall conceive, and bear a son,
and shall name him Emmanuel. ✛

Psalm 24:1-2, 3-4ab, 5-6

R. (see 7c and 10b) **Let the Lord enter; he is king of glory.**
The LORD's are the earth and its fullness;
the world and those who dwell in it.
For he founded it upon the seas
and established it upon the rivers. **R.**
Who can ascend the mountain of the LORD?
or who may stand in his holy place?
One whose hands are sinless, whose heart is clean,
who desires not what is vain. **R.**
He shall receive a blessing from the LORD,
a reward from God his savior.
Such is the race that seeks for him,
that seeks the face of the God of Jacob. **R.**

✝ *Romans 1:1-7*
Jesus Christ, descended from David, is the Son of God.

Paul, a slave of Christ Jesus,
called to be an apostle and set apart for the gospel of God,
which he promised previously through his prophets in the holy
Scriptures,
the gospel about his Son, descended from David according to the
flesh,
but established as Son of God in power
according to the Spirit of holiness
through resurrection from the dead, Jesus Christ our Lord.
Through him we have received the grace of apostleship,
to bring about the obedience of faith,
for the sake of his name, among all the Gentiles,
among whom are you also, who are called to belong to Jesus
Christ;
to all the beloved of God in Rome, called to be holy.
Grace to you and peace from God our Father
and the Lord Jesus Christ. ✛

Matthew 1:23

R. Alleluia, alleluia.

The virgin shall conceive, and bear a son,
and they shall name him Emmanuel. **R.**

† *Matthew 1:18-24*
Jesus will be born of Mary, the betrothed of Joseph, a son of David.

This is how the birth of Jesus Christ came about.
When his mother Mary was betrothed to Joseph,
but before they lived together,
she was found with child through the Holy Spirit.
Joseph her husband, since he was a righteous man,
yet unwilling to expose her to shame,
decided to divorce her quietly.
Such was his intention when, behold,
the angel of the Lord appeared to him in a dream and said,
"Joseph, son of David,
do not be afraid to take Mary your wife into your home.
For it is through the Holy Spirit
that this child has been conceived in her.
She will bear a son and you are to name him Jesus,
because he will save his people from their sins."
All this took place to fulfill what the Lord had said through the
prophet:
Behold, the virgin shall conceive and bear a son,
and they shall name him Emmanuel,
which means "God is with us."
When Joseph awoke,
he did as the angel of the Lord had commanded him
and took his wife into his home. ✛

MONDAY, DECEMBER 19
ADVENT WEEKDAY

† *Judges 13:2-7, 24-25a*
The birth of Samson is announced by an angel.

There was a certain man Zorah, of the clan of the Danites,
whose name was Manoah.
His wife was barren and had borne no children.
An angel of the LORD appeared to the woman and said to her,
"Though you are barren and have had no children,
yet you will conceive and bear a son.
Now, then, be careful to take no wine or strong drink
and to eat nothing unclean.
As for the son you will conceive and bear,

no razor shall touch his head,
for this boy is to be consecrated to God from the womb.
It is he who will begin the deliverance of Israel
from the power of the Philistines."

The woman went and told her husband,
"A man of God came to me;
he had the appearance of an angel of God, terrible indeed.
I did not ask him where he came from, nor did he tell me his name.
But he said to me,
'You will be with child and will bear a son.
So take neither wine nor strong drink, and eat nothing unclean.
For the boy shall be consecrated to God from the womb,
until the day of his death.'"

The woman bore a son and named him Samson.
The boy grew up and the Lord blessed him;
the Spirit of the LORD stirred him. ✛

Psalm 71:3-4a, 5-6ab, 16-17

R. (see 8) **My mouth shall be filled with your praise, and I will
sing your glory!**
Be my rock of refuge,
a stronghold to give me safety,
for you are my rock and my fortress.
O my God, rescue me from the hand of the wicked. **R.**
For you are my hope, O LORD;
my trust, O God, from my youth.
On you I depend from birth;
from my mother's womb you are my strength. **R.**
I will treat of the mighty works of the LORD;
O God, I will tell of your singular justice.
O God, you have taught me from my youth,
and till the present I proclaim your wondrous deeds. **R.**

R. Alleluia, alleluia.
O Root of Jesse's stem,
sign of God's love for all his people:
come to save us without delay! **R.**

† *Luke 1:5-25*
The birth of John the Baptist is announced by Gabriel.

In the days of Herod, King of Judea,
there was a priest named Zechariah
of the priestly division of Abijah;
his wife was from the daughters of Aaron,

and her name was Elizabeth.
Both were righteous in the eyes of God,
  observing all the commandments
  and ordinances of the Lord blamelessly.
But they had no child, because Elizabeth was barren
  and both were advanced in years.

Once when he was serving as priest
  in his division's turn before God,
  according to the practice of the priestly service,
  he was chosen by lot
  to enter the sanctuary of the Lord to burn incense.
Then, when the whole assembly of the people was praying outside
  at the hour of the incense offering,
  the angel of the Lord appeared to him,
  standing at the right of the altar of incense.
Zechariah was troubled by what he saw, and fear came upon him.

But the angel said to him, "Do not be afraid, Zechariah,
  because your prayer has been heard.
Your wife Elizabeth will bear you a son,
  and you shall name him John.
And you will have joy and gladness,
  and many will rejoice at his birth,
  for he will be great in the sight of the Lord.
He will drink neither wine nor strong drink.
He will be filled with the Holy Spirit even from his mother's womb,
  and he will turn many of the children of Israel
  to the Lord their God.
He will go before him in the spirit and power of Elijah
  to turn the hearts of fathers toward children
  and the disobedient to the understanding of the righteous,
  to prepare a people fit for the Lord."

Then Zechariah said to the angel,
  "How shall I know this?
For I am an old man, and my wife is advanced in years."
And the angel said to him in reply,
  "I am Gabriel, who stand before God.
I was sent to speak to you and to announce to you this good news.
But now you will be speechless and unable to talk
  until the day these things take place,
  because you did not believe my words,
  which will be fulfilled at their proper time."
Meanwhile the people were waiting for Zechariah

and were amazed that he stayed so long in the sanctuary.
But when he came out, he was unable to speak to them,
  and they realized that he had seen a vision in the sanctuary.
He was gesturing to them but remained mute.

Then, when his days of ministry were completed, he went home.

After this time his wife Elizabeth conceived,
  and she went into seclusion for five months, saying,
  "So has the Lord done for me at a time when he has seen fit
  to take away my disgrace before others." ✛

TUESDAY, DECEMBER 20
ADVENT WEEKDAY

✝ *Isaiah 7:10-14*
Behold, the virgin shall be with child.

The LORD spoke to Ahaz:
Ask for a sign from the LORD, your God;
  let it be deep as the nether world, or high as the sky!
But Ahaz answered,
  "I will not ask! I will not tempt the LORD!"
Then Isaiah said:
  Listen, O house of David!
Is it not enough for you to weary men,
  must you also weary my God?
Therefore the Lord himself will give you this sign:
  the virgin shall conceive and bear a son,
  and shall name him Emmanuel. ✛

Psalm 24:1-2, 3-4ab, 5-6
R. (see 7c and 10b) **Let the Lord enter; he is the king of glory.**
The LORD's are the earth and its fullness;
  the world and those who dwell in it.
For he founded it upon the seas
  and established it upon the rivers. **R.**
Who can ascend the mountain of the LORD?
  or who may stand in his holy place?
He whose hands are sinless, whose heart is clean,
  who desires not what is vain. **R.**
He shall receive a blessing from the LORD,
  a reward from God his savior.
Such is the race that seeks for him,
  that seeks the face of the God of Jacob. **R.**

R. Alleluia, alleluia.
O Key of David,
opening the gates of God's eternal Kingdom:
come and free the prisoners of darkness! **R.**

✝ *Luke 1:26-38*
You will conceive in your womb and bear a son.

In the sixth month,
    the angel Gabriel was sent from God
    to a town of Galilee called Nazareth,
    to a virgin betrothed to a man named Joseph,
    of the house of David,
    and the virgin's name was Mary.
And coming to her, he said,
    "Hail, full of grace! The Lord is with you."
But she was greatly troubled at what was said
    and pondered what sort of greeting this might be.
Then the angel said to her,
    "Do not be afraid, Mary,
    for you have found favor with God.
Behold, you will conceive in your womb and bear a son,
    and you shall name him Jesus.
He will be great and will be called Son of the Most High,
    and the Lord God will give him the throne of David his father,
    and he will rule over the house of Jacob forever,
    and of his Kingdom there will be no end."

But Mary said to the angel,
    "How can this be,
    since I have no relations with a man?"
And the angel said to her in reply,
    "The Holy Spirit will come upon you,
    and the power of the Most High will overshadow you.
Therefore the child to be born
    will be called holy, the Son of God.
And behold, Elizabeth, your relative,
    has also conceived a son in her old age,
    and this is the sixth month for her who was called barren;
    for nothing will be impossible for God."

Mary said, "Behold, I am the handmaid of the Lord.
May it be done to me according to your word."
    Then the angel departed from her. ✝

WEDNESDAY, DECEMBER 21
ADVENT WEEKDAY, ST. PETER CANISIUS

† *Song of Songs 2:8-14* (or *Zephaniah 3:14-18a*)
Hark! my lover comes, springing across the mountains.

Hark! my lover—here he comes
   springing across the mountains,
   leaping across the hills.
My lover is like a gazelle
   or a young stag.
Here he stands behind our wall,
   gazing through the windows,
   peering through the lattices.
My lover speaks; he says to me,
   "Arise, my beloved, my dove, my beautiful one,
   and come!
For see, the winter is past,
   the rains are over and gone.
The flowers appear on the earth,
   the time of pruning the vines has come,
   and the song of the dove is heard in our land.
The fig tree puts forth its figs,
   and the vines, in bloom, give forth fragrance.
Arise, my beloved, my beautiful one,
   and come!

"O my dove in the clefts of the rock,
   in the secret recesses of the cliff,
Let me see you,
   let me hear your voice,
For your voice is sweet,
   and you are lovely." †

Psalm 33:2-3, 11-12, 20-21

R. (1a; 3a) **Exult, you just, in the Lord! Sing to him a new song.**

Give thanks to the LORD on the harp;
   with the ten-stringed lyre chant his praises.
Sing to him a new song;
   pluck the strings skillfully, with shouts of gladness. **R.**
But the plan of the LORD stands forever;
   the design of his heart, through all generations.
Blessed the nation whose God is the LORD,
   the people he has chosen for his own inheritance. **R.**
Our soul waits for the LORD,

who is our help and our shield,
For in him our hearts rejoice;
  in his holy name we trust. **R.**

R. Alleluia, alleluia.
O Emmanuel, our King and Giver of Law:
come to save us, Lord our God! **R.**

† Luke 1:39-45
And how does this happen to me,
that the mother of my Lord should come to me?

$\mathbf{M}$ary set out in those days
  and traveled to the hill country in haste
  to a town of Judah,
  where she entered the house of Zechariah
  and greeted Elizabeth.
When Elizabeth heard Mary's greeting,
  the infant leaped in her womb,
  and Elizabeth, filled with the Holy Spirit,
  cried out in a loud voice and said,
  "Most blessed are you among women,
  and blessed is the fruit of your womb.
And how does this happen to me,
  that the mother of my Lord should come to me?
For at the moment the sound of your greeting reached my ears,
  the infant in my womb leaped for joy.
Blessed are you who believed
  that what was spoken to you by the Lord
  would be fulfilled." ✛

THURSDAY, DECEMBER 22
ADVENT WEEKDAY

† 1 Samuel 1:24-28
Hannah gives thanks for the birth of Samuel.

$\mathbf{I}$n those days,
Hannah brought Samuel with her,
  along with a three-year-old bull,
  an ephah of flour, and a skin of wine,
  and presented him at the temple of the LORD in Shiloh.
After the boy's father had sacrificed the young bull,
  Hannah, his mother, approached Eli and said:
  "Pardon, my lord!
As you live, my lord,
  I am the woman who stood near you here, praying to the LORD.
I prayed for this child, and the LORD granted my request.

Now I, in turn, give him to the LORD;
  as long as he lives, he shall be dedicated to the LORD."
She left Samuel there. ✛

1 Samuel 2:1, 4-5, 6-7, 8abcd
R. (see 1a) **My heart exults in the Lord, my Savior.**
"My heart exults in the LORD,
  my horn is exalted in my God.
I have swallowed up my enemies;
  I rejoice in my victory." **R.**
"The bows of the mighty are broken,
  while the tottering gird on strength.
The well-fed hire themselves out for bread,
  while the hungry batten on spoil.
The barren wife bears seven sons,
  while the mother of many languishes." **R.**
"The LORD puts to death and gives life;
  he casts down to the nether world;
  he raises up again.
The LORD makes poor and makes rich,
  he humbles, he also exalts." **R.**
"He raises the needy from the dust;
  from the dung heap he lifts up the poor,
To seat them with nobles
  and make a glorious throne their heritage." **R.**

R. Alleluia, alleluia.
O King of all nations and keystone of the Church:
come and save man, whom you formed from the dust! **R.**

† Luke 1:46-56
The Mighty One has done great things for me.

Mary said:

"My soul proclaims the greatness of the Lord;
  my spirit rejoices in God my savior.
  for he has looked upon his lowly servant.
From this day all generations will call me blessed;
  the Almighty has done great things for me,
  and holy is his Name.
He has mercy on those who fear him
  in every generation.
He has shown the strength of his arm,
  and has scattered the proud in their conceit.
He has cast down the mighty from their thrones
  and has lifted up the lowly.

He has filled the hungry with good things,
  and the rich he has sent away empty.
He has come to the help of his servant Israel
  for he remembered his promise of mercy,
  the promise he made to our fathers,
  to Abraham and his children for ever."

Mary remained with Elizabeth about three months
and then returned to her home. ✛

FRIDAY, DECEMBER 23
ADVENT WEEKDAY, ST. JOHN OF KANTY

† *Malachi 3:1-4, 23-24*
I will send you Elijah, the prophet, before the day of the Lord comes.

Thus says the Lord GOD:
Lo, I am sending my messenger
  to prepare the way before me;
And suddenly there will come to the temple
  the LORD whom you seek,
And the messenger of the covenant whom you desire.
  Yes, he is coming, says the LORD of hosts.
But who will endure the day of his coming?
  And who can stand when he appears?
For he is like the refiner's fire,
  or like the fuller's lye.
He will sit refining and purifying silver,
  and he will purify the sons of Levi,
Refining them like gold or like silver
  that they may offer due sacrifice to the LORD.
Then the sacrifice of Judah and Jerusalem
  will please the LORD,
  as in the days of old, as in years gone by.

Lo, I will send you
  Elijah, the prophet,
Before the day of the LORD comes,
  the great and terrible day,
To turn the hearts of the fathers to their children,
  and the hearts of the children to their fathers,
Lest I come and strike
  the land with doom. ✛

Psalm 25:4-5ab, 8-9, 10 and 14
R. (see Luke 21:28) **Lift up your heads and see; your redemption is near at hand.**

Your ways, O Lord, make known to me;
  teach me your paths,
Guide me in your truth and teach me,
  for you are God my savior. **R.**
Good and upright is the Lord;
  thus he shows sinners the way.
He guides the humble to justice,
  he teaches the humble his way. **R.**
All the paths of the Lord are kindness and constancy
  toward those who keep his covenant and his decrees.
The friendship of the Lord is with those who fear him,
  and his covenant, for their instruction. **R.**

R. Alleluia, alleluia.
O King of all nations and keystone of the Church;
come and save man, whom you formed from the dust! **R.**

† *Luke 1:57-66*
The birth of John the Baptist.

When the time arrived for Elizabeth to have her child
  she gave birth to a son.
Her neighbors and relatives heard
  that the Lord had shown his great mercy toward her,
  and they rejoiced with her.
When they came on the eighth day to circumcise the child,
  they were going to call him Zechariah after his father,
  but his mother said in reply,
  "No. He will be called John."
But they answered her,
  "There is no one among your relatives who has this name."
So they made signs, asking his father what he wished him to be
    called.
He asked for a tablet and wrote, "John is his name,"
  and all were amazed.
Immediately his mouth was opened, his tongue freed,
  and he spoke blessing God.
Then fear came upon all their neighbors,
  and all these matters were discussed
  throughout the hill country of Judea.
All who heard these things took them to heart, saying,
  "What, then, will this child be?"
For surely the hand of the Lord was with him. ✛

SATURDAY, DECEMBER 24
ADVENT WEEKDAY (MORNING)

✝ 2 Samuel 7:1-5, 8b-12, 14a, 16
The Kingdom of David shall endure forever in the sight of the Lord.

When King David was settled in his palace,
and the LORD had given him rest from his enemies on every side,
he said to Nathan the prophet,
"Here I am living in a house of cedar,
while the ark of God dwells in a tent!"
Nathan answered the king,
"Go, do whatever you have in mind,
for the LORD is with you."
But that night the LORD spoke to Nathan and said:
"Go, tell my servant David, 'Thus says the LORD:
Should you build me a house to dwell in?

"'It was I who took you from the pasture
and from the care of the flock
to be commander of my people Israel.
I have been with you wherever you went,
and I have destroyed all your enemies before you.
And I will make you famous like the great ones of the earth.
I will fix a place for my people Israel;
I will plant them so that they may dwell in their place
without further disturbance.
Neither shall the wicked continue to afflict them as they did of old,
since the time I first appointed judges over my people Israel.
I will give you rest from all your enemies.
The LORD also reveals to you
that he will establish a house for you.
And when your time comes and you rest with your ancestors,
I will raise up your heir after you, sprung from your loins,
and I will make his Kingdom firm.
I will be a father to him,
and he shall be a son to me.
Your house and your Kingdom shall endure forever before me;
your throne shall stand firm forever.'" ✛

Psalm 89:2-3, 4-5, 27 and 29
R. (2) **For ever I will sing the goodness of the Lord.**
The favors of the LORD I will sing forever;
through all generations my mouth shall proclaim your faithfulness.
For you have said, "My kindness is established forever";
in heaven you have confirmed your faithfulness. **R.**

"I have made a covenant with my chosen one,
   I have sworn to David my servant:
Forever will I confirm your posterity
   and establish your throne for all generations." **R.**
"He shall say of me, 'You are my father,
   my God, the rock, my savior.'
Forever I will maintain my kindness toward him,
   and my covenant with him stands firm." **R.**

R. Alleluia, alleluia.
O Radiant Dawn,
splendor of eternal light, sun of justice:
come and shine on those who dwell in darkness and in the shadow
     of death. **R.**

† Luke 1:67-79
The daybreak from on high has visited us.

Zechariah his father, filled with the Holy Spirit, prophesied, saying:

"Blessed be the Lord, the God of Israel;
   for he has come to his people and set them free.
He has raised up for us a mighty Savior,
   born of the house of his servant David.
Through his prophets he promised of old
   that he would save us from our enemies,
   from the hands of all who hate us.
He promised to show mercy to our fathers
   and to remember his holy covenant.
This was the oath he swore to our father Abraham:
   to set us free from the hand of our enemies,
   free to worship him without fear,
   holy and righteous in his sight
     all the days of our life.
You, my child, shall be called the prophet of the Most High,
   for you will go before the Lord to prepare his way,
   to give his people knowledge of salvation
   by the forgiveness of their sins.
In the tender compassion of our God
   the dawn from on high shall break upon us,
   to shine on those who dwell in darkness and the shadow of
     death,
   and to guide our feet into the way of peace."✛

SUNDAY, DECEMBER 25
THE NATIVITY OF THE LORD (CHRISTMAS)

Below are readings for Mass During the Night and Mass During the Day. For Vigil Mass:
Isaiah 62:1-5 • Psalm 89:4-5, 16-17, 27 and 29 • Acts 13:16-17, 22-25 • Matthew 1:1-25 or
1:18-25; At Dawn: Isaiah 62:11-12 • Psalm 97:1 and 6, 11-12 • Titus 3:4-7 • Luke 2:15-20

† Isaiah 9:1-6
A son is given us.

The people who walked in darkness
   have seen a great light;
upon those who dwelt in the land of gloom
   a light has shone.
You have brought them abundant joy
   and great rejoicing,
as they rejoice before you as at the harvest,
   as people make merry when dividing spoils.
For the yoke that burdened them,
   the pole on their shoulder,
and the rod of their taskmaster
   you have smashed, as on the day of Midian.
For every boot that tramped in battle,
   every cloak rolled in blood,
   will be burned as fuel for flames.
For a child is born to us, a son is given us;
   upon his shoulder dominion rests.
They name him Wonder-Counselor, God-Hero,
   Father-Forever, Prince of Peace.
His dominion is vast
   and forever peaceful,
from David's throne, and over his kingdom,
   which he confirms and sustains
by judgment and justice,
   both now and forever.
The zeal of the LORD of hosts will do this! ✛

Psalm 96:1-2a, 2b-3, 11-12, 13

R. (Luke 2:11) **Today is born our Savior, Christ the Lord.**
Sing to the LORD a new song;
   sing to the LORD, all you lands.
Sing to the LORD; bless his name. **R.**
Announce his salvation, day after day.
   Tell his glory among the nations;
   among all peoples, his wondrous deeds. **R.**
Let the heavens be glad and the earth rejoice;
   let the sea and what fills it resound;

let the plains be joyful and all that is in them!
Then shall all the trees of the forest exult. **R.**
They shall exult before the LORD, for he comes;
   for he comes to rule the earth.
He shall rule the world with justice
   and the peoples with his constancy. **R.**

† *Titus 2:11-14*
The grace of God has appeared to all.

Beloved:
The grace of God has appeared, saving all
   and training us to reject godless ways and worldly desires
   and to live temperately, justly, and devoutly in this age,
   as we await the blessed hope,
   the appearance of the glory of our great God
   and savior Jesus Christ,
   who gave himself for us to deliver us from all lawlessness
   and to cleanse for himself a people as his own,
   eager to do what is good. ✛

Luke 2:10-11
R. Alleluia, alleluia.
I proclaim to you good news of great joy:
today a Savior is born for us,
Christ the Lord. **R.**

† *Luke 2:1-14*
Today a Savior has been born for you.

In those days a decree went out from Caesar Augustus
   that the whole world should be enrolled.
This was the first enrollment,
   when Quirinius was governor of Syria.
So all went to be enrolled, each to his own town.
And Joseph too went up from Galilee from the town of Nazareth
   to Judea, to the city of David that is called Bethlehem,
   because he was of the house and family of David,
   to be enrolled with Mary, his betrothed, who was with child.
While they were there,
   the time came for her to have her child,
   and she gave birth to her firstborn son.
She wrapped him in swaddling clothes and laid him in a manger,
   because there was no room for them in the inn.

Now there were shepherds in that region living in the fields
   and keeping the night watch over their flock.

The angel of the Lord appeared to them
  and the glory of the Lord shone around them,
  and they were struck with great fear.
The angel said to them,
  "Do not be afraid;
  for behold, I proclaim to you good news of great joy
  that will be for all the people.
For today in the city of David
  a savior has been born for you who is Christ and Lord.
And this will be a sign for you:
  you will find an infant wrapped in swaddling clothes
  and lying in a manger."
And suddenly there was a multitude of the heavenly host with the
    angel,
  praising God and saying:
    "Glory to God in the highest
    and on earth peace to those on whom his favor rests." ✛

Mass during the Day

✝ *Isaiah 52:7-10*
All the ends of the earth will behold the salvation of our God.

How beautiful upon the mountains
  are the feet of him who brings glad tidings,
announcing peace, bearing good news,
  announcing salvation, and saying to Zion,
  "Your God is King!"

Hark! Your sentinels raise a cry,
  together they shout for joy,
for they see directly, before their eyes,
  the LORD restoring Zion.
Break out together in song,
  O ruins of Jerusalem!
For the LORD comforts his people,
  he redeems Jerusalem.
The LORD has bared his holy arm
  in the sight of all the nations;
all the ends of the earth will behold
  the salvation of our God. ✛

Psalm 98:1bcde, 2-3ab, 3cd-4, 5-6
R. (3c) **All the ends of the earth have seen the saving power
  of God.**
Sing to the LORD a new song,
  for he has done wondrous deeds;

his right hand has won victory for him,
 his holy arm. **R.**
The LORD has made his salvation known:
 in the sight of the nations he has revealed his justice.
He has remembered his kindness and his faithfulness
 toward the house of Israel. **R.**
All the ends of the earth have seen
 the salvation by our God.
Sing joyfully to the LORD, all you lands;
 break into song; sing praise. **R.**
Sing praise to the LORD with the harp,
 with the harp and melodious song.
With trumpets and the sound of the horn
 sing joyfully before the King, the LORD. **R.**

† *Hebrews 1:1-6*
God has spoken to us through the Son.

Brothers and sisters:
In times past, God spoke in partial and various ways
 to our ancestors through the prophets;
 in these last days, he has spoken to us through the Son,
 whom he made heir of all things
 and through whom he created the universe,
 who is the refulgence of his glory, the very imprint of his being,
 and who sustains all things by his mighty word.
 When he had accomplished purification from sins,
 he took his seat at the right hand of the Majesty on high,
 as far superior to the angels
 as the name he has inherited is more excellent than theirs.

For to which of the angels did God ever say:
You are my son; this day I have begotten you?
Or again:
I will be a father to him, and he shall be a son to me?
And again, when he leads the firstborn into the world, he says:
Let all the angels of God worship him. ✢

R. Alleluia, alleluia.
A holy day has dawned upon us.
Come, you nations, and adore the Lord.
For today a great light has come upon the earth. **R.**

† *John 1:1-18* (or *John 1:1-5, 9-14*)
The Word became flesh and made his dwelling among us.

In the beginning was the Word,

and the Word was with God,
and the Word was God.
He was in the beginning with God.
All things came to be through him,
and without him nothing came to be.
What came to be through him was life,
and this life was the light of the human race;
the light shines in the darkness,
and the darkness has not overcome it.
A man named John was sent from God.
He came for testimony, to testify to the light,
so that all might believe through him.
He was not the light,
but came to testify to the light.
The true light, which enlightens everyone, was coming into the
world.
He was in the world,
and the world came to be through him,
but the world did not know him.
He came to what was his own,
but his own people did not accept him.

But to those who did accept him
he gave power to become children of God,
to those who believe in his name,
who were born not by natural generation
nor by human choice nor by a man's decision
but of God.
And the Word became flesh
and made his dwelling among us,
and we saw his glory,
the glory as of the Father's only Son,
full of grace and truth.
John testified to him and cried out, saying,
"This was he of whom I said,
'The one who is coming after me ranks ahead of me
because he existed before me.'"
From his fullness we have all received,
grace in place of grace,
because while the law was given through Moses,
grace and truth came through Jesus Christ.
No one has ever seen God.
The only Son, God, who is at the Father's side,
has revealed him. ✛

MONDAY, DECEMBER 26
St. Stephen

† *Acts 6:8-10; 7:54-59*
I see the heavens opened.

Stephen, filled with grace and power,
   was working great wonders and signs among the people.
Certain members of the so-called Synagogue of Freedmen,
   Cyrenians, and Alexandrians,
   and people from Cilicia and Asia,
   came forward and debated with Stephen,
   but they could not withstand the wisdom
      and the spirit with which he spoke.

When they heard this, they were infuriated,
   and they ground their teeth at him.
But he, filled with the Holy Spirit,
   looked up intently to heaven
   and saw the glory of God and Jesus standing
      at the right hand of God,
   and he said,
   "Behold, I see the heavens opened and the Son of Man
   standing at the right hand of God."
But they cried out in a loud voice, covered their ears,
   and rushed upon him together.
They threw him out of the city, and began to stone him.
The witnesses laid down their cloaks
   at the feet of a young man named Saul.
As they were stoning Stephen, he called out
   "Lord Jesus, receive my spirit." ✝

Psalm 31:3cd-4, 6 and 8ab, 16bc and 17
R. (6) **Into your hands, O Lord, I commend my spirit.**
Be my rock of refuge,
   a stronghold to give me safety.
You are my rock and my fortress;
   for your name's sake you will lead and guide me. **R.**
Into your hands I commend my spirit;
   you will redeem me, O Lord, O faithful God.
I will rejoice and be glad because of your mercy. **R.**
Rescue me from the clutches of my enemies and my persecutors,
Let your face shine upon your servant;
   save me in your kindness. **R.**

Psalm 118:26a, 27a
R. Alleluia, alleluia.
Blessed is he who comes in the name of the LORD:
the LORD is God and has given us light. **R.**

† *Matthew 10:17-22*
For it will not be you who speak but the Spirit of your Father.

Jesus said to his disciples:
"Beware of men, for they will hand you over to courts
　and scourge you in their synagogues,
　and you will be led before governors and kings for my sake
　as a witness before them and the pagans.
When they hand you over,
　do not worry about how you are to speak
　or what you are to say.
You will be given at that moment what you are to say.
For it will not be you who speak
　but the Spirit of your Father speaking through you.
Brother will hand over brother to death,
　and the father his child;
　children will rise up against parents and have them put to death.
You will be hated by all because of my name,
　but whoever endures to the end will be saved." ✛

TUESDAY, DECEMBER 27
ST. JOHN

† *1 John 1:1-4*
What we have seen and heard we proclaim now to you.

Beloved:
　What was from the beginning,
　what we have heard,
　what we have seen with our eyes,
　what we looked upon
　and touched with our hands
　concerns the Word of life—
　for the life was made visible;
　we have seen it and testify to it
　and proclaim to you the eternal life
　that was with the Father and was made visible to us—
　what we have seen and heard
　we proclaim now to you,
　so that you too may have fellowship with us;
　for our fellowship is with the Father

and with his Son, Jesus Christ.
We are writing this so that our joy may be complete. ✛

Psalm 97:1-2, 5-6, 11-12
R. (12) **Rejoice in the Lord, you just!**
The LORD is king; let the earth rejoice;
  let the many isles be glad.
Clouds and darkness are around him,
  justice and judgment are the foundation of his throne. **R.**
The mountains melt like wax before the LORD,
  before the LORD of all the earth.
The heavens proclaim his justice,
  and all peoples see his glory. **R.**
Light dawns for the just;
  and gladness, for the upright of heart.
Be glad in the LORD, you just,
  and give thanks to his holy name. **R.**

See Te Deum
R. Alleluia, alleluia.
We praise you, O God,
we acclaim you as Lord;
the glorious company of Apostles praise you. **R.**

✝ *John 20:1a, 2-8*
The other disciple ran faster than Peter and arrived at the tomb first.

On the first day of the week,
  Mary Magdalene ran and went to Simon Peter
  and to the other disciple whom Jesus loved, and told them,
  "They have taken the Lord from the tomb,
  and we do not know where they put him."
So Peter and the other disciple went out and came to the tomb.
They both ran, but the other disciple ran faster than Peter
  and arrived at the tomb first;
  he bent down and saw the burial cloths there, but did not go in.
When Simon Peter arrived after him,
  he went into the tomb and saw the burial cloths there,
  and the cloth that had covered his head,
  not with the burial cloths but rolled up in a separate place.
Then the other disciple also went in,
  the one who had arrived at the tomb first,
  and he saw and believed. ✛

WEDNESDAY, DECEMBER 28
THE HOLY INNOCENTS

† *1 John 1:5—2:2*
The Blood of his Son Jesus Christ cleanses us from all sin.

Beloved:
This is the message that we have heard from Jesus Christ
  and proclaim to you:
  God is light, and in him there is no darkness at all.
If we say, "We have fellowship with him,"
  while we continue to walk in darkness,
  we lie and do not act in truth.
But if we walk in the light as he is in the light,
  then we have fellowship with one another,
  and the Blood of his Son Jesus cleanses us from all sin.
If we say, "We are without sin,"
  we deceive ourselves, and the truth is not in us.
If we acknowledge our sins, he is faithful and just
  and will forgive our sins and cleanse us from every wrongdoing.
If we say, "We have not sinned," we make him a liar,
  and his word is not in us.

My children, I am writing this to you
  so that you may not commit sin.
But if anyone does sin, we have an Advocate with the Father,
  Jesus Christ the righteous one.
He is expiation for our sins,
  and not for our sins only but for those of the whole world. ✛

Psalm 124:2-3, 4-5, 7b-8
R. (7) **Our soul has been rescued like a bird from the fowler's
  snare.**
Had not the LORD been with us—
When men rose up against us,
  then would they have swallowed us alive,
When their fury was inflamed against us. **R.**
Then would the waters have overwhelmed us;
The torrent would have swept over us;
  over us then would have swept the raging waters. **R.**
Broken was the snare,
  and we were freed.
Our help is in the name of the LORD,
  who made heaven and earth. **R.**

See Te Deum
R. Alleluia, alleluia.
We praise you, O God,
we acclaim you as Lord;
the white-robed army of martyrs praise you. **R.**

† *Matthew 2:13-18*
He ordered the massacre of all boys in Bethlehem.

When the magi had departed, behold,
the angel of the Lord appeared to Joseph in a dream and said,
"Rise, take the child and his mother, flee to Egypt,
and stay there until I tell you.
Herod is going to search for the child to destroy him."
Joseph rose and took the child and his mother by night
and departed for Egypt.
He stayed there until the death of Herod,
that what the Lord had said through the prophet might be fulfilled,
Out of Egypt I called my son.

When Herod realized that he had been deceived by the magi,
he became furious.
He ordered the massacre of all the boys in Bethlehem and its vicinity
two years old and under,
in accordance with the time he had ascertained from the magi.
Then was fulfilled what had been said through Jeremiah the prophet:

A voice was heard in Ramah,
sobbing and loud lamentation;
Rachel weeping for her children,
and she would not be consoled,
since they were no more. ✝

THURSDAY, DECEMBER 29
FIFTH DAY WITHIN THE OCTAVE OF THE NATIVITY OF THE LORD, ST. THOMAS BECKET

† *1 John 2:3-11*
Those who love their brother remain in the light.

Beloved:
The way we may be sure that we know Jesus
is to keep his commandments.
Whoever says, "I know him," but does not keep his commandments
is a liar, and the truth is not in him.
But whoever keeps his word,
the love of God is truly perfected in him.
This is the way we may know that we are in union with him:
whoever claims to abide in him ought to walk just as he walked.

Beloved, I am writing no new commandment to you
   but an old commandment that you had from the beginning.
The old commandment is the word that you have heard.
And yet I do write a new commandment to you,
   which holds true in him and among you,
   for the darkness is passing away,
   and the true light is already shining.
Whoever says he is in the light,
   yet hates his brother, is still in the darkness.
Whoever loves his brother remains in the light,
   and there is nothing in him to cause a fall.
Whoever hates his brother is in darkness;
   he walks in darkness
   and does not know where he is going
   because the darkness has blinded his eyes. ✛

Psalm 96:1-2a, 2b-3, 5b-6
R. (11a) Let the heavens be glad and the earth rejoice!
Sing to the LORD a new song;
   sing to the LORD, all you lands.
Sing to the LORD; bless his name. **R.**
Announce his salvation, day after day.
Tell his glory among the nations;
   among all peoples, his wondrous deeds. **R.**
The LORD made the heavens.
Splendor and majesty go before him;
   praise and grandeur are in his sanctuary. **R.**

Luke 2:32
R. Alleluia, alleluia.
A light of revelation to the Gentiles
and glory for your people Israel. **R.**

† *Luke 2:22-35*
This is the light of revelation to the Gentiles.

When the days were completed for their purification
   according to the law of Moses,
   the parents of Jesus took him up to Jerusalem
   to present him to the Lord,
   just as it is written in the law of the Lord,
   Every male that opens the womb shall be consecrated to the Lord,
   and to offer the sacrifice of
   a pair of turtledoves or two young pigeons,
   in accordance with the dictate in the law of the Lord.

Now there was a man in Jerusalem whose name was Simeon.

This man was righteous and devout,
  awaiting the consolation of Israel,
  and the Holy Spirit was upon him.
It had been revealed to him by the Holy Spirit
  that he should not see death
  before he had seen the Christ of the Lord.
He came in the Spirit into the temple;
  and when the parents brought in the child Jesus
  to perform the custom of the law in regard to him,
  he took him into his arms and blessed God, saying:

"Lord, now let your servant go in peace;
  your word has been fulfilled:
my own eyes have seen the salvation
  which you prepared in the sight of every people,
a light to reveal you to the nations
  and the glory of your people Israel."

The child's father and mother were amazed at what was said about
    him;
  and Simeon blessed them and said to Mary his mother,
  "Behold, this child is destined
  for the fall and rise of many in Israel,
  and to be a sign that will be contradicted
  (and you yourself a sword will pierce)
  so that the thoughts of many hearts may be revealed." ✝

FRIDAY, DECEMBER 30
THE HOLY FAMILY OF JESUS, MARY AND JOSEPH

✝ Sirach 3:2-6, 12-14 (or Colossians 3:12-21 or 3:12-17)
Those who fear the Lord honor their parents.

God sets a father in honor over his children;
  a mother's authority he confirms over her sons.
Whoever honors his father atones for sins,
  and preserves himself from them.
When he prays, he is heard;
  he stores up riches who reveres his mother.
Whoever honors his father is gladdened by children,
  and, when he prays, is heard.
Whoever reveres his father will live a long life;
  he who obeys his father brings comfort to his mother.

My son, take care of your father when he is old;
  grieve him not as long as he lives.
Even if his mind fail, be considerate of him;

revile him not all the days of his life;
kindness to a father will not be forgotten,
    firmly planted against the debt of your sins
    —a house raised in justice to you. ✛

Psalm 128:1-2, 3, 4-5

R. (see 1) **Blessed are those who fear the Lord and walk in his ways.**

Blessed is everyone who fears the LORD,
    who walks in his ways!
For you shall eat the fruit of your handiwork;
    blessed shall you be, and favored. **R.**
Your wife shall be like a fruitful vine
    in the recesses of your home;
your children like olive plants
    around your table. **R.**
Behold, thus is the man blessed
    who fears the LORD.
The LORD bless you from Zion:
    may you see the prosperity of Jerusalem
    all the days of your life. **R.**

Colossians 3:15a, 16a

R. Alleluia, alleluia.

Let the peace of Christ control your hearts;
let the word of Christ dwell in you richly. **R.**

† Matthew 2:13-15, 19-23
Take the child and his mother, and flee into Egypt.

When the magi had departed, behold,
    the angel of the Lord appeared to Joseph in a dream and said,
    "Rise, take the child and his mother, flee to Egypt,
    and stay there until I tell you.
Herod is going to search for the child to destroy him."
Joseph rose and took the child and his mother by night
    and departed for Egypt.
He stayed there until the death of Herod,
    that what the Lord had said through the prophet might be fulfilled,
    Out of Egypt I called my son.

When Herod had died, behold,
    the angel of the Lord appeared in a dream
    to Joseph in Egypt and said,
    "Rise, take the child and his mother and go to the land of Israel,
    for those who sought the child's life are dead."
He rose, took the child and his mother,

and went to the land of Israel.
But when he heard that Archelaus was ruling over Judea
  in place of his father Herod,
  he was afraid to go back there.
And because he had been warned in a dream,
  he departed for the region of Galilee.
He went and dwelt in a town called Nazareth,
  so that what had been spoken through the prophets
  might be fulfilled,
  He shall be called a Nazorean. ✛

SATURDAY, DECEMBER 31
SEVENTH DAY WITHIN THE OCTAVE OF THE NATIVITY OF THE LORD, ST. POPE SYLVESTER I

✝ *1 John 2:18-21*
*You have the anointing that comes from the Holy One,
and you have all knowledge.*

Children, it is the last hour;
  and just as you heard that the antichrist was coming,
  so now many antichrists have appeared.
Thus we know this is the last hour.
They went out from us, but they were not really of our number;
  if they had been, they would have remained with us.
Their desertion shows that none of them was of our number.
But you have the anointing that comes from the Holy One,
  and you all have knowledge.
I write to you not because you do not know the truth
  but because you do, and because every lie is alien to the truth. ✛

Psalm 96:1-2a, 11-12, 13
R. (11a) **Let the heavens be glad and the earth rejoice!**
Sing to the LORD a new song;
  sing to the LORD, all you lands.
Sing to the LORD; bless his name;
  announce his salvation, day after day. **R.**
Let the heavens be glad and the earth rejoice;
  let the sea and what fills it resound;
  let the plains be joyful and all that is in them!
Then shall all the trees of the forest exult before the LORD. **R.**
The LORD comes,
  he comes to rule the earth.
He shall rule the world with justice
  and the peoples with his constancy. **R.**

John 1:14a, 12a

R. Alleluia, alleluia.

The Word of God became flesh and dwelt among us.
To those who accepted him
he gave power to become the children of God. **R.**

† *John 1:1-18*
The Word became flesh.

In the beginning was the Word,
and the Word was with God,
and the Word was God.
He was in the beginning with God.
All things came to be through him,
and without him nothing came to be.
What came to be through him was life,
and this life was the light of the human race;
the light shines in the darkness,
and the darkness has not overcome it.

A man named John was sent from God.
He came for testimony, to testify to the light,
so that all might believe through him.
He was not the light,
but came to testify to the light.
The true light, which enlightens everyone, was coming into the
world.

He was in the world,
and the world came to be through him,
but the world did not know him.
He came to what was his own,
but his own people did not accept him.

But to those who did accept him
he gave power to become children of God,
to those who believe in his name,
who were born not by natural generation
nor by human choice nor by a man's decision
but of God.

And the Word became flesh
and made his dwelling among us,
and we saw his glory,
the glory as of the Father's only-begotten Son,
full of grace and truth.

John testified to him and cried out, saying,
"This was he of whom I said,
'The one who is coming after me ranks ahead of me
because he existed before me.'"
From his fullness we have all received,
grace in place of grace,
because while the law was given through Moses,
grace and truth came through Jesus Christ.
No one has ever seen God.
The only-begotten Son, God, who is at the Father's side,
has revealed him. ✛

SUNDAY, JANUARY 1, 2023
THE OCTAVE DAY OF THE NATIVITY OF THE LORD,
SOLEMNITY OF MARY, THE HOLY MOTHER OF GOD

† *Numbers 6:22-27*
They shall invoke my name upon the Israelites, and I will bless them.

The LORD said to Moses:
"Speak to Aaron and his sons and tell them:
This is how you shall bless the Israelites.
Say to them:
The LORD bless you and keep you!
The LORD let his face shine upon
you, and be gracious to you!
The LORD look upon you kindly and
give you peace!
So shall they invoke my name upon the Israelites,
and I will bless them." ✛

Psalm 67:2-3, 5, 6, 8
R. (2a) **May God bless us in his mercy.**
May God have pity on us and bless us;
may he let his face shine upon us.
So may your way be known upon earth;
among all nations, your salvation. **R.**
May the nations be glad and exult
because you rule the peoples in equity;
the nations on the earth you guide. **R.**
May the peoples praise you, O God;
may all the peoples praise you!
May God bless us,
and may all the ends of the earth fear him! **R.**

† *Galatians 4:4-7*
God sent his Son, born of a woman.

Brothers and sisters:
When the fullness of time had come, God sent his Son,
  born of a woman, born under the law,
  to ransom those under the law,
  so that we might receive adoption as sons.
As proof that you are sons,
  God sent the Spirit of his Son into our hearts,
  crying out, "Abba, Father!"
So you are no longer a slave but a son,
  and if a son then also an heir, through God. ✛

Hebrews 1:1-2
R. Alleluia, alleluia.
In the past God spoke to our ancestors through the prophets;
in these last days, he has spoken to us through the Son. **R.**

† *Luke 2:16-21*
They found Mary and Joseph and the infant.
When the eight days were completed, he was named Jesus.

The shepherds went in haste to Bethlehem and found Mary and
  Joseph,
  and the infant lying in the manger.
When they saw this,
  they made known the message
  that had been told them about this child.
All who heard it were amazed
  by what had been told them by the shepherds.
And Mary kept all these things,
  reflecting on them in her heart.
Then the shepherds returned,
  glorifying and praising God
  for all they had heard and seen,
  just as it had been told to them.

When eight days were completed for his circumcision,
  he was named Jesus, the name given him by the angel
  before he was conceived in the womb. ✛

MONDAY, JANUARY 2
St. Basil the Great and St. Gregory Nazianzen

† *1 John 2:22-28*
Let what you heard from the beginning remain in you.

Beloved:
Who is the liar?
Whoever denies that Jesus is the Christ.
Whoever denies the Father and the Son, this is the antichrist.
Anyone who denies the Son does not have the Father,
 but whoever confesses the Son has the Father as well.

Let what you heard from the beginning remain in you.
If what you heard from the beginning remains in you,
 then you will remain in the Son and in the Father.
And this is the promise that he made us: eternal life.
I write you these things about those who would deceive you.
As for you,
 the anointing that you received from him remains in you,
 so that you do not need anyone to teach you.
But his anointing teaches you about everything and is true and not
  false;
 just as it taught you, remain in him.

And now, children, remain in him,
 so that when he appears we may have confidence
 and not be put to shame by him at his coming. ✛

Psalm 98:1, 2-3ab, 3cd-4
**R. (3cd) All the ends of the earth have seen the saving power
 of God.**
Sing to the Lord a new song,
 for he has done wondrous deeds;
His right hand has won victory for him,
 his holy arm. **R.**
The Lord has made his salvation known:
 in the sight of the nations he has revealed his justice.
He has remembered his kindness and his faithfulness
 toward the house of Israel. **R.**
All the ends of the earth have seen
 the salvation by our God.
Sing joyfully to the Lord, all you lands;
 break into song; sing praise. **R.**

Hebrews 1:1-2
R. Alleluia, alleluia

In times past, God spoke to our ancestors through the prophets:
in these last days, he has spoken to us through his Son. **R.**

✝ *John 1:19-28*
There is one who is coming after me.

This is the testimony of John.
When the Jews from Jerusalem sent priests and Levites to him
    to ask him, "Who are you?"
He admitted and did not deny it, but admitted,
    "I am not the Christ."
So they asked him,
    "What are you then? Are you Elijah?"
And he said, "I am not."
"Are you the Prophet?"
He answered, "No."
So they said to him,
    "Who are you, so we can give an answer to those who sent us?
What do you have to say for yourself?"
He said:
    "I am *the voice of one crying out in the desert,*
    'Make straight the way of the Lord,'
    as Isaiah the prophet said."
Some Pharisees were also sent.
They asked him,
    "Why then do you baptize
    if you are not the Christ or Elijah or the Prophet?"
John answered them,
    "I baptize with water;
    but there is one among you whom you do not recognize,
    the one who is coming after me,
    whose sandal strap I am not worthy to untie."
This happened in Bethany across the Jordan,
    where John was baptizing. ✛

TUESDAY, JANUARY 3
CHRISTMAS WEEKDAY, THE MOST HOLY NAME OF JESUS

✝ *1 John 2:29—3:6*
No one who remains in him sins.

If you consider that God is righteous,
    you also know that everyone who acts in righteousness
    is begotten by him.

See what love the Father has bestowed on us
    that we may be called the children of God.

Yet so we are.
The reason the world does not know us is that it did not know him.
Beloved, we are God's children now;
　what we shall be has not yet been revealed.
We do know that when it is revealed we shall be like him,
　for we shall see him as he is.
Everyone who has this hope based on him makes himself pure,
　as he is pure.

Everyone who commits sin commits lawlessness,
　for sin is lawlessness.
You know that he was revealed to take away sins,
　and in him there is no sin.
No one who remains in him sins;
　no one who sins has seen him or known him. ✢

Psalm 98:1, 3cd-4, 5-6
R. (3cd) **All the ends of the earth have seen the saving power of God.**
Sing to the LORD a new song,
　for he has done wondrous deeds;
His right hand has won victory for him,
　his holy arm. **R.**
All the ends of the earth have seen
　the salvation by our God.
Sing joyfully to the LORD, all you lands;
　break into song; sing praise. **R.**
Sing praise to the LORD with the harp,
　with the harp and melodious song.
With trumpets and the sound of the horn
　sing joyfully before the King, the LORD. **R.**

John 1:14a, 12a
R. Alleluia, alleluia.
The Word of God became flesh and dwelt among us.
To those who accepted him
he gave power to become the children of God. **R.**

† John 1:29-34
Behold the Lamb of God.

John the Baptist saw Jesus coming toward him and said,
　"Behold, the Lamb of God, who takes away the sin of the world.
He is the one of whom I said,
　'A man is coming after me who ranks ahead of me
　because he existed before me.'
I did not know him,

but the reason why I came baptizing with water
was that he might be made known to Israel."
John testified further, saying,
"I saw the Spirit come down like a dove from the sky
and remain upon him.
I did not know him,
but the one who sent me to baptize with water told me,
'On whomever you see the Spirit come down and remain,
he is the one who will baptize with the Holy Spirit.'
Now I have seen and testified that he is the Son of God." ✢

WEDNESDAY, JANUARY 4
St. Elizabeth Ann Seton

† *1 John 3:7-10*
Those who are begotten by God commit no sin.

Children, let no one deceive you.
The person who acts in righteousness is righteous,
    just as he is righteous.
Whoever sins belongs to the Devil,
    because the Devil has sinned from the beginning.
Indeed, the Son of God was revealed to destroy the works of the Devil.
No one who is begotten by God commits sin,
    because God's seed remains in him;
    he cannot sin because he is begotten by God.
In this way,
    the children of God and the children of the Devil are made plain;
    no one who fails to act in righteousness belongs to God,
    nor anyone who does not love his brother. ✢

Psalm 98:1, 7-8, 9

R. (3cd) **All the ends of the earth have seen the saving power
    of God.**
Sing to the LORD a new song,
    for he has done wondrous deeds;
His right hand has won victory for him,
    his holy arm. **R.**
Let the sea and what fills it resound,
    the world and those who dwell in it;
Let the rivers clap their hands,
    the mountains shout with them for joy before the LORD. **R.**
The LORD comes;
    he comes to rule the earth;
He will rule the world with justice
    and the peoples with equity. **R.**

Hebrews 1:1-2

R. Alleluia, alleluia

In the past, God spoke to our ancestors through the prophets:
in these last days, he has spoken to us through the Son. **R.**

† John 1:35-42
We have found the Messiah.

John was standing with two of his disciples,
  and as he watched Jesus walk by, he said,
  "Behold, the Lamb of God."
The two disciples heard what he said and followed Jesus.
Jesus turned and saw them following him and said to them,
  "What are you looking for?"
They said to him, "Rabbi" (which translated means Teacher),
  "where are you staying?"
He said to them, "Come, and you will see."
So they went and saw where he was staying,
  and they stayed with him that day.
It was about four in the afternoon.
Andrew, the brother of Simon Peter,
  was one of the two who heard John and followed Jesus.
He first found his own brother Simon and told him,
  "We have found the Messiah," which is translated Christ.
Then he brought him to Jesus.
Jesus looked at him and said,
  "You are Simon the son of John;
  you will be called Cephas," which is translated Peter. ✝

THURSDAY, JANUARY 5
St. John Neumann

† 1 John 3:11-21
We have passed from death to life because we love our brothers.

Beloved:
This is the message you have heard from the beginning:
  we should love one another,
  unlike Cain who belonged to the Evil One
  and slaughtered his brother.
Why did he slaughter him?
Because his own works were evil,
  and those of his brother righteous.
Do not be amazed, then, brothers and sisters, if the world hates you.
We know that we have passed from death to life
  because we love our brothers.
Whoever does not love remains in death.

Everyone who hates his brother is a murderer,
  and you know that no murderer has eternal life remaining in him.
The way we came to know love
  was that he laid down his life for us;
  so we ought to lay down our lives for our brothers.
If someone who has worldly means
  sees a brother in need and refuses him compassion,
  how can the love of God remain in him?
Children, let us love not in word or speech
  but in deed and truth.

Now this is how we shall know that we belong to the truth
  and reassure our hearts before him
  in whatever our hearts condemn,
  for God is greater than our hearts and knows everything.
Beloved, if our hearts do not condemn us,
  we have confidence in God. ✛

Psalm 100:1b-2, 3, 4, 5

R. (2a) **Let all the earth cry out to God with joy.**

Sing joyfully to the LORD, all you lands;
  serve the LORD with gladness;
  come before him with joyful song. **R.**
Know that the LORD is God;
  he made us, his we are;
  his people, the flock he tends. **R.**
Enter his gates with thanksgiving,
  his courts with praise;
Give thanks to him; bless his name. **R.**
The LORD is good:
  the LORD, whose kindness endures forever,
  and his faithfulness, to all generations. **R.**

R. Alleluia, alleluia.

A holy day has dawned upon us.
Come, you nations, and adore the Lord.
Today a great light has come upon the earth. **R.**

† *John 1:43-51*
You are the Son of God; you are the King of Israel.

Jesus decided to go to Galilee, and he found Philip.
And Jesus said to him, "Follow me."
Now Philip was from Bethsaida, the town of Andrew and Peter.
Philip found Nathanael and told him,
  "We have found the one about whom Moses wrote in the law,
  and also the prophets, Jesus, son of Joseph, from Nazareth."

But Nathanael said to him,
  "Can anything good come from Nazareth?"
Philip said to him, "Come and see."
Jesus saw Nathanael coming toward him and said of him,
  "Here is a true child of Israel.
There is no duplicity in him."
Nathanael said to him, "How do you know me?"
Jesus answered and said to him,
  "Before Philip called you, I saw you under the fig tree."
Nathanael answered him,
  "Rabbi, you are the Son of God; you are the King of Israel."
Jesus answered and said to him,
  "Do you believe
because I told you that I saw you under the fig tree?
You will see greater things than this."
And he said to him, "Amen, amen, I say to you,
  you will see the sky opened and the angels of God
  ascending and descending on the Son of Man." ✛

FRIDAY, JANUARY 6
CHRISTMAS WEEKDAY, ST. ANDRÉ BESSETTE

† *1 John 5:5-13*
The Spirit, the water, and the Blood.

Beloved:
Who indeed is the victor over the world
  but the one who believes that Jesus is the Son of God?

This is the one who came through water and Blood, Jesus Christ,
  not by water alone, but by water and Blood.
The Spirit is the one who testifies,
  and the Spirit is truth.
So there are three that testify,
  the Spirit, the water, and the Blood,
  and the three are of one accord.
If we accept human testimony,
  the testimony of God is surely greater.
Now the testimony of God is this,
  that he has testified on behalf of his Son.
Whoever believes in the Son of God
  has this testimony within himself.
Whoever does not believe God has made him a liar
  by not believing the testimony God has given about his Son.
And this is the testimony:
  God gave us eternal life,

and this life is in his Son.
Whoever possesses the Son has life;
 whoever does not possess the Son of God does not have life.

I write these things to you so that you may know
 that you have eternal life,
 you who believe in the name of the Son of God. ✛

Psalm 147:12-13, 14-15, 19-20

R. (12a) **Praise the Lord, Jerusalem.** *(or* **Alleluia.***)*

Glorify the LORD, O Jerusalem;
 praise your God, O Zion.
For he has strengthened the bars of your gates;
 he has blessed your children within you. **R.**
He has granted peace in your borders;
 with the best of wheat he fills you.
He sends forth his command to the earth;
 swiftly runs his word! **R.**
He has proclaimed his word to Jacob,
 his statutes and his ordinances to Israel.
He has not done thus for any other nation;
 his ordinances he has not made known to them. Alleluia. **R.**

See Mark 9:6

R. Alleluia, alleluia.

The heavens were opened and the voice of the Father thundered:
This is my beloved Son. Listen to him. **R.**

*✝ **Mark 1:7-11** (or Luke 3:23–38 or 3:23, 31–34, 36, 38)*
You are my beloved Son; with you I am well pleased.

This is what John the Baptist proclaimed:
 "One mightier than I is coming after me.
I am not worthy to stoop and loosen the thongs of his sandals.
I have baptized you with water;
 he will baptize you with the Holy Spirit."

It happened in those days that Jesus came from Nazareth of Galilee
 and was baptized in the Jordan by John.
On coming up out of the water he saw the heavens being torn open
 and the Spirit, like a dove, descending upon him.
And a voice came from the heavens,
 "You are my beloved Son; with you I am well pleased." ✛

SATURDAY, JANUARY 7
CHRISTMAS WEEKDAY, ST. RAYMOND OF PENYAFORT

† *1 John 5:14-21*
God hears us in regard to whatever we ask.

Beloved:
We have this confidence in God
   that if we ask anything according to his will, he hears us.
And if we know that he hears us in regard to whatever we ask,
   we know that what we have asked him for is ours.
If anyone sees his brother sinning, if the sin is not deadly,
   he should pray to God and he will give him life.
This is only for those whose sin is not deadly.
There is such a thing as deadly sin,
   about which I do not say that you should pray.
All wrongdoing is sin, but there is sin that is not deadly.

We know that no one begotten by God sins;
   but the one begotten by God he protects,
   and the Evil One cannot touch him.
We know that we belong to God,
   and the whole world is under the power of the Evil One.
We also know that the Son of God has come
   and has given us discernment to know the one who is true.
And we are in the one who is true, in his Son Jesus Christ.
He is the true God and eternal life.
Children, be on your guard against idols. ✛

   Psalm 149:1-2, 3-4, 5-6a, 9b
R. (see 4a) **The Lord takes delight in his people.** (*or* **Alleluia.**)
Sing to the LORD a new song
   of praise in the assembly of the faithful.
Let Israel be glad in their maker,
   let the children of Zion rejoice in their king. **R.**
Let them praise his name in the festive dance,
   let them sing praise to him with timbrel and harp.
For the LORD loves his people,
   and he adorns the lowly with victory. **R.**
Let the faithful exult in glory;
   let them sing for joy upon their couches;
let the high praises of God be in their throats.
   This is the glory of all his faithful. Alleluia. **R.**

Luke 7:16

R. Alleluia, alleluia.

A great prophet has arisen in our midst
and God has visited his people. **R.**

† *John 2:1-11*
Jesus did this as the beginning of his signs at Cana in Galilee.

There was a wedding at Cana in Galilee,
and the mother of Jesus was there.
Jesus and his disciples were also invited to the wedding.
When the wine ran short,
the mother of Jesus said to him,
"They have no wine."
And Jesus said to her,
"Woman, how does your concern affect me?
My hour has not yet come."
His mother said to the servers,
"Do whatever he tells you."
Now there were six stone water jars there for Jewish ceremonial
washings,
each holding twenty to thirty gallons.
Jesus told them,
"Fill the jars with water."
So they filled them to the brim.
Then he told them,
"Draw some out now and take it to the headwaiter."
So they took it.
And when the headwaiter tasted the water that had become wine,
without knowing where it came from
(although the servers who had drawn the water knew),
the headwaiter called the bridegroom and said to him,
"Everyone serves good wine first,
and then when people have drunk freely, an inferior one;
but you have kept the good wine until now."
Jesus did this as the beginning of his signs at Cana in Galilee
and so revealed his glory,
and his disciples began to believe in him. ✛

SUNDAY, JANUARY 8
THE EPIPHANY OF THE LORD

† *Isaiah 60:1-6*
The glory of the Lord shines upon you.

Rise up in splendor, Jerusalem! Your light has come,
the glory of the Lord shines upon you.

See, darkness covers the earth,
   and thick clouds cover the peoples;
but upon you the LORD shines,
   and over you appears his glory.
Nations shall walk by your light,
   and kings by your shining radiance.
Raise your eyes and look about;
   they all gather and come to you:
your sons come from afar,
   and your daughters in the arms of their nurses.

Then you shall be radiant at what you see,
   your heart shall throb and overflow,
for the riches of the sea shall be emptied out before you,
   the wealth of nations shall be brought to you.
Caravans of camels shall fill you,
   dromedaries from Midian and Ephah;
all from Sheba shall come
   bearing gold and frankincense,
   and proclaiming the praises of the LORD. ✙

Psalm 72:1-2, 7-8, 10-11, 12-13
R. (see 11) **Lord, every nation on earth will adore you.**
O God, with your judgment endow the king,
   and with your justice, the king's son;
he shall govern your people with justice
   and your afflicted ones with judgment. **R.**
Justice shall flower in his days,
   and profound peace, till the moon be no more.
May he rule from sea to sea,
   and from the River to the ends of the earth. **R.**
The kings of Tarshish and the Isles shall offer gifts;
   the kings of Arabia and Seba shall bring tribute.
All kings shall pay him homage,
   all nations shall serve him. **R.**
For he shall rescue the poor when he cries out,
   and the afflicted when he has no one to help him.
He shall have pity for the lowly and the poor;
   the lives of the poor he shall save. **R.**

† *Ephesians 3:2-3a, 5-6*
Now it has been revealed that the Gentiles are coheirs of the promise.

Brothers and sisters:
You have heard of the stewardship of God's grace
   that was given to me for your benefit,

namely, that the mystery was made known to me by revelation.
It was not made known to people in other generations
as it has now been revealed
to his holy apostles and prophets by the Spirit:
that the Gentiles are coheirs, members of the same body,
and copartners in the promise in Christ Jesus through the gospel. ✛

Matthew 2:2
R. Alleluia, alleluia.
We saw his star at its rising
and have come to do him homage. **R.**

✝ Matthew 2:1-12

We saw his star at its rising and have come to do him homage.

When Jesus was born in Bethlehem of Judea,
in the days of King Herod,
behold, magi from the east arrived in Jerusalem, saying,
"Where is the newborn king of the Jews?
We saw his star at its rising
and have come to do him homage."
When King Herod heard this,
he was greatly troubled,
and all Jerusalem with him.
Assembling all the chief priests and the scribes of the people,
he inquired of them where the Christ was to be born.
They said to him, "In Bethlehem of Judea,
for thus it has been written through the prophet:
And you, Bethlehem, land of Judah,
are by no means least among the rulers of Judah;
since from you shall come a ruler,
who is to shepherd my people Israel."
Then Herod called the magi secretly
and ascertained from them the time of the star's appearance.
He sent them to Bethlehem and said,
"Go and search diligently for the child.
When you have found him, bring me word,
that I too may go and do him homage."
After their audience with the king they set out.
And behold, the star that they had seen at its rising preceded them,
until it came and stopped over the place where the child was.
They were overjoyed at seeing the star,
and on entering the house
they saw the child with Mary his mother.
They prostrated themselves and did him homage.
Then they opened their treasures

and offered him gifts of gold, frankincense, and myrrh.
And having been warned in a dream not to return to Herod,
they departed for their country by another way. ✛

MONDAY, JANUARY 9
THE BAPTISM OF THE LORD

✝Isaiah 42:1-4, 6-7 (or Acts 10:34-38)
Behold my servant with whom I am well pleased.

Thus says the LORD:
Here is my servant whom I uphold,
   my chosen one with whom I am pleased,
upon whom I have put my spirit;
   he shall bring forth justice to the nations,
not crying out, not shouting,
   not making his voice heard in the street.
A bruised reed he shall not break,
   and a smoldering wick he shall not quench,
until he establishes justice on the earth;
   the coastlands will wait for his teaching.

I, the LORD, have called you for the victory of justice,
   I have grasped you by the hand;
I formed you, and set you
   as a covenant of the people,
   a light for the nations,
to open the eyes of the blind,
   to bring out prisoners from confinement,
   and from the dungeon, those who live in darkness. ✛

Psalm 29:1bc-2, 3ac-4, 3b and 9c-10
R. (11b) The Lord will bless his people with peace.
Give to the LORD, you sons of God,
   give to the LORD glory and praise,
Give to the LORD the glory due his name;
   adore the LORD in holy attire. **R.**
The voice of the LORD is over the waters,
   the LORD, over vast waters.
The voice of the LORD is mighty;
   the voice of the LORD is majestic. **R.**
The God of glory thunders,
   and in his temple all say, "Glory!"
The LORD is enthroned above the flood;
   the LORD is enthroned as king forever. **R.**

See Mark 9:7
R. Alleluia, alleluia.
The heavens were opened and the voice of the Father thundered:
This is my beloved Son, listen to him. **R.**

✝ Matthew 3:13-17
After Jesus was baptized, he saw the Spirit of God coming upon him.

Jesus came from Galilee to John at the Jordan
  to be baptized by him.
John tried to prevent him, saying,
  "I need to be baptized by you,
  and yet you are coming to me?"
Jesus said to him in reply,
  "Allow it now, for thus it is fitting for us
  to fulfill all righteousness."
Then he allowed him.
After Jesus was baptized,
  he came up from the water and behold,
  the heavens were opened for him,
  and he saw the Spirit of God descending like a dove
  and coming upon him.
And a voice came from the heavens, saying,
  "This is my beloved Son, with whom I am well pleased." ✛

TUESDAY, JANUARY 10
WEEKDAY (FIRST WEEK IN ORDINARY TIME)
When the Baptism of the Lord occurs on Monday of the First Week in Ordinary Time,
the readings assigned to Monday may be joined to those of Tuesday
so that the opening of each book will be read.)

✝ Hebrews 2:5-12 *(or Hebrews 1:1-6 and 2:5-12)*
He made the one who leads them to their salvation perfect through suffering.

It was not to angels that God subjected the world to come,
  of which we are speaking.
Instead, someone has testified somewhere:

  What is man that you are mindful of him,
    or the son of man that you care for him?
  You made him for a little while lower than the angels;
    you crowned him with glory and honor,
    subjecting all things under his feet.

In "subjecting" all things to him,
  he left nothing not "subject to him."
Yet at present we do not see "all things subject to him,"
  but we do see Jesus "crowned with glory and honor"

because he suffered death,
he who "for a little while" was made "lower than the angels,"
that by the grace of God he might taste death for everyone.

For it was fitting that he,
for whom and through whom all things exist,
in bringing many children to glory,
should make the leader to their salvation perfect through suffering.
He who consecrates
and those who are being consecrated all have one origin.
Therefore, he is not ashamed to call them "brothers" saying:

*I will proclaim your name to my brethren,
in the midst of the assembly I will praise you.* ✚

Psalm 8:2ab and 5, 6-7, 8-9 (or Psalm 97:1 and 2b, 6 and 7c, 9)
R. (see 7) **You have given your Son rule over the works of
your hands.**
O LORD, our Lord,
how glorious is your name over all the earth!
What is man that you should be mindful of him,
or the son of man that you should care for him? **R.**
You have made him little less than the angels,
and crowned him with glory and honor.
You have given him rule over the works of your hands,
putting all things under his feet. **R.**
All sheep and oxen,
yes, and the beasts of the field,
The birds of the air, the fishes of the sea,
and whatever swims the paths of the seas. **R.**

See 1 Thessalonians 2:13
R. Alleluia, alleluia.
Receive the word of God, not as the word of men,
but as it truly is, the word of God. **R.**

✝ ***Mark 1:21-28*** *(or Mark 1:14-20 and 1:21-28)*
Jesus taught them as one having authority.

Jesus came to Capernaum with his followers,
and on the sabbath he entered the synagogue and taught.
The people were astonished at his teaching,
for he taught them as one having authority and not as the scribes.
In their synagogue was a man with an unclean spirit;
he cried out, "What have you to do with us, Jesus of Nazareth?
Have you come to destroy us?
I know who you are—the Holy One of God!"

Jesus rebuked him and said, "Quiet! Come out of him!"
The unclean spirit convulsed him and with a loud cry came out of
    him.
All were amazed and asked one another,
    "What is this?
A new teaching with authority.
He commands even the unclean spirits and they obey him."
His fame spread everywhere throughout the whole region of Galilee. ✛

WEDNESDAY, JANUARY 11
WEEKDAY

† Hebrews 2:14-18
*He had to become like his brothers and sisters in every way,
that he might be merciful.*

Since the children share in blood and Flesh,
    Jesus likewise shared in them,
    that through death he might destroy the one
    who has the power of death, that is, the Devil,
    and free those who through fear of death
    had been subject to slavery all their life.

Surely he did not help angels
    but rather the descendants of Abraham;
    therefore, he had to become like his brothers and sisters in every
        way,
    that he might be a merciful and faithful high priest before God
    to expiate the sins of the people.
Because he himself was tested through what he suffered,
    he is able to help those who are being tested. ✛

Psalm 105:1-2, 3-4, 6-7, 8-9
R. (8a) **The Lord remembers his covenant for ever.**
    *(or **Alleluia**.)*
Give thanks to the LORD, invoke his name;
    make known among the nations his deeds.
Sing to him, sing his praise,
    proclaim all his wondrous deeds. **R.**
Glory in his holy name;
    rejoice, O hearts that seek the LORD!
Look to the LORD in his strength;
    seek to serve him constantly. **R.**
You descendants of Abraham, his servants,
    sons of Jacob, his chosen ones!
He, the LORD, is our God;
    throughout the earth his judgments prevail. **R.**

He remembers forever his covenant
  which he made binding for a thousand generations—
Which he entered into with Abraham
  and by his oath to Isaac. **R.**

   John 10:27
R. Alleluia, alleluia.
My sheep hear my voice, says the Lord.
I know them, and they follow me. **R.**

† *Mark 1:29-39*
Jesus cured many who were sick with various diseases.

On leaving the synagogue
  Jesus entered the house of Simon and Andrew with James and
    John.
Simon's mother-in-law lay sick with a fever.
They immediately told him about her.
He approached, grasped her hand, and helped her up.
Then the fever left her and she waited on them.

When it was evening, after sunset,
  they brought to him all who were ill or possessed by demons.
The whole town was gathered at the door.
He cured many who were sick with various diseases,
  and he drove out many demons,
  not permitting them to speak because they knew him.

Rising very early before dawn,
  he left and went off to a deserted place, where he prayed.
Simon and those who were with him pursued him
  and on finding him said, "Everyone is looking for you."
He told them, "Let us go on to the nearby villages
  that I may preach there also.
For this purpose have I come."
So he went into their synagogues, preaching and driving out demons
  throughout the whole of Galilee. ✛

THURSDAY, JANUARY 12
WEEKDAY

† *Hebrews 3:7-14*
Encourage yourselves daily while it is still "today."

The Holy Spirit says:
  Oh, that today you would hear his voice,
    "Harden not your hearts as at the rebellion
    in the day of testing in the desert,

where your ancestors tested and tried me
and saw my works for forty years.
Because of this I was provoked with that generation
and I said, 'They have always been of erring heart,
and they do not know my ways.'
As I swore in my wrath,
'They shall not enter into my rest.'"
Take care, brothers and sisters,
that none of you may have an evil and unfaithful heart,
so as to forsake the living God.
Encourage yourselves daily while it is still "today,"
so that none of you may grow hardened by the deceit of sin.
We have become partners of Christ
if only we hold the beginning of the reality firm until the end. ✛

Psalm 95:6-7ab, 7c-9, 10-11
R. (8) **If today you hear his voice, harden not your hearts.**
Come, let us bow down in worship;
let us kneel before the LORD who made us.
For he is our God,
and we are the people he shepherds, the flock he guides. **R.**
Oh, that today you would hear his voice:
"Harden not your hearts as at Meribah,
as in the day of Massah in the desert,
Where your fathers tempted me;
they tested me though they had seen my works." **R.**
Forty years I was wearied of that generation;
I said: "This people's heart goes astray,
they do not know my ways."
Therefore I swore in my anger:
"They shall never enter my rest." **R.**

See Matthew 4:23
R. Alleluia, alleluia.
Jesus preached the Gospel of the Kingdom
and cured every disease among the people. **R.**

† *Mark 1:40-45*
The leprosy left him, and he was made clean.

A leper came to him and kneeling down begged him and said,
"If you wish, you can make me clean."
Moved with pity, he stretched out his hand,
touched the leper, and said to him,
"I do will it. Be made clean."
The leprosy left him immediately, and he was made clean.
Then, warning him sternly, he dismissed him at once.

Then he said to him, "See that you tell no one anything,
but go, show yourself to the priest
and offer for your cleansing what Moses prescribed;
that will be proof for them."
The man went away and began to publicize the whole matter.
He spread the report abroad
so that it was impossible for Jesus to enter a town openly.
He remained outside in deserted places,
and people kept coming to him from everywhere. ✝

FRIDAY, JANUARY 13
WEEKDAY, ST. HILARY

✝ *Hebrews 4:1-5, 11*
Let us strive to enter into that rest.

Let us be on our guard
while the promise of entering into his rest remains,
that none of you seem to have failed.
For in fact we have received the Good News just as our ancestors did.
But the word that they heard did not profit them,
for they were not united in faith with those who listened.
For we who believed enter into that rest,
just as he has said:

As I swore in my wrath,
"They shall not enter into my rest,"

and yet his works were accomplished
at the foundation of the world.
For he has spoken somewhere about the seventh day in this manner,
And God rested on the seventh day from all his works;
and again, in the previously mentioned place,
They shall not enter into my rest.

Therefore, let us strive to enter into that rest,
so that no one may fall after the same example of disobedience. ✝

Psalm 78:3 and 4bc, 6c-7, 8
R. (see 7b) **Do not forget the works of the Lord!**
What we have heard and know,
and what our fathers have declared to us,
we will declare to the generation to come
The glorious deeds of the LORD and his strength. **R.**
That they too may rise and declare to their sons
that they should put their hope in God,
And not forget the deeds of God

but keep his commands. **R.**
And not be like their fathers,
   a generation wayward and rebellious,
A generation that kept not its heart steadfast
   nor its spirit faithful toward God. **R.**

Luke 7:16
R. Alleluia, alleluia.
A great prophet has arisen in our midst
and God has visited his people. **R.**

✝ Mark 2:1-12
The Son of Man has authority to forgive sins on earth.

When Jesus returned to Capernaum after some days,
   it became known that he was at home.
Many gathered together so that there was no longer room for them,
   not even around the door,
   and he preached the word to them.
They came bringing to him a paralytic carried by four men.
Unable to get near Jesus because of the crowd,
   they opened up the roof above him.
After they had broken through,
   they let down the mat on which the paralytic was lying.
When Jesus saw their faith, he said to him,
   "Child, your sins are forgiven."
Now some of the scribes were sitting there asking themselves,
   "Why does this man speak that way? He is blaspheming.
Who but God alone can forgive sins?"
Jesus immediately knew in his mind what
   they were thinking to themselves,
   so he said, "Why are you thinking such things in your hearts?
Which is easier, to say to the paralytic,
   'Your sins are forgiven,'
   or to say, 'Rise, pick up your mat and walk'?
But that you may know
   that the Son of Man has authority to forgive sins on earth"
   —he said to the paralytic,
   "I say to you, rise, pick up your mat, and go home."
He rose, picked up his mat at once,
   and went away in the sight of everyone.
They were all astounded
   and glorified God, saying, "We have never seen anything like this." ✛

SATURDAY, JANUARY 14
Weekday, *[BVM]*

† *Hebrews 4:12-16*
Let us confidently approach the throne of grace.

The word of God is living and effective,
   sharper than any two-edged sword,
   penetrating even between soul and spirit,
   joints and marrow,
   and able to discern reflections and thoughts of the heart.
No creature is concealed from him,
   but everything is naked and exposed to the eyes of him
   to whom we must render an account.

Since we have a great high priest who has passed through the
      heavens,
   Jesus, the Son of God,
   let us hold fast to our confession.
For we do not have a high priest
   who is unable to sympathize with our weaknesses,
   but one who has similarly been tested in every way,
   yet without sin.
So let us confidently approach the throne of grace
   to receive mercy and to find grace for timely help. ✛

Psalm 19:8, 9, 10, 15

R. (see John 6:63c) **Your words, Lord, are Spirit and life.**
The law of the LORD is perfect,
   refreshing the soul;
The decree of the LORD is trustworthy,
   giving wisdom to the simple. **R.**
The precepts of the LORD are right,
   rejoicing the heart;
The command of the LORD is clear,
   enlightening the eye. **R.**
The fear of the LORD is pure,
   enduring forever;
The ordinances of the LORD are true,
   all of them just. **R.**
Let the words of my mouth and the thought of my heart
   find favor before you,
   O LORD, my rock and my redeemer. **R.**

Luke 4:18
R. Alleluia, alleluia.
The Lord sent me to bring glad tidings to the poor
and to proclaim liberty to captives. **R.**

† *Mark 2:13-17*
I did not come to call the righteous but sinners.

Jesus went out along the sea.
All the crowd came to him and he taught them.
As he passed by, he saw Levi, son of Alphaeus,
    sitting at the customs post.
Jesus said to him, "Follow me."
And he got up and followed Jesus.
While he was at table in his house,
    many tax collectors and sinners sat with Jesus and his disciples;
    for there were many who followed him.
Some scribes who were Pharisees saw that Jesus was eating with
      sinners
    and tax collectors and said to his disciples,
    "Why does he eat with tax collectors and sinners?"
Jesus heard this and said to them,
    "Those who are well do not need a physician, but the sick do.
I did not come to call the righteous but sinners." ✛

SUNDAY, JANUARY 15
SECOND SUNDAY IN ORDINARY TIME

† *Isaiah 49:3, 5-6*
I will make you a light to the nations,
that my salvation may reach to the ends of the earth.

The LORD said to me: You are my servant,
    Israel, through whom I show my glory.
Now the LORD has spoken
    who formed me as his servant from the womb,
that Jacob may be brought back to him
    and Israel gathered to him;
and I am made glorious in the sight of the LORD,
    and my God is now my strength!
It is too little, the LORD says, for you to be my servant,
    to raise up the tribes of Jacob,
    and restore the survivors of Israel;
I will make you a light to the nations,
    that my salvation may reach to the ends of the earth. ✛

Psalm 40:2 and 4, 7-8a, 8b-9, 10

R. (8a and 9a) **Here am I, Lord; I come to do your will.**

I have waited, waited for the LORD,
  and he stooped toward me and heard my cry.
And he put a new song into my mouth,
  a hymn to our God. **R.**
Sacrifice or offering you wished not,
  but ears open to obedience you gave me.
Holocausts or sin-offerings you sought not;
  then said I, "Behold I come." **R.**
"In the written scroll it is prescribed for me,
to do your will, O my God, is my delight,
  and your law is within my heart!" **R.**
I announced your justice in the vast assembly;
  I did not restrain my lips, as you, O LORD, know. **R.**

† *1 Corinthians 1:1-3*
Grace to you and peace from God our Father and the Lord Jesus Christ.

Paul, called to be an apostle of Christ Jesus by the will of God,
  and Sosthenes our brother,
  to the church of God that is in Corinth,
  to you who have been sanctified in Christ Jesus, called to be holy,
  with all those everywhere who call upon the name of our Lord
    Jesus Christ, their Lord and ours.
Grace to you and peace from God our Father
  and the Lord Jesus Christ. ✚

John 1:14a, 12a

R. Alleluia, alleluia.
The Word of God became flesh and dwelt among us.
To those who accepted him,
he gave power to become children of God. **R.**

† *John 1:29-34*
Behold, the Lamb of God who takes away the sin of the world.

John the Baptist saw Jesus coming toward him and said,
  "Behold, the Lamb of God, who takes away the sin of the world.
He is the one of whom I said,
  'A man is coming after me who ranks ahead of me
  because he existed before me.'
I did not know him,
  but the reason why I came baptizing with water
  was that he might be made known to Israel."
John testified further, saying,
  "I saw the Spirit come down like a dove from heaven

and remain upon him.
I did not know him,
but the one who sent me to baptize with water told me,
'On whomever you see the Spirit come down and remain,
he is the one who will baptize with the Holy Spirit.'
Now I have seen and testified that he is the Son of God."✣

MONDAY, JANUARY 16
WEEKDAY

† *Hebrews 5:1-10*
Son though he was, he learned obedience from what he suffered.

Brothers and sisters:
Every high priest is taken from among men
and made their representative before God,
to offer gifts and sacrifices for sins.
He is able to deal patiently with the ignorant and erring,
for he himself is beset by weakness
and so, for this reason, must make sin offerings for himself
as well as for the people.
No one takes this honor upon himself
but only when called by God,
just as Aaron was.
In the same way,
it was not Christ who glorified himself in becoming high priest,
but rather the one who said to him:
You are my Son:
this day I have begotten you;
just as he says in another place,
You are a priest forever
according to the order of Melchizedek.
In the days when he was in the Flesh,
he offered prayers and supplications with loud cries and tears
to the one who was able to save him from death,
and he was heard because of his reverence.
Son though he was, he learned obedience from what he suffered;
and when he was made perfect,
he became the source of eternal salvation for all who obey him. ✣

Psalm 110:1, 2, 3, 4
R. (4b) **You are a priest for ever, in the line of Melchizedek.**
The Lord said to my Lord: "Sit at my right hand
till I make your enemies your footstool." **R.**
The scepter of your power the Lord will stretch forth from Zion:
"Rule in the midst of your enemies." **R.**

"Yours is princely power in the day of your birth, in holy splendor;
    before the daystar, like the dew, I have begotten you." **R.**
The LORD has sworn, and he will not repent:
    "You are a priest forever, according to the order of Melchizedek." **R.**

Hebrews 4:12
R. Alleluia, alleluia.
The word of God is living and effective,
able to discern reflections and thoughts of the heart. **R.**

† *Mark 2:18-22*
The bridegroom is with them.

The disciples of John and of the Pharisees were accustomed to fast.
People came to Jesus and objected,
    "Why do the disciples of John and the disciples of the Pharisees
        fast,
    but your disciples do not fast?"
Jesus answered them,
    "Can the wedding guests fast while the bridegroom is with them?
As long as they have the bridegroom with them they cannot fast.
But the days will come when the bridegroom is taken away from
        them,
    and then they will fast on that day.
No one sews a piece of unshrunken cloth on an old cloak.
If he does, its fullness pulls away,
    the new from the old, and the tear gets worse.
Likewise, no one pours new wine into old wineskins.
Otherwise, the wine will burst the skins,
    and both the wine and the skins are ruined.
Rather, new wine is poured into fresh wineskins." ✛

TUESDAY, JANUARY 17
ST. ANTHONY

† *Hebrews 6:10-20*
This hope we have as an anchor sure and firm.

Brothers and sisters:
God is not unjust so as to overlook your work
    and the love you have demonstrated for his name
    by having served and continuing to serve the holy ones.
We earnestly desire each of you to demonstrate the same eagerness
    for the fulfillment of hope until the end,
    so that you may not become sluggish, but imitators of those who,
    through faith and patience, are inheriting the promises.

When God made the promise to Abraham,

since he had no one greater by whom to swear, *he swore by himself,*
and said, *I will indeed bless you and multiply you.*
And so, after patient waiting, Abraham obtained the promise.
Now, men swear by someone greater than themselves;
for them an oath serves as a guarantee
and puts an end to all argument.
So when God wanted to give the heirs of his promise
an even clearer demonstration of the immutability of his purpose,
he intervened with an oath,
so that by two immutable things,
in which it was impossible for God to lie,
we who have taken refuge might be strongly encouraged
to hold fast to the hope that lies before us.
This we have as an anchor of the soul,
sure and firm, which reaches into the interior behind the veil,
where Jesus has entered on our behalf as forerunner,
becoming high priest forever
according to the order of Melchizedek. ✢

Psalm 111:1-2, 4-5, 9 and 10c
R. (5) **The Lord will remember his covenant for ever.**
(or **Alleluia.***)*
I will give thanks to the LORD with all my heart
in the company and assembly of the just.
Great are the works of the LORD,
exquisite in all their delights. **R.**
He has won renown for his wondrous deeds;
gracious and merciful is the LORD.
He has given food to those who fear him;
he will forever be mindful of his covenant. **R.**
He has sent deliverance to his people;
he has ratified his covenant forever;
holy and awesome is his name.
His praise endures forever. **R.**

See Ephesians 1:17-18
R. Alleluia, alleluia.
May the Father of our Lord Jesus Christ
enlighten the eyes of our hearts,
that we may know what is the hope
that belongs to our call. **R.**

† *Mark 2:23-28*
The sabbath was made for people, not people for the sabbath.

As Jesus was passing through a field of grain on the sabbath,

his disciples began to make a path while picking the heads of grain.
At this the Pharisees said to him,
"Look, why are they doing what is unlawful on the sabbath?"
He said to them,
"Have you never read what David did
when he was in need and he and his companions were hungry?
How he went into the house of God when Abiathar was high priest
and ate the bread of offering that only the priests could lawfully eat,
and shared it with his companions?"
Then he said to them,
"The sabbath was made for man, not man for the sabbath.
That is why the Son of Man is lord even of the sabbath." ✛

WEDNESDAY, JANUARY 18
WEEKDAY

† Hebrews 7:1-3, 15-17
You are a priest forever according to the order of Melchizedek.

*M*elchizedek, king of Salem and priest of God Most High,
   met Abraham as he returned from his defeat of the kings
   and *blessed him.*
And Abraham apportioned to him *a tenth of everything.*
His name first means righteous king,
   and he was also "king of Salem," that is, king of peace.
Without father, mother, or ancestry,
   without beginning of days or end of life,
   thus made to resemble the Son of God, he remains a priest forever.

It is even more obvious if another priest is raised up
   after the likeness of Melchizedek, who has become so,
   not by a law expressed in a commandment concerning physical
      descent
   but by the power of a life that cannot be destroyed.
For it is testified:

You are a priest forever according to the order of Melchizedek. ✛

   Psalm 110:1, 2, 3, 4

R. (4b) **You are a priest for ever, in the line of Melchizedek.**
The LORD said to my Lord: "Sit at my right hand
   till I make your enemies your footstool." **R.**
The scepter of your power the LORD will stretch forth from Zion:
   "Rule in the midst of your enemies." **R.**
"Yours is princely power in the day of your birth, in holy splendor;
   before the daystar, like the dew, I have begotten you." **R.**
The LORD has sworn, and he will not repent:

"You are a priest forever, according to the order of Melchizedek." **R.**

See Matthew 4:23

R. Alleluia, alleluia.
Jesus preached the Gospel of the Kingdom
and cured every disease among the people. **R.**

† *Mark 3:1-6*
Is it lawful on the sabbath to save life rather than to destroy it?

Jesus entered the synagogue.
There was a man there who had a withered hand.
They watched Jesus closely
   to see if he would cure him on the sabbath
   so that they might accuse him.
He said to the man with the withered hand,
   "Come up here before us."
Then he said to the Pharisees,
   "Is it lawful to do good on the sabbath rather than to do evil,
   to save life rather than to destroy it?"
But they remained silent.
Looking around at them with anger
   and grieved at their hardness of heart,
   Jesus said to the man, "Stretch out your hand."
He stretched it out and his hand was restored.
The Pharisees went out and immediately took counsel
   with the Herodians against him to put him to death. ✛

THURSDAY, JANUARY 19
WEEKDAY

† *Hebrews 7:25—8:6*
He offered sacrifice once for all when he offered himself.

Jesus is always able to save those who approach God through him,
   since he lives forever to make intercession for them.

It was fitting that we should have such a high priest:
   holy, innocent, undefiled, separated from sinners,
   higher than the heavens.
He has no need, as did the high priests,
   to offer sacrifice day after day,
   first for his own sins and then for those of the people;
   he did that once for all when he offered himself.
For the law appoints men subject to weakness to be high priests,
   but the word of the oath, which was taken after the law,
   appoints a son, who has been made perfect forever.

The main point of what has been said is this:

we have such a high priest,
   who has taken his seat at the right hand of the throne
   of the Majesty in heaven, a minister of the sanctuary
   and of the true tabernacle that the Lord, not man, set up.
Now every high priest is appointed to offer gifts and sacrifices;
   thus the necessity for this one also to have something to offer.
If then he were on earth, he would not be a priest,
   since there are those who offer gifts according to the law.
They worship in a copy and shadow of the heavenly sanctuary,
   as Moses was warned when he was about to erect the tabernacle.
For God says, "See that you make everything
   according to the pattern shown you on the mountain."
Now he has obtained so much more excellent a ministry
   as he is mediator of a better covenant,
   enacted on better promises. ✛

Psalm 40:7-8a, 8b-9, 10, 17

R. (8a and 9a) **Here am I, Lord; I come to do your will.**
Sacrifice or oblation you wished not,
   but ears open to obedience you gave me.
Burnt offerings or sin-offerings you sought not;
   then said I, "Behold I come." **R.**
"In the written scroll it is prescribed for me,
To do your will, O my God, is my delight,
   and your law is within my heart!" **R.**
I announced your justice in the vast assembly;
   I did not restrain my lips, as you, O LORD, know. **R.**
May all who seek you
   exult and be glad in you,
And may those who love your salvation
   say ever, "The LORD be glorified." **R.**

See 2 Timothy 1:10

R. Alleluia, alleluia.
Our Savior Jesus Christ has destroyed death
and brought life to light through the Gospel. **R.**

✛ *Mark 3:7-12*

The unclean spirits shouted, "You are the Son of God,"
but Jesus warned them sternly not to make him known.

Jesus withdrew toward the sea with his disciples.
A large number of people followed from Galilee and from Judea.
Hearing what he was doing,
   a large number of people came to him also from Jerusalem,
   from Idumea, from beyond the Jordan,
   and from the neighborhood of Tyre and Sidon.

He told his disciples to have a boat ready for him because of the
crowd,
so that they would not crush him.
He had cured many and, as a result, those who had diseases
were pressing upon him to touch him.
And whenever unclean spirits saw him they would fall down before
him
and shout, "You are the Son of God."
He warned them sternly not to make him known. ✛

FRIDAY, JANUARY 20
WEEKDAY, ST. POPE FABIAN, ST. SEBASTIAN

† *Hebrews 8:6-13*
He is mediator of a better covenant.

Brothers and sisters:
Now our high priest has obtained so much more excellent a ministry
as he is mediator of a better covenant,
enacted on better promises.

For if that first covenant had been faultless,
no place would have been sought for a second one.
But he finds fault with them and says:
Behold, the days are coming, says the Lord,
when I will conclude a new covenant with the house of
Israel and the house of Judah.
It will not be like the covenant I made with their fathers
the day I took them by the hand to lead
them forth from the land of Egypt;
for they did not stand by my covenant
and I ignored them, says the Lord.
But this is the covenant I will establish with the house of Israel
after those days, says the Lord:
I will put my laws in their minds
and I will write them upon their hearts.
I will be their God,
and they shall be my people.
And they shall not teach, each one his fellow citizen and kin, saying,
"Know the Lord,"
for all shall know me, from least to greatest.
For I will forgive their evildoing
and remember their sins no more.

When he speaks of a "new" covenant,
he declares the first one obsolete.

And what has become obsolete
   and has grown old is close to disappearing. ✛

Psalm 85:8 and 10, 11-12, 13-14
R. (11a) **Kindness and truth shall meet.**
Show us, O LORD, your mercy,
   and grant us your salvation.
Near indeed is his salvation to those who fear him,
   glory dwelling in our land. **R.**
Kindness and truth shall meet;
   justice and peace shall kiss.
Truth shall spring out of the earth,
   and justice shall look down from heaven. **R.**
The LORD himself will give his benefits;
   our land shall yield its increase.
Justice shall walk before him,
   and salvation, along the way of his steps. **R.**

2 Corinthians 5:19
R. Alleluia, alleluia.
God was reconciling the world to himself in Christ,
and entrusting to us the message of reconciliation. **R.**

† *Mark 3:13-19*
Jesus summoned those whom he wanted and they came to him.

Jesus went up the mountain and summoned those whom he wanted
   and they came to him.
He appointed Twelve, whom he also named Apostles,
   that they might be with him
   and he might send them forth to preach
   and to have authority to drive out demons:
He appointed the Twelve:
   Simon, whom he named Peter;
   James, son of Zebedee,
   and John the brother of James, whom he named Boanerges,
   that is, sons of thunder;
   Andrew, Philip, Bartholomew,
   Matthew, Thomas, James the son of Alphaeus;
   Thaddeus, Simon the Cananean,
   and Judas Iscariot who betrayed him. ✛

SATURDAY, JANUARY 21
St. Agnes

† *Hebrews 9:2-3, 11-14*
He entered once for all into the sanctuary with his own Blood.

A tabernacle was constructed, the outer one,
   in which were the lampstand, the table, and the bread of offering;
   this is called the Holy Place.
Behind the second veil was the tabernacle called the Holy of Holies.

But when Christ came as high priest of the good things that have
      come to be,
   passing through the greater and more perfect tabernacle not made
      by hands,
   that is, not belonging to this creation,
   he entered once for all into the sanctuary,
   not with the blood of goats and calves but with his own Blood,
   thus obtaining eternal redemption.
For if the blood of goats and bulls and the sprinkling of a heifer's
      ashes
   can sanctify those who are defiled
   so that their flesh is cleansed,
   how much more will the Blood of Christ,
   who through the eternal spirit offered himself unblemished to God,
   cleanse our consciences from dead works to worship the living God. ✛

Psalm 47:2-3, 6-7, 8-9

R. (6) **God mounts his throne to shouts of joy: a blare of
   trumpets for the Lord.**
All you peoples, clap your hands,
   shout to God with cries of gladness,
For the Lord, the Most High, the awesome,
   is the great king over all the earth. **R.**
God mounts his throne amid shouts of joy;
   the Lord, amid trumpet blasts.
Sing praise to God, sing praise;
   sing praise to our king, sing praise. **R.**
For king of all the earth is God:
   sing hymns of praise.
God reigns over the nations,
   God sits upon his holy throne. **R.**

See Acts 16:14b

R. Alleluia, alleluia.
Open our hearts, O Lord,
to listen to the words of your Son. **R.**

† Mark 3:20-21
They said, "He is out of his mind."

Jesus came with his disciples into the house.
Again the crowd gathered,
  making it impossible for them even to eat.
When his relatives heard of this they set out to seize him,
  for they said, "He is out of his mind." ✙

SUNDAY, JANUARY 22
THIRD SUNDAY IN ORDINARY TIME

† Isaiah 8:23—9:3
In Galilee of the Gentiles, the people have seen a great light.

First the LORD degraded the land of Zebulun
  and the land of Naphtali;
  but in the end he has glorified the seaward road,
  the land west of the Jordan,
  the District of the Gentiles.

Anguish has taken wing, dispelled is darkness:
    for there is no gloom where but now there was distress.
The people who walked in darkness
    have seen a great light;
  upon those who dwelt in the land of gloom
      a light has shone.
You have brought them abundant joy
    and great rejoicing,
  as they rejoice before you as at the harvest,
    as people make merry when dividing spoils.
For the yoke that burdened them,
    the pole on their shoulder,
  and the rod of their taskmaster
    you have smashed, as on the day of Midian. ✙

Psalm 27:1, 4, 13-14
R. (1a) **The Lord is my light and my salvation.**
The LORD is my light and my salvation;
  whom should I fear?
The LORD is my life's refuge;
  of whom should I be afraid? **R.**
One thing I ask of the LORD;
  this I seek:
to dwell in the house of the LORD
  all the days of my life,
that I may gaze on the loveliness of the LORD

and contemplate his temple. **R.**
I believe that I shall see the bounty of the LORD
in the land of the living.
Wait for the LORD with courage;
be stouthearted, and wait for the LORD. **R.**

† *1 Corinthians 1:10-13, 17*
That all of you may agree in what you say,
and that there be no divisions among you.

I urge you, brothers and sisters, in the name of our Lord Jesus
Christ,
that all of you agree in what you say,
and that there be no divisions among you,
but that you be united in the same mind and in the same purpose.
For it has been reported to me about you, my brothers and sisters,
by Chloe's people, that there are rivalries among you.
I mean that each of you is saying,
"I belong to Paul," or "I belong to Apollos,"
or "I belong to Cephas," or "I belong to Christ."
Is Christ divided?
Was Paul crucified for you?
Or were you baptized in the name of Paul?
For Christ did not send me to baptize but to preach the gospel,
and not with the wisdom of human eloquence,
so that the cross of Christ might not be emptied of its meaning. ✛

See Matthew 4:23
R. Alleluia, alleluia.
Jesus proclaimed the Gospel of the kingdom
and cured every disease among the people. **R.**

† *Matthew 4:12-23* (or Matthew 4:12-17)
Jesus went to Capernaum, so that what had been said
through Isaiah might be fulfilled.

When Jesus heard that John had been arrested,
he withdrew to Galilee.
He left Nazareth and went to live in Capernaum by the sea,
in the region of Zebulun and Naphtali,
that what had been said through Isaiah the prophet
might be fulfilled:
Land of Zebulun and land of Naphtali,
the way to the sea, beyond the Jordan,
Galilee of the Gentiles,
the people who sit in darkness have seen a great light,
on those dwelling in a land overshadowed by death
light has arisen.

From that time on, Jesus began to preach and say,
  "Repent, for the kingdom of heaven is at hand."

As he was walking by the Sea of Galilee, he saw two brothers,
  Simon who is called Peter, and his brother Andrew,
  casting a net into the sea; they were fishermen.
He said to them,
  "Come after me, and I will make you fishers of men."
At once they left their nets and followed him.
He walked along from there and saw two other brothers,
  James, the son of Zebedee, and his brother John.
They were in a boat, with their father Zebedee, mending their nets.
He called them, and immediately they left their boat and their father
  and followed him.
He went around all of Galilee,
  teaching in their synagogues, proclaiming the gospel of the kingdom,
  and curing every disease and illness among the people. ✛

MONDAY, JANUARY 23
DAY OF PRAYER FOR THE LEGAL PROTECTION OF UNBORN CHILDREN, ST. VINCENT, ST. MARIANNE COPE

† *Hebrews 9:15, 24-28*
Christ who offered once to take away the sins of many,
will appear a second time to those who eagerly await him.

Christ is mediator of a new covenant:
  since a death has taken place
  for deliverance from transgressions under the first covenant,
  those who are called may receive the promised eternal inheritance.

For Christ did not enter into a sanctuary made by hands,
  a copy of the true one, but heaven itself,
  that he might now appear before God on our behalf.
Not that he might offer himself repeatedly,
  as the high priest enters each year into the sanctuary
  with blood that is not his own;
  if that were so, he would have had to suffer repeatedly
  from the foundation of the world.
But now once for all he has appeared at the end of the ages
  to take away sin by his sacrifice.
Just as it is appointed that human beings die once,
  and after this the judgment, so also Christ,
  offered once to take away the sins of many,
  will appear a second time, not to take away sin
  but to bring salvation to those who eagerly await him. ✛

Psalm 98:1bcde, 2-3ab, 3cd-4, 5-6

R. (1a) Sing to the Lord a new song, for he has done marvelous deeds.

Sing to the LORD a new song,
   for he has done wondrous deeds;
His right hand has won victory for him,
   his holy arm. **R.**

The LORD has made his salvation known:
   in the sight of the nations he has revealed his justice.
He has remembered his kindness and his faithfulness
   toward the house of Israel. **R.**

All the ends of the earth have seen
   the salvation by our God.
Sing joyfully to the LORD, all you lands;
   break into song; sing praise. **R.**

Sing praise to the LORD with the harp,
   with the harp and melodious song.
With trumpets and the sound of the horn
   sing joyfully before the King, the LORD. **R.**

See *2 Timothy 1:10*

R. Alleluia, alleluia.
Our Savior Jesus Christ has destroyed death
and brought life to light through the Gospel. **R.**

† *Mark 3:22-30*
It is the end of Satan.

The scribes who had come from Jerusalem said of Jesus,
   "He is possessed by Beelzebul," and
   "By the prince of demons he drives out demons."

Summoning them, he began to speak to them in parables,
   "How can Satan drive out Satan?
If a kingdom is divided against itself, that kingdom cannot stand.
And if a house is divided against itself,
   that house will not be able to stand.
And if Satan has risen up against himself and is divided,
   he cannot stand;
   that is the end of him.
But no one can enter a strong man's house to plunder his property
   unless he first ties up the strong man.
Then he can plunder his house.
Amen, I say to you, all sins and all blasphemies
   that people utter will be forgiven them.
But whoever blasphemes against the Holy Spirit
   will never have forgiveness,

but is guilty of an everlasting sin."
For they had said, "He has an unclean spirit." ✢

or, for the Day of Prayer
Any of the following readings: Genesis 1:1—2:2 (41) or 2 Maccabees 7:1, 20-31 (vol. II, 499) •
Isaiah 49:1-6 (587) • Romans 11:33-36 (121) • Ephesians 1:3-14 (104) •
Ephesians 3:14-21 (vol. III, 476) • Colossians 1:12-20 (162) • 1 John 3:11-21 (208) •
Matthew 18:1-5, 10, 12-14 (414) • Mark 9:30-37 (134) • Luke 1:39-56 (622) • Luke
17:11-19 (144) • Luke 23:35-43 (162) • John 1:1-5, 9-14, 16-18 (755) • John 6:24-35 (113), or
the *Lectionary for Mass* (volume IV), the Mass "For Peace and Justice," numbers 887-891.

Readings from the Mass "For Peace and Justice"

† *James 3:13-18*
The fruit of righteousness is sown in peace for those who cultivate peace.

Beloved:
Who among you is wise and understanding?
Let him show his works by a good life
 in the humility that comes from wisdom.
But if you have bitter jealousy and selfish ambition in your hearts,
 do not boast and be false to the truth.
Wisdom of this kind does not come down from above
 but is earthly, unspiritual, demonic.
For where jealousy and selfish ambition exist,
 there is disorder and every foul practice.
But the wisdom from above is first of all pure,
 the peaceable, gentle, compliant,
 full of mercy and good fruits,
 without inconstancy or insincerity.
And the fruit of righteousness is sown in peace
 for those who cultivate peace. ✢

Psalm 85:9 and 10, 11-12, 13-14
R. (9b) The Lord speaks of peace to his people.
I will hear what God proclaims;
 the LORD—for he proclaims peace.
Near indeed is his salvation to those who fear him,
 glory dwelling in our land. **R.**
Kindness and truth shall meet;
 justice and peace shall kiss.
Truth shall spring out of the earth,
 and justice shall look down from heaven. **R.**
The LORD himself will give his benefits;
 our land shall yield its increase.
Justice shall walk before him,
 and salvation, along the way of his steps. **R.**

John 14:27

R. Alleluia, alleluia.
Peace I leave with you, says the Lord,
my peace I give to you. **R.**

✝ *John 14:23-29*
My peace I give to you.

Jesus said to his disciple, Jude:
"Whoever loves me will keep my word,
   and my Father will love him,
   and we will come to him and make our dwelling with him.
Whoever does not love me does not keep my words;
   yet the word you hear is not mine
   but that of the Father who sent me.

"I have told you this while I am with you.
The Advocate, the Holy Spirit—
   that the Father will send in my name—
   he will teach you everything
   and remind you of all that I told you.
Peace I leave with you; my peace I give to you.
Not as the world gives do I give it to you.
Do not let your hearts be troubled or afraid.
You heard me tell you,
   'I am going away and I will come back to you.'
If you loved me,
   you would rejoice that I am going to the Father;
   for the Father is greater than I.
And now I have told you this before it happens,
   so that when it happens you may believe." ✝

TUESDAY, JANUARY 24
St. Francis de Sales

✝ *Hebrews 10:1-10*
Behold, I come to do your will, O God.

Brothers and sisters:
Since the law has only a shadow of the good things to come,
   and not the very image of them, it can never make perfect
   those who come to worship by the same sacrifices
   that they offer continually each year.
Otherwise, would not the sacrifices have ceased to be offered,
   since the worshipers, once cleansed, would no longer
   have had any consciousness of sins?
But in those sacrifices there is only a yearly remembrance of sins,

for it is impossible that the blood of bulls and goats
take away sins.
For this reason, when he came into the world, he said:

Sacrifice and offering you did not desire,
*   but a body you prepared for me;*
in burnt offerings and sin offerings you took no delight.
Then I said, As is written of me in the scroll,
*   Behold, I come to do your will, O God.*

First he says, *Sacrifices and offerings,*
burnt offerings and sin offerings,
you neither desired nor delighted in.

These are offered according to the law.
Then he says, *Behold, I come to do your will.*
He takes away the first to establish the second.
By this "will," we have been consecrated
    through the offering of the Body of Jesus Christ once for all. ✛

Psalm 40:2 and 4ab, 7-8a, 10, 11
R. (8a and 9a) **Here am I Lord; I come to do your will.**
I have waited, waited for the LORD,
    and he stooped toward me.
And he put a new song into my mouth,
    a hymn to our God. **R.**
Sacrifice or oblation you wished not,
    but ears open to obedience you gave me.
Burnt offerings or sin-offerings you sought not;
    then said I, "Behold I come." **R.**
I announced your justice in the vast assembly;
    I did not restrain my lips, as you, O LORD, know. **R.**
Your justice I kept not hid within my heart;
    your faithfulness and your salvation I have spoken of;
I have made no secret of your kindness and your truth
    in the vast assembly. **R.**

See Matthew 11:25
R. Alleluia, alleluia.
Blessed are you, Father, Lord of heaven and earth;
you have revealed to little ones the mysteries of the Kingdom. **R.**

† *Mark 3:31-35*
Whoever does the will of God is my brother and sister and mother.

The mother of Jesus and his brothers arrived at the house.
Standing outside, they sent word to Jesus and called him.
A crowd seated around him told him,

"Your mother and your brothers and your sisters
    are outside asking for you."
But he said to them in reply,
    "Who are my mother and my brothers?"
And looking around at those seated in the circle he said,
    "Here are my mother and my brothers.
For whoever does the will of God
    is my brother and sister and mother." ✛

WEDNESDAY, JANUARY 25
THE CONVERSION OF ST. PAUL

✝Acts 22:3-16 (or Acts 9:1-22)
Get up and have yourself baptized and your sins washed away,
calling upon the name of Jesus.

Paul addressed the people in these words:
"I am a Jew, born in Tarsus in Cilicia,
    but brought up in this city.
At the feet of Gamaliel I was educated strictly in our ancestral law
    and was zealous for God, just as all of you are today.
I persecuted this Way to death,
    binding both men and women and delivering them to prison.
Even the high priest and the whole council of elders
    can testify on my behalf.
For from them I even received letters to the brothers
    and set out for Damascus to bring back to Jerusalem
    in chains for punishment those there as well.

"On that journey as I drew near to Damascus,
    about noon a great light from the sky suddenly shone around me.
I fell to the ground and heard a voice saying to me,
    'Saul, Saul, why are you persecuting me?'
I replied, 'Who are you, sir?'
And he said to me,
    'I am Jesus the Nazorean whom you are persecuting.'
My companions saw the light
    but did not hear the voice of the one who spoke to me.
I asked, 'What shall I do, sir?'
The Lord answered me, 'Get up and go into Damascus,
    and there you will be told about everything
    appointed for you to do.'
Since I could see nothing because of the brightness of that light,
    I was led by hand by my companions and entered Damascus.

"A certain Ananias, a devout observer of the law,
    and highly spoken of by all the Jews who lived there,

came to me and stood there and said,
  'Saul, my brother, regain your sight.'
And at that very moment I regained my sight and saw him.
Then he said,
  'The God of our ancestors designated you to know his will,
  to see the Righteous One, and to hear the sound of his voice;
  for you will be his witness before all
  to what you have seen and heard.
Now, why delay?
Get up and have yourself baptized and your sins washed away,
  calling upon his name.'" ✛

Psalm 117:1bc, 2
**R. (Mark 16:15) Go out to all the world and tell the Good
    News. (or Alleluia, alleluia.)**
Praise the LORD, all you nations;
  glorify him, all you peoples! **R.**
For steadfast is his kindness toward us,
  and the fidelity of the LORD endures forever. **R.**

See John 15:16
R. Alleluia, alleluia.
I chose you from the world,
to go and bear fruit that will last, says the Lord. **R.**

† Mark 16:15-18
Go out to all the world and tell the Good News.

Jesus appeared to the Eleven and said to them:
"Go into the whole world
  and proclaim the Gospel to every creature.
Whoever believes and is baptized will be saved;
  whoever does not believe will be condemned.
These signs will accompany those who believe:
  in my name they will drive out demons,
  they will speak new languages.
They will pick up serpents with their hands,
  and if they drink any deadly thing, it will not harm them.
They will lay hands on the sick, and they will recover." ✛

THURSDAY, JANUARY 26
ST. TIMOTHY AND ST. TITUS

† 2 Timothy 1:1-8 (or Titus 1:1-5)
I recall your sincere faith.

Paul, an Apostle of Christ Jesus by the will of God
  for the promise of life in Christ Jesus,

to Timothy, my dear child:
grace, mercy, and peace from God the Father
and Christ Jesus our Lord.

I am grateful to God,
  whom I worship with a clear conscience as my ancestors did,
  as I remember you constantly in my prayers, night and day.
I yearn to see you again, recalling your tears,
  so that I may be filled with joy,
  as I recall your sincere faith
  that first lived in your grandmother Lois
  and in your mother Eunice
  and that I am confident lives also in you.

For this reason, I remind you to stir into flame
  the gift of God that you have through the imposition of my hands.
For God did not give us a spirit of cowardice
  but rather of power and love and self-control.
So do not be ashamed of your testimony to our Lord,
  nor of me, a prisoner for his sake;
  but bear your share of hardship for the Gospel
  with the strength that comes from God. ✝

Psalm 96:1-2a, 2b-3, 7-8a, 10

R. (3) Proclaim God's marvelous deeds to all the nations.
Sing to the LORD a new song;
  sing to the LORD, all you lands.
Sing to the LORD; bless his name. **R.**
Announce his salvation, day after day.
Tell his glory among the nations;
  among all peoples, his wondrous deeds. **R.**
Give to the LORD, you families of nations,
  give to the LORD glory and praise;
  give to the LORD the glory due his name! **R.**
Say among the nations: The LORD is king.
He has made the world firm, not to be moved;
  he governs the peoples with equity. **R.**

Psalm 119:105

R. Alleluia, alleluia.
A lamp to my feet is your word,
a light to my path. **R.**

† *Mark 4:21-25*

A lamp is to be placed on a lampstand. The measure with which
you measure will be measured out to you.

Jesus said to his disciples,
  "Is a lamp brought in to be placed under a bushel basket
  or under a bed,
  and not to be placed on a lampstand?
For there is nothing hidden except to be made visible;
  nothing is secret except to come to light.
Anyone who has ears to hear ought to hear."
He also told them, "Take care what you hear.
The measure with which you measure will be measured out to you,
  and still more will be given to you.
To the one who has, more will be given;
  from the one who has not, even what he has will be taken away." ✛

FRIDAY, JANUARY 27
WEEKDAY, ST. ANGELA MERICI

† *Hebrews 10:32-39*
Do not throw away your confidence. it will have a great reward.

Remember the days past when, after you had been enlightened,
  you endured a great contest of suffering.
At times you were publicly exposed to abuse and affliction;
  at other times you associated yourselves with those so treated.
You even joined in the sufferings of those in prison
  and joyfully accepted the confiscation of your property,
  knowing that you had a better and lasting possession.
Therefore, do not throw away your confidence;
  it will have great recompense.
You need endurance to do the will of God and receive what he has
    promised.

  For, after just a brief moment,
    he who is to come shall come;
    he shall not delay.
  But my just one shall live by faith,
    and if he draws back I take no pleasure in him.

We are not among those who draw back and perish,
  but among those who have faith and will possess life. ✛

  Psalm 37:3-4, 5-6, 23-24, 39-40
R. (39a) The salvation of the just comes from the Lord.
Trust in the LORD and do good,
  that you may dwell in the land and be fed in security.

Take delight in the L<small>ORD</small>,
  and he will grant you your heart's requests. **R.**
Commit to the L<small>ORD</small> your way;
  trust in him, and he will act.
He will make justice dawn for you like the light;
  bright as the noonday shall be your vindication. **R.**
By the L<small>ORD</small> are the steps of a man made firm,
  and he approves his way.
Though he fall, he does not lie prostrate,
  for the hand of the L<small>ORD</small> sustains him. **R.**
The salvation of the just is from the L<small>ORD</small>;
  he is their refuge in time of distress.
And the L<small>ORD</small> helps them and delivers them;
  he delivers them from the wicked and saves them,
  because they take refuge in him. **R.**

  See Matthew 11:25
R. Alleluia, alleluia.
Blessed are you, Father, Lord of heaven and earth;
you have revealed to little ones the mysteries of the Kingdom. **R.**

✝ Mark 4:26-34
*A man scatters seed on the land and would sleep and
the seed would sprout and grow, he knows not how.*

Jesus said to the crowds:
"This is how it is with the Kingdom of God;
  it is as if a man were to scatter seed on the land
  and would sleep and rise night and day
  and the seed would sprout and grow,
  he knows not how.
Of its own accord the land yields fruit,
  first the blade, then the ear, then the full grain in the ear.
And when the grain is ripe, he wields the sickle at once,
  for the harvest has come."

He said,
  "To what shall we compare the Kingdom of God,
  or what parable can we use for it?
It is like a mustard seed that, when it is sown in the ground,
  is the smallest of all the seeds on the earth.
But once it is sown, it springs up and becomes the largest of plants
  and puts forth large branches,
  so that the birds of the sky can dwell in its shade."
With many such parables
  he spoke the word to them as they were able to understand it.

Without parables he did not speak to them,
  but to his own disciples he explained everything in private. ✝

SATURDAY, JANUARY 28
St. Thomas Aquinas

✝ *Hebrews 11:1-2, 8-19*
He was looking forward to the city whose architect and maker is God.

Brothers and sisters:
Faith is the realization of what is hoped for
  and evidence of things not seen.
Because of it the ancients were well attested.

By faith Abraham obeyed when he was called to go out to a place
  that he was to receive as an inheritance;
  he went out, not knowing where he was to go.
By faith he sojourned in the promised land as in a foreign country,
  dwelling in tents with Isaac and Jacob, heirs of the same promise;
  for he was looking forward to the city with foundations,
  whose architect and maker is God.
By faith he received power to generate,
  even though he was past the normal age
  —and Sarah herself was sterile—
  for he thought that the one who had made the promise was trust-
    worthy.
So it was that there came forth from one man,
  himself as good as dead,
descendants as numerous as the stars in the sky
and as countless as the sands on the seashore.

All these died in faith.
They did not receive what had been promised
  but saw it and greeted it from afar
  and acknowledged themselves to be strangers and aliens on earth,
  for those who speak thus show that they are seeking a homeland.
If they had been thinking of the land from which they had come,
  they would have had opportunity to return.
But now they desire a better homeland, a heavenly one.
Therefore, God is not ashamed to be called their God,
  for he has prepared a city for them.
By faith Abraham, when put to the test, offered up Isaac,
  and he who had received the promises was ready to offer his only
    son,
  of whom it was said,
  Through Isaac descendants shall bear your name.

He reasoned that God was able to raise even from the dead,
  and he received Isaac back as a symbol. ✛

Luke 1:69-70, 71-72, 73-75

**R. (see 68) Blessed be the Lord the God of Israel; he has come
  to his people.**
He has raised up for us a mighty savior,
  born of the house of his servant David. **R.**
Through his holy prophets he promised of old
    that he would save us from our sins,
    from the hands of all who hate us.
He promised to show mercy to our fathers
    and to remember his holy covenant. **R.**
This was the oath he swore to our father Abraham:
    to set us free from the bonds of our enemies,
    free to worship him without fear,
    holy and righteous in his sight
    all the days of our life. **R.**

John 3:16

R. Alleluia, alleluia.
God so loved the world that he gave his only-begotten Son,
so that everyone who believes in him might have eternal life. **R.**

† Mark 4:35-41
Who then is this whom even wind and sea obey?

On that day, as evening drew on, Jesus said to his disciples:
"Let us cross to the other side."
Leaving the crowd, they took Jesus with them in the boat just as he
  was.
And other boats were with him.
A violent squall came up and waves were breaking over the boat,
  so that it was already filling up.
Jesus was in the stern, asleep on a cushion.
They woke him and said to him,
  "Teacher, do you not care that we are perishing?"
He woke up,
  rebuked the wind,
    and said to the sea, "Quiet! Be still!"
The wind ceased and there was great calm.
Then he asked them, "Why are you terrified?
Do you not yet have faith?"
They were filled with great awe and said to one another,
  "Who then is this whom even wind and sea obey?" ✛

SUNDAY, JANUARY 29
FOURTH SUNDAY IN ORDINARY TIME

† *Zephaniah 2:3; 3:12-13*
I will leave in your midst a people humble and lowly.

Seek the LORD, all you humble of the earth,
who have observed his law;
seek justice, seek humility;
perhaps you may be sheltered
on the day of the LORD's anger.

But I will leave as a remnant in your midst
a people humble and lowly,
who shall take refuge in the name of the LORD:
the remnant of Israel.
They shall do no wrong
and speak no lies;
nor shall there be found in their mouths
a deceitful tongue;
they shall pasture and couch their flocks
with none to disturb them. ✛

Psalm 146:6c-7, 8-9a, 9bc-10

R. (Matthew 5:3) **Blessed are the poor in spirit; the kingdom of heaven is theirs!** *(or* **Alleluia***.)*

The LORD keeps faith forever,
secures justice for the oppressed,
gives food to the hungry.
The LORD sets captives free. **R.**
The LORD gives sight to the blind;
the LORD raises up those who were bowed down.
The LORD loves the just;
the LORD protects strangers. **R.**
The fatherless and the widow the LORD sustains,
but the way of the wicked he thwarts.
The LORD shall reign forever;
your God, O Zion, through all generations. Alleluia. **R.**

† *1 Corinthians 1:26-31*
God chose the weak of the world.

Consider your own calling, brothers and sisters.
Not many of you were wise by human standards,
not many were powerful,
not many were of noble birth.
Rather, God chose the foolish of the world to shame the wise,

and God chose the weak of the world to shame the strong,
and God chose the lowly and despised of the world,
those who count for nothing,
to reduce to nothing those who are something,
so that no human being might boast before God.
It is due to him that you are in Christ Jesus,
who became for us wisdom from God,
as well as righteousness, sanctification, and redemption,
so that, as it is written,
"Whoever boasts, should boast in the Lord." ✝

Matthew 5:12a
R. Alleluia, alleluia.
Rejoice and be glad;
your reward will be great in heaven. **R.**

† *Matthew 5:1-12a*
Blessed are the poor in spirit.

When Jesus saw the crowds, he went up the mountain,
and after he had sat down, his disciples came to him.
He began to teach them, saying:
"Blessed are the poor in spirit,
for theirs is the kingdom of heaven.
Blessed are they who mourn,
for they will be comforted.
Blessed are the meek,
for they will inherit the land.
Blessed are they who hunger and thirst for righteousness,
for they will be satisfied.
Blessed are the merciful,
for they will be shown mercy.
Blessed are the clean of heart,
for they will see God.
Blessed are the peacemakers,
for they will be called children of God.
Blessed are they who are persecuted for the sake of righteousness,
for theirs is the kingdom of heaven.
Blessed are you when they insult you and persecute you
and utter every kind of evil against you falsely because of me.
Rejoice and be glad,
for your reward will be great in heaven." ✝

MONDAY, JANUARY 30
WEEKDAY

† *Hebrews 11:32-40*
By faith they conquered kingdoms.
God had foreseen something better for us.

Brothers and sisters:
What more shall I say?
I have not time to tell of Gideon, Barak, Samson, Jephthah,
of David and Samuel and the prophets,
who by faith conquered kingdoms,
did what was righteous, obtained the promises;
they closed the mouths of lions, put out raging fires,
escaped the devouring sword;
out of weakness they were made powerful, became strong in battle,
and turned back foreign invaders.
Women received back their dead through resurrection.
Some were tortured and would not accept deliverance,
in order to obtain a better resurrection.
Others endured mockery, scourging, even chains and imprisonment.
They were stoned, sawed in two, put to death at sword's point;
they went about in skins of sheep or goats,
needy, afflicted, tormented.
The world was not worthy of them.
They wandered about in deserts and on mountains,
in caves and in crevices in the earth.

Yet all these, though approved because of their faith,
did not receive what had been promised.
God had foreseen something better for us,
so that without us they should not be made perfect. ✛

Psalm 31:20, 21, 22, 23, 24
**R. (25) Let your hearts take comfort, all who hope in the
    Lord.**
How great is the goodness, O LORD,
    which you have in store for those who fear you,
And which, toward those who take refuge in you,
    you show in the sight of the children of men. **R.**
You hide them in the shelter of your presence
    from the plottings of men;
You screen them within your abode
    from the strife of tongues. **R.**
Blessed be the LORD whose wondrous mercy
    he has shown me in a fortified city. **R.**
Once I said in my anguish,

"I am cut off from your sight";
Yet you heard the sound of my pleading
 when I cried out to you. **R.**
Love the LORD, all you his faithful ones!
 The LORD keeps those who are constant,
 but more than requites those who act proudly. **R.**

Luke 7:16

R. Alleluia, alleluia.
A great prophet has arisen in our midst
and God has visited his people. **R.**

✝ Mark 5:1-20

Unclean spirit, come out of the man!

Jesus and his disciples came to the other side of the sea,
 to the territory of the Gerasenes.
When he got out of the boat,
 at once a man from the tombs who had an unclean spirit met him.
The man had been dwelling among the tombs,
 and no one could restrain him any longer, even with a chain.
In fact, he had frequently been bound with shackles and chains,
 but the chains had been pulled apart by him and the shackles
  smashed,
 and no one was strong enough to subdue him.
Night and day among the tombs and on the hillsides
 he was always crying out and bruising himself with stones.
Catching sight of Jesus from a distance,
 he ran up and prostrated himself before him,
 crying out in a loud voice,
 "What have you to do with me, Jesus, Son of the Most High God?
I adjure you by God, do not torment me!"
(He had been saying to him, "Unclean spirit, come out of the man!")
He asked him, "What is your name?"
He replied, "Legion is my name. There are many of us."
And he pleaded earnestly with him,
 not to drive them away from that territory.

Now a large herd of swine was feeding there on the hillside.
And they pleaded with him,
 "Send us into the swine. Let us enter them."
And he let them, and the unclean spirits came out and entered the
 swine.
The herd of about two thousand rushed down a steep bank into the
 sea,
 where they were drowned.

The swineherds ran away and reported the incident in the town
  and throughout the countryside.
And people came out to see what had happened.
As they approached Jesus,
  they caught sight of the man who had been possessed by Legion,
  sitting there clothed and in his right mind.
And they were seized with fear.
Those who witnessed the incident explained to them what had
    happened
  to the possessed man and to the swine.
Then they began to beg him to leave their district.
As he was getting into the boat,
  the man who had been possessed pleaded to remain with him.
But Jesus would not permit him but told him instead,
  "Go home to your family and announce to them
  all that the Lord in his pity has done for you."
Then the man went off and began to proclaim in the Decapolis
  what Jesus had done for him; and all were amazed. ✝

TUESDAY, JANUARY 31
St. John Bosco

✝ *Hebrews 12:1-4*
Let us persevere in running the race that lies before us.

Brothers and sisters:
Since we are surrounded by so great a cloud of witnesses,
  let us rid ourselves of every burden and sin that clings to us
  and persevere in running the race that lies before us
  while keeping our eyes fixed on Jesus,
  the leader and perfecter of faith.
For the sake of the joy that lay before him
  Jesus endured the cross, despising its shame,
  and has taken his seat at the right of the throne of God.
Consider how he endured such opposition from sinners,
  in order that you may not grow weary and lose heart.
In your struggle against sin
  you have not yet resisted to the point of shedding blood. ✝

Psalm 22:26b-27, 28 and 30, 31-32
R. (see 27b) **They will praise you, Lord, who long for you.**
I will fulfill my vows before those who fear him.
The lowly shall eat their fill;
  they who seek the Lord shall praise him:
  "May your hearts be ever merry!" **R.**
All the ends of the earth

shall remember and turn to the LORD;
All the families of the nations
   shall bow down before him.
To him alone shall bow down
   all who sleep in the earth;
Before him shall bend
   all who go down into the dust. **R.**
And to him my soul shall live;
   my descendants shall serve him.
Let the coming generation be told of the LORD
   that they may proclaim to a people yet to be born
   the justice he has shown. **R.**

   Matthew 8:17
R. Alleluia, alleluia.
Christ took away our infirmities
and bore our diseases. **R.**

† Mark 5:21-43
Little girl, I say to you, arise!

When Jesus had crossed again in the boat to the other side,
   a large crowd gathered around him, and he stayed close to the sea.
One of the synagogue officials, named Jairus, came forward.
Seeing him he fell at his feet and pleaded earnestly with him, saying,
   "My daughter is at the point of death.
Please, come lay your hands on her
   that she may get well and live."
He went off with him
   and a large crowd followed him.

There was a woman afflicted with hemorrhages for twelve years.
She had suffered greatly at the hands of many doctors
   and had spent all that she had.
Yet she was not helped but only grew worse.
She had heard about Jesus and came up behind him in the crowd
   and touched his cloak.
She said, "If I but touch his clothes, I shall be cured."
Immediately her flow of blood dried up.
She felt in her body that she was healed of her affliction.
Jesus, aware at once that power had gone out from him,
   turned around in the crowd and asked, "Who has touched my
      clothes?"
But his disciples said to him,
   "You see how the crowd is pressing upon you,
   and yet you ask, Who touched me?"

And he looked around to see who had done it.
The woman, realizing what had happened to her,
　approached in fear and trembling.
She fell down before Jesus and told him the whole truth.
He said to her, "Daughter, your faith has saved you.
Go in peace and be cured of your affliction."

While he was still speaking,
　people from the synagogue official's house arrived and said,
　"Your daughter has died; why trouble the teacher any longer?"
Disregarding the message that was reported,
　Jesus said to the synagogue official,
　"Do not be afraid; just have faith."
He did not allow anyone to accompany him inside
　except Peter, James, and John, the brother of James.
When they arrived at the house of the synagogue official,
　he caught sight of a commotion,
　people weeping and wailing loudly.
So he went in and said to them,
　"Why this commotion and weeping?
The child is not dead but asleep."
And they ridiculed him.
Then he put them all out.
He took along the child's father and mother
　and those who were with him
　and entered the room where the child was.
He took the child by the hand and said to her, *"Talitha koum,"*
　which means, "Little girl, I say to you, arise!"
The girl, a child of twelve, arose immediately and walked around.
At that they were utterly astounded.
He gave strict orders that no one should know this
　and said that she should be given something to eat. ✙

WEDNESDAY, FEBRUARY 1
WEEKDAY

† Hebrews 12:4-7, 11-15
The Lord disciplines those he loves.

Brothers and sisters:
In your struggle against sin
　you have not yet resisted to the point of shedding blood.
You have also forgotten the exhortation addressed to you as children:

*My son, do not disdain the discipline of the Lord
　or lose heart when reproved by him;*

for whom the Lord loves, he disciplines;
he scourges every son he acknowledges.

Endure your trials as "discipline";
God treats you as his sons.
For what "son" is there whom his father does not discipline?
At the time, all discipline seems a cause not for joy but for pain,
yet later it brings the peaceful fruit of righteousness
to those who are trained by it.

So strengthen your drooping hands and your weak knees.
Make straight paths for your feet,
that what is lame may not be dislocated but healed.

Strive for peace with everyone,
and for that holiness without which no one will see the Lord.
See to it that no one be deprived of the grace of God,
that no bitter root spring up and cause trouble,
through which many may become defiled. ✛

Psalm 103:1-2, 13-14, 17-18a
R. (see 17) **The Lord's kindness is everlasting to those who
fear him.**
Bless the LORD, O my soul;
and all my being, bless his holy name.
Bless the LORD, O my soul,
and forget not all his benefits. **R.**
As a father has compassion on his children,
so the LORD has compassion on those who fear him,
For he knows how we are formed;
he remembers that we are dust. **R.**
But the kindness of the LORD is from eternity
to eternity toward those who fear him,
And his justice toward children's children
among those who keep his covenant. **R.**

John 10:27
R. Alleluia, alleluia.
My sheep hear my voice, says the Lord;
I know them, and they follow me. **R.**

† *Mark 6:1-6*
A prophet is not without honor except in his native place.

Jesus departed from there and came to his native place,
accompanied by his disciples.
When the sabbath came he began to teach in the synagogue,
and many who heard him were astonished.

They said, "Where did this man get all this?
What kind of wisdom has been given him?
What mighty deeds are wrought by his hands!
Is he not the carpenter, the son of Mary,
   and the brother of James and Joseph and Judas and Simon?
And are not his sisters here with us?"
And they took offense at him.
Jesus said to them,
   "A prophet is not without honor except in his native place
   and among his own kin and in his own house."
So he was not able to perform any mighty deed there,
   apart from curing a few sick people by laying his hands on them.
He was amazed at their lack of faith. ✢

THURSDAY, FEBRUARY 2
THE PRESENTATION OF THE LORD

✝ *Malachi 3:1-4*
There will come to the temple the Lord whom you seek.

Thus says the Lord GOD:
Lo, I am sending my messenger
   to prepare the way before me;
And suddenly there will come to the temple
   the LORD whom you seek,
And the messenger of the covenant whom you desire.
   Yes, he is coming, says the LORD of hosts.
But who will endure the day of his coming?
   And who can stand when he appears?
For he is like the refiner's fire,
   or like the fuller's lye.
He will sit refining and purifying silver,
   and he will purify the sons of Levi,
Refining them like gold or like silver
   that they may offer due sacrifice to the LORD.
Then the sacrifice of Judah and Jerusalem
   will please the LORD,
   as in the days of old, as in years gone by. ✢

Psalm 24:7, 8, 9, 10
R. (8) **Who is this king of glory? It is the Lord!**
Lift up, O gates, your lintels;
   reach up, you ancient portals,
   that the king of glory may come in! **R.**
Who is this king of glory?
   The LORD, strong and mighty,

the LORD, mighty in battle. **R.**
Lift up, O gates, your lintels;
   reach up, you ancient portals,
   that the king of glory may come in! **R.**
Who is this king of glory?
   The LORD of hosts; he is the king of glory. **R.**

† *Hebrews 2:14-18*
He had to become like his brothers and sisters in every way.

Since the children share in blood and flesh,
   Jesus likewise shared in them,
   that through death he might destroy the one
   who has the power of death, that is, the Devil,
   and free those who through fear of death
   had been subject to slavery all their life.
Surely he did not help angels
   but rather the descendants of Abraham;
   therefore, he had to become like his brothers and sisters
   in every way,
   that he might be a merciful and faithful high priest before God
   to expiate the sins of the people.
Because he himself was tested through what he suffered,
   he is able to help those who are being tested. ✛

Luke 2:32
R. Alleluia, alleluia.
A light of revelation to the Gentiles,
and glory for your people Israel. **R.**

† *Luke 2:22-40* *(or Luke 2:22-32)*
My eyes have seen your salvation.

When the days were completed for their purification
   according to the law of Moses,
   Mary and Joseph took Jesus up to Jerusalem
   to present him to the Lord,
   just as it is written in the law of the Lord,
   Every male that opens the womb shall be consecrated to the Lord,
   and to offer the sacrifice of
   a pair of turtledoves or two young pigeons,
   in accordance with the dictate in the law of the Lord.

Now there was a man in Jerusalem whose name was Simeon.
This man was righteous and devout,
   awaiting the consolation of Israel,
   and the Holy Spirit was upon him.

It had been revealed to him by the Holy Spirit
   that he should not see death
   before he had seen the Christ of the Lord.
He came in the Spirit into the temple;
   and when the parents brought in the child Jesus
   to perform the custom of the law in regard to him,
   he took him into his arms and blessed God, saying:

   "Now, Master, you may let your servant go
      in peace, according to your word,
   for my eyes have seen your salvation,
      which you prepared in sight of all the peoples:
   a light for revelation to the Gentiles,
      and glory for your people Israel."

The child's father and mother were amazed at what was said about
      him;
   and Simeon blessed them and said to Mary his mother,
   "Behold, this child is destined
   for the fall and rise of many in Israel,
   and to be a sign that will be contradicted
   —and you yourself a sword will pierce—
   so that the thoughts of many hearts may be revealed."
There was also a prophetess, Anna,
   the daughter of Phanuel, of the tribe of Asher.
She was advanced in years,
   having lived seven years with her husband after her marriage,
   and then as a widow until she was eighty-four.
She never left the temple,
   but worshiped night and day with fasting and prayer.
And coming forward at that very time,
   she gave thanks to God and spoke about the child
   to all who were awaiting the redemption of Jerusalem.

When they had fulfilled all the prescriptions
   of the law of the Lord,
   they returned to Galilee, to their own town of Nazareth.
The child grew and became strong, filled with wisdom;
   and the favor of God was upon him. ✛

FRIDAY, FEBRUARY 3
WEEKDAY, ST. BLAISE, ST. ANSGAR

† *Hebrews 13:1-8*
Jesus Christ is the same yesterday, today, and forever.

Let brotherly love continue.
Do not neglect hospitality,
   for through it some have unknowingly entertained angels.
Be mindful of prisoners as if sharing their imprisonment,
   and of the ill-treated as of yourselves,
   for you also are in the body.
Let marriage be honored among all
   and the marriage bed be kept undefiled,
   for God will judge the immoral and adulterers.
Let your life be free from love of money
   but be content with what you have,
   for he has said, *I will never forsake you or abandon you.*
Thus we may say with confidence:

   The Lord is my helper,
   and I will not be afraid.
   What can anyone do to me?

Remember your leaders who spoke the word of God to you.
Consider the outcome of their way of life and imitate their faith.
Jesus Christ is the same yesterday, today, and forever. ✦

Psalm 27:1, 3, 5, 8b-9abc
R. (1a) **The Lord is my light and my salvation.**
The LORD is my light and my salvation;
   whom should I fear?
The LORD is my life's refuge;
   of whom should I be afraid? **R.**
Though an army encamp against me,
   my heart will not fear;
Though war be waged upon me,
   even then will I trust. **R.**
For he will hide me in his abode
   in the day of trouble;
He will conceal me in the shelter of his tent,
   he will set me high upon a rock. **R.**
Your presence, O LORD, I seek.
   Hide not your face from me;
do not in anger repel your servant.
   You are my helper: cast me not off. **R.**

See Luke 8:15

R. Alleluia, alleluia.

Blessed are they who have kept the word with a generous heart,
and yield a harvest through perseverance. **R.**

† *Mark 6:14-29*

It is John whom I beheaded. He has been raised up.

King Herod heard about Jesus, for his fame had become widespread,
and people were saying,
"John the Baptist has been raised from the dead;
that is why mighty powers are at work in him."
Others were saying, "He is Elijah";
still others, "He is a prophet like any of the prophets."
But when Herod learned of it, he said,
"It is John whom I beheaded. He has been raised up."

Herod was the one who had John arrested and bound in prison
on account of Herodias,
the wife of his brother Philip, whom he had married.
John had said to Herod,
"It is not lawful for you to have your brother's wife."
Herodias harbored a grudge against him
and wanted to kill him but was unable to do so.
Herod feared John, knowing him to be a righteous and holy man,
and kept him in custody.
When he heard him speak he was very much perplexed,
yet he liked to listen to him.
Herodias had an opportunity one day when Herod, on his birthday,
gave a banquet for his courtiers, his military officers,
and the leading men of Galilee.
His own daughter came in and performed a dance
that delighted Herod and his guests.
The king said to the girl,
"Ask of me whatever you wish and I will grant it to you."
He even swore many things to her,
"I will grant you whatever you ask of me,
even to half of my kingdom."
She went out and said to her mother,
"What shall I ask for?"
Her mother replied, "The head of John the Baptist."
The girl hurried back to the king's presence and made her request,
"I want you to give me at once on a platter
the head of John the Baptist."
The king was deeply distressed,
but because of his oaths and the guests

he did not wish to break his word to her.
So he promptly dispatched an executioner
    with orders to bring back his head.
He went off and beheaded him in the prison.
He brought in the head on a platter
    and gave it to the girl.
The girl in turn gave it to her mother.
When his disciples heard about it,
    they came and took his body and laid it in a tomb. ✙

SATURDAY, FEBRUARY 4
WEEKDAY, *[BVM]*

†*Hebrews 13:15-17, 20-21*
May the God of peace, who brought up from the dead the great shepherd,
furnish you with all that is good.

Brothers and sisters:
Through Jesus, let us continually offer God a sacrifice of praise,
    that is, the fruit of lips that confess his name.
Do not neglect to do good and to share what you have;
    God is pleased by sacrifices of that kind.

Obey your leaders and defer to them,
    for they keep watch over you and will have to give an account,
    that they may fulfill their task with joy and not with sorrow,
    for that would be of no advantage to you.

May the God of peace, who brought up from the dead
    the great shepherd of the sheep
    by the Blood of the eternal covenant, Jesus our Lord,
    furnish you with all that is good, that you may do his will.
May he carry out in you what is pleasing to him through Jesus
        Christ,
    to whom be glory forever and ever. Amen. ✙

Psalm 23:1b-3a, 3b-4, 5, 6
R. (1) **The Lord is my shepherd; there is nothing I shall want.**
The LORD is my shepherd; I shall not want.
    In verdant pastures he gives me repose.
Beside restful waters he leads me;
    he refreshes my soul. **R.**
He guides me in right paths
    for his name's sake.
Even though I walk in the dark valley
    I fear no evil; for you are at my side
With your rod and your staff

that give me courage. **R.**
You spread the table before me
  in the sight of my foes;
You anoint my head with oil;
  my cup overflows. **R.**
Only goodness and kindness follow me
  all the days of my life;
And I shall dwell in the house of the LORD
  for years to come. **R.**

John 10:27
R. Alleluia, alleluia.
My sheep hear my voice, says the Lord;
I know them, and they follow me. **R.**

† *Mark 6:30-34*
They were like sheep without a shepherd.

The Apostles gathered together with Jesus
  and reported all they had done and taught.
He said to them,
  "Come away by yourselves to a deserted place and rest a while."
People were coming and going in great numbers,
  and they had no opportunity even to eat.
So they went off in the boat by themselves to a deserted place.
People saw them leaving and many came to know about it.
They hastened there on foot from all the towns
  and arrived at the place before them.

When Jesus disembarked and saw the vast crowd,
  his heart was moved with pity for them,
  for they were like sheep without a shepherd;
  and he began to teach them many things. ✛

SUNDAY, FEBRUARY 5
FIFTH SUNDAY IN ORDINARY TIME

† *Isaiah 58:7-10*
Your light shall break forth like the dawn.

Thus says the LORD:
  Share your bread with the hungry,
    shelter the oppressed and the homeless;
  clothe the naked when you see them,
    and do not turn your back on your own.
  Then your light shall break forth like the dawn,
    and your wound shall quickly be healed;
  your vindication shall go before you,

and the glory of the LORD shall be your rear guard.
Then you shall call, and the LORD will answer,
   you shall cry for help, and he will say: Here I am!
If you remove from your midst oppression,
   false accusation and malicious speech;
if you bestow your bread on the hungry
   and satisfy the afflicted;
then light shall rise for you in the darkness,
   and the gloom shall become for you like midday. ✣

Psalm 112:4-5, 6-7, 8-9

R. (4a) **The just man is a light in darkness to the upright.**
   (or **Alleluia.***)*

Light shines through the darkness for the upright;
   he is gracious and merciful and just.
Well for the man who is gracious and lends,
   who conducts his affairs with justice. **R.**
He shall never be moved;
   the just one shall be in everlasting remembrance.
An evil report he shall not fear;
   his heart is firm, trusting in the LORD. **R.**
His heart is steadfast; he shall not fear.
   Lavishly he gives to the poor;
his justice shall endure forever;
   his horn shall be exalted in glory. **R.**

† *1 Corinthians 2:1-5*
I have announced to you the mystery of Christ crucified.

When I came to you, brothers and sisters,
   proclaiming the mystery of God,
   I did not come with sublimity of words or of wisdom.
For I resolved to know nothing while I was with you
   except Jesus Christ, and him crucified.
I came to you in weakness and fear and much trembling,
   and my message and my proclamation
   were not with persuasive words of wisdom,
   but with a demonstration of Spirit and power,
   so that your faith might rest not on human wisdom
   but on the power of God. ✣

John 8:12

R. Alleluia, alleluia.
I am the light of the world, says the Lord;
   whoever follows me will have the light of life. **R.**

† *Matthew 5:13-16*
You are the light of the world.

Jesus said to his disciples:
  "You are the salt of the earth.
But if salt loses its taste, with what can it be seasoned?
It is no longer good for anything
  but to be thrown out and trampled underfoot.
You are the light of the world.
A city set on a mountain cannot be hidden.
Nor do they light a lamp and then put it under a bushel basket;
  it is set on a lampstand,
  where it gives light to all in the house.
Just so, your light must shine before others,
  that they may see your good deeds
  and glorify your heavenly Father." ✝

MONDAY, FEBRUARY 6
ST. PAUL MIKI AND COMPANIONS

† *Genesis 1:1-19*
God spoke, and it was done.

In the beginning, when God created the heavens and the earth,
  the earth was a formless wasteland, and darkness covered the
    abyss,
  while a mighty wind swept over the waters.

Then God said,
  "Let there be light," and there was light.
God saw how good the light was.
God then separated the light from the darkness.
God called the light "day," and the darkness he called "night."
Thus evening came, and morning followed—the first day.

Then God said,
  "Let there be a dome in the middle of the waters,
  to separate one body of water from the other."
And so it happened:
  God made the dome,
  and it separated the water above the dome from the water below it.
God called the dome "the sky."
Evening came, and morning followed—the second day.

Then God said,
  "Let the water under the sky be gathered into a single basin,
  so that the dry land may appear."

And so it happened:
   the water under the sky was gathered into its basin,
   and the dry land appeared.
God called the dry land "the earth,"
   and the basin of the water he called "the sea."
God saw how good it was.
Then God said,
   "Let the earth bring forth vegetation:
   every kind of plant that bears seed
   and every kind of fruit tree on earth
   that bears fruit with its seed in it."
And so it happened:
   the earth brought forth every kind of plant that bears seed
   and every kind of fruit tree on earth that
   bears fruit with its seed in it.
God saw how good it was.
Evening came, and morning followed—the third day.

Then God said:
   "Let there be lights in the dome of the sky,
   to separate day from night.
Let them mark the fixed times, the days and the years,
   and serve as luminaries in the dome of the sky,
   to shed light upon the earth."
And so it happened:
   God made the two great lights,
   the greater one to govern the day,
   and the lesser one to govern the night;
   and he made the stars.
God set them in the dome of the sky,
   to shed light upon the earth,
   to govern the day and the night,
   and to separate the light from the darkness.
God saw how good it was.
Evening came, and morning followed—the fourth day. ✚

   Psalm 104:1-2a, 5-6, 10 and 12, 24 and 35c
R. (31b) **May the Lord be glad in his works.**
Bless the LORD, O my soul!
   O LORD, my God, you are great indeed!
You are clothed with majesty and glory,
   robed in light as with a cloak. **R.**
You fixed the earth upon its foundation,
   not to be moved forever;
With the ocean, as with a garment, you covered it;

above the mountains the waters stood. **R.**
You send forth springs into the watercourses
   that wind among the mountains.
Beside them the birds of heaven dwell;
   from among the branches they send forth their song. **R.**
How manifold are your works, O LORD!
   In wisdom you have wrought them all—
   the earth is full of your creatures;
Bless the LORD, O my soul! Alleluia. **R.**

   See Matthew 4:23
R. Alleluia, alleluia.
Jesus preached the Gospel of the Kingdom
and cured every disease among the people. **R.**

✝ *Mark 6:53-56*
As many as touched it were healed.

After making the crossing to the other side of the sea,
   Jesus and his disciples came to land at Gennesaret
   and tied up there.
As they were leaving the boat, people immediately recognized him.
They scurried about the surrounding country
   and began to bring in the sick on mats
   to wherever they heard he was.
Whatever villages or towns or countryside he entered,
   they laid the sick in the marketplaces
   and begged him that they might touch only the tassel on his cloak;
and as many as touched it were healed. ✝

TUESDAY, FEBRUARY 7
WEEKDAY

✝ *Genesis 1:20—2:4a*
Let us make man in our own image, after our likeness.

God said,
   "Let the water teem with an abundance of living creatures,
   and on the earth let birds fly beneath the dome of the sky."
And so it happened:
   God created the great sea monsters
   and all kinds of swimming creatures with which the water teems,
   and all kinds of winged birds.
God saw how good it was, and God blessed them, saying,
   "Be fertile, multiply, and fill the water of the seas;
   and let the birds multiply on the earth."
Evening came, and morning followed–the fifth day.

Then God said,
"Let the earth bring forth all kinds of living creatures:
cattle, creeping things, and wild animals of all kinds."
And so it happened:
God made all kinds of wild animals, all kinds of cattle,
and all kinds of creeping things of the earth.
God saw how good it was.
Then God said:
"Let us make man in our image, after our likeness.
Let them have dominion over the fish of the sea,
the birds of the air, and the cattle,
and over all the wild animals
and all the creatures that crawl on the ground."

God created man in his image;
in the divine image he created him;
male and female he created them.

God blessed them, saying:
"Be fertile and multiply;
fill the earth and subdue it.
Have dominion over the fish of the sea, the birds of the air,
and all the living things that move on the earth."
God also said:
"See, I give you every seed-bearing plant all over the earth
and every tree that has seed-bearing fruit on it to be your food;
and to all the animals of the land, all the birds of the air,
and all the living creatures that crawl on the ground,
I give all the green plants for food."
And so it happened.
God looked at everything he had made, and he found it very good.
Evening came, and morning followed—the sixth day.

Thus the heavens and the earth and all their array were completed.
Since on the seventh day God was finished with the work he had
been doing,
he rested on the seventh day from all the work he had undertaken.
So God blessed the seventh day and made it holy,
because on it he rested from all the work he had done in creation.

Such is the story of the heavens and the earth at their creation. ✙

Psalm 8:4-5, 6-7, 8-9
R. (2ab) O Lord, our God, how wonderful your name in all the earth!
When I behold your heavens, the work of your fingers,

the moon and the stars which you set in place—
What is man that you should be mindful of him,
  or the son of man that you should care for him? **R.**
You have made him little less than the angels,
  and crowned him with glory and honor.
You have given him rule over the works of your hands,
  putting all things under his feet. **R.**
All sheep and oxen,
  yes, and the beasts of the field,
The birds of the air, the fishes of the sea,
  and whatever swims the paths of the seas. **R.**

  Psalm 119:36, 29b
R. Alleluia, alleluia.
Incline my heart, O God, to your decrees;
and favor me with your law. **R.**

† *Mark 7:1-13*
You disregard God's commandment but cling to human tradition.

When the Pharisees with some scribes who had come from Jerusalem
  gathered around Jesus,
    they observed that some of his disciples ate their meals
    with unclean, that is, unwashed, hands.
(For the Pharisees and, in fact, all Jews,
  do not eat without carefully washing their hands,
  keeping the tradition of the elders.)
And on coming from the marketplace
  they do not eat without purifying themselves.
And there are many other things that they have traditionally observed,
  the purification of cups and jugs and kettles and beds.)
So the Pharisees and scribes questioned him,
  "Why do your disciples not follow the tradition of the elders
  but instead eat a meal with unclean hands?"
He responded,
  "Well did Isaiah prophesy about you hypocrites,
  as it is written:

*This people honors me with their lips,
    but their hearts are far from me;
  In vain do they worship me,
    teaching as doctrines human precepts.*

You disregard God's commandment but cling to human tradition."
He went on to say,
  "How well you have set aside the commandment of God
  in order to uphold your tradition!

For Moses said,
  Honor your father and your mother,
  and *Whoever curses father or mother shall die.*
Yet you say,
  'If someone says to father or mother,
  "Any support you might have had from me is *qorban*"'
  (meaning, dedicated to God),
  you allow him to do nothing more for his father or mother.
You nullify the word of God
  in favor of your tradition that you have handed on.
And you do many such things." ✛

WEDNESDAY, FEBRUARY 8
Weekday, St. Jerome Emiliani, St. Josephine Bakhita

† *Genesis 2:4b-9, 15-17*
*The Lord God planted a garden in Eden and placed there
the man whom he had formed.*

At the time when the Lord God made the earth and the heavens—
  while as yet there was no field shrub on earth
  and no grass of the field had sprouted,
  for the Lord God had sent no rain upon the earth
  and there was no man to till the soil,
  but a stream was welling up out of the earth
  and was watering all the surface of the ground—
  the Lord God formed man out of the clay of the ground
  and blew into his nostrils the breath of life,
  and so man became a living being.

Then the Lord God planted a garden in Eden, in the east,
  and he placed there the man whom he had formed.
Out of the ground the Lord God made various trees grow
  that were delightful to look at and good for food,
  with the tree of life in the middle of the garden
  and the tree of the knowledge of good and evil.

The Lord God then took the man
  and settled him in the garden of Eden,
  to cultivate and care for it.
The Lord God gave man this order:
  "You are free to eat from any of the trees of the garden
  except the tree of knowledge of good and evil.
From that tree you shall not eat;
  the moment you eat from it you are surely doomed to die." ✛

Psalm 104:1-2a, 27-28, 29bc-30

R. (1a) **O bless the Lord, my soul!**

Bless the LORD, O my soul!
O LORD, my God, you are great indeed!
You are clothed with majesty and glory,
  robed in light as with a cloak. **R.**
All creatures look to you
  to give them food in due time.
When you give it to them, they gather it;
  when you open your hand, they are filled with good things. **R.**
If you take away their breath, they perish
  and return to their dust.
When you send forth your spirit, they are created,
  and you renew the face of the earth. **R.**

See John 17:17b, 17a

R. Alleluia, alleluia.

Your word, O Lord, is truth:
consecrate us in the truth. **R.**

† Mark 7:14-23

What comes out of the man, that is what defiles him.

Jesus summoned the crowd again and said to them,
  "Hear me, all of you, and understand.
Nothing that enters one from outside can defile that person;
  but the things that come out from within are what defile."

When he got home away from the crowd
  his disciples questioned him about the parable.
He said to them,
  "Are even you likewise without understanding?
Do you not realize that everything
  that goes into a person from outside cannot defile,
  since it enters not the heart but the stomach
  and passes out into the latrine?"
(Thus he declared all foods clean.)
"But what comes out of the man, that is what defiles him.
From within the man, from his heart,
  come evil thoughts, unchastity, theft, murder,
  adultery, greed, malice, deceit,
  licentiousness, envy, blasphemy, arrogance, folly.
All these evils come from within and they defile." ✛

THURSDAY, FEBRUARY 9
WEEKDAY

† *Genesis 2:18-25*
The LORD God brought her to Adam,
and the two of them became one flesh.

The LORD God said:
"It is not good for the man to be alone.
I will make a suitable partner for him."
So the LORD God formed out of the ground
    various wild animals and various birds of the air,
    and he brought them to the man to see what he would call them;
    whatever the man called each of them would be its name.
The man gave names to all the cattle,
    all the birds of the air, and all the wild animals;
    but none proved to be the suitable partner for the man.

So the LORD God cast a deep sleep on the man,
    and while he was asleep, he took out one of his ribs
    and closed up its place with flesh.
The LORD God then built up into a woman
    the rib that he had taken from the man.
When he brought her to the man, the man said:

    "This one, at last, is bone of my bones
        and flesh of my flesh;
    this one shall be called 'woman,'
        for out of 'her man' this one has been taken."

That is why a man leaves his father and mother
    and clings to his wife,
    and the two of them become one flesh.

The man and his wife were both naked, yet they felt no shame. ✛

Psalm 128:1-2, 3, 4-5
R. (see 1a) **Blessed are those who fear the Lord.**
Blessed are you who fear the LORD,
    who walk in his ways!
For you shall eat the fruit of your handiwork;
    blessed shall you be, and favored. **R.**
Your wife shall be like a fruitful vine
    in the recesses of your home;
Your children like olive plants
    around your table. **R.**
Behold, thus is the man blessed
    who fears the LORD.

The LORD bless you from Zion:
  may you see the prosperity of Jerusalem
  all the days of your life. **R.**

James 1:21bc
R. Alleluia, alleluia.
Humbly welcome the word that has been planted in you
and is able to save your souls. **R.**

† Mark 7:24-30
The dogs under the table eat the children's scraps.

Jesus went to the district of Tyre.
He entered a house and wanted no one to know about it,
  but he could not escape notice.
Soon a woman whose daughter had an unclean spirit heard about
    him.
She came and fell at his feet.
The woman was a Greek, a Syrophoenician by birth,
  and she begged him to drive the demon out of her daughter.
He said to her, "Let the children be fed first.
For it is not right to take the food of the children
  and throw it to the dogs."
She replied and said to him,
  "Lord, even the dogs under the table eat the children's scraps."
Then he said to her, "For saying this, you may go.
The demon has gone out of your daughter."
When the woman went home, she found the child lying in bed
  and the demon gone. ✠

FRIDAY, FEBRUARY 10
ST. SCHOLASTICA

† Genesis 3:1-8
You will be like gods, knowing what is good and what is evil.

Now the serpent was the most cunning of all the animals
  that the LORD God had made.
The serpent asked the woman,
  "Did God really tell you not to eat
  from any of the trees in the garden?"
The woman answered the serpent:
  "We may eat of the fruit of the trees in the garden;
  it is only about the fruit of the tree
  in the middle of the garden that God said,
  'You shall not eat it or even touch it, lest you die.'"
But the serpent said to the woman:
  "You certainly will not die!

No, God knows well that the moment you eat of it
    your eyes will be opened and you will be like gods
    who know what is good and what is evil."
The woman saw that the tree was good for food,
    pleasing to the eyes, and desirable for gaining wisdom.
So she took some of its fruit and ate it;
    and she also gave some to her husband, who was with her,
    and he ate it.
Then the eyes of both of them were opened,
    and they realized that they were naked;
    so they sewed fig leaves together
    and made loincloths for themselves.

When they heard the sound of the LORD God moving about in the
        garden
    at the breezy time of the day,
    the man and his wife hid themselves from the LORD God
    among the trees of the garden. ✛

Psalm 32:1-2, 5, 6, 7
R. (1a) **Blessed are those whose sins are forgiven.**
Blessed is he whose fault is taken away,
    whose sin is covered.
Blessed the man to whom the LORD imputes not guilt,
    in whose spirit there is no guile. **R.**
Then I acknowledged my sin to you,
    my guilt I covered not.
I said, "I confess my faults to the LORD,"
    and you took away the guilt of my sin. **R.**
For this shall every faithful man pray to you
    in time of stress.
Though deep waters overflow,
    they shall not reach him. **R.**
You are my shelter; from distress you will preserve me;
    with glad cries of freedom you will ring me round. **R.**

See Acts 16:14b
R. Alleluia, alleluia.
Open our hearts, O Lord,
to listen to the words of your Son. **R.**

† *Mark 7:31-37*
He makes the deaf hear and the mute speak.

Jesus left the district of Tyre
    and went by way of Sidon to the Sea of Galilee,
    into the district of the Decapolis.

And people brought to him a deaf man who had a speech impediment
and begged him to lay his hand on him.
He took him off by himself away from the crowd.
He put his finger into the man's ears
and, spitting, touched his tongue;
then he looked up to heaven and groaned, and said to him,
"Ephphatha!" (that is, "Be opened!")
And immediately the man's ears were opened,
his speech impediment was removed,
and he spoke plainly.
He ordered them not to tell anyone.
But the more he ordered them not to,
the more they proclaimed it.
They were exceedingly astonished and they said,
"He has done all things well.
He makes the deaf hear and the mute speak." ✢

SATURDAY, FEBRUARY 11
WEEKDAY, OUR LADY OF LOURDES, *[BVM]*

† *Genesis 3:9-24*
God banished him from the garden of Eden to till the ground.

The LORD God called to Adam and asked him, "Where are you?"
He answered, "I heard you in the garden;
but I was afraid, because I was naked,
so I hid myself."
Then he asked, "Who told you that you were naked?
You have eaten, then,
from the tree of which I had forbidden you to eat!"
The man replied, "The woman whom you put here with me—
she gave me fruit from the tree, and so I ate it."
The LORD God then asked the woman,
"Why did you do such a thing?"
The woman answered, "The serpent tricked me into it, so I ate it."

Then the LORD God said to the serpent:

"Because you have done this, you shall be banned
from all the animals
and from all the wild creatures;
On your belly shall you crawl,
and dirt shall you eat
all the days of your life.
I will put enmity between you and the woman,
and between your offspring and hers;

He will strike at your head,
    while you strike at his heel."

To the woman he said:

"I will intensify the pangs of your childbearing;
    in pain shall you bring forth children.
Yet your urge shall be for your husband,
    and he shall be your master."

To the man he said: "Because you listened to your wife
    and ate from the tree of which I had forbidden you to eat,

"Cursed be the ground because of you!
    In toil shall you eat its yield
    all the days of your life.
Thorns and thistles shall it bring forth to you,
    as you eat of the plants of the field.
By the sweat of your face
    shall you get bread to eat,
Until you return to the ground,
    from which you were taken;
For you are dirt,
    and to dirt you shall return."

The man called his wife Eve,
    because she became the mother of all the living.

For the man and his wife the LORD God made leather garments,
    with which he clothed them.
Then the LORD God said: "See! The man has become like one of us,
    knowing what is good and what is evil!
Therefore, he must not be allowed to put out his hand
    to take fruit from the tree of life also,
    and thus eat of it and live forever."
The LORD God therefore banished him from the garden of Eden,
    to till the ground from which he had been taken.
When he expelled the man,
    he settled him east of the garden of Eden;
    and he stationed the cherubim and the fiery revolving sword,
    to guard the way to the tree of life. ✛

    Psalm 90:2, 3-4abc, 5-6, 12-13
R. (1) In every age, O Lord, you have been our refuge.
Before the mountains were begotten
    and the earth and the world were brought forth,
    from everlasting to everlasting you are God. **R.**

You turn man back to dust,
  saying, "Return, O children of men."
For a thousand years in your sight
  are as yesterday, now that it is past,
  or as a watch of the night. **R.**
You make an end of them in their sleep;
  the next morning they are like the changing grass,
Which at dawn springs up anew,
  but by evening wilts and fades. **R.**
Teach us to number our days aright,
  that we may gain wisdom of heart.
Return, O LORD! How long?
  Have pity on your servants! **R.**

Matthew 4:4b
R. Alleluia, alleluia.
One does not live on bread alone,
but on every word that comes forth from the mouth of God. **R.**

† *Mark 8:1-10*
They ate and were satisfied.

In those days when there again was a great crowd without any-
    thing to eat,
  Jesus summoned the disciples and said,
  "My heart is moved with pity for the crowd,
  because they have been with me now for three days
  and have nothing to eat.
If I send them away hungry to their homes,
  they will collapse on the way,
  and some of them have come a great distance."
His disciples answered him, "Where can anyone get enough bread
  to satisfy them here in this deserted place?"
Still he asked them, "How many loaves do you have?"
They replied, "Seven."
He ordered the crowd to sit down on the ground.
Then, taking the seven loaves he gave thanks, broke them,
  and gave them to his disciples to distribute,
  and they distributed them to the crowd.
They also had a few fish.
He said the blessing over them
  and ordered them distributed also.
They ate and were satisfied.
They picked up the fragments left over—seven baskets.
There were about four thousand people.

He dismissed the crowd and got into the boat with his disciples
and came to the region of Dalmanutha. ✛

SUNDAY, FEBRUARY 12
SIXTH SUNDAY IN ORDINARY TIME

† Sirach 15:15-20
No one does he command to act unjustly.

If you choose you can keep the commandments, they will save you;
  if you trust in God, you too shall live;
he has set before you fire and water;
  to whichever you choose, stretch forth your hand.
Before man are life and death, good and evil,
  whichever he chooses shall be given him.
Immense is the wisdom of the Lord;
  he is mighty in power, and all-seeing.
The eyes of God are on those who fear him;
  he understands man's every deed.
No one does he command to act unjustly,
  to none does he give license to sin. ✛

Psalm 119:1-2, 4-5, 17-18, 33-34
R. (1b) **Blessed are they who follow the law of the Lord!**
Blessed are they whose way is blameless,
  who walk in the law of the LORD.
Blessed are they who observe his decrees,
  who seek him with all their heart. **R.**
You have commanded that your precepts
  be diligently kept.
Oh, that I might be firm in the ways
  of keeping your statutes! **R.**
Be good to your servant, that I may live
  and keep your words.
Open my eyes, that I may consider
  the wonders of your law. **R.**
Instruct me, O LORD, in the way of your statutes,
  that I may exactly observe them.
Give me discernment, that I may observe your law
  and keep it with all my heart. **R.**

† 1 Corinthians 2:6-10
God predestined wisdom before the ages for our glory.

Brothers and sisters:
We speak a wisdom to those who are mature,
  not a wisdom of this age,

nor of the rulers of this age who are passing away.
Rather, we speak God's wisdom, mysterious, hidden,
  which God predetermined before the ages for our glory,
  and which none of the rulers of this age knew;
  or, if they had known it,
  they would not have crucified the Lord of glory.
But as it is written:
  What eye has not seen, and ear has not heard,
    and what has not entered the human heart,
    what God has prepared for those who love him,
  this God has revealed to us through the Spirit.

For the Spirit scrutinizes everything, even the depths of God. ✝

  See Matthew 11:25
R. Alleluia, alleluia.
Blessed are you, Father, Lord of heaven and earth;
you have revealed to little ones the mysteries of the kingdom. **R.**

  ✝ ***Matthew 5:17-37*** *(or Matthew 5:20-22a, 27-28, 33-34a, 37)*
    So it was said to your ancestors; but I say this to you.

Jesus said to his disciples:
  "Do not think that I have come to abolish the law or the prophets.
I have come not to abolish but to fulfill.
Amen, I say to you, until heaven and earth pass away,
  not the smallest letter or the smallest part of a letter
  will pass from the law,
  until all things have taken place.
Therefore, whoever breaks one of the least of these commandments
  and teaches others to do so
  will be called least in the kingdom of heaven.
But whoever obeys and teaches these commandments
  will be called greatest in the kingdom of heaven.
I tell you, unless your righteousness surpasses
  that of the scribes and Pharisees,
  you will not enter the kingdom of heaven.

"You have heard that it was said to your ancestors,
  You shall not kill; and whoever kills will be liable to judgment.
But I say to you,
  whoever is angry with his brother
  will be liable to judgment;
  and whoever says to his brother, 'Raqa,'
  will be answerable to the Sanhedrin;
  and whoever says, 'You fool,'
  will be liable to fiery Gehenna.

Therefore, if you bring your gift to the altar,
   and there recall that your brother
   has anything against you,
   leave your gift there at the altar,
   go first and be reconciled with your brother,
   and then come and offer your gift.
Settle with your opponent quickly while on the way to court.
Otherwise your opponent will hand you over to the judge,
   and the judge will hand you over to the guard,
   and you will be thrown into prison.
Amen, I say to you,
   you will not be released until you have paid the last penny.

"You have heard that it was said,
   You shall not commit adultery.
But I say to you,
   everyone who looks at a woman with lust
   has already committed adultery with her in his heart.
If your right eye causes you to sin,
   tear it out and throw it away.
It is better for you to lose one of your members
   than to have your whole body thrown into Gehenna.
And if your right hand causes you to sin,
   cut it off and throw it away.
It is better for you to lose one of your members
   than to have your whole body go into Gehenna.

"It was also said,
   Whoever divorces his wife must give her a bill of divorce.
But I say to you,
   whoever divorces his wife—unless the marriage is unlawful—
   causes her to commit adultery,
   and whoever marries a divorced woman commits adultery.

"Again you have heard that it was said to your ancestors,
   Do not take a false oath,
   but make good to the Lord all that you vow.
But I say to you, do not swear at all;
   not by heaven, for it is God's throne;
   nor by the earth, for it is his footstool;
   nor by Jerusalem, for it is the city of the great King.
Do not swear by your head,
   for you cannot make a single hair white or black.
Let your 'Yes' mean 'Yes,' and your 'No' mean 'No.'
Anything more is from the evil one." ✦

MONDAY, FEBRUARY 13
WEEKDAY

† *Genesis 4:1-15, 25*
Cain attacked his brother Abel and killed him.

The man had relations with his wife Eve,
and she conceived and bore Cain, saying,
"I have produced a man with the help of the LORD."
Next she bore his brother Abel.
Abel became a keeper of flocks, and Cain a tiller of the soil.
In the course of time Cain brought an offering to the LORD
from the fruit of the soil,
while Abel, for his part,
brought one of the best firstlings of his flock.
The LORD looked with favor on Abel and his offering,
but on Cain and his offering he did not.
Cain greatly resented this and was crestfallen.
So the LORD said to Cain:
"Why are you so resentful and crestfallen?
If you do well, you can hold up your head;
but if not, sin is a demon lurking at the door:
his urge is toward you, yet you can be his master."

Cain said to his brother Abel, "Let us go out in the field."
When they were in the field,
Cain attacked his brother Abel and killed him.
Then the LORD asked Cain, "Where is your brother Abel?"
He answered, "I do not know.
Am I my brother's keeper?"
The LORD then said: "What have you done!
Listen: your brother's blood cries out to me from the soil!
Therefore you shall be banned from the soil
that opened its mouth to receive
your brother's blood from your hand.
If you till the soil, it shall no longer give you its produce.
You shall become a restless wanderer on the earth."
Cain said to the LORD: "My punishment is too great to bear.
Since you have now banished me from the soil,
and I must avoid your presence
and become a restless wanderer on the earth,
anyone may kill me at sight."
"Not so!" the LORD said to him.
"If anyone kills Cain, Cain shall be avenged sevenfold."
So the LORD put a mark on Cain, lest anyone should kill him at sight.

Adam again had relations with his wife,
and she gave birth to a son whom she called Seth.
"God has granted me more offspring in place of Abel," she said,
"because Cain slew him." ✛

Psalm 50:1 and 8, 16bc-17, 20-21
R. (14a) **Offer to God a sacrifice of praise.**
God the LORD has spoken and summoned the earth,
from the rising of the sun to its setting.
"Not for your sacrifices do I rebuke you,
for your burnt offerings are before me always." **R.**
"Why do you recite my statutes,
and profess my covenant with your mouth
Though you hate discipline
and cast my words behind you?" **R.**
"You sit speaking against your brother;
against your mother's son you spread rumors.
When you do these things, shall I be deaf to it?
Or do you think that I am like yourself?
I will correct you by drawing them up before your eyes." **R.**

John 14:6
R. Alleluia, alleluia.
I am the way and the truth and the life, says the Lord;
no one comes to the Father except through me. **R.**

† *Mark 8:11-13*
Why does this generation seek a sign?

The Pharisees came forward and began to argue with Jesus,
seeking from him a sign from heaven to test him.
He sighed from the depth of his spirit and said,
"Why does this generation seek a sign?
Amen, I say to you, no sign will be given to this generation."
Then he left them, got into the boat again,
and went off to the other shore. ✛

TUESDAY, FEBRUARY 14
ST. CYRIL, ST. MONK AND ST. METHODIUS

† *Genesis 6:5-8; 7:1-5, 10*
I will wipe out from the earth the men whom I have created.

When the LORD saw how great was man's wickedness on earth,
and how no desire that his heart conceived
was ever anything but evil,
he regretted that he had made man on the earth,
and his heart was grieved.

So the Lord said:
"I will wipe out from the earth the men whom I have created,
and not only the men,
but also the beasts and the creeping things and the birds of the air,
for I am sorry that I made them."
But Noah found favor with the Lord.

Then the Lord said to Noah:
"Go into the ark, you and all your household,
for you alone in this age have I found to be truly just.
Of every clean animal, take with you seven pairs,
a male and its mate;
and of the unclean animals, one pair,
a male and its mate;
likewise, of every clean bird of the air, seven pairs,
a male and a female,
and of all the unclean birds, one pair,
a male and a female.
Thus you will keep their issue alive over all the earth.
Seven days from now I will bring rain down on the earth
for forty days and forty nights,
and so I will wipe out from the surface of the earth
every moving creature that I have made."
Noah did just as the Lord had commanded him.

As soon as the seven days were over,
the waters of the flood came upon the earth. ✛

Psalm 29:1bc, 2, 3ac-4, 3b and 9c-10
R. (11b) The Lord will bless his people with peace.
Give to the Lord, you sons of God,
give to the Lord glory and praise,
Give to the Lord the glory due his name;
adore the Lord in holy attire. **R.**
The voice of the Lord is over the waters,
the Lord, over vast waters.
The voice of the Lord is mighty;
the voice of the Lord is majestic. **R.**
The God of glory thunders,
and in his temple all say, "Glory!"
The Lord is enthroned above the flood;
the Lord is enthroned as king forever. **R.**

John 14:23
R. Alleluia, alleluia.
Whoever loves me will keep my word, says the Lord;
and my Father will love him
and we will come to him. **R.**

† *Mark 8:14-21*
Watch out, guard against the leaven of the Pharisees and the leaven of Herod.

The disciples had forgotten to bring bread,
  and they had only one loaf with them in the boat.
Jesus enjoined them, "Watch out,
  guard against the leaven of the Pharisees
  and the leaven of Herod."
They concluded among themselves that
  it was because they had no bread.
When he became aware of this he said to them,
  "Why do you conclude that it is because you have no bread?
Do you not yet understand or comprehend?
Are your hearts hardened?
Do you have eyes and not see, ears and not hear?
And do you not remember,
  when I broke the five loaves for the five thousand,
  how many wicker baskets full of fragments you picked up?"
They answered him, "Twelve."
"When I broke the seven loaves for the four thousand,
  how many full baskets of fragments did you pick up?"
They answered him, "Seven."
He said to them, "Do you still not understand?" ✛

WEDNESDAY, FEBRUARY 15
WEEKDAY

† *Genesis 8:6-13, 20-22*
Noah saw that the surface of the ground was drying up.

At the end of forty days Noah opened the hatch he had made in the
    ark,
  and he sent out a raven,
  to see if the waters had lessened on the earth.
It flew back and forth until the waters dried off from the earth.
Then he sent out a dove,
  to see if the waters had lessened on the earth.
But the dove could find no place to alight and perch,
  and it returned to him in the ark,
  for there was water all over the earth.
Putting out his hand, he caught the dove

and drew it back to him inside the ark.
He waited seven days more and again sent the dove out from the ark.
In the evening the dove came back to him,
    and there in its bill was a plucked-off olive leaf!
So Noah knew that the waters had lessened on the earth.
He waited still another seven days
    and then released the dove once more;
    and this time it did not come back.

In the six hundred and first year of Noah's life,
    in the first month, on the first day of the month,
    the water began to dry up on the earth.
Noah then removed the covering of the ark
    and saw that the surface of the ground was drying up.

Noah built an altar to the LORD,
    and choosing from every clean animal and every clean bird,
    he offered burnt offerings on the altar.
When the LORD smelled the sweet odor, he said to himself:
    "Never again will I doom the earth because of man
    since the desires of man's heart are evil from the start;
    nor will I ever again strike down all living beings, as I have done.
    As long as the earth lasts,
        seedtime and harvest,
        cold and heat,
    Summer and winter,
        and day and night
        shall not cease." ✛

Psalm 116:12-13, 14-15, 18-19
R. (17a) **To you, Lord, I will offer a sacrifice of praise.**
    (*or* **Alleluia.***)*
How shall I make a return to the LORD
    for all the good he has done for me?
The cup of salvation I will take up,
    and I will call upon the name of the LORD. **R.**
My vows to the LORD I will pay
    in the presence of all his people.
Precious in the eyes of the LORD
    is the death of his faithful ones. **R.**
My vows to the LORD I will pay
    in the presence of all his people,
In the courts of the house of the LORD,
    in your midst, O Jerusalem. **R.**

See Ephesians 1:17-18
R. Alleluia, alleluia.
May the Father of our Lord Jesus Christ
enlighten the eyes of our hearts,
that we may know what is the hope
that belongs to his call. **R.**

† *Mark 8:22-26*
His sight was restored and he could see everything distinctly.

When Jesus and his disciples arrived at Bethsaida,
people brought to him a blind man and begged Jesus to touch him.
He took the blind man by the hand and led him outside the village.
Putting spittle on his eyes he laid his hands on the man and asked,
"Do you see anything?"
Looking up the man replied, "I see people looking like trees and
walking."
Then he laid hands on the man's eyes a second time and he saw
clearly;
his sight was restored and he could see everything distinctly.
Then he sent him home and said, "Do not even go into the village." ✢

THURSDAY, FEBRUARY 16
WEEKDAY

† *Genesis 9:1-13*
I set my bow in the clouds to serve as a sign
of the covenant between me and the earth.

God blessed Noah and his sons and said to them:
"Be fertile and multiply and fill the earth.
Dread fear of you shall come upon all the animals of the earth
and all the birds of the air,
upon all the creatures that move about on the ground
and all the fishes of the sea;
into your power they are delivered.
Every creature that is alive shall be yours to eat;
I give them all to you as I did the green plants.
Only flesh with its lifeblood still in it you shall not eat.
For your own lifeblood, too, I will demand an accounting:
from every animal I will demand it,
and from one man in regard to his fellow man
I will demand an accounting for human life.

If anyone sheds the blood of man,
by man shall his blood be shed;
For in the image of God
has man been made.

Be fertile, then, and multiply;
   abound on earth and subdue it."

God said to Noah and to his sons with him:
   "See, I am now establishing my covenant with you
   and your descendants after you
   and with every living creature that was with you:
   all the birds, and the various tame and wild animals
   that were with you and came out of the ark.
I will establish my covenant with you,
   that never again shall all bodily creatures be destroyed
   by the waters of a flood;
   there shall not be another flood to devastate the earth."
God added:
   "This is the sign that I am giving for all ages to come,
   of the covenant between me and you
   and every living creature with you:
   I set my bow in the clouds to serve as a sign
   of the covenant between me and the earth." ✢

Psalm 102:16-18, 19-21, 29 and 22-23

R. (20b) From heaven the Lord looks down on the earth.
The nations shall revere your name, O LORD,
   and all the kings of the earth your glory,
When the LORD has rebuilt Zion
   and appeared in his glory;
When he has regarded the prayer of the destitute,
   and not despised their prayer. **R.**
Let this be written for the generation to come,
   and let his future creatures praise the LORD:
"The LORD looked down from his holy height,
   from heaven he beheld the earth,
To hear the groaning of the prisoners,
   to release those doomed to die." **R.**
The children of your servants shall abide,
   and their posterity shall continue in your presence,
That the name of the LORD may be declared in Zion,
   and his praise, in Jerusalem,
When the peoples gather together,
   and the kingdoms, to serve the LORD. **R.**

See John 6:63c, 68c

R. Alleluia, alleluia.
Your words, Lord, are Spirit and life;
you have the words of everlasting life. **R.**

† *Mark 8:27-33*
You are the Christ. The Son of Man must suffer much.

Jesus and his disciples set out
  for the villages of Caesarea Philippi.
Along the way he asked his disciples,
  "Who do people say that I am?"
They said in reply,
  "John the Baptist, others Elijah,
  still others one of the prophets."
And he asked them,
  "But who do you say that I am?"
Peter said to him in reply,
  "You are the Christ."
Then he warned them not to tell anyone about him.

He began to teach them
  that the Son of Man must suffer greatly
  and be rejected by the elders, the chief priests, and the scribes,
  and be killed, and rise after three days.
He spoke this openly.
Then Peter took him aside and began to rebuke him.
At this he turned around and, looking at his disciples,
  rebuked Peter and said, "Get behind me, Satan.
You are thinking not as God does, but as human beings do." ✢

FRIDAY, FEBRUARY 17
WEEKDAY, THE SEVEN HOLY FOUNDERS OF THE SERVITE ORDER

† *Genesis 11:1-9*
Let us go down and there confuse their language.

The whole world spoke the same language, using the same words.
While the people were migrating in the east,
  they came upon a valley in the land of Shinar and settled there.
They said to one another,
  "Come, let us mold bricks and harden them with fire."
They used bricks for stone, and bitumen for mortar.
Then they said, "Come, let us build ourselves a city
  and a tower with its top in the sky,
  and so make a name for ourselves;
  otherwise we shall be scattered all over the earth."

The LORD came down to see the city and the tower
  that they had built.
Then the LORD said: "If now, while they are one people,
  all speaking the same language,

they have started to do this,
nothing will later stop them from doing whatever they presume to
    do.
Let us then go down and there confuse their language,
so that one will not understand what another says."
Thus the LORD scattered them from there all over the earth,
and they stopped building the city.
That is why it was called Babel,
because there the LORD confused the speech of all the world.
It was from that place that he scattered them all over the earth. ✢

    Psalm 33:10-11, 12-13, 14-15

R. (12) **Blessed the people the Lord has chosen to be his own.**
The LORD brings to nought the plans of nations;
he foils the designs of peoples.
But the plan of the LORD stands forever;
the design of his heart, through all generations. **R.**
Blessed the nation whose God is the LORD,
the people he has chosen for his own inheritance.
From heaven the LORD looks down;
he sees all mankind. **R.**
From his fixed throne he beholds
all who dwell on the earth,
He who fashioned the heart of each,
he who knows all their works. **R.**

    John 15:15b

R. Alleluia, alleluia.
I call you my friends, says the Lord,
for I have made known to you all that the Father has told me. **R.**

† Mark 8:34—9:1
*Those who lose their lives for my sake
and that of the Gospel, will save them.*

Jesus summoned the crowd with his disciples and said to them,
"Whoever wishes to come after me must deny himself,
take up his cross, and follow me.
For whoever wishes to save his life will lose it,
but whoever loses his life for my sake
and that of the Gospel will save it.
What profit is there for one to gain the whole world
and forfeit his life?
What could one give in exchange for his life?
Whoever is ashamed of me and of my words
in this faithless and sinful generation,
the Son of Man will be ashamed of

when he comes in his Father's glory with the holy angels."

He also said to them,
"Amen, I say to you,
there are some standing here who will not taste death
until they see that the Kingdom of God has come in power." ✛

SATURDAY, FEBRUARY 18
WEEKDAY, *[BVM]*

† *Hebrews 11:1-7*
*By faith we understand that the universe was
ordered by the word of God.*

Brothers and sisters:
Faith is the realization of what is hoped for
    and evidence of things not seen.
Because of it the ancients were well attested.
By faith we understand that the universe was ordered by the word
        of God,
    so that what is visible came into being through the invisible.
By faith Abel offered to God a sacrifice greater than Cain's.
Through this, he was attested to be righteous,
    God bearing witness to his gifts,
    and through this, though dead, he still speaks.
By faith Enoch was taken up so that he should not see death,
    and *he was found no more because God had taken him.*
Before he was taken up, he was attested to have pleased God.
But without faith it is impossible to please him,
    for anyone who approaches God must believe that he exists
    and that he rewards those who seek him.
By faith Noah, warned about what was not yet seen,
    with reverence built an ark for the salvation of his household.
Through this, he condemned the world
    and inherited the righteousness that comes through faith. ✛

Psalm 145:2-3, 4-5, 10-11
R. (see 1) **I will praise your name for ever, Lord.**
Every day will I bless you,
    and I will praise your name forever and ever.
Great is the LORD and highly to be praised;
    his greatness is unsearchable. **R.**
Generation after generation praises your works
    and proclaims your might.
They speak of the splendor of your glorious majesty
    and tell of your wondrous works. **R.**
Let all your works give you thanks, O LORD,

and let your faithful ones bless you.
Let them discourse of the glory of your Kingdom
   and speak of your might. **R.**

See Mark 9:6
R. Alleluia, alleluia.
The heavens were opened and the voice of the Father thundered:
This is my beloved Son. Listen to him. **R.**

† *Mark 9:2-13*
Jesus was transfigured before them.

Jesus took Peter, James, and John
   and led them up a high mountain apart by themselves.
And he was transfigured before them,
   and his clothes became dazzling white,
   such as no fuller on earth could bleach them.
Then Elijah appeared to them along with Moses,
   and they were conversing with Jesus.
Then Peter said to Jesus in reply,
   "Rabbi, it is good that we are here!
Let us make three tents:
   one for you, one for Moses, and one for Elijah."
He hardly knew what to say, they were so terrified.
Then a cloud came, casting a shadow over them;
   then from the cloud came a voice,
   "This is my beloved Son. Listen to him."
Suddenly, looking around, the disciples no longer saw anyone
   but Jesus alone with them.

As they were coming down from the mountain,
   he charged them not to relate what they had seen to anyone,
   except when the Son of Man had risen from the dead.
So they kept the matter to themselves,
   questioning what rising from the dead meant.
Then they asked him,
   "Why do the scribes say that Elijah must come first?"
He told them, "Elijah will indeed come first and restore all things,
   yet how is it written regarding the Son of Man
   that he must suffer greatly and be treated with contempt?
But I tell you that Elijah has come
   and they did to him whatever they pleased,
   as it is written of him." ✝

SUNDAY, FEBRUARY 19
SEVENTH SUNDAY IN ORDINARY TIME

† *Leviticus 19:1-2, 17-18*
You shall love your neighbor as yourself.

The LORD said to Moses,
"Speak to the whole Israelite community and tell them:
Be holy, for I, the LORD, your God, am holy.

"You shall not bear hatred for your brother or sister in your heart.
Though you may have to reprove your fellow citizen,
   do not incur sin because of him.
Take no revenge and cherish no grudge against any of your people.
You shall love your neighbor as yourself.
I am the LORD." ✛

Psalm 103:1-2, 3-4, 8 and 10, 12-13
R. (8a) **The Lord is kind and merciful.**
Bless the LORD, O my soul;
   and all my being, bless his holy name.
Bless the LORD, O my soul,
   and forget not all his benefits. **R.**
He pardons all your iniquities,
   heals all your ills.
He redeems your life from destruction,
   crowns you with kindness and compassion. **R.**
Merciful and gracious is the LORD,
   slow to anger and abounding in kindness.
Not according to our sins does he deal with us,
   nor does he requite us according to our crimes. **R.**
As far as the east is from the west,
   so far has he put our transgressions from us.
As a father has compassion on his children,
   so the Lord has compassion on those who fear him. **R.**

† *1 Corinthians 3:16-23*
All things belong to you, and you to Christ, and Christ to God.

Brothers and sisters:
Do you not know that you are the temple of God,
   and that the Spirit of God dwells in you?
If anyone destroys God's temple, God will destroy that person;
   for the temple of God, which you are, is holy.

Let no one deceive himself.
If any one among you considers himself wise in this age,
   let him become a fool, so as to become wise.

For the wisdom of this world is foolishness in the eyes of God,
  for it is written:
    God catches the wise in their own ruses,
and again:
    The Lord knows the thoughts of the wise,
      that they are vain.
So let no one boast about human beings, for everything belongs to
  you,
  Paul or Apollos or Cephas,
  or the world or life or death,
  or the present or the future:
  all belong to you, and you to Christ, and Christ to God. ✝

  1 John 2:5
R. Alleluia, alleluia.
Whoever keeps the word of Christ,
the love of God is truly perfected in him. **R.**

✝ *Matthew 5:38-48*
Love your enemies.

Jesus said to his disciples:
  "You have heard that it was said,
  An eye for an eye and a tooth for a tooth.
But I say to you, offer no resistance to one who is evil.
When someone strikes you on your right cheek,
  turn the other one as well.
If anyone wants to go to law with you over your tunic,
  hand over your cloak as well.
Should anyone press you into service for one mile,
  go for two miles.
Give to the one who asks of you,
  and do not turn your back on one who wants to borrow.

"You have heard that it was said,
  You shall love your neighbor and hate your enemy.
But I say to you, love your enemies
  and pray for those who persecute you,
    that you may be children of your heavenly Father,
    for he makes his sun rise on the bad and the good,
    and causes rain to fall on the just and the unjust.
For if you love those who love you, what recompense will you have?
Do not the tax collectors do the same?
And if you greet your brothers only,
  what is unusual about that?

Do not the pagans do the same?
So be perfect, just as your heavenly Father is perfect." ✚

MONDAY, FEBRUARY 20
WEEKDAY

† *Sirach 1:1-10*
Before all things else wisdom was created.

All wisdom comes from the LORD
and with him it remains forever, and is before all time.
The sand of the seashore, the drops of rain,
the days of eternity: who can number these?
Heaven's height, earth's breadth,
the depths of the abyss: who can explore these?
Before all things else wisdom was created;
and prudent understanding, from eternity.
The word of God on high is the fountain of wisdom
and her ways are everlasting.
To whom has wisdom's root been revealed?
Who knows her subtleties?
To whom has the discipline of wisdom been revealed?
And who has understood the multiplicity of her ways?
There is but one, wise and truly awe-inspiring,
seated upon his throne:
There is but one, Most High
all-powerful creator-king and truly awe-inspiring one,
seated upon his throne and he is the God of dominion.
It is the LORD; he created her through the Holy Spirit,
has seen her and taken note of her.
He has poured her forth upon all his works,
upon every living thing according to his bounty;
he has lavished her upon his friends. ✚

Psalm 93:1ab, 1cd-2, 5
R. (1a) **The Lord is king; he is robed in majesty.**
The LORD is king, in splendor robed;
robed is the LORD and girt about with strength. **R.**
And he has made the world firm,
not to be moved.
Your throne stands firm from of old;
from everlasting you are, O LORD. **R.**
Your decrees are worthy of trust indeed:
holiness befits your house,
O LORD, for length of days. **R.**

See *2 Timothy 1:10*

R. Alleluia, alleluia.

Our Savior Jesus Christ has destroyed death
and brought life to light through the Gospel. **R.**

† *Mark 9:14-29*
I do believe, help my unbelief!

As Jesus came down from the mountain with Peter, James, John
   and approached the other disciples,
   they saw a large crowd around them and scribes arguing with
      them.
Immediately on seeing him,
   the whole crowd was utterly amazed.
They ran up to him and greeted him.
He asked them, "What are you arguing about with them?"
Someone from the crowd answered him,
   "Teacher, I have brought to you my son possessed by a mute spirit.
Wherever it seizes him, it throws him down;
   he foams at the mouth, grinds his teeth, and becomes rigid.
I asked your disciples to drive it out, but they were unable to do so."
He said to them in reply,
   "O faithless generation, how long will I be with you?
How long will I endure you? Bring him to me."
They brought the boy to him.
And when he saw him,
   the spirit immediately threw the boy into convulsions.
As he fell to the ground, he began to roll around
   and foam at the mouth.
Then he questioned his father,
   "How long has this been happening to him?"
He replied, "Since childhood.
It has often thrown him into fire and into water to kill him.
But if you can do anything, have compassion on us and help us."
Jesus said to him,
   "'If you can!' Everything is possible to one who has faith."
Then the boy's father cried out, "I do believe, help my unbelief!"
Jesus, on seeing a crowd rapidly gathering,
   rebuked the unclean spirit and said to it,
   "Mute and deaf spirit, I command you:
   come out of him and never enter him again!"
Shouting and throwing the boy into convulsions, it came out.
He became like a corpse, which caused many to say, "He is dead!"
But Jesus took him by the hand, raised him, and he stood up.
When he entered the house, his disciples asked him in private,

"Why could we not drive the spirit out?"
He said to them, "This kind can only come out through prayer." ✛

TUESDAY, FEBRUARY 21
WEEKDAY, ST. PETER DAMIAN

✝ Sirach 2:1-11
Prepare yourself for trials.

My son, when you come to serve the LORD,
   stand in justice and fear,
   prepare yourself for trials.
Be sincere of heart and steadfast,
   incline your ear and receive the word of understanding,
   undisturbed in time of adversity.
Wait on God, with patience, cling to him, forsake him not;
   thus will you be wise in all your ways.
Accept whatever befalls you,
   when sorrowful, be steadfast,
   and in crushing misfortune be patient;
For in fire gold and silver are tested,
   and worthy people in the crucible of humiliation.
Trust God and God will help you;
   trust in him, and he will direct your way;
   keep his fear and grow old therein.

You who fear the LORD, wait for his mercy,
   turn not away lest you fall.
You who fear the LORD, trust him,
   and your reward will not be lost.
You who fear the LORD, hope for good things,
   for lasting joy and mercy.
You who fear the LORD, love him,
   and your hearts will be enlightened.
Study the generations long past and understand;
   has anyone hoped in the LORD and been disappointed?
Has anyone persevered in his commandments and been forsaken?
   has anyone called upon him and been rebuffed?
Compassionate and merciful is the LORD;
   he forgives sins, he saves in time of trouble
   and he is a protector to all who seek him in truth. ✛

Psalm 37:3-4, 18-19, 27-28, 39-40
R. (see 5) **Commit your life to the Lord, and he will help you.**
Trust in the LORD and do good,
   that you may dwell in the land and be fed in security.
Take delight in the LORD,

and he will grant you your heart's requests. **R.**
The LORD watches over the lives of the wholehearted;
   their inheritance lasts forever.
They are not put to shame in an evil time;
   in days of famine they have plenty. **R.**
Turn from evil and do good,
   that you may abide forever;
For the LORD loves what is right,
   and forsakes not his faithful ones. **R.**
The salvation of the just is from the LORD;
   he is their refuge in time of distress.
And the LORD helps them and delivers them;
   he delivers them from the wicked and saves them,
   because they take refuge in him. **R.**

Galatians 6:14
R. Alleluia, alleluia.
May I never boast except in the Cross of our Lord Jesus Christ,
through which the world has been crucified to me and I to the
   world. **R.**

† *Mark 9:30-37*
The Son of Man is to be handed over.
Whoever wishes to be first, shall be last of all.

Jesus and his disciples left from there and began a journey through
   Galilee,
   but he did not wish anyone to know about it.
He was teaching his disciples and telling them,
   "The Son of Man is to be handed over to men
   and they will kill him,
   and three days after his death the Son of Man will rise."
But they did not understand the saying,
   and they were afraid to question him.

They came to Capernaum and, once inside the house,
   he began to ask them,
   "What were you arguing about on the way?"
But they remained silent.
For they had been discussing among themselves on the way
   who was the greatest.
Then he sat down, called the Twelve, and said to them,
   "If anyone wishes to be first,
   he shall be the last of all and the servant of all."
Taking a child, he placed it in their midst,
   and putting his arms around it, he said to them,

"Whoever receives one child such as this in my name, receives me;
and whoever receives me,
receives not me but the One who sent me." ✢

WEDNESDAY, FEBRUARY 22
ASH WEDNESDAY

† *Joel 2:12-18*
Rend your hearts, not your garments.

Even now, says the LORD,
   return to me with your whole heart,
   with fasting, and weeping, and mourning;
Rend your hearts, not your garments,
   and return to the LORD, your God.
For gracious and merciful is he,
   slow to anger, rich in kindness,
   and relenting in punishment.
Perhaps he will again relent
   and leave behind him a blessing,
Offerings and libations
   for the LORD, your God.

Blow the trumpet in Zion!
   proclaim a fast,
   call an assembly;
Gather the people,
   notify the congregation;
Assemble the elders,
   gather the children
   and the infants at the breast;
Let the bridegroom quit his room
   and the bride her chamber.
Between the porch and the altar
   let the priests, the ministers of the LORD, weep,
And say, "Spare, O LORD, your people,
   and make not your heritage a reproach,
   with the nations ruling over them!
Why should they say among the peoples,
   'Where is their God?'"

Then the LORD was stirred to concern for his land
   and took pity on his people. ✢

   Psalm 51:3-4, 5-6ab, 12-13, 14 and 17
R. (see 3a) **Be merciful, O Lord, for we have sinned.**
Have mercy on me, O God, in your goodness;

in the greatness of your compassion wipe out my offense.
Thoroughly wash me from my guilt
  and of my sin cleanse me. **R.**
For I acknowledge my offense,
  and my sin is before me always:
"Against you only have I sinned,
  and done what is evil in your sight." **R.**
A clean heart create for me, O God,
  and a steadfast spirit renew within me.
Cast me not out from your presence,
  and your Holy Spirit take not from me. **R.**
Give me back the joy of your salvation,
  and a willing spirit sustain in me.
O LORD, open my lips,
  and my mouth shall proclaim your praise. **R.**

† *2 Corinthians 5:20—6:2*
Be reconciled to God. Behold, now is the acceptable time.

Brothers and sisters:
We are ambassadors for Christ,
  as if God were appealing through us.
We implore you on behalf of Christ,
  be reconciled to God.
For our sake he made him to be sin who did not know sin,
  so that we might become the righteousness of God in him.

Working together, then,
  we appeal to you not to receive the grace of God in vain.
For he says:

  In an acceptable time I heard you,
    and on the day of salvation I helped you.

Behold, now is a very acceptable time;
  behold, now is the day of salvation. ✛

  See Psalm 95:8
R. Glory and praise to you, Lord Jesus Christ!
If today you hear his voice,
harden not your hearts. **R.**

† *Matthew 6:1-6, 16-18*
Your Father who sees in secret will repay you.

Jesus said to his disciples:
  "Take care not to perform righteous deeds
  in order that people may see them;

otherwise, you will have no recompense from your heavenly Father.
When you give alms,
   do not blow a trumpet before you,
   as the hypocrites do in the synagogues and in the streets
   to win the praise of others.
Amen, I say to you,
   they have received their reward.
But when you give alms,
   do not let your left hand know what your right is doing,
   so that your almsgiving may be secret.
And your Father who sees in secret will repay you.

"When you pray,
   do not be like the hypocrites,
   who love to stand and pray in the synagogues and on street corners
   so that others may see them.
Amen, I say to you,
   they have received their reward.
But when you pray, go to your inner room,
   close the door, and pray to your Father in secret.
And your Father who sees in secret will repay you.

"When you fast,
   do not look gloomy like the hypocrites.
They neglect their appearance,
   so that they may appear to others to be fasting.
Amen, I say to you, they have received their reward.
But when you fast,
   anoint your head and wash your face,
   so that you may not appear to be fasting,
   except to your Father who is hidden.
And your Father who sees what is hidden will repay you." ✚

THURSDAY, FEBRUARY 23
THURSDAY AFTER ASH WEDNESDAY, ST. POLYCARP

† Deuteronomy 30:15-20
Behold, I set before you the blessing and the curse (Deuteronomy 11:26).

Moses said to the people:
   "Today I have set before you
   life and prosperity, death and doom.
If you obey the commandments of the LORD, your God,
   which I enjoin on you today,
   loving him, and walking in his ways,
   and keeping his commandments, statutes and decrees,

you will live and grow numerous,
and the LORD, your God,
will bless you in the land you are entering to occupy.
If, however, you turn away your hearts and will not listen,
but are led astray and adore and serve other gods,
I tell you now that you will certainly perish;
you will not have a long life
on the land that you are crossing the Jordan to enter and occupy.
I call heaven and earth today to witness against you:
I have set before you life and death,
the blessing and the curse.
Choose life, then,
that you and your descendants may live, by loving the LORD, your
God,
heeding his voice, and holding fast to him.
For that will mean life for you,
a long life for you to live on the land that the LORD swore
he would give to your fathers Abraham, Isaac and Jacob." ✛

Psalm 1:1-2, 3, 4 and 6

R. (40:5a) **Blessed are they who hope in the Lord.**
Blessed the man who follows not
the counsel of the wicked
Nor walks in the way of sinners,
nor sits in the company of the insolent,
But delights in the law of the LORD
and meditates on his law day and night. **R.**
He is like a tree
planted near running water,
That yields its fruit in due season,
and whose leaves never fade.
Whatever he does, prospers. **R.**
Not so the wicked, not so;
they are like chaff which the wind drives away.
For the LORD watches over the way of the just,
but the way of the wicked vanishes. **R.**

Matthew 4:17

R. Glory and praise to you, Lord Jesus Christ!
Repent, says the Lord;
the Kingdom of heaven is at hand. **R.**

† *Luke 9:22-25*
Whoever loses his life for my sake will save it.

Jesus said to his disciples:
"The Son of Man must suffer greatly and be rejected

by the elders, the chief priests, and the scribes,
and be killed and on the third day be raised."

Then he said to all,
    "If anyone wishes to come after me, he must deny himself
and take up his cross daily and follow me.
For whoever wishes to save his life will lose it,
    but whoever loses his life for my sake will save it.
What profit is there for one to gain the whole world
    yet lose or forfeit himself?" ✛

FRIDAY, FEBRUARY 24
FRIDAY AFTER ASH WEDNESDAY

† *Isaiah 58:1-9a*
Is this the manner of fasting I wish?

Thus says the Lord GOD:
Cry out full-throated and unsparingly,
    lift up your voice like a trumpet blast;
Tell my people their wickedness,
    and the house of Jacob their sins.
They seek me day after day,
    and desire to know my ways,
Like a nation that has done what is just
    and not abandoned the law of their God;
They ask me to declare what is due them,
    pleased to gain access to God.
"Why do we fast, and you do not see it?
    afflict ourselves, and you take no note of it?"

Lo, on your fast day you carry out your own pursuits,
    and drive all your laborers.
Yes, your fast ends in quarreling and fighting,
    striking with wicked claw.
Would that today you might fast
    so as to make your voice heard on high!
Is this the manner of fasting I wish,
    of keeping a day of penance:
That a man bow his head like a reed
    and lie in sackcloth and ashes?
Do you call this a fast,
    a day acceptable to the LORD?
This, rather, is the fasting that I wish:
    releasing those bound unjustly,
    untying the thongs of the yoke;

Setting free the oppressed,
  breaking every yoke;
Sharing your bread with the hungry,
  sheltering the oppressed and the homeless;
Clothing the naked when you see them,
  and not turning your back on your own.
Then your light shall break forth like the dawn,
  and your wound shall quickly be healed;
Your vindication shall go before you,
  and the glory of the LORD shall be your rear guard.
Then you shall call, and the LORD will answer,
  you shall cry for help, and he will say: Here I am! ✢

Psalm 51:3-4, 5-6ab, 18-19

R. (19b) A heart contrite and humbled, O God, you will not spurn.

Have mercy on me, O God, in your goodness;
  in the greatness of your compassion wipe out my offense.
Thoroughly wash me from my guilt
  and of my sin cleanse me. **R.**
For I acknowledge my offense,
  and my sin is before me always:
"Against you only have I sinned,
  and done what is evil in your sight." **R.**
For you are not pleased with sacrifices;
  should I offer a burnt offering, you would not accept it.
My sacrifice, O God, is a contrite spirit;
  a heart contrite and humbled, O God, you will not spurn. **R.**

See Amos 5:14

R. Glory and praise to you, Lord Jesus Christ!
Seek good and not evil so that you may live,
and the LORD will be with you. **R.**

† *Matthew 9:14-15*
When the bridegroom is taken from them, then they will fast.

The disciples of John approached Jesus and said,
  "Why do we and the Pharisees fast much,
  but your disciples do not fast?"
Jesus answered them, "Can the wedding guests mourn
  as long as the bridegroom is with them?
The days will come when the bridegroom is taken away from them,
  and then they will fast." ✢

SATURDAY, FEBRUARY 25
SATURDAY AFTER ASH WEDNESDAY

† *Isaiah 58:9b-14*

If you bestow your bread on the hungry,
then light shall rise for you in the darkness.

Thus says the LORD:
If you remove from your midst oppression,
   false accusation and malicious speech;
If you bestow your bread on the hungry
   and satisfy the afflicted;
Then light shall rise for you in the darkness,
   and the gloom shall become for you like midday;
Then the LORD will guide you always
   and give you plenty even on the parched land.
He will renew your strength,
   and you shall be like a watered garden,
   like a spring whose water never fails.
The ancient ruins shall be rebuilt for your sake,
   and the foundations from ages past you shall raise up;
"Repairer of the breach," they shall call you,
   "Restorer of ruined homesteads."

If you hold back your foot on the sabbath
   from following your own pursuits on my holy day;
If you call the sabbath a delight,
   and the LORD's holy day honorable;
If you honor it by not following your ways,
   seeking your own interests, or speaking with malice—
Then you shall delight in the LORD,
   and I will make you ride on the heights of the earth;
I will nourish you with the heritage of Jacob, your father,
   for the mouth of the LORD has spoken. ✛

Psalm 86:1-2, 3-4, 5-6

R. (11ab) **Teach me your way, O Lord, that I may walk in your**
   truth.
Incline your ear, O LORD; answer me,
   for I am afflicted and poor.
Keep my life, for I am devoted to you;
   save your servant who trusts in you.
   You are my God. **R.**
Have mercy on me, O LORD,
   for to you I call all the day.
Gladden the soul of your servant,
   for to you, O LORD, I lift up my soul. **R.**

For you, O LORD, are good and forgiving,
  abounding in kindness to all who call upon you.
Hearken, O LORD, to my prayer
  and attend to the sound of my pleading. **R.**

  Ezekiel 33:11
R. Glory and praise to you, Lord Jesus Christ!
I take no pleasure in the death of the wicked man, says the Lord,
but rather in his conversion, that he may live. **R.**

† *Luke 5:27-32*
I have not come to call righteous to repentance but sinners.

Jesus saw a tax collector named Levi sitting at the customs post.
He said to him, "Follow me."
And leaving everything behind, he got up and followed him.
Then Levi gave a great banquet for him in his house,
  and a large crowd of tax collectors
  and others were at table with them.
The Pharisees and their scribes complained to his disciples, saying,
  "Why do you eat and drink with tax collectors and sinners?"
Jesus said to them in reply,
  "Those who are healthy do not need a physician, but the sick do.
I have not come to call the righteous to repentance but sinners." ✚

SUNDAY, FEBRUARY 26
FIRST SUNDAY OF LENT

† *Genesis 2:7-9; 3:1-7*
The creation of our first parents, and sin.

The LORD God formed man out of the clay of the ground
  and blew into his nostrils the breath of life,
  and so man became a living being.

Then the LORD God planted a garden in Eden, in the east,
  and placed there the man whom he had formed.
Out of the ground the LORD God made various trees grow
  that were delightful to look at and good for food,
  with the tree of life in the middle of the garden
  and the tree of the knowledge of good and evil.

Now the serpent was the most cunning of all the animals
  that the LORD God had made.
The serpent asked the woman,
  "Did God really tell you not to eat
  from any of the trees in the garden?"
The woman answered the serpent:

"We may eat of the fruit of the trees in the garden;
    it is only about the fruit of the tree
    in the middle of the garden that God said,
    'You shall not eat it or even touch it, lest you die.'"
But the serpent said to the woman:
    "You certainly will not die!
No, God knows well that the moment you eat of it
    your eyes will be opened and you will be like gods
    who know what is good and what is evil."
The woman saw that the tree was good for food,
    pleasing to the eyes, and desirable for gaining wisdom.
So she took some of its fruit and ate it;
    and she also gave some to her husband, who was with her,
    and he ate it.
Then the eyes of both of them were opened,
    and they realized that they were naked;
    so they sewed fig leaves together
    and made loincloths for themselves. ✝

Psalm 51:3-4, 5-6ab, 12-13, 14 and 17

R. (see 3a) **Be merciful, O Lord, for we have sinned.**
Have mercy on me, O God, in your goodness;
    in the greatness of your compassion wipe out my offense.
Thoroughly wash me from my guilt
    and of my sin cleanse me. **R.**
For I acknowledge my offense,
    and my sin is before me always:
"Against you only have I sinned,
    and done what is evil in your sight." **R.**
A clean heart create for me, O God,
    and a steadfast spirit renew within me.
Cast me not out from your presence,
    and your Holy Spirit take not from me. **R.**
Give me back the joy of your salvation,
    and a willing spirit sustain in me.
O Lord, open my lips,
    and my mouth shall proclaim your praise. **R.**

*✝ **Romans 5:12-19** (or Romans 5:12, 17-19)*
Where sin increased, there grace increased all the more.

Brothers and sisters:
Through one man sin entered the world,
    and through sin, death,
    and thus death came to all men, inasmuch as all sinned—
    for up to the time of the law, sin was in the world,

though sin is not accounted when there is no law.
But death reigned from Adam to Moses,
  even over those who did not sin
  after the pattern of the trespass of Adam,
  who is the type of the one who was to come.

But the gift is not like the transgression.
For if by the transgression of the one, the many died,
  how much more did the grace of God
  and the gracious gift of the one man Jesus Christ
  overflow for the many.
And the gift is not like the result of the one who sinned.
For after one sin there was the judgment that brought condemnation;
  but the gift, after many transgressions, brought acquittal.
For if, by the transgression of the one,
  death came to reign through that one,
  how much more will those who receive the abundance of grace
  and of the gift of justification
  come to reign in life through the one Jesus Christ.
In conclusion, just as through one transgression
  condemnation came upon all,
  so, through one righteous act,
  acquittal and life came to all.
For just as through the disobedience of the one man
  the many were made sinners,
  so, through the obedience of the one,
  the many will be made righteous. ✢

Matthew 4:4b
R. Glory and praise to you, Lord Jesus Christ!
One does not live on bread alone,
but on every word that comes forth from the mouth of God. **R.**

✝ *Matthew 4:1-11*
Jesus fasted for forty days and forty nights and was tempted.

At that time Jesus was led by the Spirit into the desert
  to be tempted by the devil.
He fasted for forty days and forty nights,
  and afterwards he was hungry.
The tempter approached and said to him,
  "If you are the Son of God,
  command that these stones become loaves of bread."
He said in reply,
  "It is written:
  One does not live on bread alone,

but on every word that comes forth
from the mouth of God."

Then the devil took him to the holy city,
   and made him stand on the parapet of the temple,
   and said to him, "If you are the Son of God, throw yourself down.
For it is written:
   He will command his angels concerning you
      and with their hands they will support you,
   lest you dash your foot against a stone."
Jesus answered him,
   "Again it is written,
   You shall not put the Lord, your God, to the test."

Then the devil took him up to a very high mountain,
   and showed him all the kingdoms of the world in their magnificence,
   and he said to him, "All these I shall give to you,
   if you will prostrate yourself and worship me."
At this, Jesus said to him,
   "Get away, Satan!
It is written:
   The Lord, your God, shall you worship
      and him alone shall you serve."

Then the devil left him and, behold,
   angels came and ministered to him. ✛

MONDAY, FEBRUARY 27
LENTEN WEEKDAY, ST. GREGORY OF NAREK

† *Leviticus 19:1-2, 11-18*
Judge your fellow man justly.

The LORD said to Moses,
   "Speak to the whole assembly of the children of Israel and tell
      them:
   Be holy, for I, the LORD, your God, am holy.

"You shall not steal.
You shall not lie or speak falsely to one another.
You shall not swear falsely by my name,
   thus profaning the name of your God.
I am the LORD.

"You shall not defraud or rob your neighbor.
You shall not withhold overnight the wages of your day laborer.
You shall not curse the deaf,
   or put a stumbling block in front of the blind,

but you shall fear your God.
I am the LORD.

"You shall not act dishonestly in rendering judgment.
Show neither partiality to the weak nor deference to the mighty,
   but judge your fellow men justly.
You shall not go about spreading slander among your kin;
   nor shall you stand by idly when your neighbor's life is at stake.
I am the LORD.

"You shall not bear hatred for your brother in your heart.
Though you may have to reprove him,
   do not incur sin because of him.
Take no revenge and cherish no grudge against your fellow
      countrymen.
You shall love your neighbor as yourself.
I am the LORD." ✢

   Psalm 19:8, 9, 10, 15
R. (John 6:63b) **Your words, Lord, are Spirit and life.**
The law of the LORD is perfect,
   refreshing the soul.
The decree of the LORD is trustworthy,
   giving wisdom to the simple. **R.**
The precepts of the LORD are right,
   rejoicing the heart.
The command of the LORD is clear,
   enlightening the eye. **R.**
The fear of the LORD is pure,
   enduring forever;
The ordinances of the LORD are true,
   all of them just. **R.**
Let the words of my mouth and the thought of my heart
   find favor before you,
   O LORD, my rock and my redeemer. **R.**

   2 Corinthians 6:2b
R. Glory and praise to you, Lord Jesus Christ!
Behold, now is a very acceptable time;
behold, now is the day of salvation. **R.**

✝ *Matthew 25:31-46*
Whatever you have done to the very least of my brothers, you have done to me.

Jesus said to his disciples:
   "When the Son of Man comes in his glory,
   and all the angels with him,

he will sit upon his glorious throne,
  and all the nations will be assembled before him.
And he will separate them one from another,
  as a shepherd separates the sheep from the goats.
He will place the sheep on his right and the goats on his left.
Then the king will say to those on his right,
  'Come, you who are blessed by my Father.
Inherit the kingdom prepared for you from the foundation of the
    world.
For I was hungry and you gave me food,
  I was thirsty and you gave me drink,
  a stranger and you welcomed me,
  naked and you clothed me,
  ill and you cared for me,
  in prison and you visited me.'
Then the righteous will answer him and say,
  'Lord, when did we see you hungry and feed you,
  or thirsty and give you drink?
When did we see you a stranger and welcome you,
  or naked and clothe you?
When did we see you ill or in prison, and visit you?'
And the king will say to them in reply,
  'Amen, I say to you, whatever you did
  for one of these least brothers of mine, you did for me.'
Then he will say to those on his left,
  'Depart from me, you accursed,
  into the eternal fire prepared for the Devil and his angels.
For I was hungry and you gave me no food,
  I was thirsty and you gave me no drink,
  a stranger and you gave me no welcome,
  naked and you gave me no clothing,
  ill and in prison, and you did not care for me.'
Then they will answer and say,
  'Lord, when did we see you hungry or thirsty
  or a stranger or naked or ill or in prison,
  and not minister to your needs?'
He will answer them, 'Amen, I say to you,
  what you did not do for one of these least ones,
  you did not do for me.'
And these will go off to eternal punishment,
  but the righteous to eternal life." ✛

TUESDAY, FEBRUARY 28
LENTEN WEEKDAY

† *Isaiah 55:10-11*
My word will do whatever I will.

Thus says the LORD:
Just as from the heavens
    the rain and snow come down
And do not return there
    till they have watered the earth,
    making it fertile and fruitful,
Giving seed to the one who sows
    and bread to the one who eats,
So shall my word be
    that goes forth from my mouth;
It shall not return to me void,
    but shall do my will,
    achieving the end for which I sent it. ✛

Psalm 34:4-5, 6-7, 16-17, 18-19
R. (18b) **From all their distress God rescues the just.**
Glorify the LORD with me,
    let us together extol his name.
I sought the LORD, and he answered me
    and delivered me from all my fears. **R.**
Look to him that you may be radiant with joy,
    and your faces may not blush with shame.
When the poor one called out, the LORD heard,
    and from all his distress he saved him. **R.**
The LORD has eyes for the just,
    and ears for their cry.
The LORD confronts the evildoers,
    to destroy remembrance of them from the earth. **R.**
When the just cry out, the LORD hears them,
    and from all their distress he rescues them.
The LORD is close to the brokenhearted;
    and those who are crushed in spirit he saves. **R.**

Matthew 4:4b
R. Glory and praise to you, Lord Jesus Christ!
One does not live on bread alone,
but on every word that comes forth from the mouth of God. **R.**

† *Matthew 6:7-15*
This is how you are to pray.

Jesus said to his disciples:

"In praying, do not babble like the pagans,
who think that they will be heard because of their many words.
Do not be like them.
Your Father knows what you need before you ask him.

"This is how you are to pray:

Our Father who art in heaven,
hallowed be thy name,
thy Kingdom come,
thy will be done,
on earth as it is in heaven.
Give us this day our daily bread;
and forgive us our trespasses,
as we forgive those who trespass against us;
and lead us not into temptation,
but deliver us from evil.

"If you forgive men their transgressions,
your heavenly Father will forgive you.
But if you do not forgive men,
neither will your Father forgive your transgressions." ✛

WEDNESDAY, MARCH 1
LENTEN WEEKDAY

† *Jonah 3:1-10*
The Ninevites turned from their evil way.

The word of the LORD came to Jonah a second time:
"Set out for the great city of Nineveh,
and announce to it the message that I will tell you."
So Jonah made ready and went to Nineveh,
according to the LORD's bidding.
Now Nineveh was an enormously large city;
it took three days to go through it.
Jonah began his journey through the city,
and had gone but a single day's walk announcing,
"Forty days more and Nineveh shall be destroyed,"
when the people of Nineveh believed God;
they proclaimed a fast
and all of them, great and small, put on sackcloth.

When the news reached the king of Nineveh,
he rose from his throne, laid aside his robe,
covered himself with sackcloth, and sat in the ashes.
Then he had this proclaimed throughout Nineveh,

by decree of the king and his nobles:
"Neither man nor beast, neither cattle nor sheep,
shall taste anything;
they shall not eat, nor shall they drink water.
Man and beast shall be covered with sackcloth and call loudly to
    God;
every man shall turn from his evil way
and from the violence he has in hand.
Who knows, God may relent and forgive, and withhold his blazing
    wrath,
so that we shall not perish."
When God saw by their actions how they turned from their evil way,
he repented of the evil that he had threatened to do to them;
he did not carry it out. ✛

Psalm 51:3-4, 12-13, 18-19

**R. (19b) A heart contrite and humbled, O God, you will not
    spurn.**
Have mercy on me, O God, in your goodness;
in the greatness of your compassion wipe out my offense.
Thoroughly wash me from my guilt
and of my sin cleanse me. **R.**
A clean heart create for me, O God,
and a steadfast spirit renew within me.
Cast me not out from your presence,
and your Holy Spirit take not from me. **R.**
For you are not pleased with sacrifices;
should I offer a burnt offering, you would not accept it.
My sacrifice, O God, is a contrite spirit;
a heart contrite and humbled, O God, you will not spurn. **R.**

Joel 2:12-13

R. Glory and praise to you, Lord Jesus Christ!
Even now, says the LORD,
return to me with your whole heart
for I am gracious and merciful. **R.**

† *Luke 11:29-32*
No sign will be given to this generation except the sign of Jonah.

While still more people gathered in the crowd, Jesus said to them,
"This generation is an evil generation;
it seeks a sign, but no sign will be given it,
except the sign of Jonah.
Just as Jonah became a sign to the Ninevites,
so will the Son of Man be to this generation.

At the judgment
    the queen of the south will rise with the men of this generation
    and she will condemn them,
    because she came from the ends of the earth
    to hear the wisdom of Solomon,
    and there is something greater than Solomon here.
At the judgment the men of Nineveh will arise with this generation
    and condemn it,
    because at the preaching of Jonah they repented,
    and there is something greater than Jonah here." ✛

THURSDAY, MARCH 2
LENTEN WEEKDAY

† Esther C:12, 14-16, 23-25
I have no protector other than you, Lord.

Queen Esther, seized with mortal anguish,
    had recourse to the LORD.
She lay prostrate upon the ground, together with her handmaids,
    from morning until evening, and said:
    "God of Abraham, God of Isaac, and God of Jacob, blessed are you.
Help me, who am alone and have no help but you,
    for I am taking my life in my hand.
As a child I used to hear from the books of my forefathers
    that you, O LORD, always free those who are pleasing to you.
Now help me, who am alone and have no one but you,
    O LORD, my God.

"And now, come to help me, an orphan.
Put in my mouth persuasive words in the presence of the lion
    and turn his heart to hatred for our enemy,
    so that he and those who are in league with him may perish.
Save us from the hand of our enemies;
    turn our mourning into gladness
    and our sorrows into wholeness." ✛

    Psalm 138:1-2ab, 2cde-3, 7c-8
R. (3a) **Lord, on the day I called for help, you answered me.**
I will give thanks to you, O LORD, with all my heart,
    for you have heard the words of my mouth;
    in the presence of the angels I will sing your praise;
I will worship at your holy temple
    and give thanks to your name. **R.**
Because of your kindness and your truth;
    for you have made great above all things
    your name and your promise.

When I called, you answered me;
  you built up strength within me. **R.**
Your right hand saves me.
The LORD will complete what he has done for me;
  your kindness, O LORD, endures forever;
  forsake not the work of your hands. **R.**

  Psalm 51:12a, 14a
R. Glory and praise to you, Lord Jesus Christ!
A clean heart create for me, God;
give me back the joy of your salvation. **R.**

† *Matthew 7:7-12*
Everyone who asks, receives.

Jesus said to his disciples:
  "Ask and it will be given to you;
  seek and you will find;
  knock and the door will be opened to you.
For everyone who asks, receives; and the one who seeks, finds;
  and to the one who knocks, the door will be opened.
Which one of you would hand his son a stone
  when he asked for a loaf of bread,
  or a snake when he asked for a fish?
If you then, who are wicked,
  know how to give good gifts to your children,
  how much more will your heavenly Father give good things
  to those who ask him.

"Do to others whatever you would have them do to you.
This is the law and the prophets." ✛

FRIDAY, MARCH 3
LENTEN WEEKDAY, ST. KATHARINE DREXEL

† *Ezekiel 18:21-28*
*Do I derive any pleasure from the death of the wicked and not rejoice
when he turns from his evil way that he may live?*

Thus says the Lord GOD:
If the wicked man turns away from all the sins he committed,
  if he keeps all my statutes and does what is right and just,
  he shall surely live, he shall not die.
None of the crimes he committed shall be remembered against him;
  he shall live because of the virtue he has practiced.
Do I indeed derive any pleasure from the death of the wicked?
  says the Lord GOD.

Do I not rather rejoice when he turns from his evil way
    that he may live?

And if the virtuous man turns from the path of virtue to do evil,
    the same kind of abominable things that the wicked man does,
    can he do this and still live?
None of his virtuous deeds shall be remembered,
    because he has broken faith and committed sin;
    because of this, he shall die.
You say, "The LORD's way is not fair!"
Hear now, house of Israel:
    Is it my way that is unfair, or rather, are not your ways unfair?
When someone virtuous turns away from virtue to commit iniquity,
        and dies,
    it is because of the iniquity he committed that he must die.
But if the wicked, turning from the wickedness he has committed,
    does what is right and just,
    he shall preserve his life;
    since he has turned away from all the sins that he committed,
    he shall surely live, he shall not die. ✝

Psalm 130:1-2, 3-4, 5-7a, 7bc-8
R. (3) **If you, O Lord, mark iniquities, who can stand?**
Out of the depths I cry to you, O LORD;
    LORD, hear my voice!
Let your ears be attentive
    to my voice in supplication. **R.**
If you, O LORD, mark iniquities,
    LORD, who can stand?
But with you is forgiveness,
    that you may be revered. **R.**
I trust in the LORD;
    my soul trusts in his word.
My soul waits for the LORD
    more than sentinels wait for the dawn.
    Let Israel wait for the LORD. **R.**
For with the LORD is kindness
    and with him is plenteous redemption;
And he will redeem Israel
    from all their iniquities. **R.**

Ezekiel 18:31
R. Glory and praise to you, Lord Jesus Christ!
Cast away from you all the crimes you have committed, says the
        Lord,
and make for yourselves a new heart and a new spirit. **R.**

† *Matthew 5:20-26*
Go first and be reconciled with your brother.

Jesus said to his disciples:
"I tell you,
   unless your righteousness surpasses that
   of the scribes and Pharisees,
   you will not enter into the Kingdom of heaven.

"You have heard that it was said to your ancestors,
   You shall not kill; and whoever kills will be liable to judgment.
But I say to you, whoever is angry with his brother
   will be liable to judgment,
   and whoever says to his brother, *Raqa,*
   will be answerable to the Sanhedrin,
   and whoever says, 'You fool,' will be liable to fiery Gehenna.
Therefore, if you bring your gift to the altar,
   and there recall that your brother
   has anything against you,
   leave your gift there at the altar,
   go first and be reconciled with your brother,
   and then come and offer your gift.
Settle with your opponent quickly while on the way to court.
Otherwise your opponent will hand you over to the judge,
   and the judge will hand you over to the guard,
   and you will be thrown into prison.
Amen, I say to you,
   you will not be released until you have paid the last penny." ✛

SATURDAY, MARCH 4
LENTEN WEEKDAY, ST. CASIMIR

† *Deuteronomy 26:16-19*
You will be a people sacred to the Lord God.

Moses spoke to the people, saying:
   "This day the LORD, your God,
   commands you to observe these statutes and decrees.
Be careful, then,
   to observe them with all your heart and with all your soul.
Today you are making this agreement with the LORD:
   he is to be your God and you are to walk in his ways
   and observe his statutes, commandments and decrees,
   and to hearken to his voice.
And today the LORD is making this agreement with you:
   you are to be a people peculiarly his own, as he promised you;
   and provided you keep all his commandments,

he will then raise you high in praise and renown and glory
above all other nations he has made,
and you will be a people sacred to the LORD, your God,
as he promised." ✛

Psalm 119:1-2, 4-5, 7-8
R. (1b) Blessed are they who follow the law of the Lord!
Blessed are they whose way is blameless,
    who walk in the law of the LORD.
Blessed are they who observe his decrees,
    who seek him with all their heart. **R.**
You have commanded that your precepts
    be diligently kept.
Oh, that I might be firm in the ways
    of keeping your statutes! **R.**
I will give you thanks with an upright heart,
    when I have learned your just ordinances.
I will keep your statutes;
    do not utterly forsake me. **R.**

2 Corinthians 6:2b
R. Glory and praise to you, Lord Jesus Christ!
Behold, now is a very acceptable time;
behold, now is the day of salvation. **R.**

† *Matthew 5:43-48*
Be perfect, just as your heavenly Father is perfect.

Jesus said to his disciples:
    "You have heard that it was said,
    You shall love your neighbor and hate your enemy.
But I say to you, love your enemies,
    and pray for those who persecute you,
    that you may be children of your heavenly Father,
    for he makes his sun rise on the bad and the good,
    and causes rain to fall on the just and the unjust.
For if you love those who love you, what recompense will you have?
Do not the tax collectors do the same?
And if you greet your brothers and sisters only,
    what is unusual about that?
Do not the pagans do the same?
So be perfect, just as your heavenly Father is perfect." ✛

SUNDAY, MARCH 5
SECOND SUNDAY OF LENT

† *Genesis 12:1-4a*
The call of Abraham, the father of God's people.

The LORD said to Abram:
"Go forth from the land of your kinsfolk
and from your father's house to a land that I will show you.

"I will make of you a great nation,
    and I will bless you;
I will make your name great,
    so that you will be a blessing.
I will bless those who bless you
    and curse those who curse you.
All the communities of the earth
    shall find blessing in you."

Abram went as the LORD directed him. ✛

Psalm 33:4-5, 18-19, 20 and 22
R. (22) **Lord, let your mercy be on us, as we place our trust in you.**
Upright is the word of the LORD,
    and all his works are trustworthy.
He loves justice and right;
    of the kindness of the LORD the earth is full. **R.**
See, the eyes of the LORD are upon those who fear him,
    upon those who hope for his kindness,
to deliver them from death
    and preserve them in spite of famine. **R.**
Our soul waits for the LORD,
    who is our help and our shield.
May your kindness, O LORD, be upon us
    who have put our hope in you. **R.**

† *2 Timothy 1:8b-10*
God has saved us and called us to be holy.

Beloved:
Bear your share of hardship for the gospel
    with the strength that comes from God.

He saved us and called us to a holy life,
    not according to our works
    but according to his own design
    and the grace bestowed on us in Christ Jesus before time began,

but now made manifest
through the appearance of our savior Christ Jesus,
who destroyed death and brought life and immortality
to light through the gospel. ✛

See Matthew 17:5
R. Glory and praise to you, Lord Jesus Christ!
From the shining cloud the Father's voice is heard:
This is my beloved Son, hear him. **R.**

† *Matthew 17:1-9*
Jesus' face shone like the sun.

Jesus took Peter, James, and John his brother,
and led them up a high mountain by themselves.
And he was transfigured before them;
his face shone like the sun
and his clothes became white as light.
And behold, Moses and Elijah appeared to them,
conversing with him.
Then Peter said to Jesus in reply,
"Lord, it is good that we are here.
If you wish, I will make three tents here,
one for you, one for Moses, and one for Elijah."
While he was still speaking, behold,
a bright cloud cast a shadow over them,
then from the cloud came a voice that said,
"This is my beloved Son, with whom I am well pleased;
listen to him."
When the disciples heard this, they fell prostrate
and were very much afraid.
But Jesus came and touched them, saying,
"Rise, and do not be afraid."
And when the disciples raised their eyes,
they saw no one else but Jesus alone.

As they were coming down from the mountain,
Jesus charged them,
"Do not tell the vision to anyone
until the Son of Man has been raised from the dead." ✛

MONDAY, MARCH 6
LENTEN WEEKDAY

† *Daniel 9:4b-10*
We have sinned, been wicked and done evil.

"**L**ord, great and awesome God,
　you who keep your merciful covenant toward those who love you
　and observe your commandments!
We have sinned, been wicked and done evil;
　we have rebelled and departed from your commandments and
　　　your laws.
We have not obeyed your servants the prophets,
　who spoke in your name to our kings, our princes,
　our fathers, and all the people of the land.
Justice, O Lord, is on your side;
　we are shamefaced even to this day:
　we, the men of Judah, the residents of Jerusalem,
　and all Israel, near and far,
　in all the countries to which you have scattered them
　because of their treachery toward you.
O LORD, we are shamefaced, like our kings, our princes, and our
　　　fathers,
　for having sinned against you.
But yours, O Lord, our God, are compassion and forgiveness!
Yet we rebelled against you
　and paid no heed to your command, O LORD, our God,
　to live by the law you gave us through your servants the
　　　prophets." ✢

　Psalm 79:8, 9, 11 and 13
R. (see 103:10a) **Lord, do not deal with us according to our
　sins.**
Remember not against us the iniquities of the past;
　may your compassion quickly come to us,
　for we are brought very low. **R.**
Help us, O God our savior,
　because of the glory of your name;
Deliver us and pardon our sins
　for your name's sake. **R.**
Let the prisoners' sighing come before you;
　with your great power free those doomed to death.
Then we, your people and the sheep of your pasture,
　will give thanks to you forever;
　through all generations we will declare your praise. **R.**

See John 6:63c, 68c

R. Glory and praise to you, Lord Jesus Christ!
Your words, Lord, are Spirit and life;
you have the words of everlasting life. **R.**

† *Luke 6:36-38*
Forgive and you will be forgiven.

Jesus said to his disciples:
"Be merciful, just as your Father is merciful.

"Stop judging and you will not be judged.
Stop condemning and you will not be condemned.
Forgive and you will be forgiven.
Give and gifts will be given to you;
a good measure, packed together, shaken down, and overflowing,
will be poured into your lap.
For the measure with which you measure
will in return be measured out to you." ✛

TUESDAY, MARCH 7
LENTEN WEEKDAY, ST. PERPETUA AND ST. FELICITY

† *Isaiah 1:10, 16-20*
Learn to do good; make justice your aim.

Hear the word of the LORD,
princes of Sodom!
Listen to the instruction of our God,
people of Gomorrah!

Wash yourselves clean!
Put away your misdeeds from before my eyes;
cease doing evil; learn to do good.
Make justice your aim: redress the wronged,
hear the orphan's plea, defend the widow.

Come now, let us set things right,
says the LORD:
Though your sins be like scarlet,
they may become white as snow;
Though they be crimson red,
they may become white as wool.
If you are willing, and obey,
you shall eat the good things of the land;
But if you refuse and resist,
the sword shall consume you:
for the mouth of the LORD has spoken! ✛

Psalm 50:8-9, 16bc-17, 21 and 23

R. (23b) To the upright I will show the saving power of God.

"Not for your sacrifices do I rebuke you,
  for your burnt offerings are before me always.
I take from your house no bullock,
  no goats out of your fold." **R.**

"Why do you recite my statutes,
  and profess my covenant with your mouth,
Though you hate discipline
  and cast my words behind you?" **R.**

"When you do these things, shall I be deaf to it?
  Or do you think that I am like yourself?
I will correct you by drawing them up before your eyes.
He that offers praise as a sacrifice glorifies me;
  and to him that goes the right way I will show the salvation of
    God." **R.**

Ezekiel 18:31

R. Glory and praise to you, Lord Jesus Christ!

Cast away from you all the crimes you have committed, says the
    Lord,
and make for yourselves a new heart and a new spirit. **R.**

† Matthew 23:1-12
They preach but they do not practice.

Jesus spoke to the crowds and to his disciples, saying,
  "The scribes and the Pharisees
  have taken their seat on the chair of Moses.
Therefore, do and observe all things whatsoever they tell you,
  but do not follow their example.
For they preach but they do not practice.
They tie up heavy burdens hard to carry
  and lay them on people's shoulders,
  but they will not lift a finger to move them.
All their works are performed to be seen.
They widen their phylacteries and lengthen their tassels.
They love places of honor at banquets, seats of honor in synagogues,
  greetings in marketplaces, and the salutation 'Rabbi.'
As for you, do not be called 'Rabbi.'
You have but one teacher, and you are all brothers.
Call no one on earth your father;
  you have but one Father in heaven.
Do not be called 'Master';
  you have but one master, the Christ.
The greatest among you must be your servant.

Whoever exalts himself will be humbled;
  but whoever humbles himself will be exalted." ✝

WEDNESDAY, MARCH 8
LENTEN WEEKDAY, ST. JOHN OF GOD

✝ *Jeremiah 18:18-20*
Come, let us persecute him.

The people of Judah and the citizens of Jerusalem said,
  "Come, let us contrive a plot against Jeremiah.
It will not mean the loss of instruction from the priests,
  nor of counsel from the wise, nor of messages from the prophets.
And so, let us destroy him by his own tongue;
  let us carefully note his every word."

Heed me, O LORD,
  and listen to what my adversaries say.
Must good be repaid with evil
  that they should dig a pit to take my life?
Remember that I stood before you
  to speak in their behalf,
  to turn away your wrath from them. ✝

Psalm 31:5-6, 14, 15-16
R. (17b) **Save me, O Lord, in your kindness.**
You will free me from the snare they set for me,
  for you are my refuge.
Into your hands I commend my spirit;
  you will redeem me, O LORD, O faithful God. **R.**
I hear the whispers of the crowd, that frighten me from every side,
as they consult together against me, plotting to take my life. **R.**
But my trust is in you, O LORD;
  I say, "You are my God."
In your hands is my destiny; rescue me
  from the clutches of my enemies and my persecutors. **R.**

John 8:12
R. Glory and praise to you, Lord Jesus Christ!
I am the light of the world, says the Lord;
whoever follows me will have the light of life. **R.**

✝ *Matthew 20:17-28*
They will condemn the Son of Man to death.

As Jesus was going up to Jerusalem,
  he took the Twelve disciples aside by themselves,
  and said to them on the way,

"Behold, we are going up to Jerusalem,
and the Son of Man will be handed over to the chief priests
and the scribes,
and they will condemn him to death,
and hand him over to the Gentiles
to be mocked and scourged and crucified,
and he will be raised on the third day."

Then the mother of the sons of Zebedee approached Jesus with her
    sons
and did him homage, wishing to ask him for something.
He said to her, "What do you wish?"
She answered him,
    "Command that these two sons of mine sit,
    one at your right and the other at your left, in your kingdom."
Jesus said in reply,
    "You do not know what you are asking.
Can you drink the chalice that I am going to drink?"
They said to him, "We can."
He replied,
    "My chalice you will indeed drink,
    but to sit at my right and at my left,
    this is not mine to give
    but is for those for whom it has been prepared by my Father."
When the ten heard this,
    they became indignant at the two brothers.
But Jesus summoned them and said,
    "You know that the rulers of the Gentiles lord it over them,
    and the great ones make their authority over them felt.
But it shall not be so among you.
Rather, whoever wishes to be great among you shall be your servant;
    whoever wishes to be first among you shall be your slave.
Just so, the Son of Man did not come to be served but to serve
    and to give his life as a ransom for many." ✠

THURSDAY, MARCH 9
LENTEN WEEKDAY, ST. FRANCES OF ROME

† Jeremiah 17:5-10
A curse on those who trust in mortals;
a blessing on those who trust in the Lord God.

Thus says the LORD:
Cursed is the man who trusts in human beings,
    who seeks his strength in flesh,
    whose heart turns away from the LORD.

He is like a barren bush in the desert
  that enjoys no change of season,
But stands in a lava waste,
  a salt and empty earth.
Blessed is the man who trusts in the LORD,
  whose hope is the LORD.
He is like a tree planted beside the waters
  that stretches out its roots to the stream:
It fears not the heat when it comes,
  its leaves stay green;
In the year of drought it shows no distress,
  but still bears fruit.
More tortuous than all else is the human heart,
  beyond remedy; who can understand it?
I, the LORD, alone probe the mind
  and test the heart,
To reward everyone according to his ways,
  according to the merit of his deeds. ✛

Psalm 1:1-2, 3, 4 and 6

R. (40:5a) **Blessed are they who hope in the Lord.**

Blessed the man who follows not
  the counsel of the wicked
Nor walks in the way of sinners,
  nor sits in the company of the insolent,
But delights in the law of the LORD
  and meditates on his law day and night. **R.**

He is like a tree
  planted near running water,
That yields its fruit in due season,
  and whose leaves never fade.
  Whatever he does, prospers. **R.**

Not so, the wicked, not so;
  they are like chaff which the wind drives away.
For the LORD watches over the way of the just,
  but the way of the wicked vanishes. **R.**

See Luke 8:15

R. Glory and praise to you, Lord Jesus Christ!

Blessed are they who have kept the word with a generous heart
and yield a harvest through perseverance. **R.**

† *Luke 16:19-31*

Good things came to you and bad things to Lazarus;
now he is comforted while you are in agony.

Jesus said to the Pharisees:
"There was a rich man who dressed in purple garments and fine
    linen
  and dined sumptuously each day.
And lying at his door was a poor man named Lazarus, covered with
    sores,
  who would gladly have eaten his fill of the scraps
  that fell from the rich man's table.
Dogs even used to come and lick his sores.
When the poor man died,
  he was carried away by angels to the bosom of Abraham.
The rich man also died and was buried,
  and from the netherworld, where he was in torment,
  he raised his eyes and saw Abraham far off
  and Lazarus at his side.
And he cried out, 'Father Abraham, have pity on me.
Send Lazarus to dip the tip of his finger in water and cool my
    tongue,
  for I am suffering torment in these flames.'
Abraham replied, 'My child,
  remember that you received what was good during your lifetime
  while Lazarus likewise received what was bad;
  but now he is comforted here, whereas you are tormented.
Moreover, between us and you a great chasm is established
  to prevent anyone from crossing
  who might wish to go from our side to yours
  or from your side to ours.'
He said, 'Then I beg you, father, send him
  to my father's house,
  for I have five brothers, so that he may warn them,
  lest they too come to this place of torment.'
But Abraham replied, 'They have Moses and the prophets.
Let them listen to them.'
He said, 'Oh no, father Abraham,
  but if someone from the dead goes to them, they will repent.'
Then Abraham said,
  'If they will not listen to Moses and the prophets,
  neither will they be persuaded
  if someone should rise from the dead.'" ✛

FRIDAY, MARCH 10
LENTEN WEEKDAY

† *Genesis 37:3-4, 12-13a, 17b-28a*
Here comes the man of dreams; let us kill him.

Israel loved Joseph best of all his sons,
  for he was the child of his old age;
  and he had made him a long tunic.
When his brothers saw that their father loved him best of all his
    sons,
  they hated him so much that they would not even greet him.

One day, when his brothers had gone
  to pasture their father's flocks at Shechem,
  Israel said to Joseph,
  "Your brothers, you know, are tending our flocks at Shechem.
Get ready; I will send you to them."

So Joseph went after his brothers and caught up with them in Dothan.
They noticed him from a distance,
  and before he came up to them, they plotted to kill him.
They said to one another: "Here comes that master dreamer!
Come on, let us kill him and throw him into one of the cisterns here;
  we could say that a wild beast devoured him.
We shall then see what comes of his dreams."

When Reuben heard this,
  he tried to save him from their hands, saying,
  "We must not take his life.
Instead of shedding blood," he continued,
  "just throw him into that cistern there in the desert;
  but do not kill him outright."
His purpose was to rescue him from their hands
  and return him to his father.
So when Joseph came up to them,
  they stripped him of the long tunic he had on;
  then they took him and threw him into the cistern,
  which was empty and dry.

They then sat down to their meal.
Looking up, they saw a caravan of Ishmaelites coming from Gilead,
  their camels laden with gum, balm and resin
  to be taken down to Egypt.
Judah said to his brothers:
  "What is to be gained by killing our brother and concealing his
    blood?

Rather, let us sell him to these Ishmaelites,
  instead of doing away with him ourselves.
After all, he is our brother, our own flesh."
His brothers agreed.
They sold Joseph to the Ishmaelites for twenty pieces of silver. ✛

Psalm 105:16-17, 18-19, 20-21
R. (5a) Remember the marvels the Lord has done.
When the Lᴏʀᴅ called down a famine on the land
  and ruined the crop that sustained them,
He sent a man before them,
  Joseph, sold as a slave. **R.**
They had weighed him down with fetters,
  and he was bound with chains,
Till his prediction came to pass
  and the word of the Lᴏʀᴅ proved him true. **R.**
The king sent and released him,
  the ruler of the peoples set him free.
He made him lord of his house
  and ruler of all his possessions. **R.**

John 3:16
R. Glory and praise to you, Lord Jesus Christ!
God so loved the world that he gave his only-begotten Son;
so that everyone who believes in him might have eternal life. **R.**

† *Matthew 21:33-43, 45-46*
This is the heir; let us kill him.

Jesus said to the chief priests and the elders of the people:
"Hear another parable.
There was a landowner who planted a vineyard,
  put a hedge around it,
  dug a wine press in it, and built a tower.
Then he leased it to tenants and went on a journey.
When vintage time drew near,
  he sent his servants to the tenants to obtain his produce.
But the tenants seized the servants and one they beat,
  another they killed, and a third they stoned.
Again he sent other servants, more numerous than the first ones,
  but they treated them in the same way.
Finally, he sent his son to them,
  thinking, 'They will respect my son.'
But when the tenants saw the son, they said to one another,
  'This is the heir.
Come, let us kill him and acquire his inheritance.'
They seized him, threw him out of the vineyard, and killed him.

What will the owner of the vineyard do to those tenants when he
   comes?"
They answered him,
   "He will put those wretched men to a wretched death
   and lease his vineyard to other tenants
   who will give him the produce at the proper times."
Jesus said to them, "Did you never read in the Scriptures:

The stone that the builders rejected
   has become the cornerstone;
by the Lord has this been done,
   and it is wonderful in our eyes?

Therefore, I say to you,
   the Kingdom of God will be taken away from you
   and given to a people that will produce its fruit."
When the chief priests and the Pharisees heard his parables,
   they knew that he was speaking about them.
And although they were attempting to arrest him,
   they feared the crowds, for they regarded him as a prophet. ✛

SATURDAY, MARCH 11
LENTEN WEEKDAY

† Micah 7:14-15, 18-20
God will cast our sins into the depths of the sea.

Shepherd your people with your staff,
   the flock of your inheritance,
That dwells apart in a woodland,
   in the midst of Carmel.
Let them feed in Bashan and Gilead,
   as in the days of old;
As in the days when you came from the land of Egypt,
   show us wonderful signs.

Who is there like you, the God who removes guilt
   and pardons sin for the remnant of his inheritance;
Who does not persist in anger forever,
   but delights rather in clemency,
And will again have compassion on us,
   treading underfoot our guilt?
You will cast into the depths of the sea all our sins;
You will show faithfulness to Jacob,
   and grace to Abraham,
As you have sworn to our fathers
   from days of old. ✛

Psalm 103:1-2, 3-4, 9-10, 11-12

R. (8a) **The Lord is kind and merciful.**

Bless the LORD, O my soul;
  and all my being, bless his holy name.
Bless the LORD, O my soul,
  and forget not all his benefits. **R.**

He pardons all your iniquities,
  he heals all your ills.
He redeems your life from destruction,
  he crowns you with kindness and compassion. **R.**

He will not always chide,
  nor does he keep his wrath forever.
Not according to our sins does he deal with us,
  nor does he requite us according to our crimes. **R.**

For as the heavens are high above the earth,
  so surpassing is his kindness toward those who fear him.
As far as the east is from the west,
  so far has he put our transgressions from us. **R.**

Luke 15:18

R. Glory and praise to you, Lord Jesus Christ!

I will get up and go to my father and shall say to him,
Father, I have sinned against heaven and against you. **R.**

† *Luke 15:1-3, 11-32*

Your brother was dead and has come to life.

Tax collectors and sinners were all drawing near to listen to Jesus,
  but the Pharisees and scribes began to complain, saying,
  "This man welcomes sinners and eats with them."
So to them Jesus addressed this parable.

"A man had two sons, and the younger son said to his father,
  'Father, give me the share of your estate that should come to me.'
So the father divided the property between them.
After a few days, the younger son collected all his belongings
  and set off to a distant country
  where he squandered his inheritance on a life of dissipation.
When he had freely spent everything,
  a severe famine struck that country,
  and he found himself in dire need.
So he hired himself out to one of the local citizens
  who sent him to his farm to tend the swine.
And he longed to eat his fill of the pods on which the swine fed,
  but nobody gave him any.
Coming to his senses he thought,

'How many of my father's hired workers
have more than enough food to eat,
but here am I, dying from hunger.
I shall get up and go to my father and I shall say to him,
"Father, I have sinned against heaven and against you.
I no longer deserve to be called your son;
treat me as you would treat one of your hired workers."'
So he got up and went back to his father.
While he was still a long way off,
his father caught sight of him, and was filled with compassion.
He ran to his son, embraced him and kissed him.
His son said to him,
'Father, I have sinned against heaven and against you;
I no longer deserve to be called your son.'
But his father ordered his servants,
'Quickly, bring the finest robe and put it on him;
put a ring on his finger and sandals on his feet.
Take the fattened calf and slaughter it.
Then let us celebrate with a feast,
because this son of mine was dead, and has come to life again;
he was lost, and has been found.'
Then the celebration began.
Now the older son had been out in the field
and, on his way back, as he neared the house,
he heard the sound of music and dancing.
He called one of the servants and asked what this might mean.
The servant said to him,
'Your brother has returned
and your father has slaughtered the fattened calf
because he has him back safe and sound.'
He became angry,
and when he refused to enter the house,
his father came out and pleaded with him.
He said to his father in reply,
'Look, all these years I served you
and not once did I disobey your orders;
yet you never gave me even a young goat to feast on with my
    friends.
But when your son returns
who swallowed up your property with prostitutes,
for him you slaughter the fattened calf.'
He said to him,
'My son, you are here with me always;
everything I have is yours.

But now we must celebrate and rejoice,
   because your brother was dead and has come to life again;
   he was lost and has been found." ✛

SUNDAY, MARCH 12
THIRD SUNDAY OF LENT

✝ Exodus 17:3-7
Give us water, so that we may drink.

In those days, in their thirst for water,
   the people grumbled against Moses,
   saying, "Why did you ever make us leave Egypt?
Was it just to have us die here of thirst
   with our children and our livestock?"
So Moses cried out to the LORD,
   "What shall I do with this people?
A little more and they will stone me!"
The LORD answered Moses,
   "Go over there in front of the people,
   along with some of the elders of Israel,
   holding in your hand, as you go,
   the staff with which you struck the river.
I will be standing there in front of you on the rock in Horeb.
Strike the rock, and the water will flow from it
   for the people to drink."
This Moses did, in the presence of the elders of Israel.
The place was called Massah and Meribah,
   because the Israelites quarreled there
   and tested the LORD, saying,
"Is the LORD in our midst or not?" ✛

Psalm 95:1-2, 6-7, 8-9
R. (8) If today you hear his voice, harden not your hearts.
Come, let us sing joyfully to the LORD;
   let us acclaim the Rock of our salvation.
Let us come into his presence with thanksgiving;
   let us joyfully sing psalms to him. **R.**
Come, let us bow down in worship;
   let us kneel before the LORD who made us.
For he is our God,
   and we are the people he shepherds, the flock he guides. **R.**
Oh, that today you would hear his voice:
   "Harden not your hearts as at Meribah,
   as in the day of Massah in the desert,

where your fathers tempted me;
    they tested me though they had seen my works." **R.**

✝ *Romans 5:1-2, 5-8*

The love of God has been poured into our hearts
through the Holy Spirit that has been given to us.

Brothers and sisters:
Since we have been justified by faith,
    we have peace with God through our Lord Jesus Christ,
    through whom we have gained access by faith
    to this grace in which we stand,
    and we boast in hope of the glory of God.

And hope does not disappoint,
    because the love of God has been poured out into our hearts
    through the Holy Spirit who has been given to us.
For Christ, while we were still helpless,
    died at the appointed time for the ungodly.
Indeed, only with difficulty does one die for a just person,
    though perhaps for a good person one might even find courage to
        die.
But God proves his love for us
    in that while we were still sinners Christ died for us. ✛

    See John 4:42, 15
R. Glory and praise to you, Lord Jesus Christ!
Lord, you are truly the Savior of the world;
give me living water, that I may never thirst again. **R.**

✝ *John 4:5-42* (or John 4:5-15, 19b-26, 39a, 40-42)

The water that I shall give will become a spring of eternal life.

Jesus came to a town of Samaria called Sychar,
    near the plot of land that Jacob had given to his son Joseph.
Jacob's well was there.
Jesus, tired from his journey, sat down there at the well.
It was about noon.

A woman of Samaria came to draw water.
Jesus said to her,
    "Give me a drink."
His disciples had gone into the town to buy food.
The Samaritan woman said to him,
    "How can you, a Jew, ask me, a Samaritan woman, for a drink?"
—For Jews use nothing in common with Samaritans.—
Jesus answered and said to her,
    "If you knew the gift of God

and who is saying to you, 'Give me a drink,'
you would have asked him
and he would have given you living water."
The woman said to him,
"Sir, you do not even have a bucket and the cistern is deep;
where then can you get this living water?
Are you greater than our father Jacob,
who gave us this cistern and drank from it himself
with his children and his flocks?"
Jesus answered and said to her,
"Everyone who drinks this water will be thirsty again;
but whoever drinks the water I shall give will never thirst;
the water I shall give will become in him
a spring of water welling up to eternal life."
The woman said to him,
"Sir, give me this water, so that I may not be thirsty
or have to keep coming here to draw water."

Jesus said to her,
"Go call your husband and come back."
The woman answered and said to him,
"I do not have a husband."
Jesus answered her,
"You are right in saying, 'I do not have a husband.'
For you have had five husbands,
and the one you have now is not your husband.
What you have said is true."
The woman said to him,
"Sir, I can see that you are a prophet.
Our ancestors worshiped on this mountain;
but you people say that the place to worship is in Jerusalem."
Jesus said to her,
"Believe me, woman, the hour is coming
when you will worship the Father
neither on this mountain nor in Jerusalem.
You people worship what you do not understand;
we worship what we understand,
because salvation is from the Jews.
But the hour is coming, and is now here,
when true worshipers will worship the Father in Spirit and truth;
and indeed the Father seeks such people to worship him.
God is Spirit, and those who worship him
must worship in Spirit and truth."
The woman said to him,

"I know that the Messiah is coming, the one called the Christ;
   when he comes, he will tell us everything."
Jesus said to her,
   "I am he, the one speaking with you."

At that moment his disciples returned,
   and were amazed that he was talking with a woman,
   but still no one said, "What are you looking for?"
   or "Why are you talking with her?"
The woman left her water jar
   and went into the town and said to the people,
   "Come see a man who told me everything I have done.
Could he possibly be the Christ?"
They went out of the town and came to him.
Meanwhile, the disciples urged him, "Rabbi, eat."
But he said to them,
   "I have food to eat of which you do not know."
So the disciples said to one another,
   "Could someone have brought him something to eat?"
Jesus said to them,
   "My food is to do the will of the one who sent me
   and to finish his work.
Do you not say, 'In four months the harvest will be here'?
I tell you, look up and see the fields ripe for the harvest.
The reaper is already receiving payment
   and gathering crops for eternal life,
   so that the sower and reaper can rejoice together.
For here the saying is verified that 'One sows and another reaps.'
I sent you to reap what you have not worked for;
   others have done the work,
   and you are sharing the fruits of their work."

Many of the Samaritans of that town began to believe in him
   because of the word of the woman who testified,
   "He told me everything I have done."
When the Samaritans came to him,
   they invited him to stay with them;
   and he stayed there two days.
Many more began to believe in him because of his word,
   and they said to the woman,
   "We no longer believe because of your word;
   for we have heard for ourselves,
   and we know that this is truly the savior of the world." ✟

MONDAY, MARCH 13
LENTEN WEEKDAY

† 2 Kings 5:1-15ab (or any day this week, Exodus 17:1-7)
There were many people with leprosy in Israel,
but none were made clean, except Naaman the Syrian (Luke 4:27).

Naaman, the army commander of the king of Aram,
   was highly esteemed and respected by his master,
   for through him the LORD had brought victory to Aram.
But valiant as he was, the man was a leper.
Now the Arameans had captured in a raid on the land of Israel
   a little girl, who became the servant of Naaman's wife.
"If only my master would present himself to the prophet in Samaria,"
   she said to her mistress, "he would cure him of his leprosy."
Naaman went and told his lord
   just what the slave girl from the land of Israel had said.
"Go," said the king of Aram.
"I will send along a letter to the king of Israel."
So Naaman set out, taking along ten silver talents,
   six thousand gold pieces, and ten festal garments.
To the king of Israel he brought the letter, which read:
   "With this letter I am sending my servant Naaman to you,
   that you may cure him of his leprosy."

When he read the letter,
   the king of Israel tore his garments and exclaimed:
   "Am I a god with power over life and death,
   that this man should send someone to me to be cured of leprosy?
Take note! You can see he is only looking for a quarrel with me!"
When Elisha, the man of God,
   heard that the king of Israel had torn his garments,
   he sent word to the king:
   "Why have you torn your garments?
Let him come to me and find out
   that there is a prophet in Israel."

Naaman came with his horses and chariots
   and stopped at the door of Elisha's house.
The prophet sent him the message:
   "Go and wash seven times in the Jordan,
   and your flesh will heal, and you will be clean."
But Naaman went away angry, saying,
   "I thought that he would surely come out and stand there
   to invoke the LORD his God,
   and would move his hand over the spot,

and thus cure the leprosy.
Are not the rivers of Damascus, the Abana and the Pharpar,
    better than all the waters of Israel?
Could I not wash in them and be cleansed?"
With this, he turned about in anger and left.

But his servants came up and reasoned with him.
"My father," they said,
    "if the prophet had told you to do something extraordinary,
    would you not have done it?
All the more now, since he said to you,
    'Wash and be clean,' should you do as he said."
So Naaman went down and plunged into the Jordan seven times
    at the word of the man of God.
His flesh became again like the flesh of a little child, and he was clean.

He returned with his whole retinue to the man of God.
On his arrival he stood before him and said,
    "Now I know that there is no God in all the earth,
    except in Israel." ✛

*Psalms 42:2, 3; 43:3, 4 (or any day this week, Psalm 95:1-2,
6-7ab, 7c-9)*

R. (see 42:3) **Athirst is my soul for the living God. When shall I
go and behold the face of God?**
As the hind longs for the running waters,
    so my soul longs for you, O God. **R.**
Athirst is my soul for God, the living God.
    When shall I go and behold the face of God? **R.**
Send forth your light and your fidelity;
    they shall lead me on
And bring me to your holy mountain,
    to your dwelling-place. **R.**
Then will I go in to the altar of God,
    the God of my gladness and joy;
Then will I give you thanks upon the harp,
    O God, my God! **R.**

See Psalm 130:5, 7
R. Glory and praise to you, Lord Jesus Christ!
I hope in the LORD, I trust in his word;
with him there is kindness and plenteous redemption. **R.**

*†**Luke 4:24-30** (or any day this week, John 4:5-42)*
Like Elijah and Elisha, Jesus was sent not only to the Jews.

Jesus said to the people in the synagogue at Nazareth:

"Amen, I say to you,
  no prophet is accepted in his own native place.
Indeed, I tell you, there were many widows in Israel
  in the days of Elijah
    when the sky was closed for three and a half years
    and a severe famine spread over the entire land.
It was to none of these that Elijah was sent,
  but only to a widow in Zarephath in the land of Sidon.
Again, there were many lepers in Israel
  during the time of Elisha the prophet;
    yet not one of them was cleansed, but only Naaman the Syrian."
When the people in the synagogue heard this,
  they were all filled with fury.
They rose up, drove him out of the town,
  and led him to the brow of the hill
  on which their town had been built,
    to hurl him down headlong.
But he passed through the midst of them and went away. ✛

TUESDAY, MARCH 14
LENTEN WEEKDAY

† Daniel 3:25, 34-43
We ask you to receive us with humble and contrite hearts.

Azariah stood up in the fire and prayed aloud:

"For your name's sake, O Lord, do not deliver us up forever,
  or make void your covenant.
Do not take away your mercy from us,
  for the sake of Abraham, your beloved,
  Isaac your servant, and Israel your holy one,
To whom you promised to multiply their offspring
  like the stars of heaven,
  or the sand on the shore of the sea.
For we are reduced, O Lord, beyond any other nation,
  brought low everywhere in the world this day
  because of our sins.
We have in our day no prince, prophet, or leader,
  no burnt offering, sacrifice, oblation, or incense,
  no place to offer first fruits, to find favor with you.
But with contrite heart and humble spirit
  let us be received;
As though it were burnt offerings of rams and bullocks,
  or thousands of fat lambs,
So let our sacrifice be in your presence today

as we follow you unreservedly;
  for those who trust in you cannot be put to shame.
And now we follow you with our whole heart,
  we fear you and we pray to you.
Do not let us be put to shame,
  but deal with us in your kindness and great mercy.
Deliver us by your wonders,
  and bring glory to your name, O Lord." ✛

Psalm 25:4-5ab, 6 and 7bc, 8-9

R. (6a) **Remember your mercies, O Lord.**

Your ways, O LORD, make known to me;
  teach me your paths,
Guide me in your truth and teach me,
  for you are God my savior. **R.**
Remember that your compassion, O LORD,
  and your kindness are from of old.
In your kindness remember me,
  because of your goodness, O LORD. **R.**
Good and upright is the LORD;
  thus he shows sinners the way.
He guides the humble to justice,
  he teaches the humble his way. **R.**

Joel 2:12-13

R. Glory and praise to you, Lord Jesus Christ!

Even now, says the LORD,
return to me with your whole heart;
for I am gracious and merciful. **R.**

† Matthew 18:21-35
Unless each of you forgives your brother and sister,
the Father will not forgive you.

Peter approached Jesus and asked him,
  "Lord, if my brother sins against me,
  how often must I forgive him?
As many as seven times?"
Jesus answered, "I say to you, not seven times but seventy-seven
    times.
That is why the Kingdom of heaven may be likened to a king
  who decided to settle accounts with his servants.
When he began the accounting,
  a debtor was brought before him who owed him a huge amount.
Since he had no way of paying it back,
  his master ordered him to be sold,
  along with his wife, his children, and all his property,

in payment of the debt.
At that, the servant fell down, did him homage, and said,
  'Be patient with me, and I will pay you back in full.'
Moved with compassion the master of that servant
  let him go and forgave him the loan.
When that servant had left, he found one of his fellow servants
  who owed him a much smaller amount.
He seized him and started to choke him, demanding,
  'Pay back what you owe.'
Falling to his knees, his fellow servant begged him,
  'Be patient with me, and I will pay you back.'
But he refused.
Instead, he had him put in prison
  until he paid back the debt.
Now when his fellow servants saw what had happened,
  they were deeply disturbed, and went to their master
  and reported the whole affair.
His master summoned him and said to him, 'You wicked servant!
I forgave you your entire debt because you begged me to.
Should you not have had pity on your fellow servant,
  as I had pity on you?'
Then in anger his master handed him over to the torturers
  until he should pay back the whole debt.
So will my heavenly Father do to you,
  unless each of you forgives your brother from your heart." ✛

WEDNESDAY, MARCH 15
LENTEN WEEKDAY

† *Deuteronomy 4:1, 5-9*
Keep the commandments and your work will be complete.

Moses spoke to the people and said:
"Now, Israel, hear the statutes and decrees
  which I am teaching you to observe,
    that you may live, and may enter in and take possession of the land
    which the LORD, the God of your fathers, is giving you.
Therefore, I teach you the statutes and decrees
  as the LORD, my God, has commanded me,
    that you may observe them in the land you are entering to occupy.
Observe them carefully,
  for thus will you give evidence
  of your wisdom and intelligence to the nations,
  who will hear of all these statutes and say,
    'This great nation is truly a wise and intelligent people.'
For what great nation is there

that has gods so close to it as the LORD, our God, is to us
whenever we call upon him?
Or what great nation has statutes and decrees
that are as just as this whole law
which I am setting before you today?

"However, take care and be earnestly on your guard
not to forget the things which your own eyes have seen,
nor let them slip from your memory as long as you live,
but teach them to your children and to your children's children." ✝

Psalm 147:12-13, 15-16, 19-20
R. (12a) **Praise the Lord, Jerusalem.**
Glorify the LORD, O Jerusalem;
praise your God, O Zion.
For he has strengthened the bars of your gates;
he has blessed your children within you. **R.**
He sends forth his command to the earth;
swiftly runs his word!
He spreads snow like wool;
frost he strews like ashes. **R.**
He has proclaimed his word to Jacob,
his statutes and his ordinances to Israel.
He has not done thus for any other nation;
his ordinances he has not made known to them. **R.**

See John 6:63c, 68c
R. **Glory and praise to you, Lord Jesus Christ!**
Your words, Lord, are Spirit and life;
you have the words of everlasting life. **R.**

† *Matthew 5:17-19*
Whoever keeps and teaches the law will be called great.

Jesus said to his disciples:
"Do not think that I have come to abolish the law or the prophets.
I have come not to abolish but to fulfill.
Amen, I say to you, until heaven and earth pass away,
not the smallest letter or the smallest part of a letter
will pass from the law,
until all things have taken place.
Therefore, whoever breaks one of the least of these commandments
and teaches others to do so
will be called least in the Kingdom of heaven.
But whoever obeys and teaches these commandments
will be called greatest in the Kingdom of heaven." ✝

THURSDAY, MARCH 16
LENTEN WEEKDAY

† *Jeremiah 7:23-28*
This is the nation that will not listen to the voice of the LORD God.

Thus says the LORD:
This is what I commanded my people:
 Listen to my voice;
  then I will be your God and you shall be my people.
Walk in all the ways that I command you,
 so that you may prosper.

But they obeyed not, nor did they pay heed.
They walked in the hardness of their evil hearts
 and turned their backs, not their faces, to me.
From the day that your fathers left the land of Egypt even to this day,
 I have sent you untiringly all my servants the prophets.
Yet they have not obeyed me nor paid heed;
 they have stiffened their necks and done worse than their fathers.
When you speak all these words to them,
 they will not listen to you either;
 when you call to them, they will not answer you.
Say to them:
 This is the nation that does not listen
 to the voice of the LORD, its God,
 or take correction.
Faithfulness has disappeared;
 the word itself is banished from their speech. ✝

Psalm 95:1b-2, 6-7, 8-9
R. (8) **If today you hear his voice, harden not your hearts.**
Come, let us sing joyfully to the LORD;
 let us acclaim the Rock of our salvation.
Let us come into his presence with thanksgiving;
 let us joyfully sing psalms to him. **R.**
Come, let us bow down in worship;
 let us kneel before the LORD who made us.
For he is our God,
 and we are the people he shepherds, the flock he guides. **R.**
Oh, that today you would hear his voice:
 "Harden not your hearts as at Meribah,
 as in the day of Massah in the desert,
Where your fathers tempted me;
 they tested me though they had seen my works." **R.**

Joel 2:12-13

R. Glory and praise to you, Lord Jesus Christ!

Even now, says the LORD,
return to me with your whole heart,
for I am gracious and merciful. **R.**

† *Luke 11:14-23*
Whoever is not with me is against me.

Jesus was driving out a demon that was mute,
and when the demon had gone out,
the mute man spoke and the crowds were amazed.
Some of them said, "By the power of Beelzebul, the prince of demons,
he drives out demons."
Others, to test him, asked him for a sign from heaven.
But he knew their thoughts and said to them,
"Every kingdom divided against itself will be laid waste
and house will fall against house.
And if Satan is divided against himself,
how will his kingdom stand?
For you say that it is by Beelzebul that I drive out demons.
If I, then, drive out demons by Beelzebul,
by whom do your own people drive them out?
Therefore they will be your judges.
But if it is by the finger of God that I drive out demons,
then the Kingdom of God has come upon you.
When a strong man fully armed guards his palace,
his possessions are safe.
But when one stronger than he attacks and overcomes him,
he takes away the armor on which he relied
and distributes the spoils.
Whoever is not with me is against me,
and whoever does not gather with me scatters." ✦

FRIDAY, MARCH 17
LENTEN WEEKDAY, ST. PATRICK

† *Hosea 14:2-10*
We will not say to the work of our hands: our god.

Thus says the LORD:
Return, O Israel, to the LORD, your God;
you have collapsed through your guilt.
Take with you words,
and return to the LORD;
Say to him, "Forgive all iniquity,
and receive what is good, that we may render

as offerings the bullocks from our stalls.
Assyria will not save us,
   nor shall we have horses to mount;
We shall say no more, 'Our god,'
   to the work of our hands;
   for in you the orphan finds compassion."

I will heal their defection, says the LORD,
   I will love them freely;
   for my wrath is turned away from them.
I will be like the dew for Israel:
   he shall blossom like the lily;
He shall strike root like the Lebanon cedar,
   and put forth his shoots.
His splendor shall be like the olive tree
   and his fragrance like the Lebanon cedar.
Again they shall dwell in his shade
   and raise grain;
They shall blossom like the vine,
   and his fame shall be like the wine of Lebanon.

Ephraim! What more has he to do with idols?
   I have humbled him, but I will prosper him.
"I am like a verdant cypress tree"—
   Because of me you bear fruit!

Let him who is wise understand these things;
   let him who is prudent know them.
Straight are the paths of the LORD,
   in them the just walk,
   but sinners stumble in them. ✝

   Psalm 81:6c-8a, 8bc-9, 10-11ab, 14 and 17
R. (see 11 and 9a) **I am the Lord your God: hear my voice.**
An unfamiliar speech I hear:
   "I relieved his shoulder of the burden;
   his hands were freed from the basket.
In distress you called, and I rescued you." **R.**
"Unseen, I answered you in thunder;
   I tested you at the waters of Meribah.
Hear, my people, and I will admonish you;
   O Israel, will you not hear me?" **R.**
"There shall be no strange god among you
   nor shall you worship any alien god.
I, the LORD, am your God
   who led you forth from the land of Egypt." **R.**

"If only my people would hear me,
  and Israel walk in my ways,
I would feed them with the best of wheat,
  and with honey from the rock I would fill them." **R.**

Matthew 4:17
R. Glory and praise to you, Lord Jesus Christ!
Repent, says the Lord;
the Kingdom of heaven is at hand. **R.**

✝ Mark 12:28-34
The Lord our God is one Lord, and you shall love the Lord your God.

One of the scribes came to Jesus and asked him,
  "Which is the first of all the commandments?"
Jesus replied, "The first is this:
  Hear, O Israel!
  The Lord our God is Lord alone!
You shall love the Lord your God with all your heart,
  with all your soul,
  with all your mind,
  and with all your strength.
The second is this:
  You shall love your neighbor as yourself.
There is no other commandment greater than these."
The scribe said to him, "Well said, teacher.
You are right in saying,
  He is One and there is no other than he.
  And *to love him with all your heart,*
  with all your understanding,
  with all your strength,
  and to love your neighbor as yourself
  is worth more than all burnt offerings and sacrifices."
And when Jesus saw that he answered with understanding,
  he said to him,
  "You are not far from the Kingdom of God."
And no one dared to ask him any more questions. ✛

SATURDAY, MARCH 18
Lenten Weekday, St. Cyril of Jerusalem

✝ Hosea 6:1-6
What I want is love, not sacrifice.

"Come, let us return to the Lord,
  it is he who has rent, but he will heal us;
  he has struck us, but he will bind our wounds.
He will revive us after two days;

on the third day he will raise us up,
to live in his presence.
Let us know, let us strive to know the LORD;
as certain as the dawn is his coming,
and his judgment shines forth like the light of day!
He will come to us like the rain,
like spring rain that waters the earth."

What can I do with you, Ephraim?
What can I do with you, Judah?
Your piety is like a morning cloud,
like the dew that early passes away.
For this reason I smote them through the prophets,
I slew them by the words of my mouth;
For it is love that I desire, not sacrifice,
and knowledge of God rather than burnt offerings. ✛

Psalm 51:3-4, 18-19, 20-21ab
R. (see Hosea 6:6) **It is mercy I desire, and not sacrifice.**
Have mercy on me, O God, in your goodness;
in the greatness of your compassion wipe out my offense.
Thoroughly wash me from my guilt
and of my sin cleanse me. **R.**
For you are not pleased with sacrifices;
should I offer a burnt offering, you would not accept it.
My sacrifice, O God, is a contrite spirit;
a heart contrite and humbled, O God, you will not spurn. **R.**
Be bountiful, O LORD, to Zion in your kindness
by rebuilding the walls of Jerusalem;
Then shall you be pleased with due sacrifices,
burnt offerings and holocausts. **R.**

Psalm 95:8
R. Glory and praise to you, Lord Jesus Christ!
If today you hear his voice,
harden not your hearts. **R.**

✝ *Luke 18:9-14*
The tax collector went home justified, not the Pharisee.

Jesus addressed this parable
to those who were convinced of their own righteousness
and despised everyone else.
"Two people went up to the temple area to pray;
one was a Pharisee and the other was a tax collector.
The Pharisee took up his position and spoke this prayer to himself,
'O God, I thank you that I am not like the rest of humanity—

greedy, dishonest, adulterous—or even like this tax collector.
I fast twice a week,
　and I pay tithes on my whole income.'
But the tax collector stood off at a distance
　and would not even raise his eyes to heaven
　but beat his breast and prayed,
　'O God, be merciful to me a sinner.'
I tell you, the latter went home justified, not the former;
　for everyone who exalts himself will be humbled,
　and the one who humbles himself will be exalted." ✛

SUNDAY, MARCH 19
FOURTH SUNDAY OF LENT

† 1 Samuel 16:1b, 6-7, 10-13a
David is anointed as king of Israel.

The LORD said to Samuel:
　"Fill your horn with oil, and be on your way.
I am sending you to Jesse of Bethlehem,
　for I have chosen my king from among his sons."

As Jesse and his sons came to the sacrifice,
　Samuel looked at Eliab and thought,
　"Surely the LORD's anointed is here before him."
But the LORD said to Samuel:
　"Do not judge from his appearance or from his lofty stature,
　because I have rejected him.
Not as man sees does God see,
　because man sees the appearance
　but the LORD looks into the heart."
In the same way Jesse presented seven sons before Samuel,
　but Samuel said to Jesse,
　"The LORD has not chosen any one of these."
Then Samuel asked Jesse,
　"Are these all the sons you have?"
Jesse replied,
　"There is still the youngest, who is tending the sheep."
Samuel said to Jesse,
　"Send for him;
　we will not begin the sacrificial banquet until he arrives here."
Jesse sent and had the young man brought to them.
He was ruddy, a youth handsome to behold
　and making a splendid appearance.
The LORD said,
　"There—anoint him, for this is the one!"

Then Samuel, with the horn of oil in hand,
  anointed David in the presence of his brothers;
  and from that day on, the spirit of the LORD rushed upon David. ✝

  Psalm 23:1-3a, 3b-4, 5, 6
R. (1) **The Lord is my shepherd; there is nothing I shall want.**
The LORD is my shepherd; I shall not want.
  In verdant pastures he gives me repose;
beside restful waters he leads me;
  he refreshes my soul. **R.**
He guides me in right paths
  for his name's sake.
Even though I walk in the dark valley
  I fear no evil; for you are at my side
With your rod and your staff
  that give me courage. **R.**
You spread the table before me
  in the sight of my foes;
you anoint my head with oil;
  my cup overflows. **R.**
Only goodness and kindness follow me
  all the days of my life;
and I shall dwell in the house of the LORD
  for years to come. **R.**

✝ *Ephesians 5:8-14*
Arise from the dead, and Christ will give you light.

Brothers and sisters:
You were once darkness,
  but now you are light in the Lord.
Live as children of light,
  for light produces every kind of goodness
  and righteousness and truth.
Try to learn what is pleasing to the Lord.
Take no part in the fruitless works of darkness;
  rather expose them, for it is shameful even to mention
  the things done by them in secret;
  but everything exposed by the light becomes visible,
  for everything that becomes visible is light.
Therefore, it says:
  "Awake, O sleeper,
  and arise from the dead,
  and Christ will give you light." ✝

John 8:12

R. Glory and praise to you, Lord Jesus Christ!

I am the light of the world, says the Lord;
whoever follows me will have the light of life. **R.**

† *John 9:1-41* (or *John 9:1, 6-9, 13-17, 34-38*)
The man who was blind went off and
washed himself and came back able to see.

As Jesus passed by he saw a man blind from birth.
His disciples asked him,
   "Rabbi, who sinned, this man or his parents,
   that he was born blind?"
Jesus answered,
   "Neither he nor his parents sinned;
   it is so that the works of God might be made visible through him.
We have to do the works of the one who sent me while it is day.
Night is coming when no one can work.
While I am in the world, I am the light of the world."
When he had said this, he spat on the ground
   and made clay with the saliva,
   and smeared the clay on his eyes,
   and said to him,
   "Go wash in the Pool of Siloam"—which means Sent—.
So he went and washed, and came back able to see.

His neighbors and those who had seen him earlier as a beggar said,
   "Isn't this the one who used to sit and beg?"
Some said, "It is,"
   but others said, "No, he just looks like him."
He said, "I am."
So they said to him, "How were your eyes opened?"
He replied,
   "The man called Jesus made clay and anointed my eyes
   and told me, 'Go to Siloam and wash.'
So I went there and washed and was able to see."
And they said to him, "Where is he?"
He said, "I don't know."

They brought the one who was once blind to the Pharisees.
Now Jesus had made clay and opened his eyes on a sabbath.
So then the Pharisees also asked him how he was able to see.
He said to them,
   "He put clay on my eyes, and I washed, and now I can see."
So some of the Pharisees said,
   "This man is not from God,

because he does not keep the sabbath."
But others said,
   "How can a sinful man do such signs?"
And there was a division among them.
So they said to the blind man again,
   "What do you have to say about him,
   since he opened your eyes?"
He said, "He is a prophet."

Now the Jews did not believe
   that he had been blind and gained his sight
   until they summoned the parents of the one who had gained his
     sight.
They asked them,
   "Is this your son, who you say was born blind?
How does he now see?"
His parents answered and said,
   "We know that this is our son and that he was born blind.
We do not know how he sees now,
   nor do we know who opened his eyes.
Ask him, he is of age;
   he can speak for himself."
His parents said this because they were afraid of the Jews,
   for the Jews had already agreed
   that if anyone acknowledged him as the Christ,
   he would be expelled from the synagogue.
For this reason his parents said,
   "He is of age; question him."

So a second time they called the man who had been blind
   and said to him, "Give God the praise!
We know that this man is a sinner."
He replied,
   "If he is a sinner, I do not know.
One thing I do know is that I was blind and now I see."
So they said to him,
   "What did he do to you?
   How did he open your eyes?"
He answered them,
   "I told you already and you did not listen.
Why do you want to hear it again?
Do you want to become his disciples, too?"
They ridiculed him and said,
   "You are that man's disciple;
   we are disciples of Moses!

We know that God spoke to Moses,
  but we do not know where this one is from."
The man answered and said to them,
  "This is what is so amazing,
  that you do not know where he is from, yet he opened my eyes.
We know that God does not listen to sinners,
  but if one is devout and does his will, he listens to him.
It is unheard of that anyone ever opened the eyes of a person born
     blind.
If this man were not from God,
  he would not be able to do anything."
They answered and said to him,
  "You were born totally in sin,
  and are you trying to teach us?"
Then they threw him out.

When Jesus heard that they had thrown him out,
  he found him and said, "Do you believe in the Son of Man?"
He answered and said,
  "Who is he, sir, that I may believe in him?"
Jesus said to him,
  "You have seen him,
  the one speaking with you is he."
He said,
  "I do believe, Lord, " and he worshiped him.
Then Jesus said,
  "I came into this world for judgment,
  so that those who do not see might see,
  and those who do see might become blind."

Some of the Pharisees who were with him heard this
  and said to him, "Surely we are not also blind, are we?"
Jesus said to them,
  "If you were blind, you would have no sin;
  but now you are saying, 'We see,' so your sin remains." ✛

MONDAY, MARCH 20
St. Joseph, Spouse of the Blessed Virgin Mary

†2 Samuel 7:4-5a, 12-14a, 16
The Lord God will give him the throne of David, his father (Luke 1:32).

The LORD spoke to Nathan and said:
"Go, tell my servant David,
  'When your time comes and you rest with your ancestors,
  I will raise up your heir after you, sprung from your loins,

and I will make his kingdom firm.
It is he who shall build a house for my name.
And I will make his royal throne firm forever.
I will be a father to him,
    and he shall be a son to me.
Your house and your kingdom shall endure forever before me;
    your throne shall stand firm forever.'" ✛

Psalm 89:2-3, 4-5, 27 and 29
R. (37) **The son of David will live for ever.**
The promises of the LORD I will sing forever;
    through all generations my mouth shall proclaim your faithfulness,
For you have said, "My kindness is established forever";
    in heaven you have confirmed your faithfulness. **R.**
"I have made a covenant with my chosen one,
    I have sworn to David my servant:
Forever will I confirm your posterity
    and establish your throne for all generations." **R.**
"He shall say of me, 'You are my father,
    my God, the Rock, my savior.'
Forever I will maintain my kindness toward him,
    and my covenant with him stands firm." **R.**

*† **Romans 4:13, 16-18, 22***
Abraham believed, hoping against hope.

Brothers and sisters:
It was not through the law
    that the promise was made to Abraham and his descendants
    that he would inherit the world,
    but through the righteousness that comes from faith.
For this reason, it depends on faith,
    so that it may be a gift,
    and the promise may be guaranteed to all his descendants,
    not to those who only adhere to the law
    but to those who follow the faith of Abraham,
    who is the father of all of us, as it is written,
    I have made you father of many nations.
He is our father in the sight of God,
    in whom he believed, who gives life to the dead
    and calls into being what does not exist.
He believed, hoping against hope,
    that he would become *the father of many nations,*
    according to what was said, *Thus shall your descendants be.*
That is why *it was credited to him as righteousness.* ✛

Psalm 84:5

R. Glory and praise to you, Lord Jesus Christ!

Blessed are those who dwell in your house, O Lord;
they never cease to praise you. **R.**

✝ Matthew 1:16, 18-21, 24a (or Luke 2:41-51a)
Joseph did as the angel of the Lord had commanded him.

Jacob was the father of Joseph, the husband of Mary.
Of her was born Jesus who is called the Christ.

Now this is how the birth of Jesus Christ came about.
When his mother Mary was betrothed to Joseph,
    but before they lived together,
    she was found with child through the Holy Spirit.
Joseph her husband, since he was a righteous man,
    yet unwilling to expose her to shame,
    decided to divorce her quietly.
Such was his intention when, behold,
    the angel of the Lord appeared to him in a dream and said,
    "Joseph, son of David,
    do not be afraid to take Mary your wife into your home.
For it is through the Holy Spirit
    that this child has been conceived in her.
She will bear a son and you are to name him Jesus,
    because he will save his people from their sins."
When Joseph awoke,
    he did as the angel of the Lord had commanded him
    and took his wife into his home. ✚

TUESDAY, MARCH 21
LENTEN WEEKDAY

✝ Ezekiel 47:1-9, 12 (or any day this week, Micah 7:7-9)
I saw water flowing from the temple, and all who were touched by it were saved
(see Roman Missal).

The angel brought me, Ezekiel,
    back to the entrance of the temple of the LORD,
    and I saw water flowing out
    from beneath the threshold of the temple toward the east,
    for the façade of the temple was toward the east;
    the water flowed down from the right side of the temple,
    south of the altar.
He led me outside by the north gate,
    and around to the outer gate facing the east,
    where I saw water trickling from the right side.
Then when he had walked off to the east

with a measuring cord in his hand,
he measured off a thousand cubits
and had me wade through the water,
which was ankle-deep.
He measured off another thousand
and once more had me wade through the water,
which was now knee-deep.
Again he measured off a thousand and had me wade;
the water was up to my waist.
Once more he measured off a thousand,
but there was now a river through which I could not wade;
for the water had risen so high it had become a river
that could not be crossed except by swimming.
He asked me, "Have you seen this, son of man?"
Then he brought me to the bank of the river, where he had me sit.
Along the bank of the river I saw very many trees on both sides.
He said to me,
"This water flows into the eastern district down upon the Arabah,
and empties into the sea, the salt waters, which it makes fresh.
Wherever the river flows,
every sort of living creature that can multiply shall live,
and there shall be abundant fish,
for wherever this water comes the sea shall be made fresh.
Along both banks of the river, fruit trees of every kind shall grow;
their leaves shall not fade, nor their fruit fail.
Every month they shall bear fresh fruit,
for they shall be watered by the flow from the sanctuary.
Their fruit shall serve for food, and their leaves for medicine." ✝

Psalm 46:2-3, 5-6, 8-9 (or any day this week,
Psalm 27:1, 7-8a, 8b-9abc, 13-14)

R. (8) **The Lord of hosts is with us; our stronghold is the God**
of Jacob.
God is our refuge and our strength,
an ever-present help in distress.
Therefore we fear not, though the earth be shaken
and mountains plunge into the depths of the sea. **R.**
There is a stream whose runlets gladden the city of God,
the holy dwelling of the Most High.
God is in its midst; it shall not be disturbed;
God will help it at the break of dawn. **R.**
The LORD of hosts is with us;
our stronghold is the God of Jacob.
Come! behold the deeds of the LORD,
the astounding things he has wrought on earth. **R.**

Psalm 51:12a, 14a
R. Glory and praise to you, Lord Jesus Christ!
A clean heart create for me, O God;
give me back the joy of your salvation. **R.**

✝ ***John 5:1-16*** *(or any day this week, John 9:1-41)*
Immediately the man became well.

There was a feast of the Jews, and Jesus went up to Jerusalem.
Now there is in Jerusalem at the Sheep Gate
  a pool called in Hebrew Bethesda, with five porticoes.
In these lay a large number of ill, blind, lame, and crippled.
One man was there who had been ill for thirty-eight years.
When Jesus saw him lying there
  and knew that he had been ill for a long time, he said to him,
  "Do you want to be well?"
The sick man answered him,
  "Sir, I have no one to put me into the pool
  when the water is stirred up;
  while I am on my way, someone else gets down there before me."
Jesus said to him, "Rise, take up your mat, and walk."
Immediately the man became well, took up his mat, and walked.

Now that day was a sabbath.
So the Jews said to the man who was cured,
  "It is the sabbath, and it is not lawful for you to carry your mat."
He answered them, "The man who made me well told me,
  'Take up your mat and walk.'"
They asked him,
  "Who is the man who told you, 'Take it up and walk'?"
The man who was healed did not know who it was,
  for Jesus had slipped away, since there was a crowd there.
After this Jesus found him in the temple area and said to him,
  "Look, you are well; do not sin any more,
  so that nothing worse may happen to you."
The man went and told the Jews
  that Jesus was the one who had made him well.
Therefore, the Jews began to persecute Jesus
  because he did this on a sabbath. ✚

WEDNESDAY, MARCH 22
LENTEN WEEKDAY

† *Isaiah 49:8-15*
I have given you as a covenant to the people, to restore the land.

Thus says the LORD:
In a time of favor I answer you,
  on the day of salvation I help you;
  and I have kept you and given you as a covenant to the people,
To restore the land
  and allot the desolate heritages,
Saying to the prisoners: Come out!
To those in darkness: Show yourselves!
Along the ways they shall find pasture,
  on every bare height shall their pastures be.
They shall not hunger or thirst,
  nor shall the scorching wind or the sun strike them;
For he who pities them leads them
  and guides them beside springs of water.
I will cut a road through all my mountains,
  and make my highways level.
See, some shall come from afar,
  others from the north and the west,
  and some from the land of Syene.
Sing out, O heavens, and rejoice, O earth,
  break forth into song, you mountains.
For the LORD comforts his people
  and shows mercy to his afflicted.

But Zion said, "The LORD has forsaken me;
  my Lord has forgotten me."
Can a mother forget her infant,
  be without tenderness for the child of her womb?
Even should she forget,
  I will never forget you. ✚

Psalm 145:8-9, 13cd-14, 17-18
R. (8a) **The Lord is gracious and merciful.**
The LORD is gracious and merciful,
  slow to anger and of great kindness.
The LORD is good to all
  and compassionate toward all his works. **R.**
The LORD is faithful in all his words
  and holy in all his works.
The LORD lifts up all who are falling

and raises up all who are bowed down. **R.**
The Lord is just in all his ways
    and holy in all his works.
The Lord is near to all who call upon him,
    to all who call upon him in truth. **R.**

John 11:25a, 26

R. Glory and praise to you, Lord Jesus Christ!
I am the resurrection and the life, says the Lord;
whoever believes in me will never die. **R.**

† *John 5:17-30*

As the Father raises the dead and gives them life,
so also does the Son give life to those whom he chooses.

Jesus answered the Jews:
"My Father is at work until now, so I am at work."
For this reason they tried all the more to kill him,
    because he not only broke the sabbath
    but he also called God his own father, making himself equal to God.

Jesus answered and said to them,
    "Amen, amen, I say to you, the Son cannot do anything on his own,
    but only what he sees the Father doing;
    for what he does, the Son will do also.
For the Father loves the Son
    and shows him everything that he himself does,
    and he will show him greater works than these,
    so that you may be amazed.
For just as the Father raises the dead and gives life,
    so also does the Son give life to whomever he wishes.
Nor does the Father judge anyone,
    but he has given all judgment to the Son,
    so that all may honor the Son just as they honor the Father.
Whoever does not honor the Son
    does not honor the Father who sent him.
Amen, amen, I say to you, whoever hears my word
    and believes in the one who sent me
    has eternal life and will not come to condemnation,
    but has passed from death to life.
Amen, amen, I say to you, the hour is coming and is now here
    when the dead will hear the voice of the Son of God,
    and those who hear will live.
For just as the Father has life in himself,
    so also he gave to the Son the possession of life in himself.
And he gave him power to exercise judgment,

because he is the Son of Man.
Do not be amazed at this,
because the hour is coming in which all who are in the tombs
will hear his voice and will come out,
those who have done good deeds
to the resurrection of life,
but those who have done wicked deeds
to the resurrection of condemnation.

"I cannot do anything on my own;
I judge as I hear, and my judgment is just,
because I do not seek my own will
but the will of the one who sent me." ✝

THURSDAY, MARCH 23
LENTEN WEEKDAY, ST. TURIBIUS OF MOGROVEJO

✝ Exodus 32:7-14
Relent in punishing your people.

The LORD said to Moses,
"Go down at once to your people
whom you brought out of the land of Egypt,
for they have become depraved.
They have soon turned aside from the way I pointed out to them,
making for themselves a molten calf and worshiping it,
sacrificing to it and crying out,
'This is your God, O Israel,
who brought you out of the land of Egypt!'"
The LORD said to Moses,
"I see how stiff-necked this people is.
Let me alone, then,
that my wrath may blaze up against them to consume them.
Then I will make of you a great nation."

But Moses implored the LORD, his God, saying,
"Why, O LORD, should your wrath blaze up against your own
people,
whom you brought out of the land of Egypt
with such great power and with so strong a hand?
Why should the Egyptians say,
'With evil intent he brought them out,
that he might kill them in the mountains
and exterminate them from the face of the earth'?
Let your blazing wrath die down;
relent in punishing your people.

Remember your servants Abraham, Isaac and Israel,
  and how you swore to them by your own self, saying,
  'I will make your descendants as numerous as the stars in the sky;
  and all this land that I promised,
  I will give your descendants as their perpetual heritage.'"
So the LORD relented in the punishment
  he had threatened to inflict on his people. ✛

Psalm 106:19-20, 21-22, 23

R. (4a) **Remember us, O Lord, as you favor your people.**
Our fathers made a calf in Horeb
  and adored a molten image;
They exchanged their glory
  for the image of a grass-eating bullock. **R.**
They forgot the God who had saved them,
  who had done great deeds in Egypt,
Wondrous deeds in the land of Ham,
  terrible things at the Red Sea. **R.**
Then he spoke of exterminating them,
  but Moses, his chosen one,
Withstood him in the breach
  to turn back his destructive wrath. **R.**

John 3:16

R. Glory and praise to you, Lord Jesus Christ!
God so loved the world that he gave his only-begotten Son,
so that everyone who believes in him might have eternal life. **R.**

† *John 5:31-47*
The one who will accuse you is Moses,
in whom you have placed your hope.

Jesus said to the Jews:
"If I testify on my own behalf, my testimony is not true.
But there is another who testifies on my behalf,
  and I know that the testimony he gives on my behalf is true.
You sent emissaries to John, and he testified to the truth.
I do not accept human testimony,
  but I say this so that you may be saved.
He was a burning and shining lamp,
  and for a while you were content to rejoice in his light.
But I have testimony greater than John's.
The works that the Father gave me to accomplish,
  these works that I perform testify on my behalf
  that the Father has sent me.
Moreover, the Father who sent me has testified on my behalf.
But you have never heard his voice nor seen his form,

and you do not have his word remaining in you,
because you do not believe in the one whom he has sent.
You search the Scriptures,
because you think you have eternal life through them;
even they testify on my behalf.
But you do not want to come to me to have life.

"I do not accept human praise;
moreover, I know that you do not have the love of God in you.
I came in the name of my Father,
but you do not accept me;
yet if another comes in his own name,
you will accept him.
How can you believe, when you accept praise from one another
and do not seek the praise that comes from the only God?
Do not think that I will accuse you before the Father:
the one who will accuse you is Moses,
in whom you have placed your hope.
For if you had believed Moses,
you would have believed me,
because he wrote about me.
But if you do not believe his writings,
how will you believe my words?" ✛

FRIDAY, MARCH 24
LENTEN WEEKDAY

✝ Wisdom 2:1a, 12-22
Let us condemn him to a shameful death.

The wicked said among themselves,
thinking not aright:
"Let us beset the just one, because he is obnoxious to us;
he sets himself against our doings,
Reproaches us for transgressions of the law
and charges us with violations of our training.
He professes to have knowledge of God
and styles himself a child of the LORD.
To us he is the censure of our thoughts;
merely to see him is a hardship for us,
Because his life is not like that of others,
and different are his ways.
He judges us debased;
he holds aloof from our paths as from things impure.
He calls blest the destiny of the just
and boasts that God is his Father.

Let us see whether his words be true;
   let us find out what will happen to him.
For if the just one be the son of God, he will defend him
   and deliver him from the hand of his foes.
With revilement and torture let us put him to the test
   that we may have proof of his gentleness
   and try his patience.
Let us condemn him to a shameful death;
   for according to his own words, God will take care of him."
These were their thoughts, but they erred;
   for their wickedness blinded them,
and they knew not the hidden counsels of God;
   neither did they count on a recompense of holiness
   nor discern the innocent souls' reward. ✛

Psalm 34:17-18, 19-20, 21 and 23
R. (19a) **The Lord is close to the brokenhearted.**
The LORD confronts the evildoers,
   to destroy remembrance of them from the earth.
When the just cry out, the LORD hears them,
   and from all their distress he rescues them. **R.**
The LORD is close to the brokenhearted;
   and those who are crushed in spirit he saves.
Many are the troubles of the just man,
   but out of them all the LORD delivers him. **R.**
He watches over all his bones;
   not one of them shall be broken.
The LORD redeems the lives of his servants;
   no one incurs guilt who takes refuge in him. **R.**

Matthew 4:4b
R. Glory and praise to you, Lord Jesus Christ!
One does not live on bread alone,
but on every word that comes forth from the mouth of God. **R.**

† *John 7:1-2, 10, 25-30*
They tried to arrest him, but his hour had not yet come.

Jesus moved about within Galilee;
   he did not wish to travel in Judea,
   because the Jews were trying to kill him.
But the Jewish feast of Tabernacles was near.

But when his brothers had gone up to the feast,
   he himself also went up, not openly but as it were in secret.

Some of the inhabitants of Jerusalem said,

"Is he not the one they are trying to kill?
And look, he is speaking openly and they say nothing to him.
Could the authorities have realized that he is the Christ?
But we know where he is from.
When the Christ comes, no one will know where he is from."
So Jesus cried out in the temple area as he was teaching and said,
    "You know me and also know where I am from.
Yet I did not come on my own,
    but the one who sent me, whom you do not know, is true.
I know him, because I am from him, and he sent me."
So they tried to arrest him,
    but no one laid a hand upon him,
    because his hour had not yet come. ✢

SATURDAY, MARCH 25
THE ANNUNCIATION OF THE LORD

† Isaiah 7:10-14; 8:10
Behold, the virgin shall conceive.

The LORD spoke to Ahaz, saying:
Ask for a sign from the LORD, your God;
    let it be deep as the nether world, or high as the sky!
But Ahaz answered,
    "I will not ask! I will not tempt the LORD!"
Then Isaiah said:
    Listen, O house of David!
Is it not enough for you to weary people,
    must you also weary my God?
Therefore the Lord himself will give you this sign:
    the virgin shall be with child, and bear a son,
    and shall name him Emmanuel,
    which means "God is with us!" ✢

Psalm 40:7-8a, 8b-9, 10, 11
R. (8a and 9a) **Here I am, Lord; I come to do your will.**
Sacrifice or oblation you wished not,
    but ears open to obedience you gave me.
Holocausts or sin-offerings you sought not;
    then said I, "Behold I come." **R.**
"In the written scroll it is prescribed for me,
To do your will, O my God, is my delight,
    and your law is within my heart!" **R.**
I announced your justice in the vast assembly;
    I did not restrain my lips, as you, O LORD, know. **R.**

Your justice I kept not hid within my heart;
   your faithfulness and your salvation I have spoken of;
I have made no secret of your kindness and your truth
   in the vast assembly. **R.**

† *Hebrews 10:4-10*
As is written of me in the scroll, behold, I come to do your will, O God.

Brothers and sisters:
It is impossible that the blood of bulls and goats
   take away sins.
For this reason, when Christ came into the world, he said:

   "Sacrifice and offering you did not desire,
      but a body you prepared for me;
   in holocausts and sin offerings you took no delight.
   Then I said, 'As is written of me in the scroll,
   behold, I come to do your will, O God.'"

First he says, "Sacrifices and offerings,
   holocausts and sin offerings,
   you neither desired nor delighted in."
These are offered according to the law.
Then he says, "Behold, I come to do your will."
He takes away the first to establish the second.
By this "will," we have been consecrated
   through the offering of the Body of Jesus Christ once for all. ✛

   John 1:14ab
R. Glory and praise to you, Lord Jesus Christ!
The Word of God became flesh and made his dwelling among us;
and we saw his glory. **R.**

† *Luke 1:26-38*
Behold, you will conceive in your womb and bear a son.

The angel Gabriel was sent from God
   to a town of Galilee called Nazareth,
   to a virgin betrothed to a man named Joseph,
   of the house of David,
   and the virgin's name was Mary.
And coming to her, he said,
   "Hail, full of grace! The Lord is with you."
But she was greatly troubled at what was said
   and pondered what sort of greeting this might be.
Then the angel said to her,
   "Do not be afraid, Mary,
   for you have found favor with God.

Behold, you will conceive in your womb and bear a son,
and you shall name him Jesus.
He will be great and will be called Son of the Most High,
and the Lord God will give him the throne of David his father,
and he will rule over the house of Jacob forever,
and of his Kingdom there will be no end."
But Mary said to the angel,
"How can this be,
since I have no relations with a man?"
And the angel said to her in reply,
"The Holy Spirit will come upon you,
and the power of the Most High will overshadow you.
Therefore the child to be born
will be called holy, the Son of God.
And behold, Elizabeth, your relative,
has also conceived a son in her old age,
and this is the sixth month for her who was called barren;
for nothing will be impossible for God."
Mary said, "Behold, I am the handmaid of the Lord.
May it be done to me according to your word."
Then the angel departed from her. ✢

SUNDAY, MARCH 26
FIFTH SUNDAY OF LENT

† *Ezekiel 37:12-14*
I will put my spirit in you that you may live.

Thus says the Lord GOD:
O my people, I will open your graves
and have you rise from them,
and bring you back to the land of Israel.
Then you shall know that I am the LORD,
when I open your graves and have you rise from them,
O my people!
I will put my spirit in you that you may live,
and I will settle you upon your land;
thus you shall know that I am the LORD.
I have promised, and I will do it, says the LORD. ✢

Psalm 130:1-2, 3-4, 5-6, 7-8
R. (7) With the Lord there is mercy and fullness of redemption.
Out of the depths I cry to you, O LORD;
LORD, hear my voice!
Let your ears be attentive
to my voice in supplication. **R.**

If you, O LORD, mark iniquities,
   LORD, who can stand?
But with you is forgiveness,
   that you may be revered. **R.**
I trust in the LORD;
   my soul trusts in his word.
More than sentinels wait for the dawn,
   let Israel wait for the LORD. **R.**
For with the LORD is kindness
   and with him is plenteous redemption;
and he will redeem Israel
   from all their iniquities. **R.**

† *Romans 8:8-11*
The Spirit of the One who raised Jesus from the dead dwells in you.

Brothers and sisters:
Those who are in the flesh cannot please God.
But you are not in the flesh;
   on the contrary, you are in the spirit,
   if only the Spirit of God dwells in you.
Whoever does not have the Spirit of Christ does not belong to him.
But if Christ is in you,
   although the body is dead because of sin,
   the spirit is alive because of righteousness.
If the Spirit of the one who raised Jesus from the dead dwells in you,
   the One who raised Christ from the dead
   will give life to your mortal bodies also,
   through his Spirit dwelling in you. ✛

John 11:25a, 26

R. Glory and praise to you, Lord Jesus Christ!
I am the resurrection and the life, says the Lord;
whoever believes in me, even if he dies, will never die. **R.**

John 11:1-45 (or *John 11:3-7, 17, 20-27, 33b-45*)
I am the resurrection and the life.

Now a man was ill, Lazarus from Bethany,
   the village of Mary and her sister Martha.
Mary was the one who had anointed the Lord with perfumed oil
   and dried his feet with her hair;
   it was her brother Lazarus who was ill.
So the sisters sent word to Jesus saying,
   "Master, the one you love is ill."
When Jesus heard this he said,
   "This illness is not to end in death,

but is for the glory of God,
that the Son of God may be glorified through it."
Now Jesus loved Martha and her sister and Lazarus.
So when he heard that he was ill,
he remained for two days in the place where he was.
Then after this he said to his disciples,
"Let us go back to Judea."
The disciples said to him,
"Rabbi, the Jews were just trying to stone you,
and you want to go back there?"
Jesus answered,
"Are there not twelve hours in a day?
If one walks during the day, he does not stumble,
because he sees the light of this world.
But if one walks at night, he stumbles,
because the light is not in him."
He said this, and then told them,
"Our friend Lazarus is asleep,
but I am going to awaken him."
So the disciples said to him,
"Master, if he is asleep, he will be saved."
But Jesus was talking about his death,
while they thought that he meant ordinary sleep.
So then Jesus said to them clearly,
"Lazarus has died.
And I am glad for you that I was not there,
that you may believe.
Let us go to him."
So Thomas, called Didymus, said to his fellow disciples,
"Let us also go to die with him."

When Jesus arrived, he found that Lazarus
had already been in the tomb for four days.
Now Bethany was near Jerusalem, only about two miles away.
And many of the Jews had come to Martha and Mary
to comfort them about their brother.
When Martha heard that Jesus was coming,
she went to meet him;
but Mary sat at home.
Martha said to Jesus,
"Lord, if you had been here,
my brother would not have died.
But even now I know that whatever you ask of God,
God will give you."

Jesus said to her,
  "Your brother will rise."
Martha said to him,
  "I know he will rise,
  in the resurrection on the last day."
Jesus told her,
  "I am the resurrection and the life;
  whoever believes in me, even if he dies, will live,
  and everyone who lives and believes in me will never die.
Do you believe this?"
She said to him, "Yes, Lord.
I have come to believe that you are the Christ, the Son of God,
  the one who is coming into the world."

When she had said this,
  she went and called her sister Mary secretly, saying,
  "The teacher is here and is asking for you."
As soon as she heard this,
  she rose quickly and went to him.
For Jesus had not yet come into the village,
  but was still where Martha had met him.
So when the Jews who were with her in the house comforting her
  saw Mary get up quickly and go out,
  they followed her,
  presuming that she was going to the tomb to weep there.
When Mary came to where Jesus was and saw him,
  she fell at his feet and said to him,
  "Lord, if you had been here,
  my brother would not have died."
When Jesus saw her weeping and the Jews who had come with her
      weeping,
  he became perturbed and deeply troubled, and said,
  "Where have you laid him?"
They said to him, "Sir, come and see."
And Jesus wept.
So the Jews said, "See how he loved him."
But some of them said,
  "Could not the one who opened the eyes of the blind man
  have done something so that this man would not have died?"

So Jesus, perturbed again, came to the tomb.
It was a cave, and a stone lay across it.
Jesus said, "Take away the stone."
Martha, the dead man's sister, said to him,
  "Lord, by now there will be a stench;

he has been dead for four days."
Jesus said to her,
"Did I not tell you that if you believe
you will see the glory of God?"
So they took away the stone.
And Jesus raised his eyes and said,
"Father, I thank you for hearing me.
I know that you always hear me;
but because of the crowd here I have said this,
that they may believe that you sent me."
And when he had said this,
he cried out in a loud voice,
"Lazarus, come out!"
The dead man came out,
tied hand and foot with burial bands,
and his face was wrapped in a cloth.
So Jesus said to them,
"Untie him and let him go."

Now many of the Jews who had come to Mary
and seen what he had done began to believe in him. ✛

MONDAY, MARCH 27
Lenten Weekday

*✝ Daniel 13:1-9, 15-17, 19-30, 33-62 (or Daniel 13:41c-62,
or any day this week, 2 Kings 4:18b-21,32-37)*
Here I am about to die, though I have done none of the things charged against me.

In Babylon there lived a man named Joakim,
who married a very beautiful and God-fearing woman, Susanna,
the daughter of Hilkiah;
her pious parents had trained their daughter
according to the law of Moses.
Joakim was very rich;
he had a garden near his house,
and the Jews had recourse to him often
because he was the most respected of them all.

That year, two elders of the people were appointed judges,
of whom the Lord said, "Wickedness has come out of Babylon:
from the elders who were to govern the people as judges."
These men, to whom all brought their cases,
frequented the house of Joakim.
When the people left at noon,
Susanna used to enter her husband's garden for a walk.

When the old men saw her enter every day for her walk,
    they began to lust for her.
They suppressed their consciences;
    they would not allow their eyes to look to heaven,
    and did not keep in mind just judgments.

One day, while they were waiting for the right moment,
    she entered the garden as usual, with two maids only.
She decided to bathe, for the weather was warm.
Nobody else was there except the two elders,
    who had hidden themselves and were watching her.
"Bring me oil and soap," she said to the maids,
    "and shut the garden doors while I bathe."

As soon as the maids had left,
    the two old men got up and hurried to her.
"Look," they said, "the garden doors are shut, and no one can see us;
    give in to our desire, and lie with us.
If you refuse, we will testify against you
    that you dismissed your maids because a young man was here
        with you."

"I am completely trapped," Susanna groaned.
"If I yield, it will be my death;
    if I refuse, I cannot escape your power.
Yet it is better for me to fall into your power without guilt
    than to sin before the Lord."
Then Susanna shrieked, and the old men also shouted at her,
    as one of them ran to open the garden doors.
When the people in the house heard the cries from the garden,
    they rushed in by the side gate to see what had happened to her.
At the accusations by the old men,
    the servants felt very much ashamed,
    for never had any such thing been said about Susanna.

When the people came to her husband Joakim the next day,
    the two wicked elders also came,
    fully determined to put Susanna to death.
Before all the people they ordered:
    "Send for Susanna, the daughter of Hilkiah,
    the wife of Joakim."
When she was sent for,
    she came with her parents, children and all her relatives.
All her relatives and the onlookers were weeping.

In the midst of the people the two elders rose up

and laid their hands on her head.
Through tears she looked up to heaven,
  for she trusted in the Lord wholeheartedly.
The elders made this accusation:
  "As we were walking in the garden alone,
  this woman entered with two girls
  and shut the doors of the garden, dismissing the girls.
A young man, who was hidden there, came and lay with her.
When we, in a corner of the garden, saw this crime,
  we ran toward them.
We saw them lying together,
  but the man we could not hold, because he was stronger than we;
  he opened the doors and ran off.
Then we seized her and asked who the young man was,
  but she refused to tell us.
We testify to this."
The assembly believed them,
  since they were elders and judges of the people,
  and they condemned her to death.

But Susanna cried aloud:
  "O eternal God, you know what is hidden
  and are aware of all things before they come to be:
  you know that they have testified falsely against me.
Here I am about to die,
  though I have done none of the things
  with which these wicked men have charged me."

The Lord heard her prayer.
As she was being led to execution,
  God stirred up the holy spirit of a young boy named Daniel,
  and he cried aloud:
  "I will have no part in the death of this woman."
All the people turned and asked him, "What is this you are saying?"
He stood in their midst and continued,
  "Are you such fools, O children of Israel!
To condemn a woman of Israel without examination
  and without clear evidence?
Return to court, for they have testified falsely against her."

Then all the people returned in haste.
To Daniel the elders said,
  "Come, sit with us and inform us,
  since God has given you the prestige of old age."
But he replied,

"Separate these two far from each other that I may examine them."

After they were separated one from the other,
    he called one of them and said:
    "How you have grown evil with age!
Now have your past sins come to term:
    passing unjust sentences, condemning the innocent,
    and freeing the guilty, although the Lord says,
    'The innocent and the just you shall not put to death.'
Now, then, if you were a witness,
    tell me under what tree you saw them together."
"Under a mastic tree," he answered.
Daniel replied, "Your fine lie has cost you your head,
    for the angel of God shall receive the sentence from him
    and split you in two."
Putting him to one side, he ordered the other one to be brought.
Daniel said to him,
    "Offspring of Canaan, not of Judah, beauty has seduced you,
    lust has subverted your conscience.
This is how you acted with the daughters of Israel,
    and in their fear they yielded to you;
    but a daughter of Judah did not tolerate your wickedness.
Now, then, tell me under what tree you surprised them together."
"Under an oak," he said.
Daniel replied, "Your fine lie has cost you also your head,
    for the angel of God waits with a sword to cut you in two
    so as to make an end of you both."

The whole assembly cried aloud,
    blessing God who saves those who hope in him.
They rose up against the two elders,
    for by their own words Daniel had convicted them of perjury.
According to the law of Moses,
    they inflicted on them
    the penalty they had plotted to impose on their neighbor:
    they put them to death.
Thus was innocent blood spared that day. ✠

    Psalm 23:1b-3a, 3b-4, 5, 6 (or any day this week,
    Psalm 17:1bcd, 6-7, 8b and 15)
R. (4ab) **Even though I walk in the dark valley I fear no evil;**
    for you are at my side.
The LORD is my shepherd; I shall not want.
    In verdant pastures he gives me repose;
Beside restful waters he leads me;

he refreshes my soul. **R.**
He guides me in right paths
  for his name's sake.
Even though I walk in the dark valley
  I fear no evil; for you are at my side
With your rod and your staff
  that give me courage. **R.**
You spread the table before me
  in the sight of my foes;
You anoint my head with oil;
  my cup overflows. **R.**
Only goodness and kindness follow me
  all the days of my life;
And I shall dwell in the house of the LORD
  for years to come. **R.**

    Ezekiel 33:11

R. Glory and praise to you, Lord Jesus Christ!
I take no pleasure in the death of the wicked man, says the Lord,
but rather in his conversion, that he may live. **R.**

       † John 8:1-11 (or any day this week, John 11:1-45)
         Let the person without sin be the first to throw a stone.

Jesus went to the Mount of Olives.
But early in the morning he arrived again in the temple area,
  and all the people started coming to him,
  and he sat down and taught them.
Then the scribes and the Pharisees brought a woman
  who had been caught in adultery
  and made her stand in the middle.
They said to him,
  "Teacher, this woman was caught
  in the very act of committing adultery.
Now in the law, Moses commanded us to stone such women.
So what do you say?"
They said this to test him,
  so that they could have some charge to bring against him.
Jesus bent down and began to write on the ground with his finger.
But when they continued asking him,
  he straightened up and said to them,
  "Let the one among you who is without sin
  be the first to throw a stone at her."
Again he bent down and wrote on the ground.
And in response, they went away one by one,
  beginning with the elders.

So he was left alone with the woman before him.
Then Jesus straightened up and said to her,
  "Woman, where are they?
Has no one condemned you?"
She replied, "No one, sir."
Then Jesus said, "Neither do I condemn you.
Go, and from now on do not sin any more." ✛

TUESDAY, MARCH 28
LENTEN WEEKDAY

† *Numbers 21:4-9*
Whoever looks at the bronze serpent, shall live.

From Mount Hor the children of Israel set out on the Red Sea road,
  to bypass the land of Edom.
But with their patience worn out by the journey,
  the people complained against God and Moses,
  "Why have you brought us up from Egypt to die in this desert,
  where there is no food or water?
We are disgusted with this wretched food!"

In punishment the LORD sent among the people saraph serpents,
  which bit the people so that many of them died.
Then the people came to Moses and said,
  "We have sinned in complaining against the LORD and you.
Pray the LORD to take the serpents away from us."
So Moses prayed for the people, and the LORD said to Moses,
  "Make a saraph and mount it on a pole,
  and whoever looks at it after being bitten will live."
Moses accordingly made a bronze serpent and mounted it on a pole,
  and whenever anyone who had been bitten by a serpent
  looked at the bronze serpent, he lived. ✛

  Psalm 102:2-3, 16-18, 19-21
R. (2) **O Lord, hear my prayer, and let my cry come to you.**
O LORD, hear my prayer,
  and let my cry come to you.
Hide not your face from me
  in the day of my distress.
Incline your ear to me;
  in the day when I call, answer me speedily. **R.**
The nations shall revere your name, O LORD,
  and all the kings of the earth your glory,
When the LORD has rebuilt Zion
  and appeared in his glory;
When he has regarded the prayer of the destitute,

and not despised their prayer. **R.**
Let this be written for the generation to come,
  and let his future creatures praise the LORD:
"The LORD looked down from his holy height,
  from heaven he beheld the earth,
To hear the groaning of the prisoners,
  to release those doomed to die." **R.**

R. Glory and praise to you, Lord Jesus Christ!
The seed is the word of God, Christ is the sower;
all who come to him will live for ever. **R.**

† *John 8:21-30*
When you have lifted up the Son of Man,
then you will know that I am he.

Jesus said to the Pharisees:
"I am going away and you will look for me,
  but you will die in your sin.
Where I am going you cannot come."
So the Jews said,
  "He is not going to kill himself, is he,
  because he said, 'Where I am going you cannot come'?"
He said to them, "You belong to what is below,
  I belong to what is above.
You belong to this world,
  but I do not belong to this world.
That is why I told you that you will die in your sins.
For if you do not believe that I AM,
  you will die in your sins."
So they said to him, "Who are you?"
Jesus said to them, "What I told you from the beginning.
I have much to say about you in condemnation.
But the one who sent me is true,
  and what I heard from him I tell the world."
They did not realize that he was speaking to them of the Father.
So Jesus said to them,
  "When you lift up the Son of Man,
  then you will realize that I AM,
  and that I do nothing on my own,
  but I say only what the Father taught me.
The one who sent me is with me.
He has not left me alone,
  because I always do what is pleasing to him."
Because he spoke this way, many came to believe in him. ✛

WEDNESDAY, MARCH 29
LENTEN WEEKDAY

† Daniel 3:14-20, 91-92, 95
The Lord has sent his angel to deliver his servants.

King Nebuchadnezzar said:
"Is it true, Shadrach, Meshach, and Abednego,
   that you will not serve my god,
   or worship the golden statue that I set up?
Be ready now to fall down and worship the statue I had made,
   whenever you hear the sound of the trumpet,
   flute, lyre, harp, psaltery, bagpipe,
   and all the other musical instruments;
   otherwise, you shall be instantly cast into the white-hot furnace;
   and who is the God who can deliver you out of my hands?"
Shadrach, Meshach, and Abednego answered King Nebuchadnezzar,
   "There is no need for us to defend ourselves before you
   in this matter.
If our God, whom we serve,
   can save us from the white-hot furnace
   and from your hands, O king, may he save us!
But even if he will not, know, O king,
   that we will not serve your god
   or worship the golden statue that you set up."

King Nebuchadnezzar's face became livid with utter rage
   against Shadrach, Meshach, and Abednego.
He ordered the furnace to be heated seven times more than usual
   and had some of the strongest men in his army
   bind Shadrach, Meshach, and Abednego
   and cast them into the white-hot furnace.

Nebuchadnezzar rose in haste and asked his nobles,
   "Did we not cast three men bound into the fire?"
"Assuredly, O king," they answered.
"But," he replied, "I see four men unfettered and unhurt,
   walking in the fire, and the fourth looks like a son of God."
Nebuchadnezzar exclaimed,
   "Blessed be the God of Shadrach, Meshach, and Abednego,
   who sent his angel to deliver the servants who trusted in him;
   they disobeyed the royal command and yielded their bodies
   rather than serve or worship any god
   except their own God." ✛

Daniel 3:52, 53, 54, 55, 56

R. (52b) **Glory and praise for ever!**

"Blessed are you, O Lord, the God of our fathers,
    praiseworthy and exalted above all forever;
And blessed is your holy and glorious name,
    praiseworthy and exalted above all for all ages." **R.**

"Blessed are you in the temple of your holy glory,
    praiseworthy and exalted above all forever." **R.**

"Blessed are you on the throne of your Kingdom,
    praiseworthy and exalted above all forever." **R.**

"Blessed are you who look into the depths
    from your throne upon the cherubim;
    praiseworthy and exalted above all forever." **R.**

"Blessed are you in the firmament of heaven,
    praiseworthy and glorious forever." **R.**

See Luke 8:15

R. Glory and praise to you, Lord Jesus Christ!

Blessed are they who have kept the word with a generous heart
and yield a harvest through perseverance. **R.**

† *John 8:31-42*

If the Son makes you free, you will be free indeed.

Jesus said to those Jews who believed in him,
    "If you remain in my word, you will truly be my disciples,
    and you will know the truth, and the truth will set you free."
They answered him, "We are descendants of Abraham
    and have never been enslaved to anyone.
How can you say, 'You will become free'?"
Jesus answered them, "Amen, amen, I say to you,
    everyone who commits sin is a slave of sin.
A slave does not remain in a household forever,
    but a son always remains.
So if the Son frees you, then you will truly be free.
I know that you are descendants of Abraham.
But you are trying to kill me,
    because my word has no room among you.
I tell you what I have seen in the Father's presence;
    then do what you have heard from the Father."

They answered and said to him, "Our father is Abraham."
Jesus said to them, "If you were Abraham's children,
    you would be doing the works of Abraham.
But now you are trying to kill me,
    a man who has told you the truth that I heard from God;

Abraham did not do this.
You are doing the works of your father!"
So they said to him, "We were not born of fornication.
We have one Father, God."
Jesus said to them, "If God were your Father, you would love me,
  for I came from God and am here;
  I did not come on my own, but he sent me." ✛

THURSDAY, MARCH 30
LENTEN WEEKDAY

† *Genesis 17:3-9*
You will be the father of a multitude of nations.

When Abram prostrated himself, God spoke to him:
"My covenant with you is this:
  you are to become the father of a host of nations.
No longer shall you be called Abram;
  your name shall be Abraham,
  for I am making you the father of a host of nations.
I will render you exceedingly fertile;
  I will make nations of you;
  kings shall stem from you.
I will maintain my covenant with you
  and your descendants after you
  throughout the ages as an everlasting pact,
  to be your God and the God of your descendants after you.
I will give to you
  and to your descendants after you
  the land in which you are now staying,
  the whole land of Canaan, as a permanent possession;
  and I will be their God."

God also said to Abraham:
  "On your part, you and your descendants after you
  must keep my covenant throughout the ages." ✛

Psalm 105:4-5, 6-7, 8-9
R. (8a) **The Lord remembers his covenant for ever.**
Look to the LORD in his strength;
  seek to serve him constantly.
Recall the wondrous deeds that he has wrought,
  his portents, and the judgments he has uttered. **R.**
You descendants of Abraham, his servants,
  sons of Jacob, his chosen ones!
He, the LORD, is our God;
  throughout the earth his judgments prevail. **R.**

He remembers forever his covenant
  which he made binding for a thousand generations—
Which he entered into with Abraham
  and by his oath to Isaac. **R.**

  Psalm 95:8
R. Glory and praise to you, Lord Jesus Christ!
If today you hear his voice,
harden not your hearts. **R.**

† *John 8:51-59*
Your father, Abraham, rejoiced because he saw my day.

Jesus said to the Jews:
"Amen, amen, I say to you,
  whoever keeps my word will never see death."
So the Jews said to him,
  "Now we are sure that you are possessed.
Abraham died, as did the prophets, yet you say,
  'Whoever keeps my word will never taste death.'
Are you greater than our father Abraham, who died?
Or the prophets, who died?
Who do you make yourself out to be?"
Jesus answered, "If I glorify myself, my glory is worth nothing;
  but it is my Father who glorifies me,
  of whom you say, 'He is our God.'
You do not know him, but I know him.
And if I should say that I do not know him,
  I would be like you a liar.
But I do know him and I keep his word.
Abraham your father rejoiced to see my day;
  he saw it and was glad."
So the Jews said to him,
  "You are not yet fifty years old and you have seen Abraham?"
Jesus said to them, "Amen, amen, I say to you,
  before Abraham came to be, I AM."
So they picked up stones to throw at him;
  but Jesus hid and went out of the temple area. ✛

FRIDAY, MARCH 31
LENTEN WEEKDAY

† *Jeremiah 20:10-13*
The Lord God is with me, a mighty hero.

I hear the whisperings of many:
  "Terror on every side!
  Denounce! let us denounce him!"

All those who were my friends
   are on the watch for any misstep of mine.
"Perhaps he will be trapped; then we can prevail,
   and take our vengeance on him."
But the LORD is with me, like a mighty champion:
   my persecutors will stumble, they will not triumph.
In their failure they will be put to utter shame,
   to lasting, unforgettable confusion.
O LORD of hosts, you who test the just,
   who probe mind and heart,
Let me witness the vengeance you take on them,
   for to you I have entrusted my cause.
Sing to the LORD,
   praise the LORD,
For he has rescued the life of the poor
   from the power of the wicked! ✝

Psalm 18:2-3a, 3bc-4, 5-6, 7

R. (see 7) In my distress I called upon the Lord, and he heard my voice.

I love you, O LORD, my strength,
   O LORD, my rock, my fortress, my deliverer. **R.**
My God, my rock of refuge,
   my shield, the horn of my salvation, my stronghold!
Praised be the LORD, I exclaim,
   and I am safe from my enemies. **R.**
The breakers of death surged round about me,
   the destroying floods overwhelmed me;
The cords of the nether world enmeshed me,
   the snares of death overtook me. **R.**
In my distress I called upon the LORD
   and cried out to my God;
From his temple he heard my voice,
   and my cry to him reached his ears. **R.**

See John 6:63c, 68c

R. Glory and praise to you, Lord Jesus Christ!
Your words, Lord, are Spirit and life;
you have the words of everlasting life. **R.**

✝ *John 10:31-42*

They wanted to arrest Jesus, but he eluded them.

The Jews picked up rocks to stone Jesus.
Jesus answered them, "I have shown you many good works from my
   Father.
For which of these are you trying to stone me?"

The Jews answered him,
"We are not stoning you for a good work but for blasphemy.
You, a man, are making yourself God."
Jesus answered them,
"Is it not written in your law, 'I said, "You are gods"'?
If it calls them gods to whom the word of God came,
and Scripture cannot be set aside,
can you say that the one
whom the Father has consecrated and sent into the world
blasphemes because I said, 'I am the Son of God'?
If I do not perform my Father's works, do not believe me;
but if I perform them, even if you do not believe me,
believe the works, so that you may realize and understand
that the Father is in me and I am in the Father."
Then they tried again to arrest him;
but he escaped from their power.

He went back across the Jordan
to the place where John first baptized, and there he remained.
Many came to him and said,
"John performed no sign,
but everything John said about this man was true."
And many there began to believe in him. ✛

SATURDAY, APRIL 1
LENTEN WEEKDAY

† *Ezekiel 37:21-28*
I will make them into one nation.

Thus says the Lord GOD:
I will take the children of Israel from among the nations
to which they have come,
and gather them from all sides to bring them back to their land.
I will make them one nation upon the land,
in the mountains of Israel,
and there shall be one prince for them all.
Never again shall they be two nations,
and never again shall they be divided into two kingdoms.

No longer shall they defile themselves with their idols,
their abominations, and all their transgressions.
I will deliver them from all their sins of apostasy,
and cleanse them so that they may be my people
and I may be their God.
My servant David shall be prince over them,

and there shall be one shepherd for them all;
   they shall live by my statutes and carefully observe my decrees.
They shall live on the land that I gave to my servant Jacob,
   the land where their fathers lived;
   they shall live on it forever,
   they, and their children, and their children's children,
   with my servant David their prince forever.
I will make with them a covenant of peace;
   it shall be an everlasting covenant with them,
   and I will multiply them, and put my sanctuary among them forever.
My dwelling shall be with them;
   I will be their God, and they shall be my people.
Thus the nations shall know that it is I, the LORD,
   who make Israel holy,
   when my sanctuary shall be set up among them forever. ✛

Jeremiah 31:10, 11-12abcd, 13

R. (see 10d) **The Lord will guard us, as a shepherd guards his flock.**

Hear the word of the LORD, O nations,
   proclaim it on distant isles, and say:
He who scattered Israel, now gathers them together,
   he guards them as a shepherd his flock. **R.**
The LORD shall ransom Jacob,
   he shall redeem him from the hand of his conqueror.
Shouting, they shall mount the heights of Zion,
   they shall come streaming to the LORD's blessings:
The grain, the wine, and the oil,
   the sheep and the oxen. **R.**
Then the virgins shall make merry and dance,
   and young men and old as well.
I will turn their mourning into joy,
   I will console and gladden them after their sorrows. **R.**

Ezekiel 18:31

R. Glory and praise to you, Lord Jesus Christ!
Cast away from you all the crimes you have committed, says the
   Lord,
and make for yourselves a new heart and a new spirit. **R.**

† *John 11:45-56*
To gather together in unity the scattered children of God.

Many of the Jews who had come to Mary
   and seen what Jesus had done began to believe in him.
But some of them went to the Pharisees

and told them what Jesus had done.
So the chief priests and the Pharisees
   convened the Sanhedrin and said,
     "What are we going to do?
This man is performing many signs.
If we leave him alone, all will believe in him,
   and the Romans will come
   and take away both our land and our nation."
But one of them, Caiaphas,
   who was high priest that year, said to them,
     "You know nothing,
   nor do you consider that it is better for you
   that one man should die instead of the people,
   so that the whole nation may not perish."
He did not say this on his own,
   but since he was high priest for that year,
   he prophesied that Jesus was going to die for the nation,
   and not only for the nation,
   but also to gather into one the dispersed children of God.
So from that day on they planned to kill him.

So Jesus no longer walked about in public among the Jews,
   but he left for the region near the desert,
   to a town called Ephraim,
   and there he remained with his disciples.

Now the Passover of the Jews was near,
   and many went up from the country to Jerusalem
   before Passover to purify themselves.
They looked for Jesus and said to one another
   as they were in the temple area, "What do you think?
That he will not come to the feast?" ✝

SUNDAY, APRIL 2
PALM SUNDAY OF THE PASSION OF THE LORD
(At the Procession with Palms)

† *Matthew 21:1-11*
Blessed is he who comes in the name of the Lord.

When Jesus and the disciples drew near Jerusalem
   and came to Bethphage on the Mount of Olives,
   Jesus sent two disciples, saying to them,
   "Go into the village opposite you,
   and immediately you will find an ass tethered,
   and a colt with her.

Untie them and bring them here to me.
And if anyone should say anything to you, reply,
   'The master has need of them.'
Then he will send them at once."
This happened so that what had been spoken through the prophet
   might be fulfilled:
   Say to daughter Zion,
   "Behold, your king comes to you,
   meek and riding on an ass,
   and on a colt, the foal of a beast of burden."
The disciples went and did as Jesus had ordered them.
They brought the ass and the colt and laid their cloaks over them,
   and he sat upon them.
The very large crowd spread their cloaks on the road,
   while others cut branches from the trees
   and strewed them on the road.
The crowds preceding him and those following
   kept crying out and saying:
   "Hosanna to the Son of David;
   blessed is the he who comes in the name of the Lord;
   hosanna in the highest."
And when he entered Jerusalem
   the whole city was shaken and asked, "Who is this?"
And the crowds replied,
   "This is Jesus the prophet, from Nazareth in Galilee." ✣

(At Mass)

† *Isaiah 50:4-7*

My face I did not shield from buffets and spitting,
knowing that I shall not be put to shame.

The Lord GOD has given me
   a well-trained tongue,
that I might know how to speak to the weary
   a word that will rouse them.
Morning after morning
   he opens my ear that I may hear;
and I have not rebelled,
   have not turned back.
I gave my back to those who beat me,
   my cheeks to those who plucked my beard;
my face I did not shield
   from buffets and spitting.

The Lord GOD is my help,

    therefore I am not disgraced;
I have set my face like flint,
    knowing that I shall not be put to shame. ✛

Psalm 22:8-9, 17-18, 19-20, 23-24

R. (2a) **My God, my God, why have you abandoned me?**
All who see me scoff at me;
    they mock me with parted lips, they wag their heads:
"He relied on the LORD; let him deliver him,
    let him rescue him, if he loves him." **R.**
Indeed, many dogs surround me,
    a pack of evildoers closes in upon me;
they have pierced my hands and my feet;
    I can count all my bones. **R.**
They divide my garments among them,
    and for my vesture they cast lots.
But you, O LORD, be not far from me;
    O my help, hasten to aid me. **R.**
I will proclaim your name to my brethren;
    in the midst of the assembly I will praise you:
"You who fear the LORD, praise him;
    all you descendants of Jacob, give glory to him;
    revere him, all you descendants of Israel!" **R.**

† *Philippians 2:6-11*
Christ humbled himself. Because of this God greatly exalted him.

Christ Jesus, though he was in the form of God,
    did not regard equality with God
    something to be grasped.
Rather, he emptied himself,
    taking the form of a slave,
    coming in human likeness;
    and found human in appearance,
    he humbled himself,
    becoming obedient to the point of death,
    even death on a cross.
Because of this, God greatly exalted him
    and bestowed on him the name
    which is above every name,
    that at the name of Jesus
    every knee should bend,
    of those in heaven and on earth and under the earth,
    and every tongue confess that
    Jesus Christ is Lord,
    to the glory of God the Father. ✛

Philippians 2:8-9

R. Glory and praise to you, Lord Jesus Christ!

Christ became obedient to the point of death,
even death on a cross.
Because of this, God greatly exalted him
and bestowed on him the name which is above every name. **R.**

✝ ***Matthew 26:14—27:66*** *(or Matthew 27:11-54)*
The Passion of our Lord Jesus Christ.

One of the Twelve, who was called Judas Iscariot,
  went to the chief priests and said,
  "What are you willing to give me
  if I hand him over to you?"
They paid him thirty pieces of silver,
  and from that time on he looked for an opportunity to hand him
    over.

On the first day of the Feast of Unleavened Bread,
  the disciples approached Jesus and said,
  "Where do you want us to prepare
  for you to eat the Passover?"
He said,
  "Go into the city to a certain man and tell him,
  'The teacher says, "My appointed time draws near;
  in your house I shall celebrate the Passover with my disciples."'"
The disciples then did as Jesus had ordered,
  and prepared the Passover.

When it was evening,
  he reclined at table with the Twelve.
And while they were eating, he said,
  "Amen, I say to you, one of you will betray me."
Deeply distressed at this,
  they began to say to him one after another,
  "Surely it is not I, Lord?"
He said in reply,
  "He who has dipped his hand into the dish with me
  is the one who will betray me.
The Son of Man indeed goes, as it is written of him,
  but woe to that man by whom the Son of Man is betrayed.
It would be better for that man if he had never been born."
Then Judas, his betrayer, said in reply,
  "Surely it is not I, Rabbi?"
He answered, "You have said so."

While they were eating,
   Jesus took bread, said the blessing,
   broke it, and giving it to his disciples said,
   "Take and eat; this is my body."
Then he took a cup, gave thanks, and gave it to them, saying,
   "Drink from it, all of you,
   for this is my blood of the covenant,
   which will be shed on behalf of many
   for the forgiveness of sins.
I tell you, from now on I shall not drink this fruit of the vine
   until the day when I drink it with you new
   in the kingdom of my Father."
Then, after singing a hymn,
   they went out to the Mount of Olives.

Then Jesus said to them,
"This night all of you will have your faith in me shaken,
   for it is written:
     I will strike the shepherd,
       and the sheep of the flock will be dispersed;
   but after I have been raised up,
   I shall go before you to Galilee."
Peter said to him in reply,
   "Though all may have their faith in you shaken,
   mine will never be."
Jesus said to him,
   "Amen, I say to you,
   this very night before the cock crows,
   you will deny me three times."
Peter said to him,
   "Even though I should have to die with you,
   I will not deny you."
And all the disciples spoke likewise.

Then Jesus came with them to a place called Gethsemane,
   and he said to his disciples,
   "Sit here while I go over there and pray."
He took along Peter and the two sons of Zebedee,
   and began to feel sorrow and distress.
Then he said to them,
   "My soul is sorrowful even to death.
Remain here and keep watch with me."
He advanced a little and fell prostrate in prayer, saying,
   "My Father, if it is possible,
   let this cup pass from me;

yet, not as I will, but as you will."
When he returned to his disciples he found them asleep.
He said to Peter,
    "So you could not keep watch with me for one hour?
Watch and pray that you may not undergo the test.
The spirit is willing, but the flesh is weak."
Withdrawing a second time, he prayed again,
    "My Father, if it is not possible that this cup pass
    without my drinking it, your will be done!"
Then he returned once more and found them asleep,
    for they could not keep their eyes open.
He left them and withdrew again and prayed a third time,
    saying the same thing again.
Then he returned to his disciples and said to them,
    "Are you still sleeping and taking your rest?
Behold, the hour is at hand
    when the Son of Man is to be handed over to sinners.
Get up, let us go.
Look, my betrayer is at hand."

While he was still speaking,
    Judas, one of the Twelve, arrived,
    accompanied by a large crowd, with swords and clubs,
    who had come from the chief priests and the elders of the people.
His betrayer had arranged a sign with them, saying,
    "The man I shall kiss is the one; arrest him."
Immediately he went over to Jesus and said,
    "Hail, Rabbi!" and he kissed him.
Jesus answered him,
    "Friend, do what you have come for."
Then stepping forward they laid hands on Jesus and arrested him.
And behold, one of those who accompanied Jesus
    put his hand to his sword, drew it,
    and struck the high priest's servant, cutting off his ear.
Then Jesus said to him,
    "Put your sword back into its sheath,
    for all who take the sword will perish by the sword.
Do you think that I cannot call upon my Father
    and he will not provide me at this moment
    with more than twelve legions of angels?
But then how would the Scriptures be fulfilled
    which say that it must come to pass in this way?"
At that hour Jesus said to the crowds,
    "Have you come out as against a robber,

with swords and clubs to seize me?
Day after day I sat teaching in the temple area,
    yet you did not arrest me.
But all this has come to pass
    that the writings of the prophets may be fulfilled."
Then all the disciples left him and fled.

Those who had arrested Jesus led him away
    to Caiaphas the high priest,
    where the scribes and the elders were assembled.
Peter was following him at a distance
    as far as the high priest's courtyard,
    and going inside he sat down with the servants to see the outcome.
The chief priests and the entire Sanhedrin
    kept trying to obtain false testimony against Jesus
    in order to put him to death,
    but they found none,
    though many false witnesses came forward.
Finally two came forward who stated,
    "This man said, 'I can destroy the temple of God
    and within three days rebuild it.'"
The high priest rose and addressed him,
    "Have you no answer?
What are these men testifying against you?"
But Jesus was silent.
Then the high priest said to him,
    "I order you to tell us under oath before the living God
    whether you are the Christ, the Son of God."
Jesus said to him in reply,
    "You have said so.
But I tell you:
    From now on you will see 'the Son of Man
    seated at the right hand of the Power'
    and 'coming on the clouds of heaven.'"
Then the high priest tore his robes and said,
    "He has blasphemed!
What further need have we of witnesses?
You have now heard the blasphemy;
    what is your opinion?"
They said in reply,
    "He deserves to die!"
Then they spat in his face and struck him,
    while some slapped him, saying,
    "Prophesy for us, Christ: who is it that struck you?"

Now Peter was sitting outside in the courtyard.
One of the maids came over to him and said,
  "You too were with Jesus the Galilean."
But he denied it in front of everyone, saying,
  "I do not know what you are talking about!"
As he went out to the gate, another girl saw him
  and said to those who were there,
  "This man was with Jesus the Nazorean."
Again he denied it with an oath,
  "I do not know the man!"
A little later the bystanders came over and said to Peter,
  "Surely you too are one of them;
  even your speech gives you away."
At that he began to curse and to swear,
  "I do not know the man."
And immediately a cock crowed.
Then Peter remembered the word that Jesus had spoken:
  "Before the cock crows you will deny me three times."
He went out and began to weep bitterly.

When it was morning,
  all the chief priests and the elders of the people
  took counsel against Jesus to put him to death.
They bound him, led him away,
  and handed him over to Pilate, the governor.

Then Judas, his betrayer, seeing that Jesus had been condemned,
  deeply regretted what he had done.
He returned the thirty pieces of silver
  to the chief priests and elders, saying,
  "I have sinned in betraying innocent blood."
They said,
  "What is that to us?
  Look to it yourself."
Flinging the money into the temple,
  he departed and went off and hanged himself.
The chief priests gathered up the money, but said,
  "It is not lawful to deposit this in the temple treasury,
  for it is the price of blood."
After consultation, they used it to buy the potter's field
  as a burial place for foreigners.
That is why that field even today is called the Field of Blood.
Then was fulfilled what had been said through Jeremiah
  the prophet,

And they took the thirty pieces of silver,
the value of a man with a price on his head,
a price set by some of the Israelites,
and they paid it out for the potter's field
just as the Lord had commanded me.

Now Jesus stood before the governor, and he questioned him,
  "Are you the king of the Jews?"
Jesus said, "You say so."
And when he was accused by the chief priests and elders,
  he made no answer.
Then Pilate said to him,
  "Do you not hear how many things they are testifying against
      you?"
But he did not answer him one word,
  so that the governor was greatly amazed.

Now on the occasion of the feast
  the governor was accustomed to release to the crowd
  one prisoner whom they wished.
And at that time they had a notorious prisoner called Barabbas.
So when they had assembled, Pilate said to them,
  "Which one do you want me to release to you,
  Barabbas, or Jesus called Christ?"
For he knew that it was out of envy
  that they had handed him over.
While he was still seated on the bench,
  his wife sent him a message,
  "Have nothing to do with that righteous man.
I suffered much in a dream today because of him."
The chief priests and the elders persuaded the crowds
  to ask for Barabbas but to destroy Jesus.
The governor said to them in reply,
  "Which of the two do you want me to release to you?"
They answered, "Barabbas!"
Pilate said to them,
  "Then what shall I do with Jesus called Christ?"
They all said,
  "Let him be crucified!"
But he said,
  "Why? What evil has he done?"
They only shouted the louder,
  "Let him be crucified!"
When Pilate saw that he was not succeeding at all,
  but that a riot was breaking out instead,

he took water and washed his hands in the sight of the crowd,
   saying, "I am innocent of this man's blood.
Look to it yourselves."
And the whole people said in reply,
   "His blood be upon us and upon our children."
Then he released Barabbas to them,
   but after he had Jesus scourged,
   he handed him over to be crucified.

Then the soldiers of the governor took Jesus inside the praetorium
   and gathered the whole cohort around him.
They stripped off his clothes
   and threw a scarlet military cloak about him.
Weaving a crown out of thorns, they placed it on his head,
   and a reed in his right hand.
And kneeling before him, they mocked him, saying,
   "Hail, King of the Jews!"
They spat upon him and took the reed
   and kept striking him on the head.
And when they had mocked him,
   they stripped him of the cloak,
   dressed him in his own clothes,
   and led him off to crucify him.

As they were going out, they met a Cyrenian named Simon;
   this man they pressed into service
   to carry his cross.

And when they came to a place called Golgotha
   —which means Place of the Skull—,
   they gave Jesus wine to drink mixed with gall.
But when he had tasted it, he refused to drink.
After they had crucified him,
   they divided his garments by casting lots;
   then they sat down and kept watch over him there.
And they placed over his head the written charge against him:
   This is Jesus, the King of the Jews.
Two revolutionaries were crucified with him,
   one on his right and the other on his left.
Those passing by reviled him, shaking their heads and saying,
   "You who would destroy the temple and rebuild it in three days,
   save yourself, if you are the Son of God,
   and come down from the cross!"
Likewise the chief priests with the scribes and elders mocked him
      and said,

"He saved others; he cannot save himself.
So he is the king of Israel!
Let him come down from the cross now,
   and we will believe in him.
He trusted in God;
   let him deliver him now if he wants him.
For he said, 'I am the Son of God.'"
The revolutionaries who were crucified with him
   also kept abusing him in the same way.

From noon onward, darkness came over the whole land
   until three in the afternoon.
And about three o'clock Jesus cried out in a loud voice,
   "Eli, Eli, lema sabachthani?"
   which means, "My God, my God, why have you forsaken me?"
Some of the bystanders who heard it said,
   "This one is calling for Elijah."
Immediately one of them ran to get a sponge;
   he soaked it in wine, and putting it on a reed,
   gave it to him to drink.
But the rest said,
   "Wait, let us see if Elijah comes to save him."
But Jesus cried out again in a loud voice,
      and gave up his spirit.

   (Here all kneel and pause for a short time.)

And behold, the veil of the sanctuary
   was torn in two from top to bottom.
The earth quaked, rocks were split, tombs were opened,
   and the bodies of many saints who had fallen asleep were raised.
And coming forth from their tombs after his resurrection,
   they entered the holy city and appeared to many.
The centurion and the men with him who were keeping watch over
      Jesus
   feared greatly when they saw the earthquake
   and all that was happening, and they said,
   "Truly, this was the Son of God!"
There were many women there, looking on from a distance,
   who had followed Jesus from Galilee, ministering to him.
Among them were Mary Magdalene and Mary the mother of James
      and Joseph,
   and the mother of the sons of Zebedee.

When it was evening,
   there came a rich man from Arimathea named Joseph,

who was himself a disciple of Jesus.
He went to Pilate and asked for the body of Jesus;
  then Pilate ordered it to be handed over.
Taking the body, Joseph wrapped it in clean linen
  and laid it in his new tomb that he had hewn in the rock.
Then he rolled a huge stone across the entrance to the tomb
  and departed.
But Mary Magdalene and the other Mary
  remained sitting there, facing the tomb.

The next day, the one following the day of preparation,
  the chief priests and the Pharisees
  gathered before Pilate and said,
  "Sir, we remember that this impostor while still alive said,
  'After three days I will be raised up.'
Give orders, then, that the grave be secured until the third day,
  lest his disciples come and steal him and say to the people,
  'He has been raised from the dead.'
This last imposture would be worse than the first."
Pilate said to them,
  "The guard is yours;
  go, secure it as best you can."
So they went and secured the tomb
  by fixing a seal to the stone and setting the guard. ✛

MONDAY, APRIL 3
MONDAY OF HOLY WEEK

† *Isaiah 42:1-7*
He will not cry out, nor make his voice heard in the street.
(First oracle of the Servant of the Lord)

Here is my servant whom I uphold,
  my chosen one with whom I am pleased,
Upon whom I have put my Spirit;
  he shall bring forth justice to the nations,
Not crying out, not shouting,
  not making his voice heard in the street.
A bruised reed he shall not break,
  and a smoldering wick he shall not quench,
Until he establishes justice on the earth;
  the coastlands will wait for his teaching.

Thus says God, the LORD,
  who created the heavens and stretched them out,
  who spreads out the earth with its crops,
Who gives breath to its people

and spirit to those who walk on it:
I, the LORD, have called you for the victory of justice,
  I have grasped you by the hand;
I formed you, and set you
  as a covenant of the people,
  a light for the nations,
To open the eyes of the blind,
  to bring out prisoners from confinement,
  and from the dungeon, those who live in darkness. ✝

  Psalm 27:1, 2, 3, 13-14

R. (1a) **The Lord is my light and my salvation.**

The LORD is my light and my salvation;
  whom should I fear?
The LORD is my life's refuge;
  of whom should I be afraid? **R.**

When evildoers come at me
  to devour my flesh,
My foes and my enemies
  themselves stumble and fall. **R.**

Though an army encamp against me,
  my heart will not fear;
Though war be waged upon me,
  even then will I trust. **R.**

I believe that I shall see the bounty of the LORD
  in the land of the living.
Wait for the LORD with courage;
  be stouthearted, and wait for the LORD. **R.**

R. Glory and praise to you, Lord Jesus Christ!
Hail to you, our King;
you alone are compassionate with our faults. **R.**

✝ *John 12:1-11*
Let her keep this for the day of my burial.

Six days before Passover Jesus came to Bethany,
  where Lazarus was, whom Jesus had raised from the dead.
They gave a dinner for him there, and Martha served,
  while Lazarus was one of those reclining at table with him.
Mary took a liter of costly perfumed oil
  made from genuine aromatic nard
  and anointed the feet of Jesus and dried them with her hair;
  the house was filled with the fragrance of the oil.
Then Judas the Iscariot, one of his disciples,
  and the one who would betray him, said,

"Why was this oil not sold for three hundred days' wages
   and given to the poor?"
He said this not because he cared about the poor
   but because he was a thief and held the money bag
   and used to steal the contributions.
So Jesus said, "Leave her alone.
Let her keep this for the day of my burial.
You always have the poor with you, but you do not always have me."

The large crowd of the Jews found out that he was there and came,
   not only because of him, but also to see Lazarus,
   whom he had raised from the dead.
And the chief priests plotted to kill Lazarus too,
   because many of the Jews were turning away
   and believing in Jesus because of him. ✛

TUESDAY, APRIL 4
TUESDAY OF HOLY WEEK

† Isaiah 49:1-6
I will make you a light to the nations, that my salvation may reach to the ends of the earth. (Second oracle of the Servant of the Lord)

Hear me, O islands,
   listen, O distant peoples.
The LORD called me from birth,
   from my mother's womb he gave me my name.
He made of me a sharp-edged sword
   and concealed me in the shadow of his arm.
He made me a polished arrow,
   in his quiver he hid me.
You are my servant, he said to me,
   Israel, through whom I show my glory.

Though I thought I had toiled in vain,
   and for nothing, uselessly, spent my strength,
Yet my reward is with the LORD,
   my recompense is with my God.
For now the LORD has spoken
   who formed me as his servant from the womb,
That Jacob may be brought back to him
   and Israel gathered to him;
And I am made glorious in the sight of the LORD,
   and my God is now my strength!
It is too little, he says, for you to be my servant,
   to raise up the tribes of Jacob,
   and restore the survivors of Israel;

I will make you a light to the nations,
that my salvation may reach to the ends of the earth. ✛

Psalm 71:1-2, 3-4a, 5ab-6ab, 15 and 17

R. (see 15ab) **I will sing of your salvation.**

In you, O LORD, I take refuge;
let me never be put to shame.
In your justice rescue me, and deliver me;
incline your ear to me, and save me. **R.**

Be my rock of refuge,
a stronghold to give me safety,
for you are my rock and my fortress.
O my God, rescue me from the hand of the wicked. **R.**

For you are my hope, O Lord;
my trust, O God, from my youth.
On you I depend from birth;
from my mother's womb you are my strength. **R.**

My mouth shall declare your justice,
day by day your salvation.
O God, you have taught me from my youth,
and till the present I proclaim your wondrous deeds. **R.**

R. Glory and praise to you, Lord Jesus Christ!
Hail to you, our King, obedient to the Father;
you were led to your crucifixion like a gentle lamb to the slaughter. **R.**

✝ John 13:21-33, 36-38
One of you will betray me; the cock will not crow before you deny me three times.

Reclining at table with his disciples, Jesus was deeply troubled
and testified,
"Amen, amen, I say to you, one of you will betray me."
The disciples looked at one another, at a loss as to whom he meant.
One of his disciples, the one whom Jesus loved,
was reclining at Jesus' side.
So Simon Peter nodded to him to find out whom he meant.
He leaned back against Jesus' chest and said to him,
"Master, who is it?"
Jesus answered,
"It is the one to whom I hand the morsel after I have dipped it."
So he dipped the morsel and took it and handed it to Judas,
son of Simon the Iscariot.
After Judas took the morsel, Satan entered him.
So Jesus said to him, "What you are going to do, do quickly."
Now none of those reclining at table realized why he said this to him.
Some thought that since Judas kept the money bag, Jesus had told
him,

"Buy what we need for the feast,"
or to give something to the poor.
So Judas took the morsel and left at once. And it was night.

When he had left, Jesus said,
"Now is the Son of Man glorified, and God is glorified in him.
If God is glorified in him, God will also glorify him in himself,
and he will glorify him at once.
My children, I will be with you only a little while longer.
You will look for me, and as I told the Jews,
'Where I go you cannot come,' so now I say it to you."

Simon Peter said to him, "Master, where are you going?"
Jesus answered him,
"Where I am going, you cannot follow me now,
though you will follow later."
Peter said to him,
"Master, why can I not follow you now?
I will lay down my life for you."
Jesus answered, "Will you lay down your life for me?
Amen, amen, I say to you, the cock will not crow
before you deny me three times." ✛

WEDNESDAY, APRIL 5
WEDNESDAY OF HOLY WEEK

† *Isaiah 50:4-9a*
My face I did not shield from buffets and spitting.
(Third oracle of the Servant of the Lord)

The Lord GOD has given me
a well-trained tongue,
That I might know how to speak to the weary
a word that will rouse them.
Morning after morning
he opens my ear that I may hear;
And I have not rebelled,
have not turned back.
I gave my back to those who beat me,
my cheeks to those who plucked my beard;
My face I did not shield
from buffets and spitting.

The Lord GOD is my help,
therefore I am not disgraced;
I have set my face like flint,
knowing that I shall not be put to shame.

He is near who upholds my right;
  if anyone wishes to oppose me,
  let us appear together.
Who disputes my right?
  Let him confront me.
See, the Lord GOD is my help;
  who will prove me wrong? ✝

Psalm 69:8-10, 21-22, 31 and 33-34

R. (14c) Lord, in your great love, answer me.
For your sake I bear insult,
  and shame covers my face.
I have become an outcast to my brothers,
  a stranger to my mother's sons,
because zeal for your house consumes me,
  and the insults of those who blaspheme you fall upon me. **R.**
Insult has broken my heart, and I am weak,
  I looked for sympathy, but there was none;
  for consolers, not one could I find.
Rather they put gall in my food,
  and in my thirst they gave me vinegar to drink. **R.**
I will praise the name of God in song,
  and I will glorify him with thanksgiving:
"See, you lowly ones, and be glad;
  you who seek God, may your hearts revive!
For the LORD hears the poor,
  and his own who are in bonds he spurns not." **R.**

R. Glory and praise to you, Lord Jesus Christ!
Hail to you, our King, obedient to the Father;
you were led to your crucifixion like a gentle lamb to the slaughter. **R.**
or
R. Glory and praise to you, Lord Jesus Christ!
Hail to you, our King;
you alone are compassionate with our errors. **R.**

✝ Matthew 26:14-25
The Son of Man indeed goes, as it is written of him,
but woe to that man by whom the Son of Man is betrayed.

One of the Twelve, who was called Judas Iscariot,
  went to the chief priests and said,
  "What are you willing to give me
  if I hand him over to you?"
They paid him thirty pieces of silver,
  and from that time on he looked for an opportunity to hand him
    over.

On the first day of the Feast of Unleavened Bread,
   the disciples approached Jesus and said,
   "Where do you want us to prepare
   for you to eat the Passover?"
He said,
   "Go into the city to a certain man and tell him,
   'The teacher says, "My appointed time draws near;
   in your house I shall celebrate the Passover with my disciples."'"
The disciples then did as Jesus had ordered,
   and prepared the Passover.

When it was evening,
   he reclined at table with the Twelve.
And while they were eating, he said,
   "Amen, I say to you, one of you will betray me."
Deeply distressed at this,
   they began to say to him one after another,
   "Surely it is not I, Lord?"
He said in reply,
   "He who has dipped his hand into the dish with me
   is the one who will betray me.
The Son of Man indeed goes, as it is written of him,
   but woe to that man by whom the Son of Man is betrayed.
It would be better for that man if he had never been born."
Then Judas, his betrayer, said in reply,
   "Surely it is not I, Rabbi?"
He answered, "You have said so." ✛

THURSDAY, APRIL 6
THURSDAY OF HOLY WEEK (HOLY THURSDAY)
EVENING MASS OF THE LORD'S SUPPER
(Readings for the Chrism Mass are:
Isaiah 61:1-3a, 6a, 8b-9 • Psalm 89:21-22, 25, 27 • Revelation 1:5-8 • Luke 4:16-21.)

† *Exodus 12:1-8, 11-14*
The law regarding the Passover meal.

The LORD said to Moses and Aaron in the land of Egypt,
   "This month shall stand at the head of your calendar;
   you shall reckon it the first month of the year.
Tell the whole community of Israel:
   On the tenth of this month every one of your families
   must procure for itself a lamb, one apiece for each household.
If a family is too small for a whole lamb,
   it shall join the nearest household in procuring one
   and shall share in the lamb

in proportion to the number of persons who partake of it.
The lamb must be a year-old male and without blemish.
You may take it from either the sheep or the goats.
You shall keep it until the fourteenth day of this month,
   and then, with the whole assembly of Israel present,
   it shall be slaughtered during the evening twilight.
They shall take some of its blood
   and apply it to the two doorposts and the lintel
   of every house in which they partake of the lamb.
That same night they shall eat its roasted flesh
   with unleavened bread and bitter herbs.

"This is how you are to eat it:
   with your loins girt, sandals on your feet and your staff in hand,
   you shall eat like those who are in flight.
It is the Passover of the LORD.
For on this same night I will go through Egypt,
   striking down every firstborn of the land, both man and beast,
   and executing judgment on all the gods of Egypt—I, the LORD!
But the blood will mark the houses where you are.
Seeing the blood, I will pass over you;
   thus, when I strike the land of Egypt,
   no destructive blow will come upon you.

"This day shall be a memorial feast for you,
   which all your generations shall celebrate
   with pilgrimage to the LORD, as a perpetual institution." ✛

Psalm 116:12-13, 15-16bc, 17-18
R. (see 1 Corinthians 10:16) **Our blessing-cup is a communion with the Blood of Christ.**
How shall I make a return to the LORD
   for all the good he has done for me?
The cup of salvation I will take up,
   and I will call upon the name of the LORD. **R.**
Precious in the eyes of the LORD
   is the death of his faithful ones.
I am your servant, the son of your handmaid;
   you have loosed my bonds. **R.**
To you will I offer sacrifice of thanksgiving,
   and I will call upon the name of the LORD.
My vows to the LORD I will pay
   in the presence of all his people. **R.**

† 1 Corinthians 11:23-26

For as often as you eat this bread and drink the cup,
you proclaim the death of the Lord.

Brothers and sisters:
I received from the Lord what I also handed on to you,
   that the Lord Jesus, on the night he was handed over,
   took bread, and, after he had given thanks,
   broke it and said, "This is my body that is for you.
Do this in remembrance of me."
In the same way also the cup, after supper, saying,
   "This cup is the new covenant in my blood.
Do this, as often as you drink it, in remembrance of me."
For as often as you eat this bread and drink the cup,
   you proclaim the death of the Lord until he comes. ✠

   John 13:34

R. Glory and praise to you, Lord Jesus Christ!
I give you a new commandment, says the Lord:
love one another as I have loved you. **R.**

† John 13:1-15

Jesus loved them to the end.

Before the feast of Passover, Jesus knew that his hour had come
   to pass from this world to the Father.
He loved his own in the world and he loved them to the end.
The devil had already induced Judas, son of Simon the Iscariot, to
      hand him over.
So, during supper,
   fully aware that the Father had put everything into his power
   and that he had come from God and was returning to God,
   he rose from supper and took off his outer garments.
He took a towel and tied it around his waist.
Then he poured water into a basin
   and began to wash the disciples' feet
   and dry them with the towel around his waist.
He came to Simon Peter, who said to him,
   "Master, are you going to wash my feet?"
Jesus answered and said to him,
   "What I am doing, you do not understand now,
   but you will understand later."
Peter said to him, "You will never wash my feet."
Jesus answered him,
   "Unless I wash you, you will have no inheritance with me."
Simon Peter said to him,
   "Master, then not only my feet, but my hands and head as well."

Jesus said to him,
  "Whoever has bathed has no need except to have his feet washed,
  for he is clean all over;
  so you are clean, but not all."
For he knew who would betray him;
  for this reason, he said, "Not all of you are clean."

So when he had washed their feet
  and put his garments back on and reclined at table again,
  he said to them, "Do you realize what I have done for you?
You call me 'teacher' and 'master,' and rightly so, for indeed I am.
If I, therefore, the master and teacher, have washed your feet,
  you ought to wash one another's feet.
I have given you a model to follow,
  so that as I have done for you, you should also do." ✝

FRIDAY, APRIL 7
FRIDAY OF THE PASSION OF THE LORD (GOOD FRIDAY)

✝ *Isaiah 52:13—53:12*
He himself was wounded for our sins. (Fourth oracle of the Servant of the Lord)

See, my servant shall prosper,
  he shall be raised high and greatly exalted.
Even as many were amazed at him—
  so marred was his look beyond human semblance
  and his appearance beyond that of the sons of man—
so shall he startle many nations,
  because of him kings shall stand speechless;
for those who have not been told shall see,
  those who have not heard shall ponder it.

Who would believe what we have heard?
  To whom has the arm of the LORD been revealed?
He grew up like a sapling before him,
  like a shoot from the parched earth;
there was in him no stately bearing to make us look at him,
  nor appearance that would attract us to him.
He was spurned and avoided by people,
  a man of suffering, accustomed to infirmity,
one of those from whom people hide their faces,
  spurned, and we held him in no esteem.

Yet it was our infirmities that he bore,
  our sufferings that he endured,
while we thought of him as stricken,
  as one smitten by God and afflicted.

But he was pierced for our offenses,
  crushed for our sins;
upon him was the chastisement that makes us whole,
  by his stripes we were healed.
We had all gone astray like sheep,
  each following his own way;
but the LORD laid upon him
  the guilt of us all.

Though he was harshly treated, he submitted
  and opened not his mouth;
like a lamb led to the slaughter
  or a sheep before the shearers,
  he was silent and opened not his mouth.
Oppressed and condemned, he was taken away,
  and who would have thought any more of his destiny?
When he was cut off from the land of the living,
  and smitten for the sin of his people,
a grave was assigned him among the wicked
  and a burial place with evildoers,
though he had done no wrong
  nor spoken any falsehood.
But the LORD was pleased
  to crush him in infirmity.

If he gives his life as an offering for sin,
  he shall see his descendants in a long life,
  and the will of the LORD shall be accomplished through him.

Because of his affliction
  he shall see the light in fullness of days;
through his suffering, my servant shall justify many,
  and their guilt he shall bear.
Therefore I will give him his portion among the great,
  and he shall divide the spoils with the mighty,
because he surrendered himself to death
  and was counted among the wicked;
and he shall take away the sins of many,
  and win pardon for their offenses. ✛

  Psalm 31:2 and 6, 12-13, 15-16, 17 and 25
R. (Luke 23:46) **Father, into your hands I commend my spirit.**
In you, O LORD, I take refuge;
  let me never be put to shame.
In your justice rescue me.
Into your hands I commend my spirit;

you will redeem me, O LORD, O faithful God. **R.**

For all my foes I am an object of reproach,
  a laughingstock to my neighbors, and a dread to my friends;
  they who see me abroad flee from me.

I am forgotten like the unremembered dead;
  I am like a dish that is broken. **R.**

But my trust is in you, O LORD;
  I say, "You are my God.

In your hands is my destiny; rescue me
  from the clutches of my enemies and my persecutors." **R.**

Let your face shine upon your servant;
  save me in your kindness.

Take courage and be stouthearted,
  all you who hope in the LORD. **R.**

† *Hebrews 4:14-16; 5:7-9*

*Jesus learned obedience and became the source
of salvation for all who obey him.*

Brothers and sisters:

Since we have a great high priest who has passed through the heavens,
  Jesus, the Son of God,
  let us hold fast to our confession.

For we do not have a high priest
  who is unable to sympathize with our weaknesses,
  but one who has similarly been tested in every way,
  yet without sin.

So let us confidently approach the throne of grace
  to receive mercy and to find grace for timely help.

In the days when Christ was in the flesh,
  he offered prayers and supplications with loud cries and tears
  to the one who was able to save him from death,
  and he was heard because of his reverence.

Son though he was, he learned obedience from what he suffered;
  and when he was made perfect,
  he became the source of eternal salvation for all who obey him. ✛

Philippians 2:8-9

R. Glory and praise to you, Lord Jesus Christ!

Christ became obedient to the point of death,
even death on a cross.

Because of this, God greatly exalted him
and bestowed on him the name which is above every other name. **R.**

† *John 18:1—19:42*
The Passion of our Lord Jesus Christ.

Jesus went out with his disciples across the Kidron valley
    to where there was a garden,
    into which he and his disciples entered.
Judas his betrayer also knew the place,
    because Jesus had often met there with his disciples.
So Judas got a band of soldiers and guards
    from the chief priests and the Pharisees
    and went there with lanterns, torches, and weapons.
Jesus, knowing everything that was going to happen to him,
    went out and said to them, "Whom are you looking for?"
They answered him, "Jesus the Nazorean."
He said to them, "I AM."
Judas his betrayer was also with them.
When he said to them, "I AM, "
    they turned away and fell to the ground.
So he again asked them,
    "Whom are you looking for?"
They said, "Jesus the Nazorean."
Jesus answered,
    "I told you that I AM.
So if you are looking for me, let these men go."
This was to fulfill what he had said,
    "I have not lost any of those you gave me."
Then Simon Peter, who had a sword, drew it,
    struck the high priest's slave, and cut off his right ear.
The slave's name was Malchus.
Jesus said to Peter,
    "Put your sword into its scabbard.
Shall I not drink the cup that the Father gave me?"

So the band of soldiers, the tribune, and the Jewish guards seized
    Jesus,
    bound him, and brought him to Annas first.
He was the father-in-law of Caiaphas,
    who was high priest that year.
It was Caiaphas who had counseled the Jews
    that it was better that one man should die rather than the people.

Simon Peter and another disciple followed Jesus.
Now the other disciple was known to the high priest,
    and he entered the courtyard of the high priest with Jesus.
But Peter stood at the gate outside.

So the other disciple, the acquaintance of the high priest,
  went out and spoke to the gatekeeper and brought Peter in.
Then the maid who was the gatekeeper said to Peter,
  "You are not one of this man's disciples, are you?"
He said, "I am not."
Now the slaves and the guards were standing around a charcoal fire
  that they had made, because it was cold,
    and were warming themselves.
Peter was also standing there keeping warm.

The high priest questioned Jesus
  about his disciples and about his doctrine.
Jesus answered him,
  "I have spoken publicly to the world.
I have always taught in a synagogue
  or in the temple area where all the Jews gather,
  and in secret I have said nothing. Why ask me?
Ask those who heard me what I said to them.
They know what I said."
When he had said this,
  one of the temple guards standing there struck Jesus and said,
  "Is this the way you answer the high priest?"
Jesus answered him,
  "If I have spoken wrongly, testify to the wrong;
  but if I have spoken rightly, why do you strike me?"
Then Annas sent him bound to Caiaphas the high priest.

Now Simon Peter was standing there keeping warm.
And they said to him,
  "You are not one of his disciples, are you?"
He denied it and said,
  "I am not."
One of the slaves of the high priest,
  a relative of the one whose ear Peter had cut off, said,
  "Didn't I see you in the garden with him?"
Again Peter denied it.
And immediately the cock crowed.

Then they brought Jesus from Caiaphas to the praetorium.
It was morning.
And they themselves did not enter the praetorium,
  in order not to be defiled so that they could eat the Passover.
So Pilate came out to them and said,
  "What charge do you bring against this man?"
They answered and said to him,

"If he were not a criminal,
we would not have handed him over to you."
At this, Pilate said to them,
"Take him yourselves, and judge him according to your law."
The Jews answered him,
"We do not have the right to execute anyone, "
in order that the word of Jesus might be fulfilled
that he said indicating the kind of death he would die.
So Pilate went back into the praetorium
and summoned Jesus and said to him,
"Are you the King of the Jews?"
Jesus answered,
"Do you say this on your own
or have others told you about me?"
Pilate answered,
"I am not a Jew, am I?
Your own nation and the chief priests handed you over to me.
What have you done?"
Jesus answered,
"My kingdom does not belong to this world.
If my kingdom did belong to this world,
my attendants would be fighting
to keep me from being handed over to the Jews.
But as it is, my kingdom is not here."
So Pilate said to him,
"Then you are a king?"
Jesus answered,
"You say I am a king.
For this I was born and for this I came into the world,
to testify to the truth.
Everyone who belongs to the truth listens to my voice."
Pilate said to him, "What is truth?"

When he had said this,
he again went out to the Jews and said to them,
"I find no guilt in him.
But you have a custom that I release one prisoner to you at Passover.
Do you want me to release to you the King of the Jews?"
They cried out again,
"Not this one but Barabbas!"
Now Barabbas was a revolutionary.

Then Pilate took Jesus and had him scourged.
And the soldiers wove a crown out of thorns and placed it on his head,
and clothed him in a purple cloak,

and they came to him and said,
  "Hail, King of the Jews!"
And they struck him repeatedly.
Once more Pilate went out and said to them,
  "Look, I am bringing him out to you,
  so that you may know that I find no guilt in him."
So Jesus came out,
  wearing the crown of thorns and the purple cloak.
And he said to them, "Behold, the man!"
When the chief priests and the guards saw him they cried out,
  "Crucify him, crucify him!"
Pilate said to them,
  "Take him yourselves and crucify him.
I find no guilt in him."
The Jews answered,
  "We have a law, and according to that law he ought to die,
  because he made himself the Son of God."
Now when Pilate heard this statement,
  he became even more afraid,
  and went back into the praetorium and said to Jesus,
  "Where are you from?"
Jesus did not answer him.
So Pilate said to him,
  "Do you not speak to me?
Do you not know that I have power to release you
  and I have power to crucify you?"
Jesus answered him,
  "You would have no power over me
  if it had not been given to you from above.
For this reason the one who handed me over to you
  has the greater sin."
Consequently, Pilate tried to release him; but the Jews cried out,
  "If you release him, you are not a Friend of Caesar.
Everyone who makes himself a king opposes Caesar."

When Pilate heard these words he brought Jesus out
  and seated him on the judge's bench
  in the place called Stone Pavement, in Hebrew, Gabbatha.
It was preparation day for Passover, and it was about noon.
And he said to the Jews,
  "Behold, your king!"
They cried out,
  "Take him away, take him away! Crucify him!"
Pilate said to them,

"Shall I crucify your king?"
The chief priests answered,
 "We have no king but Caesar."
Then he handed him over to them to be crucified.

So they took Jesus, and, carrying the cross himself,
 he went out to what is called the Place of the Skull,
 in Hebrew, Golgotha.
There they crucified him, and with him two others,
 one on either side, with Jesus in the middle.
Pilate also had an inscription written and put on the cross.
It read,
 "Jesus the Nazorean, the King of the Jews."
Now many of the Jews read this inscription,
 because the place where Jesus was crucified was near the city;
 and it was written in Hebrew, Latin, and Greek.
So the chief priests of the Jews said to Pilate,
 "Do not write 'The King of the Jews,'
 but that he said, 'I am the King of the Jews.'"
Pilate answered,
 "What I have written, I have written."

When the soldiers had crucified Jesus,
 they took his clothes and divided them into four shares,
 a share for each soldier.
They also took his tunic, but the tunic was seamless,
 woven in one piece from the top down.
So they said to one another,
 "Let's not tear it, but cast lots for it to see whose it will be,"
 in order that the passage of Scripture might be fulfilled that says:
  They divided my garments among them,
   and for my vesture they cast lots.
This is what the soldiers did.
Standing by the cross of Jesus were his mother
 and his mother's sister, Mary the wife of Clopas,
 and Mary of Magdala.
When Jesus saw his mother and the disciple there whom he loved
 he said to his mother, "Woman, behold, your son."
Then he said to the disciple,
 "Behold, your mother."
And from that hour the disciple took her into his home.

After this, aware that everything was now finished,
 in order that the Scripture might be fulfilled,
 Jesus said, "I thirst."

There was a vessel filled with common wine.
So they put a sponge soaked in wine on a sprig of hyssop
   and put it up to his mouth.
When Jesus had taken the wine, he said,
   "It is finished."
And bowing his head, he handed over the spirit.

   (Here all kneel and pause for a short time.)

Now since it was preparation day,
   in order that the bodies might not remain
      on the cross on the sabbath,
   for the sabbath day of that week was a solemn one,
   the Jews asked Pilate that their legs be broken
   and that they be taken down.
So the soldiers came and broke the legs of the first
   and then of the other one who was crucified with Jesus.
But when they came to Jesus and saw that he was already dead,
   they did not break his legs,
   but one soldier thrust his lance into his side,
   and immediately blood and water flowed out.
An eyewitness has testified, and his testimony is true;
   he knows that he is speaking the truth,
   so that you also may come to believe.
For this happened so that the Scripture passage might be fulfilled:
   Not a bone of it will be broken.
And again another passage says:
   They will look upon him whom they have pierced.

After this, Joseph of Arimathea,
   secretly a disciple of Jesus for fear of the Jews,
   asked Pilate if he could remove the body of Jesus.
And Pilate permitted it.
So he came and took his body.
Nicodemus, the one who had first come to him at night,
   also came bringing a mixture of myrrh and aloes
   weighing about one hundred pounds.
They took the body of Jesus
   and bound it with burial cloths along with the spices,
   according to the Jewish burial custom.
Now in the place where he had been crucified there was a garden,
   and in the garden a new tomb, in which no one had yet been buried.
So they laid Jesus there because of the Jewish preparation day;
   for the tomb was close by. ✛

SATURDAY, APRIL 8
HOLY SATURDAY: EASTER VIGIL MASS

Nine readings are assigned to the Easter Vigil: seven from the Old Testament and two from the New. If circumstances demand in individual cases, the number of prescribed readings may be reduced. Three selections from the Old Testament, both from the Law and the Prophets, should be read before the Epistle and Gospel. In any case, the reading from Exodus about the escape through the Red Sea (reading 3) should never be omitted.

(Other readings for the Easter Vigil liturgy are: Genesis 1:1—2:2 or Genesis 1:1, 26-31a •
Psalm 104:1-2, 5-6, 10 and 12, 13-14, 24 and 35c or Psalm 33:4-5, 6-7, 12-13, 20 and 22 •
Genesis 22:1-18 or Genesis 22:1-2, 9a, 10-13, 15-18 • Psalm 16:5 and 8, 9-10, 11 •
Isaiah 54:5-14 • Psalm 30:2 and 4, 5-6, 11-12a and 13b • Isaiah 55:1-11 • Isaiah 12:2-3,
4bcd, 5-6 • Baruch 3:9-15, 32—4:4 • Psalm 19:8, 9, 10, 11 • Ezekiel 36:16-17a, 18-28 •
Psalms 42:3, 5; 43:3, 4 or Isaiah 12:2-3, 4bcd, 5-6 or Psalm 51:12-13, 14-15, 18-19.)

† Exodus 14:15—15:1
The Israelites marched on dry land through the midst of the sea.

The LORD said to Moses, "Why are you crying out to me?
Tell the Israelites to go forward.
And you, lift up your staff and, with hand outstretched over the sea,
    split the sea in two,
    that the Israelites may pass through it on dry land.
But I will make the Egyptians so obstinate
    that they will go in after them.
Then I will receive glory through Pharaoh and all his army,
    his chariots and charioteers.
The Egyptians shall know that I am the LORD,
    when I receive glory through Pharaoh
    and his chariots and charioteers."

The angel of God, who had been leading Israel's camp,
    now moved and went around behind them.
The column of cloud also, leaving the front,
    took up its place behind them,
    so that it came between the camp of the Egyptians
    and that of Israel.
But the cloud now became dark, and thus the night passed
    without the rival camps coming any closer together
        all night long.
Then Moses stretched out his hand over the sea,
    and the LORD swept the sea
    with a strong east wind throughout the night
    and so turned it into dry land.
When the water was thus divided,
    the Israelites marched into the midst of the sea on dry land,
    with the water like a wall to their right and to their left.

The Egyptians followed in pursuit;
   all Pharaoh's horses and chariots and charioteers went after them
   right into the midst of the sea.
In the night watch just before dawn
   the LORD cast through the column of the fiery cloud
   upon the Egyptian force a glance that threw it into a panic;
   and he so clogged their chariot wheels
   that they could hardly drive.
With that the Egyptians sounded the retreat before Israel,
   because the LORD was fighting for them against the Egyptians.

Then the LORD told Moses, "Stretch out your hand over the sea,
   that the water may flow back upon the Egyptians,
   upon their chariots and their charioteers."
So Moses stretched out his hand over the sea,
   and at dawn the sea flowed back to its normal depth.
The Egyptians were fleeing head on toward the sea,
   when the LORD hurled them into its midst.
As the water flowed back,
   it covered the chariots and the charioteers of Pharaoh's whole army
   which had followed the Israelites into the sea.
Not a single one of them escaped.
But the Israelites had marched on dry land
   through the midst of the sea,
   with the water like a wall to their right and to their left.
Thus the LORD saved Israel on that day
   from the power of the Egyptians.
When Israel saw the Egyptians lying dead on the seashore
   and beheld the great power that the Lord
   had shown against the Egyptians,
   they feared the LORD and believed in him and in his servant Moses.

Then Moses and the Israelites sang this song to the LORD:
   I will sing to the LORD, for he is gloriously triumphant;
   horse and chariot he has cast into the sea. ✢

Exodus 15:1-2, 3-4, 5-6, 17-18

R. (1b) **Let us sing to the Lord; he has covered himself in glory.**

I will sing to the LORD, for he is gloriously triumphant;
   horse and chariot he has cast into the sea.
My strength and my courage is the LORD,
   and he has been my savior.
He is my God, I praise him;
   the God of my father, I extol him. **R.**

The LORD is a warrior,
   LORD is his name!
Pharaoh's chariots and army he hurled into the sea;
   the elite of his officers were submerged in the Red Sea. **R.**
The flood waters covered them,
   they sank into the depths like a stone.
Your right hand, O LORD, magnificent in power,
   your right hand, O LORD, has shattered the enemy. **R.**
You brought in the people you redeemed
   and planted them on the mountain of your inheritance—
the place where you made your seat, O LORD,
   the sanctuary, LORD, which your hands established.
The LORD shall reign forever and ever. **R.**

† *Romans 6:3-11*
Christ, raised from the dead, dies no more.

Brothers and sisters:
Are you unaware that we who were baptized into Christ Jesus
   were baptized into his death?
We were indeed buried with him through baptism into death,
   so that, just as Christ was raised from the dead
   by the glory of the Father,
   we too might live in newness of life.

For if we have grown into union with him through a death like his,
   we shall also be united with him in the resurrection.
We know that our old self was crucified with him,
   so that our sinful body might be done away with,
   that we might no longer be in slavery to sin.
For a dead person has been absolved from sin.
If, then, we have died with Christ,
   we believe that we shall also live with him.
We know that Christ, raised from the dead, dies no more;
   death no longer has power over him.
As to his death, he died to sin once and for all;
   as to his life, he lives for God.
Consequently, you too must think of yourselves as being dead to sin
   and living for God in Christ Jesus. ✛

Psalm 118:1-2, 16-17, 22-23
R. Alleluia, alleluia, alleluia.
Give thanks to the LORD, for he is good,
   for his mercy endures forever.
Let the house of Israel say,
   "His mercy endures forever." **R.**

The right hand of the LORD has struck with power;
  the right hand of the LORD is exalted.
I shall not die, but live,
  and declare the works of the LORD. **R.**
The stone which the builders rejected
  has become the cornerstone.
By the LORD has this been done;
  it is wonderful in our eyes. **R.**

† *Matthew 28:1-10*

He has been raised from the dead and is going before you to Galilee.

After the sabbath, as the first day of the week was dawning,
  Mary Magdalene and the other Mary came to see the tomb.
And behold, there was a great earthquake;
  for an angel of the Lord descended from heaven,
  approached, rolled back the stone, and sat upon it.
His appearance was like lightning
  and his clothing was white as snow.
The guards were shaken with fear of him
  and became like dead men.
Then the angel said to the women in reply,
  "Do not be afraid!
I know that you are seeking Jesus the crucified.
He is not here, for he has been raised just as he said.
Come and see the place where he lay.
Then go quickly and tell his disciples,
  'He has been raised from the dead,
  and he is going before you to Galilee;
  there you will see him.'
  Behold, I have told you."
Then they went away quickly from the tomb,
  fearful yet overjoyed,
  and ran to announce this to his disciples.
And behold, Jesus met them on their way and greeted them.
They approached, embraced his feet, and did him homage.
Then Jesus said to them, "Do not be afraid.
Go tell my brothers to go to Galilee,
  and there they will see me." ✢

SUNDAY, APRIL 9
EASTER SUNDAY OF THE RESURRECTION OF THE LORD

† *Acts of the Apostles 10:34a, 37-43*
We ate and drank with him after he rose from the dead.

Peter proceeded to speak and said:

"You know what has happened all over Judea,
beginning in Galilee after the baptism
that John preached,
how God anointed Jesus of Nazareth
with the Holy Spirit and power.
He went about doing good
and healing all those oppressed by the devil,
for God was with him.
We are witnesses of all that he did
both in the country of the Jews and in Jerusalem.
They put him to death by hanging him on a tree.
This man God raised on the third day and granted that he be visible,
not to all the people, but to us,
the witnesses chosen by God in advance,
who ate and drank with him after he rose from the dead.
He commissioned us to preach to the people
and testify that he is the one appointed by God
as judge of the living and the dead.
To him all the prophets bear witness,
that everyone who believes in him
will receive forgiveness of sins through his name." ✝

Psalm 118:1-2, 16-17, 22-23

R. (24) **This is the day the Lord has made; let us rejoice and
be glad.** *(or* **Alleluia.***)*

Give thanks to the LORD, for he is good,
for his mercy endures forever.
Let the house of Israel say,
"His mercy endures forever." **R.**
"The right hand of the LORD has struck with power;
the right hand of the LORD is exalted.
I shall not die, but live,
and declare the works of the LORD." **R.**
The stone which the builders rejected
has become the cornerstone.
By the LORD has this been done;
it is wonderful in our eyes. **R.**

*† **Colossians 3:1-4** (or 1 Corinthians 5:6b-8)*
Seek what is above, where Christ is.

Brothers and sisters:
If then you were raised with Christ, seek what is above,
where Christ is seated at the right hand of God.
Think of what is above, not of what is on earth.
For you have died, and your life is hidden with Christ in God.

When Christ your life appears,
   then you too will appear with him in glory. ✛

   SEQUENCE: Victimae paschali laudes
Christians, to the Paschal Victim
   Offer your thankful praises!
A Lamb the sheep redeems;
   Christ, who only is sinless,
   Reconciles sinners to the Father.
Death and life have contended in that combat stupendous:
   The Prince of life, who died, reigns immortal.
Speak, Mary, declaring
   What you saw, wayfaring.
"The tomb of Christ, who is living,
   The glory of Jesus' resurrection;
Bright angels attesting,
   The shroud and napkin resting.
Yes, Christ my hope is arisen;
   to Galilee he goes before you."
Christ indeed from death is risen, our new life obtaining.
   Have mercy, victor King, ever reigning!
   Amen. Alleluia.

   See 1 Corinthians 5:7b-8a
R. Alleluia, alleluia.
Christ, our paschal lamb, has been sacrificed;
let us then feast with joy in the Lord. **R.**

   ✝ ***John 20:1-9*** *(or Matthew 28:1-10 or,*
   at an afternoon or evening Mass, Luke 24:13-35)
   He had to rise from the dead.

On the first day of the week,
   Mary of Magdala came to the tomb early in the morning,
   while it was still dark,
   and saw the stone removed from the tomb.
So she ran and went to Simon Peter
   and to the other disciple whom Jesus loved, and told them,
   "They have taken the Lord from the tomb,
   and we don't know where they put him."
So Peter and the other disciple went out and came to the tomb.
They both ran, but the other disciple ran faster than Peter
   and arrived at the tomb first;
   he bent down and saw the burial cloths there, but did not go in.
When Simon Peter arrived after him,
   he went into the tomb and saw the burial cloths there,
   and the cloth that had covered his head,
   not with the burial cloths but rolled up in a separate place.
Then the other disciple also went in,

the one who had arrived at the tomb first,
and he saw and believed.
For they did not yet understand the Scripture
that he had to rise from the dead. ✛

MONDAY, APRIL 10
MONDAY WITHIN THE OCTAVE OF EASTER

† *Acts of the Apostles 2:14, 22-33*
God raised this Jesus; of this we are all witnesses.

On the day of Pentecost, Peter stood up with the Eleven,
raised his voice, and proclaimed:
"You who are Jews, indeed all of you staying in Jerusalem.
Let this be known to you, and listen to my words.

"You who are children of Israel, hear these words.
Jesus the Nazorean was a man commended to you by God
with mighty deeds, wonders, and signs,
which God worked through him in your midst, as you yourselves
know.
This man, delivered up by the set plan and foreknowledge of God,
you killed, using lawless men to crucify him.
But God raised him up, releasing him from the throes of death,
because it was impossible for him to be held by it.
For David says of him:

> *I saw the Lord ever before me,*
> *with him at my right hand I shall not be disturbed.*
> *Therefore my heart has been glad and my tongue has exulted;*
> *my flesh, too, will dwell in hope,*
> *because you will not abandon my soul to the nether world,*
> *nor will you suffer your holy one to see corruption.*
> *You have made known to me the paths of life;*
> *you will fill me with joy in your presence.*

My brothers, one can confidently say to you
about the patriarch David that he died and was buried,
and his tomb is in our midst to this day.
But since he was a prophet and knew that God had sworn an oath to
him
that he would set one of his descendants upon his throne,
he foresaw and spoke of the resurrection of the Christ,
that neither was he abandoned to the netherworld
nor did his flesh see corruption.
God raised this Jesus;
of this we are all witnesses.

Exalted at the right hand of God,
he poured forth the promise of the Holy Spirit
that he received from the Father, as you both see and hear." ✛

Psalm 16:1b-2a and 5, 7-8, 9-10, 11
R. (1) **Keep me safe, O God; you are my hope.** *(or* **Alleluia.***)*
Keep me, O God, for in you I take refuge;
I say to the LORD, "My Lord are you."
O LORD, my allotted portion and my cup,
you it is who hold fast my lot. **R.**
I bless the LORD who counsels me;
even in the night my heart exhorts me.
I set the LORD ever before me;
with him at my right hand I shall not be disturbed. **R.**
Therefore my heart is glad and my soul rejoices,
my body, too, abides in confidence;
Because you will not abandon my soul to the nether world,
nor will you suffer your faithful one to undergo corruption. **R.**
You will show me the path to life,
fullness of joys in your presence,
the delights at your right hand forever. **R.**

Psalm 118:24
R. Alleluia, alleluia.
This is the day the LORD has made;
let us be glad and rejoice in it. **R.**

† *Matthew 28:8-15*
Go tell my brothers to go to Galilee, and there they will see me.

Mary Magdalene and the other Mary went away quickly from the
tomb,
fearful yet overjoyed,
and ran to announce the news to his disciples.
And behold, Jesus met them on their way and greeted them.
They approached, embraced his feet, and did him homage.
Then Jesus said to them, "Do not be afraid.
Go tell my brothers to go to Galilee,
and there they will see me."

While they were going, some of the guard went into the city
and told the chief priests all that had happened.
The chief priests assembled with the elders and took counsel;
then they gave a large sum of money to the soldiers,
telling them, "You are to say,
'His disciples came by night and stole him while we were asleep.'
And if this gets to the ears of the governor,

we will satisfy him and keep you out of trouble."
The soldiers took the money and did as they were instructed.
And this story has circulated among the Jews to the present day. ✢

TUESDAY, APRIL 11
TUESDAY WITHIN THE OCTAVE OF EASTER

† *Acts of the Apostles 2:36-41*
Repent and be baptized, every one of you, in the name of Jesus Christ.

On the day of Pentecost, Peter said to the Jewish people,
  "Let the whole house of Israel know for certain
  that God has made him both Lord and Christ,
  this Jesus whom you crucified."

Now when they heard this, they were cut to the heart,
  and they asked Peter and the other Apostles,
  "What are we to do, my brothers?"
Peter said to them,
  "Repent and be baptized, every one of you,
  in the name of Jesus Christ, for the forgiveness of your sins;
  and you will receive the gift of the Holy Spirit.
For the promise is made to you and to your children
  and to all those far off,
  whomever the Lord our God will call."
He testified with many other arguments, and was exhorting them,
  "Save yourselves from this corrupt generation."
Those who accepted his message were baptized,
  and about three thousand persons were added that day. ✢

Psalm 33:4-5, 18-19, 20 and 22
R. (5b) **The earth is full of the goodness of the Lord.**
  *(or **Alleluia**.)*
Upright is the word of the LORD,
  and all his works are trustworthy.
He loves justice and right;
  of the kindness of the LORD the earth is full. **R.**
See, the eyes of the LORD are upon those who fear him,
  upon those who hope for his kindness,
To deliver them from death
  and preserve them in spite of famine. **R.**
Our soul waits for the LORD,
  who is our help and our shield.
May your kindness, O LORD, be upon us
  who have put our hope in you. **R.**

Psalm 118:24

R. Alleluia, alleluia.

This is the day the LORD has made;
let us be glad and rejoice in it. **R.**

† *John 20:11-18*
I have seen the Lord, and he said these things to me.

Mary Magdalene stayed outside the tomb weeping.
And as she wept, she bent over into the tomb
 and saw two angels in white sitting there,
 one at the head and one at the feet
 where the Body of Jesus had been.
And they said to her, "Woman, why are you weeping?"
She said to them, "They have taken my Lord,
 and I don't know where they laid him."
When she had said this, she turned around and saw Jesus there,
 but did not know it was Jesus.
Jesus said to her, "Woman, why are you weeping?
Whom are you looking for?"
She thought it was the gardener and said to him,
 "Sir, if you carried him away,
 tell me where you laid him,
 and I will take him."
Jesus said to her, "Mary!"
She turned and said to him in Hebrew, "Rabbouni,"
 which means Teacher.
Jesus said to her, "Stop holding on to me,
 for I have not yet ascended to the Father.
But go to my brothers and tell them,
 'I am going to my Father and your Father,
 to my God and your God.'"
Mary went and announced to the disciples,
 "I have seen the Lord,"
 and then reported what he had told her. ✛

WEDNESDAY, APRIL 12
WEDNESDAY WITHIN THE OCTAVE OF EASTER

† *Acts of the Apostles 3:1-10*
What I do have I give you: in the name of the Lord Jesus, rise and walk.

Peter and John were going up to the temple area
 for the three o'clock hour of prayer.
And a man crippled from birth was carried
 and placed at the gate of the temple called "the Beautiful Gate"
 every day

to beg for alms from the people who entered the temple.
When he saw Peter and John about to go into the temple,
  he asked for alms.
But Peter looked intently at him, as did John,
  and said, "Look at us."
He paid attention to them, expecting to receive something from
    them.
Peter said, "I have neither silver nor gold,
  but what I do have I give you:
  in the name of Jesus Christ the Nazorean, rise and walk."
Then Peter took him by the right hand and raised him up,
  and immediately his feet and ankles grew strong.
He leaped up, stood, and walked around,
  and went into the temple with them,
  walking and jumping and praising God.
When all the people saw him walking and praising God,
  they recognized him as the one
  who used to sit begging at the Beautiful Gate of the temple,
  and they were filled with amazement and astonishment
  at what had happened to him. ✚

  Psalm 105:1-2, 3-4, 6-7, 8-9
R. (3b) **Rejoice, O hearts that seek the Lord.** *(or* **Alleluia.***)*
Give thanks to the L ORD, invoke his name;
  make known among the nations his deeds.
Sing to him, sing his praise,
  proclaim all his wondrous deeds. **R.**
Glory in his holy name;
  rejoice, O hearts that seek the L ORD!
Look to the L ORD in his strength;
  seek to serve him constantly. **R.**
You descendants of Abraham, his servants,
  sons of Jacob, his chosen ones!
He, the L ORD, is our God;
  throughout the earth his judgments prevail. **R.**
He remembers forever his covenant
  which he made binding for a thousand generations—
Which he entered into with Abraham
  and by his oath to Isaac. **R.**

  Psalm 118:24
R. Alleluia, alleluia.
This is the day the L ORD has made;
let us be glad and rejoice in it. **R.**

† *Luke 24:13-35*
They recognized Jesus in the breaking of the bread.

That very day, the first day of the week,
  two of Jesus' disciples were going
  to a village seven miles from Jerusalem called Emmaus,
  and they were conversing about all the things that had occurred.
And it happened that while they were conversing and debating,
  Jesus himself drew near and walked with them,
  but their eyes were prevented from recognizing him.
He asked them,
  "What are you discussing as you walk along?"
They stopped, looking downcast.
One of them, named Cleopas, said to him in reply,
  "Are you the only visitor to Jerusalem
  who does not know of the things
  that have taken place there in these days?"
And he replied to them, "What sort of things?"
They said to him,
  "The things that happened to Jesus the Nazarene,
  who was a prophet mighty in deed and word
  before God and all the people,
  how our chief priests and rulers both handed him over
  to a sentence of death and crucified him.
But we were hoping that he would be the one to redeem Israel;
  and besides all this,
  it is now the third day since this took place.
Some women from our group, however, have astounded us:
  they were at the tomb early in the morning
  and did not find his Body;
  they came back and reported
  that they had indeed seen a vision of angels
  who announced that he was alive.
Then some of those with us went to the tomb
  and found things just as the women had described,
  but him they did not see."
And he said to them, "Oh, how foolish you are!
How slow of heart to believe all that the prophets spoke!
Was it not necessary that the Christ should suffer these things
  and enter into his glory?"
Then beginning with Moses and all the prophets,
  he interpreted to them what referred to him
  in all the Scriptures.
As they approached the village to which they were going,
  he gave the impression that he was going on farther.

But they urged him, "Stay with us,
for it is nearly evening and the day is almost over."
So he went in to stay with them.
And it happened that, while he was with them at table,
he took bread, said the blessing,
broke it, and gave it to them.
With that their eyes were opened and they recognized him,
but he vanished from their sight.
Then they said to each other,
"Were not our hearts burning within us
while he spoke to us on the way and opened the Scriptures to us?"
So they set out at once and returned to Jerusalem
where they found gathered together
the Eleven and those with them who were saying,
"The Lord has truly been raised and has appeared to Simon!"
Then the two recounted what had taken place on the way
and how he was made known to them in the breaking of the bread. ✟

THURSDAY, APRIL 13
THURSDAY WITHIN THE OCTAVE OF EASTER

† Acts of the Apostles 3:11-26
The author of life you put to death, but God raised him from the dead.

As the crippled man who had been cured clung to Peter and John,
all the people hurried in amazement toward them
in the portico called "Solomon's Portico."
When Peter saw this, he addressed the people,
"You children of Israel, why are you amazed at this,
and why do you look so intently at us
as if we had made him walk by our own power or piety?
The God of Abraham, the God of Isaac, and the God of Jacob,
the God of our fathers, has glorified his servant Jesus
whom you handed over and denied in Pilate's presence,
when he had decided to release him.
You denied the Holy and Righteous One
and asked that a murderer be released to you.
The author of life you put to death,
but God raised him from the dead; of this we are witnesses.
And by faith in his name,
this man, whom you see and know, his name has made strong,
and the faith that comes through it
has given him this perfect health,
in the presence of all of you.
Now I know, brothers and sisters,
that you acted out of ignorance, just as your leaders did;

but God has thus brought to fulfillment
what he had announced beforehand
through the mouth of all the prophets,
that his Christ would suffer.
Repent, therefore, and be converted, that your sins may be wiped
away,
and that the Lord may grant you times of refreshment
and send you the Christ already appointed for you, Jesus,
whom heaven must receive until the times of universal restoration
of which God spoke through the mouth
of his holy prophets from of old.
For Moses said:

A prophet like me will the Lord, your God, raise up for you
from among your own kin;
to him you shall listen in all that he may say to you.
Everyone who does not listen to that prophet
will be cut off from the people.

"Moreover, all the prophets who spoke,
from Samuel and those afterwards, also announced these days.
You are the children of the prophets
and of the covenant that God made with your ancestors
when he said to Abraham,
In your offspring all the families of the earth shall be blessed.
For you first, God raised up his servant and sent him to bless you
by turning each of you from your evil ways." ✝

Psalm 8:2ab and 5, 6-7, 8-9

R. (2ab) **O Lord, our God, how wonderful your name in all the**
earth! *(or* **Alleluia.***)*

O LORD, our Lord,
how glorious is your name over all the earth!
What is man that you should be mindful of him,
or the son of man that you should care for him? **R.**
You have made him little less than the angels,
and crowned him with glory and honor.
You have given him rule over the works of your hands,
putting all things under his feet. **R.**
All sheep and oxen,
yes, and the beasts of the field,
The birds of the air, the fishes of the sea,
and whatever swims the paths of the seas. **R.**

Psalm 118:24

R. Alleluia, alleluia.

This is the day the LORD has made;
let us be glad and rejoice in it. **R.**

✟ *Luke 24:35-48*

*Thus it was written that the Christ would suffer and
rise from the dead on the third day.*

The disciples of Jesus recounted what had taken place along the
    way,
and how they had come to recognize him in the breaking of bread.

While they were still speaking about this,
    he stood in their midst and said to them,
    "Peace be with you."
But they were startled and terrified
    and thought that they were seeing a ghost.
Then he said to them, "Why are you troubled?
And why do questions arise in your hearts?
Look at my hands and my feet, that it is I myself.
Touch me and see, because a ghost does not have flesh and bones
    as you can see I have."
And as he said this,
    he showed them his hands and his feet.
While they were still incredulous for joy and were amazed,
    he asked them, "Have you anything here to eat?"
They gave him a piece of baked fish;
    he took it and ate it in front of them.

He said to them,
    "These are my words that I spoke to you while I was still with you,
    that everything written about me in the law of Moses
    and in the prophets and psalms must be fulfilled."
Then he opened their minds to understand the Scriptures.
And he said to them,
    "Thus it is written that the Christ would suffer
    and rise from the dead on the third day
    and that repentance, for the forgiveness of sins,
    would be preached in his name
    to all the nations, beginning from Jerusalem.
You are witnesses of these things." ✟

FRIDAY, APRIL 14
FRIDAY WITHIN THE OCTAVE OF EASTER

† *Acts of the Apostles 4:1-12*
There is no salvation through anyone else.

After the crippled man had been cured,
  while Peter and John were still speaking to the people,
  the priests, the captain of the temple guard,
  and the Sadducees confronted them,
  disturbed that they were teaching the people
  and proclaiming in Jesus the resurrection of the dead.
They laid hands on Peter and John
  and put them in custody until the next day,
  since it was already evening.
But many of those who heard the word came to believe
  and the number of men grew to about five thousand.

On the next day, their leaders, elders, and scribes
  were assembled in Jerusalem, with Annas the high priest,
  Caiaphas, John, Alexander,
  and all who were of the high-priestly class.
They brought them into their presence and questioned them,
  "By what power or by what name have you done this?"
Then Peter, filled with the Holy Spirit, answered them,
  "Leaders of the people and elders:
  If we are being examined today
  about a good deed done to a cripple,
  namely, by what means he was saved,
  then all of you and all the people of Israel should know
  that it was in the name of Jesus Christ the Nazorean
  whom you crucified, whom God raised from the dead;
  in his name this man stands before you healed.
He is *the stone rejected by you, the builders,*
  which has become the cornerstone.
There is no salvation through anyone else,
  nor is there any other name under heaven
  given to the human race by which we are to be saved." ✛

Psalm 118:1-2 and 4, 22-24, 25-27a
**R. (22) The stone rejected by the builders has become the
  cornerstone.** *(or Alleluia.)*
Give thanks to the LORD, for he is good,
  for his mercy endures forever.
Let the house of Israel say,
  "His mercy endures forever."

Let those who fear the Lord say,
  "His mercy endures forever." **R.**
The stone which the builders rejected
  has become the cornerstone.
By the Lord has this been done;
  it is wonderful in our eyes.
This is the day the Lord has made;
  let us be glad and rejoice in it. **R.**
O Lord, grant salvation!
  O Lord, grant prosperity!
Blessed is he who comes in the name of the Lord;
  we bless you from the house of the Lord.
  The Lord is God, and he has given us light. **R.**

Psalm 118:24
R. Alleluia, alleluia.
This is the day the Lord has made;
let us be glad and rejoice in it. **R.**

† *John 21:1-14*

*Jesus came over and took the bread and gave it to them,
and in like manner the fish.*

Jesus revealed himself again to his disciples at the Sea of Tiberias.
He revealed himself in this way.
Together were Simon Peter, Thomas called Didymus,
  Nathanael from Cana in Galilee,
  Zebedee's sons, and two others of his disciples.
Simon Peter said to them, "I am going fishing."
They said to him, "We also will come with you."
So they went out and got into the boat,
  but that night they caught nothing.
When it was already dawn, Jesus was standing on the shore;
  but the disciples did not realize that it was Jesus.
Jesus said to them, "Children, have you caught anything to eat?"
They answered him, "No."
So he said to them, "Cast the net over the right side of the boat
  and you will find something."
So they cast it, and were not able to pull it in
  because of the number of fish.
So the disciple whom Jesus loved said to Peter, "It is the Lord."
When Simon Peter heard that it was the Lord,
  he tucked in his garment, for he was lightly clad,
  and jumped into the sea.
The other disciples came in the boat,
  for they were not far from shore, only about a hundred yards,

dragging the net with the fish.
When they climbed out on shore,
   they saw a charcoal fire with fish on it and bread.
Jesus said to them, "Bring some of the fish you just caught."
So Simon Peter went over and dragged the net ashore
   full of one hundred fifty-three large fish.
Even though there were so many, the net was not torn.
Jesus said to them, "Come, have breakfast."
And none of the disciples dared to ask him, "Who are you?"
   because they realized it was the Lord.
Jesus came over and took the bread and gave it to them,
   and in like manner the fish.
This was now the third time Jesus was revealed to his disciples
   after being raised from the dead. ✛

SATURDAY, APRIL 15
SATURDAY WITHIN THE OCTAVE OF EASTER

✝ *Acts of the Apostles 4:13-21*
It is impossible for us not to speak about what we have seen and heard.

Observing the boldness of Peter and John
   and perceiving them to be uneducated, ordinary men,
   the leaders, elders, and scribes were amazed,
   and they recognized them as the companions of Jesus.
Then when they saw the man who had been cured standing there
      with them,
   they could say nothing in reply.
So they ordered them to leave the Sanhedrin,
   and conferred with one another, saying,
   "What are we to do with these men?
Everyone living in Jerusalem knows that a remarkable sign
   was done through them, and we cannot deny it.
But so that it may not be spread any further among the people,
   let us give them a stern warning
   never again to speak to anyone in this name."

So they called them back
   and ordered them not to speak or teach at all in the name of Jesus.
Peter and John, however, said to them in reply,
   "Whether it is right in the sight of God
   for us to obey you rather than God, you be the judges.
It is impossible for us not to speak about what we have seen and
      heard."
After threatening them further,
   they released them,

finding no way to punish them,
on account of the people who were all praising God
for what had happened. ✛

Psalm 118:1 and 14-15ab, 16-18, 19-21
R. (21a) **I will give thanks to you, for you have answered me.**
(or **Alleluia.***)*
Give thanks to the LORD, for he is good,
  for his mercy endures forever.
My strength and my courage is the LORD,
  and he has been my savior.
The joyful shout of victory
  in the tents of the just. **R.**
"The right hand of the LORD is exalted;
  the right hand of the LORD has struck with power."
I shall not die, but live,
  and declare the works of the LORD.
Though the LORD has indeed chastised me,
  yet he has not delivered me to death. **R.**
Open to me the gates of justice;
  I will enter them and give thanks to the LORD.
This is the gate of the LORD;
  the just shall enter it.
I will give thanks to you, for you have answered me
  and have been my savior. **R.**

Psalm 118:24
R. Alleluia, alleluia.
This is the day the LORD has made;
let us be glad and rejoice in it. **R.**

† *Mark 16:9-15*
Go into the whole world and proclaim the Gospel to every creature.

When Jesus had risen, early on the first day of the week,
  he appeared first to Mary Magdalene,
  out of whom he had driven seven demons.
She went and told his companions who were mourning and weeping.
When they heard that he was alive
  and had been seen by her, they did not believe.

After this he appeared in another form
  to two of them walking along on their way to the country.
They returned and told the others;
  but they did not believe them either.

But later, as the Eleven were at table, he appeared to them
  and rebuked them for their unbelief and hardness of heart

because they had not believed those
　who saw him after he had been raised.
He said to them, "Go into the whole world
　and proclaim the Gospel to every creature." ✛

SUNDAY, APRIL 16
SECOND SUNDAY OF EASTER (OR SUNDAY OF DIVINE MERCY)

† *Acts of the Apostles 2:42-47*
All who believed were together and had all things in common.

They devoted themselves
　to the teaching of the apostles and to the communal life,
　to the breaking of bread and to the prayers.
Awe came upon everyone,
　and many wonders and signs were done through the apostles.
All who believed were together and had all things in common;
　they would sell their property and possessions
　and divide them among all according to each one's need.
Every day they devoted themselves
　to meeting together in the temple area
　and to breaking bread in their homes.
They ate their meals with exultation and sincerity of heart,
　praising God and enjoying favor with all the people.
And every day the Lord added to their number those who were being
　saved. ✛

Psalm 118:2-4, 13-15, 22-24

R. (1) **Give thanks to the Lord, for he is good, his love is everlasting.** *(or* **Alleluia.***)*

Let the house of Israel say,
　"His mercy endures forever."
Let the house of Aaron say,
　"His mercy endures forever."
Let those who fear the LORD say,
　"His mercy endures forever." **R.**
I was hard pressed and was falling,
　but the LORD helped me.
My strength and my courage is the LORD,
　and he has been my savior.
The joyful shout of victory
　in the tents of the just. **R.**
The stone which the builders rejected
　has become the cornerstone.
By the LORD has this been done;
　it is wonderful in our eyes.

This is the day the LORD has made;
  let us be glad and rejoice in it. **R.**

† *1 Peter 1:3-9*
*God has given us new birth to a living hope through
the resurrection of Jesus Christ from the dead.*

Blessed be the God and Father of our Lord Jesus Christ,
  who in his great mercy gave us a new birth to a living hope
  through the resurrection of Jesus Christ from the dead,
  to an inheritance that is imperishable, undefiled, and unfading,
  kept in heaven for you
  who by the power of God are safeguarded through faith,
  to a salvation that is ready to be revealed in the final time.
In this you rejoice, although now for a little while
  you may have to suffer through various trials,
  so that the genuineness of your faith,
  more precious than gold that is perishable even though tested by
      fire,
  may prove to be for praise, glory, and honor
  at the revelation of Jesus Christ.
Although you have not seen him you love him;
  even though you do not see him now yet believe in him,
  you rejoice with an indescribable and glorious joy,
  as you attain the goal of your faith, the salvation of your souls. ✛

John 20:29
R. Alleluia, alleluia.
You believe in me, Thomas, because you have seen me, says the Lord;
blessed are they who have not seen me, but still believe! **R.**

† *John 20:19-31*
Eight days later Jesus came and stood in their midst.

On the evening of that first day of the week,
  when the doors were locked, where the disciples were,
  for fear of the Jews,
  Jesus came and stood in their midst
  and said to them, "Peace be with you."
When he had said this, he showed them his hands and his side.
The disciples rejoiced when they saw the Lord.
Jesus said to them again, "Peace be with you.
As the Father has sent me, so I send you."
And when he had said this, he breathed on them and said to them,
  "Receive the Holy Spirit.
Whose sins you forgive are forgiven them,
  and whose sins you retain are retained."

Thomas, called Didymus, one of the Twelve,
   was not with them when Jesus came.
So the other disciples said to him, "We have seen the Lord."
But he said to them,
   "Unless I see the mark of the nails in his hands
   and put my finger into the nailmarks
   and put my hand into his side, I will not believe."

Now a week later his disciples were again inside
   and Thomas was with them.
Jesus came, although the doors were locked,
   and stood in their midst and said, "Peace be with you."
Then he said to Thomas, "Put your finger here and see my hands,
   and bring your hand and put it into my side,
   and do not be unbelieving, but believe."
Thomas answered and said to him, "My Lord and my God!"
Jesus said to him, "Have you come to believe because you have seen
      me?
Blessed are those who have not seen and have believed."

Now Jesus did many other signs in the presence of his disciples
   that are not written in this book.
But these are written that you may come to believe
   that Jesus is the Christ, the Son of God,
   and that through this belief you may have life in his name. ✝

MONDAY, APRIL 17
EASTER WEEKDAY

✝ *Acts of the Apostles 4:23-31*
*As they prayed, they were all filled with the Holy Spirit and
continued to speak the word of God with boldness.*

After their release Peter and John went back to their own people
   and reported what the chief priests and elders had told them.
And when they heard it,
   they raised their voices to God with one accord
   and said, "Sovereign Lord, maker of heaven and earth
   and the sea and all that is in them,
   you said by the Holy Spirit
   through the mouth of our father David, your servant:

*Why did the Gentiles rage
   and the peoples entertain folly?
The kings of the earth took their stand
   and the princes gathered together
   against the Lord and against his anointed.*

Indeed they gathered in this city
   against your holy servant Jesus whom you anointed,
   Herod and Pontius Pilate,
   together with the Gentiles and the peoples of Israel,
   to do what your hand and your will
   had long ago planned to take place.
And now, Lord, take note of their threats,
   and enable your servants to speak your word
   with all boldness, as you stretch forth your hand to heal,
   and signs and wonders are done
   through the name of your holy servant Jesus."
As they prayed, the place where they were gathered shook,
   and they were all filled with the Holy Spirit
   and continued to speak the word of God with boldness. ✣

   Psalm 2:1-3, 4-7a, 7b-9
R. (see 11d) **Blessed are all who take refuge in the Lord.**
   (or **Alleluia.***)*
Why do the nations rage
   and the peoples utter folly?
The kings of the earth rise up,
   and the princes conspire together
   against the LORD and against his anointed:
"Let us break their fetters
   and cast their bonds from us!" **R.**
He who is throned in heaven laughs;
   the LORD derides them.
Then in anger he speaks to them;
   he terrifies them in his wrath:
"I myself have set up my king
   on Zion, my holy mountain."
I will proclaim the decree of the LORD. **R.**
The LORD said to me, "You are my Son;
   this day I have begotten you.
Ask of me and I will give you
   the nations for an inheritance
   and the ends of the earth for your possession.
You shall rule them with an iron rod;
   you shall shatter them like an earthen dish." **R.**

   Colossians 3:1
R. Alleluia, alleluia.
If then you were raised with Christ,
seek what is above,
where Christ is seated at the right hand of God. **R.**

† *John 3:1-8*
No one can enter the Kingdom of God
without being born of water and Spirit.

There was a Pharisee named Nicodemus, a ruler of the Jews.
He came to Jesus at night and said to him,
  "Rabbi, we know that you are a teacher who has come from God,
  for no one can do these signs that you are doing
  unless God is with him."
Jesus answered and said to him,
  "Amen, amen, I say to you,
  unless one is born from above, he cannot see the Kingdom of God."
Nicodemus said to him,
  "How can a man once grown old be born again?
Surely he cannot reenter his mother's womb and be born again, can
    he?"
Jesus answered,
  "Amen, amen, I say to you,
  unless one is born of water and Spirit
  he cannot enter the Kingdom of God.
What is born of flesh is flesh
  and what is born of spirit is spirit.
Do not be amazed that I told you,
  'You must be born from above.'
The wind blows where it wills,
  and you can hear the sound it makes,
  but you do not know where it comes from or where it goes;
  so it is with everyone who is born of the Spirit." ✛

TUESDAY, APRIL 18
EASTER WEEKDAY

† *Acts of the Apostles 4:32-37*
The community of believers was of one heart and mind.

The community of believers was of one heart and mind,
  and no one claimed that any of his possessions was his own,
  but they had everything in common.
With great power the Apostles bore witness
  to the resurrection of the Lord Jesus,
  and great favor was accorded them all.
There was no needy person among them,
  for those who owned property or houses would sell them,
  bring the proceeds of the sale,
  and put them at the feet of the Apostles,
  and they were distributed to each according to need.

Thus Joseph, also named by the Apostles Barnabas
  (which is translated "son of encouragement"),
  a Levite, a Cypriot by birth,
  sold a piece of property that he owned,
  then brought the money and put it at the feet of the Apostles. ✛

  Psalm 93:1ab, 1cd-2, 5
R. (1a) The Lord is king; he is robed in majesty. *(or* **Alleluia.***)*
The Lord is king, in splendor robed;
  robed is the Lord and girt about with strength. **R.**
And he has made the world firm,
  not to be moved.
Your throne stands firm from of old;
  from everlasting you are, O Lord. **R.**
Your decrees are worthy of trust indeed:
  holiness befits your house,
  O Lord, for length of days. **R.**

  John 3:14-15
R. Alleluia, alleluia.
The Son of Man must be lifted up,
so that everyone who believes in him
may have eternal life. **R.**

† *John 3:7b-15*

*No one has gone up to heaven except the one who
has come down from heaven, the Son of Man.*

Jesus said to Nicodemus:
  "'You must be born from above.'
The wind blows where it wills, and you can hear the sound it makes,
  but you do not know where it comes from or where it goes;
  so it is with everyone who is born of the Spirit."
Nicodemus answered and said to him,
  "How can this happen?"
Jesus answered and said to him,
  "You are the teacher of Israel and you do not understand this?
Amen, amen, I say to you,
  we speak of what we know and we testify to what we have seen,
  but you people do not accept our testimony.
If I tell you about earthly things and you do not believe,
  how will you believe if I tell you about heavenly things?
No one has gone up to heaven
  except the one who has come down from heaven, the Son of Man.
And just as Moses lifted up the serpent in the desert,
  so must the Son of Man be lifted up,
  so that everyone who believes in him may have eternal life." ✛

WEDNESDAY, APRIL 19
EASTER WEEKDAY

†Acts of the Apostles 5:17-26
*The men whom you put in prison are in the temple area
and are teaching the people.*

The high priest rose up and all his companions,
   that is, the party of the Sadducees,
   and, filled with jealousy,
   laid hands upon the Apostles and put them in the public jail.
But during the night, the angel of the Lord opened the doors of the
      prison,
   led them out, and said,
   "Go and take your place in the temple area,
   and tell the people everything about this life."
When they heard this,
   they went to the temple early in the morning and taught.
When the high priest and his companions arrived,
   they convened the Sanhedrin,
   the full senate of the children of Israel,
   and sent to the jail to have them brought in.
But the court officers who went did not find them in the prison,
   so they came back and reported,
   "We found the jail securely locked
   and the guards stationed outside the doors,
   but when we opened them, we found no one inside."
When the captain of the temple guard and the chief priests heard
      this report,
   they were at a loss about them,
   as to what this would come to.
Then someone came in and reported to them,
   "The men whom you put in prison are in the temple area
   and are teaching the people."
Then the captain and the court officers went and brought them,
   but without force,
   because they were afraid of being stoned by the people. ✛

Psalm 34:2-3, 4-5, 6-7, 8-9
R. (7a) **The Lord hears the cry of the poor.** *(or* **Alleluia.***)*
I will bless the LORD at all times;
   his praise shall be ever in my mouth.
Let my soul glory in the LORD;
   the lowly will hear me and be glad. **R.**
Glorify the LORD with me,
   let us together extol his name.

I sought the LORD, and he answered me
and delivered me from all my fears. **R.**
Look to him that you may be radiant with joy,
and your faces may not blush with shame.
When the poor one called out, the LORD heard,
and from all his distress he saved him. **R.**
The angel of the LORD encamps
around those who fear him, and delivers them.
Taste and see how good the LORD is;
blessed the man who takes refuge in him. **R.**

John 3:16

R. Alleluia, alleluia.
God so loved the world that he gave his only-begotten Son,
so that everyone who believes in him might have eternal life. **R.**

† *John 3:16-21*
God sent his Son that the world might be saved through him.

God so loved the world that he gave his only-begotten Son,
so that everyone who believes in him might not perish
but might have eternal life.
For God did not send his Son into the world to condemn the world,
but that the world might be saved through him.
Whoever believes in him will not be condemned,
but whoever does not believe has already been condemned,
because he has not believed in the name of the only-begotten Son
of God.
And this is the verdict,
that the light came into the world,
but people preferred darkness to light,
because their works were evil.
For everyone who does wicked things hates the light
and does not come toward the light,
so that his works might not be exposed.
But whoever lives the truth comes to the light,
so that his works may be clearly seen as done in God. ✦

THURSDAY, APRIL 20
EASTER WEEKDAY

† *Acts of the Apostles 5:27-33*
We are witnesses of these words, as is the Holy Spirit.

When the court officers had brought the Apostles in
and made them stand before the Sanhedrin,
the high priest questioned them,
"We gave you strict orders did we not,

to stop teaching in that name.
Yet you have filled Jerusalem with your teaching
  and want to bring this man's blood upon us."
But Peter and the Apostles said in reply,
  "We must obey God rather than men.
The God of our ancestors raised Jesus,
  though you had him killed by hanging him on a tree.
God exalted him at his right hand as leader and savior
  to grant Israel repentance and forgiveness of sins.
We are witnesses of these things,
  as is the Holy Spirit whom God has given to those who obey him."

When they heard this,
  they became infuriated and wanted to put them to death. ✛

Psalm 34:2 and 9, 17-18, 19-20
R. (7a) **The Lord hears the cry of the poor.** (*or* **Alleluia.***)*
I will bless the LORD at all times;
  his praise shall be ever in my mouth.
Taste and see how good the LORD is;
  blessed the man who takes refuge in him. **R.**
The LORD confronts the evildoers,
  to destroy remembrance of them from the earth.
When the just cry out, the LORD hears them,
  and from all their distress he rescues them. **R.**
The LORD is close to the brokenhearted;
  and those who are crushed in spirit he saves.
Many are the troubles of the just man,
  but out of them all the LORD delivers him. **R.**

John 20:29
R. Alleluia, alleluia.
You believe in me, Thomas, because you have seen me, says the
    Lord;
blessed are those who have not seen, but still believe! **R.**

† *John 3:31-36*
The Father loves the Son and has given everything over to him.

The one who comes from above is above all.
The one who is of the earth is earthly and speaks of earthly things.
But the one who comes from heaven is above all.
He testifies to what he has seen and heard,
  but no one accepts his testimony.
Whoever does accept his testimony certifies that God is trustworthy.
For the one whom God sent speaks the words of God.
He does not ration his gift of the Spirit.

The Father loves the Son and has given everything over to him.
Whoever believes in the Son has eternal life,
  but whoever disobeys the Son will not see life,
  but the wrath of God remains upon him. ✛

FRIDAY, APRIL 21
EASTER WEEKDAY, ST. ANSELM

† *Acts of the Apostles 5:34-42*
*The Apostles went out rejoicing that they had been found worthy
to suffer dishonor for the sake of the name.*

A Pharisee in the Sanhedrin named Gamaliel,
  a teacher of the law, respected by all the people,
  stood up, ordered the Apostles to be put outside for a short time,
  and said to the Sanhedrin, "Fellow children of Israel,
  be careful what you are about to do to these men.
Some time ago, Theudas appeared, claiming to be someone important,
  and about four hundred men joined him, but he was killed,
  and all those who were loyal to him
  were disbanded and came to nothing.
After him came Judas the Galilean at the time of the census.
He also drew people after him,
  but he too perished and all who were loyal to him were scattered.
So now I tell you,
  have nothing to do with these men, and let them go.
For if this endeavor or this activity is of human origin,
  it will destroy itself.
But if it comes from God, you will not be able to destroy them;
  you may even find yourselves fighting against God."
They were persuaded by him.
After recalling the Apostles, they had them flogged,
  ordered them to stop speaking in the name of Jesus,
  and dismissed them.
So they left the presence of the Sanhedrin,
  rejoicing that they had been found worthy
  to suffer dishonor for the sake of the name.
And all day long, both at the temple and in their homes,
  they did not stop teaching and proclaiming the Christ, Jesus. ✛

  Psalm 27:1, 4, 13-14
R. (see 4abc) **One thing I seek: to dwell in the house of the
    Lord.** *(or* **Alleluia.***)*
The LORD is my light and my salvation;
  whom should I fear?
The LORD is my life's refuge;

of whom should I be afraid? **R.**
One thing I ask of the LORD;
  this I seek:
To dwell in the house of the LORD
  all the days of my life,
That I may gaze on the loveliness of the LORD
  and contemplate his temple. **R.**
I believe that I shall see the bounty of the LORD
  in the land of the living.
Wait for the LORD with courage;
  be stouthearted, and wait for the LORD. **R.**

   Matthew 4:4b
R. Alleluia, alleluia.
One does not live on bread alone,
but on every word that comes forth from the mouth of God. **R.**

† *John 6:1-15*

Jesus distributed to those who were reclining as much as they wanted.

Jesus went across the Sea of Galilee.
A large crowd followed him,
  because they saw the signs he was performing on the sick.
Jesus went up on the mountain,
  and there he sat down with his disciples.
The Jewish feast of Passover was near.
When Jesus raised his eyes and saw that a large crowd was coming
      to him,
  he said to Philip, "Where can we buy enough food for them to eat?"
He said this to test him,
  because he himself knew what he was going to do.
Philip answered him,
  "Two hundred days' wages worth of food would not be enough
  for each of them to have a little."
One of his disciples,
  Andrew, the brother of Simon Peter, said to him,
  "There is a boy here who has five barley loaves and two fish;
  but what good are these for so many?"
Jesus said, "Have the people recline."
Now there was a great deal of grass in that place.
So the men reclined, about five thousand in number.
Then Jesus took the loaves, gave thanks,
  and distributed them to those who were reclining,
  and also as much of the fish as they wanted.
When they had had their fill, he said to his disciples,
  "Gather the fragments left over,

so that nothing will be wasted."
So they collected them,
  and filled twelve wicker baskets with fragments
  from the five barley loaves that had been more than they could eat.
When the people saw the sign he had done, they said,
  "This is truly the Prophet, the one who is to come into the world."
Since Jesus knew that they were going to come and carry him off
  to make him king,
  he withdrew again to the mountain alone. ✣

SATURDAY, APRIL 22
EASTER WEEKDAY

† *Acts of the Apostles 6:1-7*
They chose seven men filled with the Holy Spirit.

As the number of disciples continued to grow,
  the Hellenists complained against the Hebrews
  because their widows
  were being neglected in the daily distribution.
So the Twelve called together the community of the disciples and
    said,
  "It is not right for us to neglect the word of God to serve at table.
Brothers, select from among you seven reputable men,
  filled with the Spirit and wisdom,
  whom we shall appoint to this task,
  whereas we shall devote ourselves to prayer
  and to the ministry of the word."
The proposal was acceptable to the whole community,
  so they chose Stephen, a man filled with faith and the Holy Spirit,
  also Philip, Prochorus, Nicanor, Timon, Parmenas,
  and Nicholas of Antioch, a convert to Judaism.
They presented these men to the Apostles
  who prayed and laid hands on them.
The word of God continued to spread,
  and the number of the disciples in Jerusalem increased greatly;
  even a large group of priests were becoming obedient to the faith. ✣

Psalm 33:1-2, 4-5, 18-19

R. (22) **Lord, let your mercy be on us, as we place our trust in you.** *(or* **Alleluia.***)*
Exult, you just, in the LORD;
  praise from the upright is fitting.
Give thanks to the LORD on the harp;
  with the ten-stringed lyre chant his praises. **R.**
Upright is the word of the LORD,

and all his works are trustworthy.
He loves justice and right;
   of the kindness of the L ORD the earth is full. **R.**
See, the eyes of the L ORD are upon those who fear him,
   upon those who hope for his kindness,
To deliver them from death
   and preserve them in spite of famine. **R.**

R. Alleluia, alleluia.
Christ is risen, who made all things;
he has shown mercy on all people. **R.**

† *John 6:16-21*
They saw Jesus, walking on the sea.

When it was evening, the disciples of Jesus went down to the sea,
   embarked in a boat, and went across the sea to Capernaum.
It had already grown dark, and Jesus had not yet come to them.
The sea was stirred up because a strong wind was blowing.
When they had rowed about three or four miles,
   they saw Jesus walking on the sea and coming near the boat,
   and they began to be afraid.
But he said to them, "It is I. Do not be afraid."
They wanted to take him into the boat,
   but the boat immediately arrived at the shore
   to which they were heading. ✢

SUNDAY, APRIL 23
THIRD SUNDAY OF EASTER

† *Acts of the Apostles 2:14, 22-33*
It was impossible for Jesus to be held by death.

Then Peter stood up with the Eleven,
   raised his voice, and proclaimed:
   "You who are Jews, indeed all of you staying in Jerusalem.
Let this be known to you, and listen to my words.
You who are Israelites, hear these words.
Jesus the Nazorean was a man commended to you by God
   with mighty deeds, wonders, and signs,
     which God worked through him in your midst, as you yourselves
      know.
This man, delivered up by the set plan and foreknowledge of God,
   you killed, using lawless men to crucify him.
But God raised him up, releasing him from the throes of death,
   because it was impossible for him to be held by it.
For David says of him:

I saw the Lord ever before me,
with him at my right hand I shall not be disturbed.
Therefore my heart has been glad and my tongue has exulted;
my flesh, too, will dwell in hope,
because you will not abandon my soul to the netherworld,
nor will you suffer your holy one to see corruption.
You have made known to me the paths of life;
you will fill me with joy in your presence.

"My brothers, one can confidently say to you
   about the patriarch David that he died and was buried,
   and his tomb is in our midst to this day.
But since he was a prophet and knew that God had sworn an oath to
      him
   that he would set one of his descendants upon his throne,
   he foresaw and spoke of the resurrection of the Christ,
   that neither was he abandoned to the netherworld
   nor did his flesh see corruption.
God raised this Jesus;
   of this we are all witnesses.
Exalted at the right hand of God,
   he received the promise of the Holy Spirit from the Father
   and poured him forth, as you see and hear." ✛

Psalm 16:1b-2a and 5, 7-8, 9-10, 11
R. (11a) **Lord, you will show us the path of life.** *(or* **Alleluia.***)*
Keep me, O God, for in you I take refuge;
   I say to the LORD, "My Lord are you."
O LORD, my allotted portion and my cup,
   you it is who hold fast my lot. **R.**
I bless the LORD who counsels me;
   even in the night my heart exhorts me.
I set the LORD ever before me;
   with him at my right hand I shall not be disturbed. **R.**
Therefore my heart is glad and my soul rejoices,
   my body, too, abides in confidence;
because you will not abandon my soul to the netherworld,
   nor will you suffer your faithful one to undergo corruption. **R.**
You will show me the path to life,
   abounding joy in your presence,
   the delights at your right hand forever. **R.**

† 1 Peter 1:17-21
You were saved with the precious Blood of Christ,
as with that of a spotless, unblemished lamb.

Beloved:
If you invoke as Father him who judges impartially
   according to each one's works,
     conduct yourselves with reverence during the time of your
       sojourning,
   realizing that you were ransomed from your futile conduct,
   handed on by your ancestors,
   not with perishable things like silver or gold
   but with the precious blood of Christ
   as of a spotless unblemished lamb.

He was known before the foundation of the world
   but revealed in the final time for you,
   who through him believe in God
   who raised him from the dead and gave him glory,
   so that your faith and hope are in God. ✛

   See Luke 24:32
R. Alleluia, alleluia.
Lord Jesus, open the Scriptures to us;
make our hearts burn while you speak to us. **R.**

† Luke 24:13-35
They recognized Jesus in the breaking of bread.

That very day, the first day of the week,
   two of Jesus' disciples were going
   to a village seven miles from Jerusalem called Emmaus,
   and they were conversing about all the things that had occurred.
And it happened that while they were conversing and debating,
   Jesus himself drew near and walked with them,
   but their eyes were prevented from recognizing him.
He asked them,
   "What are you discussing as you walk along?"
They stopped, looking downcast.
One of them, named Cleopas, said to him in reply,
   "Are you the only visitor to Jerusalem
   who does not know of the things
   that have taken place there in these days?"
And he replied to them, "What sort of things?"
They said to him,
   "The things that happened to Jesus the Nazarene,
   who was a prophet mighty in deed and word

before God and all the people,
how our chief priests and rulers both handed him over
to a sentence of death and crucified him.
But we were hoping that he would be the one to redeem Israel;
and besides all this,
it is now the third day since this took place.
Some women from our group, however, have astounded us:
they were at the tomb early in the morning
and did not find his body;
they came back and reported
that they had indeed seen a vision of angels
who announced that he was alive.
Then some of those with us went to the tomb
and found things just as the women had described,
but him they did not see."
And he said to them, "Oh, how foolish you are!
How slow of heart to believe all that the prophets spoke!
Was it not necessary that the Christ should suffer these things
and enter into his glory?"
Then beginning with Moses and all the prophets,
he interpreted to them what referred to him
in all the Scriptures.
As they approached the village to which they were going,
he gave the impression that he was going on farther.
But they urged him, "Stay with us,
for it is nearly evening and the day is almost over."
So he went in to stay with them.
And it happened that, while he was with them at table,
he took bread, said the blessing,
broke it, and gave it to them.
With that their eyes were opened and they recognized him,
but he vanished from their sight.
Then they said to each other,
"Were not our hearts burning within us
while he spoke to us on the way and opened the Scriptures to us?"
So they set out at once and returned to Jerusalem
where they found gathered together
the eleven and those with them who were saying,
"The Lord has truly been raised and has appeared to Simon!"
Then the two recounted
what had taken place on the way
and how he was made known to them in the breaking of bread. ✛

MONDAY, APRIL 24
Easter Weekday, St. Fidelis of Sigmaringen

† *Acts of the Apostles 6:8-15*
They could not withstand the wisdom and the Spirit with which he spoke.

Stephen, filled with grace and power,
 was working great wonders and signs among the people.
Certain members of the so-called Synagogue of Freedmen,
 Cyreneans, and Alexandrians,
 and people from Cilicia and Asia,
 came forward and debated with Stephen,
 but they could not withstand the wisdom and the Spirit with
  which he spoke.
Then they instigated some men to say,
 "We have heard him speaking blasphemous words
 against Moses and God."
They stirred up the people, the elders, and the scribes,
 accosted him, seized him,
 and brought him before the Sanhedrin.
They presented false witnesses who testified,
 "This man never stops saying things against this holy place and
  the law.
For we have heard him claim
 that this Jesus the Nazorean will destroy this place
 and change the customs that Moses handed down to us."
All those who sat in the Sanhedrin looked intently at him
 and saw that his face was like the face of an angel. ✦

Psalm 119:23-24, 26-27, 29-30
R. (1ab) **Blessed are they who follow the law of the Lord!**
 (*or* **Alleluia.***)*
Though princes meet and talk against me,
 your servant meditates on your statutes.
Yes, your decrees are my delight;
 they are my counselors. **R.**
I declared my ways, and you answered me;
 teach me your statutes.
Make me understand the way of your precepts,
 and I will meditate on your wondrous deeds. **R.**
Remove from me the way of falsehood,
 and favor me with your law.
The way of truth I have chosen;
 I have set your ordinances before me. **R.**

Matthew 4:4b

R. Alleluia, alleluia.

One does not live on bread alone
but on every word that comes forth from the mouth of God. **R.**

✝ John 6:22-29

Do not work for food that perishes but for food that endures for eternal life.

[**A**fter Jesus had fed the five thousand men, his disciples saw him
    walking on the sea.]
The next day, the crowd that remained across the sea
    saw that there had been only one boat there,
    and that Jesus had not gone along with his disciples in the boat,
    but only his disciples had left.
Other boats came from Tiberias
    near the place where they had eaten the bread
    when the Lord gave thanks.
When the crowd saw that neither Jesus nor his disciples were there,
    they themselves got into boats
    and came to Capernaum looking for Jesus.
And when they found him across the sea they said to him,
    "Rabbi, when did you get here?"
Jesus answered them and said,
    "Amen, amen, I say to you, you are looking for me
    not because you saw signs
    but because you ate the loaves and were filled.
Do not work for food that perishes
    but for the food that endures for eternal life,
    which the Son of Man will give you.
For on him the Father, God, has set his seal."
So they said to him,
    "What can we do to accomplish the works of God?"
Jesus answered and said to them,
    "This is the work of God, that you believe in the one he sent." ✛

TUESDAY, APRIL 25
ST. MARK

✝ 1 Peter 5:5b-14

Mark, my son, sends you greetings.

Beloved:
Clothe yourselves with humility
    in your dealings with one another, for:

*God opposes the proud
    but bestows favor on the humble.*

So humble yourselves under the mighty hand of God,
   that he may exalt you in due time.
Cast all your worries upon him because he cares for you.

Be sober and vigilant.
Your opponent the Devil is prowling around like a roaring lion
   looking for someone to devour.
Resist him, steadfast in faith,
   knowing that your brothers and sisters throughout the world
   undergo the same sufferings.
The God of all grace
   who called you to his eternal glory through Christ Jesus
   will himself restore, confirm, strengthen, and establish you
   after you have suffered a little.
To him be dominion forever. Amen.

I write you this briefly through Silvanus,
   whom I consider a faithful brother,
   exhorting you and testifying that this is the true grace of God.
Remain firm in it.
The chosen one at Babylon sends you greeting, as does Mark, my son.
Greet one another with a loving kiss.
Peace to all of you who are in Christ. ✛

Psalm 89:2-3, 6-7, 16-17

R. (2) **For ever I will sing the goodness of the Lord.**
   (or **Alleluia.***)*

The favors of the LORD I will sing forever;
   through all generations my mouth shall proclaim your faithfulness.
For you have said, "My kindness is established forever";
   in heaven you have confirmed your faithfulness. **R.**
The heavens proclaim your wonders, O LORD,
   and your faithfulness, in the assembly of the holy ones.
For who in the skies can rank with the LORD?
   Who is like the LORD among the sons of God? **R.**
Blessed the people who know the joyful shout;
   in the light of your countenance, O LORD, they walk.
At your name they rejoice all the day,
   and through your justice they are exalted. **R.**

1 Corinthians 1:23a-24b

R. Alleluia, alleluia.
We proclaim Christ crucified;
he is the power of God and the wisdom of God. **R.**

✝ Mark 16:15-20
Proclaim the Gospel to every creature.

Jesus appeared to the Eleven and said to them:
"Go into the whole world
  and proclaim the Gospel to every creature.
Whoever believes and is baptized will be saved;
  whoever does not believe will be condemned.
These signs will accompany those who believe:
  in my name they will drive out demons,
  they will speak new languages.
They will pick up serpents with their hands,
  and if they drink any deadly thing, it will not harm them.
They will lay hands on the sick, and they will recover."

Then the Lord Jesus, after he spoke to them,
  was taken up into heaven
  and took his seat at the right hand of God.
But they went forth and preached everywhere,
  while the Lord worked with them
  and confirmed the word through accompanying signs. ✛

WEDNESDAY, APRIL 26
EASTER WEEKDAY

✝ Acts of the Apostles 8:1b-8
They went about preaching the word.

There broke out a severe persecution of the Church in Jerusalem,
  and all were scattered
  throughout the countryside of Judea and Samaria,
  except the Apostles.
Devout men buried Stephen and made a loud lament over him.
Saul, meanwhile, was trying to destroy the Church;
  entering house after house and dragging out men and women,
  he handed them over for imprisonment.

Now those who had been scattered went about preaching the word.
Thus Philip went down to the city of Samaria
  and proclaimed the Christ to them.
With one accord, the crowds paid attention to what was said by
    Philip
  when they heard it and saw the signs he was doing.
For unclean spirits, crying out in a loud voice,
  came out of many possessed people,
  and many paralyzed and crippled people were cured.
There was great joy in that city. ✛

Psalm 66:1b-3a, 4-5, 6-7a

R. (1) **Let all the earth cry out to God with joy.** *(or* **Alleluia.***)*

Shout joyfully to God, all the earth,
   sing praise to the glory of his name;
   proclaim his glorious praise.
Say to God, "How tremendous are your deeds!" **R.**
"Let all on earth worship and sing praise to you,
   sing praise to your name!"
Come and see the works of God,
   his tremendous deeds among the children of Adam. **R.**
He has changed the sea into dry land;
   through the river they passed on foot;
   therefore let us rejoice in him.
He rules by his might forever. **R.**

See John 6:40

R. Alleluia, alleluia.

Everyone who believes in the Son has eternal life,
and I shall raise him on the last day, says the Lord. **R.**

† *John 6:35-40*

*This is the will of my Father, that all
who see the Son may have eternal life.*

Jesus said to the crowds,
   "I am the bread of life;
   whoever comes to me will never hunger,
   and whoever believes in me will never thirst.
But I told you that although you have seen me,
   you do not believe.
Everything that the Father gives me will come to me,
   and I will not reject anyone who comes to me,
   because I came down from heaven not to do my own will
   but the will of the one who sent me.
And this is the will of the one who sent me,
   that I should not lose anything of what he gave me,
   but that I should raise it on the last day.
For this is the will of my Father,
   that everyone who sees the Son and believes in him
   may have eternal life,
   and I shall raise him on the last day." **✛**

THURSDAY, APRIL 27
Easter Weekday

✝ Acts of the Apostles 8:26-40
Look, there is water. What is to prevent my being baptized?

The angel of the Lord spoke to Philip,
  "Get up and head south on the road
  that goes down from Jerusalem to Gaza, the desert route."
So he got up and set out.
Now there was an Ethiopian eunuch,
  a court official of the Candace,
  that is, the queen of the Ethiopians,
  in charge of her entire treasury,
  who had come to Jerusalem to worship, and was returning home.
Seated in his chariot, he was reading the prophet Isaiah.
The Spirit said to Philip,
  "Go and join up with that chariot."
Philip ran up and heard him reading Isaiah the prophet and said,
  "Do you understand what you are reading?"
He replied,
  "How can I, unless someone instructs me?"
So he invited Philip to get in and sit with him.
This was the Scripture passage he was reading:

  Like a sheep he was led to the slaughter,
    and as a lamb before its shearer is silent,
      so he opened not his mouth.
  In his humiliation justice was denied him.
    Who will tell of his posterity?
      For his life is taken from the earth.

Then the eunuch said to Philip in reply,
  "I beg you, about whom is the prophet saying this?
About himself, or about someone else?"
Then Philip opened his mouth and, beginning with this Scripture
      passage,
  he proclaimed Jesus to him.
As they traveled along the road
  they came to some water,
  and the eunuch said, "Look, there is water.
What is to prevent my being baptized?"
Then he ordered the chariot to stop,
  and Philip and the eunuch both went down into the water,
  and he baptized him.
When they came out of the water,

the Spirit of the Lord snatched Philip away,
and the eunuch saw him no more,
but continued on his way rejoicing.
Philip came to Azotus, and went about proclaiming the good news
to all the towns until he reached Caesarea. ✛

Psalm 66:8-9, 16-17, 20
R. (1) Let all the earth cry out to God with joy. *(or* **Alleluia.***)*
Bless our God, you peoples,
loudly sound his praise;
He has given life to our souls,
and has not let our feet slip. **R.**
Hear now, all you who fear God, while I declare
what he has done for me.
When I appealed to him in words,
praise was on the tip of my tongue. **R.**
Blessed be God who refused me not
my prayer or his kindness! **R.**

John 6:51
R. Alleluia, alleluia.
I am the living bread that came down from heaven, says the Lord;
whoever eats this bread will live forever. **R.**

✝ *John 6:44-51*
I am the living bread that came down from heaven.

Jesus said to the crowds:
"No one can come to me unless the Father who sent me draw him,
and I will raise him on the last day.
It is written in the prophets:

They shall all be taught by God.

Everyone who listens to my Father and learns from him comes to me.
Not that anyone has seen the Father
except the one who is from God;
he has seen the Father.
Amen, amen, I say to you,
whoever believes has eternal life.
I am the bread of life.
Your ancestors ate the manna in the desert, but they died;
this is the bread that comes down from heaven
so that one may eat it and not die.
I am the living bread that came down from heaven;
whoever eats this bread will live forever;

and the bread that I will give
is my Flesh for the life of the world." ✝

FRIDAY, APRIL 28
Easter Weekday, St. Peter Chanel, St. Louis Grignion de Montfort

† Acts of the Apostles 9:1-20
*This man is a chosen instrument of mine
to carry my name before the Gentiles.*

Saul, still breathing murderous threats against the disciples of the
    Lord,
    went to the high priest and asked him
    for letters to the synagogues in Damascus, that,
    if he should find any men or women who belonged to the Way,
    he might bring them back to Jerusalem in chains.
On his journey, as he was nearing Damascus,
    a light from the sky suddenly flashed around him.
He fell to the ground and heard a voice saying to him,
    "Saul, Saul, why are you persecuting me?"
He said, "Who are you, sir?"
The reply came, "I am Jesus, whom you are persecuting.
Now get up and go into the city and you will be told what you must
    do."
The men who were traveling with him stood speechless,
    for they heard the voice but could see no one.
Saul got up from the ground,
    but when he opened his eyes he could see nothing;
    so they led him by the hand and brought him to Damascus.
For three days he was unable to see, and he neither ate nor drank.

There was a disciple in Damascus named Ananias,
    and the Lord said to him in a vision, "Ananias."
He answered, "Here I am, Lord."
The Lord said to him, "Get up and go to the street called Straight
    and ask at the house of Judas for a man from Tarsus named Saul.
He is there praying,
    and in a vision he has seen a man named Ananias
    come in and lay his hands on him,
    that he may regain his sight."
But Ananias replied,
    "Lord, I have heard from many sources about this man,
    what evil things he has done to your holy ones in Jerusalem.
And here he has authority from the chief priests
    to imprison all who call upon your name."
But the Lord said to him,

"Go, for this man is a chosen instrument of mine
    to carry my name before Gentiles, kings, and children of Israel,
    and I will show him what he will have to suffer for my name."
So Ananias went and entered the house;
    laying his hands on him, he said,
    "Saul, my brother, the Lord has sent me,
    Jesus who appeared to you on the way by which you came,
    that you may regain your sight and be filled with the Holy Spirit."
Immediately things like scales fell from his eyes
    and he regained his sight.
He got up and was baptized,
    and when he had eaten, he recovered his strength.

He stayed some days with the disciples in Damascus,
    and he began at once to proclaim Jesus in the synagogues,
    that he is the Son of God. ✛

Psalm 117:1bc, 2

R. (Mark 16:15) **Go out to all the world and tell the Good
    News.** *(or* **Alleluia.***)*
Praise the LORD, all you nations;
    glorify him, all you peoples! **R.**
For steadfast is his kindness toward us,
    and the fidelity of the LORD endures forever. **R.**

John 6:56

R. Alleluia, alleluia.
Whoever eats my Flesh and drinks my Blood,
remains in me and I in him, says the Lord. **R.**

✝ *John 6:52-59*
My Flesh is true food, and my Blood is true drink.

The Jews quarreled among themselves, saying,
    "How can this man give us his Flesh to eat?"
Jesus said to them,
    "Amen, amen, I say to you,
    unless you eat the Flesh of the Son of Man and drink his Blood,
    you do not have life within you.
Whoever eats my Flesh and drinks my Blood
    has eternal life,
    and I will raise him on the last day.
For my Flesh is true food,
    and my Blood is true drink.
Whoever eats my Flesh and drinks my Blood
    remains in me and I in him.
Just as the living Father sent me

and I have life because of the Father,
  so also the one who feeds on me will have life because of me.
This is the bread that came down from heaven.
Unlike your ancestors who ate and still died,
  whoever eats this bread will live forever."
These things he said while teaching in the synagogue in Capernaum. ✙

SATURDAY, APRIL 29
St. Catherine of Siena

† *Acts of the Apostles 9:31-42*
*The Church was being built up, and with the consolation
of the Holy Spirit she grew in numbers.*

The Church throughout all Judea, Galilee, and Samaria
  was at peace.
She was being built up and walked in the fear of the Lord,
  and with the consolation of the Holy Spirit she grew in numbers.

As Peter was passing through every region,
  he went down to the holy ones living in Lydda.
There he found a man named Aeneas,
  who had been confined to bed for eight years, for he was paralyzed.
Peter said to him,
  "Aeneas, Jesus Christ heals you. Get up and make your bed."
He got up at once.
And all the inhabitants of Lydda and Sharon saw him,
  and they turned to the Lord.

Now in Joppa there was a disciple named Tabitha
  (which translated is Dorcas).
She was completely occupied with good deeds and almsgiving.
Now during those days she fell sick and died,
  so after washing her, they laid her out in a room upstairs.
Since Lydda was near Joppa,
  the disciples, hearing that Peter was there,
  sent two men to him with the request,
  "Please come to us without delay."
So Peter got up and went with them.
When he arrived, they took him to the room upstairs
  where all the widows came to him weeping
  and showing him the tunics and cloaks
  that Dorcas had made while she was with them.
Peter sent them all out and knelt down and prayed.
Then he turned to her body and said, "Tabitha, rise up."
She opened her eyes, saw Peter, and sat up.
He gave her his hand and raised her up,

and when he had called the holy ones and the widows,
he presented her alive.
This became known all over Joppa,
and many came to believe in the Lord. ✛

Psalm 116:12-13, 14-15, 16-17
R. (12) **How shall I make a return to the Lord for all the good
he has done for me?** *(or* **Alleluia.***)*
How shall I make a return to the LORD
for all the good he has done for me?
The cup of salvation I will take up,
and I will call upon the name of the LORD. **R.**
My vows to the LORD I will pay
in the presence of all his people.
Precious in the eyes of the LORD
is the death of his faithful ones. **R.**
O LORD, I am your servant;
I am your servant, the son of your handmaid;
you have loosed my bonds.
To you will I offer sacrifice of thanksgiving,
and I will call upon the name of the LORD. **R.**

See *John 6:63c, 68c*
R. Alleluia, alleluia.
Your words, Lord, are Spirit and life;
you have the words of everlasting life. **R.**

† *John 6:60-69*
To whom shall we go? You have the words of eternal life.

Many of the disciples of Jesus who were listening said,
"This saying is hard; who can accept it?"
Since Jesus knew that his disciples were murmuring about this,
he said to them, "Does this shock you?
What if you were to see the Son of Man ascending to where he was
before?
It is the Spirit that gives life, while the flesh is of no avail.
The words I have spoken to you are Spirit and life.
But there are some of you who do not believe."
Jesus knew from the beginning the ones who would not believe
and the one who would betray him.
And he said, "For this reason I have told you that no one can come
to me
unless it is granted him by my Father."

As a result of this,
many of his disciples returned to their former way of life

and no longer walked with him.
Jesus then said to the Twelve, "Do you also want to leave?"
Simon Peter answered him, "Master, to whom shall we go?
You have the words of eternal life.
We have come to believe
    and are convinced that you are the Holy One of God." ✛

SUNDAY, APRIL 30
FOURTH SUNDAY OF EASTER

† Acts of the Apostles 2:14a, 36-41
God has made Jesus both Lord and Christ.

Then Peter stood up with the Eleven,
    raised his voice, and proclaimed:
"Let the whole house of Israel know for certain
    that God has made both Lord and Christ,
    this Jesus whom you crucified."

Now when they heard this, they were cut to the heart,
    and they asked Peter and the other apostles,
    "What are we to do, my brothers?"
Peter said to them,
    "Repent and be baptized, every one of you,
    in the name of Jesus Christ for the forgiveness of your sins;
    and you will receive the gift of the Holy Spirit.
For the promise is made to you and to your children
    and to all those far off,
    whomever the Lord our God will call."
He testified with many other arguments, and was exhorting them,
    "Save yourselves from this corrupt generation."
Those who accepted his message were baptized,
    and about three thousand persons were added that day. ✛

Psalm 23:1b-3a, 3b-4, 5, 6
R. (1) **The Lord is my shepherd; there is nothing I shall want.**
    (or **Alleluia.***)*
The LORD is my shepherd; I shall not want.
    In verdant pastures he gives me repose;
beside restful waters he leads me;
    he refreshes my soul. **R.**
He guides me in right paths
    for his name's sake.
Even though I walk in the dark valley
    I fear no evil; for you are at my side.
with your rod and your staff

that give me courage. **R.**
You spread the table before me
  in the sight of my foes;
you anoint my head with oil;
  my cup overflows. **R.**
Only goodness and kindness follow me
  all the days of my life;
and I shall dwell in the house of the LORD
  for years to come. **R.**

† *1 Peter 2:20b-25*
You have returned to the shepherd and guardian of your souls.

Beloved:
If you are patient when you suffer for doing what is good,
  this is a grace before God.
For to this you have been called,
  because Christ also suffered for you,
  leaving you an example that you should follow in his footsteps.
He committed no sin, and no deceit was found in his mouth.

When he was insulted, he returned no insult;
  when he suffered, he did not threaten;
  instead, he handed himself over to the one who judges justly.
He himself bore our sins in his body upon the cross,
  so that, free from sin, we might live for righteousness.
By his wounds you have been healed.
For you had gone astray like sheep,
  but you have now returned to the shepherd and guardian of your
    souls. ✛

John 10:14
R. Alleluia, alleluia.
I am the good shepherd, says the Lord;
I know my sheep, and mine know me. **R.**

† *John 10:1-10*
I am the gate for the sheep.

Jesus said:
  "Amen, amen, I say to you,
  whoever does not enter a sheepfold through the gate
  but climbs over elsewhere is a thief and a robber.
But whoever enters through the gate is the shepherd of the sheep.
The gatekeeper opens it for him, and the sheep hear his voice,
  as the shepherd calls his own sheep by name and leads them out.
When he has driven out all his own,

he walks ahead of them, and the sheep follow him,
   because they recognize his voice.
But they will not follow a stranger;
   they will run away from him,
   because they do not recognize the voice of strangers."
Although Jesus used this figure of speech,
   the Pharisees did not realize what he was trying to tell them.

So Jesus said again, "Amen, amen, I say to you,
   I am the gate for the sheep.
All who came before me are thieves and robbers,
   but the sheep did not listen to them.
I am the gate.
Whoever enters through me will be saved,
   and will come in and go out and find pasture.
A thief comes only to steal and slaughter and destroy;
   I came so that they might have life and have it more abundantly." ✛

MONDAY, MAY 1
Easter Weekday, St. Joseph the Worker
(Readings for the St. Joseph Memorial Mass are: Genesis 1:26—2:3 or
Colossians 3:14-15, 17, 23-24 • Psalm 90:2-4, 12-13, 14 and 16 • Matthew 13:54-58)

† Acts of the Apostles 11:1-18
God has then granted life-giving repentance to the Gentiles too.

The Apostles and the brothers who were in Judea
   heard that the Gentiles too had accepted the word of God.
So when Peter went up to Jerusalem
   the circumcised believers confronted him, saying,
   "You entered the house of uncircumcised people and ate with
      them."
Peter began and explained it to them step by step, saying,
   "I was at prayer in the city of Joppa
   when in a trance I had a vision,
   something resembling a large sheet coming down,
   lowered from the sky by its four corners, and it came to me.
Looking intently into it,
   I observed and saw the four-legged animals of the earth,
   the wild beasts, the reptiles, and the birds of the sky.
I also heard a voice say to me, 'Get up, Peter. Slaughter and eat.'
But I said, 'Certainly not, sir,
   because nothing profane or unclean has ever entered my mouth.'
But a second time a voice from heaven answered,
   'What God has made clean, you are not to call profane.'
This happened three times,

and then everything was drawn up again into the sky.
Just then three men appeared at the house where we were,
  who had been sent to me from Caesarea.
The Spirit told me to accompany them without discriminating.
These six brothers also went with me,
  and we entered the man's house.
He related to us how he had seen the angel standing in his house,
    saying,
  'Send someone to Joppa and summon Simon, who is called Peter,
  who will speak words to you
  by which you and all your household will be saved.'
As I began to speak, the Holy Spirit fell upon them
  as it had upon us at the beginning,
  and I remembered the word of the Lord, how he had said,
  'John baptized with water
  but you will be baptized with the Holy Spirit.'
If then God gave them the same gift he gave to us
  when we came to believe in the Lord Jesus Christ,
  who was I to be able to hinder God?"
When they heard this,
  they stopped objecting and glorified God, saying,
  "God has then granted life-giving repentance to the Gentiles too." ✛

Psalms 42:2-3; 43:3, 4
R. (see 3a) **Athirst is my soul for the living God.** *(or* **Alleluia.***)*
As the hind longs for the running waters,
  so my soul longs for you, O God.
Athirst is my soul for God, the living God.
  When shall I go and behold the face of God? **R.**
Send forth your light and your fidelity;
  they shall lead me on
And bring me to your holy mountain,
  to your dwelling-place. **R.**
Then will I go in to the altar of God,
  the God of my gladness and joy;
Then will I give you thanks upon the harp,
  O God, my God! **R.**

John 10:14
R. Alleluia, alleluia.
I am the good shepherd, says the Lord;
I know my sheep, and mine know me. **R.**

✝ *John 10:11-18*
A good shepherd lays down his life for the sheep.

J esus said:
"I am the good shepherd.
A good shepherd lays down his life for the sheep.
A hired man, who is not a shepherd
    and whose sheep are not his own,
    sees a wolf coming and leaves the sheep and runs away,
    and the wolf catches and scatters them.
This is because he works for pay and has no concern for the sheep.
I am the good shepherd,
    and I know mine and mine know me,
    just as the Father knows me and I know the Father;
    and I will lay down my life for the sheep.
I have other sheep that do not belong to this fold.
These also I must lead, and they will hear my voice,
    and there will be one flock, one shepherd.
This is why the Father loves me,
    because I lay down my life in order to take it up again.
No one takes it from me, but I lay it down on my own.
I have power to lay it down, and power to take it up again.
This command I have received from my Father." ✛

TUESDAY, MAY 2
St. Athanasius

✝ *Acts of the Apostles 11:19-26*
*They began speaking to the Greeks as well, proclaiming
the Good News of Jesus Christ.*

T hose who had been scattered by the persecution
    that arose because of Stephen
    went as far as Phoenicia, Cyprus, and Antioch,
    preaching the word to no one but Jews.
There were some Cypriots and Cyrenians among them, however,
    who came to Antioch and began to speak to the Greeks as well,
    proclaiming the Lord Jesus.
The hand of the Lord was with them
    and a great number who believed turned to the Lord.
The news about them reached the ears of the Church in Jerusalem,
    and they sent Barnabas to go to Antioch.
When he arrived and saw the grace of God,
    he rejoiced and encouraged them all
    to remain faithful to the Lord in firmness of heart,
    for he was a good man, filled with the Holy Spirit and faith.

And a large number of people was added to the Lord.
Then he went to Tarsus to look for Saul,
  and when he had found him he brought him to Antioch.
For a whole year they met with the Church
  and taught a large number of people,
  and it was in Antioch that the disciples
  were first called Christians. ✝

   Psalm 87:1b-3, 4-5, 6-7
R. *(117:1a)* **All you nations, praise the Lord.** *(or* **Alleluia.***)*
His foundation upon the holy mountains
  the LORD loves:
The gates of Zion,
  more than any dwelling of Jacob.
Glorious things are said of you,
  O city of God! **R.**
I tell of Egypt and Babylon
  among those who know the LORD;
Of Philistia, Tyre, Ethiopia:
  "This man was born there."
And of Zion they shall say:
  "One and all were born in her;
And he who has established her
  is the Most High LORD." **R.**
They shall note, when the peoples are enrolled:
  "This man was born there."
And all shall sing, in their festive dance:
  "My home is within you." **R.**

   John 10:27
R. Alleluia, alleluia.
My sheep hear my voice, says the Lord;
I know them, and they follow me. **R.**

✝ *John 10:22-30*
The Father and I are one.

The feast of the Dedication was taking place in Jerusalem.
It was winter.
And Jesus walked about in the temple area on the Portico of Solo-
    mon.
So the Jews gathered around him and said to him,
  "How long are you going to keep us in suspense?
If you are the Christ, tell us plainly."
Jesus answered them, "I told you and you do not believe.
The works I do in my Father's name testify to me.
But you do not believe, because you are not among my sheep.

My sheep hear my voice;
 I know them, and they follow me.
I give them eternal life, and they shall never perish.
No one can take them out of my hand.
My Father, who has given them to me, is greater than all,
 and no one can take them out of the Father's hand.
The Father and I are one." ✛

WEDNESDAY, MAY 3
St. Philip and St. James

† 1 Corinthians 15:1-8
After that he appeared to James, then to all the Apostles.

I am reminding you, brothers and sisters,
 of the Gospel I preached to you,
 which you indeed received and in which you also stand.
Through it you are also being saved,
 if you hold fast to the word I preached to you,
 unless you believed in vain.
For I handed on to you as of first importance what I also received:
 that Christ died for our sins
  in accordance with the Scriptures;
 that he was buried;
 that he was raised on the third day
  in accordance with the Scriptures;
 that he appeared to Cephas, then to the Twelve.
After that, he appeared to more
 than five hundred brothers and sisters at once,
 most of whom are still living,
 though some have fallen asleep.
After that he appeared to James,
 then to all the Apostles.
Last of all, as to one born abnormally,
 he appeared to me. ✛

Psalm 19:2-3, 4-5
R. (5) **Their message goes out through all the earth.**
 (or **Alleluia.***)*
The heavens declare the glory of God;
 and the firmament proclaims his handiwork.
Day pours out the word to day;
 and night to night imparts knowledge. **R.**
Not a word nor a discourse
 whose voice is not heard;
Through all the earth their voice resounds,
 and to the ends of the world, their message. **R.**

John 14:6b, 9c
R. Alleluia, alleluia.
I am the way, the truth, and the life, says the Lord;
Philip, whoever has seen me has seen the Father. **R.**

† *John 14:6-14*
Have I been with you so long and you still do not know me?

Jesus said to Thomas, "I am the way and the truth and the life.
No one comes to the Father except through me.
If you know me, then you will also know my Father.
From now on you do know him and have seen him."
Philip said to him,
 "Master, show us the Father, and that will be enough for us."
Jesus said to him, "Have I been with you for so long a time
 and you still do not know me, Philip?
Whoever has seen me has seen the Father.
How can you say, 'Show us the Father'?
Do you not believe that I am in the Father and the Father is in me?
The words that I speak to you I do not speak on my own.
The Father who dwells in me is doing his works.
Believe me that I am in the Father and the Father is in me,
 or else, believe because of the works themselves.
Amen, amen, I say to you,
 whoever believes in me will do the works that I do,
 and will do greater ones than these,
 because I am going to the Father.
And whatever you ask in my name, I will do,
 so that the Father may be glorified in the Son.
If you ask anything of me in my name, I will do it." ✝

THURSDAY, MAY 4
EASTER WEEKDAY

† *Acts of the Apostles 13:13-25*
*From this man's descendants God, according to his promise,
has brought to Israel a savior, Jesus.*

From Paphos, Paul and his companions
 set sail and arrived at Perga in Pamphylia.
But John left them and returned to Jerusalem.
They continued on from Perga and reached Antioch in Pisidia.
On the sabbath they entered into the synagogue and took their
 seats.
After the reading of the law and the prophets,
 the synagogue officials sent word to them,

"My brothers, if one of you has a word of exhortation
    for the people, please speak."

So Paul got up, motioned with his hand, and said,
    "Fellow children of Israel and you others who are God-fearing,
        listen.
The God of this people Israel chose our ancestors
    and exalted the people during their sojourn in the land of Egypt.
With uplifted arms he led them out,
    and for about forty years he put up with them in the desert.
When he had destroyed seven nations in the land of Canaan,
    he gave them their land as an inheritance
    at the end of about four hundred and fifty years.
After these things he provided judges up to Samuel the prophet.
Then they asked for a king.
God gave them Saul, son of Kish,
    a man from the tribe of Benjamin, for forty years.
Then he removed him and raised up David as their king;
    of him he testified,
    I have found David, son of Jesse, a man after my own heart;
    he will carry out my every wish.
From this man's descendants God, according to his promise,
    has brought to Israel a savior, Jesus.
John heralded his coming by proclaiming a baptism of repentance
    to all the people of Israel;
    and as John was completing his course, he would say,
    'What do you suppose that I am? I am not he.
Behold, one is coming after me;
    I am not worthy to unfasten the sandals of his feet.'" ✛

Psalm 89:2-3, 21-22, 25 and 27
R. (2) **For ever I will sing the goodness of the Lord.**
    (or **Alleluia.***)*
The favors of the LORD I will sing forever;
    through all generations my mouth shall proclaim your faithfulness.
For you have said, "My kindness is established forever";
    in heaven you have confirmed your faithfulness. **R.**
"I have found David, my servant;
    with my holy oil I have anointed him,
That my hand may be always with him,
    and that my arm may make him strong." **R.**
"My faithfulness and my mercy shall be with him,
    and through my name shall his horn be exalted.
He shall say of me, 'You are my father,
    my God, the Rock, my savior.'" **R.**

See Revelation 1:5ab

R. Alleluia, alleluia.

Jesus Christ, you are the faithful witness,
the firstborn of the dead,
you have loved us and freed us from our sins by your Blood. **R.**

† *John 13:16-20*
Whoever receives the one I send receives me.

When Jesus had washed the disciples' feet, he said to them:
"Amen, amen, I say to you, no slave is greater than his master
  nor any messenger greater than the one who sent him.
If you understand this, blessed are you if you do it.
I am not speaking of all of you.
I know those whom I have chosen.
But so that the Scripture might be fulfilled,
  The one who ate my food has raised his heel against me.
From now on I am telling you before it happens,
  so that when it happens you may believe that I AM.
Amen, amen, I say to you, whoever receives the one I send
  receives me, and whoever receives me receives the one who sent
    me." ✛

FRIDAY, MAY 5
EASTER WEEKDAY

† *Acts of the Apostles 13:26-33*
God has fulfilled his promise by raising Jesus from the dead.

When Paul came to Antioch in Pisidia, he said in the synagogue:
"My brothers, children of the family of Abraham,
  and those others among you who are God-fearing,
  to us this word of salvation has been sent.
The inhabitants of Jerusalem and their leaders failed to recognize
    him,
  and by condemning him they fulfilled the oracles of the prophets
  that are read sabbath after sabbath.
For even though they found no grounds for a death sentence,
  they asked Pilate to have him put to death,
  and when they had accomplished all that was written about him,
  they took him down from the tree and placed him in a tomb.
But God raised him from the dead,
  and for many days he appeared to those
  who had come up with him from Galilee to Jerusalem.
These are now his witnesses before the people.
We ourselves are proclaiming this good news to you
  that what God promised our fathers

he has brought to fulfillment for us, their children, by raising up
Jesus,
as it is written in the second psalm,
You are my Son; this day I have begotten you." ✣

Psalm 2:6-7, 8-9, 10-11ab
R. (7bc) **You are my Son; this day I have begotten you.**
(or **Alleluia.***)*
"I myself have set up my king
on Zion, my holy mountain."
I will proclaim the decree of the LORD:
The LORD said to me, "You are my Son;
this day I have begotten you." **R.**
"Ask of me and I will give you
the nations for an inheritance
and the ends of the earth for your possession.
You shall rule them with an iron rod;
you shall shatter them like an earthen dish." **R.**
And now, O kings, give heed;
take warning, you rulers of the earth.
Serve the LORD with fear, and rejoice before him;
with trembling rejoice. **R.**

John 14:6
R. Alleluia, alleluia.
I am the way and the truth and the life, says the Lord;
no one comes to the Father except through me. **R.**

✝ John 14:1-6
I am the way and the truth and the life.

Jesus said to his disciples:
"Do not let your hearts be troubled.
You have faith in God; have faith also in me.
In my Father's house there are many dwelling places.
If there were not,
would I have told you that I am going to prepare a place for you?
And if I go and prepare a place for you,
I will come back again and take you to myself,
so that where I am you also may be.
Where I am going you know the way."
Thomas said to him,
"Master, we do not know where you are going;
how can we know the way?"
Jesus said to him, "I am the way and the truth and the life.
No one comes to the Father except through me." ✣

SATURDAY, MAY 6
EASTER WEEKDAY

† *Acts of the Apostles 13:44-52*
We now turn to the Gentiles.

On the following sabbath
  almost the whole city
  gathered to hear the word of the Lord.
When the Jews saw the crowds, they were filled with jealousy
  and with violent abuse contradicted what Paul said.
Both Paul and Barnabas spoke out boldly and said,
  "It was necessary that the word of God be spoken to you first,
  but since you reject it
  and condemn yourselves as unworthy of eternal life,
  we now turn to the Gentiles.
For so the Lord has commanded us,
  I have made you a light to the Gentiles,
  that you may be an instrument of salvation
  to the ends of the earth."

The Gentiles were delighted when they heard this
  and glorified the word of the Lord.
All who were destined for eternal life came to believe,
  and the word of the Lord continued to spread
  through the whole region.
The Jews, however, incited the women of prominence who were
    worshipers and the leading men of the city,
  stirred up a persecution against Paul and Barnabas,
  and expelled them from their territory.
So they shook the dust from their feet in protest against them
  and went to Iconium.
The disciples were filled with joy and the Holy Spirit. ✛

Psalm 98:1bcde, 2-3ab, 3cd-4

R. (3cd) **All the ends of the earth have seen the saving power of God.** *(or **Alleluia.**)*

Sing to the LORD a new song,
  for he has done wondrous deeds;
His right hand has won victory for him,
  his holy arm. **R.**
The LORD has made his salvation known:
  in the sight of the nations he has revealed his justice.
He has remembered his kindness and his faithfulness
  toward the house of Israel. **R.**
All the ends of the earth have seen

the salvation by our God.
Sing joyfully to the LORD, all you lands;
    break into song; sing praise. **R.**

John 8:31b-32
R. Alleluia, alleluia.
If you remain in my word, you will truly be my disciples,
and you will know the truth, says the Lord. **R.**

✝ *John 14:7-14*
Whoever has seen me has seen the Father.

Jesus said to his disciples:
"If you know me, then you will also know my Father.
From now on you do know him and have seen him."
Philip said to Jesus,
    "Master, show us the Father, and that will be enough for us."
Jesus said to him, "Have I been with you for so long a time
    and you still do not know me, Philip?
Whoever has seen me has seen the Father.
How can you say, 'Show us the Father'?
Do you not believe that I am in the Father and the Father is in me?
The words that I speak to you I do not speak on my own.
The Father who dwells in me is doing his works.
Believe me that I am in the Father and the Father is in me,
    or else, believe because of the works themselves.
Amen, amen, I say to you,
    whoever believes in me will do the works that I do,
    and will do greater ones than these,
    because I am going to the Father.
And whatever you ask in my name, I will do,
    so that the Father may be glorified in the Son.
If you ask anything of me in my name, I will do it." ✝

SUNDAY, MAY 7
FIFTH SUNDAY OF EASTER

✝ *Acts of the Apostles 6:1-7*
They chose seven men filled with the Spirit.

As the number of disciples continued to grow,
    the Hellenists complained against the Hebrews
    because their widows
    were being neglected in the daily distribution.
So the Twelve called together the community of the disciples and
        said,
    "It is not right for us to neglect the word of God to serve at table.

Brothers, select from among you seven reputable men,
  filled with the Spirit and wisdom,
  whom we shall appoint to this task,
  whereas we shall devote ourselves to prayer
  and to the ministry of the word."
The proposal was acceptable to the whole community,
  so they chose Stephen, a man filled with faith and the Holy Spirit,
  also Philip, Prochorus, Nicanor, Timon, Parmenas,
  and Nicholas of Antioch, a convert to Judaism.
They presented these men to the apostles
  who prayed and laid hands on them.
The word of God continued to spread,
  and the number of the disciples in Jerusalem increased greatly;
  even a large group of priests were becoming obedient to the
    faith. ✛

Psalm 33:1-2, 4-5, 18-19

R. (22) **Lord, let your mercy be on us, as we place our trust in
  you.** *(or* **Alleluia.***)*

Exult, you just, in the LORD;
  praise from the upright is fitting.
Give thanks to the LORD on the harp;
  with the ten-stringed lyre chant his praises. **R.**
Upright is the word of the LORD,
  and all his works are trustworthy.
He loves justice and right;
  of the kindness of the LORD the earth is full. **R.**
See, the eyes of the LORD are upon those who fear him,
  upon those who hope for his kindness,
to deliver them from death
  and preserve them in spite of famine. **R.**

† 1 Peter 2:4-9

You are a chosen race, a royal priesthood.

Beloved:
Come to him, a living stone, rejected by human beings
  but chosen and precious in the sight of God,
  and, like living stones,
  let yourselves be built into a spiritual house
  to be a holy priesthood to offer spiritual sacrifices
  acceptable to God through Jesus Christ.
For it says in Scripture:
  Behold, I am laying a stone in Zion,
  a cornerstone, chosen and precious,
  and whoever believes in it shall not be put to shame.

Therefore, its value is for you who have faith, but for those without
   faith:
The stone that the builders rejected
has become the cornerstone,
and
A stone that will make people stumble,
and a rock that will make them fall.
They stumble by disobeying the word, as is their destiny.

You are "a chosen race, a royal priesthood,
   a holy nation, a people of his own,
   so that you may announce the praises" of him
   who called you out of darkness into his wonderful light. ✦

   John 14:6
R. Alleluia, alleluia.
I am the way, the truth and the life, says the Lord;
no one comes to the Father, except through me. **R.**

† *John 14:1-12*
I am the way and the truth and the life.

Jesus said to his disciples:
   "Do not let your hearts be troubled.
You have faith in God; have faith also in me.
In my Father's house there are many dwelling places.
If there were not,
   would I have told you that I am going to prepare a place for you?
And if I go and prepare a place for you,
   I will come back again and take you to myself,
   so that where I am you also may be.
Where I am going you know the way."
Thomas said to him,
   "Master, we do not know where you are going;
   how can we know the way?"
Jesus said to him, "I am the way and the truth and the life.
No one comes to the Father except through me.
If you know me, then you will also know my Father.
From now on you do know him and have seen him."
Philip said to him,
   "Master, show us the Father, and that will be enough for us."
Jesus said to him, "Have I been with you for so long a time
   and you still do not know me, Philip?
Whoever has seen me has seen the Father.
How can you say, 'Show us the Father'?
Do you not believe that I am in the Father and the Father is in me?

The words that I speak to you I do not speak on my own.
The Father who dwells in me is doing his works.
Believe me that I am in the Father and the Father is in me,
or else, believe because of the works themselves.
Amen, amen, I say to you,
whoever believes in me will do the works that I do,
and will do greater ones than these,
because I am going to the Father." ✙

MONDAY, MAY 8
EASTER WEEKDAY

✝ Acts of the Apostles 14:5-18
*We proclaim to you Good News that you should turn
from these idols to the living God.*

There was an attempt in Iconium
by both the Gentiles and the Jews,
together with their leaders,
to attack and stone Paul and Barnabas.
They realized it,
and fled to the Lycaonian cities of Lystra and Derbe
and to the surrounding countryside,
where they continued to proclaim the Good News.

At Lystra there was a crippled man, lame from birth,
who had never walked.
He listened to Paul speaking, who looked intently at him,
saw that he had the faith to be healed,
and called out in a loud voice, "Stand up straight on your feet."
He jumped up and began to walk about.
When the crowds saw what Paul had done,
they cried out in Lycaonian,
"The gods have come down to us in human form."
They called Barnabas "Zeus" and Paul "Hermes,"
because he was the chief speaker.
And the priest of Zeus, whose temple was at the entrance to the city,
brought oxen and garlands to the gates,
for he together with the people intended to offer sacrifice.

The Apostles Barnabas and Paul tore their garments
when they heard this and rushed out into the crowd, shouting,
"Men, why are you doing this?
We are of the same nature as you, human beings.
We proclaim to you good news
that you should turn from these idols to the living God,
who made heaven and earth and sea and all that is in them.

In past generations he allowed all Gentiles to go their own ways;
    yet, in bestowing his goodness,
    he did not leave himself without witness,
    for he gave you rains from heaven and fruitful seasons,
    and filled you with nourishment and gladness for your hearts."
Even with these words, they scarcely restrained the crowds
    from offering sacrifice to them. ✛

Psalm 115:1-2, 3-4, 15-16

R. (1ab) **Not to us, O Lord, but to your name give the glory.**
    (or **Alleluia.***)*

Not to us, O Lord, not to us
    but to your name give glory
    because of your mercy, because of your truth.
Why should the pagans say,
    "Where is their God?" **R.**
Our God is in heaven;
    whatever he wills, he does.
Their idols are silver and gold,
    the handiwork of men. **R.**
May you be blessed by the Lord,
    who made heaven and earth.
Heaven is the heaven of the Lord,
    but the earth he has given to the children of men. **R.**

John 14:26

R. Alleluia, alleluia.
The Holy Spirit will teach you everything
and remind you of all I told you. **R.**

† *John 14:21-26*

The Advocate whom the Father will send will teach you everything.

Jesus said to his disciples:
"Whoever has my commandments and observes them
    is the one who loves me.
Whoever loves me will be loved by my Father,
    and I will love him and reveal myself to him."
Judas, not the Iscariot, said to him,
    "Master, then what happened that you will reveal yourself to us
    and not to the world?"
Jesus answered and said to him,
    "Whoever loves me will keep my word,
    and my Father will love him,
    and we will come to him and make our dwelling with him.
Whoever does not love me does not keep my words;

yet the word you hear is not mine
but that of the Father who sent me.

"I have told you this while I am with you.
The Advocate, the Holy Spirit
    whom the Father will send in my name—
    he will teach you everything
    and remind you of all that I told you." ✢

TUESDAY, MAY 9
EASTER WEEKDAY

✝ Acts of the Apostles 14:19-28
*They called the Church together and
reported what God had done with them.*

In those days, some Jews from Antioch and Iconium
    arrived and won over the crowds.
They stoned Paul and dragged him out of the city,
    supposing that he was dead.
But when the disciples gathered around him,
    he got up and entered the city.
On the following day he left with Barnabas for Derbe.

After they had proclaimed the good news to that city
    and made a considerable number of disciples,
    they returned to Lystra and to Iconium and to Antioch.
They strengthened the spirits of the disciples
    and exhorted them to persevere in the faith, saying,
    "It is necessary for us to undergo many hardships
    to enter the Kingdom of God."
They appointed presbyters for them in each Church and,
    with prayer and fasting, commended them to the Lord
    in whom they had put their faith.
Then they traveled through Pisidia and reached Pamphylia.
After proclaiming the word at Perga they went down to Attalia.
From there they sailed to Antioch,
    where they had been commended to the grace of God
    for the work they had now accomplished.
And when they arrived, they called the Church together
    and reported what God had done with them
    and how he had opened the door of faith to the Gentiles.
Then they spent no little time with the disciples. ✢

Psalm 145:10-11, 12-13ab, 21

R. (see 12) **Your friends make known, O Lord, the glorious splendor of your kingdom.** *(or* **Alleluia.***)*

Let all your works give you thanks, O LORD,
  and let your faithful ones bless you.
Let them discourse of the glory of your kingdom
  and speak of your might. **R.**
Making known to men your might
  and the glorious splendor of your kingdom.
Your kingdom is a kingdom for all ages,
  and your dominion endures through all generations. **R.**
May my mouth speak the praise of the LORD,
  and may all flesh bless his holy name forever and ever. **R.**

See Luke 24:46, 26

R. Alleluia, alleluia.

Christ had to suffer and to rise from the dead,
and so enter into his glory. **R.**

† *John 14:27-31a*
My peace I give to you.

Jesus said to his disciples:
"Peace I leave with you; my peace I give to you.
Not as the world gives do I give it to you.
Do not let your hearts be troubled or afraid.
You heard me tell you,
  'I am going away and I will come back to you.'
If you loved me,
  you would rejoice that I am going to the Father;
  for the Father is greater than I.
And now I have told you this before it happens,
  so that when it happens you may believe.
I will no longer speak much with you,
  for the ruler of the world is coming.
He has no power over me,
  but the world must know that I love the Father
  and that I do just as the Father has commanded me." ✚

WEDNESDAY, MAY 10
EASTER WEEKDAY, ST JOHN OF AVILA, ST. DAMIEN DE VEUSTER

† *Acts of the Apostles 15:1-6*
*They decided to go up to Jerusalem to the Apostles
and presbyters about this question.*

Some who had come down from Judea were instructing the brothers,
  "Unless you are circumcised according to the Mosaic practice,

you cannot be saved."
Because there arose no little dissension and debate
   by Paul and Barnabas with them,
   it was decided that Paul, Barnabas, and some of the others
   should go up to Jerusalem to the Apostles and presbyters
   about this question.
They were sent on their journey by the Church,
   and passed through Phoenicia and Samaria
   telling of the conversion of the Gentiles,
   and brought great joy to all the brethren.
When they arrived in Jerusalem,
   they were welcomed by the Church,
   as well as by the Apostles and the presbyters,
   and they reported what God had done with them.
But some from the party of the Pharisees who had become believers
   stood up and said, "It is necessary to circumcise them
   and direct them to observe the Mosaic law."

The Apostles and the presbyters met together to see about this
   matter. ✛

Psalm 122:1-2, 3-4ab, 4cd-5
R. (see 1) **Let us go rejoicing to the house of the Lord.**
   (or **Alleluia.***)*
I rejoiced because they said to me,
   "We will go up to the house of the Lord."
And now we have set foot
   within your gates, O Jerusalem. **R.**
Jerusalem, built as a city
   with compact unity.
To it the tribes go up,
   the tribes of the Lord. **R.**
According to the decree for Israel,
   to give thanks to the name of the Lord.
In it are set up judgment seats,
   seats for the house of David. **R.**

John 15:4a, 5b
R. Alleluia, alleluia.
Remain in me, as I remain in you, says the Lord;
whoever remains in me will bear much fruit. **R.**

✝ John 15:1-8
Whoever remains in me and I in him will bear much fruit.

Jesus said to his disciples:
"I am the true vine, and my Father is the vine grower.

He takes away every branch in me that does not bear fruit,
  and everyone that does he prunes so that it bears more fruit.
You are already pruned because of the word that I spoke to you.
Remain in me, as I remain in you.
Just as a branch cannot bear fruit on its own
  unless it remains on the vine,
  so neither can you unless you remain in me.
I am the vine, you are the branches.
Whoever remains in me and I in him will bear much fruit,
  because without me you can do nothing.
Anyone who does not remain in me
  will be thrown out like a branch and wither;
  people will gather them and throw them into a fire
  and they will be burned.
If you remain in me and my words remain in you,
  ask for whatever you want and it will be done for you.
By this is my Father glorified,
  that you bear much fruit and become my disciples." ✝

THURSDAY, MAY 11
EASTER WEEKDAY

† *Acts of the Apostles 15:7-21*
*It is my judgment, therefore, that we ought to stop troubling
the Gentiles who turn to God.*

After much debate had taken place,
  Peter got up and said to the Apostles and the presbyters,
  "My brothers, you are well aware that from early days
  God made his choice among you that through my mouth
  the Gentiles would hear the word of the Gospel and believe.
And God, who knows the heart,
  bore witness by granting them the Holy Spirit
  just as he did us.
He made no distinction between us and them,
  for by faith he purified their hearts.
Why, then, are you now putting God to the test
  by placing on the shoulders of the disciples
  a yoke that neither our ancestors nor we have been able to bear?
On the contrary, we believe that we are saved
  through the grace of the Lord Jesus, in the same way as they."
The whole assembly fell silent,
  and they listened
  while Paul and Barnabas described the signs and wonders
  God had worked among the Gentiles through them.

After they had fallen silent, James responded,
"My brothers, listen to me.
Symeon has described how God first concerned himself
with acquiring from among the Gentiles a people for his name.
The words of the prophets agree with this, as is written:

After this I shall return
and rebuild the fallen hut of David;
from its ruins I shall rebuild it
and raise it up again,
so that the rest of humanity may seek out the Lord,
even all the Gentiles on whom my name is invoked.
Thus says the Lord who accomplishes these things,
known from of old.

It is my judgment, therefore,
that we ought to stop troubling the Gentiles who turn to God,
but tell them by letter to avoid pollution from idols,
unlawful marriage, the meat of strangled animals, and blood.
For Moses, for generations now,
has had those who proclaim him in every town,
as he has been read in the synagogues every sabbath." ✛

Psalm 96:1-2a, 2b-3, 10
R. (3) Proclaim God's marvelous deeds to all the nations.
*(or **Alleluia.**)*
Sing to the LORD a new song;
sing to the LORD, all you lands.
Sing to the LORD; bless his name. **R.**
Announce his salvation, day after day.
Tell his glory among the nations;
among all peoples, his wondrous deeds. **R.**
Say among the nations: The LORD is king.
He has made the world firm, not to be moved;
he governs the peoples with equity. **R.**

John 10:27
R. Alleluia, alleluia.
My sheep hear my voice, says the Lord;
I know them, and they follow me. **R.**

✝ *John 15:9-11*
Remain in my love, that your joy might be complete.

Jesus said to his disciples:
"As the Father loves me, so I also love you.
Remain in my love.

If you keep my commandments, you will remain in my love,
    just as I have kept my Father's commandments
    and remain in his love.

"I have told you this so that
    my joy might be in you and
    your joy might be complete." ✠

FRIDAY, MAY 12
Easter Weekday, St. Nereus and St. Achilleus, St. Pancras

† *Acts of the Apostles 15:22-31*
*It is the decision of the Holy Spirit and of us not to place on you
any burden beyond these necessities.*

The Apostles and presbyters, in agreement with the whole Church,
    decided to choose representatives
    and to send them to Antioch with Paul and Barnabas.
The ones chosen were Judas, who was called Barsabbas,
    and Silas, leaders among the brothers.
This is the letter delivered by them:
"The Apostles and the presbyters, your brothers,
    to the brothers in Antioch, Syria, and Cilicia
    of Gentile origin: greetings.
Since we have heard that some of our number
    who went out without any mandate from us
    have upset you with their teachings
    and disturbed your peace of mind,
    we have with one accord decided to choose representatives
    and to send them to you along with our beloved Barnabas and
        Paul,
    who have dedicated their lives to the name of our Lord Jesus
        Christ.
So we are sending Judas and Silas
    who will also convey this same message by word of mouth:
    'It is the decision of the Holy Spirit and of us
    not to place on you any burden beyond these necessities,
    namely, to abstain from meat sacrificed to idols,
    from blood, from meats of strangled animals,
    and from unlawful marriage.
If you keep free of these,
    you will be doing what is right. Farewell.'"

And so they were sent on their journey.
Upon their arrival in Antioch
    they called the assembly together and delivered the letter.
When the people read it, they were delighted with the exhortation. ✠

Psalm 57:8-9, 10 and 12

R. (10a) **I will give you thanks among the peoples, O Lord.**
(or **Alleluia.***)*

My heart is steadfast, O God; my heart is steadfast;
   I will sing and chant praise.
Awake, O my soul; awake, lyre and harp!
   I will wake the dawn. **R.**

I will give thanks to you among the peoples, O LORD,
   I will chant your praise among the nations.
For your mercy towers to the heavens,
   and your faithfulness to the skies.
Be exalted above the heavens, O God;
   above all the earth be your glory! **R.**

John 15:15b

R. Alleluia, alleluia.

I call you my friends, says the Lord,
for I have made known to you all that the Father has told me. **R.**

† *John 15:12-17*
This is my commandment: love one another.

Jesus said to his disciples:
"This is my commandment: love one another as I love you.
No one has greater love than this,
   to lay down one's life for one's friends.
You are my friends if you do what I command you.
I no longer call you slaves,
   because a slave does not know what his master is doing.
I have called you friends,
   because I have told you everything I have heard from my Father.
It was not you who chose me, but I who chose you
   and appointed you to go and bear fruit that will remain,
   so that whatever you ask the Father in my name he may give you.
This I command you: love one another." ✝

SATURDAY, MAY 13
EASTER WEEKDAY, OUR LADY OF FATIMA

† *Acts of the Apostles 16:1-10*
Come over to Macedonia and help us.

Paul reached also Derbe and Lystra
   where there was a disciple named Timothy,
   the son of a Jewish woman who was a believer,
   but his father was a Greek.
The brothers in Lystra and Iconium spoke highly of him,

and Paul wanted him to come along with him.
On account of the Jews of that region, Paul had him circumcised,
    for they all knew that his father was a Greek.
As they traveled from city to city,
    they handed on to the people for observance the decisions
    reached by the Apostles and presbyters in Jerusalem.
Day after day the churches grew stronger in faith
    and increased in number.

They traveled through the Phrygian and Galatian territory
    because they had been prevented by the Holy Spirit
    from preaching the message in the province of Asia.
When they came to Mysia, they tried to go on into Bithynia,
    but the Spirit of Jesus did not allow them,
    so they crossed through Mysia and came down to Troas.
During the night Paul had a vision.
A Macedonian stood before him and implored him with these words,
    "Come over to Macedonia and help us."
When he had seen the vision,
    we sought passage to Macedonia at once,
    concluding that God had called us to proclaim the Good News to
    them. ✛

Psalm 100:1b-2, 3, 5

R. (2a) Let all the earth cry out to God with joy. *(or* **Alleluia.***)*
Sing joyfully to the LORD, all you lands;
    serve the LORD with gladness;
    come before him with joyful song. **R.**
Know that the LORD is God;
    he made us, his we are;
    his people, the flock he tends. **R.**
The LORD is good:
    his kindness endures forever,
    and his faithfulness, to all generations. **R.**

Colossians 3:1

R. Alleluia, alleluia.
If then you were raised with Christ,
seek what is above,
where Christ is seated at the right hand of God. **R.**

† *John 15:18-21*
You do not belong to the world, and I have chosen you out of the world.

Jesus said to his disciples:
"If the world hates you, realize that it hated me first.
If you belonged to the world, the world would love its own;

but because you do not belong to the world,
and I have chosen you out of the world,
the world hates you.
Remember the word I spoke to you,
'No slave is greater than his master.'
If they persecuted me, they will also persecute you.
If they kept my word, they will also keep yours.
And they will do all these things to you on account of my name,
because they do not know the one who sent me." ✛

SUNDAY, MAY 14
Sixth Sunday of Easter
(When the Ascension of the Lord is celebrated on the following Sunday, the Second Reading and Gospel from the Seventh Sunday of Easter may be read on the Sixth Sunday of Easter.)

† Acts of the Apostles 8:5-8, 14-17
Peter and John laid hands on them, and they received the Holy Spirit.

Philip went down to the city of Samaria
and proclaimed the Christ to them.
With one accord, the crowds paid attention to what was said by
Philip
when they heard it and saw the signs he was doing.
For unclean spirits, crying out in a loud voice,
came out of many possessed people,
and many paralyzed or crippled people were cured.
There was great joy in that city.

Now when the apostles in Jerusalem
heard that Samaria had accepted the word of God,
they sent them Peter and John,
who went down and prayed for them,
that they might receive the Holy Spirit,
for it had not yet fallen upon any of them;
they had only been baptized in the name of the Lord Jesus.
Then they laid hands on them
and they received the Holy Spirit. ✛

Psalm 66:1b-3a, 4-5, 6-7a, 16 and 20
R. (1) **Let all the earth cry out to God with joy.** *(or* **Alleluia.***)*
Shout joyfully to God, all the earth,
sing praise to the glory of his name;
proclaim his glorious praise.
Say to God, "How tremendous are your deeds!" **R.**
"Let all on earth worship and sing praise to you,
sing praise to your name!"

Come and see the works of God,
    his tremendous deeds among the children of Adam. **R.**
He has changed the sea into dry land;
    through the river they passed on foot;
    therefore let us rejoice in him.
He rules by his might forever. **R.**
Hear now, all you who fear God, while I declare
    what he has done for me.
Blessed be God who refused me not
    my prayer or his kindness! **R.**

✝ *1 Peter 3:15-18* (or 1 Peter 4:13-16)
Put to death in the flesh, Christ was raised to life in the Spirit.

Beloved:
Sanctify Christ as Lord in your hearts.
Always be ready to give an explanation
    to anyone who asks you for a reason for your hope,
    but do it with gentleness and reverence,
    keeping your conscience clear,
    so that, when you are maligned,
    those who defame your good conduct in Christ
    may themselves be put to shame.
For it is better to suffer for doing good,
    if that be the will of God, than for doing evil.
For Christ also suffered for sins once,
    the righteous for the sake of the unrighteous,
    that he might lead you to God.
Put to death in the flesh,
    he was brought to life in the Spirit. ✙

John 14:23
R. Alleluia, alleluia.
Whoever loves me will keep my word, says the Lord,
and my Father will love him and we will come to him. **R.**

✝ *John 14:15-21* (or John 17:1-11a)
I will ask the Father and he will give you another Advocate.

Jesus said to his disciples:
    "If you love me, you will keep my commandments.
And I will ask the Father,
    and he will give you another Advocate to be with you always,
    the Spirit of truth, whom the world cannot accept,
    because it neither sees nor knows him.
But you know him, because he remains with you,
    and will be in you.

I will not leave you orphans; I will come to you.
In a little while the world will no longer see me,
  but you will see me, because I live and you will live.
On that day you will realize that I am in my Father
  and you are in me and I in you.
Whoever has my commandments and observes them
  is the one who loves me.
And whoever loves me will be loved by my Father,
  and I will love him and reveal myself to him." ✛

MONDAY, MAY 15
EASTER WEEKDAY, ST. ISIDORE

✝ Acts of the Apostles 16:11-15
The Lord opened her heart to pay attention to what Paul taught.

We set sail from Troas, making a straight run for Samothrace,
  and on the next day to Neapolis, and from there to Philippi,
  a leading city in that district of Macedonia and a Roman colony.
We spent some time in that city.
On the sabbath we went outside the city gate along the river
  where we thought there would be a place of prayer.
We sat and spoke with the women who had gathered there.
One of them, a woman named Lydia, a dealer in purple cloth,
  from the city of Thyatira, a worshiper of God, listened,
  and the Lord opened her heart to pay attention
  to what Paul was saying.
After she and her household had been baptized,
  she offered us an invitation,
  "If you consider me a believer in the Lord,
  come and stay at my home," and she prevailed on us. ✛

  Psalm 149:1b-2, 3-4, 5-6a and 9b
R. (see 4a) **The Lord takes delight in his people.** *(or Alleluia.)*
Sing to the LORD a new song
  of praise in the assembly of the faithful.
Let Israel be glad in their maker,
  let the children of Zion rejoice in their king. **R.**
Let them praise his name in the festive dance,
  let them sing praise to him with timbrel and harp.
For the LORD loves his people,
  and he adorns the lowly with victory. **R.**
Let the faithful exult in glory;
  let them sing for joy upon their couches.
Let the high praises of God be in their throats.
  This is the glory of all his faithful. Alleluia. **R.**

John 15:26b, 27a
R. Alleluia, alleluia.
The Spirit of truth will testify to me, says the Lord,
and you also will testify. **R.**

† *John 15:26—16:4a*
The Spirit of truth will testify to me.

Jesus said to his disciples:
"When the Advocate comes whom I will send you from the Father,
   the Spirit of truth who proceeds from the Father,
   he will testify to me.
And you also testify,
   because you have been with me from the beginning.

"I have told you this so that you may not fall away.
They will expel you from the synagogues;
   in fact, the hour is coming when everyone who kills you
   will think he is offering worship to God.
They will do this because they have not known either the Father or
      me.
I have told you this so that when their hour comes
   you may remember that I told you." ✛

TUESDAY, MAY 16
EASTER WEEKDAY

† *Acts of the Apostles 16:22-34*
Believe in the Lord Jesus and you and your household will be saved.

The crowd in Philippi joined in the attack on Paul and Silas,
   and the magistrates had them stripped
   and ordered them to be beaten with rods.
After inflicting many blows on them,
   they threw them into prison
   and instructed the jailer to guard them securely.
When he received these instructions, he put them in the innermost
      cell
   and secured their feet to a stake.

About midnight, while Paul and Silas were praying
   and singing hymns to God as the prisoners listened,
   there was suddenly such a severe earthquake
   that the foundations of the jail shook;
   all the doors flew open, and the chains of all were pulled loose.
When the jailer woke up and saw the prison doors wide open,
   he drew his sword and was about to kill himself,
   thinking that the prisoners had escaped.

But Paul shouted out in a loud voice,
  "Do no harm to yourself; we are all here."
He asked for a light and rushed in and,
  trembling with fear, he fell down before Paul and Silas.
Then he brought them out and said,
  "Sirs, what must I do to be saved?"
And they said, "Believe in the Lord Jesus
  and you and your household will be saved."
So they spoke the word of the Lord to him and to everyone in his
    house.
He took them in at that hour of the night and bathed their wounds;
  then he and all his family were baptized at once.
He brought them up into his house and provided a meal
  and with his household rejoiced at having come to faith in God. ✠

Psalm 138:1-2ab, 2cde-3, 7c-8

R. (7c) Your right hand saves me, O Lord. *(or* **Alleluia.***)*
I will give thanks to you, O LORD, with all my heart,
  for you have heard the words of my mouth;
  in the presence of the angels I will sing your praise;
I will worship at your holy temple,
  and give thanks to your name. **R.**
Because of your kindness and your truth,
  you have made great above all things
  your name and your promise.
When I called, you answered me;
  you built up strength within me. **R.**
Your right hand saves me.
The LORD will complete what he has done for me;
  your kindness, O LORD, endures forever;
  forsake not the work of your hands. **R.**

See John 16:7, 13

R. Alleluia, alleluia.
I will send to you the Spirit of truth, says the Lord;
he will guide you to all truth. **R.**

✝ *John 16:5-11*
For if I do not go, the Advocate will not come to you.

Jesus said to his disciples:
"Now I am going to the one who sent me,
  and not one of you asks me, 'Where are you going?'
But because I told you this, grief has filled your hearts.
But I tell you the truth, it is better for you that I go.
For if I do not go, the Advocate will not come to you.

But if I go, I will send him to you.
And when he comes he will convict the world
  in regard to sin and righteousness and condemnation:
  sin, because they do not believe in me;
  righteousness, because I am going to the Father
  and you will no longer see me;
  condemnation, because the ruler of this world has been
    condemned." ✝

WEDNESDAY, MAY 17
EASTER WEEKDAY

✝ *Acts of the Apostles 17:15, 22—18:1*
What therefore you unknowingly worship, I proclaim to you.

After Paul's escorts had taken him to Athens,
  they came away with instructions for Silas and Timothy
  to join him as soon as possible.

Then Paul stood up at the Areopagus and said:
  "You Athenians, I see that in every respect
  you are very religious.
For as I walked around looking carefully at your shrines,
  I even discovered an altar inscribed, 'To an Unknown God.'
What therefore you unknowingly worship, I proclaim to you.
The God who made the world and all that is in it,
  the Lord of heaven and earth,
  does not dwell in sanctuaries made by human hands,
  nor is he served by human hands because he needs anything.
Rather it is he who gives to everyone life and breath and everything.
He made from one the whole human race
  to dwell on the entire surface of the earth,
  and he fixed the ordered seasons and the boundaries of their regions,
  so that people might seek God,
  even perhaps grope for him and find him,
  though indeed he is not far from any one of us.
For 'In him we live and move and have our being,'
  as even some of your poets have said,
  'For we too are his offspring.'
Since therefore we are the offspring of God,
  we ought not to think that the divinity is like an image
  fashioned from gold, silver, or stone by human art and imagination.
God has overlooked the times of ignorance,
  but now he demands that all people everywhere repent
  because he has established a day on which he will 'judge the world
  with justice' through a man he has appointed,

and he has provided confirmation for all
by raising him from the dead."

When they heard about resurrection of the dead,
some began to scoff, but others said,
"We should like to hear you on this some other time."
And so Paul left them.
But some did join him, and became believers.
Among them were Dionysius,
a member of the Court of the Areopagus,
a woman named Damaris, and others with them.

After this he left Athens and went to Corinth. ✛

Psalm 148:1-2, 11-12, 13, 14

R. Heaven and earth are full of your glory. *(or* **Alleluia.***)*
Praise the LORD from the heavens;
  praise him in the heights.
Praise him, all you his angels;
  praise him, all you his hosts. **R.**
Let the kings of the earth and all peoples,
  the princes and all the judges of the earth,
Young men too, and maidens,
  old men and boys. **R.**
Praise the name of the LORD,
  for his name alone is exalted;
His majesty is above earth and heaven. **R.**
He has lifted up the horn of his people;
Be this his praise from all his faithful ones,
  from the children of Israel, the people close to him.
  Alleluia. **R.**

John 14:16

R. Alleluia, alleluia.
I will ask the Father
and he will give you another Advocate
to be with you always. **R.**

✝ *John 16:12-15*

When the Spirit of truth comes, he will guide you to all truth.

Jesus said to his disciples:
"I have much more to tell you, but you cannot bear it now.
But when he comes, the Spirit of truth,
  he will guide you to all truth.
He will not speak on his own,
  but he will speak what he hears,

and will declare to you the things that are coming.
He will glorify me,
    because he will take from what is mine and declare it to you.
Everything that the Father has is mine;
    for this reason I told you that he will take from what is mine
    and declare it to you." ✛

THURSDAY, MAY 18
THE ASCENSION OF THE LORD

(If the Ascension is celebrated on the Seventh Sunday of Easter, May 21,
the readings today are for an Easter Weekday [St. Pope John I]:
Acts of the Apostles 18:1-8 • Psalm 98:1, 2-3ab, 3cd-4 • John 16:16-20 [294].)

† Acts of the Apostles 1:1-11
As the Apostles were looking on, Jesus was taken up.

In the first book, Theophilus,
    I dealt with all that Jesus did and taught
    until the day he was taken up,
    after giving instructions through the Holy Spirit
    to the apostles whom he had chosen.
He presented himself alive to them
    by many proofs after he had suffered,
    appearing to them during forty days
    and speaking about the kingdom of God.
While meeting with them,
    he enjoined them not to depart from Jerusalem,
    but to wait for "the promise of the Father
    about which you have heard me speak;
    for John baptized with water,
    but in a few days you will be baptized with the Holy Spirit."

When they had gathered together they asked him,
    "Lord, are you at this time going to restore the kingdom to Israel?"
He answered them, "It is not for you to know the times or seasons
    that the Father has established by his own authority.
But you will receive power when the Holy Spirit comes upon you,
    and you will be my witnesses in Jerusalem,
    throughout Judea and Samaria,
    and to the ends of the earth."
When he had said this, as they were looking on,
    he was lifted up, and a cloud took him from their sight.
While they were looking intently at the sky as he was going,
    suddenly two men dressed in white garments stood beside them.
They said, "Men of Galilee,
    why are you standing there looking at the sky?

This Jesus who has been taken up from you into heaven
  will return in the same way as you have seen him going into
    heaven." ✢

Psalm 47:2-3, 6-7, 8-9

R. (6) **God mounts his throne to shouts of joy: a blare of
  trumpets for the Lord.** *(or* **Alleluia.***)*

All you peoples, clap your hands,
  shout to God with cries of gladness,
For the LORD, the Most High, the awesome,
  is the great king over all the earth. **R.**
God mounts his throne amid shouts of joy;
  the LORD, amid trumpet blasts.
Sing praise to God, sing praise;
  sing praise to our king, sing praise. **R.**
For king of all the earth is God;
  sing hymns of praise.
God reigns over the nations,
  God sits upon his holy throne. **R.**

† *Ephesians 1:17-23*

God seated Jesus at his right hand in the heavens.

Brothers and sisters:
May the God of our Lord Jesus Christ, the Father of glory,
  give you a Spirit of wisdom and revelation
  resulting in knowledge of him.
May the eyes of your hearts be enlightened,
  that you may know what is the hope that belongs to his call,
  what are the riches of glory
  in his inheritance among the holy ones,
  and what is the surpassing greatness of his power
  for us who believe,
  in accord with the exercise of his great might,
  which he worked in Christ,
  raising him from the dead
  and seating him at his right hand in the heavens,
  far above every principality, authority, power, and dominion,
  and every name that is named
  not only in this age but also in the one to come.
And he put all things beneath his feet
  and gave him as head over all things to the church,
  which is his body,
  the fullness of the one who fills all things in every way. ✢

Matthew 28:19a, 20b
R. Alleluia, alleluia.
Go and teach all nations, says the Lord;
I am with you always, until the end of the world. **R.**

✝ *Matthew 28:16-20*
All power in heaven and on earth has been given to me.

The eleven disciples went to Galilee,
  to the mountain to which Jesus had ordered them.
When they saw him, they worshiped, but they doubted.
Then Jesus approached and said to them,
  "All power in heaven and on earth has been given to me.
Go, therefore, and make disciples of all nations,
  baptizing them in the name of the Father,
  and of the Son, and of the Holy Spirit,
  teaching them to observe all that I have commanded you.
And behold, I am with you always, until the end of the age."✛

FRIDAY, MAY 19
EASTER WEEKDAY

✝ *Acts of the Apostles 18:9-18*
I have many people in this city.

One night while Paul was in Corinth, the Lord said to him in a vision,
  "Do not be afraid.
Go on speaking, and do not be silent, for I am with you.
No one will attack and harm you,
  for I have many people in this city."
He settled there for a year and a half
  and taught the word of God among them.

But when Gallio was proconsul of Achaia,
  the Jews rose up together against Paul
  and brought him to the tribunal, saying,
  "This man is inducing people to worship God contrary to the law."
When Paul was about to reply, Gallio spoke to the Jews,
  "If it were a matter of some crime or malicious fraud,
  I should with reason hear the complaint of you Jews;
  but since it is a question of arguments over doctrine and titles
  and your own law, see to it yourselves.
I do not wish to be a judge of such matters."
And he drove them away from the tribunal.
They all seized Sosthenes, the synagogue official,
  and beat him in full view of the tribunal.
But none of this was of concern to Gallio.

Paul remained for quite some time,
   and after saying farewell to the brothers he sailed for Syria,
   together with Priscilla and Aquila.
At Cenchreae he had shaved his head because he had taken a vow. ✛

   Psalm 47:2-3, 4-5, 6-7
R. (8a) **God is king of all the earth.** *(or* **Alleluia.***)*
All you peoples, clap your hands,
   shout to God with cries of gladness,
For the LORD, the Most High, the awesome,
   is the great king over all the earth. **R.**
He brings people under us;
   nations under our feet.
He chooses for us our inheritance,
   the glory of Jacob, whom he loves. **R.**
God mounts his throne amid shouts of joy;
   the LORD, amid trumpet blasts.
Sing praise to God, sing praise;
   sing praise to our king, sing praise. **R.**

   See Luke 24:46, 26
R. Alleluia, alleluia.
Christ had to suffer and to rise from the dead,
and so enter into his glory. **R.**

✝ *John 16:20-23*
No one will take your joy away from you.

Jesus said to his disciples:
"Amen, amen, I say to you, you will weep and mourn,
   while the world rejoices;
   you will grieve, but your grief will become joy.
When a woman is in labor, she is in anguish because her hour has
     arrived;
   but when she has given birth to a child,
   she no longer remembers the pain because of her joy
   that a child has been born into the world.
So you also are now in anguish.
But I will see you again, and your hearts will rejoice,
   and no one will take your joy away from you.
On that day you will not question me about anything.
Amen, amen, I say to you,
   whatever you ask the Father in my name he will give you." ✛

SATURDAY, MAY 20
Easter Weekday, St. Bernardine of Siena

† *Acts of the Apostles 18:23-28*
Apollos established from the Scriptures that the Christ is Jesus.

After staying in Antioch some time,
   Paul left and traveled in orderly sequence
   through the Galatian country and Phrygia,
   bringing strength to all the disciples.

A Jew named Apollos, a native of Alexandria,
   an eloquent speaker, arrived in Ephesus.
He was an authority on the Scriptures.
He had been instructed in the Way of the Lord and,
   with ardent spirit, spoke and taught accurately about Jesus,
   although he knew only the baptism of John.
He began to speak boldly in the synagogue;
   but when Priscilla and Aquila heard him,
   they took him aside
   and explained to him the Way of God more accurately.
And when he wanted to cross to Achaia,
   the brothers encouraged him
   and wrote to the disciples there to welcome him.
After his arrival he gave great assistance
   to those who had come to believe through grace.
He vigorously refuted the Jews in public,
   establishing from the Scriptures that the Christ is Jesus. ✛

   Psalm 47:2-3, 8-9, 10
R. (8a) **God is king of all the earth.** *(or Alleluia.)*
All you peoples, clap your hands;
   shout to God with cries of gladness.
For the LORD, the Most High, the awesome,
   is the great king over all the earth. **R.**
For king of all the earth is God;
   sing hymns of praise.
God reigns over the nations,
   God sits upon his holy throne. **R.**
The princes of the peoples are gathered together
   with the people of the God of Abraham.
For God's are the guardians of the earth;
   he is supreme. **R.**

   John 16:28
R. Alleluia, alleluia.
I came from the Father and have come into the world;
now I am leaving the world and going back to the Father. **R.**

† *John 16:23b-28*

My Father loves you because you have loved me and believed in me.

Jesus said to his disciples:
"Amen, amen, I say to you,
 whatever you ask the Father in my name he will give you.
Until now you have not asked anything in my name;
 ask and you will receive, so that your joy may be complete.

"I have told you this in figures of speech.
The hour is coming when I will no longer speak to you in figures
 but I will tell you clearly about the Father.
On that day you will ask in my name,
 and I do not tell you that I will ask the Father for you.
For the Father himself loves you, because you have loved me
 and have come to believe that I came from God.
I came from the Father and have come into the world.
Now I am leaving the world and going back to the Father." ✛

SUNDAY, MAY 21
SEVENTH SUNDAY OF EASTER
(If the Ascension is celebrated today, use the readings given for Thursday, May 18.)

† *Acts of the Apostles 1:12-14*
All these devoted themselves with one accord to prayer.

After Jesus had been taken up to heaven the apostles
 returned to Jerusalem
 from the mount called Olivet, which is near Jerusalem,
 a sabbath day's journey away.

When they entered the city
 they went to the upper room where they were staying,
 Peter and John and James and Andrew,
 Philip and Thomas, Bartholomew and Matthew,
 James son of Alphaeus, Simon the Zealot,
 and Judas son of James.
All these devoted themselves with one accord to prayer,
 together with some women,
 and Mary the mother of Jesus, and his brothers. ✛

Psalm 27:1, 4, 7-8

R. (13) **I believe that I shall see the good things of the Lord in
 the land of the living.** *(or Alleluia.)*
The LORD is my light and my salvation;
 whom should I fear?
The LORD is my life's refuge;

of whom should I be afraid? **R.**

One thing I ask of the L ORD;
   this I seek:
to dwell in the house of the L ORD
   all the days of my life,
That I may gaze on the loveliness of the L ORD
   and contemplate his temple. **R.**
Hear, O Lord, the sound of my call;
   have pity on me, and answer me.
Of you my heart speaks; you my glance seeks. **R.**

† *1 Peter 4:13-16*
If you are insulted for the name of Christ, blessed are you.

Beloved:

Rejoice to the extent that you share in the sufferings of Christ,
   so that when his glory is revealed
   you may also rejoice exultantly.
If you are insulted for the name of Christ, blessed are you,
   for the Spirit of glory and of God rests upon you.
But let no one among you be made to suffer
   as a murderer, a thief, an evildoer, or as an intriguer.
But whoever is made to suffer as a Christian should not be ashamed
   but glorify God because of the name. ✛

   See John 14:18
R. Alleluia, alleluia.
I will not leave you orphans, says the Lord.
I will come back to you, and your heart will rejoice. **R.**

† *John 17:1-11a*
Father, glorify your Son.

Jesus raised his eyes to heaven and said,
   "Father, the hour has come.
Give glory to your son, so that your son may glorify you,
   just as you gave him authority over all people,
   so that your son may give eternal life to all you gave him.
Now this is eternal life,
   that they should know you, the only true God,
   and the one whom you sent, Jesus Christ.
I glorified you on earth
   by accomplishing the work that you gave me to do.
Now glorify me, Father, with you,
   with the glory that I had with you before the world began.

"I revealed your name to those whom you gave me out of the world.

They belonged to you, and you gave them to me,
   and they have kept your word.
Now they know that everything you gave me is from you,
   because the words you gave to me I have given to them,
   and they accepted them and truly understood that I came from you,
   and they have believed that you sent me.
I pray for them.
I do not pray for the world but for the ones you have given me,
   because they are yours, and everything of mine is yours
   and everything of yours is mine,
   and I have been glorified in them.
And now I will no longer be in the world,
   but they are in the world, while I am coming to you." ✛

MONDAY, MAY 22
EASTER WEEKDAY, ST. RITA OF CASCIA

✝ Acts of the Apostles 19:1-8
Did you receive the Holy Spirit when you became believers?

While Apollos was in Corinth,
   Paul traveled through the interior of the country
   and down to Ephesus where he found some disciples.
He said to them,
   "Did you receive the Holy Spirit when you became believers?"
They answered him,
   "We have never even heard that there is a Holy Spirit."
He said, "How were you baptized?"
They replied, "With the baptism of John."
Paul then said, "John baptized with a baptism of repentance,
   telling the people to believe in the one who was to come after him,
   that is, in Jesus."
When they heard this,
   they were baptized in the name of the Lord Jesus.
And when Paul laid his hands on them,
   the Holy Spirit came upon them,
   and they spoke in tongues and prophesied.
Altogether there were about twelve men.

He entered the synagogue, and for three months debated boldly
   with persuasive arguments about the Kingdom of God. ✛

   Psalm 68:2-3ab, 4-5acd, 6-7ab
R. (33a) Sing to God, O kingdoms of the earth. *(or **Alleluia.**)*
God arises; his enemies are scattered,
   and those who hate him flee before him.
As smoke is driven away, so are they driven;

as wax melts before the fire. **R.**
But the just rejoice and exult before God;
   they are glad and rejoice.
Sing to God, chant praise to his name;
   whose name is the LORD. **R.**
The father of orphans and the defender of widows
   is God in his holy dwelling.
God gives a home to the forsaken;
   he leads forth prisoners to prosperity. **R.**

   Colossians 3:1
R. Alleluia, alleluia.
If then you were raised with Christ,
seek what is above,
where Christ is seated at the right hand of God. **R.**

✛ John 16:29-33
Take courage, I have conquered the world.

The disciples said to Jesus,
   "Now you are talking plainly, and not in any figure of speech.
Now we realize that you know everything
   and that you do not need to have anyone question you.
Because of this we believe that you came from God."
Jesus answered them, "Do you believe now?
Behold, the hour is coming and has arrived
   when each of you will be scattered to his own home
   and you will leave me alone.
But I am not alone, because the Father is with me.
I have told you this so that you might have peace in me.
In the world you will have trouble,
   but take courage, I have conquered the world." ✛

TUESDAY, MAY 23
EASTER WEEKDAY

✛ Acts of the Apostles 20:17-27
I am finishing my course and the ministry that I received from the Lord Jesus.

From Miletus Paul had the presbyters
   of the Church at Ephesus summoned.
When they came to him, he addressed them,
   "You know how I lived among you
   the whole time from the day I first came to the province of Asia.
I served the Lord with all humility
   and with the tears and trials that came to me
   because of the plots of the Jews,
   and I did not at all shrink from telling you

what was for your benefit,
or from teaching you in public or in your homes.
I earnestly bore witness for both Jews and Greeks
to repentance before God and to faith in our Lord Jesus.
But now, compelled by the Spirit, I am going to Jerusalem.
What will happen to me there I do not know,
except that in one city after another
the Holy Spirit has been warning me
that imprisonment and hardships await me.
Yet I consider life of no importance to me,
if only I may finish my course
and the ministry that I received from the Lord Jesus,
to bear witness to the Gospel of God's grace.

"But now I know that none of you
to whom I preached the kingdom during my travels
will ever see my face again.
And so I solemnly declare to you this day
that I am not responsible for the blood of any of you,
for I did not shrink from proclaiming to you the entire plan of God." ✛

Psalm 68:10-11, 20-21
R. (33a) **Sing to God, O kingdoms of the earth.** *(or* **Alleluia.***)*
A bountiful rain you showered down, O God, upon your inheritance;
you restored the land when it languished;
Your flock settled in it;
in your goodness, O God, you provided it for the needy. **R.**
Blessed day by day be the Lord,
who bears our burdens; God, who is our salvation.
God is a saving God for us;
the LORD, my Lord, controls the passageways of death. **R.**

John 14:16
R. Alleluia, alleluia.
I will ask the Father
and he will give you another Advocate
to be with you always. **R.**

† *John 17:1-11a*
Father, glorify your Son.

Jesus raised his eyes to heaven and said,
"Father, the hour has come.
Give glory to your son, so that your son may glorify you,
just as you gave him authority over all people,
so that your son may give eternal life to all you gave him.
Now this is eternal life,

that they should know you, the only true God,
and the one whom you sent, Jesus Christ.
I glorified you on earth
by accomplishing the work that you gave me to do.
Now glorify me, Father, with you,
with the glory that I had with you before the world began.

"I revealed your name to those whom you gave me out of the world.
They belonged to you, and you gave them to me,
and they have kept your word.
Now they know that everything you gave me is from you,
because the words you gave to me I have given to them,
and they accepted them and truly understood that I came from you,
and they have believed that you sent me.
I pray for them.
I do not pray for the world but for the ones you have given me,
because they are yours, and everything of mine is yours
and everything of yours is mine,
and I have been glorified in them.
And now I will no longer be in the world,
but they are in the world, while I am coming to you." ✛

WEDNESDAY, MAY 24
Easter Weekday

† *Acts of the Apostles 20:28-38*
*I commend you to God who has the power to build you up
and to give you an inheritance.*

At Miletus, Paul spoke to the presbyters of the Church of Ephesus:
"Keep watch over yourselves and over the whole flock
of which the Holy Spirit has appointed you overseers,
in which you tend the Church of God
that he acquired with his own Blood.
I know that after my departure savage wolves will come among you,
and they will not spare the flock.
And from your own group, men will come forward perverting the
truth
to draw the disciples away after them.
So be vigilant and remember that for three years, night and day,
I unceasingly admonished each of you with tears.
And now I commend you to God
and to that gracious word of his that can build you up
and give you the inheritance among all who are consecrated.
I have never wanted anyone's silver or gold or clothing.
You know well that these very hands

have served my needs and my companions.
In every way I have shown you that by hard work of that sort
  we must help the weak,
  and keep in mind the words of the Lord Jesus who himself said,
  'It is more blessed to give than to receive.'"

When he had finished speaking
  he knelt down and prayed with them all.
They were all weeping loudly
  as they threw their arms around Paul and kissed him,
  for they were deeply distressed that he had said
  that they would never see his face again.
Then they escorted him to the ship. ✢

Psalm 68:29-30, 33-35a, 35bc-36ab
R. (33a) **Sing to God, O kingdoms of the earth.** *(or* **Alleluia.***)*
Show forth, O God, your power,
  the power, O God, with which you took our part;
For your temple in Jerusalem
  let the kings bring you gifts. **R.**
You kingdoms of the earth, sing to God,
  chant praise to the Lord
  who rides on the heights of the ancient heavens.
Behold, his voice resounds, the voice of power:
  "Confess the power of God!" **R.**
Over Israel is his majesty;
  his power is in the skies.
Awesome in his sanctuary is God, the God of Israel;
  he gives power and strength to his people. **R.**

See John 17:17b, 17a
R. Alleluia, alleluia.
Your word, O Lord, is truth;
consecrate us in the truth. **R.**

✝ *John 17:11b-19*
May they be one just as we are one.

Lifting up his eyes to heaven, Jesus prayed, saying:
"Holy Father, keep them in your name
  that you have given me,
  so that they may be one just as we are one.
When I was with them I protected them in your name that you gave
    me,
  and I guarded them, and none of them was lost
  except the son of destruction,
  in order that the Scripture might be fulfilled.

But now I am coming to you.
I speak this in the world
    so that they may share my joy completely.
I gave them your word, and the world hated them,
    because they do not belong to the world
    any more than I belong to the world.
I do not ask that you take them out of the world
    but that you keep them from the Evil One.
They do not belong to the world
    any more than I belong to the world.
Consecrate them in the truth.
Your word is truth.
As you sent me into the world,
    so I sent them into the world.
And I consecrate myself for them,
    so that they also may be consecrated in truth." ✝

THURSDAY, MAY 25
EASTER WEEKDAY, ST. BEDE THE VENERABLE, ST. POPE GREGORY VII, ST. MARY MAGDALENE DE' PAZZI

† *Acts of the Apostles 22:30; 23:6-11*
You must bear witness in Rome.

Wishing to determine the truth
    about why Paul was being accused by the Jews,
    the commander freed him
    and ordered the chief priests and the whole Sanhedrin to convene.
Then he brought Paul down and made him stand before them.

Paul was aware that some were Sadducees and some Pharisees,
    so he called out before the Sanhedrin,
    "My brothers, I am a Pharisee, the son of Pharisees;
    I am on trial for hope in the resurrection of the dead."
When he said this,
    a dispute broke out between the Pharisees and Sadducees,
    and the group became divided.
For the Sadducees say that there is no resurrection
    or angels or spirits,
    while the Pharisees acknowledge all three.
A great uproar occurred,
    and some scribes belonging to the Pharisee party
    stood up and sharply argued,
    "We find nothing wrong with this man.
Suppose a spirit or an angel has spoken to him?"
The dispute was so serious that the commander,

afraid that Paul would be torn to pieces by them,
ordered his troops to go down and rescue Paul from their midst
and take him into the compound.
The following night the Lord stood by him and said, "Take courage.
For just as you have borne witness to my cause in Jerusalem,
so you must also bear witness in Rome." ✠

Psalm 16:1b-2a and 5, 7-8, 9-10, 11
R. (1) **Keep me safe, O God; you are my hope.** *(or* **Alleluia.***)*
Keep me, O God, for in you I take refuge;
I say to the LORD, "My Lord are you."
O LORD, my allotted portion and my cup,
you it is who hold fast my lot. **R.**
I bless the LORD who counsels me;
even in the night my heart exhorts me.
I set the LORD ever before me;
with him at my right hand I shall not be disturbed. **R.**
Therefore my heart is glad and my soul rejoices,
my body, too, abides in confidence;
Because you will not abandon my soul to the nether world,
nor will you suffer your faithful one to undergo corruption. **R.**
You will show me the path to life,
fullness of joys in your presence,
the delights at your right hand forever. **R.**

John 17:21
R. Alleluia, alleluia.
May they all be one as you, Father, are in me and I in you,
that the world may believe that you sent me, says the Lord. **R.**

† *John 17:20-26*
May they all be one.

Lifting up his eyes to heaven, Jesus prayed saying:
"I pray not only for these,
but also for those who will believe in me through their word,
so that they may all be one,
as you, Father, are in me and I in you,
that they also may be in us,
that the world may believe that you sent me.
And I have given them the glory you gave me,
so that they may be one, as we are one,
I in them and you in me,
that they may be brought to perfection as one,
that the world may know that you sent me,
and that you loved them even as you loved me.

Father, they are your gift to me.
I wish that where I am they also may be with me,
  that they may see my glory that you gave me,
  because you loved me before the foundation of the world.
Righteous Father, the world also does not know you,
  but I know you, and they know that you sent me.
I made known to them your name and I will make it known,
  that the love with which you loved me
  may be in them and I in them." ✛

FRIDAY, MAY 26
St. Philip Neri

† *Acts of the Apostles 25:13b-21*
Jesus was dead, whom Paul claimed to be alive.

King Agrippa and Bernice arrived in Caesarea
  on a visit to Festus.
Since they spent several days there,
  Festus referred Paul's case to the king, saying,
  "There is a man here left in custody by Felix.
When I was in Jerusalem the chief priests and the elders of the Jews
  brought charges against him and demanded his condemnation.
I answered them that it was not Roman practice
  to hand over an accused person before he has faced his accusers
  and had the opportunity to defend himself against their charge.
So when they came together here, I made no delay;
  the next day I took my seat on the tribunal
  and ordered the man to be brought in.
His accusers stood around him,
  but did not charge him with any of the crimes I suspected.
Instead they had some issues with him about their own religion
  and about a certain Jesus who had died
  but who Paul claimed was alive.
Since I was at a loss how to investigate this controversy,
  I asked if he were willing to go to Jerusalem
  and there stand trial on these charges.
And when Paul appealed that he be held in custody
  for the Emperor's decision,
  I ordered him held until I could send him to Caesar." ✛

Psalm 103:1-2, 11-12, 19-20ab
R. (19a) **The Lord has established his throne in heaven.**
  *(or **Alleluia**.)*
Bless the LORD, O my soul;
  and all my being, bless his holy name.

Bless the LORD, O my soul,
  and forget not all his benefits. **R.**
For as the heavens are high above the earth,
  so surpassing is his kindness toward those who fear him.
As far as the east is from the west,
  so far has he put our transgressions from us. **R.**
The LORD has established his throne in heaven,
  and his kingdom rules over all.
Bless the LORD, all you his angels,
  you mighty in strength, who do his bidding. **R.**

John 14:26
R. Alleluia, alleluia.
The Holy Spirit will teach you everything
and remind you of all I told you. **R.**

† *John 21:15-19*

Feed my lambs, feed my sheep.

After Jesus had revealed himself to his disciples and eaten
    breakfast with them,
  he said to Simon Peter,
  "Simon, son of John, do you love me more than these?"
Simon Peter answered him, "Yes, Lord, you know that I love you."
Jesus said to him, "Feed my lambs."
He then said to Simon Peter a second time,
  "Simon, son of John, do you love me?"
Simon Peter answered him, "Yes, Lord, you know that I love you."
He said to him, "Tend my sheep."
He said to him the third time,
  "Simon, son of John, do you love me?"
Peter was distressed that he had said to him a third time,
  "Do you love me?" and he said to him,
  "Lord, you know everything; you know that I love you."
Jesus said to him, "Feed my sheep.
Amen, amen, I say to you, when you were younger,
  you used to dress yourself and go where you wanted;
  but when you grow old, you will stretch out your hands,
  and someone else will dress you
  and lead you where you do not want to go."
He said this signifying by what kind of death he would glorify God.
And when he had said this, he said to him, "Follow me." ✝

SATURDAY, MAY 27
EASTER WEEKDAY, ST. AUGUSTINE OF CANTERBURY

(Morning) ✝ *Acts of the Apostles 28:16-20, 30-31*
Paul remained at Rome, proclaiming the Kingdom of God.

When he entered Rome, Paul was allowed to live by himself,
　　with the soldier who was guarding him.

Three days later he called together the leaders of the Jews.
When they had gathered he said to them, "My brothers,
　　although I had done nothing against our people
　　or our ancestral customs,
　　I was handed over to the Romans as a prisoner from Jerusalem.
After trying my case the Romans wanted to release me,
　　because they found nothing against me deserving the death penalty.
But when the Jews objected, I was obliged to appeal to Caesar,
　　even though I had no accusation to make against my own nation.
This is the reason, then, I have requested to see you
　　and to speak with you, for it is on account of the hope of Israel
　　that I wear these chains."

He remained for two full years in his lodgings.
He received all who came to him, and with complete assurance
　　and without hindrance he proclaimed the Kingdom of God
　　and taught about the Lord Jesus Christ. ✛

Psalm 11:4, 5, 7
R. (see 7b) **The just will gaze on your face, O Lord.**
　　(or **Alleluia.***)*
The LORD is in his holy temple;
　　the LORD's throne is in heaven.
His eyes behold,
　　his searching glance is on mankind. **R.**
The LORD searches the just and the wicked;
　　the lover of violence he hates.
For the LORD is just, he loves just deeds;
　　the upright shall see his face. **R.**

John 16:7, 13
R. Alleluia, alleluia.
I will send to you the Spirit of truth, says the Lord;
he will guide you to all truth. **R.**

✝ *John 21:20-25*
This is the disciple who has written these things and his testimony is true.

Peter turned and saw the disciple following whom Jesus loved,
　　the one who had also reclined upon his chest during the supper

and had said, "Master, who is the one who will betray you?"
When Peter saw him, he said to Jesus, "Lord, what about him?"
Jesus said to him, "What if I want him to remain until I come?
What concern is it of yours?
You follow me."
So the word spread among the brothers that that disciple would not
    die.
But Jesus had not told him that he would not die,
  just "What if I want him to remain until I come?
What concern is it of yours?"

It is this disciple who testifies to these things
  and has written them, and we know that his testimony is true.
There are also many other things that Jesus did,
  but if these were to be described individually,
    I do not think the whole world would contain the books
that would be written. ✛

SUNDAY, MAY 28
PENTECOST SUNDAY

(The Pentecost Vigil Readings are: Genesis 11:1-9 or Exodus 19:3-8a, 16-20b or
Ezekiel 37:1-14 or Joel 3:1-5 • Psalm 104:1-2, 24, 35, 27-28, 29-30 • Romans 8:22-27 •
John 7:37-39. The Extended Vigil: Genesis 11:1-9 • Psalm 33:10-15 • Exodus 19:3-8a,
16-20b • Daniel 3:52-56 or Psalm 19:8-11• Ezekiel 37:1-14 • Psalm 107:2-9 • Joel 3:1-5 •
Psalm 104:1-2, 24, 35, 27-28, 29, 30 • Romans 8:22-27 • John 7:37-39 [62].)

† Acts of the Apostles 2:1-11
They were filled with the Holy Spirit and began to speak.

When the time for Pentecost was fulfilled,
  they were all in one place together.
And suddenly there came from the sky
  a noise like a strong driving wind,
  and it filled the entire house in which they were.
Then there appeared to them tongues as of fire,
  which parted and came to rest on each one of them.
And they were all filled with the Holy Spirit
  and began to speak in different tongues,
  as the Spirit enabled them to proclaim.

Now there were devout Jews from every nation under heaven
  staying in Jerusalem.
At this sound, they gathered in a large crowd,
  but they were confused
  because each one heard them speaking in his own language.
They were astounded, and in amazement they asked,
  "Are not all these people who are speaking Galileans?

Then how does each of us hear them in his native language?
We are Parthians, Medes, and Elamites,
  inhabitants of Mesopotamia, Judea and Cappadocia,
  Pontus and Asia, Phrygia and Pamphylia,
  Egypt and the districts of Libya near Cyrene,
  as well as travelers from Rome,
  both Jews and converts to Judaism, Cretans and Arabs,
  yet we hear them speaking in our own tongues
  of the mighty acts of God." ✚

  Psalm 104:1, 24, 29-30, 31, 34

R. (see 30) **Lord, send out your Spirit, and renew the face of
  the earth.** *(or Alleluia.)*
Bless the LORD, O my soul!
  O LORD, my God, you are great indeed!
How manifold are your works, O LORD!
  The earth is full of your creatures. **R.**
If you take away their breath, they perish
  and return to their dust.
When you send forth your spirit, they are created,
  and you renew the face of the earth. **R.**
May the glory of the LORD endure forever;
  may the LORD be glad in his works!
Pleasing to him be my theme;
  I will be glad in the LORD. **R.**

† *1 Corinthians 12:3b-7, 12-13*
In one Spirit we were all baptized into one body.

Brothers and sisters:
No one can say, "Jesus is Lord," except by the Holy Spirit.
There are different kinds of spiritual gifts but the same Spirit;
  there are different forms of service but the same Lord;
  there are different workings but the same God
  who produces all of them in everyone.
To each individual the manifestation of the Spirit
  is given for some benefit.

As a body is one though it has many parts,
  and all the parts of the body, though many, are one body,
  so also Christ.
For in one Spirit we were all baptized into one body,
  whether Jews or Greeks, slaves or free persons,
  and we were all given to drink of one Spirit. ✚

PENTECOST SEQUENCE: Veni, Sancte Spiritus

Come, Holy Spirit, come!
And from your celestial home
   Shed a ray of light divine!
Come, Father of the poor!
Come, source of all our store!
   Come, within our bosoms shine.
You, of comforters the best;
You, the soul's most welcome guest;
   Sweet refreshment here below;
In our labor, rest most sweet;
Grateful coolness in the heat;
   Solace in the midst of woe.
O most blessed Light divine,
Shine within these hearts of yours,
   And our inmost being fill!
Where you are not, we have naught,
Nothing good in deed or thought,
   Nothing free from taint of ill.
Heal our wounds, our strength renew;
On our dryness pour your dew;
   Wash the stains of guilt away:
Bend the stubborn heart and will;
Melt the frozen, warm the chill;
   Guide the steps that go astray.
On the faithful, who adore
And confess you, evermore
   In your sevenfold gift descend;
Give them virtue's sure reward;
Give them your salvation, Lord;
   Give them joys that never end. Amen.
   Alleluia.

R. Alleluia, alleluia.

Come, Holy Spirit, fill the hearts of your faithful
and kindle in them the fire of your love. **R.**

† *John 20:19-23*

As the Father sent me, so I send you. Receive the Holy Spirit.

On the evening of that first day of the week,
   when the doors were locked, where the disciples were,
   for fear of the Jews,
   Jesus came and stood in their midst
   and said to them, "Peace be with you."
When he had said this, he showed them his hands and his side.
The disciples rejoiced when they saw the Lord.
Jesus said to them again, "Peace be with you.
As the Father has sent me, so I send you."
And when he had said this, he breathed on them and said to them,

"Receive the Holy Spirit.
Whose sins you forgive are forgiven them,
    and whose sins you retain are retained." ✛

MONDAY, MAY 29
THE BLESSED VIRGIN MARY, MOTHER OF THE CHURCH
(EIGHTH WEEK IN ORDINARY TIME)

† Genesis 3:9-15, 20 (or Acts of the Apostles 1:12-14)
The mother of all the living.

After Adam had eaten of the tree,
    the LORD God called to him and asked him, "Where are you?"
He answered, "I heard you in the garden;
    but I was afraid, because I was naked,
    so I hid myself."
Then he asked, "Who told you that you were naked?
You have eaten, then,
    from the tree of which I had forbidden you to eat!"
The man replied, "The woman whom you put here with me—
    she gave me fruit from the tree, and so I ate it."
The LORD God then asked the woman,
    "Why did you do such a thing?"
The woman answered, "The serpent tricked me into it, so I ate it."

Then the LORD God said to the serpent:
    "Because you have done this, you shall be banned
        from all the animals
        and from all the wild creatures;
    On your belly shall you crawl,
        and dirt shall you eat
        all the days of your life.
    I will put enmity between you and the woman,
        and between your offspring and hers;
    He will strike at your head,
        while you strike at his heel."
The man called his wife Eve,
    because she became the mother of all the living. ✛

Psalm 87:1-2, 3 and 5, 6-7
R. (3) **Glorious things are told of you, O city of God.**
His foundation upon the holy mountains
    the LORD loves:
The gates of Zion,
    more than any dwelling of Jacob. **R.**
Glorious things are said of you,
    O city of God!

And of Zion they shall say:
"One and all were born in her;
And he who has established her
is the Most High LORD." **R.**
They shall note, when the peoples are enrolled:
"This man was born there."
And all shall sing, in their festive dance:
"My home is within you." **R.**

R. Alleluia, alleluia.

O happy Virgin, you gave birth to the Lord;
O blessed mother of the Church,
you warm our hearts with the Spirit of your Son Jesus Christ. **R.**

† *John 19:25-34*
Woman, behold your son. Behold your mother.

Standing by the cross of Jesus were his mother
and his mother's sister, Mary the wife of Clopas,
and Mary of Magdala.
When Jesus saw his mother and the disciple there whom he loved,
he said to his mother, "Woman, behold, your son."
Then he said to the disciple,
"Behold, your mother."
And from that hour the disciple took her into his home.
After this, aware that everything was now finished,
in order that the Scripture might be fulfilled,
Jesus said, "I thirst."
There was a vessel filled with common wine.
So they put a sponge soaked in wine on a sprig of hyssop
and put it up to his mouth.
When Jesus had taken the wine, he said,
"It is finished."
And bowing his head, he handed over the spirit.

Now since it was preparation day,
in order that the bodies might not remain on the cross on the
sabbath,
for the sabbath day of that week was a solemn one,
the Jews asked Pilate that their legs be broken
and they be taken down.
So the soldiers came and broke the legs of the first
and then of the other one who was crucified with Jesus.
But when they came to Jesus and saw that he was already dead,
they did not break his legs,

but one soldier thrust his lance into his side,
and immediately Blood and water flowed out. ✦

TUESDAY, MAY 30
WEEKDAY

† *Sirach 35:1-12*
To keep the law is a great oblation.

To keep the law is a great oblation,
　and he who observes the
　commandments sacrifices a peace offering.
In works of charity one offers fine flour,
　and when he gives alms he presents his sacrifice of praise.
To refrain from evil pleases the LORD,
　and to avoid injustice is an atonement.
Appear not before the LORD empty-handed,
　for all that you offer is in fulfillment of the precepts.
The just one's offering enriches the altar
　and rises as a sweet odor before the Most High.
The just one's sacrifice is most pleasing,
　nor will it ever be forgotten.
In a generous spirit pay homage to the LORD,
　be not sparing of freewill gifts.
With each contribution show a cheerful countenance,
　and pay your tithes in a spirit of joy.
Give to the Most High as he has given to you,
　generously, according to your means.

For the LORD is one who always repays,
　and he will give back to you sevenfold.
But offer no bribes, these he does not accept!
　Trust not in sacrifice of the fruits of extortion.
For he is a God of justice,
　who knows no favorites. ✦

Psalm 50:5-6, 7-8, 14 and 23
R. (23b) **To the upright I will show the saving power of God.**
"Gather my faithful ones before me,
　those who have made a covenant with me by sacrifice."
And the heavens proclaim his justice;
　for God himself is the judge. **R.**
"Hear, my people, and I will speak;
　Israel, I will testify against you;
　God, your God, am I.
Not for your sacrifices do I rebuke you,
　for your burnt offerings are before me always." **R.**

"Offer to God praise as your sacrifice
and fulfill your vows to the Most High.
He that offers praise as a sacrifice glorifies me;
and to him that goes the right way I will show the salvation of
God." **R.**

See Matthew 11:25
R. Alleluia, alleluia.
Blessed are you, Father, Lord of heaven and earth;
you have revealed to little ones the mysteries of the Kingdom. **R.**

† *Mark 10:28-31*
*You will receive a hundred times as much persecution in this
present age, and eternal life in the age to come.*

Peter began to say to Jesus,
"We have given up everything and followed you."
Jesus said, "Amen, I say to you,
there is no one who has given up house or brothers or sisters
or mother or father or children or lands
for my sake and for the sake of the Gospel
who will not receive a hundred times more now in this present age:
houses and brothers and sisters
and mothers and children and lands,
with persecutions, and eternal life in the age to come.
But many that are first will be last, and the last will be first." ✛

WEDNESDAY, MAY 31
THE VISITATION OF THE BLESSED VIRGIN MARY

† *Zephaniah 3:14-18a (or Romans 12:9-16)*
The King of Israel, the Lord, is in your midst.

Shout for joy, O daughter Zion!
Sing joyfully, O Israel!
Be glad and exult with all your heart,
O daughter Jerusalem!
The LORD has removed the judgment against you,
he has turned away your enemies;
The King of Israel, the LORD, is in your midst,
you have no further misfortune to fear.
On that day, it shall be said to Jerusalem:
Fear not, O Zion, be not discouraged!
The LORD, your God, is in your midst,
a mighty savior;
He will rejoice over you with gladness,
and renew you in his love,

He will sing joyfully because of you,
  as one sings at festivals. ✦

Isaiah 12:2-3, 4bcd, 5-6
R. (6) **Among you is the great and Holy One of Israel.**
God indeed is my savior;
  I am confident and unafraid.
My strength and my courage is the LORD,
  and he has been my savior.
With joy you will draw water
  at the fountain of salvation. **R.**
Give thanks to the LORD, acclaim his name;
  among the nations make known his deeds,
  proclaim how exalted is his name. **R.**
Sing praise to the LORD for his glorious achievement;
  let this be known throughout all the earth.
Shout with exultation, O city of Zion,
  for great in your midst
  is the Holy One of Israel! **R.**

See Luke 1:45
R. Alleluia, alleluia.
Blessed are you, O Virgin Mary, who believed
that what was spoken to you by the Lord would be fulfilled. **R.**

† *Luke 1:39-56*
*And how does this happen to me, that the mother
of my Lord should come to me?*

Mary set out
  and traveled to the hill country in haste
  to a town of Judah,
  where she entered the house of Zechariah
  and greeted Elizabeth.
When Elizabeth heard Mary's greeting,
  the infant leaped in her womb,
  and Elizabeth, filled with the Holy Spirit,
  cried out in a loud voice and said,
  "Most blessed are you among women,
  and blessed is the fruit of your womb.
And how does this happen to me,
  that the mother of my Lord should come to me?
For at the moment the sound of your greeting reached my ears,
  the infant in my womb leaped for joy.
Blessed are you who believed
  that what was spoken to you by the Lord
  would be fulfilled."

And Mary said:

"My soul proclaims the greatness of the Lord;
   my spirit rejoices in God my Savior,
   for he has looked with favor on his lowly servant.
From this day all generations will call me blessed:
   the Almighty has done great things for me,
   and holy is his Name.

He has mercy on those who fear him
   in every generation.
He has shown the strength of his arm,
   he has scattered the proud in their conceit.
He has cast down the mighty from their thrones,
   and has lifted up the lowly.
He has filled the hungry with good things,
   and the rich he has sent away empty.
He has come to the help of his servant Israel
   for he has remembered his promise of mercy,
   the promise he made to our fathers,
   to Abraham and his children for ever."

Mary remained with her about three months
   and then returned to her home. ✝

THURSDAY, JUNE 1
St. Justin

✝ *Sirach 42:15-25*
The glory of the Lord fills all his works.

Now will I recall God's works;
   what I have seen, I will describe.
At God's word were his works brought into being;
   they do his will as he has ordained for them.
As the rising sun is clear to all,
   so the glory of the LORD fills all his works;
Yet even God's holy ones must fail
   in recounting the wonders of the LORD,
Though God has given these, his hosts, the strength
   to stand firm before his glory.
He plumbs the depths and penetrates the heart;
   their innermost being he understands.
The Most High possesses all knowledge,
   and sees from of old the things that are to come:
He makes known the past and the future,
   and reveals the deepest secrets.

No understanding does he lack;
  no single thing escapes him.
Perennial is his almighty wisdom;
  he is from all eternity one and the same,
With nothing added, nothing taken away;
  no need of a counselor for him!
How beautiful are all his works!
  even to the spark and fleeting vision!
The universe lives and abides forever;
  to meet each need, each creature is preserved.
All of them differ, one from another,
  yet none of them has he made in vain,
For each in turn, as it comes, is good;
  can one ever see enough of their splendor? ✛

   Psalm 33:2-3, 4-5, 6-7, 8-9

R. (6a) **By the word of the Lord the heavens were made.**
Give thanks to the LORD on the harp;
  with the ten-stringed lyre chant his praises.
Sing to him a new song;
  pluck the strings skillfully, with shouts of gladness. **R.**
For upright is the word of the LORD,
  and all his works are trustworthy.
He loves justice and right;
  of the kindness of the LORD the earth is full. **R.**
By the word of the LORD the heavens were made;
  by the breath of his mouth all their host.
He gathers the waters of the sea as in a flask;
  in cellars he confines the deep. **R.**
Let all the earth fear the LORD;
  let all who dwell in the world revere him.
For he spoke, and it was made;
  he commanded, and it stood forth. **R.**

   John 8:12

R. Alleluia, alleluia.
I am the light of the world, says the Lord;
whoever follows me will have the light of life. **R.**

      †Mark 10:46-52
        Master, I want to see.

As Jesus was leaving Jericho with his disciples and a sizable crowd,
  Bartimaeus, a blind man, the son of Timaeus,
  sat by the roadside begging.
On hearing that it was Jesus of Nazareth,
  he began to cry out and say,

"Jesus, son of David, have pity on me."
And many rebuked him, telling him to be silent.
But he kept calling out all the more, "Son of David, have pity on me."
Jesus stopped and said, "Call him."
So they called the blind man, saying to him,
   "Take courage; get up, Jesus is calling you."
He threw aside his cloak, sprang up, and came to Jesus.
Jesus said to him in reply, "What do you want me to do for you?"
The blind man replied to him, "Master, I want to see."
Jesus told him, "Go your way; your faith has saved you."
Immediately he received his sight
and followed him on the way. ✢

FRIDAY, JUNE 2
WEEKDAY, ST. MARCELLINUS AND ST. PETER

† *Sirach 44:1, 9-13*
Our ancestors were merciful, and their name will live for generations.

Now will I praise those godly men,
   our ancestors, each in his own time.
But of others there is no memory,
   for when they ceased, they ceased.
And they are as though they had not lived,
   they and their children after them.
Yet these also were godly men
   whose virtues have not been forgotten;
Their wealth remains in their families,
   their heritage with their descendants;
Through God's covenant with them their family endures,
   their posterity, for their sake.

And for all time their progeny will endure,
   their glory will never be blotted out. ✢

   Psalm 149:1b-2, 3-4, 5-6a and 9b
R. (see 4a) **The Lord takes delight in his people.** *(or* **Alleluia.***)*
Sing to the LORD a new song
   of praise in the assembly of the faithful.
Let Israel be glad in their maker,
   let the children of Zion rejoice in their king. **R.**
Let them praise his name in the festive dance,
   let them sing praise to him with timbrel and harp.
For the LORD loves his people,
   and he adorns the lowly with victory. **R.**
Let the faithful exult in glory;
   let them sing for joy upon their couches;

Let the high praises of God be in their throats.
    This is the glory of all his faithful. Alleluia. **R.**

> *See John 15:16*

R. Alleluia, alleluia.
I chose you from the world,
to go and bear fruit that will last, says the Lord. **R.**

† *Mark 11:11-26*

My house will be called a house of prayer for all peoples.
Have faith in God.

Jesus entered Jerusalem and went into the temple area.
He looked around at everything and, since it was already late,
    went out to Bethany with the Twelve.

The next day as they were leaving Bethany he was hungry.
Seeing from a distance a fig tree in leaf,
    he went over to see if he could find anything on it.
When he reached it he found nothing but leaves;
    it was not the time for figs.
And he said to it in reply, "May no one ever eat of your fruit again!"
And his disciples heard it.

They came to Jerusalem,
    and on entering the temple area
    he began to drive out those selling and buying there.
He overturned the tables of the money changers
    and the seats of those who were selling doves.
He did not permit anyone to carry anything through the temple area.
Then he taught them saying, "Is it not written:

> *My house shall be called a house of prayer for all peoples?*
> *But you have made it a den of thieves.*"

The chief priests and the scribes came to hear of it
    and were seeking a way to put him to death,
    yet they feared him
    because the whole crowd was astonished at his teaching.
When evening came, they went out of the city.

Early in the morning, as they were walking along,
    they saw the fig tree withered to its roots.
Peter remembered and said to him, "Rabbi, look!
The fig tree that you cursed has withered."
Jesus said to them in reply, "Have faith in God.
Amen, I say to you, whoever says to this mountain,
    'Be lifted up and thrown into the sea,'

and does not doubt in his heart
but believes that what he says will happen,
it shall be done for him.
Therefore I tell you, all that you ask for in prayer,
believe that you will receive it and it shall be yours.
When you stand to pray,
forgive anyone against whom you have a grievance,
so that your heavenly Father may in turn
forgive you your transgressions." ✛

SATURDAY, JUNE 3
St. Charles Lwanga and Companions

✝ *Sirach 51:12cd-20*
Give me wisdom and I will give you glory.

I thank the LORD and I praise him;
I bless the name of the LORD.
When I was young and innocent,
I sought wisdom openly in my prayer.
I prayed for her before the temple,
and I will seek her until the end,
and she flourished as a grape soon ripe.
My heart delighted in her,
My feet kept to the level path
because from earliest youth I was familiar with her.
In the short time I paid heed,
I met with great instruction.
Since in this way I have profited,
I will give my teacher grateful praise.
I became resolutely devoted to her—
the good I persistently strove for.
My soul was tormented in seeking her,
My hand opened her gate
and I came to know her secrets.
I directed my soul to her,
and in cleanness I attained to her. ✛

Psalm 19:8, 9, 10, 11
R. (9ab) **The precepts of the Lord give joy to the heart.**
The law of the LORD is perfect,
refreshing the soul.
The decree of the LORD is trustworthy,
giving wisdom to the simple. **R.**
The precepts of the LORD are right,
rejoicing the heart.

The command of the Lord is clear,
  enlightening the eye. **R.**
The fear of the Lord is pure,
  enduring forever;
The ordinances of the Lord are true,
  all of them just. **R.**
They are more precious than gold,
  than a heap of purest gold;
Sweeter also than syrup
  or honey from the comb. **R.**

  See Colossians 3:16a, 17c
R. Alleluia, alleluia.
Let the word of Christ dwell in you richly;
giving thanks to God the Father through him. **R.**

† *Mark 11:27-33*
By what authority are you doing these things?

Jesus and his disciples returned once more to Jerusalem.
As he was walking in the temple area,
  the chief priests, the scribes, and the elders
  approached him and said to him,
"By what authority are you doing these things?
Or who gave you this authority to do them?"
Jesus said to them, "I shall ask you one question.
Answer me, and I will tell you by what authority I do these things.
Was John's baptism of heavenly or of human origin? Answer me."
They discussed this among themselves and said,
  "If we say, 'Of heavenly origin,' he will say,
  'Then why did you not believe him?'
But shall we say, 'Of human origin'?"—
  they feared the crowd,
  for they all thought John really was a prophet.
So they said to Jesus in reply, "We do not know."
Then Jesus said to them,
  "Neither shall I tell you by what authority I do these things." ✛

SUNDAY, JUNE 4
THE MOST HOLY TRINITY

† *Exodus 34:4b-6, 8-9*
The Lord, the Lord, a merciful and gracious God.

Early in the morning Moses went up Mount Sinai
  as the Lord had commanded him,
  taking along the two stone tablets.

Having come down in a cloud, the Lord stood with Moses there
  and proclaimed his name, "Lord."
Thus the Lord passed before him and cried out,
  "The Lord, the Lord, a merciful and gracious God,
  slow to anger and rich in kindness and fidelity."
Moses at once bowed down to the ground in worship.
Then he said, "If I find favor with you, O Lord,
  do come along in our company.
This is indeed a stiff-necked people; yet pardon our wickedness and
    sins,
  and receive us as your own." ✢

Daniel 3:52, 53, 54, 55, 56
R. (52b) **Glory and praise for ever!**
Blessed are you, O Lord, the God of our fathers,
  praiseworthy and exalted above all forever;
And blessed is your holy and glorious name,
  praiseworthy and exalted above all for all ages. **R.**
Blessed are you in the temple of your holy glory,
  praiseworthy and glorious above all forever. **R.**
Blessed are you on the throne of your kingdom,
  praiseworthy and exalted above all forever. **R.**
Blessed are you who look into the depths
  from your throne upon the cherubim,
  praiseworthy and exalted above all forever. **R.**

✝ *2 Corinthians 13:11-13*
*The grace of Jesus Christ and the love of God
and the fellowship of the Holy Spirit.*

Brothers and sisters, rejoice.
Mend your ways, encourage one another,
  agree with one another, live in peace,
  and the God of love and peace will be with you.
Greet one another with a holy kiss.
All the holy ones greet you.

The grace of the Lord Jesus Christ
  and the love of God
  and the fellowship of the Holy Spirit be with all of you. ✢

See Revelation 1:8
R. Alleluia, alleluia.
Glory to the Father, the Son, and the Holy Spirit;
to God who is, who was, and who is to come. **R.**

† *John 3:16-18*
God sent his Son that the world might be saved through him.

God so loved the world that he gave his only Son,
  so that everyone who believes in him might not perish
  but might have eternal life.
For God did not send his Son into the world to condemn the world,
  but that the world might be saved through him.
Whoever believes in him will not be condemned,
  but whoever does not believe has already been condemned,
  because he has not believed in the name of the only Son of God. ✛

MONDAY, JUNE 5
St. Boniface (Ninth Week in Ordinary Time)

† *Tobit 1:3; 2:1b-8*
Tobit walked on the paths of truth and righteousness.

I, Tobit, have walked all the days of my life
  on the paths of truth and righteousness.
I performed many charitable works for my kinsmen and my people
  who had been deported with me to Nineveh, in Assyria.

On our festival of Pentecost, the feast of Weeks,
  a fine dinner was prepared for me, and I reclined to eat.
The table was set for me,
  and when many different dishes were placed before me,
  I said to my son Tobiah: "My son,
  go out and try to find a poor man
  from among our kinsmen exiled here in Nineveh.
If he is a sincere worshiper of God, bring him back with you,
  so that he can share this meal with me.
Indeed, son, I shall wait for you to come back."

Tobiah went out to look for some poor kinsman of ours.
When he returned he exclaimed, "Father!"
I said to him, "What is it, son?"
He answered, "Father, one of our people has been murdered!
His body lies in the market place where he was just strangled!"
I sprang to my feet, leaving the dinner untouched;
  and I carried the dead man from the street
  and put him in one of the rooms,
  so that I might bury him after sunset.
Returning to my own quarters, I washed myself and ate my food in
    sorrow.
I was reminded of the oracle
  pronounced by the prophet Amos against Bethel:

"All your festivals shall be turned into mourning,
   and all your songs into lamentation."

And I wept.
Then at sunset I went out, dug a grave, and buried him.

The neighbors mocked me, saying to one another:
   "He is still not afraid!
Once before he was hunted down for execution
   because of this very thing;
   yet now that he has scarcely escaped,
   here he is again burying the dead!" ✛

Psalm 112:1b-2, 3b-4, 5-6
R. (1b) **Blessed the man who fears the Lord.** *(or* **Alleluia.***)*
Blessed the man who fears the LORD,
   who greatly delights in his commands.
His posterity shall be mighty upon the earth;
   the upright generation shall be blessed. **R.**
His generosity shall endure forever.
Light shines through the darkness for the upright;
   he is gracious and merciful and just. **R.**
Well for the man who is gracious and lends,
   who conducts his affairs with justice;
He shall never be moved;
   the just man shall be in everlasting remembrance. **R.**

See Revelation 1:5ab
R. Alleluia, alleluia.
Jesus Christ, you are the faithful witness,
the firstborn of the dead;
you have loved us and freed us from our sins by your Blood. **R.**

✝ *Mark 12:1-12*
*They seized the beloved son, killed him,
and threw him out of the vineyard.*

Jesus began to speak to the chief priests, the scribes,
   and the elders in parables.
"A man planted a vineyard, put a hedge around it,
   dug a wine press, and built a tower.
Then he leased it to tenant farmers and left on a journey.
At the proper time he sent a servant to the tenants
   to obtain from them some of the produce of the vineyard.
But they seized him, beat him,
   and sent him away empty-handed.
Again he sent them another servant.

And that one they beat over the head and treated shamefully.
He sent yet another whom they killed.
So, too, many others; some they beat, others they killed.
He had one other to send, a beloved son.
He sent him to them last of all, thinking, 'They will respect my son.'
But those tenants said to one another, 'This is the heir.
Come, let us kill him, and the inheritance will be ours.'
So they seized him and killed him,
  and threw him out of the vineyard.
What then will the owner of the vineyard do?
He will come, put the tenants to death,
  and give the vineyard to others.
Have you not read this Scripture passage:

> *The stone that the builders rejected*
>   *has become the cornerstone;*
> *by the Lord has this been done,*
>   *and it is wonderful in our eyes?"*

They were seeking to arrest him, but they feared the crowd,
  for they realized that he had addressed the parable to them.
So they left him and went away. ✛

TUESDAY, JUNE 6
WEEKDAY, ST. NORBERT

† Tobit 2:9-14
I was deprived of eyesight.

On the night of Pentecost, after I had buried the dead,
  I, Tobit, went into my courtyard
  to sleep next to the courtyard wall.
My face was uncovered because of the heat.
I did not know there were birds perched on the wall above me,
  till their warm droppings settled in my eyes, causing cataracts.
I went to see some doctors for a cure
  but the more they anointed my eyes with various salves,
  the worse the cataracts became,
  until I could see no more.
For four years I was deprived of eyesight, and
  all my kinsmen were grieved at my condition.
Ahiqar, however, took care of me for two years,
  until he left for Elymais.

At that time, my wife Anna worked for hire
  at weaving cloth, the kind of work women do.
When she sent back the goods to their owners, they would pay her.

Late in winter on the seventh of Dystrus,
    she finished the cloth and sent it back to the owners.
They paid her the full salary
    and also gave her a young goat for the table.
On entering my house the goat began to bleat.

I called to my wife and said: "Where did this goat come from?
Perhaps it was stolen! Give it back to its owners;
    we have no right to eat stolen food!"
She said to me, "It was given to me as a bonus over and above my
        wages."
Yet I would not believe her,
    and told her to give it back to its owners.
I became very angry with her over this.
So she retorted: "Where are your charitable deeds now?
Where are your virtuous acts?
See! Your true character is finally showing itself!" ✙

Psalm 112:1-2, 7-8, 9
R. (see 7c) **The heart of the just one is firm, trusting in the
    Lord.** *(or* **Alleluia.***)*
Blessed the man who fears the LORD,
    who greatly delights in his commands.
His posterity shall be mighty upon the earth;
    the upright generation shall be blessed. **R.**
An evil report he shall not fear;
    his heart is firm, trusting in the LORD.
His heart is steadfast; he shall not fear
    till he looks down upon his foes. **R.**
Lavishly he gives to the poor;
    his generosity shall endure forever;
    his horn shall be exalted in glory. **R.**

See Ephesians 1:17-18
R. Alleluia, alleluia.
May the Father of our Lord Jesus Christ
enlighten the eyes of our hearts,
that we may know what is the hope
that belongs to his call. **R.**

† *Mark 12:13-17*
Repay to Caesar what belongs to Caesar and to God what belongs to God.

Some Pharisees and Herodians were sent
    to Jesus to ensnare him in his speech.
They came and said to him,
    "Teacher, we know that you are a truthful man

and that you are not concerned with anyone's opinion.
You do not regard a person's status
    but teach the way of God in accordance with the truth.
Is it lawful to pay the census tax to Caesar or not?
Should we pay or should we not pay?"
Knowing their hypocrisy he said to them,
    "Why are you testing me?
Bring me a denarius to look at."
They brought one to him and he said to them,
    "Whose image and inscription is this?"
They replied to him, "Caesar's."
So Jesus said to them,
    "Repay to Caesar what belongs to Caesar
    and to God what belongs to God."
They were utterly amazed at him. ✛

WEDNESDAY, JUNE 7
WEEKDAY

† *Tobit 3:1-11a, 16-17a*
*The prayer of these two petitioners was heard
in the glorious presence of Almighty God.*

Grief-stricken in spirit, I, Tobit, groaned and wept aloud.
Then with sobs I began to pray:

"You are righteous, O Lord,
    and all your deeds are just;
All your ways are mercy and truth;
    you are the judge of the world.
And now, O Lord, may you be mindful of me,
    and look with favor upon me.
Punish me not for my sins,
    nor for my inadvertent offenses,
    nor for those of my ancestors.

"We sinned against you,
    and disobeyed your commandments.
So you handed us over to plundering, exile, and death,
    till you made us the talk and reproach of all the nations
    among whom you had dispersed us.

"Yes, your judgments are many and true
    in dealing with me as my sins
    and those of my ancestors deserve.
For we have not kept your commandments,
    nor have we trodden the paths of truth before you.

"So now, deal with me as you please,
    and command my life breath to be taken from me,
    that I may go from the face of the earth into dust.
It is better for me to die than to live,
    because I have heard insulting calumnies,
    and I am overwhelmed with grief.

"Lord, command me to be delivered from such anguish;
    let me go to the everlasting abode;
    Lord, refuse me not.
For it is better for me to die
    than to endure so much misery in life,
    and to hear these insults!"

On the same day, at Ecbatana in Media,
    it so happened that Raguel's daughter Sarah
    also had to listen to abuse,
    from one of her father's maids.
For she had been married to seven husbands,
    but the wicked demon Asmodeus killed them off
    before they could have intercourse with her,
    as it is prescribed for wives.
So the maid said to her:
    "You are the one who strangles your husbands!
Look at you!
You have already been married seven times,
    but you have had no joy with any one of your husbands.
Why do you beat us? Is it on account of your seven husbands,
Because they are dead?
May we never see a son or daughter of yours!"

The girl was deeply saddened that day,
    and she went into an upper chamber of her house,
    where she planned to hang herself.

But she reconsidered, saying to herself:
    "No! People would level this insult against my father:
'You had only one beloved daughter,
    but she hanged herself because of ill fortune!'
And thus would I cause my father in his old age
    to go down to the nether world laden with sorrow.
It is far better for me not to hang myself,
    but to beg the Lord to have me die,
    so that I need no longer live to hear such insults."

At that time, then, she spread out her hands,

and facing the window, poured out her prayer:

"Blessed are you, O Lord, merciful God,
and blessed is your holy and honorable name.
Blessed are you in all your works for ever!"

At that very time,
the prayer of these two suppliants
was heard in the glorious presence of Almighty God.
So Raphael was sent to heal them both:
to remove the cataracts from Tobit's eyes,
so that he might again see God's sunlight;
and to marry Raguel's daughter Sarah to Tobit's son Tobiah,
and then drive the wicked demon Asmodeus from her. ✛

Psalm 25:2-3, 4-5ab, 6 and 7bc, 8-9
R. (1) **To you, O Lord, I lift my soul.**
In you I trust; let me not be put to shame,
let not my enemies exult over me.
No one who waits for you shall be put to shame;
those shall be put to shame who heedlessly break faith. **R.**
Your ways, O LORD, make known to me;
teach me your paths,
Guide me in your truth and teach me,
for you are God my savior. **R.**
Remember that your compassion, O LORD,
and your kindness are from of old.
In your kindness remember me,
because of your goodness, O LORD. **R.**
Good and upright is the LORD;
thus he shows sinners the way.
He guides the humble to justice,
he teaches the humble his way. **R.**

John 11:25a, 26
R. Alleluia, alleluia.
I am the resurrection and the life, says the Lord;
whoever believes in me will never die. **R.**

†*Mark 12:18-27*
He is not God of the dead but of the living.

Some Sadducees, who say there is no resurrection,
came to Jesus and put this question to him, saying,
"Teacher, Moses wrote for us,
If someone's brother dies, leaving a wife but no child,
his brother must take the wife

and raise up descendants for his brother.
Now there were seven brothers.
The first married a woman and died, leaving no descendants.
So the second brother married her and died, leaving no descendants,
and the third likewise.
And the seven left no descendants.
Last of all the woman also died.
At the resurrection when they arise whose wife will she be?
For all seven had been married to her."
Jesus said to them, "Are you not misled
because you do not know the Scriptures or the power of God?
When they rise from the dead,
they neither marry nor are given in marriage,
but they are like the angels in heaven.
As for the dead being raised,
have you not read in the Book of Moses,
in the passage about the bush, how God told him,
I am the God of Abraham, the God of Isaac,
and the God of Jacob?
He is not God of the dead but of the living.
You are greatly misled." ✛

THURSDAY, JUNE 8
WEEKDAY

✝ *Tobit 6:10-11; 7:1bcde, 9-17; 8:4-9a*
Call down your mercy on me and her and
allow us to live together to a happy old age.

When the angel Raphael and Tobiah had entered Media
and were getting close to Ecbatana,
Raphael said to the boy,
"Tobiah, my brother!"
He replied: "Here I am!"
He said: "Tonight we must stay with Raguel, who is a relative of
yours.
He has a daughter named Sarah."

So he brought him to the house of Raguel,
whom they found seated by his courtyard gate.
They greeted him first.
He said to them, "Greetings to you too, brothers!
Good health to you, and welcome!"
And he brought them into his home.

Raguel slaughtered a ram from the flock
and gave them a cordial reception.

When they had bathed and reclined to eat, Tobiah said to Raphael,
"Brother Azariah, ask Raguel to let me marry
my kinswoman Sarah."
Raguel overheard the words; so he said to the boy:
"Eat and drink and be merry tonight,
for no man is more entitled
to marry my daughter Sarah than you, brother.
Besides, not even I have the right to give her to anyone but you,
because you are my closest relative.
But I will explain the situation to you very frankly.
I have given her in marriage to seven men,
all of whom were kinsmen of ours,
and all died on the very night they approached her.
But now, son, eat and drink.
I am sure the Lord will look after you both."
Tobiah answered,
"I will eat or drink nothing until you set aside what belongs to me."

Raguel said to him: "I will do it.
She is yours according to the decree of the Book of Moses.
Your marriage to her has been decided in heaven!
Take your kinswoman;
from now on you are her love, and she is your beloved.
She is yours today and ever after.
And tonight, son, may the Lord of heaven prosper you both.
May he grant you mercy and peace."
Then Raguel called his daughter Sarah, and she came to him.
He took her by the hand and gave her to Tobiah with the words:
"Take her according to the law.
According to the decree written in the Book of Moses
she is your wife.
Take her and bring her back safely to your father.
And may the God of heaven grant both of you peace and prosperity."
Raguel then called Sarah's mother and told her to bring a scroll,
so that he might draw up a marriage contract
stating that he gave Sarah to Tobiah as his wife
according to the decree of the Mosaic law.
Her mother brought the scroll,
and Raguel drew up the contract, to which they affixed their seals.

Afterward they began to eat and drink.
Later Raguel called his wife Edna and said,
"My love, prepare the other bedroom and bring the girl there."
She went and made the bed in the room, as she was told,
and brought the girl there.

After she had cried over her, she wiped away the tears and said:
"Be brave, my daughter.
May the Lord grant you joy in place of your grief.
Courage, my daughter."
Then she left.

When the girl's parents left the bedroom
and closed the door behind them,
Tobiah arose from bed and said to his wife,
"My love, get up.
Let us pray and beg our Lord to have mercy on us
and to grant us deliverance."
She got up, and they started to pray
and beg that deliverance might be theirs.
And they began to say:

"Blessed are you, O God of our fathers,
praised be your name forever and ever.
Let the heavens and all your creation
praise you forever.
You made Adam and you gave him his wife Eve
to be his help and support;
and from these two the human race descended.
You said, 'It is not good for the man to be alone;
let us make him a partner like himself.'
Now, Lord, you know that I take this wife of mine
not because of lust,
but for a noble purpose.
Call down your mercy on me and on her,
and allow us to live together to a happy old age."

They said together, "Amen, amen," and went to bed for the night. ✛

Psalm 128:1-2, 3, 4-5
R. (see 1a) **Blessed are those who fear the Lord.**
Blessed are you who fear the LORD,
who walk in his ways!
For you shall eat the fruit of your handiwork;
blessed shall you be, and favored. **R.**
Your wife shall be like a fruitful vine
in the recesses of your home;
Your children like olive plants
around your table. **R.**
Behold, thus is the man blessed
who fears the LORD.

The L<small>ORD</small> bless you from Zion:
may you see the prosperity of Jerusalem
all the days of your life. **R.**

See 2 Timothy 1:10
R. Alleluia, alleluia.
Our Savior Jesus Christ has destroyed death
and brought life to light through the Gospel. **R.**

† *Mark 12:28-34*
There is no commandment greater than these.

One of the scribes came to Jesus and asked him,
"Which is the first of all the commandments?"
Jesus replied, "The first is this:
Hear, O Israel!
The Lord our God is Lord alone!
You shall love the Lord your God with all your heart,
with all your soul, with all your mind,
and with all your strength.
The second is this:
You shall love your neighbor as yourself.
There is no other commandment greater than these."
The scribe said to him, "Well said, teacher.
You are right in saying,
He is One and there is no other than he.
And *to love him with all your heart,*
with all your understanding,
with all your strength,
and to love your neighbor as yourself
is worth more than all burnt offerings and sacrifices."
And when Jesus saw that he answered with understanding,
he said to him, "You are not far from the Kingdom of God."
And no one dared to ask him any more questions. ✛

FRIDAY, JUNE 9
W<small>EEKDAY</small>, S<small>T</small>. E<small>PHREM</small>

† *Tobit 11:5-17*
God himself scourged me and behold, I now see my son Tobiah!

Anna sat watching the road by which her son was to come.
When she saw him coming, she exclaimed to his father,
"Tobit, your son is coming, and the man who traveled with him!"

Raphael said to Tobiah before he reached his father:
"I am certain that his eyes will be opened.
Smear the fish gall on them.

This medicine will make the cataracts shrink and peel off from his
    eyes;
    then your father will again be able to see the light of day."

Then Anna ran up to her son, threw her arms around him,
    and said to him,
    "Now that I have seen you again, son, I am ready to die!"
And she sobbed aloud.

Tobit got up and stumbled out through the courtyard gate.
Tobiah went up to him with the fish gall in his hand,
    and holding him firmly, blew into his eyes.
"Courage, father," he said.
Next he smeared the medicine on his eyes, and it made them smart.
Then, beginning at the corners of Tobit's eyes,
    Tobiah used both hands to peel off the cataracts.

When Tobit saw his son, he threw his arms around him and wept.
He exclaimed, "I can see you, son, the light of my eyes!"
Then he said:

"Blessed be God,
    and praised be his great name,
    and blessed be all his holy angels.
May his holy name be praised
    throughout all the ages,
Because it was he who scourged me,
    and it is he who has had mercy on me.
Behold, I now see my son Tobiah!"

Then Tobit went back in, rejoicing and praising God with full voice
    for everything that had happened.
Tobiah told his father that
    the Lord God had granted him a successful journey;
    that he had brought back the money;
    and that he had married Raguel's daughter Sarah,
    who would arrive shortly,
    for she was approaching the gate of Nineveh.

Tobit and Anna rejoiced
    and went out to the gate of Nineveh
    to meet their daughter-in-law.
When the people of Nineveh saw Tobit walking along briskly,
    with no one leading him by the hand, they were amazed.
Before them all Tobit proclaimed
    how God had mercifully restored sight to his eyes.

When Tobit reached Sarah, the wife of his son Tobiah,
　　he greeted her: "Welcome, my daughter!
Blessed be your God for bringing you to us, daughter!
Blessed is your father, and blessed is my son Tobiah,
　　and blessed are you, daughter!
Welcome to your home with blessing and joy.
Come in, daughter!"
That day there was joy for all the Jews who lived in Nineveh. ✛

Psalm 146:1b-2, 6c-7, 8-9a, 9bc-10
R. (1b) **Praise the Lord, my soul!** *(or* **Alleluia.***)*
Praise the Lord, O my soul;
　　I will praise the Lord all my life;
　　I will sing praise to my God while I live. **R.**
The Lord keeps faith forever,
　　secures justice for the oppressed,
　　gives food to the hungry.
The Lord sets captives free. **R.**
The Lord gives sight to the blind.
The Lord raises up those who are bowed down;
　　the Lord loves the just.
The Lord protects strangers. **R.**
The fatherless and the widow he sustains,
　　but the way of the wicked he thwarts
The Lord shall reign forever,
　　your God, O Zion, through all generations! Alleluia. **R.**

John 14:23
R. Alleluia, alleluia.
Whoever loves me will keep my word,
and my Father will love him
and we will come to him. **R.**

† *Mark 12:35-37*
How do the scribes claim that the Christ is the son of David?

As Jesus was teaching in the temple area he said,
　　"How do the scribes claim that the Christ is the son of David?
David himself, inspired by the Holy Spirit, said:

The Lord said to my lord,
'Sit at my right hand
until I place your enemies under your feet.'

David himself calls him 'lord';
　　so how is he his son?"
The great crowd heard this with delight.

SATURDAY, JUNE 10
WEEKDAY, *[BVM]*

† *Tobit 12:1, 5-15, 20*
So now praise God. Behold, I am about to ascend to him who sent me.

Tobit called his son Tobiah and said to him,
"Son, see to it that you give what is due to the man
who made the journey with you; give him a bonus too."
So he called Raphael and said,
"Take as your wages half of all that you have brought back,
and go in peace."

Raphael called the two men aside privately and said to them:
"Thank God! Give him the praise and the glory.
Before all the living,
acknowledge the many good things he has done for you,
by blessing and extolling his name in song.
Honor and proclaim God's deeds,
and do not be slack in praising him.
A king's secret it is prudent to keep,
but the works of God are to be declared and made known.
Praise them with due honor.
Do good, and evil will not find its way to you.
Prayer and fasting are good,
but better than either is almsgiving accompanied by righteousness.
A little with righteousness is better than abundance with wickedness.
It is better to give alms than to store up gold;
for almsgiving saves one from death and expiates every sin.
Those who regularly give alms shall enjoy a full life;
but those habitually guilty of sin are their own worst enemies.

"I will now tell you the whole truth;
I will conceal nothing at all from you.
I have already said to you,
'A king's secret it is prudent to keep,
but the works of God are to be made known with due honor.'
I can now tell you that when you, Tobit, and Sarah prayed,
it was I who presented and read the record of your prayer
before the Glory of the Lord;
and I did the same thing when you used to bury the dead.
When you did not hesitate to get up
and leave your dinner in order to go and bury the dead,
I was sent to put you to the test.
At the same time, however,
God commissioned me to heal you and your daughter-in-law Sarah.

I am Raphael, one of the seven angels
  who enter and serve before the Glory of the Lord."

"So now get up from the ground and praise God.
Behold, I am about to ascend to him who sent me;
  write down all these things that have happened to you." ✛

Tobit 13:2, 6efgh, 7, 8
R. (1b) **Blessed be God, who lives for ever.**
He scourges and then has mercy;
  he casts down to the depths of the nether world,
  and he brings up from the great abyss.
No one can escape his hand. **R.**
So now consider what he has done for you,
  and praise him with full voice.
Bless the Lord of righteousness,
  and exalt the King of ages. **R.**
In the land of my exile I praise him
  and show his power and majesty to a sinful nation. **R.**
Bless the Lord, all you his chosen ones,
  and may all of you praise his majesty.
Celebrate days of gladness, and give him praise. **R.**

Matthew 5:3
R. Alleluia, alleluia.
Blessed are the poor in spirit;
for theirs is the Kingdom of heaven. **R.**

† Mark 12:38-44
This poor widow has given more than all others.

In the course of his teaching Jesus said,
  "Beware of the scribes, who like to go around in long robes
  and accept greetings in the marketplaces,
  seats of honor in synagogues,
  and places of honor at banquets.
They devour the houses of widows and, as a pretext,
  recite lengthy prayers.
They will receive a very severe condemnation."

He sat down opposite the treasury
  and observed how the crowd put money into the treasury.
Many rich people put in large sums.
A poor widow also came and put in two small coins worth a few
      cents.
Calling his disciples to himself, he said to them,
  "Amen, I say to you, this poor widow put in more

than all the other contributors to the treasury.
For they have all contributed from their surplus wealth,
but she, from her poverty, has contributed all she had,
her whole livelihood." ✝

SUNDAY, JUNE 11
THE MOST HOLY BODY AND BLOOD OF CHRIST (CORPUS CHRISTI)

✝ *Deuteronomy 8:2-3, 14b-16a*
He gave you a food unknown to you and your fathers.

Moses said to the people:
"Remember how for forty years now the LORD, your God,
has directed all your journeying in the desert,
so as to test you by affliction
and find out whether or not it was your intention
to keep his commandments.
He therefore let you be afflicted with hunger,
and then fed you with manna,
a food unknown to you and your fathers,
in order to show you that not by bread alone does one live,
but by every word that comes forth from the mouth of the LORD.

"Do not forget the LORD, your God,
who brought you out of the land of Egypt,
that place of slavery;
who guided you through the vast and terrible desert
with its saraph serpents and scorpions,
its parched and waterless ground;
who brought forth water for you from the flinty rock
and fed you in the desert with manna,
a food unknown to your fathers." ✝

Psalm 147:12-13, 14-15, 19-20
R. Praise the Lord, Jerusalem. *(or **Alleluia**.)*
Glorify the LORD, O Jerusalem;
    praise your God, O Zion.
For he has strengthened the bars of your gates;
    he has blessed your children within you. **R.**
He has granted peace in your borders;
    with the best of wheat he fills you.
He sends forth his command to the earth;
    swiftly runs his word! **R.**
He has proclaimed his word to Jacob,
    his statutes and his ordinances to Israel.
He has not done thus for any other nation;

his ordinances he has not made known to them.
Alleluia. **R.**

✝ *1 Corinthians 10:16-17*
The bread is one, and we, though many, are one body.

Brothers and sisters:
The cup of blessing that we bless,
  is it not a participation in the blood of Christ?
The bread that we break,
  is it not a participation in the body of Christ?
Because the loaf of bread is one,
  we, though many, are one body,
  for we all partake of the one loaf. ✛

The sequence Laud, O Zion (Lauda Sion), *or the shorter form beginning with the verse* Lo! the angel's food is given, *may be sung optionally before the Alleluia.*

John 6:51
R. Alleluia, alleluia.
I am the living bread that came down from heaven, says the Lord;
whoever eats this bread will live forever. **R.**

✝ *John 6:51-58*
My flesh is true food, and my blood is true drink.

Jesus said to the Jewish crowds:
  "I am the living bread that came down from heaven;
  whoever eats this bread will live forever;
  and the bread that I will give
  is my flesh for the life of the world."

The Jews quarreled among themselves, saying,
  "How can this man give us his flesh to eat?"
Jesus said to them,
  "Amen, amen, I say to you,
  unless you eat the flesh of the Son of Man and drink his blood,
  you do not have life within you.
Whoever eats my flesh and drinks my blood
  has eternal life,
  and I will raise him on the last day.
For my flesh is true food,
  and my blood is true drink.
Whoever eats my flesh and drinks my blood
  remains in me and I in him.
Just as the living Father sent me
  and I have life because of the Father,

so also the one who feeds on me
will have life because of me.
This is the bread that came down from heaven.
Unlike your ancestors who ate and still died,
whoever eats this bread will live forever." ✠

MONDAY, JUNE 12
WEEKDAY (TENTH WEEK IN ORDINARY TIME)

✝ 2 Corinthians 1:1-7

*God encourages us that we ourselves may be able to encourage
those who are in any affliction.*

Paul, an Apostle of Christ Jesus by the will of God,
and Timothy our brother,
to the Church of God that is at Corinth,
with all the holy ones throughout Achaia:
grace to you and peace from God our Father and the Lord Jesus
Christ.

Blessed be the God and Father of our Lord Jesus Christ,
the Father of compassion and the God of all encouragement,
who encourages us in our every affliction,
so that we may be able to encourage
those who are in any affliction
with the encouragement with which we ourselves are encouraged
by God.
For as Christ's sufferings overflow to us,
so through Christ does our encouragement also overflow.
If we are afflicted,
it is for your encouragement and salvation;
if we are encouraged,
it is for your encouragement,
which enables you to endure the same sufferings that we suffer.
Our hope for you is firm,
for we know that as you share in the sufferings,
you also share in the encouragement. ✠

Psalm 34:2-3, 4-5, 6-7, 8-9

R. (9a) **Taste and see the goodness of the Lord.**
I will bless the LORD at all times;
his praise shall be ever in my mouth.
Let my soul glory in the LORD;
the lowly will hear me and be glad. **R.**
Glorify the LORD with me,
let us together extol his name.
I sought the LORD, and he answered me

and delivered me from all my fears. **R.**
Look to him that you may be radiant with joy,
  and your faces may not blush with shame.
When the poor one called out, the LORD heard,
  and from all his distress he saved him. **R.**
The angel of the LORD encamps
  around those who fear him, and delivers them.
Taste and see how good the LORD is;
  blessed the man who takes refuge in him. **R.**

Matthew 5:12a
R. Alleluia, alleluia.
Rejoice and be glad;
for your reward will be great in heaven. **R.**

† *Matthew 5:1-12*
Blessed are the poor in spirit.

When Jesus saw the crowds, he went up the mountain,
  and after he had sat down, his disciples came to him.
He began to teach them, saying:

  "Blessed are the poor in spirit,
    for theirs is the Kingdom of heaven.
  Blessed are they who mourn,
    for they will be comforted.
  Blessed are the meek,
    for they will inherit the land.
  Blessed are they who hunger and thirst for righteousness,
    for they will be satisfied.
  Blessed are the merciful,
    for they will be shown mercy.
  Blessed are the clean of heart,
    for they will see God.
  Blessed are the peacemakers,
    for they will be called children of God.
  Blessed are they who are persecuted for the sake of righteousness,
    for theirs is the Kingdom of heaven.
Blessed are you when they insult you and persecute you
  and utter every kind of evil against you falsely because of me.
Rejoice and be glad,
  for your reward will be great in heaven.
Thus they persecuted the prophets who were before you." ✛

TUESDAY, JUNE 13
St. Anthony of Padua

✝ *2 Corinthians 1:18-22*
Jesus was not yes and no, but yes has always been in him.

Brothers and sisters:
As God is faithful, our word to you is not "yes" and "no."
For the Son of God, Jesus Christ, who was proclaimed to you by us,
    Silvanus and Timothy and me,
    was not "yes" and "no," but "yes" has been in him.
For however many are the promises of God, their Yes is in him;
    therefore, the Amen from us also goes through him to God for
        glory.
But the one who gives us security with you in Christ
    and who anointed us is God;
    he has also put his seal upon us
    and given the Spirit in our hearts as a first installment. ✝

Psalm 119:129, 130, 131, 132, 133, 135
R. (135a) **Lord, let your face shine on me.**
Wonderful are your decrees;
    therefore I observe them. **R.**
The revelation of your words sheds light,
    gives understanding to the simple. **R.**
I gasp with open mouth
    in my yearning for your commands. **R.**
Turn to me in pity
    as you turn to those who love your name. **R.**
Steady my footsteps according to your promise,
    and let no iniquity rule over me. **R.**
Let your countenance shine upon your servant,
    and teach me your statutes. **R.**

Matthew 5:16
R. Alleluia, alleluia.
Let your light shine before others
that they may see your good deeds and glorify your heavenly Father. **R.**

✝ *Matthew 5:13-16*
You are the light of the world.

Jesus said to his disciples:
"You are the salt of the earth.
But if salt loses its taste, with what can it be seasoned?
It is no longer good for anything
    but to be thrown out and trampled underfoot.
You are the light of the world.

A city set on a mountain cannot be hidden.
Nor do they light a lamp and then put it under a bushel basket;
   it is set on a lampstand,
   where it gives light to all in the house.
Just so, your light must shine before others,
   that they may see your good deeds
   and glorify your heavenly Father." ✛

WEDNESDAY, JUNE 14
WEEKDAY

†2 Corinthians 3:4-11
*He has qualified us as ministers of a new covenant,
not of the letter but of spirit.*

Brothers and sisters:
Such confidence we have through Christ toward God.
Not that of ourselves we are qualified to take credit
   for anything as coming from us;
   rather, our qualification comes from God,
   who has indeed qualified us as ministers of a new covenant,
   not of letter but of spirit;
   for the letter brings death, but the Spirit gives life.

Now if the ministry of death, carved in letters on stone, was so glorious
   that the children of Israel could not look intently at the face of
      Moses
   because of its glory that was going to fade,
   how much more will the ministry of the Spirit be glorious?
For if the ministry of condemnation was glorious,
   the ministry of righteousness will abound much more in glory.
Indeed, what was endowed with glory
   has come to have no glory in this respect
   because of the glory that surpasses it.
For if what was going to fade was glorious,
   how much more will what endures be glorious. ✛

Psalm 99:5, 6, 7, 8, 9
R. (see 9c) **Holy is the Lord our God.**
Extol the LORD, our God,
   and worship at his footstool;
   holy is he! **R.**
Moses and Aaron were among his priests,
   and Samuel, among those who called upon his name;
   they called upon the LORD, and he answered them. **R.**
From the pillar of cloud he spoke to them;
   they heard his decrees and the law he gave them. **R.**

O LORD, our God, you answered them;
    a forgiving God you were to them,
    though requiting their misdeeds. **R.**
Extol the LORD, our God,
    and worship at his holy mountain;
    for holy is the LORD, our God. **R.**

    Psalm 25:4b, 5a
R. Alleluia, alleluia.
Teach me your paths, my God,
and guide me in your truth. **R.**

† *Matthew 5:17-19*
I have come not to abolish the law, but to fulfill it.

Jesus said to his disciples:
"Do not think that I have come to abolish the law or the prophets.
I have come not to abolish but to fulfill.
Amen, I say to you, until heaven and earth pass away,
    not the smallest letter or the smallest part of a letter
    will pass from the law,
    until all things have taken place.
Therefore, whoever breaks one of the least of these commandments
    and teaches others to do so
    will be called least in the Kingdom of heaven.
But whoever obeys and teaches these commandments
    will be called greatest in the Kingdom of heaven." ✢

THURSDAY, JUNE 15
WEEKDAY

† *2 Corinthians 3:15–4:1, 3-6*
*God has shone in our hearts to bring
to light the knowledge of the glory of God.*

Brothers and sisters:
To this day, whenever Moses is read,
    a veil lies over the hearts of the children of Israel,
    but whenever a person turns to the Lord the veil is removed.
Now the Lord is the Spirit and where the Spirit of the Lord is,
    there is freedom.
All of us, gazing with unveiled face on the glory of the Lord,
    are being transformed into the same image from glory to glory,
    as from the Lord who is the Spirit.

Therefore, since we have this ministry through the mercy shown us,
    we are not discouraged.
And even though our Gospel is veiled,

it is veiled for those who are perishing,
in whose case the god of this age
has blinded the minds of the unbelievers,
so that they may not see the light of the Gospel
of the glory of Christ, who is the image of God.
For we do not preach ourselves but Jesus Christ as Lord,
and ourselves as your slaves for the sake of Jesus.
For God who said, *Let light shine out of darkness*,
has shone in our hearts to bring to light
the knowledge of the glory of God
on the face of Jesus Christ. ✛

Psalm 85:9ab and 10, 11-12, 13-14

R. (see 10b) **The glory of the Lord will dwell in our land.**
I will hear what God proclaims;
the LORD—for he proclaims peace to his people.
Near indeed is his salvation to those who fear him,
glory dwelling in our land. **R.**
Kindness and truth shall meet;
justice and peace shall kiss.
Truth shall spring out of the earth,
and justice shall look down from heaven. **R.**
The LORD himself will give his benefits;
our land shall yield its increase.
Justice shall walk before him,
and salvation, along the way of his steps. **R.**

John 13:34

R. Alleluia, alleluia.
I give you a new commandment:
love one another as I have loved you. **R.**

† *Matthew 5:20-26*

Whoever is angry with his brother will be liable to judgment.

Jesus said to his disciples:
"I tell you, unless your righteousness surpasses that
of the scribes and Pharisees,
you will not enter into the Kingdom of heaven.

"You have heard that it was said to your ancestors,
You shall not kill; and whoever kills will be liable to judgment.
But I say to you, whoever is angry with his brother
will be liable to judgment,
and whoever says to his brother, *Raqa*,
will be answerable to the Sanhedrin,
and whoever says, 'You fool,' will be liable to fiery Gehenna.

Therefore, if you bring your gift to the altar,
   and there recall that your brother
   has anything against you,
   leave your gift there at the altar,
   go first and be reconciled with your brother,
   and then come and offer your gift.
Settle with your opponent quickly while on the way to court with him.
Otherwise your opponent will hand you over to the judge,
   and the judge will hand you over to the guard,
   and you will be thrown into prison.
Amen, I say to you,
   you will not be released until you have paid the last penny." ✝

FRIDAY, JUNE 16
THE MOST SACRED HEART OF JESUS

✝Deuteronomy 7:6-11
The Lord set his heart on you and chose you.

Moses said to the people:
   "You are a people sacred to the LORD, your God;
   he has chosen you from all the nations on the face of the earth
   to be a people peculiarly his own.
It was not because you are the largest of all nations
   that the LORD set his heart on you and chose you,
   for you are really the smallest of all nations.
It was because the LORD loved you
   and because of his fidelity to the oath he had sworn your fathers,
   that he brought you out with his strong hand
   from the place of slavery,
   and ransomed you from the hand of Pharaoh, king of Egypt.
Understand, then, that the LORD, your God, is God indeed,
   the faithful God who keeps his merciful covenant
   down to the thousandth generation
   toward those who love him and keep his commandments,
   but who repays with destruction a person who hates him;
   he does not dally with such a one,
   but makes them personally pay for it.
You shall therefore carefully observe the commandments,
   the statutes and the decrees that I enjoin on you today." ✝

   Psalm 103:1-2, 3-4, 8, 10
R. (see 17) **The Lord's kindness is everlasting to those who
   fear him.**
Bless the LORD, O my soul;
   all my being, bless his holy name.

Bless the LORD, O my soul;
   and forget not all his benefits. **R.**
He pardons all your iniquities,
   heals all your ills.
He redeems your life from destruction,
   crowns you with kindness and compassion. **R.**
Merciful and gracious is the LORD,
   slow to anger and abounding in kindness.
Not according to our sins does he deal with us,
   nor does he requite us according to our crimes. **R.**

† *1 John 4:7-16*
God loved us.

Beloved, let us love one another,
   because love is of God;
   everyone who loves is begotten by God and knows God.
Whoever is without love does not know God, for God is love.
In this way the love of God was revealed to us:
   God sent his only Son into the world
   so that we might have life through him.
In this is love:
   not that we have loved God, but that he loved us
   and sent his Son as expiation for our sins.
Beloved, if God so loved us,
   we also must love one another.
No one has ever seen God.
Yet, if we love one another, God remains in us,
   and his love is brought to perfection in us.

This is how we know that we remain in him and he in us,
   that he has given us of his Spirit.
Moreover, we have seen and testify
   that the Father sent his Son as savior of the world.
Whoever acknowledges that Jesus is the Son of God,
   God remains in him and he in God.
We have come to know and to believe in the love God has for us.

God is love, and whoever remains in love
   remains in God and God in him. ✛

   Matthew 11:29ab
R. Alleluia, alleluia.
Take my yoke upon you, says the Lord;
and learn from me, for I am meek and humble of heart. **R.**

† *Matthew 11:25-30*
I am meek and humble of heart.

At that time Jesus exclaimed:
"I give praise to you, Father, Lord of heaven and earth,
for although you have hidden these things
from the wise and the learned
you have revealed them to little ones.
Yes, Father, such has been your gracious will.
All things have been handed over to me by my Father.
No one knows the Son except the Father,
and no one knows the Father except the Son
and anyone to whom the Son wishes to reveal him.

"Come to me, all you who labor and are burdened,
and I will give you rest.
Take my yoke upon you and learn from me,
for I am meek and humble of heart;
and you will find rest for yourselves.
For my yoke is easy, and my burden light." ✝

SATURDAY, JUNE 17
THE IMMACULATE HEART OF THE BLESSED VIRGIN MARY

† *2 Corinthians 5:14-21*
For our sake, he made him to be sin who did not know sin.

Brothers and sisters:
The love of Christ impels us,
once we have come to the conviction that one died for all;
therefore, all have died.
He indeed died for all,
so that those who live might no longer live for themselves
but for him who for their sake died and was raised.

Consequently, from now on we regard no one according to the flesh;
even if we once knew Christ according to the flesh,
yet now we know him so no longer.
So whoever is in Christ is a new creation:
the old things have passed away;
behold, new things have come.
And all this is from God,
who has reconciled us to himself through Christ
and given us the ministry of reconciliation,
namely, God was reconciling the world to himself in Christ,
not counting their trespasses against them
and entrusting to us the message of reconciliation.

So we are ambassadors for Christ,
  as if God were appealing through us.
We implore you on behalf of Christ,
  be reconciled to God.
For our sake he made him to be sin who did not know sin,
  so that we might become the righteousness of God in him. ✛

Psalm 103:1-2, 3-4, 9-10, 11-12
R. (8a) **The Lord is kind and merciful.**
Bless the LORD, O my soul;
  and all my being, bless his holy name.
Bless the LORD, O my soul,
  and forget not all his benefits. **R.**
He pardons all your iniquities,
  he heals all your ills.
He redeems your life from destruction,
  he crowns you with kindness and compassion. **R.**
He will not always chide,
  nor does he keep his wrath forever.
Not according to our sins does he deal with us,
  nor does he requite us according to our crimes. **R.**
For as the heavens are high above the earth,
  so surpassing is his kindness toward those who fear him.
As far as the east is from the west,
  so far has he put our transgressions from us. **R.**

See Luke 2:19
R. Alleluia, alleluia.
Blessed is the Virgin Mary who kept the word of God
and pondered it in her heart. **R.**

† *Luke 2:41-51*
His mother kept all these things in her heart.

Each year Jesus' parents went to Jerusalem for the feast of Passover,
  and when he was twelve years old,
  they went up according to festival custom.
After they had completed its days, as they were returning,
  the boy Jesus remained behind in Jerusalem,
  but his parents did not know it.
Thinking that he was in the caravan,
  they journeyed for a day
  and looked for him among their relatives and acquaintances,
  but not finding him,
  they returned to Jerusalem to look for him.
After three days they found him in the temple,
  sitting in the midst of the teachers,

listening to them and asking them questions,
and all who heard him were astounded
at his understanding and his answers.
When his parents saw him,
they were astonished,
and his mother said to him,
"Son, why have you done this to us?
Your father and I have been looking for you with great anxiety."
And he said to them,
"Why were you looking for me?
Did you not know that I must be in my Father's house?"
But they did not understand what he said to them.
He went down with them and came to Nazareth,
and was obedient to them;
and his mother kept all these things in her heart. ✛

SUNDAY, JUNE 18
ELEVENTH SUNDAY IN ORDINARY TIME

† *Exodus 19:2-6a*
You shall be to me a kingdom of priests, a holy nation.

In those days, the Israelites came to the desert of Sinai and pitched
camp.
While Israel was encamped here in front of the mountain,
Moses went up the mountain to God.
Then the LORD called to him and said,
"Thus shall you say to the house of Jacob;
tell the Israelites:
You have seen for yourselves how I treated the Egyptians
and how I bore you up on eagle wings
and brought you here to myself.
Therefore, if you hearken to my voice and keep my covenant,
you shall be my special possession,
dearer to me than all other people,
though all the earth is mine.
You shall be to me a kingdom of priests, a holy nation." ✛

Psalm 100:1-2, 3, 5
R. (3c) **We are his people: the sheep of his flock.**
Sing joyfully to the LORD, all you lands;
serve the LORD with gladness;
come before him with joyful song. **R.**
Know that the LORD is God;
he made us, his we are;
his people, the flock he tends. **R.**

The LORD is good:
  his kindness endures forever,
  and his faithfulness to all generations. **R.**

† *Romans 5:6-11*

*If we were reconciled to God through the death of his Son,
how much more will we be saved by his life.*

Brothers and sisters:
Christ, while we were still helpless,
  yet died at the appointed time for the ungodly.
Indeed, only with difficulty does one die for a just person,
  though perhaps for a good person
  one might even find courage to die.
But God proves his love for us
  in that while we were still sinners Christ died for us.
How much more then, since we are now justified by his blood,
  will we be saved through him from the wrath.

Indeed, if, while we were enemies,
  we were reconciled to God through the death of his Son,
  how much more, once reconciled,
  will we be saved by his life.
Not only that,
  but we also boast of God through our Lord Jesus Christ,
  through whom we have now received reconciliation. ✛

Mark 1:15

R. Alleluia, alleluia.
The kingdom of God is at hand.
Repent and believe in the Gospel. **R.**

† *Matthew 9:36—10:8*

Jesus summoned his twelve disciples and sent them out.

At the sight of the crowds, Jesus' heart was moved with pity for
    them
  because they were troubled and abandoned,
  like sheep without a shepherd.
Then he said to his disciples,
  "The harvest is abundant but the laborers are few;
  so ask the master of the harvest
  to send out laborers for his harvest."

Then he summoned his twelve disciples
  and gave them authority over unclean spirits
  to drive them out and to cure every disease and every illness.
The names of the twelve apostles are these:

first, Simon called Peter, and his brother Andrew;
James, the son of Zebedee, and his brother John;
Philip and Bartholomew, Thomas and Matthew the tax collector;
James, the son of Alphaeus, and Thaddeus;
Simon from Cana, and Judas Iscariot who betrayed him.

Jesus sent out these twelve after instructing them thus,
"Do not go into pagan territory or enter a Samaritan town.
Go rather to the lost sheep of the house of Israel.
As you go, make this proclamation: 'The kingdom of heaven is at hand.'
Cure the sick, raise the dead, cleanse lepers, drive out demons.
Without cost you have received; without cost you are to give." ✛

MONDAY, JUNE 19
WEEKDAY, ST. ROMUALD

✝ *2 Corinthians 6:1-10*
In everything we commend ourselves as ministers of God.

Brothers and sisters:
As your fellow workers, we appeal to you
   not to receive the grace of God in vain.
For he says:

> *In an acceptable time I heard you,*
>   *and on the day of salvation I helped you.*

Behold, now is a very acceptable time;
   behold, now is the day of salvation.
We cause no one to stumble in anything,
   in order that no fault may be found with our ministry;
   on the contrary, in everything we commend ourselves
   as ministers of God, through much endurance,
   in afflictions, hardships, constraints,
   beatings, imprisonments, riots,
   labors, vigils, fasts;
   by purity, knowledge, patience, kindness,
   in the Holy Spirit, in unfeigned love, in truthful speech,
   in the power of God;
   with weapons of righteousness at the right and at the left;
   through glory and dishonor, insult and praise.
We are treated as deceivers and yet are truthful;
   as unrecognized and yet acknowledged;
   as dying and behold we live;
   as chastised and yet not put to death;
   as sorrowful yet always rejoicing;

as poor yet enriching many;
as having nothing and yet possessing all things. ✛

Psalm 98:1, 2b-3ab, 3cd-4

R. (2a) **The Lord has made known his salvation.**
Sing to the LORD a new song,
    for he has done wondrous deeds;
His right hand has won victory for him,
    his holy arm. **R.**
In the sight of the nations he has revealed his justice.
He has remembered his kindness and his faithfulness
    toward the house of Israel. **R.**
All the ends of the earth have seen
    the salvation by our God.
Sing joyfully to the LORD, all you lands;
    break into song; sing praise. **R.**

Psalm 119:105

R. Alleluia, alleluia.
A lamp to my feet is your word,
a light to my path. **R.**

† *Matthew 5:38-42*
But I say to you, offer no resistance to one who is evil.

Jesus said to his disciples:
"You have heard that it was said,
    An eye for an eye and a tooth for a tooth.
But I say to you, offer no resistance to one who is evil.
When someone strikes you on your right cheek,
    turn the other one to him as well.
If anyone wants to go to law with you over your tunic,
    hand him your cloak as well.
Should anyone press you into service for one mile,
    go with him for two miles.
Give to the one who asks of you,
    and do not turn your back on one who wants to borrow." ✛

TUESDAY, JUNE 20
WEEKDAY

† *2 Corinthians 8:1-9*
Christ became poor for your sake.

We want you to know, brothers and sisters, of the grace of God
    that has been given to the churches of Macedonia,
for in a severe test of affliction,
    the abundance of their joy and their profound poverty

overflowed in a wealth of generosity on their part.
For according to their means, I can testify,
    and beyond their means, spontaneously,
    they begged us insistently for the favor of taking part
    in the service to the holy ones,
    and this, not as we expected,
    but they gave themselves first to the Lord
    and to us through the will of God,
    so that we urged Titus that, as he had already begun,
    he should also complete for you this gracious act also.
Now as you excel in every respect,
    in faith, discourse, knowledge, all earnestness,
    and in the love we have for you,
    may you excel in this gracious act also.

I say this not by way of command,
    but to test the genuineness of your love
    by your concern for others.
For you know the gracious act of our Lord Jesus Christ,
    that for your sake he became poor although he was rich,
    so that by his poverty you might become rich. ✝

Psalm 146:2, 5-6ab, 6c-7, 8-9a
R. (1b) **Praise the Lord, my soul!** *(or* **Alleluia.***)*
Praise the LORD, my soul!
    I will praise the LORD all my life;
    I will sing praise to my God while I live. **R.**
Blessed he whose help is the God of Jacob,
    whose hope is in the LORD, his God,
Who made heaven and earth,
    the sea and all that is in them. **R.**
Who keeps faith forever,
    secures justice for the oppressed,
    gives food to the hungry.
The LORD sets captives free. **R.**
The LORD gives sight to the blind.
The LORD raises up those who were bowed down;
    the LORD loves the just.
The LORD protects strangers. **R.**

John 13:34
R. Alleluia, alleluia.
I give you a new commandment:
love one another as I have loved you. **R.**

† *Matthew 5:43-48*
Love your enemies.

Jesus said to his disciples:
"You have heard that it was said,
You shall love your neighbor and hate your enemy.
But I say to you, love your enemies
and pray for those who persecute you,
that you may be children of your heavenly Father,
for he makes his sun rise on the bad and the good,
and causes rain to fall on the just and the unjust.
For if you love those who love you, what recompense will you have?
Do not the tax collectors do the same?
And if you greet your brothers only,
what is unusual about that?
Do not the pagans do the same?
So be perfect, just as your heavenly Father is perfect." ✛

WEDNESDAY, JUNE 21
St. Aloysius Gonzaga

† *2 Corinthians 9:6-11*
God loves a cheerful giver.

Brothers and sisters, consider this:
whoever sows sparingly will also reap sparingly,
and whoever sows bountifully will also reap bountifully.
Each must do as already determined, without sadness or compulsion,
for God loves a cheerful giver.
Moreover, God is able to make every grace abundant for you,
so that in all things, always having all you need,
you may have an abundance for every good work.
As it is written:

He scatters abroad, he gives to the poor;
his righteousness endures forever.

The one who supplies seed to the sower and bread for food
will supply and multiply your seed
and increase the harvest of your righteousness.

You are being enriched in every way for all generosity,
which through us produces thanksgiving to God. ✛

Psalm 112:1bc-2, 3-4, 9
R. (1b) **Blessed the man who fears the Lord.** *(or* **Alleluia.***)*
Blessed the man who fears the Lord,
who greatly delights in his commands.

His posterity shall be mighty upon the earth;
   the upright generation shall be blessed. **R.**
Wealth and riches shall be in his house;
   his generosity shall endure forever.
Light shines through the darkness for the upright;
   he is gracious and merciful and just. **R.**
Lavishly he gives to the poor;
   his generosity shall endure forever;
   his horn shall be exalted in glory. **R.**

   John 14:23
R. Alleluia, alleluia.
Whoever loves me will keep my word,
and my Father will love him
and we will come to him. **R.**

† *Matthew 6:1-6, 16-18*

And your Father who sees what is hidden will repay you.

Jesus said to his disciples:
   "Take care not to perform righteous deeds
   in order that people may see them;
   otherwise, you will have no recompense from your heavenly Father.
When you give alms, do not blow a trumpet before you,
   as the hypocrites do in the synagogues and in the streets
   to win the praise of others.
Amen, I say to you, they have received their reward.
But when you give alms,
   do not let your left hand know what your right is doing,
   so that your almsgiving may be secret.
And your Father who sees in secret will repay you.

"When you pray, do not be like the hypocrites,
   who love to stand and pray in the synagogues and on street corners
   so that others may see them.
Amen, I say to you, they have received their reward.
But when you pray, go to your inner room, close the door,
   and pray to your Father in secret.
And your Father who sees in secret will repay you.

"When you fast, do not look gloomy like the hypocrites.
They neglect their appearance,
   so that they may appear to others to be fasting.
Amen, I say to you, they have received their reward.
But when you fast, anoint your head and wash your face,
   so that you may not appear to others to be fasting,

except to your Father who is hidden.
And your Father who sees what is hidden will repay you." ✛

THURSDAY, JUNE 22
Weekday, St. Paulinus of Nola,
St. John Fisher and St. Thomas More

† *2 Corinthians 11:1-11*
I preached the Gospel of God to you without charge.

Brothers and sisters:
If only you would put up with a little foolishness from me!
Please put up with me.
For I am jealous of you with the jealousy of God,
    since I betrothed you to one husband
    to present you as a chaste virgin to Christ.
But I am afraid that, as the serpent deceived Eve by his cunning,
    your thoughts may be corrupted
    from a sincere and pure commitment to Christ.
For if someone comes and preaches another Jesus than the one we
        preached,
    or if you receive a different spirit from the one you received
    or a different gospel from the one you accepted,
    you put up with it well enough.
For I think that I am not in any way inferior to these "superapostles."
Even if I am untrained in speaking, I am not so in knowledge;
    in every way we have made this plain to you in all things.

Did I make a mistake when I humbled myself so that you might be
        exalted,
    because I preached the Gospel of God to you without charge?
I plundered other churches by accepting from them
    in order to minister to you.
And when I was with you and in need, I did not burden anyone,
    for the brothers who came from Macedonia
    supplied my needs.
So I refrained and will refrain from burdening you in any way.
By the truth of Christ in me,
    this boast of mine shall not be silenced
    in the regions of Achaia.
And why? Because I do not love you?
God knows I do! ✛

Psalm 111:1b-2, 3-4, 7-8
R. (7a) **Your works, O Lord, are justice and truth.** *(or* **Alleluia.***)*
I will give thanks to the LORD with all my heart
    in the company and assembly of the just.

Great are the works of the LORD,
  exquisite in all their delights. **R.**
Majesty and glory are his work,
  and his justice endures forever.
He has won renown for his wondrous deeds;
  gracious and merciful is the LORD. **R.**
The works of his hands are faithful and just;
  sure are all his precepts,
Reliable forever and ever,
  wrought in truth and equity. **R.**

Romans 8:15bc
R. Alleluia, alleluia.
You have received a spirit of adoption as sons
through which we cry: Abba! Father! **R.**

† *Matthew 6:7-15*
This is how you are to pray.

Jesus said to his disciples:
"In praying, do not babble like the pagans,
  who think that they will be heard because of their many words.
Do not be like them.
Your Father knows what you need before you ask him.

"This is how you are to pray:

  'Our Father who art in heaven,
    hallowed be thy name,
    thy Kingdom come,
  thy will be done,
    on earth as it is in heaven.
  Give us this day our daily bread;
  and forgive us our trespasses,
    as we forgive those who trespass against us;
  and lead us not into temptation,
    but deliver us from evil.'

"If you forgive others their transgressions,
  your heavenly Father will forgive you.
But if you do not forgive others,
  neither will your Father forgive your transgressions." †

FRIDAY, JUNE 23
WEEKDAY

† *2 Corinthians 11:18, 21-30*

Apart from these things, there is the daily pressure upon me
of my anxiety for all the churches.

Brothers and sisters:
Since many boast according to the flesh, I too will boast.
To my shame I say that we were too weak!

But what anyone dares to boast of
  (I am speaking in foolishness)
  I also dare.
Are they Hebrews? So am I.
Are they children of Israel? So am I.
Are they descendants of Abraham? So am I.
Are they ministers of Christ?
(I am talking like an insane person).
I am still more, with far greater labors,
  far more imprisonments, far worse beatings,
and numerous brushes with death.
Five times at the hands of the Jews
  I received forty lashes minus one.
Three times I was beaten with rods, once I was stoned,
  three times I was shipwrecked,
  I passed a night and a day on the deep;
  on frequent journeys, in dangers from rivers,
  dangers from robbers, dangers from my own race,
  dangers from Gentiles, dangers in the city,
  dangers in the wilderness, dangers at sea,
  dangers among false brothers;
  in toil and hardship, through many sleepless nights,
  through hunger and thirst, through frequent fastings,
  through cold and exposure.
And apart from these things, there is the daily pressure upon me
  of my anxiety for all the churches.
Who is weak, and I am not weak?
Who is led to sin, and I am not indignant?

If I must boast, I will boast of the things that show my weakness. ✛

Psalm 34:2-3, 4-5, 6-7
R. (see 18b) **From all their distress God rescues the just.**
I will bless the LORD at all times;
  his praise shall be ever in my mouth.
Let my soul glory in the LORD;

the lowly will hear me and be glad. **R.**
Glorify the LORD with me,
  let us together extol his name.
I sought the LORD, and he answered me
  and delivered me from all my fears. **R.**
Look to him that you may be radiant with joy,
  and your faces may not blush with shame.
When the poor one called out, the LORD heard,
  and from all his distress he saved him. **R.**

Matthew 5:3
R. Alleluia, alleluia.
Blessed are the poor in spirit;
for theirs is the Kingdom of heaven. **R.**

† *Matthew 6:19-23*
For where your treasure is, there also will your heart be.

Jesus said to his disciples:
"Do not store up for yourselves treasures on earth,
  where moth and decay destroy, and thieves break in and steal.
But store up treasures in heaven,
  where neither moth nor decay destroys, nor thieves break in and
    steal.
For where your treasure is, there also will your heart be.

"The lamp of the body is the eye.
If your eye is sound, your whole body will be filled with light;
  but if your eye is bad, your whole body will be in darkness.
And if the light in you is darkness, how great will the darkness be." ✛

SATURDAY, JUNE 24
THE NATIVITY OF ST. JOHN THE BAPTIST
(The Vigil Readings for the Nativity of John the Baptist are Jeremiah 1:4-10 •
Psalm 71:1-2, 3-4a, 5-6ab, 15ab and 17 • 1 Peter 1:8-12 • Luke 1:5-17 [586].)

† *Isaiah 49:1-6*
I will make you a light to the nations.

Hear me, O coastlands,
  listen, O distant peoples.
The LORD called me from birth,
  from my mother's womb he gave me my name.
He made of me a sharp-edged sword
  and concealed me in the shadow of his arm.
He made me a polished arrow,
  in his quiver he hid me.

You are my servant, he said to me,
   Israel, through whom I show my glory.

Though I thought I had toiled in vain,
   and for nothing, uselessly, spent my strength,
yet my reward is with the LORD,
   my recompense is with my God.
For now the LORD has spoken
   who formed me as his servant from the womb,
that Jacob may be brought back to him
   and Israel gathered to him;
and I am made glorious in the sight of the LORD,
   and my God is now my strength!
It is too little, he says, for you to be my servant,
   to raise up the tribes of Jacob,
   and restore the survivors of Israel;
I will make you a light to the nations,
   that my salvation may reach to the ends of the earth. ✛

   Psalm 139:1b-3, 13-14ab, 14c-15

R. (14) **I praise you, for I am wonderfully made.**

O LORD, you have probed me, you know me:
   you know when I sit and when I stand;
   you understand my thoughts from afar.
My journeys and my rest you scrutinize,
   with all my ways you are familiar. **R.**
Truly you have formed my inmost being;
   you knit me in my mother's womb.
I give you thanks that I am fearfully, wonderfully made;
   wonderful are your works. **R.**
My soul also you knew full well;
   nor was my frame unknown to you
When I was made in secret,
   when I was fashioned in the depths of the earth. **R.**

† *Acts 13:22-26*

John heralded his coming by proclaiming a baptism of repentance.

In those days, Paul said:
"God raised up David as king;
   of him God testified,
   I have found David, son of Jesse, a man after my own heart;
   he will carry out my every wish.
From this man's descendants God, according to his promise,
   has brought to Israel a savior, Jesus.
John heralded his coming by proclaiming a baptism of repentance

to all the people of Israel;
and as John was completing his course, he would say,
'What do you suppose that I am? I am not he.
Behold, one is coming after me;
I am not worthy to unfasten the sandals of his feet.'

"My brothers, sons of the family of Abraham,
and those others among you who are God-fearing,
to us this word of salvation has been sent." ✛

See Luke 1:76

R. Alleluia, alleluia.
You, child, will be called prophet of the Most High,
for you will go before the Lord to prepare his way. **R.**

✛ *Luke 1:57-66, 80*
John is his name.

When the time arrived for Elizabeth to have her child
she gave birth to a son.
Her neighbors and relatives heard
that the Lord had shown his great mercy toward her,
and they rejoiced with her.
When they came on the eighth day to circumcise the child,
they were going to call him Zechariah after his father,
but his mother said in reply,
"No. He will be called John."
But they answered her,
"There is no one among your relatives who has this name."
So they made signs, asking his father what he wished him to be
called.
He asked for a tablet and wrote, "John is his name,"
and all were amazed.
Immediately his mouth was opened, his tongue freed,
and he spoke blessing God.
Then fear came upon all their neighbors,
and all these matters were discussed
throughout the hill country of Judea.
All who heard these things took them to heart, saying,
"What, then, will this child be?"
For surely the hand of the Lord was with him.
The child grew and became strong in spirit,
and he was in the desert until the day
of his manifestation to Israel. ✛

SUNDAY, JUNE 25
TWELFTH SUNDAY IN ORDINARY TIME

†*Jeremiah 20:10-13*
He has rescued the life of the poor from the power of the wicked.

Jeremiah said:
"I hear the whisperings of many:
   'Terror on every side!
   Denounce! let us denounce him!'
All those who were my friends
   are on the watch for any misstep of mine.
'Perhaps he will be trapped; then we can prevail,
   and take our vengeance on him.'
But the LORD is with me, like a mighty champion:
   my persecutors will stumble, they will not triumph.
In their failure they will be put to utter shame,
   to lasting, unforgettable confusion.
O LORD of hosts, you who test the just,
   who probe mind and heart,
let me witness the vengeance you take on them,
   for to you I have entrusted my cause.
Sing to the LORD,
   praise the LORD,
for he has rescued the life of the poor
   from the power of the wicked!" ✢

Psalm 69:8-10, 14, 17, 33-35
R. (14c) **Lord, in your great love, answer me.**
For your sake I bear insult,
   and shame covers my face.
I have become an outcast to my brothers,
   a stranger to my mother's children,
Because zeal for your house consumes me,
   and the insults of those who blaspheme you fall upon me. **R.**
I pray to you, O LORD,
   for the time of your favor, O God!
In your great kindness answer me
   with your constant help.
Answer me, O LORD, for bounteous is your kindness;
   in your great mercy turn toward me. **R.**
"See, you lowly ones, and be glad;
   you who seek God, may your hearts revive!
For the LORD hears the poor,
   and his own who are in bonds he spurns not.

Let the heavens and the earth praise him,
  the seas and whatever moves in them!" **R.**

† *Romans 5:12-15*
The gift is not like the transgression.

Brothers and sisters:
Through one man sin entered the world,
  and through sin, death,
  and thus death came to all men, inasmuch as all sinned—
  for up to the time of the law, sin was in the world,
  though sin is not accounted when there is no law.
But death reigned from Adam to Moses,
  even over those who did not sin
  after the pattern of the trespass of Adam,
  who is the type of the one who was to come.

But the gift is not like the transgression.
For if by the transgression of the one the many died,
  how much more did the grace of God
  and the gracious gift of the one man Jesus Christ
  overflow for the many. ✢

John 15:26b, 27a
R. Alleluia, alleluia.
The Spirit of truth will testify to me, says the Lord;
and you also will testify. **R.**

† *Matthew 10:26-33*
Do not be afraid of those who kill the body.

Jesus said to the Twelve:
  "Fear no one.
Nothing is concealed that will not be revealed,
  nor secret that will not be known.
What I say to you in the darkness, speak in the light;
  what you hear whispered, proclaim on the housetops.
And do not be afraid of those who kill the body but cannot kill the
    soul;
  rather, be afraid of the one who can destroy
  both soul and body in Gehenna.
Are not two sparrows sold for a small coin?
Yet not one of them falls to the ground without your Father's
    knowledge.
Even all the hairs of your head are counted.
So do not be afraid; you are worth more than many sparrows.
Everyone who acknowledges me before others
  I will acknowledge before my heavenly Father.

But whoever denies me before others,
  I will deny before my heavenly Father." ✙

MONDAY, JUNE 26
WEEKDAY

† *Genesis 12:1-9*
Abraham went as the Lord directed him.

The LORD said to Abram:
"Go forth from the land of your kinsfolk
  and from your father's house to a land that I will show you.

  "I will make of you a great nation,
    and I will bless you;
  I will make your name great,
    so that you will be a blessing.
  I will bless those who bless you
    and curse those who curse you.
  All the communities of the earth
    shall find blessing in you."

Abram went as the LORD directed him, and Lot went with him.
Abram was seventy-five years old when he left Haran.
Abram took his wife, Sarai, his brother's son Lot,
  all the possessions that they had accumulated,
  and the persons they had acquired in Haran,
  and they set out for the land of Canaan.
When they came to the land of Canaan, Abram passed through the land
  as far as the sacred place at Shechem,
  by the terebinth of Moreh.
(The Canaanites were then in the land.)

The LORD appeared to Abram and said,
  "To your descendants I will give this land."
So Abram built an altar there to the LORD who had appeared to him.
From there he moved on to the hill country east of Bethel,
  pitching his tent with Bethel to the west and Ai to the east.
He built an altar there to the LORD and invoked the LORD by name.
Then Abram journeyed on by stages to the Negeb. ✙

  Psalm 33:12-13, 18-19, 20 and 22
R. (12) **Blessed the people the Lord has chosen to be his own.**
Blessed the nation whose God is the LORD,
  the people he has chosen for his own inheritance.
From heaven the LORD looks down;
  he sees all mankind. **R.**

See, the eyes of the LORD are upon those who fear him,
  upon those who hope for his kindness,
To deliver them from death
  and preserve them in spite of famine. **R.**
Our soul waits for the LORD,
  who is our help and our shield.
May your kindness, O LORD, be upon us
  who have put our hope in you. **R.**

  Hebrews 4:12
R. Alleluia, alleluia.
The word of God is living and effective,
able to discern reflections and thoughts of the heart. **R.**

† *Matthew 7:1-5*
Remove the wooden beam from your eye first.

Jesus said to his disciples:
"Stop judging, that you may not be judged.
For as you judge, so will you be judged,
  and the measure with which you measure will be measured out to
    you.
Why do you notice the splinter in your brother's eye,
  but do not perceive the wooden beam in your own eye?
How can you say to your brother,
  'Let me remove that splinter from your eye,'
  while the wooden beam is in your eye?
You hypocrite, remove the wooden beam from your eye first;
  then you will see clearly
  to remove the splinter from your brother's eye." ✝

TUESDAY, JUNE 27
WEEKDAY, ST. CYRIL OF ALEXANDRIA

† *Genesis 13:2, 5-18*
Let there be no strife between you and me, for we are brothers.

Abram was very rich in livestock, silver, and gold.

Lot, who went with Abram, also had flocks and herds and tents,
  so that the land could not support them if they stayed together;
  their possessions were so great that they could not dwell together.
There were quarrels between the herdsmen of Abram's livestock
  and those of Lot's.
(At this time the Canaanites and the Perizzites
  were occupying the land.)

So Abram said to Lot:

"Let there be no strife between you and me,
  or between your herdsmen and mine, for we are kinsmen.
Is not the whole land at your disposal?
Please separate from me.
If you prefer the left, I will go to the right;
  if you prefer the right, I will go to the left."
Lot looked about and saw how well watered
  the whole Jordan Plain was as far as Zoar,
  like the LORD's own garden, or like Egypt.
(This was before the LORD had destroyed Sodom and Gomorrah.)
Lot, therefore, chose for himself the whole Jordan Plain
  and set out eastward.
Thus they separated from each other;
  Abram stayed in the land of Canaan,
  while Lot settled among the cities of the Plain,
  pitching his tents near Sodom.
Now the inhabitants of Sodom were very wicked
  in the sins they committed against the LORD.

After Lot had left, the LORD said to Abram:
  "Look about you, and from where you are,
  gaze to the north and south, east and west;
  all the land that you see I will give to you
  and your descendants forever.
I will make your descendants like the dust of the earth;
  if anyone could count the dust of the earth,
  your descendants too might be counted.
Set forth and walk about in the land, through its length and
      breadth,
  for to you I will give it."
Abram moved his tents and went on to settle
  near the terebinth of Mamre, which is at Hebron.
There he built an altar to the LORD. ✛

  Psalm 15:2-3a, 3bc-4ab, 5
R. (1b) **He who does justice will live in the presence of the
    Lord.**
He who walks blamelessly and does justice;
  who thinks the truth in his heart
  and slanders not with his tongue. **R.**
Who harms not his fellow man,
  nor takes up a reproach against his neighbor;
By whom the reprobate is despised,
  while he honors those who fear the LORD. **R.**
Who lends not his money at usury

and accepts no bribe against the innocent.
He who does these things
shall never be disturbed. **R.**

John 8:12
R. Alleluia, alleluia.
I am the light of the world, says the Lord;
whoever follows me will have the light of life. **R.**

† *Matthew 7:6, 12-14*
Do to others whatever you would have them do to you.

Jesus said to his disciples:
"Do not give what is holy to dogs, or throw your pearls before swine,
    lest they trample them underfoot, and turn and tear you to pieces.

"Do to others whatever you would have them do to you.
This is the Law and the Prophets.

"Enter through the narrow gate;
    for the gate is wide and the road broad that leads to destruction,
    and those who enter through it are many.
How narrow the gate and constricted the road that leads to life.
And those who find it are few." ✛

WEDNESDAY, JUNE 28
St. Irenaeus

† *Genesis 15:1-12, 17-18*
*Abraham believed God, and it was credited to him as righteousness
(Romans 4:3b), and the Lord made a covenant with him.*

The word of the Lord came to Abram in a vision:

"Fear not, Abram!
    I am your shield;
    I will make your reward very great."

But Abram said,
    "O Lord God, what good will your gifts be,
    if I keep on being childless
    and have as my heir the steward of my house, Eliezer?"
Abram continued,
    "See, you have given me no offspring,
    and so one of my servants will be my heir."
Then the word of the Lord came to him:
    "No, that one shall not be your heir;
    your own issue shall be your heir."
He took him outside and said:

"Look up at the sky and count the stars, if you can.
Just so," he added, "shall your descendants be."
Abram put his faith in the LORD,
  who credited it to him as an act of righteousness.

He then said to him,
  "I am the LORD who brought you from Ur of the Chaldeans
  to give you this land as a possession."
"O Lord GOD," he asked,
  "how am I to know that I shall possess it?"
He answered him,
  "Bring me a three-year-old heifer, a three-year-old she-goat,
  a three-year-old ram, a turtledove, and a young pigeon."
Abram brought him all these, split them in two,
  and placed each half opposite the other;
  but the birds he did not cut up.
Birds of prey swooped down on the carcasses,
  but Abram stayed with them.
As the sun was about to set, a trance fell upon Abram,
  and a deep, terrifying darkness enveloped him.

When the sun had set and it was dark,
  there appeared a smoking fire pot and a flaming torch,
  which passed between those pieces.
It was on that occasion that the LORD made a covenant with Abram,
  saying: "To your descendants I give this land,
  from the Wadi of Egypt to the Great River the Euphrates." ✛

Psalm 105:1-2, 3-4, 6-7, 8-9
R. (8a) **The Lord remembers his covenant for ever.**
  (or **Alleluia.***)*
Give thanks to the LORD, invoke his name;
  make known among the nations his deeds.
Sing to him, sing his praise,
  proclaim all his wondrous deeds. **R.**
Glory in his holy name;
  rejoice, O hearts that seek the LORD!
Look to the LORD in his strength;
  seek to serve him constantly. **R.**
You descendants of Abraham, his servants,
  sons of Jacob, his chosen ones!
He, the LORD, is our God;
  throughout the earth his judgments prevail. **R.**
He remembers forever his covenant
  which he made binding for a thousand generations—

Which he entered into with Abraham
  and by his oath to Isaac. **R.**

John 15:4a, 5b
R. Alleluia, alleluia.
Remain in me, as I remain in you, says the Lord;
whoever remains in me will bear much fruit. **R.**

✝ *Matthew 7:15-20*
By their fruits you will know them.

Jesus said to his disciples:
"Beware of false prophets, who come to you in sheep's clothing,
  but underneath are ravenous wolves.
By their fruits you will know them.
Do people pick grapes from thornbushes, or figs from thistles?
Just so, every good tree bears good fruit,
  and a rotten tree bears bad fruit.
A good tree cannot bear bad fruit,
  nor can a rotten tree bear good fruit.
Every tree that does not bear good fruit will be cut down
  and thrown into the fire.
So by their fruits you will know them." ✝

THURSDAY, JUNE 29
St. Peter and St. Paul
(Readings for the Vigil Mass are: Acts 3:1-10 • Psalm 19:2-3, 4-5 •
Galatians 1:11-20 • John 21:15-19 [590].)

✝ *Acts 12:1-11*
Now I know for certain that the Lord rescued me from the hand of Herod.

In those days, King Herod laid hands upon some members of the
  Church to harm them.
He had James, the brother of John, killed by the sword,
  and when he saw that this was pleasing to the Jews
  he proceeded to arrest Peter also.
—It was the feast of Unleavened Bread.—
He had him taken into custody and put in prison
  under the guard of four squads of four soldiers each.
He intended to bring him before the people after Passover.
Peter thus was being kept in prison,
  but prayer by the Church was fervently being made
  to God on his behalf.

On the very night before Herod was to bring him to trial,
  Peter, secured by double chains,
  was sleeping between two soldiers,

while outside the door guards kept watch on the prison.
Suddenly the angel of the Lord stood by him,
    and a light shone in the cell.
He tapped Peter on the side and awakened him, saying,
    "Get up quickly."
The chains fell from his wrists.
The angel said to him, "Put on your belt and your sandals."
He did so.
Then he said to him, "Put on your cloak and follow me."
So he followed him out,
    not realizing that what was happening through the angel was real;
    he thought he was seeing a vision.
They passed the first guard, then the second,
    and came to the iron gate leading out to the city,
    which opened for them by itself.
They emerged and made their way down an alley,
    and suddenly the angel left him.
Then Peter recovered his senses and said,
    "Now I know for certain
    that the Lord sent his angel
    and rescued me from the hand of Herod
    and from all that the Jewish people had been expecting." ✚

Psalm 34:2-3, 4-5, 6-7, 8-9

R. (5) **The angel of the Lord will rescue those who fear him.**

I will bless the LORD at all times;
    his praise shall be ever in my mouth.
Let my soul glory in the LORD;
    the lowly will hear me and be glad. **R.**

Glorify the LORD with me,
    let us together extol his name.
I sought the LORD, and he answered me
    and delivered me from all my fears. **R.**

Look to him that you may be radiant with joy,
    and your faces may not blush with shame.
When the poor one called out, the LORD heard,
    and from all his distress he saved him. **R.**

The angel of the LORD encamps
    around those who fear him, and delivers them.
Taste and see how good the LORD is;
    blessed the man who takes refuge in him. **R.**

† *2 Timothy 4:6-8, 17-18*

From now on the crown of righteousness awaits me.

I, Paul, am already being poured out like a libation,
 and the time of my departure is at hand.
I have competed well; I have finished the race;
 I have kept the faith.
From now on the crown of righteousness awaits me,
 which the Lord, the just judge,
 will award to me on that day, and not only to me,
 but to all who have longed for his appearance.

The Lord stood by me and gave me strength,
 so that through me the proclamation might be completed
 and all the Gentiles might hear it.
And I was rescued from the lion's mouth.
The Lord will rescue me from every evil threat
 and will bring me safe to his heavenly Kingdom.
To him be glory forever and ever. Amen. ✛

Matthew 16:18
R. Alleluia, alleluia.
You are Peter and upon this rock I will build my Church,
and the gates of the netherworld shall not prevail against it. **R.**

† *Matthew 16:13-19*

You are Peter, and I will give you the keys to the Kingdom of heaven.

When Jesus went into the region of Caesarea Philippi
 he asked his disciples,
 "Who do people say that the Son of Man is?"
They replied, "Some say John the Baptist, others Elijah,
 still others Jeremiah or one of the prophets."
He said to them, "But who do you say that I am?"
Simon Peter said in reply,
 "You are the Christ, the Son of the living God."
Jesus said to him in reply, "Blessed are you, Simon son of Jonah.
For flesh and blood has not revealed this to you, but my heavenly
 Father.
And so I say to you, you are Peter,
 and upon this rock I will build my Church,
 and the gates of the netherworld shall not prevail against it.
I will give you the keys to the Kingdom of heaven.
Whatever you bind on earth shall be bound in heaven;
 and whatever you loose on earth shall be loosed in heaven." ✛

FRIDAY, JUNE 30
WEEKDAY, THE FIRST MARTYRS OF THE HOLY ROMAN CHURCH

† *Genesis 17:1, 9-10, 15-22*
Every male among you shall be circumcised: thus is my covenant with you.
Sarah shall bear you a son.

When Abram was ninety-nine years old, the LORD appeared to him
and said: "I am God the Almighty.
Walk in my presence and be blameless."

God also said to Abraham:
"On your part, you and your descendants after you
must keep my covenant throughout the ages.
This is my covenant with you and your descendants after you
that you must keep:
every male among you shall be circumcised."

God further said to Abraham:
"As for your wife Sarai, do not call her Sarai;
her name shall be Sarah.
I will bless her, and I will give you a son by her.
Him also will I bless; he shall give rise to nations,
and rulers of peoples shall issue from him."
Abraham prostrated himself and laughed as he said to himself,
"Can a child be born to a man who is a hundred years old?
Or can Sarah give birth at ninety?"
Then Abraham said to God,
"Let but Ishmael live on by your favor!"
God replied: "Nevertheless, your wife Sarah is to bear you a son,
and you shall call him Isaac.
I will maintain my covenant with him as an everlasting pact,
to be his God and the God of his descendants after him.
As for Ishmael, I am heeding you: I hereby bless him.
I will make him fertile and will multiply him exceedingly.
He shall become the father of twelve chieftains,
and I will make of him a great nation.
But my covenant I will maintain with Isaac,
whom Sarah shall bear to you by this time next year."
When he had finished speaking with him, God departed from
Abraham. ✦

Psalm 128:1-2, 3, 4-5
R. (4) See how the Lord blesses those who fear him.
Blessed are you who fear the LORD,
who walk in his ways!
For you shall eat the fruit of your handiwork;

blessed shall you be, and favored. **R.**
Your wife shall be like a fruitful vine
    in the recesses of your home;
Your children like olive plants
    around your table. **R.**
Behold, thus is the man blessed
    who fears the LORD.
The LORD bless you from Zion:
    may you see the prosperity of Jerusalem
    all the days of your life. **R.**

   Matthew 8:17
R. Alleluia, alleluia.
Christ took away our infirmities
and bore our diseases. **R.**

† *Matthew 8:1-4*
If you wish, you can make me clean.

When Jesus came down from the mountain, great crowds followed
    him.
And then a leper approached, did him homage, and said,
    "Lord, if you wish, you can make me clean."
He stretched out his hand, touched him, and said,
    "I will do it. Be made clean."
His leprosy was cleansed immediately.
Then Jesus said to him, "See that you tell no one,
    but go show yourself to the priest,
    and offer the gift that Moses prescribed;
    that will be proof for them." ✛

SATURDAY, JULY 1
WEEKDAY, ST. JUNÍPERO SERRA, *[BVM]*

† *Genesis 18:1-15*
*Is anything too marvelous for the Lord to do? I will surely return
to you and Sarah will then have a son.*

The LORD appeared to Abraham by the Terebinth of Mamre,
    as Abraham sat in the entrance of his tent,
    while the day was growing hot.
Looking up, he saw three men standing nearby.
When he saw them, he ran from the entrance of the tent to greet
    them;
    and bowing to the ground, he said:
    "Sir, if I may ask you this favor,
    please do not go on past your servant.
Let some water be brought, that you may bathe your feet,

and then rest yourselves under the tree.
Now that you have come this close to your servant,
    let me bring you a little food, that you may refresh yourselves;
    and afterward you may go on your way."
The men replied, "Very well, do as you have said."

Abraham hastened into the tent and told Sarah,
    "Quick, three measures of fine flour!
Knead it and make rolls."
He ran to the herd, picked out a tender, choice steer,
    and gave it to a servant, who quickly prepared it.
Then Abraham got some curds and milk,
    as well as the steer that had been prepared,
    and set these before them;
    and he waited on them under the tree while they ate.

They asked him, "Where is your wife Sarah?"
He replied, "There in the tent."
One of them said, "I will surely return to you about this time next
        year,
    and Sarah will then have a son."
Sarah was listening at the entrance of the tent, just behind him.
Now Abraham and Sarah were old, advanced in years,
    and Sarah had stopped having her womanly periods.
So Sarah laughed to herself and said,
    "Now that I am so withered and my husband is so old,
    am I still to have sexual pleasure?"
But the LORD said to Abraham: "Why did Sarah laugh and say,
    'Shall I really bear a child, old as I am?'
Is anything too marvelous for the LORD to do?
At the appointed time, about this time next year, I will return to you,
    and Sarah will have a son."
Because she was afraid, Sarah dissembled, saying, "I didn't laugh."
But he replied, "Yes you did." ✛

Luke 1:46-47, 48-49, 50 and 53, 54-55
R. (see 54b) **The Lord has remembered his mercy.**
"My soul proclaims the greatness of the Lord,
    my spirit rejoices in God my Savior." **R.**
"For he has looked with favor on his lowly servant.
From this day all generations will call me blessed:
    the Almighty has done great things for me,
    and holy is his Name." **R.**
"He has mercy on those who fear him
    in every generation.

He has filled the hungry with good things,
   and the rich he has sent away empty." **R.**
"He has come to the help of his servant Israel
   for he has remembered his promise of mercy,
The promise he made to our fathers,
   to Abraham and his children for ever." **R.**

Matthew 8:17
R. Alleluia, alleluia.
Christ took away our infirmities
and bore our diseases. **R.**

† *Matthew 8:5-17*

*Many will come from east and west and will recline
with Abraham, Isaac and Jacob.*

When Jesus entered Capernaum,
   a centurion approached him and appealed to him, saying,
   "Lord, my servant is lying at home paralyzed, suffering dreadfully."
He said to him, "I will come and cure him."
The centurion said in reply,
   "Lord, I am not worthy to have you enter under my roof;
   only say the word and my servant will be healed.
   For I too am a man subject to authority,
   with soldiers subject to me.
And I say to one, 'Go,' and he goes;
   and to another, 'Come here,' and he comes;
   and to my slave, 'Do this,' and he does it."
When Jesus heard this, he was amazed and said to those following
     him,
   "Amen, I say to you, in no one in Israel have I found such faith.
I say to you, many will come from the east and the west,
   and will recline with Abraham, Isaac, and Jacob
   at the banquet in the Kingdom of heaven,
   but the children of the Kingdom
   will be driven out into the outer darkness,
   where there will be wailing and grinding of teeth."
And Jesus said to the centurion,
   "You may go; as you have believed, let it be done for you."
And at that very hour his servant was healed.

Jesus entered the house of Peter,
   and saw his mother-in-law lying in bed with a fever.
He touched her hand, the fever left her,
   and she rose and waited on him.

When it was evening, they brought him many
   who were possessed by demons,
   and he drove out the spirits by a word and cured all the sick,
   to fulfill what had been said by Isaiah the prophet:

> *He took away our infirmities*
> *and bore our diseases.* ✛

SUNDAY, JULY 2
THIRTEENTH SUNDAY IN ORDINARY TIME

† *2 Kings 4:8-11, 14-16a*
Elisha is a holy man of God, let him remain.

One day Elisha came to Shunem,
   where there was a woman of influence, who urged him to dine
     with her.
Afterward, whenever he passed by, he used to stop there to dine.
So she said to her husband, "I know that Elisha is a holy man of God.
Since he visits us often, let us arrange a little room on the roof
   and furnish it for him with a bed, table, chair, and lamp,
   so that when he comes to us he can stay there."
Sometime later Elisha arrived and stayed in the room overnight.

Later Elisha asked, "Can something be done for her?"
His servant Gehazi answered, "Yes!
   She has no son, and her husband is getting on in years."
Elisha said, "Call her."
When the woman had been called and stood at the door,
   Elisha promised, "This time next year
   you will be fondling a baby son." ✛

Psalm 89:2-3, 16-17, 18-19
R. (2a) **For ever I will sing the goodness of the Lord.**
The promises of the LORD I will sing forever,
   through all generations my mouth shall proclaim your faithfulness.
For you have said, "My kindness is established forever";
   in heaven you have confirmed your faithfulness. **R.**
Blessed the people who know the joyful shout;
   in the light of your countenance, O LORD, they walk.
At your name they rejoice all the day,
   and through your justice they are exalted. **R.**
You are the splendor of their strength,
   and by your favor our horn is exalted.
For to the LORD belongs our shield,
   and the Holy One of Israel, our king. **R.**

† *Romans 6:3-4, 8-11*

Buried with Christ in baptism, we shall walk in the newness of life.

Brothers and sisters:
Are you unaware that we who were baptized into Christ Jesus
    were baptized into his death?
We were indeed buried with him through baptism into death,
    so that, just as Christ was raised from the dead
    by the glory of the Father,
    we too might live in newness of life.

If, then, we have died with Christ,
    we believe that we shall also live with him.
We know that Christ, raised from the dead, dies no more;
    death no longer has power over him.
As to his death, he died to sin once and for all;
    as to his life, he lives for God.
Consequently, you too must think of yourselves as dead to sin
    and living for God in Christ Jesus. ✛

1 Peter 2:9
R. Alleluia, alleluia.
You are a chosen race, a royal priesthood, a holy nation;
announce the praises of him who called you out of darkness into his
    wonderful light. **R.**

† *Matthew 10:37-42*

Whoever does not take up his cross is not worthy of me.
Whoever receives you, receives me.

Jesus said to his apostles:
    "Whoever loves father or mother more than me is not worthy of me,
    and whoever loves son or daughter more than me is not worthy of
        me;
    and whoever does not take up his cross
    and follow after me is not worthy of me.
Whoever finds his life will lose it,
    and whoever loses his life for my sake will find it.

"Whoever receives you receives me,
    and whoever receives me receives the one who sent me.
Whoever receives a prophet because he is a prophet
    will receive a prophet's reward,
    and whoever receives a righteous man
    because he is a righteous man
    will receive a righteous man's reward.
And whoever gives only a cup of cold water

to one of these little ones to drink
because the little one is a disciple—
amen, I say to you, he will surely not lose his reward." ✛

MONDAY, JULY 3
St. Thomas

†Ephesians 2:19-22
Built upon the foundation of the Apostles.

Brothers and sisters:
You are no longer strangers and sojourners,
    but you are fellow citizens with the holy ones
    and members of the household of God,
    built upon the foundation of the Apostles and prophets,
    with Christ Jesus himself as the capstone.
Through him the whole structure is held together
    and grows into a temple sacred in the Lord;
    in him you also are being built together
    into a dwelling place of God in the Spirit. ✛

Psalm 117:1bc, 2
R. (Mark 16:15) **Go out to all the world and tell the Good
    News.**
Praise the Lord, all you nations;
    glorify him, all you peoples! **R.**
For steadfast is his kindness for us,
    and the fidelity of the Lord endures forever. **R.**

John 20:29
R. Alleluia, alleluia.
You believe in me, Thomas, because you have seen me, says the Lord;
blessed are those who have not seen, but still believe! **R.**

†John 20:24-29
My Lord and my God!

Thomas, called Didymus, one of the Twelve,
    was not with them when Jesus came.
So the other disciples said to him, "We have seen the Lord."
But Thomas said to them,
    "Unless I see the mark of the nails in his hands
    and put my finger into the nailmarks
    and put my hand into his side, I will not believe."
Now a week later his disciples were again inside
    and Thomas was with them.
Jesus came, although the doors were locked,
    and stood in their midst and said, "Peace be with you."

Then he said to Thomas, "Put your finger here and see my hands,
  and bring your hand and put it into my side,
  and do not be unbelieving, but believe."
Thomas answered and said to him, "My Lord and my God!"
Jesus said to him, "Have you come to believe because you have seen
      me?
Blessed are those who have not seen and have believed." ✛

TUESDAY, JULY 4
WEEKDAY, INDEPENDENCE DAY, U.S.A.

(For Independence Day, any readings from the *Lectionary for Mass,*
volume IV, the Mass "For the Country or a City," numbers 882–886, or
"For Peace and Justice," numbers 887–891.)

† Genesis 19:15-29
The Lord God rained down sulphurous fire upon Sodom and Gomorrah.

As dawn was breaking, the angels urged Lot on, saying, "On your
      way!
Take with you your wife and your two daughters who are here,
  or you will be swept away in the punishment of Sodom."
When he hesitated, the men, by the LORD's mercy,
  seized his hand and the hands of his wife and his two daughters
  and led them to safety outside the city.
As soon as they had been brought outside, he was told:
  "Flee for your life!
Don't look back or stop anywhere on the Plain.
Get off to the hills at once, or you will be swept away."
  "Oh, no, my lord!" Lot replied,
"You have already thought enough of your servant
  to do me the great kindness of intervening to save my life.
But I cannot flee to the hills to keep the disaster from overtaking me,
  and so I shall die.
Look, this town ahead is near enough to escape to.
It's only a small place.
Let me flee there—it's a small place, is it not?—
  that my life may be saved."
"Well, then," he replied,
  "I will also grant you the favor you now ask.
I will not overthrow the town you speak of.
Hurry, escape there!
I cannot do anything until you arrive there."
That is why the town is called Zoar.

The sun was just rising over the earth as Lot arrived in Zoar;
  at the same time the LORD rained down sulphurous fire

upon Sodom and Gomorrah
from the LORD out of heaven.
He overthrew those cities and the whole Plain,
together with the inhabitants of the cities
and the produce of the soil.
But Lot's wife looked back, and she was turned into a pillar of salt.

Early the next morning Abraham went to the place
where he had stood in the LORD's presence.
As he looked down toward Sodom and Gomorrah
and the whole region of the Plain,
he saw dense smoke over the land rising like fumes from a furnace.

Thus it came to pass: when God destroyed the Cities of the Plain,
he was mindful of Abraham by sending Lot away from the upheaval
by which God overthrew the cities where Lot had been living. ✛

Psalm 26:2-3, 9-10, 11-12
R. (3a) O Lord, your mercy is before my eyes.
Search me, O LORD, and try me;
test my soul and my heart.
For your mercy is before my eyes,
and I walk in your truth. **R.**
Gather not my soul with those of sinners,
nor with men of blood my life.
On their hands are crimes,
and their right hands are full of bribes. **R.**
But I walk in integrity;
redeem me, and have mercy on me.
My foot stands on level ground;
in the assemblies I will bless the LORD. **R.**

Psalm 130:5
R. Alleluia, alleluia.
I trust in the LORD;
my soul trusts in his word. **R.**

† Matthew 8:23-27
Jesus rebuked the winds and the sea, and there was great calm.

As Jesus got into a boat, his disciples followed him.
Suddenly a violent storm came up on the sea,
so that the boat was being swamped by waves;
but he was asleep.
They came and woke him, saying,
"Lord, save us! We are perishing!"
He said to them, "Why are you terrified, O you of little faith?"

Then he got up, rebuked the winds and the sea,
and there was great calm.
The men were amazed and said, "What sort of man is this,
whom even the winds and the sea obey?" ✛

WEDNESDAY, JULY 5
WEEKDAY, ST. ANTHONY ZACCARIA, ST. ELIZABETH OF PORTUGAL

† *Genesis 21:5, 8-20a*
No son of that slave is going to share the inheritance with my son Isaac!

Abraham was a hundred years old when his son Isaac was born to
him.
Isaac grew, and on the day of the child's weaning
Abraham held a great feast.

Sarah noticed the son whom Hagar the Egyptian
had borne to Abraham
playing with her son Isaac;
so she demanded of Abraham:
"Drive out that slave and her son!
No son of that slave is going to share the inheritance
with my son Isaac!"
Abraham was greatly distressed,
especially on account of his son Ishmael.
But God said to Abraham: "Do not be distressed about the boy
or about your slave woman.
Heed the demands of Sarah, no matter what she is asking of you;
for it is through Isaac that descendants shall bear your name.
As for the son of the slave woman,
I will make a great nation of him also,
since he too is your offspring."

Early the next morning Abraham got some bread and a skin of water
and gave them to Hagar.
Then, placing the child on her back, he sent her away.
As she roamed aimlessly in the wilderness of Beer-sheba,
the water in the skin was used up.
So she put the child down under a shrub,
and then went and sat down opposite him, about a bowshot away;
for she said to herself, "Let me not watch to see the child die."
As she sat opposite Ishmael, he began to cry.
God heard the boy's cry,
and God's messenger called to Hagar from heaven:
"What is the matter, Hagar?
Don't be afraid; God has heard the boy's cry in this plight of his.

Arise, lift up the boy and hold him by the hand;
   for I will make of him a great nation."
Then God opened her eyes, and she saw a well of water.
She went and filled the skin with water, and then let the boy drink.

God was with the boy as he grew up. ✛

Psalm 34:7-8, 10-11, 12-13
R. (7a) **The Lord hears the cry of the poor.**
When the poor one called out, the LORD heard,
   and from all his distress he saved him.
The angel of the LORD encamps
   around those who fear him, and delivers them. **R.**
Fear the LORD, you his holy ones,
   for nought is lacking to those who fear him.
The great grow poor and hungry;
   but those who seek the LORD want for no good thing. **R.**
Come, children, hear me;
   I will teach you the fear of the LORD.
Which of you desires life,
   and takes delight in prosperous days? **R.**

James 1:18
R. Alleluia, alleluia.
The Father willed to give us birth by the word of truth
that we may be a kind of firstfruits of his creatures. **R.**

† Matthew 8:28-34
Have you come here to torment us before the appointed time?

When Jesus came to the territory of the Gadarenes,
   two demoniacs who were coming from the tombs met him.
They were so savage that no one could travel by that road.
They cried out, "What have you to do with us, Son of God?
Have you come here to torment us before the appointed time?"
Some distance away a herd of many swine was feeding.
The demons pleaded with him,
   "If you drive us out, send us into the herd of swine."
And he said to them, "Go then!"
They came out and entered the swine,
   and the whole herd rushed down the steep bank into the sea
   where they drowned.
The swineherds ran away,
   and when they came to the town they reported everything,
   including what had happened to the demoniacs.
Thereupon the whole town came out to meet Jesus,
   and when they saw him they begged him to leave their district. ✛

THURSDAY, JULY 6
WEEKDAY, ST. MARIA GORETTI

† *Genesis 22:1b-19*
The sacrifice of Abraham, our father in faith.

God put Abraham to the test.
He called to him, "Abraham!"
"Here I am," he replied.
Then God said: "Take your son Isaac, your only one, whom you love,
   and go to the land of Moriah.
There you shall offer him up as a burnt offering
   on a height that I will point out to you."
Early the next morning Abraham saddled his donkey,
   took with him his son Isaac, and two of his servants as well,
   and with the wood that he had cut for the burnt offering,
   set out for the place of which God had told him.

On the third day Abraham got sight of the place from afar.
Then he said to his servants: "Both of you stay here with the donkey,
   while the boy and I go on over yonder.
We will worship and then come back to you."
Thereupon Abraham took the wood for the burnt offering
   and laid it on his son Isaac's shoulders,
   while he himself carried the fire and the knife.
As the two walked on together, Isaac spoke to his father Abraham:
   "Father!" he said.
"Yes, son," he replied.
Isaac continued, "Here are the fire and the wood,
   but where is the sheep for the burnt offering?"
"Son," Abraham answered,
   "God himself will provide the sheep for the burnt offering."
Then the two continued going forward.

When they came to the place of which God had told him,
   Abraham built an altar there and arranged the wood on it.
Next he tied up his son Isaac,
   and put him on top of the wood on the altar.
Then he reached out and took the knife to slaughter his son.
But the LORD's messenger called to him from heaven,
   "Abraham, Abraham!"
"Here I am," he answered.
"Do not lay your hand on the boy," said the messenger.
"Do not do the least thing to him.
I know now how devoted you are to God,
   since you did not withhold from me your own beloved son."

As Abraham looked about,
he spied a ram caught by its horns in the thicket.
So he went and took the ram
and offered it up as a burnt offering in place of his son.
Abraham named the site Yahweh-yireh;
hence people now say, "On the mountain the LORD will see."
Again the LORD's messenger called to Abraham from heaven and said:
"I swear by myself, declares the LORD,
that because you acted as you did
in not withholding from me your beloved son,
I will bless you abundantly
and make your descendants as countless
as the stars of the sky and the sands of the seashore;
your descendants shall take possession
of the gates of their enemies,
and in your descendants all the nations of the earth
shall find blessing—all this because you obeyed my command."

Abraham then returned to his servants,
and they set out together for Beer-sheba,
where Abraham made his home. ✛

Psalm 115:1-2, 3-4, 5-6, 8-9
R. (9) **I will walk in the presence of the Lord, in the land of
the living.** *(or* **Alleluia.***)*
Not to us, O LORD, not to us
but to your name give glory
because of your kindness, because of your truth.
Why should the pagans say,
"Where is their God?" **R.**
Our God is in heaven;
whatever he wills, he does.
Their idols are silver and gold,
the handiwork of men. **R.**
They have mouths but speak not;
they have eyes but see not;
They have ears but hear not;
they have noses but smell not. **R.**
Their makers shall be like them,
everyone who trusts in them.
The house of Israel trusts in the LORD;
he is their help and their shield. **R.**

2 Corinthians 5:19

R. Alleluia, alleluia.

God was reconciling the world to himself in Christ
and entrusting to us the message of reconciliation. **R.**

† *Matthew 9:1-8*
They glorified God who had given such authority to men.

After entering a boat, Jesus made the crossing, and came into his
     own town.
And there people brought to him a paralytic lying on a stretcher.
When Jesus saw their faith, he said to the paralytic,
     "Courage, child, your sins are forgiven."
At that, some of the scribes said to themselves,
     "This man is blaspheming."
Jesus knew what they were thinking, and said,
     "Why do you harbor evil thoughts?
Which is easier, to say, 'Your sins are forgiven,'
     or to say, 'Rise and walk'?
But that you may know that the Son of Man
     has authority on earth to forgive sins"—
he then said to the paralytic,
     "Rise, pick up your stretcher, and go home."
He rose and went home.
When the crowds saw this they were struck with awe
     and glorified God who had given such authority to men. ✛

FRIDAY, JULY 7
WEEKDAY

† *Genesis 23:1-4, 19; 24:1-8, 62-67*
In his love for Rebekah, Isaac found solace
after the death of his mother Sarah.

The span of Sarah's life was one hundred and twenty-seven years.
She died in Kiriatharba (that is, Hebron)
     in the land of Canaan,
     and Abraham performed the customary mourning rites for her.
Then he left the side of his dead one and addressed the Hittites:
     "Although I am a resident alien among you,
     sell me from your holdings a piece of property for a burial ground,
     that I may bury my dead wife."

After the transaction, Abraham buried his wife Sarah
     in the cave of the field of Machpelah,
     facing Mamre (that is, Hebron) in the land of Canaan.

Abraham had now reached a ripe old age,

and the Lord had blessed him in every way.
Abraham said to the senior servant of his household,
   who had charge of all his possessions:
   "Put your hand under my thigh,
   and I will make you swear by the Lord,
   the God of heaven and the God of earth,
   that you will not procure a wife for my son
   from the daughters of the Canaanites among whom I live,
   but that you will go to my own land and to my kindred
   to get a wife for my son Isaac."
The servant asked him:
   "What if the woman is unwilling to follow me to this land?
Should I then take your son back to the land from which you
     migrated?"
"Never take my son back there for any reason," Abraham told him.
"The Lord, the God of heaven,
   who took me from my father's house and the land of my kin,
   and who confirmed by oath the promise he then made to me,
   'I will give this land to your descendants'—
   he will send his messenger before you,
   and you will obtain a wife for my son there.
If the woman is unwilling to follow you,
   you will be released from this oath.
But never take my son back there!"

A long time later, Isaac went to live in the region of the Negeb.
One day toward evening he went out…in the field,
   and as he looked around, he noticed that camels were approaching.
Rebekah, too, was looking about, and when she saw him,
   she alighted from her camel and asked the servant,
   "Who is the man out there, walking through the fields toward us?"
"That is my master," replied the servant.
Then she covered herself with her veil.

The servant recounted to Isaac all the things he had done.
Then Isaac took Rebekah into his tent;
   he married her, and thus she became his wife.
In his love for her, Isaac found solace
   after the death of his mother Sarah. ✛

   Psalm 106:1b-2, 3-4a, 4b-5
R. (1b) **Give thanks to the Lord, for he is good.**
Give thanks to the Lord, for he is good,
   for his mercy endures forever.
Who can tell the mighty deeds of the Lord,
   or proclaim all his praises? **R.**

Blessed are they who observe what is right,
who do always what is just.
Remember us, O LORD, as you favor your people. **R.**
Visit me with your saving help,
That I may see the prosperity of your chosen ones,
rejoice in the joy of your people,
and glory with your inheritance. **R.**

Matthew 11:28
R. Alleluia, alleluia.
Come to me, all you who labor and are burdened,
and I will give you rest, says the Lord. **R.**

† *Matthew 9:9-13*
Those who are well do not need a physician;
I desire mercy, not sacrifice.

As Jesus passed by,
he saw a man named Matthew sitting at the customs post.
He said to him, "Follow me."
And he got up and followed him.
While he was at table in his house,
many tax collectors and sinners came
and sat with Jesus and his disciples.
The Pharisees saw this and said to his disciples,
"Why does your teacher eat with tax collectors and sinners?"
He heard this and said,
"Those who are well do not need a physician, but the sick do.
Go and learn the meaning of the words,
I desire mercy, not sacrifice.
I did not come to call the righteous but sinners." ✢

SATURDAY, JULY 8
WEEKDAY, *[BVM]*

† *Genesis 27:1-5, 15-29*
Jacob displaced his brother and usurped his blessing (Genesis 27:36).

When Isaac was so old that his eyesight had failed him,
he called his older son Esau and said to him, "Son!"
"Yes father!" he replied.
Isaac then said, "As you can see, I am so old
that I may now die at any time.
Take your gear, therefore—your quiver and bow—
and go out into the country to hunt some game for me.
With your catch prepare an appetizing dish for me, such as I like,
and bring it to me to eat,
so that I may give you my special blessing before I die."

Rebekah had been listening
  while Isaac was speaking to his son Esau.
So, when Esau went out into the country
  to hunt some game for his father,
  Rebekah [then] took the best clothes of her older son Esau
  that she had in the house,
  and gave them to her younger son Jacob to wear;
  and with the skins of the kids she covered up his hands
  and the hairless parts of his neck.
Then she handed her son Jacob the appetizing dish
  and the bread she had prepared.

Bringing them to his father, Jacob said, "Father!"
"Yes?" replied Isaac. "Which of my sons are you?"
Jacob answered his father: "I am Esau, your first-born.
I did as you told me.
Please sit up and eat some of my game,
  so that you may give me your special blessing."
But Isaac asked, "How did you succeed so quickly, son?"
He answered,
  "The LORD, your God, let things turn out well with me."
Isaac then said to Jacob,
  "Come closer, son, that I may feel you,
  to learn whether you really are my son Esau or not."
So Jacob moved up closer to his father.
When Isaac felt him, he said,
  "Although the voice is Jacob's, the hands are Esau's."
(He failed to identify him because his hands were hairy,
  like those of his brother Esau;
  so in the end he gave him his blessing.)
Again he asked Jacob, "Are you really my son Esau?"
"Certainly," Jacob replied.
Then Isaac said, "Serve me your game, son, that I may eat of it
  and then give you my blessing."
Jacob served it to him, and Isaac ate;
  he brought him wine, and he drank.
Finally his father Isaac said to Jacob,
  "Come closer, son, and kiss me."
As Jacob went up and kissed him,
  Isaac smelled the fragrance of his clothes.
With that, he blessed him saying,

  "Ah, the fragrance of my son
    is like the fragrance of a field
    that the LORD has blessed!

"May God give to you
 of the dew of the heavens
And of the fertility of the earth
 abundance of grain and wine.

"Let peoples serve you,
 and nations pay you homage;
Be master of your brothers,
 and may your mother's sons bow down to you.
Cursed be those who curse you,
 and blessed be those who bless you." ✛

Psalm 135:1b-2, 3-4, 5-6
R. (3a) **Praise the Lord for the Lord is good!** *(or* **Alleluia.***)*
Praise the name of the Lord;
 Praise, you servants of the Lord
Who stand in the house of the Lord,
 in the courts of the house of our God. **R.**
Praise the Lord, for the Lord is good;
 sing praise to his name, which we love;
For the Lord has chosen Jacob for himself,
 Israel for his own possession. **R.**
For I know that the Lord is great;
 our Lord is greater than all gods.
All that the Lord wills he does
 in heaven and on earth,
 in the seas and in all the deeps. **R.**

John 10:27
R. Alleluia, alleluia.
My sheep hear my voice, says the Lord;
I know them, and they follow me. **R.**

† *Matthew 9:14-17*
Can the wedding guests mourn as long as the bridegroom is with them?

The disciples of John approached Jesus and said,
 "Why do we and the Pharisees fast much,
 but your disciples do not fast?"
Jesus answered them, "Can the wedding guests mourn
 as long as the bridegroom is with them?
The days will come when the bridegroom is taken away from them,
 and then they will fast.
No one patches an old cloak with a piece of unshrunken cloth,
 for its fullness pulls away from the cloak and the tear gets worse.
People do not put new wine into old wineskins.

Otherwise the skins burst, the wine spills out, and the skins are
ruined.
Rather, they pour new wine into fresh wineskins, and both are
preserved." ✛

SUNDAY, JULY 9
FOURTEENTH SUNDAY IN ORDINARY TIME

†*Zechariah 9:9-10*
See, your king comes to you humbly.

Thus says the LORD:
Rejoice heartily, O daughter Zion,
  shout for joy, O daughter Jerusalem!
See, your king shall come to you;
  a just savior is he,
meek, and riding on an ass,
  on a colt, the foal of an ass.
He shall banish the chariot from Ephraim,
  and the horse from Jerusalem;
the warrior's bow shall be banished,
  and he shall proclaim peace to the nations.
His dominion shall be from sea to sea,
  and from the River to the ends of the earth. ✛

Psalm 145:1-2, 8-9, 10-11, 13-14
R. (see 1) **I will praise your name for ever, my king and my
  God.** (*or* **Alleluia.**)
I will extol you, O my God and King,
  and I will bless your name forever and ever.
Every day will I bless you,
  and I will praise your name forever and ever. **R.**
The LORD is gracious and merciful,
  slow to anger and of great kindness.
The LORD is good to all
  and compassionate toward all his works. **R.**
Let all your works give you thanks, O LORD,
  and let your faithful ones bless you.
Let them discourse of the glory of your kingdom
  and speak of your might. **R.**
The LORD is faithful in all his words
  and holy in all his works.
The LORD lifts up all who are falling
  and raises up all who are bowed down. **R.**

† *Romans 8:9, 11-13*

If by the Spirit you put to death the deeds of the body, you will live.

Brothers and sisters:
You are not in the flesh;
   on the contrary, you are in the spirit,
   if only the Spirit of God dwells in you.
Whoever does not have the Spirit of Christ does not belong to him.
If the Spirit of the one who raised Jesus from the dead dwells in
     you,
   the one who raised Christ from the dead
   will give life to your mortal bodies also,
   through his Spirit that dwells in you.
Consequently, brothers and sisters,
   we are not debtors to the flesh,
   to live according to the flesh.
For if you live according to the flesh, you will die,
   but if by the Spirit you put to death the deeds of the body,
   you will live. ✛

See Matthew 11:25

R. Alleluia, alleluia.
Blessed are you, Father, Lord of heaven and earth;
you have revealed to little ones the mysteries of the kingdom. **R.**

† *Matthew 11:25-30*

I am meek and humble of heart.

At that time Jesus exclaimed:
   "I give praise to you, Father, Lord of heaven and earth,
   for although you have hidden these things
   from the wise and the learned
   you have revealed them to little ones.
Yes, Father, such has been your gracious will.
All things have been handed over to me by my Father.
No one knows the Son except the Father,
   and no one knows the Father except the Son
   and anyone to whom the Son wishes to reveal him.

"Come to me, all you who labor and are burdened,
   and I will give you rest.
Take my yoke upon you and learn from me,
   for I am meek and humble of heart;
   and you will find rest for yourselves.
For my yoke is easy, and my burden light." ✛

MONDAY, JULY 10
WEEKDAY

† *Genesis 28:10-22a*

Jacob had a dream: a stairway rested on the ground and
God's messengers were going up and down on it and the Lord was speaking.

Jacob departed from Beer-sheba and proceeded toward Haran.
When he came upon a certain shrine, as the sun had already set,
   he stopped there for the night.
Taking one of the stones at the shrine, he put it under his head
   and lay down to sleep at that spot.
Then he had a dream: a stairway rested on the ground,
   with its top reaching to the heavens;
   and God's messengers were going up and down on it.
And there was the LORD standing beside him and saying:
   "I, the LORD, am the God of your forefather Abraham
   and the God of Isaac;
   the land on which you are lying
   I will give to you and your descendants.
These shall be as plentiful as the dust of the earth,
   and through them you shall spread out east and west, north and
      south.
In you and your descendants
   all the nations of the earth shall find blessing.
Know that I am with you;
   I will protect you wherever you go,
   and bring you back to this land.
I will never leave you until I have done what I promised you."

When Jacob awoke from his sleep, he exclaimed,
   "Truly, the LORD is in this spot, although I did not know it!"
In solemn wonder he cried out: "How awesome is this shrine!
This is nothing else but an abode of God,
   and that is the gateway to heaven!"
Early the next morning Jacob took the stone
   that he had put under his head,
   set it up as a memorial stone, and poured oil on top of it.
He called the site Bethel,
   whereas the former name of the town had been Luz.

Jacob then made this vow: "If God remains with me,
   to protect me on this journey I am making
   and to give me enough bread to eat and clothing to wear,
   and I come back safe to my father's house, the LORD shall be my
      God.

This stone that I have set up as a memorial stone shall be God's
    abode." ✢

Psalm 91:1-2, 3-4, 14-15ab
R. (see 2b) **In you, my God, I place my trust.**
You who dwell in the shelter of the Most High,
  who abide in the shadow of the Almighty,
Say to the LORD, "My refuge and my fortress,
  my God, in whom I trust." **R.**
For he will rescue you from the snare of the fowler,
  from the destroying pestilence.
With his pinions he will cover you,
  and under his wings you shall take refuge. **R.**
Because he clings to me, I will deliver him;
  I will set him on high because he acknowledges my name.
He shall call upon me, and I will answer him;
  I will be with him in distress. **R.**

See 2 Timothy 1:10
R. Alleluia, alleluia.
Our Savior Jesus Christ has destroyed death
and brought life to light through the Gospel. **R.**

✝ Matthew 9:18-26
My daughter has just died, but come and she will live.

While Jesus was speaking, an official came forward,
  knelt down before him, and said,
  "My daughter has just died.
But come, lay your hand on her, and she will live."
Jesus rose and followed him, and so did his disciples.
A woman suffering hemorrhages for twelve years came up behind
    him
  and touched the tassel on his cloak.
She said to herself, "If only I can touch his cloak, I shall be cured."
Jesus turned around and saw her, and said,
  "Courage, daughter! Your faith has saved you."
And from that hour the woman was cured.

When Jesus arrived at the official's house
  and saw the flute players and the crowd who were making a
    commotion,
  he said, "Go away! The girl is not dead but sleeping."
And they ridiculed him.
When the crowd was put out, he came and took her by the hand,
  and the little girl arose.
And news of this spread throughout all that land. ✢

TUESDAY, JULY 11
St. Benedict

✝ Genesis 32:23-33
*You shall be spoken of as Israel, because you have contended
with God and have prevailed.*

In the course of the night, Jacob arose, took his two wives,
    with the two maidservants and his eleven children,
    and crossed the ford of the Jabbok.
After he had taken them across the stream
    and had brought over all his possessions,
    Jacob was left there alone.
Then some man wrestled with him until the break of dawn.
When the man saw that he could not prevail over him,
    he struck Jacob's hip at its socket,
    so that the hip socket was wrenched as they wrestled.
The man then said, "Let me go, for it is daybreak."
But Jacob said, "I will not let you go until you bless me."
The man asked, "What is your name?"
He answered, "Jacob."
Then the man said,
    "You shall no longer be spoken of as Jacob, but as Israel,
    because you have contended with divine and human beings
    and have prevailed."
Jacob then asked him, "Do tell me your name, please."
He answered, "Why should you want to know my name?"
With that, he bade him farewell.
Jacob named the place Peniel,
    "Because I have seen God face to face," he said,
    "yet my life has been spared."

At sunrise, as he left Penuel,
    Jacob limped along because of his hip.
That is why, to this day, the children of Israel do not eat
    the sciatic muscle that is on the hip socket,
    inasmuch as Jacob's hip socket was struck at the sciatic muscle. ✝

Psalm 17:1bcd, 2-3, 6-7ab, 8b and 15
R. (15a) **In justice, I shall behold your face, O Lord.**
Hear, O Lord, a just suit;
    attend to my outcry;
    hearken to my prayer from lips without deceit. **R.**
From you let my judgment come;
    your eyes behold what is right.
Though you test my heart, searching it in the night,
    though you try me with fire, you shall find no malice in me. **R.**

I call upon you, for you will answer me, O God;
  incline your ear to me; hear my word.
Show your wondrous mercies,
  O savior of those who flee from their foes. **R.**
Hide me in the shadow of your wings.
I in justice shall behold your face;
  on waking, I shall be content in your presence. **R.**

John 10:14
R. Alleluia, alleluia.
I am the good shepherd, says the Lord;
I know my sheep, and mine know me. **R.**

† *Matthew 9:32-38*
The harvest is abundant but the laborers are few.

A demoniac who could not speak was brought to Jesus,
  and when the demon was driven out the mute man spoke.
The crowds were amazed and said,
  "Nothing like this has ever been seen in Israel."
But the Pharisees said,
  "He drives out demons by the prince of demons."

Jesus went around to all the towns and villages,
  teaching in their synagogues,
  proclaiming the Gospel of the Kingdom,
  and curing every disease and illness.
At the sight of the crowds, his heart was moved with pity for them
  because they were troubled and abandoned,
  like sheep without a shepherd.
Then he said to his disciples,
  "The harvest is abundant but the laborers are few;
  so ask the master of the harvest
  to send out laborers for his harvest." ✝

WEDNESDAY, JULY 12
WEEKDAY

† *Genesis 41:55-57; 42:5-7a, 17-24a*
Alas, we are being punished because of our brother.

When hunger came to be felt throughout the land of Egypt
  and the people cried to Pharaoh for bread,
  Pharaoh directed all the Egyptians to go to Joseph
  and do whatever he told them.
When the famine had spread throughout the land,
  Joseph opened all the cities that had grain
  and rationed it to the Egyptians,

since the famine had gripped the land of Egypt.
In fact, all the world came to Joseph to obtain rations of grain,
    for famine had gripped the whole world.

The sons of Israel were among those
    who came to procure rations.

It was Joseph, as governor of the country,
    who dispensed the rations to all the people.
When Joseph's brothers came and knelt down before him
    with their faces to the ground,
    he recognized them as soon as he saw them.
But Joseph concealed his own identity from them
    and spoke sternly to them.

With that, he locked them up in the guardhouse for three days.

On the third day Joseph said to his brothers:
    "Do this, and you shall live; for I am a God-fearing man.
If you have been honest,
    only one of your brothers need be confined in this prison,
    while the rest of you may go
    and take home provisions for your starving families.
But you must come back to me with your youngest brother.
Your words will thus be verified, and you will not die."
To this they agreed.
To one another, however, they said:
    "Alas, we are being punished because of our brother.
We saw the anguish of his heart when he pleaded with us,
    yet we paid no heed;
    that is why this anguish has now come upon us."
Reuben broke in,
    "Did I not tell you not to do wrong to the boy?
But you would not listen!
Now comes the reckoning for his blood."
The brothers did not know, of course,
    that Joseph understood what they said,
    since he spoke with them through an interpreter.
But turning away from them, he wept. ✚

Psalm 33:2-3, 10-11, 18-19

**R. (22) Lord, let your mercy be on us, as we place our trust in
    you.**

Give thanks to the Lord on the harp;
    with the ten-stringed lyre chant his praises.
Sing to him a new song;

pluck the strings skillfully, with shouts of gladness. **R.**
The LORD brings to nought the plans of nations;
  he foils the designs of peoples.
But the plan of the LORD stands forever;
  the design of his heart, through all generations. **R.**
But see, the eyes of the LORD are upon those who fear him,
  upon those who hope for his kindness,
To deliver them from death
  and preserve them in spite of famine. **R.**

  Mark 1:15
R. Alleluia, alleluia.
The Kingdom of God is at hand:
repent and believe in the Gospel. **R.**

† *Matthew 10:1-7*
Go rather to the lost sheep of the house of Israel.

Jesus summoned his Twelve disciples
  and gave them authority over unclean spirits to drive them out
  and to cure every disease and every illness.
The names of the Twelve Apostles are these:
  first, Simon called Peter, and his brother Andrew;
  James, the son of Zebedee, and his brother John;
  Philip and Bartholomew,
  Thomas and Matthew the tax collector;
  James, the son of Alphaeus, and Thaddeus;
  Simon the Cananean, and Judas Iscariot
  who betrayed Jesus.

Jesus sent out these Twelve after instructing them thus,
  "Do not go into pagan territory or enter a Samaritan town.
Go rather to the lost sheep of the house of Israel.
As you go, make this proclamation: 'The Kingdom of heaven is at
    hand.'" ✝

THURSDAY, JULY 13
WEEKDAY, ST. HENRY

† *Genesis 44:18-21, 23b-29; 45:1-5*
It was really for the sake of saving lives that God sent me here ahead of you.

Judah approached Joseph and said: "I beg you, my lord,
  let your servant speak earnestly to my lord,
  and do not become angry with your servant,
  for you are the equal of Pharaoh.
My lord asked your servants, 'Have you a father, or another brother?'
So we said to my lord, 'We have an aged father,

and a young brother, the child of his old age.
This one's full brother is dead,
  and since he is the only one by that mother who is left,
  his father dotes on him.'
Then you told your servants,
  'Bring him down to me that my eyes may look on him.
Unless your youngest brother comes back with you,
  you shall not come into my presence again.'
When we returned to your servant our father,
  we reported to him the words of my lord.

"Later, our father told us to come back and buy some food for the
    family.
So we reminded him, 'We cannot go down there;
  only if our youngest brother is with us can we go,
  for we may not see the man if our youngest brother is not with us.'
Then your servant our father said to us,
  'As you know, my wife bore me two sons.
One of them, however, disappeared, and I had to conclude
  that he must have been torn to pieces by wild beasts;
  I have not seen him since.
If you now take this one away from me, too,
  and some disaster befalls him,
  you will send my white head down to the nether world in grief.'"

Joseph could no longer control himself
  in the presence of all his attendants,
  so he cried out, "Have everyone withdraw from me!"
Thus no one else was about when he made himself known to his
    brothers.
But his sobs were so loud that the Egyptians heard him,
  and so the news reached Pharaoh's palace.
"I am Joseph," he said to his brothers.
"Is my father still in good health?"
But his brothers could give him no answer,
  so dumbfounded were they at him.

"Come closer to me," he told his brothers.
When they had done so, he said:
  "I am your brother Joseph, whom you once sold into Egypt.
But now do not be distressed,
  and do not reproach yourselves for having sold me here.
It was really for the sake of saving lives
  that God sent me here ahead of you." ✦

Psalm 105:16-17, 18-19, 20-21

R. (5a) **Remember the marvels the Lord has done.**
*(or **Alleluia.**)*

When the LORD called down a famine on the land
  and ruined the crop that sustained them,
He sent a man before them,
  Joseph, sold as a slave. **R.**
They had weighed him down with fetters,
  and he was bound with chains,
Till his prediction came to pass
  and the word of the LORD proved him true. **R.**
The king sent and released him,
  the ruler of the peoples set him free.
He made him lord of his house
  and ruler of all his possessions. **R.**

Mark 1:15

R. Alleluia, alleluia.
The Kingdom of God is at hand:
repent and believe in the Gospel. **R.**

† *Matthew 10:7-15*

Without cost you have received; without cost you are to give.

Jesus said to his Apostles:
"As you go, make this proclamation:
  'The Kingdom of heaven is at hand.'
Cure the sick, raise the dead,
  cleanse the lepers, drive out demons.
Without cost you have received; without cost you are to give.
Do not take gold or silver or copper for your belts;
  no sack for the journey, or a second tunic,
  or sandals, or walking stick.
The laborer deserves his keep.
Whatever town or village you enter, look for a worthy person in it,
  and stay there until you leave.
As you enter a house, wish it peace.
If the house is worthy,
  let your peace come upon it;
  if not, let your peace return to you.
Whoever will not receive you or listen to your words—
  go outside that house or town and shake the dust from your feet.
Amen, I say to you, it will be more tolerable
  for the land of Sodom and Gomorrah on the day of judgment
  than for that town." ✛

FRIDAY, JULY 14
St. Kateri Tekakwitha

† *Genesis 46:1-7, 28-30*
At last I can die, now that I have seen for myself that Joseph is still alive.

Israel set out with all that was his.
When he arrived at Beer-sheba,
　he offered sacrifices to the God of his father Isaac.
There God, speaking to Israel in a vision by night, called,
　"Jacob! Jacob!"
He answered, "Here I am."
Then he said: "I am God, the God of your father.
Do not be afraid to go down to Egypt,
　for there I will make you a great nation.
Not only will I go down to Egypt with you;
　I will also bring you back here, after Joseph has closed your eyes."

So Jacob departed from Beer-sheba,
　and the sons of Israel
　put their father and their wives and children
　on the wagons that Pharaoh had sent for his transport.
They took with them their livestock
　and the possessions they had acquired in the land of Canaan.
Thus Jacob and all his descendants migrated to Egypt.
His sons and his grandsons, his daughters and his granddaughters—
　all his descendants—he took with him to Egypt.

Israel had sent Judah ahead to Joseph,
　so that he might meet him in Goshen.
On his arrival in the region of Goshen,
　Joseph hitched the horses to his chariot
　and rode to meet his father Israel in Goshen.
As soon as Joseph saw him, he flung himself on his neck
　and wept a long time in his arms.
And Israel said to Joseph, "At last I can die,
　now that I have seen for myself that Joseph is still alive." †

Psalm 37:3-4, 18-19, 27-28, 39-40
R. (39a) The salvation of the just comes from the Lord.
Trust in the LORD and do good,
　that you may dwell in the land and be fed in security.
Take delight in the LORD,
　and he will grant you your heart's requests. **R.**
The LORD watches over the lives of the wholehearted;
　their inheritance lasts forever.
They are not put to shame in an evil time;

in days of famine they have plenty. **R.**
Turn from evil and do good,
   that you may abide forever;
For the LORD loves what is right,
   and forsakes not his faithful ones. **R.**
The salvation of the just is from the LORD;
   he is their refuge in time of distress.
And the LORD helps them and delivers them;
    he delivers them from the wicked and saves them,
    because they take refuge in him. **R.**

    John 16:13a; 14:26d
R. Alleluia, alleluia.
When the Spirit of truth comes,
he will guide you to all truth
and remind you of all I told you. **R.**

† *Matthew 10:16-23*
*For it will not be you who speak, but the Spirit
of your Father speaking through you.*

Jesus said to his Apostles:
"Behold, I am sending you like sheep in the midst of wolves;
   so be shrewd as serpents and simple as doves.
But beware of men,
   for they will hand you over to courts
   and scourge you in their synagogues,
   and you will be led before governors and kings for my sake
   as a witness before them and the pagans.
When they hand you over,
   do not worry about how you are to speak
   or what you are to say.
You will be given at that moment what you are to say.
For it will not be you who speak
   but the Spirit of your Father speaking through you.
Brother will hand over brother to death,
   and the father his child;
   children will rise up against parents and have them put to death.
You will be hated by all because of my name,
   but whoever endures to the end will be saved.
When they persecute you in one town, flee to another.
Amen, I say to you, you will not finish the towns of Israel
   before the Son of Man comes." ✝

SATURDAY, JULY 15
St. Bonaventure

† *Genesis 49:29-32; 50:15-26a*
God will surely take care of you and lead you out of this land.

Jacob gave his sons this charge:
"Since I am about to be taken to my people,
   bury me with my fathers in the cave that lies
   in the field of Ephron the Hittite,
   the cave in the field of Machpelah,
   facing on Mamre, in the land of Canaan,
   the field that Abraham bought from Ephron the Hittite
   for a burial ground.
There Abraham and his wife Sarah are buried,
   and so are Isaac and his wife Rebekah,
   and there, too, I buried Leah—
   the field and the cave in it
   that had been purchased from the Hittites."

Now that their father was dead,
   Joseph's brothers became fearful and thought,
   "Suppose Joseph has been nursing a grudge against us
   and now plans to pay us back in full for all the wrong we did him!"
So they approached Joseph and said:
   "Before your father died, he gave us these instructions:
   'You shall say to Joseph, Jacob begs you
   to forgive the criminal wrongdoing of your brothers,
   who treated you so cruelly.'
Please, therefore, forgive the crime that we,
   the servants of your father's God, committed."
When they spoke these words to him, Joseph broke into tears.
Then his brothers proceeded to fling themselves down before him
   and said, "Let us be your slaves!"
But Joseph replied to them:
   "Have no fear. Can I take the place of God?
Even though you meant harm to me, God meant it for good,
   to achieve his present end, the survival of many people.
Therefore have no fear.
I will provide for you and for your children."
By thus speaking kindly to them, he reassured them.

Joseph remained in Egypt, together with his father's family.
He lived a hundred and ten years.
He saw Ephraim's children to the third generation,

and the children of Manasseh's son Machir
were also born on Joseph's knees.

Joseph said to his brothers: "I am about to die.
God will surely take care of you and lead you out of this land to the
  land
  that he promised on oath to Abraham, Isaac and Jacob."
Then, putting the sons of Israel under oath, he continued,
  "When God thus takes care of you,
  you must bring my bones up with you from this place."
Joseph died at the age of a hundred and ten. ✛

Psalm 105:1-2, 3-4, 6-7

R. (see Psalm 69:33) **Be glad you lowly ones; may your hearts**
  be glad!
Give thanks to the LORD, invoke his name;
  make known among the nations his deeds.
Sing to him, sing his praise,
  proclaim all his wondrous deeds. **R.**
Glory in his holy name;
  rejoice, O hearts that seek the LORD!
Look to the LORD in his strength;
  seek to serve him constantly. **R.**
You descendants of Abraham, his servants,
  sons of Jacob, his chosen ones!
He, the LORD, is our God;
  throughout the earth his judgments prevail. **R.**

1 Peter 4:14

R. Alleluia, alleluia.
If you are insulted for the name of Christ, blessed are you,
for the Spirit of God rests upon you. **R.**

† *Matthew 10:24-33*
Do not be afraid of those who kill the body.

Jesus said to his Apostles:
"No disciple is above his teacher,
  no slave above his master.
It is enough for the disciple that he become like his teacher,
  for the slave that he become like his master.
If they have called the master of the house Beelzebul,
  how much more those of his household!

"Therefore do not be afraid of them.
Nothing is concealed that will not be revealed,
  nor secret that will not be known.

What I say to you in the darkness, speak in the light;
  what you hear whispered, proclaim on the housetops.
And do not be afraid of those who kill the body but cannot kill the
    soul;
  rather, be afraid of the one who can destroy
  both soul and body in Gehenna.
Are not two sparrows sold for a small coin?
Yet not one of them falls to the ground without your Father's
    knowledge.
Even all the hairs of your head are counted.
So do not be afraid; you are worth more than many sparrows.
Everyone who acknowledges me before others
  I will acknowledge before my heavenly Father.
But whoever denies me before others,
  I will deny before my heavenly Father." ✛

SUNDAY, JULY 16
FIFTEENTH SUNDAY IN ORDINARY TIME

† *Isaiah 55:10-11*
The rain makes the earth fruitful.

Thus says the LORD:
Just as from the heavens
  the rain and snow come down
and do not return there
  till they have watered the earth,
  making it fertile and fruitful,
giving seed to the one who sows
  and bread to the one who eats,
so shall my word be
  that goes forth from my mouth;
my word shall not return to me void,
  but shall do my will,
  achieving the end for which I sent it. ✛

Psalm 65:10, 11, 12-13, 14
R. (Luke 8:8) **The seed that falls on good ground will yield a
    fruitful harvest.**
You have visited the land and watered it;
  greatly have you enriched it.
God's watercourses are filled;
  you have prepared the grain. **R.**
Thus have you prepared the land: drenching its furrows,
  breaking up its clods,
softening it with showers,

blessing its yield. **R.**
You have crowned the year with your bounty,
   and your paths overflow with a rich harvest;
the untilled meadows overflow with it,
   and rejoicing clothes the hills. **R.**
The fields are garmented with flocks
   and the valleys blanketed with grain.
   They shout and sing for joy. **R.**

† *Romans 8:18-23*
Creation awaits the revelation of the children of God.

Brothers and sisters:
I consider that the sufferings of this present time are as nothing
   compared with the glory to be revealed for us.
For creation awaits with eager expectation
   the revelation of the children of God;
   for creation was made subject to futility,
   not of its own accord but because of the one who subjected it,
   in hope that creation itself
   would be set free from slavery to corruption
   and share in the glorious freedom of the children of God.
We know that all creation is groaning in labor pains even until now;
   and not only that, but we ourselves,
   who have the firstfruits of the Spirit,
   we also groan within ourselves
   as we wait for adoption, the redemption of our bodies. ✢

R. Alleluia, alleluia.
The seed is the word of God, Christ is the sower.
All who come to him will have life forever. **R.**

† *Matthew 13:1-23* (or *Matthew 13:1-9*)
A sower went out to sow.

On that day, Jesus went out of the house and sat down by the sea.
Such large crowds gathered around him
   that he got into a boat and sat down,
   and the whole crowd stood along the shore.
And he spoke to them at length in parables, saying:
   "A sower went out to sow.
And as he sowed, some seed fell on the path,
   and birds came and ate it up.
Some fell on rocky ground, where it had little soil.
It sprang up at once because the soil was not deep,
   and when the sun rose it was scorched,
   and it withered for lack of roots.

Some seed fell among thorns, and the thorns grew up and choked it.
But some seed fell on rich soil, and produced fruit,
    a hundred or sixty or thirtyfold.
Whoever has ears ought to hear.”

The disciples approached him and said,
“Why do you speak to them in parables?”
He said to them in reply,
    “Because knowledge of the mysteries of the kingdom of heaven
    has been granted to you, but to them it has not been granted.
To anyone who has, more will be given and he will grow rich;
    from anyone who has not, even what he has will be taken away.
This is why I speak to them in parables, because
    they look but do not see and hear but do not listen or understand.
Isaiah’s prophecy is fulfilled in them, which says:
    You shall indeed hear but not understand,
        you shall indeed look but never see.
    Gross is the heart of this people,
        they will hardly hear with their ears,
        they have closed their eyes,
        lest they see with their eyes
        and hear with their ears
    and understand with their hearts and be converted,
        and I heal them.

“But blessed are your eyes, because they see,
    and your ears, because they hear.
Amen, I say to you, many prophets and righteous people
    longed to see what you see but did not see it,
    and to hear what you hear but did not hear it.

“Hear then the parable of the sower.
The seed sown on the path is the one
    who hears the word of the kingdom without understanding it,
    and the evil one comes and steals away
    what was sown in his heart.
The seed sown on rocky ground
    is the one who hears the word and receives it at once with joy.
But he has no root and lasts only for a time.
When some tribulation or persecution comes because of the word,
    he immediately falls away.
The seed sown among thorns is the one who hears the word,
    but then worldly anxiety and the lure of riches choke the word
    and it bears no fruit.
But the seed sown on rich soil

is the one who hears the word and understands it,
who indeed bears fruit and yields a hundred or sixty or thirtyfold." ✛

MONDAY, JULY 17
WEEKDAY

† *Exodus 1:8-14, 22*
Come, let us deal shrewdly with them to stop their increase.

A new king, who knew nothing of Joseph, came to power in Egypt.
He said to his subjects, "Look how numerous and powerful
the people of the children of Israel are growing, more so than we
ourselves!
Come, let us deal shrewdly with them to stop their increase;
otherwise, in time of war they too may join our enemies
to fight against us, and so leave our country."

Accordingly, taskmasters were set over the children of Israel
to oppress them with forced labor.
Thus they had to build for Pharaoh
the supply cities of Pithom and Raamses.
Yet the more they were oppressed,
the more they multiplied and spread.
The Egyptians, then, dreaded the children of Israel
and reduced them to cruel slavery,
making life bitter for them with hard work in mortar and brick
and all kinds of field work—the whole cruel fate of slaves.

Pharaoh then commanded all his subjects,
"Throw into the river every boy that is born to the Hebrews,
but you may let all the girls live." ✛

Psalm 124:1b-3, 4-6, 7-8
R. (8a) **Our help is in the name of the Lord.**
Had not the LORD been with us—
let Israel say, had not the LORD been with us—
When men rose up against us,
then would they have swallowed us alive,
When their fury was inflamed against us. **R.**
Then would the waters have overwhelmed us;
The torrent would have swept over us;
over us then would have swept
the raging waters.
Blessed be the LORD, who did not leave us
a prey to their teeth. **R.**
We were rescued like a bird
from the fowlers' snare;

Broken was the snare,
   and we were freed.
Our help is in the name of the LORD,
   who made heaven and earth. **R.**

   Matthew 5:10
R. Alleluia, alleluia.
Blessed are they who are persecuted for the sake of righteousness,
for theirs is the Kingdom of heaven. **R.**

✝ Matthew 10:34—11:1
I have come to bring not peace, but the sword.

Jesus said to his Apostles:
"Do not think that I have come to bring peace upon the earth.
I have come to bring not peace but the sword.
For I have come to set
   a man against his father,
      a daughter against her mother,
   and a daughter-in-law against her mother-in-law;
      and one's enemies will be those of his household.

"Whoever loves father or mother more than me is not worthy of me,
   and whoever loves son or daughter more than me is not worthy of
      me;
   and whoever does not take up his cross
   and follow after me is not worthy of me.
Whoever finds his life will lose it,
   and whoever loses his life for my sake will find it.

"Whoever receives you receives me,
   and whoever receives me receives the one who sent me.
Whoever receives a prophet because he is a prophet
   will receive a prophet's reward,
   and whoever receives a righteous man
   because he is righteous
   will receive a righteous man's reward.
And whoever gives only a cup of cold water
   to one of these little ones to drink
   because he is a disciple—
   amen, I say to you, he will surely not lose his reward."

When Jesus finished giving these commands to his Twelve disciples,
   he went away from that place to teach and to preach in their
      towns. ✝

TUESDAY, JULY 18
WEEKDAY, ST. CAMILLUS DE LELLIS

† *Exodus 2:1-15a*
She called him Moses for she said, "I drew him out of the water."
After Moses had grown up, he visited his people.

A certain man of the house of Levi married a Levite woman,
  who conceived and bore a son.
Seeing that he was a goodly child, she hid him for three months.
When she could hide him no longer, she took a papyrus basket,
  daubed it with bitumen and pitch,
  and putting the child in it,
  placed it among the reeds on the river bank.
His sister stationed herself at a distance
  to find out what would happen to him.

Pharaoh's daughter came down to the river to bathe,
  while her maids walked along the river bank.
Noticing the basket among the reeds, she sent her handmaid to
    fetch it.
On opening it, she looked, and lo, there was a baby boy, crying!
She was moved with pity for him and said,
  "It is one of the Hebrews' children."
Then his sister asked Pharaoh's daughter,
  "Shall I go and call one of the Hebrew women
  to nurse the child for you?"
"Yes, do so," she answered.
So the maiden went and called the child's own mother.
Pharaoh's daughter said to her,
  "Take this child and nurse it for me, and I will repay you."
The woman therefore took the child and nursed it.
When the child grew, she brought him to Pharaoh's daughter,
  who adopted him as her son and called him Moses;
  for she said, "I drew him out of the water."

On one occasion, after Moses had grown up,
  when he visited his kinsmen and witnessed their forced labor,
  he saw an Egyptian striking a Hebrew, one of his own kinsmen.
Looking about and seeing no one,
  he slew the Egyptian and hid him in the sand.
The next day he went out again, and now two Hebrews were fighting!
So he asked the culprit,
  "Why are you striking your fellow Hebrew?"
But the culprit replied,
  "Who has appointed you ruler and judge over us?

Are you thinking of killing me as you killed the Egyptian?"
Then Moses became afraid and thought,
  "The affair must certainly be known."

Pharaoh, too, heard of the affair and sought to put Moses to death.
But Moses fled from him and stayed in the land of Midian. ✢

  Psalm 69:3, 14, 30-31, 33-34
R. (see 33) **Turn to the Lord in your need, and you will live.**
I am sunk in the abysmal swamp
  where there is no foothold;
I have reached the watery depths;
  the flood overwhelms me. **R.**
But I pray to you, O LORD,
  for the time of your favor, O God!
In your great kindness answer me
  with your constant help. **R.**
But I am afflicted and in pain;
  let your saving help, O God, protect me;
I will praise the name of God in song,
  and I will glorify him with thanksgiving. **R.**
"See, you lowly ones, and be glad;
  you who seek God, may your hearts revive!
For the LORD hears the poor,
  and his own who are in bonds he spurns not." **R.**

  Psalm 95:8
R. Alleluia, alleluia.
If today you hear his voice,
harden not your hearts. **R.**

† *Matthew 11:20-24*
*It will be more tolerable for Tyre and Sidon and
for the land of Sodom on the day of judgment than for you.*

Jesus began to reproach the towns
  where most of his mighty deeds had been done,
  since they had not repented.
"Woe to you, Chorazin! Woe to you, Bethsaida!
For if the mighty deeds done in your midst
  had been done in Tyre and Sidon,
  they would long ago have repented in sackcloth and ashes.
But I tell you, it will be more tolerable
  for Tyre and Sidon on the day of judgment than for you.
And as for you, Capernaum:

  *Will you be exalted to heaven?
    You will go down to the netherworld.*

For if the mighty deeds done in your midst had been done in Sodom,
it would have remained until this day.
But I tell you, it will be more tolerable
for the land of Sodom on the day of judgment than for you." ✝

WEDNESDAY, JULY 19
WEEKDAY

✝ *Exodus 3:1-6, 9-12*
The angel of the Lord appeared to Moses in the burning bush.

Moses was tending the flock of his father-in-law Jethro, the priest
of Midian.
Leading the flock across the desert, he came to Horeb,
the mountain of God.
There an angel of the LORD appeared to him in fire
flaming out of a bush.
As he looked on, he was surprised to see that the bush,
though on fire, was not consumed.
So Moses decided,
"I must go over to look at this remarkable sight,
and see why the bush is not burned."

When the LORD saw him coming over to look at it more closely,
God called out to him from the bush, "Moses! Moses!"
He answered, "Here I am."
God said, "Come no nearer!
Remove the sandals from your feet,
for the place where you stand is holy ground.
I am the God of your father," he continued,
"the God of Abraham, the God of Isaac, the God of Jacob.
The cry of the children of Israel has reached me,
and I have truly noted that the Egyptians are oppressing them.
Come, now! I will send you to Pharaoh to lead my people,
the children of Israel, out of Egypt."

But Moses said to God,
"Who am I that I should go to Pharaoh
and lead the children of Israel out of Egypt?"
He answered, "I will be with you;
and this shall be your proof that it is I who have sent you:
when you bring my people out of Egypt,
you will worship God on this very mountain." ✝

Psalm 103:1b-2, 3-4, 6-7

R. (8a) **The Lord is kind and merciful.**

Bless the LORD, O my soul;
and all my being, bless his holy name.
Bless the LORD, O my soul,
and forget not all his benefits. **R.**

He pardons all your iniquities,
he heals all your ills.
He redeems your life from destruction,
he crowns you with kindness and compassion. **R.**

The LORD secures justice
and the rights of all the oppressed.
He has made known his ways to Moses,
and his deeds to the children of Israel. **R.**

Matthew 11:25

R. Alleluia, alleluia.

Blessed are you, Father, Lord of heaven and earth,
you have revealed to little ones the mysteries of the Kingdom. **R.**

† *Matthew 11:25-27*
Although you have hidden these things from the wise and the learned
you have revealed them to the childlike.

At that time Jesus exclaimed:
"I give praise to you, Father, Lord of heaven and earth,
for although you have hidden these things
from the wise and the learned
you have revealed them to the childlike.
Yes, Father, such has been your gracious will.
All things have been handed over to me by my Father.
No one knows the Son except the Father,
and no one knows the Father except the Son
and anyone to whom the Son wishes to reveal him." ✛

THURSDAY, JULY 20
WEEKDAY, ST. APOLLINARIS

† *Exodus 3:13-20*
I AM WHO AM. I AM has sent me to you.

Moses, hearing the voice of the LORD from the burning bush, said
to him,
"When I go to the children of Israel and say to them,
'The God of your fathers has sent me to you,'
if they ask me, 'What is his name?' what am I to tell them?"
God replied, "I am who am."
Then he added, "This is what you shall tell the children of Israel:

I AM sent me to you."

God spoke further to Moses, "Thus shall you say to the children of
   Israel:
The LORD, the God of your fathers,
the God of Abraham, the God of Isaac, the God of Jacob,
has sent me to you.

"This is my name forever;
   this my title for all generations.

"Go and assemble the elders of Israel, and tell them:
The LORD, the God of your fathers,
the God of Abraham, Isaac, and Jacob,
has appeared to me and said:
I am concerned about you
and about the way you are being treated in Egypt;
so I have decided to lead you up out of the misery of Egypt
into the land of the Canaanites, Hittites, Amorites,
Perizzites, Hivites, and Jebusites,
a land flowing with milk and honey.

"Thus they will heed your message.
Then you and the elders of Israel
   shall go to the king of Egypt and say to him:
The LORD, the God of the Hebrews, has sent us word.
Permit us, then, to go a three-days' journey in the desert,
   that we may offer sacrifice to the LORD, our God.

"Yet I know that the king of Egypt will not allow you to go
   unless he is forced.
I will stretch out my hand, therefore,
   and smite Egypt by doing all kinds of wondrous deeds there.
After that he will send you away." ✙

   Psalm 105:1 and 5, 8-9, 24-25, 26-27
R. (8a) **The Lord remembers his covenant for ever.**
   (or **Alleluia.***)*
Give thanks to the LORD, invoke his name;
   make known among the nations his deeds.
Recall the wondrous deeds that he has wrought,
   his portents, and the judgments he has uttered. **R.**
He remembers forever his covenant
   which he made binding for a thousand generations—
Which he entered into with Abraham
   and by his oath to Isaac. **R.**
He greatly increased his people

and made them stronger than their foes,
Whose hearts he changed, so that they hated his people,
   and dealt deceitfully with his servants. **R.**
He sent Moses his servant;
   Aaron, whom he had chosen.
They wrought his signs among them,
   and wonders in the land of Ham. **R.**

Matthew 11:28
R. Alleluia, alleluia.
Come to me, all you who labor and are burdened,
and I will give you rest, says the Lord. **R.**

† *Matthew 11:28-30*
I am meek and humble of heart.

Jesus said:
"Come to me, all you who labor and are burdened,
   and I will give you rest.
Take my yoke upon you and learn from me,
   for I am meek and humble of heart;
   and you will find rest for yourselves.
For my yoke is easy, and my burden light." ✛

FRIDAY, JULY 21
WEEKDAY, ST. LAWRENCE OF BRINDISI

† *Exodus 11:10—12:14*
It shall be slaughtered during the evening twilight.
Seeing the blood, I will pass over you.

Although Moses and Aaron performed various wonders
   in Pharaoh's presence,
   the LORD made Pharaoh obstinate,
   and he would not let the children of Israel leave his land.

The LORD said to Moses and Aaron in the land of Egypt,
   "This month shall stand at the head of your calendar;
   you shall reckon it the first month of the year.
Tell the whole community of Israel: On the tenth of this month
   every one of your families must procure for itself a lamb,
   one apiece for each household.
If a family is too small for a whole lamb,
   it shall join the nearest household in procuring one
   and shall share in the lamb
   in proportion to the number of persons who partake of it.
The lamb must be a year-old male and without blemish.
You may take it from either the sheep or the goats.

You shall keep it until the fourteenth day of this month, and then,
with the whole assembly of Israel present,
it shall be slaughtered during the evening twilight.
They shall take some of its blood
and apply it to the two doorposts and the lintel
of every house in which they partake of the lamb.
That same night they shall eat its roasted flesh
with unleavened bread and bitter herbs.
It shall not be eaten raw or boiled, but roasted whole,
with its head and shanks and inner organs.
None of it must be kept beyond the next morning;
whatever is left over in the morning shall be burned up.

"This is how you are to eat it:
with your loins girt, sandals on your feet and your staff in hand,
you shall eat like those who are in flight.
It is the Passover of the LORD.
For on this same night I will go through Egypt,
striking down every first-born of the land, both man and beast,
and executing judgment on all the gods of Egypt—I, the LORD!
But the blood will mark the houses where you are.
Seeing the blood, I will pass over you;
thus, when I strike the land of Egypt,
no destructive blow will come upon you.

"This day shall be a memorial feast for you,
which all your generations shall celebrate
with pilgrimage to the LORD, as a perpetual institution." ✝

Psalm 116:12-13, 15 and 16bc, 17-18

**R. (13) I will take the cup of salvation, and call on the name
of the Lord.**

How shall I make a return to the LORD
for all the good he has done for me?
The cup of salvation I will take up,
and I will call upon the name of the LORD. **R.**
Precious in the eyes of the LORD
is the death of his faithful ones.
I am your servant, the son of your handmaid;
you have loosed my bonds. **R.**
To you will I offer sacrifice of thanksgiving,
and I will call upon the name of the LORD.
My vows to the LORD I will pay
in the presence of all his people. **R.**

John 10:27
R. Alleluia, alleluia.
My sheep hear my voice, says the Lord,
I know them, and they follow me. **R.**

† *Matthew 12:1-8*
The Son of Man is Lord of the sabbath.

J esus was going through a field of grain on the sabbath.
His disciples were hungry
   and began to pick the heads of grain and eat them.
When the Pharisees saw this, they said to him,
   "See, your disciples are doing what is unlawful to do on the sabbath."
He said to them, "Have you not read what David did
   when he and his companions were hungry,
   how he went into the house of God and ate the bread of offering,
   which neither he nor his companions
   but only the priests could lawfully eat?
Or have you not read in the law that on the sabbath
   the priests serving in the temple violate the sabbath
   and are innocent?
I say to you, something greater than the temple is here.
If you knew what this meant, *I desire mercy, not sacrifice,*
   you would not have condemned these innocent men.
For the Son of Man is Lord of the sabbath." ✛

SATURDAY, JULY 22
St. Mary Magdalene

† *Song of Songs 3:1-4b* (or *2 Corinthians 5:14-17*)
I have found him who my heart loves.

T he Bride says:
On my bed at night I sought him
   whom my heart loves—
   I sought him but I did not find him.
I will rise then and go about the city;
   in the streets and crossings I will seek
Him whom my heart loves.
   I sought him but I did not find him.
The watchmen came upon me,
   as they made their rounds of the city:
   Have you seen him whom my heart loves?
I had hardly left them
   when I found him whom my heart loves. ✛

Psalm 63:2, 3-4, 5-6, 8-9

R. (2) **My soul is thirsting for you, O Lord my God.**

O God, you are my God whom I seek;
   for you my flesh pines and my soul thirsts
   like the earth, parched, lifeless and without water. **R.**
Thus have I gazed toward you in the sanctuary
   to see your power and your glory,
For your kindness is a greater good than life;
   my lips shall glorify you. **R.**
Thus will I bless you while I live;
   lifting up my hands, I will call upon your name.
As with the riches of a banquet shall my soul be satisfied,
   and with exultant lips my mouth shall praise you. **R.**
You are my help,
   and in the shadow of your wings I shout for joy.
My soul clings fast to you;
   your right hand upholds me. **R.**

R. Alleluia, alleluia.

Tell us, Mary, what did you see on the way?
I saw the glory of the risen Christ, I saw his empty tomb. **R.**

† *John 20:1-2, 11-18*

Woman, why are you weeping? Whom are you looking for?

On the first day of the week,
   Mary Magdalene came to the tomb early in the morning,
   while it was still dark,
   and saw the stone removed from the tomb.
So she ran and went to Simon Peter
   and to the other disciple whom Jesus loved, and told them,
   "They have taken the Lord from the tomb,
   and we don't know where they put him."

Mary stayed outside the tomb weeping.
And as she wept, she bent over into the tomb
   and saw two angels in white sitting there,
   one at the head and one at the feet
   where the Body of Jesus had been.
And they said to her, "Woman, why are you weeping?"
She said to them, "They have taken my Lord,
   and I don't know where they laid him."
When she had said this, she turned around and saw Jesus there,
   but did not know it was Jesus.
Jesus said to her, "Woman, why are you weeping?
Whom are you looking for?"

She thought it was the gardener and said to him,
   "Sir, if you carried him away,
   tell me where you laid him,
   and I will take him."
Jesus said to her, "Mary!"
She turned and said to him in Hebrew,
   "Rabbouni," which means Teacher.
Jesus said to her,
   "Stop holding on to me, for I have not yet ascended to the Father.
But go to my brothers and tell them,
   'I am going to my Father and your Father,
   to my God and your God.'"
Mary Magdalene went and announced to the disciples,
   "I have seen the Lord,"
   and then reported what he told her. ✛

SUNDAY, JULY 23
SIXTEENTH SUNDAY IN ORDINARY TIME

† Wisdom 12:13, 16-19
You give repentance for sins.

There is no god besides you who have the care of all,
   that you need show you have not unjustly condemned.
For your might is the source of justice;
   your mastery over all things makes you lenient to all.
For you show your might when the perfection of your power is
     disbelieved;
   and in those who know you, you rebuke temerity.
But though you are master of might, you judge with clemency,
   and with much lenience you govern us;
   for power, whenever you will, attends you.
And you taught your people, by these deeds,
   that those who are just must be kind;
and you gave your children good ground for hope
   that you would permit repentance for their sins. ✛

Psalm 86:5-6, 9-10, 15-16
R. (5a) **Lord, you are good and forgiving.**
You, O LORD, are good and forgiving,
   abounding in kindness to all who call upon you.
Hearken, O LORD, to my prayer
   and attend to the sound of my pleading. **R.**
All the nations you have made shall come
   and worship you, O LORD,
   and glorify your name.

For you are great, and you do wondrous deeds;
   you alone are God. **R.**
You, O LORD, are a God merciful and gracious,
   slow to anger, abounding in kindness and fidelity.
Turn toward me, and have pity on me;
   give your strength to your servant. **R.**

† *Romans 8:26-27*
The Spirit intercedes with inexpressible groanings.

Brothers and sisters:
The Spirit comes to the aid of our weakness;
   for we do not know how to pray as we ought,
   but the Spirit himself intercedes with inexpressible groanings.
And the one who searches hearts
   knows what is the intention of the Spirit,
   because he intercedes for the holy ones
   according to God's will. ✝

See Matthew 11:25
R. Alleluia, alleluia.
Blessed are you, Father, Lord of heaven and earth;
you have revealed to little ones the mysteries of the kingdom. **R.**

† *Matthew 13:24-43* (or Matthew 13:24-30)
Let them grow together until harvest.

Jesus proposed another parable to the crowds, saying:
"The kingdom of heaven may be likened
   to a man who sowed good seed in his field.
While everyone was asleep his enemy came
   and sowed weeds all through the wheat, and then went off.
When the crop grew and bore fruit, the weeds appeared as well.
The slaves of the householder came to him and said,
   'Master, did you not sow good seed in your field?
Where have the weeds come from?'
He answered, 'An enemy has done this.'
His slaves said to him,
   'Do you want us to go and pull them up?'
He replied, 'No, if you pull up the weeds
   you might uproot the wheat along with them.
Let them grow together until harvest;
   then at harvest time I will say to the harvesters,
   "First collect the weeds and tie them in bundles for burning;
   but gather the wheat into my barn."'"

He proposed another parable to them.

"The kingdom of heaven is like a mustard seed
  that a person took and sowed in a field.
It is the smallest of all the seeds,
  yet when full-grown it is the largest of plants.
It becomes a large bush,
  and the 'birds of the sky come and dwell in its branches.'"

He spoke to them another parable.
"The kingdom of heaven is like yeast
  that a woman took and mixed with three measures of wheat flour
  until the whole batch was leavened."

All these things Jesus spoke to the crowds in parables.
He spoke to them only in parables,
  to fulfill what had been said through the prophet:
    I will open my mouth in parables,
      I will announce what has lain hidden from the foundation of
        the world.

Then, dismissing the crowds, he went into the house.
His disciples approached him and said,
  "Explain to us the parable of the weeds in the field."
He said in reply, "He who sows good seed is the Son of Man,
  the field is the world, the good seed the children of the kingdom.
The weeds are the children of the evil one,
  and the enemy who sows them is the devil.
The harvest is the end of the age, and the harvesters are angels.
Just as weeds are collected and burned up with fire,
  so will it be at the end of the age.
The Son of Man will send his angels,
  and they will collect out of his kingdom
  all who cause others to sin and all evildoers.
They will throw them into the fiery furnace,
  where there will be wailing and grinding of teeth.
Then the righteous will shine like the sun
  in the kingdom of their Father.
Whoever has ears ought to hear." ✛

MONDAY, JULY 24
WEEKDAY, ST. SHARBEL MAKHLŪF

† *Exodus 14:5-18*
They will know that I am the Lord when I receive glory through Pharaoh.

When it was reported to the king of Egypt
  that the people had fled,
Pharaoh and his servants changed their minds about them.

They exclaimed, "What have we done!
Why, we have released Israel from our service!"
So Pharaoh made his chariots ready and mustered his soldiers—
   six hundred first-class chariots
   and all the other chariots of Egypt, with warriors on them all.
So obstinate had the LORD made Pharaoh
   that he pursued the children of Israel
   even while they were marching away in triumph.
The Egyptians, then, pursued them;
   Pharaoh's whole army, his horses, chariots and charioteers,
   caught up with them as they lay encamped by the sea,
   at Pi-hahiroth, in front of Baal-zephon.

Pharaoh was already near when the children of Israel looked up
   and saw that the Egyptians were on the march in pursuit of them.
In great fright they cried out to the LORD.
And they complained to Moses,
   "Were there no burial places in Egypt
   that you had to bring us out here to die in the desert?
Why did you do this to us?
Why did you bring us out of Egypt?
Did we not tell you this in Egypt, when we said,
   'Leave us alone. Let us serve the Egyptians'?
Far better for us to be the slaves of the Egyptians
   than to die in the desert."
But Moses answered the people,
   "Fear not! Stand your ground,
   and you will see the victory the LORD will win for you today.
These Egyptians whom you see today you will never see again.
The LORD himself will fight for you; you have only to keep still."

Then the LORD said to Moses, "Why are you crying out to me?
Tell the children of Israel to go forward.
And you, lift up your staff and, with hand outstretched over the sea,
   split the sea in two,
   that the children of Israel may pass through it on dry land.
But I will make the Egyptians so obstinate
   that they will go in after them.
Then I will receive glory through Pharaoh and all his army,
   his chariots and charioteers.
The Egyptians shall know that I am the LORD,
   when I receive glory through Pharaoh
   and his chariots and charioteers." ✛

Exodus 15:1bc-2, 3-4, 5-6

R. (1b) **Let us sing to the Lord; he has covered himself in glory.**

I will sing to the LORD, for he is gloriously triumphant;
    horse and chariot he has cast into the sea.
My strength and my courage is the LORD,
    and he has been my savior.
He is my God, I praise him;
    the God of my father, I extol him. **R.**
The LORD is a warrior,
    LORD is his name!
Pharaoh's chariots and army he hurled into the sea;
    the elite of his officers were submerged in the Red Sea. **R.**
The flood waters covered them,
    they sank into the depths like a stone.
Your right hand, O LORD, magnificent in power,
    your right hand, O LORD, has shattered the enemy. **R.**

Psalm 95:8

R. Alleluia, alleluia.

If today you hear his voice,
harden not your hearts. **R.**

† Matthew 12:38-42

*At the judgment the queen of the south will arise
with this generation and condemn it.*

Some of the scribes and Pharisees said to Jesus,
    "Teacher, we wish to see a sign from you."
He said to them in reply,
    "An evil and unfaithful generation seeks a sign,
    but no sign will be given it
    except the sign of Jonah the prophet.
Just as Jonah was in the belly of the whale three days and three nights,
    so will the Son of Man be in the heart of the earth
    three days and three nights.
At the judgment, the men of Nineveh will arise with this generation
    and condemn it, because they repented at the preaching of Jonah;
    and there is something greater than Jonah here.
At the judgment the queen of the south will arise with this generation
    and condemn it, because she came from the ends of the earth
    to hear the wisdom of Solomon;
    and there is something greater than Solomon here." ✛

TUESDAY, JULY 25
St. James

† *2 Corinthians 4:7-15*
Always carrying about in the body the dying of Jesus.

Brothers and sisters:
We hold this treasure in earthen vessels,
   that the surpassing power may be of God and not from us.
We are afflicted in every way, but not constrained;
   perplexed, but not driven to despair;
   persecuted, but not abandoned;
   struck down, but not destroyed;
   always carrying about in the body the dying of Jesus,
   so that the life of Jesus may also be manifested in our body.
For we who live are constantly being given up to death
   for the sake of Jesus,
   so that the life of Jesus may be manifested in our mortal flesh.

So death is at work in us, but life in you.
Since, then, we have the same spirit of faith,
   according to what is written, *I believed, therefore I spoke,*
   we too believe and therefore speak,
   knowing that the one who raised the Lord Jesus
   will raise us also with Jesus
   and place us with you in his presence.
Everything indeed is for you,
   so that the grace bestowed in abundance on more and more people
   may cause the thanksgiving to overflow for the glory of God. **✚**

   Psalm 126:1bc-2ab, 2cd-3, 4-5, 6
R. (5) **Those who sow in tears shall reap rejoicing.**
When the LORD brought back the captives of Zion,
   we were like men dreaming.
Then our mouth was filled with laughter,
   and our tongue with rejoicing. **R.**
Then they said among the nations,
   "The LORD has done great things for them."
The LORD has done great things for us;
   we are glad indeed. **R.**
Restore our fortunes, O LORD,
   like the torrents in the southern desert.
Those that sow in tears
   shall reap rejoicing. **R.**
Although they go forth weeping,
   carrying the seed to be sown,

They shall come back rejoicing,
   carrying their sheaves. **R.**

   See John 15:16
R. Alleluia, alleluia.
I chose you from the world,
to go and bear fruit that will last, says the Lord. **R.**

✝ *Matthew 20:20-28*
You will drink my chalice.

The mother of the sons of Zebedee approached Jesus with her sons
   and did him homage, wishing to ask him for something.
He said to her,
   "What do you wish?"
She answered him,
   "Command that these two sons of mine sit,
   one at your right and the other at your left, in your Kingdom."
Jesus said in reply,
   "You do not know what you are asking.
Can you drink the chalice that I am going to drink?"
They said to him, "We can."
He replied,
   "My chalice you will indeed drink,
   but to sit at my right and at my left, this is not mine to give
   but is for those for whom it has been prepared by my Father."
When the ten heard this,
   they became indignant at the two brothers.
But Jesus summoned them and said,
   "You know that the rulers of the Gentiles lord it over them,
   and the great ones make their authority over them felt.
But it shall not be so among you.
Rather, whoever wishes to be great among you shall be your servant;
   whoever wishes to be first among you shall be your slave.
Just so, the Son of Man did not come to be served
   but to serve and to give his life as a ransom for many." ✛

WEDNESDAY, JULY 26
ST. JOACHIM AND ST. ANNE

✝ *Exodus 16:1-5, 9-15*
I will rain down bread from heaven for you.

The children of Israel set out from Elim,
   and came into the desert of Sin,
   which is between Elim and Sinai,
   on the fifteenth day of the second month
   after their departure from the land of Egypt.

Here in the desert the whole assembly of the children of Israel
   grumbled against Moses and Aaron.
The children of Israel said to them,
   "Would that we had died at the LORD's hand in the land of Egypt,
   as we sat by our fleshpots and ate our fill of bread!
But you had to lead us into this desert
   to make the whole community die of famine!"

Then the LORD said to Moses,
   "I will now rain down bread from heaven for you.
Each day the people are to go out and gather their daily portion;
   thus will I test them,
   to see whether they follow my instructions or not.
On the sixth day, however, when they prepare what they bring in,
   let it be twice as much as they gather on the other days."

Then Moses said to Aaron, "Tell the whole congregation
   of the children of Israel:
   Present yourselves before the LORD,
   for he has heard your grumbling."
When Aaron announced this to the whole assembly of the children
      of Israel,
   they turned toward the desert, and lo,
   the glory of the LORD appeared in the cloud!
The LORD spoke to Moses and said,
   "I have heard the grumbling of the children of Israel.
Tell them: In the evening twilight you shall eat flesh,
   and in the morning you shall have your fill of bread,
   so that you may know that I, the LORD, am your God."

In the evening quail came up and covered the camp.
In the morning a dew lay all about the camp,
   and when the dew evaporated, there on the surface of the desert
   were fine flakes like hoarfrost on the ground.
On seeing it, the children of Israel asked one another, "What is
      this?"
   for they did not know what it was.
But Moses told them,
   "This is the bread which the Lord has given you to eat." ✚

   Psalm 78:18-19, 23-24, 25-26, 27-28
R. (24b) The Lord gave them bread from heaven.
They tempted God in their hearts
   by demanding the food they craved.
Yes, they spoke against God, saying,
   "Can God spread a table in the desert?" **R.**

Yet he commanded the skies above
  and the doors of heaven he opened;
He rained manna upon them for food
  and gave them heavenly bread. **R.**
Man ate the bread of angels,
  food he sent them in abundance.
He stirred up the east wind in the heavens,
  and by his power brought on the south wind. **R.**
And he rained meat upon them like dust,
  and, like the sand of the sea, winged fowl,
Which fell in the midst of their camp
  round about their tents. **R.**

R. Alleluia, alleluia.
The seed is the word of God, Christ is the sower;
all who come to him will live for ever. **R.**

✝ *Matthew 13:1-9*
The seed produced grain a hundredfold.

On that day, Jesus went out of the house and sat down by the sea.
Such large crowds gathered around him
  that he got into a boat and sat down,
  and the whole crowd stood along the shore.
And he spoke to them at length in parables, saying:
  "A sower went out to sow.
And as he sowed, some seed fell on the path,
  and birds came and ate it up.
Some fell on rocky ground, where it had little soil.
It sprang up at once because the soil was not deep,
  and when the sun rose it was scorched,
  and it withered for lack of roots.
Some seed fell among thorns, and the thorns grew up and choked it.
But some seed fell on rich soil, and produced fruit,
  a hundred or sixty or thirtyfold.
Whoever has ears ought to hear." ✛

THURSDAY, JULY 27
WEEKDAY

✝ *Exodus 19:1-2, 9-11, 16-20b*
The LORD descended on Mount Sinai before the eyes of all the people.

In the third month after their departure from the land of Egypt,
  on its first day, the children of Israel came to the desert of Sinai.
After the journey from Rephidim to the desert of Sinai,
  they pitched camp.

While Israel was encamped here in front of the mountain,
    the LORD told Moses,
    "I am coming to you in a dense cloud,
    so that when the people hear me speaking with you,
    they may always have faith in you also."
When Moses, then, had reported to the LORD the response of the
      people,
    the LORD added, "Go to the people
    and have them sanctify themselves today and tomorrow.
Make them wash their garments and be ready for the third day;
    for on the third day the LORD will come down on Mount Sinai
    before the eyes of all the people."

On the morning of the third day
    there were peals of thunder and lightning,
    and a heavy cloud over the mountain,
    and a very loud trumpet blast,
    so that all the people in the camp trembled.
But Moses led the people out of the camp to meet God,
    and they stationed themselves at the foot of the mountain.
Mount Sinai was all wrapped in smoke,
    for the LORD came down upon it in fire.
The smoke rose from it as though from a furnace,
    and the whole mountain trembled violently.
The trumpet blast grew louder and louder, while Moses was speaking
    and God answering him with thunder.

When the LORD came down to the top of Mount Sinai,
    he summoned Moses to the top of the mountain. ✢

    Daniel 3:52, 53, 54, 55, 56
R. (52b) **Glory and praise for ever!**
"Blessed are you, O Lord, the God of our fathers,
    praiseworthy and exalted above all forever;
And blessed is your holy and glorious name,
    praiseworthy and exalted above all for all ages." **R.**
"Blessed are you in the temple of your holy glory,
    praiseworthy and glorious above all forever." **R.**
"Blessed are you on the throne of your Kingdom,
    praiseworthy and exalted above all forever." **R.**
"Blessed are you who look into the depths
    from your throne upon the cherubim,
    praiseworthy and exalted above all forever." **R.**
"Blessed are you in the firmament of heaven,
    praiseworthy and glorious forever." **R.**

See Matthew 11:25

R. Alleluia, alleluia.

Blessed are you, Father, Lord of heaven and earth;
you have revealed to little ones the mysteries of the Kingdom. **R.**

✝ *Matthew 13:10-17*

*Because knowledge of the mysteries of the Kingdom of heaven
has been granted to you, but to them it has not been granted.*

The disciples approached Jesus and said,
"Why do you speak to the crowd in parables?"
He said to them in reply,
"Because knowledge of the mysteries of the Kingdom of heaven
has been granted to you, but to them it has not been granted.
To anyone who has, more will be given and he will grow rich;
from anyone who has not, even what he has will be taken away.
This is why I speak to them in parables, because
they look but do not see and hear but do not listen or understand.
Isaiah's prophecy is fulfilled in them, which says:

You shall indeed hear but not understand,
you shall indeed look but never see.
Gross is the heart of this people,
they will hardly hear with their ears,
they have closed their eyes,
lest they see with their eyes
and hear with their ears
and understand with their hearts and be converted
and I heal them.

"But blessed are your eyes, because they see,
and your ears, because they hear.
Amen, I say to you, many prophets and righteous people
longed to see what you see but did not see it,
and to hear what you hear but did not hear it." ✝

FRIDAY, JULY 28
WEEKDAY

✝ *Exodus 20:1-17*
The law was given through Moses.

In those days:
God delivered all these commandments:

"I, the LORD, am your God,
who brought you out of the land of Egypt, that place of slavery.
You shall not have other gods besides me.

You shall not carve idols for yourselves
  in the shape of anything in the sky above
  or on the earth below or in the waters beneath the earth;
  you shall not bow down before them or worship them.
For I, the LORD, your God, am a jealous God,
  inflicting punishment for their fathers' wickedness
  on the children of those who hate me,
  down to the third and fourth generation;
  but bestowing mercy down to the thousandth generation
  on the children of those who love me and keep my commandments.

"You shall not take the name of the LORD, your God, in vain.
For the LORD will not leave unpunished
  him who takes his name in vain.

"Remember to keep holy the sabbath day.
Six days you may labor and do all your work,
  but the seventh day is the sabbath of the LORD, your God.
No work may be done then either by you, or your son or daughter,
  or your male or female slave, or your beast,
  or by the alien who lives with you.
In six days the LORD made the heavens and the earth,
  the sea and all that is in them;
  but on the seventh day he rested.
That is why the LORD has blessed the sabbath day and made it holy.

"Honor your father and your mother,
  that you may have a long life in the land
  which the LORD, your God, is giving you.

"You shall not kill.

"You shall not commit adultery.

"You shall not steal.

"You shall not bear false witness against your neighbor.

"You shall not covet your neighbor's house.
You shall not covet your neighbor's wife,
  nor his male or female slave, nor his ox or ass,
  nor anything else that belongs to him." ✛

   Psalm 19:8, 9, 10, 11
R. (John 6:68c) **Lord, you have the words of everlasting life.**
The law of the LORD is perfect,
  refreshing the soul;
The decree of the LORD is trustworthy,

giving wisdom to the simple. **R.**
The precepts of the LORD are right,
  rejoicing the heart;
The command of the LORD is clear,
  enlightening the eye. **R.**
The fear of the LORD is pure,
  enduring forever;
The ordinances of the LORD are true,
  all of them just. **R.**
They are more precious than gold,
  than a heap of purest gold;
Sweeter also than syrup
  or honey from the comb. **R.**

  See Luke 8:15
R. Alleluia, alleluia.
Blessed are they who have kept the word with a generous heart
and yield a harvest through perseverance. **R.**

† *Matthew 13:18-23*
The one who hears the word and understands it will bear much fruit.

Jesus said to his disciples:
  "Hear the parable of the sower.
The seed sown on the path is the one who hears the word of the
    Kingdom
  without understanding it,
  and the Evil One comes and steals away
  what was sown in his heart.
The seed sown on rocky ground
  is the one who hears the word and receives it at once with joy.
But he has no root and lasts only for a time.
When some tribulation or persecution comes because of the word,
  he immediately falls away.
The seed sown among thorns is the one who hears the word,
  but then worldly anxiety and the lure of riches choke the word
  and it bears no fruit.
But the seed sown on rich soil
  is the one who hears the word and understands it,
  who indeed bears fruit and yields a hundred or sixty or thirtyfold." ✛

SATURDAY, JULY 29
STS. MARTHA, MARY AND LAZARUS

† *Exodus 24:3-8*
This is the blood of the covenant that the LORD has made with you.

When Moses came to the people

and related all the words and ordinances of the LORD,
they all answered with one voice,
"We will do everything that the LORD has told us."
Moses then wrote down all the words of the LORD and,
rising early the next day,
he erected at the foot of the mountain an altar
and twelve pillars for the twelve tribes of Israel.
Then, having sent certain young men of the children of Israel
to offer burnt offerings and sacrifice young bulls
as peace offerings to the LORD,
Moses took half of the blood and put it in large bowls;
the other half he splashed on the altar.
Taking the book of the covenant, he read it aloud to the people,
who answered, "All that the LORD has said, we will heed and do."
Then he took the blood and sprinkled it on the people, saying,
"This is the blood of the covenant
that the LORD has made with you
in accordance with all these words of his." ✛

Psalm 50:1b-2, 5-6, 14-15

R. (14a) **Offer to God a sacrifice of praise.**
God the LORD has spoken and summoned the earth,
from the rising of the sun to its setting.
From Zion, perfect in beauty,
God shines forth. **R.**
"Gather my faithful ones before me,
those who have made a covenant with me by sacrifice."
And the heavens proclaim his justice;
for God himself is the judge. **R.**
"Offer to God praise as your sacrifice
and fulfill your vows to the Most High;
Then call upon me in time of distress;
I will rescue you, and you shall glorify me." **R.**

John 8:12

R. Alleluia, alleluia.
I am the light of the world, says the Lord;
whoever follows me will have the light of life. **R.**

† *John 11:19-27* (or *Luke 10:38-42)*
I have come to believe that you are the Christ, the Son of God.

Many of the Jews had come to Martha and Mary
to comfort them about their brother [Lazarus, who had died].
When Martha heard that Jesus was coming,
she went to meet him;
but Mary sat at home.

Martha said to Jesus,
  "Lord, if you had been here,
  my brother would not have died.
But even now I know that whatever you ask of God,
  God will give you."
Jesus said to her,
  "Your brother will rise."
Martha said to him,
  "I know he will rise,
  in the resurrection on the last day."
Jesus told her,
  "I am the resurrection and the life;
  whoever believes in me, even if he dies, will live,
  and anyone who lives and believes in me will never die.
Do you believe this?"
She said to him, "Yes, Lord.
I have come to believe that you are the Christ, the Son of God,
  the one who is coming into the world." ✛

SUNDAY, JULY 30
SEVENTEENTH SUNDAY IN ORDINARY TIME

† *1 Kings 3:5, 7-12*
You have asked for wisdom.

The LORD appeared to Solomon in a dream at night.
God said, "Ask something of me and I will give it to you."
Solomon answered:
  "O LORD, my God, you have made me, your servant, king
  to succeed my father David;
  but I am a mere youth, not knowing at all how to act.
I serve you in the midst of the people whom you have chosen,
  a people so vast that it cannot be numbered or counted.
Give your servant, therefore, an understanding heart
  to judge your people and to distinguish right from wrong.
For who is able to govern this vast people of yours?"

The LORD was pleased that Solomon made this request.
So God said to him:
  "Because you have asked for this—
  not for a long life for yourself,
  nor for riches,
  nor for the life of your enemies,
  but for understanding so that you may know what is right—
  I do as you requested.
I give you a heart so wise and understanding

that there has never been anyone like you up to now,
and after you there will come no one to equal you." ✣

Psalm 119:57 and 72, 76-77, 127-128, 129-130
R. (97a) Lord, I love your commands.
I have said, O Lᴏʀᴅ, that my part
    is to keep your words.
The law of your mouth is to me more precious
    than thousands of gold and silver pieces. **R.**
Let your kindness comfort me
    according to your promise to your servants.
Let your compassion come to me that I may live,
    for your law is my delight. **R.**
For I love your command
    more than gold, however fine.
For in all your precepts I go forward;
    every false way I hate. **R.**
Wonderful are your decrees;
    therefore I observe them.
The revelation of your words sheds light,
    giving understanding to the simple. **R.**

† *Romans 8:28-30*
God predestined us to be conformed to the image of his Son.

Brothers and sisters:
We know that all things work for good for those who love God,
    who are called according to his purpose.
For those he foreknew he also predestined
    to be conformed to the image of his Son,
    so that he might be the firstborn
    among many brothers and sisters.
And those he predestined he also called;
    and those he called he also justified;
    and those he justified he also glorified. ✣

See Matthew 11:25
R. Alleluia, alleluia.
Blessed are you Father, Lord of heaven and earth;
for you have revealed to little ones the mysteries of the kingdom. **R.**

† *Matthew 13:44-52* (or *Matthew 13:44-46*)
He sells all that he has and buys the field.

Jesus said to his disciples:
    "The kingdom of heaven is like a treasure buried in a field,
    which a person finds and hides again,
    and out of joy goes and sells all that he has and buys that field.

Again, the kingdom of heaven is like a merchant
    searching for fine pearls.
When he finds a pearl of great price,
    he goes and sells all that he has and buys it.
Again, the kingdom of heaven is like a net thrown into the sea,
    which collects fish of every kind.
When it is full they haul it ashore
    and sit down to put what is good into buckets.
What is bad they throw away.
Thus it will be at the end of the age.
The angels will go out and separate the wicked from the righteous
    and throw them into the fiery furnace,
    where there will be wailing and grinding of teeth.

"Do you understand all these things?"
They answered, "Yes."
And he replied,
    "Then every scribe who has been instructed in the kingdom of
        heaven
    is like the head of a household
    who brings from his storeroom both the new and the old."✛

MONDAY, JULY 31
St. Ignatius of Loyola

† *Exodus 32:15-24, 30-34*
*This people has indeed committed a grave sin,
in making a god of gold for themselves.*

Moses turned and came down the mountain
    with the two tablets of the commandments in his hands,
    tablets that were written on both sides, front and back;
    tablets that were made by God,
    having inscriptions on them that were engraved by God himself.
Now, when Joshua heard the noise of the people shouting,
    he said to Moses, "That sounds like a battle in the camp."
But Moses answered, "It does not sound like cries of victory,
    nor does it sound like cries of defeat;
    the sounds that I hear are cries of revelry."
As he drew near the camp, he saw the calf and the dancing.
With that, Moses' wrath flared up, so that he threw the tablets down
    and broke them on the base of the mountain.
Taking the calf they had made, he fused it in the fire
    and then ground it down to powder,
    which he scattered on the water and made the children of Israel
        drink.

Moses asked Aaron, "What did this people ever do to you
   that you should lead them into so grave a sin?"
Aaron replied, "Let not my lord be angry.
You know well enough how prone the people are to evil.
They said to me, 'Make us a god to be our leader;
   as for the man Moses who brought us out of the land of Egypt,
   we do not know what has happened to him.'
So I told them, 'Let anyone who has gold jewelry take it off.'
They gave it to me, and I threw it into the fire, and this calf came
    out."

On the next day Moses said to the people,
   "You have committed a grave sin.
I will go up to the LORD, then;
   perhaps I may be able to make atonement for your sin."
So Moses went back to the LORD and said,
   "Ah, this people has indeed committed a grave sin
   in making a god of gold for themselves!
If you would only forgive their sin!
If you will not, then strike me out of the book that you have written."
The LORD answered, "Him only who has sinned against me
   will I strike out of my book.
Now, go and lead the people to the place I have told you.
My angel will go before you.
When it is time for me to punish, I will punish them for their sin." ✠

   Psalm 106:19-20, 21-22, 23
R. (1a) **Give thanks to the Lord, for he is good.**
Our fathers made a calf in Horeb
   and adored a molten image;
They exchanged their glory
   for the image of a grass-eating bullock. **R.**
They forgot the God who had saved them,
   who had done great deeds in Egypt,
Wondrous deeds in the land of Ham,
   terrible things at the Red Sea. **R.**
Then he spoke of exterminating them,
   but Moses, his chosen one,
Withstood him in the breach
   to turn back his destructive wrath. **R.**

   James 1:18
R. Alleluia, alleluia.
The Father willed to give us birth by the word of truth
that we may be a kind of firstfruits of his creatures. **R.**

✝ *Matthew 13:31-35*
*The mustard seed becomes a large bush and
the birds of the sky come and dwell in its branches.*

Jesus proposed a parable to the crowds.
"The Kingdom of heaven is like a mustard seed
   that a person took and sowed in a field.
It is the smallest of all the seeds,
   yet when full-grown it is the largest of plants.
It becomes a large bush,
   and the *birds of the sky come and dwell in its branches.*"

He spoke to them another parable.
"The Kingdom of heaven is like yeast
   that a woman took and mixed with three measures of wheat flour
   until the whole batch was leavened."

All these things Jesus spoke to the crowds in parables.
He spoke to them only in parables,
   to fulfill what had been said through the prophet:

I will open my mouth in parables,
   I will announce what has lain hidden from the foundation of the
     world. ✝

TUESDAY, AUGUST 1
ST. ALPHONSUS LIGUORI

✝ *Exodus 33:7-11; 34:5b-9, 28*
The Lord spoke to Moses face to face.

The tent, which was called the meeting tent,
   Moses used to pitch at some distance away, outside the camp.
Anyone who wished to consult the LORD
   would go to this meeting tent outside the camp.
Whenever Moses went out to the tent, the people would all rise
   and stand at the entrance of their own tents,
   watching Moses until he entered the tent.
As Moses entered the tent, the column of cloud would come down
   and stand at its entrance while the LORD spoke with Moses.
On seeing the column of cloud stand at the entrance of the tent,
   all the people would rise and worship
   at the entrance of their own tents.
The LORD used to speak to Moses face to face,
   as one man speaks to another.
Moses would then return to the camp,
   but his young assistant, Joshua, son of Nun,
   would not move out of the tent.

Moses stood there with the LORD and proclaimed his name, "LORD."
Thus the LORD passed before him and cried out,
"The LORD, the LORD, a merciful and gracious God,
slow to anger and rich in kindness and fidelity,
continuing his kindness for a thousand generations,
and forgiving wickedness and crime and sin;
yet not declaring the guilty guiltless,
but punishing children and grandchildren
to the third and fourth generation for their fathers' wickedness!"
Moses at once bowed down to the ground in worship.
Then he said, "If I find favor with you, O LORD,
do come along in our company.
This is indeed a stiff-necked people;
yet pardon our wickedness and sins,
and receive us as your own."

So Moses stayed there with the LORD for forty days and forty nights,
without eating any food or drinking any water,
and he wrote on the tablets the words of the covenant,
the ten commandments. ✛

Psalm 103:6-7, 8-9, 10-11, 12-13
R. (8a) **The Lord is kind and merciful.**
The LORD secures justice
and the rights of all the oppressed.
He has made known his ways to Moses,
and his deeds to the children of Israel. **R.**
Merciful and gracious is the LORD,
slow to anger and abounding in kindness.
He will not always chide,
nor does he keep his wrath forever. **R.**
Not according to our sins does he deal with us,
nor does he requite us according to our crimes.
For as the heavens are high above the earth,
so surpassing is his kindness toward those who fear him. **R.**
As far as the east is from the west,
so far has he put our transgressions from us.
As a father has compassion on his children,
so the LORD has compassion on those who fear him. **R.**

R. Alleluia, alleluia.
The seed is the word of God, Christ is the sower;
all who come to him will live for ever. **R.**

✝ *Matthew 13:36-43*
Just as the weeds are collected now and burned up with fire,
so will it be at the end of the age.

Jesus dismissed the crowds and went into the house.
His disciples approached him and said,
  "Explain to us the parable of the weeds in the field."
He said in reply, "He who sows good seed is the Son of Man,
  the field is the world, the good seed the children of the Kingdom.
The weeds are the children of the Evil One,
  and the enemy who sows them is the Devil.
The harvest is the end of the age, and the harvesters are angels.
Just as weeds are collected and burned up with fire,
  so will it be at the end of the age.
The Son of Man will send his angels,
  and they will collect out of his Kingdom
  all who cause others to sin and all evildoers.
They will throw them into the fiery furnace,
  where there will be wailing and grinding of teeth.
Then the righteous will shine like the sun
  in the Kingdom of their Father.
Whoever has ears ought to hear." ✛

WEDNESDAY, AUGUST 2
WEEKDAY, ST. EUSEBIUS OF VERCELLI, ST. PETER JULIAN EYMARD

✝ *Exodus 34:29-35*
Seeing the face of Moses, they were afraid to come near him.

As Moses came down from Mount Sinai
  with the two tablets of the commandments in his hands,
  he did not know that the skin of his face had become radiant
  while he conversed with the LORD.
When Aaron, then, and the other children of Israel saw Moses
  and noticed how radiant the skin of his face had become,
  they were afraid to come near him.
Only after Moses called to them did Aaron
  and all the rulers of the community come back to him.
Moses then spoke to them.
Later on, all the children of Israel came up to him,
  and he enjoined on them all that the LORD
  had told him on Mount Sinai.
When he finished speaking with them,
  he put a veil over his face.
Whenever Moses entered the presence of the LORD to converse with
    him,

he removed the veil until he came out again.
On coming out, he would tell the children of Israel
  all that had been commanded.
Then the children of Israel would see
  that the skin of Moses' face was radiant;
  so he would again put the veil over his face
  until he went in to converse with the LORD. ✠

Psalm 99:5, 6, 7, 9

R. (see 9c) Holy is the Lord our God.

Extol the LORD, our God,
  and worship at his footstool;
  holy is he! **R.**
Moses and Aaron were among his priests,
  and Samuel, among those who called upon his name;
  they called upon the LORD, and he answered them. **R.**
From the pillar of cloud he spoke to them;
  they heard his decrees and the law he gave them. **R.**
Extol the LORD, our God,
  and worship at his holy mountain;
  for holy is the LORD, our God. **R.**

John 15:15b

R. Alleluia, alleluia.

I call you my friends, says the Lord,
for I have made known to you all that the Father has told me. **R.**

✝ Matthew 13:44-46
He sells all he has and buys that field.

Jesus said to his disciples:
"The Kingdom of heaven is like a treasure buried in a field,
  which a person finds and hides again,
  and out of joy goes and sells all that he has and buys that field.
Again, the Kingdom of heaven is like a merchant
  searching for fine pearls.
When he finds a pearl of great price,
  he goes and sells all that he has and buys it." ✠

THURSDAY, AUGUST 3
WEEKDAY

✝ Exodus 40:16-21, 34-38
*The cloud covered the meeting tent and
the glory of the LORD filled the Dwelling.*

Moses did exactly as the LORD had commanded him.
On the first day of the first month of the second year

the Dwelling was erected.
It was Moses who erected the Dwelling.
He placed its pedestals, set up its boards, put in its bars,
  and set up its columns.
He spread the tent over the Dwelling
  and put the covering on top of the tent,
  as the LORD had commanded him.
He took the commandments and put them in the ark;
  he placed poles alongside the ark and set the propitiatory upon it.
He brought the ark into the Dwelling and hung the curtain veil,
  thus screening off the ark of the commandments,
  as the LORD had commanded him.

Then the cloud covered the meeting tent,
  and the glory of the LORD filled the Dwelling.
Moses could not enter the meeting tent,
  because the cloud settled down upon it
  and the glory of the LORD filled the Dwelling.
Whenever the cloud rose from the Dwelling,
  the children of Israel would set out on their journey.
But if the cloud did not lift, they would not go forward;
  only when it lifted did they go forward.
In the daytime the cloud of the LORD was seen over the Dwelling;
  whereas at night, fire was seen in the cloud
  by the whole house of Israel
  in all the stages of their journey. ✝

Psalm 84:3, 4, 5-6a and 8a, 11
R. (2) **How lovely is your dwelling place, O Lord, mighty God!**
My soul yearns and pines
  for the courts of the LORD.
My heart and my flesh
  cry out for the living God. **R.**
Even the sparrow finds a home,
  and the swallow a nest
  in which she puts her young—
Your altars, O LORD of hosts,
  my king and my God! **R.**
Blessed they who dwell in your house!
  continually they praise you.
Blessed the men whose strength you are!
They go from strength to strength. **R.**
I had rather one day in your courts
  than a thousand elsewhere;

I had rather lie at the threshold of the house of my God
   than dwell in the tents of the wicked. **R.**

   See Acts 16:14b
R. Alleluia, alleluia.
Open our hearts, O Lord,
to listen to the words of your Son. **R.**

✝ *Matthew 13:47-53*
They put what is good into buckets, what is bad they throw away.

Jesus said to the disciples:
"The Kingdom of heaven is like a net thrown into the sea,
   which collects fish of every kind.
When it is full they haul it ashore
   and sit down to put what is good into buckets.
What is bad they throw away.
Thus it will be at the end of the age.
The angels will go out and separate the wicked from the righteous
   and throw them into the fiery furnace,
   where there will be wailing and grinding of teeth."

"Do you understand all these things?"
They answered, "Yes."
And he replied,
   "Then every scribe who has been instructed in the Kingdom of
      heaven
   is like the head of a household who brings from his storeroom
   both the new and the old."
When Jesus finished these parables, he went away from there. ✝

FRIDAY, AUGUST 4
St. John Vianney

✝ *Leviticus 23:1, 4-11, 15-16, 27, 34b-37*
*These are the festivals of the LORD on which
you shall proclaim a sacred assembly.*

The LORD said to Moses,
   "These are the festivals of the LORD which you shall celebrate
   at their proper time with a sacred assembly.
The Passover of the LORD falls on the fourteenth day of the first
      month,
   at the evening twilight.
The fifteenth day of this month is the LORD's feast of Unleavened
      Bread.
For seven days you shall eat unleavened bread.
On the first of these days you shall hold a sacred assembly

and do no sort of work.
On each of the seven days you shall offer an oblation to the LORD.
Then on the seventh day you shall again hold a sacred assembly
and do no sort of work."

The LORD said to Moses, "Speak to the children of Israel and tell
them:
When you come into the land which I am giving you,
and reap your harvest,
you shall bring a sheaf of the first fruits of your harvest
to the priest, who shall wave the sheaf before the LORD
that it may be acceptable for you.
On the day after the sabbath the priest shall do this.

"Beginning with the day after the sabbath,
the day on which you bring the wave-offering sheaf,
you shall count seven full weeks,
and then on the day after the seventh week, the fiftieth day,
you shall present the new cereal offering to the LORD.

"The tenth of this seventh month is the Day of Atonement,
when you shall hold a sacred assembly and mortify yourselves
and offer an oblation to the LORD.

"The fifteenth day of this seventh month is the LORD's feast of
Booths,
which shall continue for seven days.
On the first day there shall be a sacred assembly,
and you shall do no sort of work.
For seven days you shall offer an oblation to the LORD,
and on the eighth day you shall again hold a sacred assembly
and offer an oblation to the LORD.
On that solemn closing you shall do no sort of work.

"These, therefore, are the festivals of the LORD
on which you shall proclaim a sacred assembly,
and offer as an oblation to the LORD burnt offerings and cereal
offerings,
sacrifices and libations, as prescribed for each day." ✛

Psalm 81:3-4, 5-6, 10-11ab
R. (2a) **Sing with joy to God our help.**
Take up a melody, and sound the timbrel,
the pleasant harp and the lyre.
Blow the trumpet at the new moon,
at the full moon, on our solemn feast. **R.**
For it is a statute in Israel,

an ordinance of the God of Jacob,
Who made it a decree for Joseph
  when he came forth from the land of Egypt. **R.**
There shall be no strange god among you
  nor shall you worship any alien god.
I, the LORD, am your God
  who led you forth from the land of Egypt. **R.**

1 Peter 1:25
R. Alleluia, alleluia.
The word of the Lord remains forever;
this is the word that has been proclaimed to you. **R.**

† *Matthew 13:54-58*
*Is he not the carpenter's son? Where did this man
get such wisdom and mighty deeds?*

Jesus came to his native place and taught the people in their
  synagogue.
They were astonished and said,
  "Where did this man get such wisdom and mighty deeds?"
Is he not the carpenter's son?
Is not his mother named Mary
  and his brothers James, Joseph, Simon, and Judas?
Are not his sisters all with us?
Where did this man get all this?"
And they took offense at him.
But Jesus said to them,
  "A prophet is not without honor except in his native place
  and in his own house."
And he did not work many mighty deeds there
  because of their lack of faith. ✝

SATURDAY, AUGUST 5
WEEKDAY, THE DEDICATION OF THE BASILICA OF ST. MARY MAJOR, [BVM]

† *Leviticus 25:1, 8-17*
*In the year of the jubilee you shall return,
everyone of you, to your own property.*

The LORD said to Moses on Mount Sinai,
  "Seven weeks of years shall you count—seven times seven years—
  so that the seven cycles amount to forty-nine years.
Then, on the tenth day of the seventh month, let the trumpet resound;
  on this, the Day of Atonement, the trumpet blast shall re-echo
  throughout your land.
This fiftieth year you shall make sacred
  by proclaiming liberty in the land for all its inhabitants.

It shall be a jubilee for you,
   when every one of you shall return to his own property,
   every one to his own family estate.
In this fiftieth year, your year of jubilee,
   you shall not sow, nor shall you reap the aftergrowth
   or pick the grapes from the untrimmed vines.
Since this is the jubilee, which shall be sacred for you,
   you may not eat of its produce,
   except as taken directly from the field.

"In this year of jubilee, then,
   every one of you shall return to his own property.
Therefore, when you sell any land to your neighbor
   or buy any from him, do not deal unfairly.
On the basis of the number of years since the last jubilee
   shall you purchase the land from your neighbor;
   and so also, on the basis of the number of years for crops,
   shall he sell it to you.
When the years are many, the price shall be so much the more;
   when the years are few, the price shall be so much the less.
For it is really the number of crops that he sells you.
Do not deal unfairly, then; but stand in fear of your God.
I, the Lord, am your God." ✛

Psalm 67:2-3, 5, 7-8
R. (4) **O God, let all the nations praise you!**
May God have pity on us and bless us;
   may he let his face shine upon us.
So may your way be known upon earth;
   among all nations, your salvation. **R.**
May the nations be glad and exult
   because you rule the peoples in equity;
   the nations on the earth you guide. **R.**
The earth has yielded its fruits;
   God, our God, has blessed us.
May God bless us,
   and may all the ends of the earth fear him! **R.**

Matthew 5:10
R. Alleluia, alleluia.
Blessed are they who are persecuted for the sake of righteousness
for theirs is the Kingdom of heaven. **R.**

† *Matthew 14:1-12*
Herod had John beheaded; John's disciples came and told Jesus.

Herod the tetrarch heard of the reputation of Jesus

and said to his servants, "This man is John the Baptist.
He has been raised from the dead;
　that is why mighty powers are at work in him."

Now Herod had arrested John, bound him, and put him in prison
　on account of Herodias, the wife of his brother Philip,
　for John had said to him,
　"It is not lawful for you to have her."
Although he wanted to kill him, he feared the people,
　for they regarded him as a prophet.
But at a birthday celebration for Herod,
　the daughter of Herodias performed a dance before the guests
　and delighted Herod so much
　that he swore to give her whatever she might ask for.
Prompted by her mother, she said,
　"Give me here on a platter the head of John the Baptist."
The king was distressed,
　but because of his oaths and the guests who were present,
　he ordered that it be given, and he had John beheaded in the
　　　prison.
His head was brought in on a platter and given to the girl,
　who took it to her mother.
His disciples came and took away the corpse
　and buried him; and they went and told Jesus. ✢

SUNDAY, AUGUST 6
THE TRANSFIGURATION OF THE LORD

† Daniel 7:9-10, 13-14
His clothing was snow bright.

As I watched:
　Thrones were set up
　　and the Ancient One took his throne.
　His clothing was bright as snow,
　　and the hair on his head as white as wool;
　his throne was flames of fire,
　　with wheels of burning fire.
　A surging stream of fire
　　flowed out from where he sat;
　Thousands upon thousands were ministering to him,
　　and myriads upon myriads attended him.
The court was convened and the books were opened.

As the visions during the night continued, I saw:

One like a Son of man coming,
   on the clouds of heaven;
When he reached the Ancient One
   and was presented before him,
The one like a Son of man received dominion, glory, and kingship;
   all peoples, nations, and languages serve him.
His dominion is an everlasting dominion
   that shall not be taken away,
   his kingship shall not be destroyed. ✤

Psalm 97:1-2, 5-6, 9
R. (1a and 9a) **The Lord is king, the Most High over all the earth.**
The LORD is king; let the earth rejoice;
   let the many islands be glad.
Clouds and darkness are round about him,
   justice and judgment are the foundation of his throne. **R.**
The mountains melt like wax before the LORD,
   before the LORD of all the earth.
The heavens proclaim his justice,
   and all peoples see his glory. **R.**
Because you, O LORD, are the Most High over all the earth,
   exalted far above all gods. **R.**

† *2 Peter 1:16-19*
We ourselves heard this voice come from heaven.

Beloved:
We did not follow cleverly devised myths
   when we made known to you
   the power and coming of our Lord Jesus Christ,
   but we had been eyewitnesses of his majesty.
For he received honor and glory from God the Father
   when that unique declaration came to him from the majestic glory,
   "This is my Son, my beloved, with whom I am well pleased."
We ourselves heard this voice come from heaven
   while we were with him on the holy mountain.
Moreover, we possess the prophetic message that is altogether reliable.
You will do well to be attentive to it,
   as to a lamp shining in a dark place,
   until day dawns and the morning star rises in your hearts. ✤

Matthew 17:5c
R. Alleluia, alleluia.
This is my beloved Son, with whom I am well pleased;
listen to him. **R.**

† *Matthew 17:1-9*
His face shone like the sun.

Jesus took Peter, James, and his brother, John,
   and led them up a high mountain by themselves.
And he was transfigured before them;
   his face shone like the sun
   and his clothes became white as light.
And behold, Moses and Elijah appeared to them,
   conversing with him.
Then Peter said to Jesus in reply,
   "Lord, it is good that we are here.
If you wish, I will make three tents here,
   one for you, one for Moses, and one for Elijah."
While he was still speaking, behold,
   a bright cloud cast a shadow over them,
   then from the cloud came a voice that said,
   "This is my beloved Son, with whom I am well pleased;
   listen to him."
When the disciples heard this, they fell prostrate
   and were very much afraid.
But Jesus came and touched them, saying,
   "Rise, and do not be afraid."
And when the disciples raised their eyes,
   they saw no one else but Jesus alone.

As they were coming down from the mountain,
   Jesus charged them,
   "Do not tell the vision to anyone
   until the Son of Man has been raised from the dead." ✛

MONDAY, AUGUST 7
WEEKDAY (EIGHTEENTH WEEK IN ORDINARY TIME), ST. POPE SIXTUS II AND COMPANIONS, ST. CAJETAN

† *Numbers 11:4b-15*
I cannot carry all this people by myself.

The children of Israel lamented,
   "Would that we had meat for food!
We remember the fish we used to eat without cost in Egypt,
   and the cucumbers, the melons, the leeks,
   the onions, and the garlic.
But now we are famished;
   we see nothing before us but this manna."

Manna was like coriander seed and had the color of resin.

When they had gone about and gathered it up,
    the people would grind it between millstones or pound it in a mortar,
    then cook it in a pot and make it into loaves,
    which tasted like cakes made with oil.
At night, when the dew fell upon the camp, the manna also fell.

When Moses heard the people, family after family,
    crying at the entrance of their tents,
    so that the LORD became very angry, he was grieved.
"Why do you treat your servant so badly?" Moses asked the LORD.
"Why are you so displeased with me
    that you burden me with all this people?
Was it I who conceived all this people?
Or was it I who gave them birth,
    that you tell me to carry them at my bosom,
    like a foster father carrying an infant,
    to the land you have promised under oath to their fathers?
Where can I get meat to give to all this people?
For they are crying to me,
    'Give us meat for our food.'
I cannot carry all this people by myself,
    for they are too heavy for me.
If this is the way you will deal with me,
    then please do me the favor of killing me at once,
    so that I need no longer face this distress." ✝

Psalm 81:12-13, 14-15, 16-17
R. (2a) **Sing with joy to God our help.**
"My people heard not my voice,
    and Israel obeyed me not;
So I gave them up to the hardness of their hearts;
    they walked according to their own counsels." **R.**
"If only my people would hear me,
    and Israel walk in my ways,
Quickly would I humble their enemies;
    against their foes I would turn my hand." **R.**
"Those who hated the LORD would seek to flatter me,
    but their fate would endure forever,
While Israel I would feed with the best of wheat,
    and with honey from the rock I would fill them." **R.**

Matthew 4:4
R. Alleluia, alleluia.
One does not live on bread alone,
but on every word that comes forth from the mouth of God. **R.**

† *Matthew 14:13-21*

Looking up to heaven, he said the blessing and gave the loaves to the disciples,
who in turn gave them to the crowds.

When Jesus heard of the death of John the Baptist,
  he withdrew in a boat to a deserted place by himself.
The crowds heard of this and followed him on foot from their towns.
When he disembarked and saw the vast crowd,
  his heart was moved with pity for them, and he cured their sick.
When it was evening, the disciples approached him and said,
  "This is a deserted place and it is already late;
  dismiss the crowds so that they can go to the villages
  and buy food for themselves."
He said to them, "There is no need for them to go away;
  give them some food yourselves."
But they said to him,
  "Five loaves and two fish are all we have here."
Then he said, "Bring them here to me,"
  and he ordered the crowds to sit down on the grass.
Taking the five loaves and the two fish, and looking up to heaven,
  he said the blessing, broke the loaves,
  and gave them to the disciples,
  who in turn gave them to the crowds.
They all ate and were satisfied,
  and they picked up the fragments left over—
  twelve wicker baskets full.
Those who ate were about five thousand men,
  not counting women and children. ✝

TUESDAY, AUGUST 8
ST. DOMINIC

† *Numbers 12:1-13*

Not so with my servant Moses!
Why, then, did you not fear to speak against him?

Miriam and Aaron spoke against Moses on the pretext
  of the marriage he had contracted with a Cushite woman.
They complained, "Is it through Moses alone that the LORD speaks?
Does he not speak through us also?"
And the LORD heard this.
Now, Moses himself was by far the meekest man on the face of the
    earth.
So at once the LORD said to Moses and Aaron and Miriam,
  "Come out, you three, to the meeting tent."
And the three of them went.
Then the LORD came down in the column of cloud,

and standing at the entrance of the tent,
    called Aaron and Miriam.
When both came forward, he said,
    "Now listen to the words of the LORD:

Should there be a prophet among you,
    in visions will I reveal myself to him,
    in dreams will I speak to him;
not so with my servant Moses!
Throughout my house he bears my trust:
    face to face I speak to him;
    plainly and not in riddles.
The presence of the LORD he beholds.

Why, then, did you not fear to speak against my servant Moses?"

So angry was the LORD against them that when he departed,
    and the cloud withdrew from the tent,
    there was Miriam, a snow-white leper!
When Aaron turned and saw her a leper, he said to Moses,
    "Ah, my lord! Please do not charge us with the sin
    that we have foolishly committed!
Let her not thus be like the stillborn babe
    that comes forth from its mother's womb
    with its flesh half consumed."
Then Moses cried to the LORD, "Please, not this! Pray, heal her!" ✛

Psalm 51:3-4, 5-6ab, 6cd-7, 12-13
R. (see 3a) **Be merciful, O Lord, for we have sinned.**
Have mercy on me, O God, in your goodness;
    in the greatness of your compassion wipe out my offense.
Thoroughly wash me from my guilt
    and of my sin cleanse me. **R.**
For I acknowledge my offense;
    and my sin is before me always:
"Against you only have I sinned;
    and done what is evil in your sight." **R.**
That you may be justified in your sentence,
    vindicated when you condemn.
Indeed, in guilt was I born,
    and in sin my mother conceived me. **R.**
A clean heart create for me, O God,
    and a steadfast spirit renew within me.
Cast me not off from your presence,
    and your Holy Spirit take not from me. **R.**

John 1:49b

R. Alleluia, alleluia.
Rabbi, you are the Son of God;
you are the King of Israel. **R.**

† Matthew 14:22-36 (or Matthew 15:1-2, 10-14)
Command me to come to you on the water.

Jesus made the disciples get into a boat
  and precede him to the other side of the sea,
  while he dismissed the crowds.
After doing so, he went up on the mountain by himself to pray.
When it was evening he was there alone.
Meanwhile the boat, already a few miles offshore,
  was being tossed about by the waves, for the wind was against it.
During the fourth watch of the night,
  he came toward them, walking on the sea.
When the disciples saw him walking on the sea they were terrified.
"It is a ghost," they said, and they cried out in fear.
At once Jesus spoke to them, "Take courage, it is I; do not be afraid."
Peter said to him in reply,
  "Lord, if it is you, command me to come to you on the water."
He said, "Come."
Peter got out of the boat and began to walk on the water toward
      Jesus.
But when he saw how strong the wind was he became frightened;
  and, beginning to sink, he cried out, "Lord, save me!"
Immediately Jesus stretched out his hand and caught him,
  and said to him, "O you of little faith, why did you doubt?"
After they got into the boat, the wind died down.
Those who were in the boat did him homage, saying,
  "Truly, you are the Son of God."

After making the crossing, they came to land at Gennesaret.
When the men of that place recognized him,
  they sent word to all the surrounding country.
People brought to him all those who were sick
  and begged him that they might touch only the tassel on his cloak,
  and as many as touched it were healed. ✛

WEDNESDAY, AUGUST 9
WEEKDAY, ST. TERESA BENEDICTA OF THE CROSS

† Numbers 13:1-2, 25—14:1, 26-29a, 34-35
They despised the desirable land (Psalm 106:24).

The LORD said to Moses [in the desert of Paran],

"Send men to reconnoiter the land of Canaan,
    which I am giving the children of Israel.
You shall send one man from each ancestral tribe,
    all of them princes."

After reconnoitering the land for forty days they returned,
    met Moses and Aaron and the whole congregation of the children
        of Israel
    in the desert of Paran at Kadesh,
    made a report to them all,
    and showed the fruit of the country
    to the whole congregation.
They told Moses: "We went into the land to which you sent us.
It does indeed flow with milk and honey, and here is its fruit.
However, the people who are living in the land are fierce,
    and the towns are fortified and very strong.
Besides, we saw descendants of the Anakim there.
Amalekites live in the region of the Negeb;
    Hittites, Jebusites, and Amorites dwell in the highlands,
    and Canaanites along the seacoast and the banks of the Jordan."

Caleb, however, to quiet the people toward Moses, said,
    "We ought to go up and seize the land, for we can certainly do so."
But the men who had gone up with him said,
    "We cannot attack these people; they are too strong for us."
So they spread discouraging reports among the children of Israel
    about the land they had scouted, saying,
    "The land that we explored is a country that consumes its
        inhabitants.
And all the people we saw there are huge, veritable giants
    (the Anakim were a race of giants);
    we felt like mere grasshoppers, and so we must have seemed to
        them."

At this, the whole community broke out with loud cries,
    and even in the night the people wailed.

The LORD said to Moses and Aaron:
    "How long will this wicked assembly grumble against me?
I have heard the grumblings of the children of Israel against me.
Tell them: By my life, says the LORD,
    I will do to you just what I have heard you say.
Here in the desert shall your dead bodies fall.
Forty days you spent in scouting the land;
    forty years shall you suffer for your crimes:
    one year for each day.

Thus you will realize what it means to oppose me.
I, the LORD, have sworn to do this
   to all this wicked assembly that conspired against me:
   here in the desert they shall die to the last man." ✛

Psalm 106:6-7ab, 13-14, 21-22, 23
R. (4a) Remember us, O Lord, as you favor your people.
We have sinned, we and our fathers;
   we have committed crimes; we have done wrong.
Our fathers in Egypt
   considered not your wonders. **R.**
But soon they forgot his works;
   they waited not for his counsel.
They gave way to craving in the desert
   and tempted God in the wilderness. **R.**
They forgot the God who had saved them,
   who had done great deeds in Egypt,
Wondrous deeds in the land of Ham,
   terrible things at the Red Sea. **R.**
Then he spoke of exterminating them,
   but Moses, his chosen one,
Withstood him in the breach
   to turn back his destructive wrath. **R.**

Luke 7:16
R. Alleluia, alleluia.
A great prophet has arisen in our midst
and God has visited his people. **R.**

† *Matthew 15:21-28*
O woman, great is your faith!

At that time Jesus withdrew to the region of Tyre and Sidon.
And behold, a Canaanite woman of that district came and called out,
   "Have pity on me, Lord, Son of David!
My daughter is tormented by a demon."
But he did not say a word in answer to her.
His disciples came and asked him,
   "Send her away, for she keeps calling out after us."
He said in reply,
   "I was sent only to the lost sheep of the house of Israel."
But the woman came and did him homage, saying, "Lord, help me."
He said in reply,
   "It is not right to take the food of the children
   and throw it to the dogs."
She said, "Please, Lord, for even the dogs eat the scraps
   that fall from the table of their masters."

Then Jesus said to her in reply,
"O woman, great is your faith!
Let it be done for you as you wish."
And her daughter was healed from that hour. ✛

THURSDAY, AUGUST 10
St. Lawrence

✛ *2 Corinthians 9:6-10*
God loves a cheerful giver.

Brothers and sisters:
Whoever sows sparingly will also reap sparingly,
   and whoever sows bountifully will also reap bountifully.
Each must do as already determined, without sadness or compulsion,
   for God loves a cheerful giver.
Moreover, God is able to make every grace abundant for you,
   so that in all things, always having all you need,
   you may have an abundance for every good work.
As it is written:

He scatters abroad, he gives to the poor;
   his righteousness endures forever.

The one who supplies seed to the sower and bread for food
   will supply and multiply your seed
   and increase the harvest of your righteousness. ✛

Psalm 112:1-2, 5-6, 7-8, 9
R. (5) **Blessed the man who is gracious and lends to those in
   need.**
Blessed the man who fears the LORD,
   who greatly delights in his commands.
His posterity shall be mighty upon the earth;
   the upright generation shall be blessed. **R.**
Well for the man who is gracious and lends,
   who conducts his affairs with justice;
He shall never be moved;
   the just one shall be in everlasting remembrance. **R.**
An evil report he shall not fear;
   his heart is firm, trusting in the LORD.
His heart is steadfast; he shall not fear
   till he looks down upon his foes. **R.**
Lavishly he gives to the poor,
   his generosity shall endure forever;
   his horn shall be exalted in glory. **R.**

John 8:12bc

R. Alleluia, alleluia.

Whoever follows me will not walk in darkness
but will have the light of life, says the Lord. **R.**

† *John 12:24-26*
The Father will honor whoever serves me.

Jesus said to his disciples:
"Amen, amen, I say to you,
    unless a grain of wheat falls to the ground and dies,
    it remains just a grain of wheat;
    but if it dies, it produces much fruit.
Whoever loves his life loses it,
    and whoever hates his life in this world
    will preserve it for eternal life.
Whoever serves me must follow me,
    and where I am, there also will my servant be.
The Father will honor whoever serves me." ✛

FRIDAY, AUGUST 11
St. Clare

† *Deuteronomy 4:32-40*
For love of your fathers the Lord chose their descendants.

Moses said to the people:
"Ask now of the days of old, before your time,
    ever since God created man upon the earth;
    ask from one end of the sky to the other:
    Did anything so great ever happen before?
Was it ever heard of?
Did a people ever hear the voice of God
    speaking from the midst of fire, as you did, and live?
Or did any god venture to go and take a nation for himself
    from the midst of another nation,
    by testings, by signs and wonders, by war,
    with his strong hand and outstretched arm, and by great terrors,
    all of which the LORD, your God,
    did for you in Egypt before your very eyes?
All this you were allowed to see
    that you might know the LORD is God and there is no other.
Out of the heavens he let you hear his voice to discipline you;
    on earth he let you see his great fire,
    and you heard him speaking out of the fire.
For love of your fathers he chose their descendants
    and personally led you out of Egypt by his great power,

driving out of your way nations greater and mightier than you,
so as to bring you in
and to make their land your heritage, as it is today.
This is why you must now know, and fix in your heart,
   that the LORD is God in the heavens above and on earth below,
   and that there is no other.
You must keep his statutes and commandments which I enjoin on
     you today,
   that you and your children after you may prosper,
   and that you may have long life on the land
   which the LORD, your God, is giving you forever." ✛

Psalm 77:12-13, 14-15, 16 and 21

R. (12a) **I remember the deeds of the Lord.**

I remember the deeds of the LORD;
   yes, I remember your wonders of old.
And I meditate on your works;
   your exploits I ponder. **R.**
O God, your way is holy;
   what great god is there like our God?
You are the God who works wonders;
   among the peoples you have made known your power. **R.**
With your strong arm you redeemed your people,
   the sons of Jacob and Joseph.
You led your people like a flock
   under the care of Moses and Aaron. **R.**

Matthew 5:10

R. Alleluia, alleluia.

Blessed are they who are persecuted for the sake of righteousness;
for theirs is the Kingdom of heaven. **R.**

† *Matthew 16:24-28*
What can one give in exchange for one's life?

Jesus said to his disciples,
   "Whoever wishes to come after me must deny himself,
   take up his cross, and follow me.
For whoever wishes to save his life will lose it,
   but whoever loses his life for my sake will find it.
What profit would there be for one to gain the whole world
   and forfeit his life?
Or what can one give in exchange for his life?
For the Son of Man will come with his angels in his Father's glory,
   and then he will repay each according to his conduct.
Amen, I say to you, there are some standing here

who will not taste death
until they see the Son of Man coming in his Kingdom." ✝

SATURDAY, AUGUST 12
WEEKDAY, ST. JANE FRANCES DE CHANTAL, *[BVM]*

✝ *Deuteronomy 6:4-13*
You shall love the LORD, your God, with all your heart.

Moses said to the people:
"Hear, O Israel! The LORD is our God, the LORD alone!
Therefore, you shall love the LORD, your God,
   with all your heart,
   and with all your soul,
   and with all your strength.
Take to heart these words which I enjoin on you today.
Drill them into your children.
Speak of them at home and abroad, whether you are busy or at rest.
Bind them at your wrist as a sign
   and let them be as a pendant on your forehead.
Write them on the doorposts of your houses and on your gates.

"When the LORD, your God, brings you into the land which he swore
   to your fathers: Abraham, Isaac and Jacob,
   that he would give you,
   a land with fine, large cities that you did not build,
   with houses full of goods of all sorts that you did not garner,
   with cisterns that you did not dig,
   with vineyards and olive groves that you did not plant;
   and when, therefore, you eat your fill,
   take care not to forget the LORD,
   who brought you out of the land of Egypt, that place of slavery.
The LORD, your God, shall you fear;
   him shall you serve, and by his name shall you swear." ✝

   Psalm 18:2-3a, 3bc-4, 47 and 51
R. (2) **I love you, Lord, my strength.**
I love you, O LORD, my strength,
   O LORD, my rock, my fortress, my deliverer. **R.**
My God, my rock of refuge,
   my shield, the horn of my salvation, my stronghold!
Praised be the LORD, I exclaim!
   And I am safe from my enemies. **R.**
The LORD live! And blessed be my Rock!
   Extolled be God my savior!
You who gave great victories to your king,

and showed kindness to your anointed,
to David and his posterity forever. **R.**

See 2 Timothy 1:10
R. Alleluia, alleluia.
Our Savior Jesus Christ has destroyed death
and brought life to light through the Gospel. **R.**

† *Matthew 17:14-20*
If you have faith, nothing will be impossible for you.

A man came up to Jesus, knelt down before him, and said,
"Lord, have pity on my son, who is a lunatic and suffers severely;
often he falls into fire, and often into water.
I brought him to your disciples, but they could not cure him."
Jesus said in reply,
"O faithless and perverse generation, how long will I be with you?
How long will I endure you?
Bring the boy here to me."
Jesus rebuked him and the demon came out of him,
and from that hour the boy was cured.
Then the disciples approached Jesus in private and said,
"Why could we not drive it out?"
He said to them, "Because of your little faith.
Amen, I say to you, if you have faith the size of a mustard seed,
you will say to this mountain,
'Move from here to there,' and it will move.
Nothing will be impossible for you." ✛

SUNDAY, AUGUST 13
NINETEENTH SUNDAY IN ORDINARY TIME

† *1 Kings 19:9a, 11-13a*
Go outside and stand on the mountain before the Lord.

At the mountain of God, Horeb,
Elijah came to a cave where he took shelter.
Then the LORD said to him,
"Go outside and stand on the mountain before the LORD;
the LORD will be passing by."
A strong and heavy wind was rending the mountains
and crushing rocks before the LORD—
but the LORD was not in the wind.
After the wind there was an earthquake—
but the LORD was not in the earthquake.
After the earthquake there was fire—
but the LORD was not in the fire.

After the fire there was a tiny whispering sound.
When he heard this,
    Elijah hid his face in his cloak
    and went and stood at the entrance of the cave. ✛

Psalm 85:9ab and 10, 11-12, 13-14

R. (8) **Lord, let us see your kindness, and grant us your salvation.**

I will hear what God proclaims;
    the LORD—for he proclaims peace.
Near indeed is his salvation to those who fear him,
    glory dwelling in our land. **R.**
Kindness and truth shall meet;
    justice and peace shall kiss.
Truth shall spring out of the earth,
    and justice shall look down from heaven. **R.**
The LORD himself will give his benefits;
    our land shall yield its increase.
Justice shall walk before him,
    and prepare the way of his steps. **R.**

✝ *Romans 9:1-5*
I could wish that I were accursed for the sake of my own people.

Brothers and sisters:
I speak the truth in Christ, I do not lie;
    my conscience joins with the Holy Spirit in bearing me witness
    that I have great sorrow and constant anguish in my heart.
For I could wish that I myself were accursed and cut off from Christ
    for the sake of my own people,
    my kindred according to the flesh.
They are Israelites;
    theirs the adoption, the glory, the covenants,
    the giving of the law, the worship, and the promises;
    theirs the patriarchs, and from them,
    according to the flesh, is the Christ,
    who is over all, God blessed forever. Amen. ✛

See Psalm 130:5

R. Alleluia, alleluia.
I wait for the Lord;
my soul waits for his word. **R.**

✝ *Matthew 14:22-33*
Command me to come to you on the water.

After he had fed the people, Jesus made the disciples get into a
    boat

and precede him to the other side,
while he dismissed the crowds.
After doing so, he went up on the mountain by himself to pray.
When it was evening he was there alone.
Meanwhile the boat, already a few miles offshore,
was being tossed about by the waves, for the wind was against it.
During the fourth watch of the night,
he came toward them walking on the sea.
When the disciples saw him walking on the sea they were terrified.
"It is a ghost," they said, and they cried out in fear.
At once Jesus spoke to them, "Take courage, it is I; do not be afraid."
Peter said to him in reply,
"Lord, if it is you, command me to come to you on the water."
He said, "Come."
Peter got out of the boat and began to walk on the water toward
Jesus.
But when he saw how strong the wind was he became frightened;
and, beginning to sink, he cried out, "Lord, save me!"
Immediately Jesus stretched out his hand and caught Peter,
and said to him, "O you of little faith, why did you doubt?"
After they got into the boat, the wind died down.
Those who were in the boat did him homage, saying,
"Truly, you are the Son of God." ✣

MONDAY, AUGUST 14
St. Maximilian Kolbe

† *Deuteronomy 10:12-22*
Circumcise your hearts. Befriend the alien,
for you were once aliens yourselves.

Moses said to the people:
"And now, Israel, what does the LORD, your God, ask of you
but to fear the LORD, your God, and follow his ways exactly,
to love and serve the LORD, your God,
with all your heart and all your soul,
to keep the commandments and statutes of the LORD
which I enjoin on you today for your own good?
Think! The heavens, even the highest heavens,
belong to the LORD, your God,
as well as the earth and everything on it.
Yet in his love for your fathers the LORD was so attached to them
as to choose you, their descendants,
in preference to all other peoples, as indeed he has now done.
Circumcise your hearts, therefore, and be no longer stiff-necked.
For the LORD, your God, is the God of gods,

the LORD of lords, the great God, mighty and awesome,
who has no favorites, accepts no bribes;
who executes justice for the orphan and the widow,
and befriends the alien, feeding and clothing him.
So you too must befriend the alien,
for you were once aliens yourselves in the land of Egypt.
The LORD, your God, shall you fear, and him shall you serve;
hold fast to him and swear by his name.
He is your glory, he, your God,
who has done for you those great and terrible things
which your own eyes have seen.
Your ancestors went down to Egypt seventy strong,
and now the LORD, your God,
has made you as numerous as the stars of the sky." ✢

Psalm 147:12-13, 14-15, 19-20
R. (12a) **Praise the Lord, Jerusalem.**
Glorify the LORD, O Jerusalem;
praise your God, O Zion.
For he has strengthened the bars of your gates;
he has blessed your children within you. **R.**
He has granted peace in your borders;
with the best of wheat he fills you.
He sends forth his command to the earth;
swiftly runs his word! **R.**
He has proclaimed his word to Jacob,
his statutes and his ordinances to Israel.
He has not done thus for any other nation;
his ordinances he has not made known to them. Alleluia. **R.**

See *2 Thessalonians 2:14*
R. Alleluia, alleluia.
God has called you through the Gospel
to possess the glory of our Lord Jesus Christ. **R.**

† *Matthew 17:22-27*
They will kill him and he will be raised.
The subjects are exempt from the tax.

As Jesus and his disciples were gathering in Galilee,
Jesus said to them,
"The Son of Man is to be handed over to men,
and they will kill him, and he will be raised on the third day."
And they were overwhelmed with grief.

When they came to Capernaum,
the collectors of the temple tax approached Peter and said,

"Does not your teacher pay the temple tax?"
"Yes," he said.
When he came into the house, before he had time to speak,
   Jesus asked him, "What is your opinion, Simon?
From whom do the kings of the earth take tolls or census tax?
From their subjects or from foreigners?"
When he said, "From foreigners," Jesus said to him,
   "Then the subjects are exempt.
But that we may not offend them, go to the sea, drop in a hook,
   and take the first fish that comes up.
Open its mouth and you will find a coin worth twice the temple tax.
Give that to them for me and for you." ✛

TUESDAY, AUGUST 15
THE ASSUMPTION OF THE BLESSED VIRGIN MARY
(Readings for the Vigil Mass are: 1 Chronicles 15:3-4, 15-16; 16:1-2 • Psalm 132:6-7,
9-10, 13-14 • 1 Corinthians 15:54b-57 • Luke 11:27-28 [621].)

† *Revelation 11:19a; 12:1-6a, 10ab*
A woman clothed with the sun, with the moon beneath her feet.

God's temple in heaven was opened,
   and the ark of his covenant could be seen in the temple.

A great sign appeared in the sky, a woman clothed with the sun,
   with the moon under her feet,
   and on her head a crown of twelve stars.
She was with child and wailed aloud in pain as she labored to give
     birth.
Then another sign appeared in the sky;
   it was a huge red dragon, with seven heads and ten horns,
   and on its heads were seven diadems.
Its tail swept away a third of the stars in the sky
   and hurled them down to the earth.
Then the dragon stood before the woman about to give birth,
   to devour her child when she gave birth.
She gave birth to a son, a male child,
   destined to rule all the nations with an iron rod.
Her child was caught up to God and his throne.
The woman herself fled into the desert
   where she had a place prepared by God.

Then I heard a loud voice in heaven say:
   "Now have salvation and power come,
     and the Kingdom of our God
     and the authority of his Anointed One." ✛

Psalm 45:10, 11, 12, 16

R. (10bc) **The queen stands at your right hand, arrayed in
    gold.**

The queen takes her place at your right hand in gold of Ophir. **R.**

Hear, O daughter, and see; turn your ear,
    forget your people and your father's house. **R.**

So shall the king desire your beauty;
    for he is your lord. **R.**

They are borne in with gladness and joy;
    they enter the palace of the king. **R.**

† *1 Corinthians 15:20-27*
Christ, the firstfruits; then those who belong to him.

Brothers and sisters:

Christ has been raised from the dead,
    the firstfruits of those who have fallen asleep.

For since death came through man,
    the resurrection of the dead came also through man.

For just as in Adam all die,
    so too in Christ shall all be brought to life,
    but each one in proper order:
    Christ the firstfruits;
    then, at his coming, those who belong to Christ;
    then comes the end,
    when he hands over the Kingdom to his God and Father,
    when he has destroyed every sovereignty
    and every authority and power.

For he must reign until he has put all his enemies under his feet.

The last enemy to be destroyed is death,
    for "he subjected everything under his feet." ✛

R. Alleluia, alleluia.

Mary is taken up to heaven;
a chorus of angels exults. **R.**

† *Luke 1:39-56*
*The Almighty has done great things for me;
he has raised up the lowly.*

Mary set out
    and traveled to the hill country in haste
    to a town of Judah,
    where she entered the house of Zechariah
    and greeted Elizabeth.

When Elizabeth heard Mary's greeting,
    the infant leaped in her womb,

and Elizabeth, filled with the Holy Spirit,
cried out in a loud voice and said,
"Blessed are you among women,
and blessed is the fruit of your womb.
And how does this happen to me,
that the mother of my Lord should come to me?
For at the moment the sound of your greeting reached my ears,
the infant in my womb leaped for joy.
Blessed are you who believed
that what was spoken to you by the Lord
would be fulfilled."

And Mary said:

"My soul proclaims the greatness of the Lord;
my spirit rejoices in God my Savior,
for he has looked with favor on his lowly servant.
From this day all generations will call me blessed:
the Almighty has done great things for me
and holy is his Name.
He has mercy on those who fear him
in every generation.
He has shown the strength of his arm,
and has scattered the proud in their conceit.
He has cast down the mighty from their thrones,
and has lifted up the lowly.
He has filled the hungry with good things,
and the rich he has sent away empty.
He has come to the help of his servant Israel,
for he has remembered his promise of mercy,
the promise he made to our fathers,
to Abraham and his children forever."

Mary remained with her about three months
and then returned to her home. ✛

WEDNESDAY, AUGUST 16
WEEKDAY, ST. STEPHEN OF HUNGARY

† *Deuteronomy 34:1-12*
*There Moses died as the LORD had said, and since then
no prophet has arisen in Israel like him.*

Moses went up from the plains of Moab to Mount Nebo,
the headland of Pisgah which faces Jericho,
and the LORD showed him all the land—
Gilead, and as far as Dan, all Naphtali,

the land of Ephraim and Manasseh,
all the land of Judah as far as the Western Sea,
the Negeb, the circuit of the Jordan
with the lowlands at Jericho, city of palms,
and as far as Zoar.
The LORD then said to him,
"This is the land
which I swore to Abraham, Isaac, and Jacob
that I would give to their descendants.
I have let you feast your eyes upon it, but you shall not cross over."
So there, in the land of Moab, Moses, the servant of the LORD,
died as the LORD had said; and he was buried in the ravine
opposite Beth-peor in the land of Moab,
but to this day no one knows the place of his burial.
Moses was one hundred and twenty years old when he died,
yet his eyes were undimmed and his vigor unabated.
For thirty days the children of Israel wept for Moses
in the plains of Moab, till they had completed
the period of grief and mourning for Moses.

Now Joshua, son of Nun, was filled with the spirit of wisdom,
since Moses had laid his hands upon him;
and so the children of Israel gave him their obedience,
thus carrying out the LORD's command to Moses.

Since then no prophet has arisen in Israel like Moses,
whom the LORD knew face to face.
He had no equal in all the signs and wonders
the LORD sent him to perform in the land of Egypt
against Pharaoh and all his servants and against all his land,
and for the might and the terrifying power
that Moses exhibited in the sight of all Israel. ✛

Psalm 66:1-3a, 5 and 8, 16-17
R. (see 20a and 10b) **Blessed be God who filled my soul with fire!**
Shout joyfully to God, all the earth;
sing praise to the glory of his name;
proclaim his glorious praise.
Say to God: "How tremendous are your deeds!" **R.**
Come and see the works of God,
his tremendous deeds among the children of Adam.
Bless our God, you peoples;
loudly sound his praise. **R.**
Hear now, all you who fear God, while I declare

what he has done for me.
When I appealed to him in words,
praise was on the tip of my tongue. **R.**

2 Corinthians 5:19
R. Alleluia, alleluia.
God was reconciling the world to himself in Christ,
and entrusting to us the message of reconciliation. **R.**

† *Matthew 18:15-20*
If your brother listens to you, you have won him over.

Jesus said to his disciples:
"If your brother sins against you,
go and tell him his fault between you and him alone.
If he listens to you, you have won over your brother.
If he does not listen,
take one or two others along with you,
so that every fact may be established
on the testimony of two or three witnesses.
If he refuses to listen to them, tell the Church.
If he refuses to listen even to the Church,
then treat him as you would a Gentile or a tax collector.
Amen, I say to you,
whatever you bind on earth shall be bound in heaven,
and whatever you loose on earth shall be loosed in heaven.
Again, amen, I say to you, if two of you agree on earth
about anything for which they are to pray,
it shall be granted to them by my heavenly Father.
For where two or three are gathered together in my name,
there am I in the midst of them." ✛

THURSDAY, AUGUST 17
WEEKDAY

† *Joshua 3:7-10a, 11, 13-17*
The ark of the covenant of the LORD will precede you into the Jordan.

The LORD said to Joshua,
"Today I will begin to exalt you in the sight of all Israel,
that they may know I am with you, as I was with Moses.
Now command the priests carrying the ark of the covenant
to come to a halt in the Jordan
when you reach the edge of the waters."

So Joshua said to the children of Israel,
"Come here and listen to the words of the LORD, your God.
This is how you will know that there is a living God in your midst,

who at your approach will dispossess the Canaanites.
The ark of the covenant of the LORD of the whole earth
  will precede you into the Jordan.
When the soles of the feet of the priests carrying the ark of the LORD,
  the Lord of the whole earth,
  touch the water of the Jordan, it will cease to flow;
  for the water flowing down from upstream will halt in a solid bank."

The people struck their tents to cross the Jordan,
  with the priests carrying the ark of the covenant ahead of them.
No sooner had these priestly bearers of the ark
  waded into the waters at the edge of the Jordan,
  which overflows all its banks
  during the entire season of the harvest,
  than the waters flowing from upstream halted,
  backing up in a solid mass for a very great distance indeed,
  from Adam, a city in the direction of Zarethan;
  while those flowing downstream toward the Salt Sea of the Arabah
  disappeared entirely.
Thus the people crossed over opposite Jericho.
While all Israel crossed over on dry ground,
  the priests carrying the ark of the covenant of the LORD
  remained motionless on dry ground in the bed of the Jordan
  until the whole nation had completed the passage. ✛

Psalm 114:1-2, 3-4, 5-6
R. Alleluia!
When Israel came forth from Egypt,
  the house of Jacob from a people of alien tongue,
Judah became his sanctuary,
  Israel his domain. **R.**
The sea beheld and fled;
  Jordan turned back.
The mountains skipped like rams,
  the hills like the lambs of the flock. **R.**
Why is it, O sea, that you flee?
  O Jordan, that you turn back?
You mountains, that you skip like rams?
  You hills, like the lambs of the flock? **R.**

Psalm 119:135
R. Alleluia, alleluia.
Let your countenance shine upon your servant
and teach me your statutes. **R.**

† *Matthew 18:21—19:1*

I say to you, not seven times but seventy-seven times.

Peter approached Jesus and asked him,
"Lord, if my brother sins against me,
how often must I forgive him?
As many as seven times?"
Jesus answered, "I say to you, not seven times but seventy-seven
times.
That is why the Kingdom of heaven may be likened to a king
who decided to settle accounts with his servants.
When he began the accounting,
a debtor was brought before him who owed him a huge amount.
Since he had no way of paying it back,
his master ordered him to be sold,
along with his wife, his children, and all his property,
in payment of the debt.
At that, the servant fell down, did him homage, and said,
'Be patient with me, and I will pay you back in full.'
Moved with compassion the master of that servant
let him go and forgave him the loan.
When that servant had left, he found one of his fellow servants
who owed him a much smaller amount.
He seized him and started to choke him, demanding,
'Pay back what you owe.'
Falling to his knees, his fellow servant begged him,
'Be patient with me, and I will pay you back.'
But he refused.
Instead, he had the fellow servant put in prison
until he paid back the debt.
Now when his fellow servants saw what had happened,
they were deeply disturbed,
and went to their master and reported the whole affair.
His master summoned him and said to him, 'You wicked servant!
I forgave you your entire debt because you begged me to.
Should you not have had pity on your fellow servant,
as I had pity on you?'
Then in anger his master handed him over to the torturers
until he should pay back the whole debt.
So will my heavenly Father do to you,
unless each of you forgives his brother from his heart."

When Jesus finished these words, he left Galilee
and went to the district of Judea across the Jordan. ✚

FRIDAY, AUGUST 18
WEEKDAY

† *Joshua 24:1-13*

I brought your father Abraham from the region beyond the River;
I led you out of Egypt, I brought you to your land.

Joshua gathered together all the tribes of Israel at Shechem,
   summoning their elders, their leaders,
   their judges and their officers.
When they stood in ranks before God, Joshua addressed all the
      people:
"Thus says the LORD, the God of Israel:
In times past your fathers, down to Terah,
   father of Abraham and Nahor,
   dwelt beyond the River and served other gods.
But I brought your father Abraham from the region beyond the
      River
   and led him through the entire land of Canaan.
I made his descendants numerous, and gave him Isaac.
To Isaac I gave Jacob and Esau.
To Esau I assigned the mountain region of Seir in which to settle,
   while Jacob and his children went down to Egypt.

"Then I sent Moses and Aaron, and smote Egypt with the prodigies
   which I wrought in her midst.
Afterward I led you out of Egypt, and when you reached the sea,
   the Egyptians pursued your fathers to the Red Sea
   with chariots and horsemen.
Because they cried out to the LORD,
   he put darkness between your people and the Egyptians,
   upon whom he brought the sea so that it engulfed them.
After you witnessed what I did to Egypt,
   and dwelt a long time in the desert,
   I brought you into the land of the Amorites
   who lived east of the Jordan.
They fought against you, but I delivered them into your power.
You took possession of their land, and I destroyed them,
   the two kings of the Amorites, before you.
Then Balak, son of Zippor, king of Moab,
   prepared to war against Israel.
He summoned Balaam, son of Beor, to curse you;
   but I would not listen to Balaam.
On the contrary, he had to bless you, and I saved you from him.
Once you crossed the Jordan and came to Jericho,
   the men of Jericho fought against you,

but I delivered them also into your power.
And I sent the hornets ahead of you that drove them
  (the Amorites, Perizzites, Canaanites,
  Hittites, Girgashites, Hivites and Jebusites)
  out of your way; it was not your sword or your bow.

"I gave you a land that you had not tilled
  and cities that you had not built, to dwell in;
  you have eaten of vineyards and olive groves
  which you did not plant." ✚

Psalm 136:1-3, 16-18, 21-22 and 24
R. His mercy endures forever.
Give thanks to the LORD, for he is good,
  for his mercy endures forever;
Give thanks to the God of gods,
  for his mercy endures forever;
Give thanks to the LORD of lords,
  for his mercy endures forever. **R.**
Who led his people through the wilderness,
  for his mercy endures forever;
Who smote great kings,
  for his mercy endures forever;
And slew powerful kings,
  for his mercy endures forever. **R.**
And made their land a heritage,
  for his mercy endures forever;
The heritage of Israel his servant,
  for his mercy endures forever;
And freed us from our foes,
  for his mercy endures forever. **R.**

See 1 Thessalonians 2:13
R. Alleluia, alleluia.
Receive the word of God, not as the word of men,
but, as it truly is, the word of God. **R.**

† *Matthew 19:3-12*
Because of the hardness of your hearts Moses allowed you to divorce your wives,
but from the beginning it was not so.

Some Pharisees approached Jesus, and tested him, saying,
  "Is it lawful for a man to divorce his wife for any cause whatever?"
He said in reply, "Have you not read that from the beginning
  the Creator *made them male and female* and said,
  For this reason a man shall leave his father and mother
  and be joined to his wife, and the two shall become one flesh?

So they are no longer two, but one flesh.
Therefore, what God has joined together, man must not separate."
They said to him, "Then why did Moses command
  that the man give the woman a bill of divorce and dismiss her?"
He said to them, "Because of the hardness of your hearts
  Moses allowed you to divorce your wives,
  but from the beginning it was not so.
I say to you, whoever divorces his wife
  (unless the marriage is unlawful)
  and marries another commits adultery."
His disciples said to him,
  "If that is the case of a man with his wife,
  it is better not to marry."
He answered, "Not all can accept this word,
  but only those to whom that is granted.
Some are incapable of marriage because they were born so;
  some, because they were made so by others;
  some, because they have renounced marriage
  for the sake of the Kingdom of heaven.
Whoever can accept this ought to accept it." ✢

SATURDAY, AUGUST 19
WEEKDAY, ST. JOHN EUDES, [BVM]

† Joshua 24:14-29
Decide today whom you will serve.

Joshua gathered together all the tribes of Israel at Shechem,
  and addressed them, saying:
  "Fear the LORD and serve him completely and sincerely.
Cast out the gods your fathers served beyond the River and in
    Egypt,
  and serve the LORD.
If it does not please you to serve the LORD,
  decide today whom you will serve,
  the gods your fathers served beyond the River
  or the gods of the Amorites in whose country you are dwelling.
As for me and my household, we will serve the LORD."

But the people answered, "Far be it from us to forsake the LORD
  for the service of other gods.
For it was the LORD, our God,
  who brought us and our fathers up out of the land of Egypt,
  out of a state of slavery.
He performed those great miracles before our very eyes

and protected us along our entire journey and among all the
    peoples
through whom we passed.
At our approach the Lord drove out all the peoples,
    including the Amorites who dwelt in the land.
Therefore we also will serve the Lord, for he is our God."

Joshua in turn said to the people,
    "You may not be able to serve the Lord, for he is a holy God;
    he is a jealous God who will not forgive
    your transgressions or your sins.
If, after the good he has done for you,
    you forsake the Lord and serve strange gods,
    he will do evil to you and destroy you."

But the people answered Joshua, "We will still serve the Lord."
Joshua therefore said to the people,
    "You are your own witnesses that you have chosen to serve the
        Lord."
They replied, "We are, indeed!"
Joshua continued:
    "Now, therefore, put away the strange gods that are among you
    and turn your hearts to the Lord, the God of Israel."
Then the people promised Joshua,
    "We will serve the Lord, our God, and obey his voice."

So Joshua made a covenant with the people that day
    and made statutes and ordinances for them at Shechem,
    which he recorded in the book of the law of God.
Then he took a large stone and set it up there under the oak
    that was in the sanctuary of the Lord.
And Joshua said to all the people, "This stone shall be our witness,
    for it has heard all the words which the Lord spoke to us.
It shall be a witness against you, should you wish to deny your
        God."
Then Joshua dismissed the people, each to his own heritage.

After these events, Joshua, son of Nun, servant of the Lord,
    died at the age of a hundred and ten. ✛

Psalm 16:1b-2a and 5, 7-8, 11
R. (see 5a) **You are my inheritance, O Lord.**
Keep me, O God, for in you I take refuge;
    I say to the Lord, "My Lord are you."
O Lord, my allotted portion and my cup,
    you it is who hold fast my lot. **R.**

I bless the LORD who counsels me;
  even in the night my heart exhorts me.
I set the LORD ever before me;
  with him at my right hand I shall not be disturbed. **R.**
You will show me the path to life,
  fullness of joys in your presence,
  the delights at your right hand forever. **R.**

See *Matthew 11:25*
R. Alleluia, alleluia.
Blessed are you, Father, Lord of heaven and earth;
you have revealed to little ones the mysteries of the Kingdom. **R.**

✝ *Matthew 19:13-15*
Let the children come to me, and do not prevent them;
for the Kingdom of heaven belongs to such as these.

Children were brought to Jesus
  that he might lay his hands on them and pray.
The disciples rebuked them, but Jesus said,
  "Let the children come to me, and do not prevent them;
  for the Kingdom of heaven belongs to such as these."
After he placed his hands on them, he went away. ✝

SUNDAY, AUGUST 20
TWENTIETH SUNDAY IN ORDINARY TIME

✝ *Isaiah 56:1, 6-7*
I will bring foreigners to my holy mountain.

Thus says the LORD:
Observe what is right, do what is just;
  for my salvation is about to come,
  my justice, about to be revealed.

The foreigners who join themselves to the LORD,
  ministering to him,
loving the name of the LORD,
  and becoming his servants—
all who keep the sabbath free from profanation
  and hold to my covenant,
them I will bring to my holy mountain
  and make joyful in my house of prayer;
their burnt offerings and sacrifices
  will be acceptable on my altar,
for my house shall be called
  a house of prayer for all peoples. ✝

Psalm 67:2-3, 5, 6 and 8
R. (4) **O God, let all the nations praise you!**
May God have pity on us and bless us;
   may he let his face shine upon us.
So may your way be known upon earth;
   among all nations, your salvation. **R.**
May the nations be glad and exult
   because you rule the peoples in equity;
   the nations on the earth you guide. **R.**
May the peoples praise you, O God;
   may all the peoples praise you!
May God bless us,
   and may all the ends of the earth fear him! **R.**

✝ *Romans 11:13-15, 29-32*
The gifts and the call of God for Israel are irrevocable.

Brothers and sisters:
I am speaking to you Gentiles.
Inasmuch as I am the apostle to the Gentiles,
   I glory in my ministry in order to make my race jealous
   and thus save some of them.
For if their rejection is the reconciliation of the world,
   what will their acceptance be but life from the dead?

For the gifts and the call of God are irrevocable.
Just as you once disobeyed God
   but have now received mercy because of their disobedience,
   so they have now disobeyed in order that,
   by virtue of the mercy shown to you,
   they too may now receive mercy.
For God delivered all to disobedience,
   that he might have mercy upon all. ✝

See Matthew 4:23
R. Alleluia, alleluia.
Jesus proclaimed the Gospel of the kingdom
and cured every disease among the people. **R.**

✝ *Matthew 15:21-28*
O woman, great is your faith!

At that time, Jesus withdrew to the region of Tyre and Sidon.
And behold, a Canaanite woman of that district came and called out,
   "Have pity on me, Lord, Son of David!
My daughter is tormented by a demon."
But Jesus did not say a word in answer to her.

Jesus' disciples came and asked him,
"Send her away, for she keeps calling out after us."
He said in reply,
"I was sent only to the lost sheep of the house of Israel."
But the woman came and did Jesus homage, saying, "Lord, help me."
He said in reply,
"It is not right to take the food of the children
and throw it to the dogs."
She said, "Please, Lord, for even the dogs eat the scraps
that fall from the table of their masters."
Then Jesus said to her in reply,
"O woman, great is your faith!
Let it be done for you as you wish."
And the woman's daughter was healed from that hour. ✢

MONDAY, AUGUST 21
St. Pope Pius X

† *Judges 2:11-19*
When the LORD raised up judges, they did not listen.

The children of Israel offended the LORD by serving the Baals.
Abandoning the LORD, the God of their fathers,
who led them out of the land of Egypt,
they followed the other gods of the various nations around them,
and by their worship of these gods provoked the LORD.

Because they had thus abandoned him and served Baal and the
Ashtaroth,
the anger of the LORD flared up against Israel,
and he delivered them over to plunderers who despoiled them.
He allowed them to fall into the power of their enemies round about
whom they were no longer able to withstand.
Whatever they undertook, the LORD turned into disaster for them,
as in his warning he had sworn he would do,
till they were in great distress.
Even when the LORD raised up judges to deliver them
from the power of their despoilers,
they did not listen to their judges,
but abandoned themselves to the worship of other gods.
They were quick to stray from the way their fathers had taken,
and did not follow their example of obedience
to the commandments of the LORD.
Whenever the LORD raised up judges for them, he would be with the
judge
and save them from the power of their enemies

as long as the judge lived;
   it was thus the LORD took pity on their distressful cries
   of affliction under their oppressors.
But when the judge died,
   they would relapse and do worse than their ancestors,
   following other gods in service and worship,
   relinquishing none of their evil practices or stubborn conduct. ✝

   Psalm 106:34-35, 36-37, 39-40, 43ab and 44
R. (4a) **Remember us, O Lord, as you favor your people.**
They did not exterminate the peoples,
   as the LORD had commanded them,
But mingled with the nations
   and learned their works. **R.**
They served their idols,
   which became a snare for them.
They sacrificed their sons
   and their daughters to demons. **R.**
They became defiled by their works,
   and wanton in their crimes.
And the LORD grew angry with his people,
   and abhorred his inheritance. **R.**
Many times did he rescue them,
   but they embittered him with their counsels.
Yet he had regard for their affliction
   when he heard their cry. **R.**

   Matthew 5:3
R. Alleluia, alleluia.
Blessed are the poor in spirit;
for theirs is the Kingdom of heaven. **R.**

† *Matthew 19:16-22*
*If you wish to be perfect, go, sell what you have
and you will have treasure in heaven.*

A young man approached Jesus and said,
   "Teacher, what good must I do to gain eternal life?"
He answered him, "Why do you ask me about the good?
There is only One who is good.
If you wish to enter into life, keep the commandments."
He asked him, "Which ones?"
And Jesus replied, *"You shall not kill;
   you shall not commit adultery;
   you shall not steal;
   you shall not bear false witness;
   honor your father and your mother;*

and *you shall love your neighbor as yourself."*
The young man said to him,
"All of these I have observed. What do I still lack?"
Jesus said to him, "If you wish to be perfect, go,
sell what you have and give to the poor,
and you will have treasure in heaven.
Then come, follow me."
When the young man heard this statement, he went away sad,
for he had many possessions. ✢

TUESDAY, AUGUST 22
THE QUEENSHIP OF THE BLESSED VIRGIN MARY

† *Judges 6:11-24a*
Go and save Israel; it is I who send you.

The angel of the LORD came and sat under the terebinth in Ophrah
that belonged to Joash the Abiezrite.
While his son Gideon was beating out wheat in the wine press
to save it from the Midianites,
the angel of the LORD appeared to him and said,
"The LORD is with you, O champion!"
Gideon said to him, "My Lord, if the LORD is with us,
why has all this happened to us?
Where are his wondrous deeds of which our fathers
told us when they said, 'Did not the LORD bring us up from Egypt?'
For now the LORD has abandoned us
and has delivered us into the power of Midian."
The LORD turned to him and said, "Go with the strength you have
and save Israel from the power of Midian.
It is I who send you."
But Gideon answered him, "Please, my lord, how can I save Israel?
My family is the lowliest in Manasseh,
and I am the most insignificant in my father's house."
"I shall be with you," the LORD said to him,
"and you will cut down Midian to the last man."
Gideon answered him, "If I find favor with you,
give me a sign that you are speaking with me.
Do not depart from here, I pray you, until I come back to you
and bring out my offering and set it before you."
He answered, "I will await your return."

So Gideon went off and prepared a kid and a measure of flour
in the form of unleavened cakes.
Putting the meat in a basket and the broth in a pot,
he brought them out to him under the terebinth

and presented them.
The angel of God said to him, "Take the meat and unleavened cakes
 and lay them on this rock; then pour out the broth."
When he had done so,
 the angel of the LORD stretched out the tip of the staff he held,
 and touched the meat and unleavened cakes.
Thereupon a fire came up from the rock
 that consumed the meat and unleavened cakes,
 and the angel of the LORD disappeared from sight.
Gideon, now aware that it had been the angel of the LORD,
 said, "Alas, Lord GOD,
 that I have seen the angel of the LORD face to face!"
The LORD answered him,
 "Be calm, do not fear. You shall not die."
So Gideon built there an altar to the LORD
 and called it Yahweh-shalom. ✛

 Psalm 85:9, 11-12, 13-14
R. (see 9b) **The Lord speaks of peace to his people.**
I will hear what God proclaims;
 the LORD—for he proclaims peace
To his people, and to his faithful ones,
 and to those who put in him their hope. **R.**
Kindness and truth shall meet;
 justice and peace shall kiss.
Truth shall spring out of the earth,
 and justice shall look down from heaven. **R.**
The LORD himself will give his benefits;
 our land shall yield its increase.
Justice shall walk before him,
 and salvation, along the way of his steps. **R.**

 2 Corinthians 8:9
R. Alleluia, alleluia.
Jesus Christ became poor although he was rich
so that by his poverty you might become rich. **R.**

† *Matthew 19:23-30*
*It is easier for a camel to pass through the eye of a needle than
for one who is rich to enter the Kingdom of God.*

Jesus said to his disciples:
"Amen, I say to you, it will be hard for one who is rich
 to enter the Kingdom of heaven.
Again I say to you,
 it is easier for a camel to pass through the eye of a needle
 than for one who is rich to enter the Kingdom of God."

When the disciples heard this, they were greatly astonished and said,
  "Who then can be saved?"
Jesus looked at them and said,
  "For men this is impossible,
  but for God all things are possible."
Then Peter said to him in reply,
  "We have given up everything and followed you.
What will there be for us?"
Jesus said to them, "Amen, I say to you
  that you who have followed me, in the new age,
  when the Son of Man is seated on his throne of glory,
  will yourselves sit on twelve thrones,
  judging the twelve tribes of Israel.
And everyone who has given up houses or brothers or sisters
  or father or mother or children or lands
  for the sake of my name will receive a hundred times more,
  and will inherit eternal life.
But many who are first will be last, and the last will be first." ✛

WEDNESDAY, AUGUST 23
WEEKDAY, ST. ROSE OF LIMA

† *Judges 9:6-15*
It is said: The king will reign over us,
when the LORD God reigns among you (1 Samuel 12:12).

All the citizens of Shechem and all Beth-millo came together
  and proceeded to make Abimelech king
  by the terebinth at the memorial pillar in Shechem.

When this was reported to him,
  Jotham went to the top of Mount Gerizim and, standing there,
  cried out to them in a loud voice:
  "Hear me, citizens of Shechem, that God may then hear you!
Once the trees went to anoint a king over themselves.
So they said to the olive tree, 'Reign over us.'
But the olive tree answered them, 'Must I give up my rich oil,
  whereby men and gods are honored,
  and go to wave over the trees?'
Then the trees said to the fig tree, 'Come; you reign over us!'
But the fig tree answered them,
  'Must I give up my sweetness and my good fruit,
  and go to wave over the trees?'
Then the trees said to the vine, 'Come you, and reign over us.'
But the vine answered them,
  'Must I give up my wine that cheers gods and men,

and go to wave over the trees?'
Then all the trees said to the buckthorn, 'Come; you reign over us!'
But the buckthorn replied to the trees,
   'If you wish to anoint me king over you in good faith,
   come and take refuge in my shadow.
Otherwise, let fire come from the buckthorn
   and devour the cedars of Lebanon.'" ✛

Psalm 21:2-3, 4-5, 6-7

R. (2a) **Lord, in your strength the king is glad.**

O LORD, in your strength the king is glad;
   in your victory how greatly he rejoices!
You have granted him his heart's desire;
   you refused not the wish of his lips. **R.**

For you welcomed him with goodly blessings,
   you placed on his head a crown of pure gold.
He asked life of you: you gave him
   length of days forever and ever. **R.**

Great is his glory in your victory;
   majesty and splendor you conferred upon him.
You made him a blessing forever,
   you gladdened him with the joy of your face. **R.**

Hebrews 4:12

R. Alleluia, alleluia.

The word of God is living and effective,
able to discern the reflections and thoughts of the heart. **R.**

† *Matthew 20:1-16*
Are you envious because I am generous?

Jesus told his disciples this parable:
"The Kingdom of heaven is like a landowner
   who went out at dawn to hire laborers for his vineyard.
After agreeing with them for the usual daily wage,
   he sent them into his vineyard.
Going out about nine o'clock,
   he saw others standing idle in the marketplace,
   and he said to them, 'You too go into my vineyard,
   and I will give you what is just.'
So they went off.
And he went out again around noon,
   and around three o'clock, and did likewise.
Going out about five o'clock,
   he found others standing around, and said to them,
   'Why do you stand here idle all day?'
They answered, 'Because no one has hired us.'

He said to them, 'You too go into my vineyard.'
When it was evening the owner of the vineyard said to his foreman,
  'Summon the laborers and give them their pay,
  beginning with the last and ending with the first.'
When those who had started about five o'clock came,
  each received the usual daily wage.
So when the first came, they thought that they would receive more,
  but each of them also got the usual wage.
And on receiving it they grumbled against the landowner, saying,
  'These last ones worked only one hour,
  and you have made them equal to us,
  who bore the day's burden and the heat.'
He said to one of them in reply,
  'My friend, I am not cheating you.
Did you not agree with me for the usual daily wage?
Take what is yours and go.
What if I wish to give this last one the same as you?
Or am I not free to do as I wish with my own money?
Are you envious because I am generous?'
Thus, the last will be first, and the first will be last." ✝

THURSDAY, AUGUST 24
St. Bartholomew

✝ *Revelation 21:9b-14*
On the foundation of the city were inscribed the names
of the twelve Apostles of the Lamb.

The angel spoke to me, saying,
  "Come here.
I will show you the bride, the wife of the Lamb."
He took me in spirit to a great, high mountain
  and showed me the holy city Jerusalem
  coming down out of heaven from God.
It gleamed with the splendor of God.
Its radiance was like that of a precious stone,
  like jasper, clear as crystal.
It had a massive, high wall,
  with twelve gates where twelve angels were stationed
  and on which names were inscribed,
  the names of the twelve tribes of the children of Israel.
There were three gates facing east,
  three north, three south, and three west.
The wall of the city had twelve courses of stones as its foundation,
  on which were inscribed the twelve names
  of the twelve Apostles of the Lamb. ✝

Psalm 145:10-11, 12-13, 17-18

R. (12) **Your friends make known, O Lord, the glorious splendor of your Kingdom.**

Let all your works give you thanks, O LORD,
    and let your faithful ones bless you.
Let them discourse of the glory of your Kingdom
    and speak of your might. **R.**

Making known to men your might
    and the glorious splendor of your Kingdom.
Your Kingdom is a Kingdom for all ages,
    and your dominion endures through all generations. **R.**

The LORD is just in all his ways
    and holy in all his works.
The LORD is near to all who call upon him,
    to all who call upon him in truth. **R.**

John 1:49b

R. Alleluia, alleluia.

Rabbi, you are the Son of God;
you are the King of Israel. **R.**

† *John 1:45-51*

Here is a true child of Israel. There is no duplicity in him.

Philip found Nathanael and told him,
    "We have found the one about whom Moses wrote in the law,
    and also the prophets, Jesus son of Joseph, from Nazareth."
But Nathanael said to him,
    "Can anything good come from Nazareth?"
Philip said to him, "Come and see."
Jesus saw Nathanael coming toward him and said of him,
    "Here is a true child of Israel.
There is no duplicity in him."
Nathanael said to him, "How do you know me?"
Jesus answered and said to him,
    "Before Philip called you, I saw you under the fig tree."
Nathanael answered him,
    "Rabbi, you are the Son of God; you are the King of Israel."
Jesus answered and said to him,
    "Do you believe
    because I told you that I saw you under the fig tree?
You will see greater things than this."
And he said to him, "Amen, amen, I say to you,
    you will see heaven opened and the angels of God
    ascending and descending on the Son of Man." ✛

FRIDAY, AUGUST 25
WEEKDAY, ST. LOUIS, ST. JOSEPH CALASANZ

† *Ruth 1:1, 3-6, 14b-16, 22*
Naomi returned with the Moabite daughter-in-law, Ruth, to Bethlehem.

Once in the time of the judges there was a famine in the land;
so a man from Bethlehem of Judah
departed with his wife and two sons
to reside on the plateau of Moab.
Elimelech, the husband of Naomi, died,
and she was left with her two sons, who married Moabite women,
one named Orpah, the other Ruth.
When they had lived there about ten years,
both Mahlon and Chilion died also,
and the woman was left with neither her two sons nor her husband.
She then made ready to go back from the plateau of Moab
because word reached her there
that the LORD had visited his people and given them food.

Orpah kissed her mother-in-law good-bye, but Ruth stayed with her.

Naomi said, "See now!
Your sister-in-law has gone back to her people and her god.
Go back after your sister-in-law!"
But Ruth said, "Do not ask me to abandon or forsake you!
For wherever you go, I will go, wherever you lodge I will lodge,
your people shall be my people, and your God my God."

Thus it was that Naomi returned
with the Moabite daughter-in-law, Ruth,
who accompanied her back from the plateau of Moab.
They arrived in Bethlehem at the beginning of the barley harvest. ✛

Psalm 146:5-6ab, 6c-7, 8-9a, 9bc-10

R. (1b) **Praise the Lord, my soul!**
Blessed is he whose help is the God of Jacob,
whose hope is in the LORD, his God,
Who made heaven and earth,
the sea and all that is in them. **R.**
The LORD keeps faith forever,
secures justice for the oppressed,
gives food to the hungry.
The LORD sets captives free. **R.**
The LORD gives sight to the blind.
The LORD raises up those who were bowed down;
The LORD loves the just.

The LORD protects strangers. **R.**
The fatherless and the widow he sustains,
   but the way of the wicked he thwarts.
The LORD shall reign forever;
   your God, O Zion, through all generations. Alleluia. **R.**

   Psalm 25:4b, 5a
R. Alleluia, alleluia.
Teach me your paths, my God,
guide me in your truth. **R.**

† *Matthew 22:34-40*
You shall love the Lord, your God, with all your heart
and your neighbor as yourself.

When the Pharisees heard that Jesus had silenced the Sadducees,
   they gathered together, and one of them,
   a scholar of the law, tested him by asking,
   "Teacher, which commandment in the law is the greatest?"
He said to him,
   "You shall love the Lord, your God, with all your heart,
   with all your soul, and with all your mind.
This is the greatest and the first commandment.
The second is like it:
   You shall love your neighbor as yourself.
The whole law and the prophets depend on these two command-
   ments." ✤

SATURDAY, AUGUST 26
WEEKDAY, *[BVM]*

† *Ruth 2:1-3, 8-11; 4:13-17*
The LORD has not failed to provide you today with an heir.
He was the father of Jesse, the father of David.

Naomi had a prominent kinsman named Boaz,
   of the clan of her husband Elimelech.
Ruth the Moabite said to Naomi,
   "Let me go and glean ears of grain in the field
   of anyone who will allow me that favor."
Naomi said to her, "Go, my daughter," and she went.
The field she entered to glean after the harvesters
   happened to be the section belonging to Boaz
   of the clan of Elimelech.

Boaz said to Ruth, "Listen, my daughter!
Do not go to glean in anyone else's field;
   you are not to leave here.

Stay here with my women servants.
Watch to see which field is to be harvested, and follow them;
   I have commanded the young men to do you no harm.
When you are thirsty, you may go and drink from the vessels
   the young men have filled."
Casting herself prostrate upon the ground, Ruth said to him,
   "Why should I, a foreigner, be favored with your notice?"
Boaz answered her:
   "I have had a complete account of what you have done
   for your mother-in-law after your husband's death;
   you have left your father and your mother and the land of your
     birth,
   and have come to a people whom you did not know previously."

Boaz took Ruth.
When they came together as man and wife,
   the LORD enabled her to conceive and she bore a son.
Then the women said to Naomi,
   "Blessed is the LORD who has not failed
   to provide you today with an heir!
May he become famous in Israel!
He will be your comfort and the support of your old age,
   for his mother is the daughter-in-law who loves you.
She is worth more to you than seven sons!"
Naomi took the child, placed him on her lap, and became his nurse.
And the neighbor women gave him his name,
   at the news that a grandson had been born to Naomi.
They called him Obed.
He was the father of Jesse, the father of David. ✝

   Psalm 128:1b-2, 3, 4, 5
R. (4) **See how the Lord blesses those who fear him.**
Blessed are you who fear the LORD,
   who walk in his ways!
For you shall eat the fruit of your handiwork;
   blessed shall you be, and favored. **R.**
Your wife shall be like a fruitful vine
   in the recesses of your home;
Your children like olive plants
   around your table. **R.**
Behold, thus is the man blessed
   who fears the LORD. **R.**
The LORD bless you from Zion:
   may you see the prosperity of Jerusalem
   all the days of your life. **R.**

Matthew 23:9b, 10b
R. Alleluia, alleluia.
You have but one Father in heaven;
you have but one master, the Christ. **R.**

† *Matthew 23:1-12*
They preach but they do not practice.

Jesus spoke to the crowds and to his disciples, saying,
"The scribes and the Pharisees
have taken their seat on the chair of Moses.
Therefore, do and observe all things whatsoever they tell you,
but do not follow their example.
For they preach but they do not practice.
They tie up heavy burdens hard to carry
and lay them on people's shoulders,
but they will not lift a finger to move them.
All their works are performed to be seen.
They widen their phylacteries and lengthen their tassels.
They love places of honor at banquets, seats of honor in synagogues,
greetings in marketplaces, and the salutation 'Rabbi.'
As for you, do not be called 'Rabbi.'
You have but one teacher, and you are all brothers.
Call no one on earth your father;
you have but one Father in heaven.
Do not be called 'Master';
you have but one master, the Christ.
The greatest among you must be your servant.
Whoever exalts himself will be humbled;
but whoever humbles himself will be exalted." ✛

SUNDAY, AUGUST 27
TWENTY-FIRST SUNDAY IN ORDINARY TIME

† *Isaiah 22:19-23*
I will place the key of the house of David upon his shoulder.

Thus says the LORD to Shebna, master of the palace:
"I will thrust you from your office
and pull you down from your station.
On that day I will summon my servant
Eliakim, son of Hilkiah;
I will clothe him with your robe,
and gird him with your sash,
and give over to him your authority.
He shall be a father to the inhabitants of Jerusalem,
and to the house of Judah.

I will place the key of the House of David on Eliakim's shoulder;
  when he opens, no one shall shut;
  when he shuts, no one shall open.
I will fix him like a peg in a sure spot,
  to be a place of honor for his family." ✝

Psalm 138:1-2a, 2bc and 3, 6 and 8bc
R. (8bc) Lord, your love is eternal; do not forsake the work of your hands.
I will give thanks to you, O LORD, with all my heart,
  for you have heard the words of my mouth;
in the presence of the angels I will sing your praise;
  I will worship at your holy temple. **R.**
I will give thanks to your name,
  because of your kindness and your truth:
when I called, you answered me;
  you built up strength within me. **R.**
The LORD is exalted, yet the lowly he sees,
  and the proud he knows from afar.
Your kindness, O LORD, endures forever;
  forsake not the work of your hands. **R.**

✝ Romans 11:33-36
From God and through him and for him are all things.

Oh, the depth of the riches and wisdom and knowledge of God!
How inscrutable are his judgments and how unsearchable his ways!
  For who has known the mind of the Lord
    or who has been his counselor?
  Or who has given the Lord anything
    that he may be repaid?
For from him and through him and for him are all things.
To him be glory forever. Amen. ✝

Matthew 16:18
R. Alleluia, alleluia.
You are Peter and upon this rock I will build my Church
and the gates of the netherworld shall not prevail against it. **R.**

✝ Matthew 16:13-20
You are Peter, and to you I will give the keys of the kingdom of heaven.

Jesus went into the region of Caesarea Philippi and
  he asked his disciples,
  "Who do people say that the Son of Man is?"
They replied, "Some say John the Baptist, others Elijah,
  still others Jeremiah or one of the prophets."
He said to them, "But who do you say that I am?"

Simon Peter said in reply,
  "You are the Christ, the Son of the living God."
Jesus said to him in reply,
  "Blessed are you, Simon son of Jonah.
For flesh and blood has not revealed this to you, but my heavenly
    Father.
And so I say to you, you are Peter,
  and upon this rock I will build my church,
  and the gates of the netherworld shall not prevail against it.
I will give you the keys to the kingdom of heaven.
Whatever you bind on earth shall be bound in heaven;
  and whatever you loose on earth shall be loosed in heaven."
Then he strictly ordered his disciples
  to tell no one that he was the Christ. ✛

MONDAY, AUGUST 28
St. Augustine

† 1 Thessalonians 1:1-5, 8b-10
You turned to God from idols to await his Son,
whom he raised from the dead.

Paul, Silvanus, and Timothy to the Church of the Thessalonians
  in God the Father and the Lord Jesus Christ:
  grace to you and peace.

We give thanks to God always for all of you,
  remembering you in our prayers,
  unceasingly calling to mind your work of faith and labor of love
  and endurance in hope of our Lord Jesus Christ,
  before our God and Father,
  knowing, brothers and sisters loved by God, how you were chosen.
For our Gospel did not come to you in word alone,
  but also in power and in the Holy Spirit and with much conviction.
You know what sort of people we were among you for your sake.
In every place your faith in God has gone forth,
  so that we have no need to say anything.
For they themselves openly declare about us
  what sort of reception we had among you,
  and how you turned to God from idols
  to serve the living and true God and to await his Son from heaven,
  whom he raised from the dead, Jesus,
  who delivers us from the coming wrath. ✛

Psalm 149:1b-2, 3-4, 5-6a and 9b
R. (see 4a) **The Lord takes delight in his people.** *(or* **Alleluia.***)*
Sing to the LORD a new song
   of praise in the assembly of the faithful.
Let Israel be glad in their maker,
   let the children of Zion rejoice in their king. **R.**
Let them praise his name in the festive dance,
   let them sing praise to him with timbrel and harp.
For the LORD loves his people,
   and he adorns the lowly with victory. **R.**
Let the faithful exult in glory;
   let them sing for joy upon their couches;
Let the high praises of God be in their throats.
   This is the glory of all his faithful. Alleluia! **R.**

John 10:27
R. Alleluia, alleluia.
My sheep hear my voice, says the Lord;
I know them, and they follow me. **R.**

† *Matthew 23:13-22*
Woe to you, blind guides.

Jesus said to the crowds and to his disciples:
"Woe to you, scribes and Pharisees, you hypocrites.
You lock the Kingdom of heaven before men.
You do not enter yourselves,
   nor do you allow entrance to those trying to enter.

"Woe to you, scribes and Pharisees, you hypocrites.
You traverse sea and land to make one convert,
   and when that happens you make him a child of Gehenna
   twice as much as yourselves.

"Woe to you, blind guides, who say,
   'If one swears by the temple, it means nothing,
   but if one swears by the gold of the temple, one is obligated.'
Blind fools, which is greater, the gold,
   or the temple that made the gold sacred?
And you say, 'If one swears by the altar, it means nothing,
   but if one swears by the gift on the altar, one is obligated.'
You blind ones, which is greater, the gift,
   or the altar that makes the gift sacred?
One who swears by the altar swears by it and all that is upon it;
   one who swears by the temple swears by it
   and by him who dwells in it;

one who swears by heaven swears by the throne of God
and by him who is seated on it." ✛

TUESDAY, AUGUST 29
THE PASSION OF ST. JOHN THE BAPTIST

† 1 Thessalonians 2:1-8
*We were determined to share with you not only the Gospel of God,
but our very selves as well.*

You yourselves know, brothers and sisters,
  that our reception among you was not without effect.
Rather, after we had suffered and been insolently treated,
  as you know, in Philippi,
  we drew courage through our God
  to speak to you the Gospel of God with much struggle.
Our exhortation was not from delusion or impure motives,
  nor did it work through deception.
But as we were judged worthy by God to be entrusted with the Gospel,
  that is how we speak,
  not as trying to please men,
  but rather God, who judges our hearts.
Nor, indeed, did we ever appear with flattering speech, as you know,
  or with a pretext for greed—God is witness—
  nor did we seek praise from men,
  either from you or from others,
  although we were able to impose our weight as Apostles of Christ.
Rather, we were gentle among you,
  as a nursing mother cares for her children.
With such affection for you, we were determined to share with you
  not only the Gospel of God, but our very selves as well,
  so dearly beloved had you become to us. ✛

Psalm 139:1-3, 4-6
R. (1) **You have searched me and you know me, Lord.**
O LORD, you have probed me and you know me;
  you know when I sit and when I stand;
  you understand my thoughts from afar.
My journeys and my rest you scrutinize,
  with all my ways you are familiar. **R.**
Even before a word is on my tongue,
  behold, O LORD, you know the whole of it.
Behind me and before, you hem me in
  and rest your hand upon me.
Such knowledge is too wonderful for me;
  too lofty for me to attain. **R.**

Matthew 5:10

R. Alleluia, alleluia.

Blessed are those who are persecuted for the sake of righteousness,
for theirs is the Kingdom of heaven. **R.**

† *Mark 6:17-29*

I want you to give me at once on a platter the head of John the Baptist.

Herod was the one who had John the Baptist arrested and bound
    in prison
  on account of Herodias,
    the wife of his brother Philip, whom he had married.
John had said to Herod,
    "It is not lawful for you to have your brother's wife."
Herodias harbored a grudge against him
    and wanted to kill him but was unable to do so.
Herod feared John, knowing him to be a righteous and holy man,
    and kept him in custody.
When he heard him speak he was very much perplexed,
    yet he liked to listen to him.
She had an opportunity one day when Herod, on his birthday,
    gave a banquet for his courtiers,
    his military officers, and the leading men of Galilee.
Herodias' own daughter came in
    and performed a dance that delighted Herod and his guests.
The king said to the girl,
    "Ask of me whatever you wish and I will grant it to you."
He even swore many things to her,
    "I will grant you whatever you ask of me,
    even to half of my kingdom."
She went out and said to her mother,
    "What shall I ask for?"
She replied, "The head of John the Baptist."
The girl hurried back to the king's presence and made her request,
    "I want you to give me at once
    on a platter the head of John the Baptist."
The king was deeply distressed,
    but because of his oaths and the guests
    he did not wish to break his word to her.
So he promptly dispatched an executioner with orders
    to bring back his head.
He went off and beheaded him in the prison.
He brought in the head on a platter and gave it to the girl.
The girl in turn gave it to her mother.

When his disciples heard about it,
they came and took his body and laid it in a tomb. ✣

WEDNESDAY, AUGUST 30
WEEKDAY

† 1 Thessalonians 2:9-13
Working night and day we proclaimed to you the Gospel of God.

You recall, brothers and sisters, our toil and drudgery.
Working night and day in order not to burden any of you,
we proclaimed to you the Gospel of God.
You are witnesses, and so is God,
how devoutly and justly and blamelessly
we behaved toward you believers.
As you know, we treated each one of you as a father treats his children,
exhorting and encouraging you and insisting
that you walk in a manner worthy of the God
who calls you into his Kingdom and glory.

And for this reason we too give thanks to God unceasingly,
that, in receiving the word of God from hearing us,
you received it not as the word of men, but as it truly is,
the word of God,
which is now at work in you who believe. ✣

Psalm 139:7-8, 9-10, 11-12ab
R. (1) You have searched me and you know me, Lord.
Where can I go from your spirit?
From your presence where can I flee?
If I go up to the heavens, you are there;
if I sink to the nether world, you are present there. **R.**
If I take the wings of the dawn,
if I settle at the farthest limits of the sea,
Even there your hand shall guide me,
and your right hand hold me fast. **R.**
If I say, "Surely the darkness shall hide me,
and night shall be my light"—
For you darkness itself is not dark,
and night shines as the day. **R.**

R. Alleluia, alleluia.
Whoever keeps the word of Christ,
the love of God is truly perfected in him. **R.**

† *Matthew 23:27-32*
You are the children of those who murdered the prophets.

Jesus said,
"Woe to you, scribes and Pharisees, you hypocrites.
You are like whitewashed tombs, which appear beautiful on the
    outside,
    but inside are full of dead men's bones and every kind of filth.
Even so, on the outside you appear righteous,
    but inside you are filled with hypocrisy and evildoing.

"Woe to you, scribes and Pharisees, you hypocrites.
You build the tombs of the prophets
    and adorn the memorials of the righteous,
    and you say, 'If we had lived in the days of our ancestors,
    we would not have joined them in shedding the prophets' blood.'
Thus you bear witness against yourselves
    that you are the children of those who murdered the prophets;
    now fill up what your ancestors measured out!" ✛

THURSDAY, AUGUST 31
WEEKDAY

† *1 Thessalonians 3:7-13*
May the Lord make you increase and abound
in love for one another and for all.

We have been reassured about you, brothers and sisters,
    in our every distress and affliction, through your faith.
For we now live, if you stand firm in the Lord.

What thanksgiving, then, can we render to God for you,
    for all the joy we feel on your account before our God?
Night and day we pray beyond measure to see you in person
    and to remedy the deficiencies of your faith.
Now may God himself, our Father, and our Lord Jesus
    direct our way to you, and may the Lord make you increase
    and abound in love for one another and for all,
    just as we have for you,
    so as to strengthen your hearts,
    to be blameless in holiness before our God and Father
    at the coming of our Lord Jesus with all his holy ones. Amen. ✛

Psalm 90:3-5a, 12-13, 14 and 17
R. (14) **Fill us with your love, O Lord, and we will sing for joy!**
You turn man back to dust,
    saying, "Return, O children of men."
For a thousand years in your sight

are as yesterday, now that it is past,
or as a watch of the night. **R.**
Teach us to number our days aright,
that we may gain wisdom of heart.
Return, O LORD! How long?
Have pity on your servants! **R.**
Fill us at daybreak with your kindness,
that we may shout for joy and gladness all our days.
And may the gracious care of the LORD our God be ours;
prosper the work of our hands for us!
Prosper the work of our hands! **R.**

Matthew 24:42a, 44
R. Alleluia, alleluia.
Stay awake!
For you do not know when the Son of Man will come. **R.**

† *Matthew 24:42-51*
Stay awake!

Jesus said to his disciples:
"Stay awake!
For you do not know on which day your Lord will come.
Be sure of this: if the master of the house
had known the hour of night when the thief was coming,
he would have stayed awake
and not let his house be broken into.
So too, you also must be prepared,
for at an hour you do not expect, the Son of Man will come.

"Who, then, is the faithful and prudent servant,
whom the master has put in charge of his household
to distribute to them their food at the proper time?
Blessed is that servant whom his master on his arrival finds doing so.
Amen, I say to you, he will put him in charge of all his property.
But if that wicked servant says to himself, 'My master is long delayed,'
and begins to beat his fellow servants,
and eat and drink with drunkards,
the servant's master will come on an unexpected day
and at an unknown hour and will punish him severely
and assign him a place with the hypocrites,
where there will be wailing and grinding of teeth." ✝

FRIDAY, SEPTEMBER 1
WEEKDAY

† *1 Thessalonians 4:1-8*
This is the will of God, your holiness.

Brothers and sisters,
  we earnestly ask and exhort you in the Lord Jesus that,
  as you received from us
  how you should conduct yourselves to please God—
  and as you are conducting yourselves—
  you do so even more.
For you know what instructions we gave you through the Lord Jesus.

This is the will of God, your holiness:
  that you refrain from immorality,
  that each of you know how to acquire a wife for himself
  in holiness and honor, not in lustful passion
  as do the Gentiles who do not know God;
  not to take advantage of or exploit a brother or sister in this matter,
  for the Lord is an avenger in all these things,
  as we told you before and solemnly affirmed.
For God did not call us to impurity but to holiness.
Therefore, whoever disregards this,
  disregards not a human being but God,
  who also gives his Holy Spirit to you. †

Psalm 97:1 and 2b, 5-6, 10, 11-12
R. (12a) Rejoice in the Lord, you just!
The LORD is king; let the earth rejoice;
  let the many isles be glad.
  Justice and judgment are the foundation of his throne. **R.**
The mountains melt like wax before the LORD,
  before the LORD of all the earth.
The heavens proclaim his justice,
  and all peoples see his glory. **R.**
The LORD loves those who hate evil;
  he guards the lives of his faithful ones;
  from the hand of the wicked he delivers them. **R.**
Light dawns for the just;
  and gladness, for the upright of heart.
Be glad in the LORD, you just,
  and give thanks to his holy name. **R.**

Luke 21:36

R. Alleluia, alleluia.

Be vigilant at all times and pray,
that you may have the strength to stand before the Son of Man. **R.**

† *Matthew 25:1-13*

Behold, the bridegroom! Come out to meet him!

Jesus told his disciples this parable:
"The Kingdom of heaven will be like ten virgins
  who took their lamps and went out to meet the bridegroom.
Five of them were foolish and five were wise.
The foolish ones, when taking their lamps,
  brought no oil with them,
  but the wise brought flasks of oil with their lamps.
Since the bridegroom was long delayed,
  they all became drowsy and fell asleep.
At midnight, there was a cry,
  'Behold, the bridegroom! Come out to meet him!'
Then all those virgins got up and trimmed their lamps.
The foolish ones said to the wise,
  'Give us some of your oil,
  for our lamps are going out.'
But the wise ones replied,
  'No, for there may not be enough for us and you.
Go instead to the merchants and buy some for yourselves.'
While they went off to buy it,
  the bridegroom came
  and those who were ready went into the wedding feast with him.
Then the door was locked.
Afterwards the other virgins came and said,
  'Lord, Lord, open the door for us!'
But he said in reply,
  'Amen, I say to you, I do not know you.'
Therefore, stay awake,
  for you know neither the day nor the hour." ✦

Time to Order
Reading God's Word 2024.

Available September 2023.

An order form is available on the last page of this book.

SATURDAY, SEPTEMBER 2
WEEKDAY, *[BVM]*

† *1 Thessalonians 4:9-11*
You have been taught by God to love one another.

Brothers and sisters:
On the subject of fraternal charity
　you have no need for anyone to write you,
　for you yourselves have been taught by God to love one another.
Indeed, you do this for all the brothers throughout Macedonia.
Nevertheless we urge you, brothers and sisters, to progress even
　　more,
　and to aspire to live a tranquil life,
　to mind your own affairs,
　and to work with your own hands,
　as we instructed you. ✛

Psalm 98:1bcde, 7-8, 9

R. (9) **The Lord comes to rule the earth with justice.**
Sing to the LORD a new song,
　for he has done wondrous deeds;
His right hand has won victory for him,
　his holy arm. **R.**
Let the sea and what fills it resound,
　the world and those who dwell in it;
Let the rivers clap their hands,
　the mountains shout with them for joy. **R.**
Before the LORD, for he comes,
　for he comes to rule the earth;
He will rule the world with justice
　and the peoples with equity. **R.**

John 13:34

R. Alleluia, alleluia.
I give you a new commandment:
love one another as I have loved you. **R.**

† *Matthew 25:14-30*
Since you have been faithful in small matters, come, share your master's joy.

Jesus told his disciples this parable:
"A man going on a journey
　called in his servants and entrusted his possessions to them.
To one he gave five talents; to another, two; to a third, one—
　to each according to his ability.
Then he went away.

Immediately the one who received five talents went and traded with
    them,
  and made another five.
Likewise, the one who received two made another two.
But the man who received one went off and dug a hole in the ground
  and buried his master's money.
After a long time
  the master of those servants came back and settled accounts with
    them.
The one who had received five talents
  came forward bringing the additional five.
He said, 'Master, you gave me five talents.
See, I have made five more.'
His master said to him, 'Well done, my good and faithful servant.
Since you were faithful in small matters,
  I will give you great responsibilities.
Come, share your master's joy.'
Then the one who had received two talents also came forward and
    said,
  'Master, you gave me two talents.
See, I have made two more.'
His master said to him, 'Well done, my good and faithful servant.
Since you were faithful in small matters,
  I will give you great responsibilities.
Come, share your master's joy.'
Then the one who had received the one talent came forward and said,
  'Master, I knew you were a demanding person,
  harvesting where you did not plant
  and gathering where you did not scatter;
  so out of fear I went off and buried your talent in the ground.
Here it is back.'
His master said to him in reply, 'You wicked, lazy servant!
So you knew that I harvest where I did not plant
  and gather where I did not scatter?
Should you not then have put my money in the bank
  so that I could have got it back with interest on my return?
Now then! Take the talent from him and give it to the one with ten.
For to everyone who has,
  more will be given and he will grow rich;
  but from the one who has not,
  even what he has will be taken away.
And throw this useless servant into the darkness outside,
  where there will be wailing and grinding of teeth.'" ✛

SUNDAY, SEPTEMBER 3
TWENTY-SECOND SUNDAY IN ORDINARY TIME

† *Jeremiah 20:7-9*
The word of the LORD has brought me derision.

You duped me, O LORD, and I let myself be duped;
　　you were too strong for me, and you triumphed.
All the day I am an object of laughter;
　　everyone mocks me.

Whenever I speak, I must cry out,
　　violence and outrage is my message;
the word of the LORD has brought me
　　derision and reproach all the day.

I say to myself, I will not mention him,
　　I will speak in his name no more.
But then it becomes like fire burning in my heart,
　　imprisoned in my bones;
I grow weary holding it in, I cannot endure it. ✛

Psalm 63:2, 3-4, 5-6, 8-9

R. (2b) My soul is thirsting for you, O Lord my God.
O God, you are my God whom I seek;
　　for you my flesh pines and my soul thirsts
　　like the earth, parched, lifeless and without water. **R.**
Thus have I gazed toward you in the sanctuary
　　to see your power and your glory,
for your kindness is a greater good than life;
　　my lips shall glorify you. **R.**
Thus will I bless you while I live;
　　lifting up my hands, I will call upon your name.
As with the riches of a banquet shall my soul be satisfied,
　　and with exultant lips my mouth shall praise you. **R.**
You are my help,
　　and in the shadow of your wings I shout for joy.
My soul clings fast to you;
　　your right hand upholds me. **R.**

† *Romans 12:1-2*
Offer your bodies as a living sacrifice.

I urge you, brothers and sisters, by the mercies of God,
　　to offer your bodies as a living sacrifice,
　　holy and pleasing to God, your spiritual worship.
Do not conform yourselves to this age
　　but be transformed by the renewal of your mind,

that you may discern what is the will of God,
what is good and pleasing and perfect. ✛

See Ephesians 1:17-18
R. Alleluia, alleluia.
May the Father of our Lord Jesus Christ
enlighten the eyes of our hearts,
that we may know what is the hope
that belongs to our call. **R.**

† *Matthew 16:21-27*
Whoever wishes to come after me must deny himself.

Jesus began to show his disciples
that he must go to Jerusalem and suffer greatly
from the elders, the chief priests, and the scribes,
and be killed and on the third day be raised.
Then Peter took Jesus aside and began to rebuke him,
"God forbid, Lord! No such thing shall ever happen to you."
He turned and said to Peter,
"Get behind me, Satan! You are an obstacle to me.
You are thinking not as God does, but as human beings do."

Then Jesus said to his disciples,
"Whoever wishes to come after me must deny himself,
take up his cross, and follow me.
For whoever wishes to save his life will lose it,
but whoever loses his life for my sake will find it.
What profit would there be for one to gain the whole world
and forfeit his life?
Or what can one give in exchange for his life?
For the Son of Man will come with his angels in his Father's glory,
and then he will repay all according to his conduct." ✛

MONDAY, SEPTEMBER 4
WEEKDAY

† *1 Thessalonians 4:13-18*
God, through Jesus, will bring with him those who have fallen asleep.

We do not want you to be unaware, brothers and sisters,
about those who have fallen asleep,
so that you may not grieve like the rest, who have no hope.
For if we believe that Jesus died and rose,
so too will God, through Jesus,
bring with him those who have fallen asleep.
Indeed, we tell you this, on the word of the Lord,
that we who are alive, who are left until the coming of the Lord,

will surely not precede those who have fallen asleep.

For the Lord himself, with a word of command,
    with the voice of an archangel and with the trumpet of God,
    will come down from heaven,
    and the dead in Christ will rise first.
Then we who are alive, who are left,
    will be caught up together with them in the clouds
    to meet the Lord in the air.
Thus we shall always be with the Lord.
Therefore, console one another with these words. ✝

Psalm 96:1 and 3, 4-5, 11-12, 13

R. (13b) The Lord comes to judge the earth.

Sing to the LORD a new song;
    sing to the LORD, all you lands.
Tell his glory among the nations;
    among all peoples, his wondrous deeds. **R.**
For great is the LORD and highly to be praised;
    awesome is he, beyond all gods.
For all the gods of the nations are things of nought,
    but the LORD made the heavens. **R.**
Let the heavens be glad and the earth rejoice;
    let the sea and what fills it resound;
    let the plains be joyful and all that is in them!
Then shall all the trees of the forest exult. **R.**
Before the LORD, for he comes;
    for he comes to rule the earth.
He shall rule the world with justice
    and the peoples with his constancy. **R.**

See Luke 4:18

R. Alleluia, alleluia.

The Spirit of the Lord is upon me;
he has sent me to bring glad tidings to the poor. **R.**

✝ *Luke 4:16-30*

He has sent me to bring glad tidings to the poor.
No prophet is accepted in his own native place.

Jesus came to Nazareth, where he had grown up,
    and went according to his custom
    into the synagogue on the sabbath day.
He stood up to read and was handed a scroll of the prophet Isaiah.
He unrolled the scroll and found the passage where it was written:

> *The Spirit of the Lord is upon me,*
> *because he has anointed me*

to bring glad tidings to the poor.
He has sent me to proclaim liberty to captives
and recovery of sight to the blind,
to let the oppressed go free,
and to proclaim a year acceptable to the Lord.

Rolling up the scroll,
he handed it back to the attendant and sat down,
and the eyes of all in the synagogue looked intently at him.
He said to them,
"Today this Scripture passage is fulfilled in your hearing."
And all spoke highly of him
and were amazed at the gracious words that came from his mouth.
They also asked, "Is this not the son of Joseph?"
He said to them, "Surely you will quote me this proverb,
'Physician, cure yourself,' and say, 'Do here in your native place
the things that we heard were done in Capernaum.'"
And he said,
"Amen, I say to you, no prophet is accepted in his own native
place.
Indeed, I tell you,
there were many widows in Israel in the days of Elijah
when the sky was closed for three and a half years
and a severe famine spread over the entire land.
It was to none of these that Elijah was sent,
but only to a widow in Zarephath in the land of Sidon.
Again, there were many lepers in Israel
during the time of Elisha the prophet;
yet not one of them was cleansed, but only Naaman the Syrian."
When the people in the synagogue heard this,
they were all filled with fury.
They rose up, drove him out of the town,
and led him to the brow of the hill
on which their town had been built, to hurl him down headlong.
But he passed through the midst of them and went away. ✛

TUESDAY, SEPTEMBER 5
WEEKDAY

† *1 Thessalonians 5:1-6, 9-11*
Jesus Christ died for us so that we may live together with him.

Concerning times and seasons, brothers and sisters,
you have no need for anything to be written to you.
For you yourselves know very well
that the day of the Lord will come like a thief at night.

When people are saying, "Peace and security,"
   then sudden disaster comes upon them,
   like labor pains upon a pregnant woman,
   and they will not escape.

But you, brothers and sisters, are not in darkness,
   for that day to overtake you like a thief.
For all of you are children of the light
   and children of the day.
We are not of the night or of darkness.
Therefore, let us not sleep as the rest do,
   but let us stay alert and sober.
For God did not destine us for wrath,
   but to gain salvation through our Lord Jesus Christ,
   who died for us, so that whether we are awake or asleep
   we may live together with him.
Therefore, encourage one another and build one another up,
   as indeed you do. ✛

Psalm 27:1, 4, 13-14

R. (13) I believe that I shall see the good things of the Lord in the land of the living.

The LORD is my light and my salvation;
   whom should I fear?
The LORD is my life's refuge;
   of whom should I be afraid? **R.**
One thing I ask of the LORD;
   this I seek:
To dwell in the house of the LORD
   all the days of my life,
That I may gaze on the loveliness of the LORD
   and contemplate his temple. **R.**
I believe that I shall see the bounty of the LORD
   in the land of the living.
Wait for the LORD with courage;
   be stouthearted, and wait for the LORD. **R.**

Luke 7:16

R. Alleluia, alleluia.

A great prophet has arisen in our midst
and God has visited his people. **R.**

✝ *Luke 4:31-37*
I know who you are—the Holy One of God!

Jesus went down to Capernaum, a town of Galilee.
He taught them on the sabbath,

and they were astonished at his teaching
because he spoke with authority.
In the synagogue there was a man with the spirit of an unclean
        demon,
    and he cried out in a loud voice,
    "What have you to do with us, Jesus of Nazareth?
Have you come to destroy us?
I know who you are–the Holy One of God!"
Jesus rebuked him and said, "Be quiet! Come out of him!"
Then the demon threw the man down in front of them
    and came out of him without doing him any harm.
They were all amazed and said to one another,
    "What is there about his word?
For with authority and power he commands the unclean spirits,
    and they come out."
And news of him spread everywhere in the surrounding region. ✢

WEDNESDAY, SEPTEMBER 6
WEEKDAY

† *Colossians 1:1-8*
The Gospel has come to you just as in the whole world.

Paul, an Apostle of Christ Jesus by the will of God,
    and Timothy our brother,
    to the holy ones and faithful brothers and sisters in Christ in
        Colossae:
    grace to you and peace from God our Father.

We always give thanks to God, the Father of our Lord Jesus Christ,
    when we pray for you,
    for we have heard of your faith in Christ Jesus
    and the love that you have for all the holy ones
    because of the hope reserved for you in heaven.
Of this you have already heard
    through the word of truth, the Gospel, that has come to you.
Just as in the whole world it is bearing fruit and growing,
    so also among you,
    from the day you heard it and came to know the grace of God in
        truth,
    as you learned it from Epaphras our beloved fellow slave,
    who is a trustworthy minister of Christ on your behalf
    and who also told us of your love in the Spirit. ✢

Psalm 52:10, 11
R. (10) **I trust in the mercy of God for ever.**
I, like a green olive tree

in the house of God,
Trust in the mercy of God
　forever and ever. **R.**
I will thank you always for what you have done,
　and proclaim the goodness of your name
　before your faithful ones. **R.**

　Luke 4:18
R. Alleluia, alleluia.
The Lord sent me to bring glad tidings to the poor
and to proclaim liberty to captives. **R.**

† *Luke 4:38-44*

*To the other towns also I must proclaim the Good News of the Kingdom of God,
because for this purpose I have been sent.*

After Jesus left the synagogue, he entered the house of Simon.
Simon's mother-in-law was afflicted with a severe fever,
　and they interceded with him about her.
He stood over her, rebuked the fever, and it left her.
She got up immediately and waited on them.

At sunset, all who had people sick with various diseases
　brought them to him.
He laid his hands on each of them and cured them.
And demons also came out from many, shouting, "You are the Son of
　God."
But he rebuked them and did not allow them to speak
　because they knew that he was the Christ.

At daybreak, Jesus left and went to a deserted place.
The crowds went looking for him, and when they came to him,
　they tried to prevent him from leaving them.
But he said to them, "To the other towns also
　I must proclaim the good news of the Kingdom of God,
　because for this purpose I have been sent."
And he was preaching in the synagogues of Judea. ✛

THURSDAY, SEPTEMBER 7
WEEKDAY

† *Colossians 1:9-14*

*God delivered us from the power of darkness and transferred
us to the Kingdom of his beloved Son.*

Brothers and sisters:
From the day we heard about you, we do not cease praying for you
　and asking that you may be filled with the knowledge of God's will
　through all spiritual wisdom and understanding

to walk in a manner worthy of the Lord,
so as to be fully pleasing, in every good work bearing fruit
and growing in the knowledge of God,
strengthened with every power, in accord with his glorious might,
for all endurance and patience,
with joy giving thanks to the Father, who has made you fit to
    share
in the inheritance of the holy ones in light.
He delivered us from the power of darkness
and transferred us to the Kingdom of his beloved Son,
in whom we have redemption, the forgiveness of sins. ✛

Psalm 98:2-3ab, 3cd-4, 5-6

R. (2) **The Lord has made known his salvation.**

The LORD has made his salvation known:
    in the sight of the nations he has revealed his justice.
He has remembered his kindness and his faithfulness
    toward the house of Israel. **R.**
All the ends of the earth have seen
    the salvation by our God.
Sing joyfully to the LORD, all you lands;
    break into song; sing praise. **R.**
Sing praise to the LORD with the harp,
    with the harp and melodious song.
With trumpets and the sound of the horn
    sing joyfully before the King, the LORD. **R.**

Matthew 4:19

R. Alleluia, alleluia.

Come after me, says the Lord,
and I will make you fishers of men. **R.**

† *Luke 5:1-11*

They left everything and followed Jesus.

While the crowd was pressing in on Jesus and listening to the
    word of God,
    he was standing by the Lake of Gennesaret.
He saw two boats there alongside the lake;
    the fishermen had disembarked and were washing their nets.
Getting into one of the boats, the one belonging to Simon,
    he asked him to put out a short distance from the shore.
Then he sat down and taught the crowds from the boat.
After he had finished speaking, he said to Simon,
    "Put out into deep water and lower your nets for a catch."
Simon said in reply,
    "Master, we have worked hard all night and have caught nothing,

but at your command I will lower the nets."
When they had done this, they caught a great number of fish
   and their nets were tearing.
They signaled to their partners in the other boat
   to come to help them.
They came and filled both boats
   so that the boats were in danger of sinking.
When Simon Peter saw this, he fell at the knees of Jesus and said,
   "Depart from me, Lord, for I am a sinful man."
For astonishment at the catch of fish they had made seized him
   and all those with him,
   and likewise James and John, the sons of Zebedee,
   who were partners of Simon.
Jesus said to Simon, "Do not be afraid;
   from now on you will be catching men."
When they brought their boats to the shore,
   they left everything and followed him. ✛

FRIDAY, SEPTEMBER 8
THE NATIVITY OF THE BLESSED VIRGIN MARY

✛ Micah 5:1-4a (or Romans 8:28-30)
The time when she who is to give birth has borne.

The LORD says:
   You, Bethlehem-Ephrathah,
      too small to be among the clans of Judah,
   From you shall come forth for me
      one who is to be ruler in Israel;
   Whose origin is from of old,
      from ancient times.
   (Therefore the Lord will give them up, until the time
      when she who is to give birth has borne,
   And the rest of his brethren shall return
      to the children of Israel.)
   He shall stand firm and shepherd his flock
      by the strength of the LORD,
      in the majestic name of the LORD, his God;
   And they shall remain, for now his greatness
      shall reach to the ends of the earth;
      he shall be peace. ✛

Psalm 13:6ab, 6c
R. (Isaiah 61:10) **With delight I rejoice in the Lord.**
Though I trusted in your mercy,
   let my heart rejoice in your salvation. **R.**

Let me sing of the LORD, "He has been good to me." **R.**

R. Alleluia, alleluia.
Blessed are you, holy Virgin Mary, deserving of all praise;
from you rose the sun of justice, Christ our God. **R.**

✝Matthew 1:1-16, 18-23 (or Matthew 1:18-23)
For it is through the Holy Spirit that this child has been conceived in her.

The Book of the genealogy of Jesus Christ,
  the son of David, the son of Abraham.

Abraham became the father of Isaac,
  Isaac the father of Jacob,
  Jacob the father of Judah and his brothers.
Judah became the father of Perez and Zerah,
  whose mother was Tamar.
Perez became the father of Hezron,
  Hezron the father of Ram,
  Ram the father of Amminadab.
Amminadab became the father of Nahshon,
  Nahshon the father of Salmon,
  Salmon the father of Boaz,
  whose mother was Rahab.
Boaz became the father of Obed,
  whose mother was Ruth.
Obed became the father of Jesse,
  Jesse the father of David the king.

David became the father of Solomon,
  whose mother had been the wife of Uriah.
Solomon became the father of Rehoboam,
  Rehoboam the father of Abijah,
  Abijah the father of Asaph.
Asaph became the father of Jehoshaphat,
  Jehoshaphat the father of Joram,
  Joram the father of Uzziah.
Uzziah became the father of Jotham,
  Jotham the father of Ahaz,
  Ahaz the father of Hezekiah.
Hezekiah became the father of Manasseh,
  Manasseh the father of Amos,
  Amos the father of Josiah.
Josiah became the father of Jechoniah and his brothers
  at the time of the Babylonian exile.

After the Babylonian exile,

Jechoniah became the father of Shealtiel,
   Shealtiel the father of Zerubbabel,
   Zerubbabel the father of Abiud.
Abiud became the father of Eliakim,
   Eliakim the father of Azor,
   Azor the father of Zadok.
Zadok became the father of Achim,
   Achim the father of Eliud,
   Eliud the father of Eleazar.
Eleazar became the father of Matthan,
   Matthan the father of Jacob,
   Jacob the father of Joseph, the husband of Mary.
Of her was born Jesus who is called the Christ.

Now this is how the birth of Jesus Christ came about.
When his mother Mary was betrothed to Joseph,
   but before they lived together,
   she was found with child through the Holy Spirit.
Joseph her husband, since he was a righteous man,
   yet unwilling to expose her to shame,
   decided to divorce her quietly.
Such was his intention when, behold,
   the angel of the Lord appeared to him in a dream and said,
   "Joseph, son of David,
   do not be afraid to take Mary your wife into your home.
For it is through the Holy Spirit
   that this child has been conceived in her.
She will bear a son and you are to name him Jesus,
   because he will save his people from their sins."
All this took place to fulfill
   what the Lord had said through the prophet:

> *Behold, the virgin shall be with child and bear a son,*
> *and they shall name him Emmanuel,*

which means "God is with us." ✛

SATURDAY, SEPTEMBER 9
St. Peter Claver

† Colossians 1:21-23
Christ has now reconciled you to present
you holy and unblemished before him.

Brothers and sisters:
You once were alienated and hostile in mind because of evil deeds;
   God has now reconciled you

in the fleshly Body of Christ through his death,
to present you holy, without blemish,
and irreproachable before him,
provided that you persevere in the faith,
firmly grounded, stable,
and not shifting from the hope of the Gospel that you heard,
which has been preached to every creature under heaven,
of which I, Paul, am a minister. ✛

Psalm 54:3-4, 6 and 8

R. (6) **God himself is my help.**

O God, by your name save me,
   and by your might defend my cause.
O God, hear my prayer;
   hearken to the words of my mouth. **R.**
Behold, God is my helper;
   the Lord sustains my life.
Freely will I offer you sacrifice;
   I will praise your name, O Lord, for its goodness. **R.**

John 14:6

R. Alleluia, alleluia.

I am the way and the truth and the life, says the Lord;
no one comes to the Father except through me. **R.**

† *Luke 6:1-5*

Why are you doing what is unlawful on the sabbath?

While Jesus was going through a field of grain on a sabbath,
   his disciples were picking the heads of grain,
   rubbing them in their hands, and eating them.
Some Pharisees said,
   "Why are you doing what is unlawful on the sabbath?"
Jesus said to them in reply,
   "Have you not read what David did
   when he and those who were with him were hungry?
How he went into the house of God, took the bread of offering,
   which only the priests could lawfully eat,
   ate of it, and shared it with his companions?"
Then he said to them, "The Son of Man is lord of the sabbath." ✛

SUNDAY, SEPTEMBER 10
TWENTY-THIRD SUNDAY IN ORDINARY TIME

† *Ezekiel 33:7-9*

If you do not speak out to dissuade the wicked from his way,
I will hold you responsible for his death.

Thus says the LORD:
　You, son of man, I have appointed watchman for the house of
　　Israel;
　when you hear me say anything, you shall warn them for me.
If I tell the wicked, "O wicked one, you shall surely die,"
　and you do not speak out to dissuade the wicked from his way,
　the wicked shall die for his guilt,
　but I will hold you responsible for his death.
But if you warn the wicked,
　trying to turn him from his way,
　and he refuses to turn from his way,
　he shall die for his guilt,
　but you shall save yourself. ✛

Psalm 95:1-2, 6-7ab, 7c-9

R. (8) **If today you hear his voice, harden not your hearts.**
Come, let us sing joyfully to the LORD;
　let us acclaim the rock of our salvation.
Let us come into his presence with thanksgiving;
　let us joyfully sing psalms to him. **R.**
Come, let us bow down in worship;
　let us kneel before the LORD who made us.
For he is our God,
　and we are the people he shepherds, the flock he guides. **R.**
Oh, that today you would hear his voice:
　"Harden not your hearts as at Meribah,
　as in the day of Massah in the desert,
where your fathers tempted me;
　they tested me though they had seen my works." **R.**

† *Romans 13:8-10*

Love is the fulfillment of the law.

Brothers and sisters:
Owe nothing to anyone, except to love one another;
　for the one who loves another has fulfilled the law.
The commandments, "You shall not commit adultery;
　you shall not kill; you shall not steal; you shall not covet,"
　and whatever other commandment there may be,
　are summed up in this saying, namely,

"You shall love your neighbor as yourself."
Love does no evil to the neighbor;
  hence, love is the fulfillment of the law. ✛

   2 Corinthians 5:19
R. Alleluia, alleluia.
God was reconciling the world to himself in Christ
and entrusting to us the message of reconciliation. **R.**

† *Matthew 18:15-20*
If your brother or sister listens to you, you have won them over.

Jesus said to his disciples:
  "If your brother sins against you,
  go and tell him his fault between you and him alone.
If he listens to you, you have won over your brother.
If he does not listen,
  take one or two others along with you,
  so that 'every fact may be established
  on the testimony of two or three witnesses.'
If he refuses to listen to them, tell the church.
If he refuses to listen even to the church,
  then treat him as you would a Gentile or a tax collector.
Amen, I say to you,
  whatever you bind on earth shall be bound in heaven,
  and whatever you loose on earth shall be loosed in heaven.
Again, amen, I say to you,
  if two of you agree on earth
  about anything for which they are to pray,
  it shall be granted to them by my heavenly Father.
For where two or three are gathered together in my name,
  there am I in the midst of them." ✛

MONDAY, SEPTEMBER 11
WEEKDAY

† *Colossians 1:24—2:3*
*I am a minister of the Church to bring to completion
the mystery hidden from ages past.*

Brothers and sisters:
I rejoice in my sufferings for your sake,
  and in my flesh I am filling up
  what is lacking in the afflictions of Christ
  on behalf of his Body, which is the Church,
  of which I am a minister
  in accordance with God's stewardship given to me
  to bring to completion for you the word of God,

the mystery hidden from ages and from generations past.
But now it has been manifested to his holy ones,
   to whom God chose to make known the riches of the glory
   of this mystery among the Gentiles;
   it is Christ in you, the hope for glory.
It is he whom we proclaim,
   admonishing everyone and teaching everyone with all wisdom,
   that we may present everyone perfect in Christ.
For this I labor and struggle,
   in accord with the exercise of his power working within me.

For I want you to know how great a struggle I am having for you
   and for those in Laodicea
   and all who have not seen me face to face,
   that their hearts may be encouraged
   as they are brought together in love,
   to have all the richness of assured understanding,
   for the knowledge of the mystery of God, Christ,
   in whom are hidden all the treasures of wisdom and knowledge. ✛

   Psalm 62:6-7, 9
R. (8) In God is my safety and my glory.
Only in God be at rest, my soul,
   for from him comes my hope.
He only is my rock and my salvation,
   my stronghold; I shall not be disturbed. **R.**
Trust in him at all times, O my people!
   Pour out your hearts before him;
   God is our refuge! **R.**

   John 10:27
R. Alleluia, alleluia.
My sheep hear my voice, says the Lord;
I know them, and they follow me. **R.**

† *Luke 6:6-11*
*The scribes and the Pharisees watched him closely
to see if he would cure on the sabbath.*

On a certain sabbath Jesus went into the synagogue and taught,
   and there was a man there whose right hand was withered.
The scribes and the Pharisees watched him closely
   to see if he would cure on the sabbath
   so that they might discover a reason to accuse him.
But he realized their intentions
   and said to the man with the withered hand,
   "Come up and stand before us."

And he rose and stood there.
Then Jesus said to them,
  "I ask you, is it lawful to do good on the sabbath
  rather than to do evil,
  to save life rather than to destroy it?"
Looking around at them all, he then said to him,
  "Stretch out your hand."
He did so and his hand was restored.
But they became enraged
  and discussed together what they might do to Jesus. ✛

TUESDAY, SEPTEMBER 12
WEEKDAY, THE MOST HOLY NAME OF MARY

† Colossians 2:6-15
*God brought you to life along with Christ having
forgiven us all our transgressions.*

Brothers and sisters:
As you received Christ Jesus the Lord, walk in him,
  rooted in him and built upon him
  and established in the faith as you were taught,
  abounding in thanksgiving.
See to it that no one captivate you with an empty, seductive philosophy
  according to the tradition of men,
  according to the elemental powers of the world
  and not according to Christ.

For in him dwells the whole fullness of the deity bodily,
  and you share in this fullness in him,
  who is the head of every principality and power.
In him you were also circumcised
  with a circumcision not administered by hand,
  by stripping off the carnal body, with the circumcision of Christ.
You were buried with him in baptism,
  in which you were also raised with him
  through faith in the power of God,
  who raised him from the dead.
And even when you were dead in transgressions
  and the uncircumcision of your flesh,
  he brought you to life along with him,
  having forgiven us all our transgressions;
  obliterating the bond against us, with its legal claims,
  which was opposed to us,
  he also removed it from our midst, nailing it to the cross;
  despoiling the principalities and the powers,

he made a public spectacle of them,
leading them away in triumph by it. ✛

Psalm 145:1b-2, 8-9, 10-11

R. (9) **The Lord is compassionate toward all his works.**
I will extol you, O my God and King,
 and I will bless your name forever and ever.
Every day will I bless you,
 and I will praise your name forever and ever. **R.**
The LORD is gracious and merciful,
 slow to anger and of great kindness.
The LORD is good to all
 and compassionate toward all his works. **R.**
Let all your works give you thanks, O LORD,
 and let your faithful ones bless you.
Let them discourse of the glory of your Kingdom
 and speak of your might. **R.**

See *John 15:16*

R. Alleluia, alleluia.
I chose you from the world,
that you may go and bear fruit that will last, says the Lord. **R.**

† *Luke 6:12-19*
He spent the night in prayer. He chose Twelve, whom he also named Apostles.

Jesus departed to the mountain to pray,
 and he spent the night in prayer to God.
When day came, he called his disciples to himself,
 and from them he chose Twelve, whom he also named Apostles:
 Simon, whom he named Peter, and his brother Andrew,
 James, John, Philip, Bartholomew,
 Matthew, Thomas, James the son of Alphaeus,
 Simon who was called a Zealot,
 and Judas the son of James,
 and Judas Iscariot, who became a traitor.

And he came down with them and stood on a stretch of level ground.
A great crowd of his disciples and a large number of the people
 from all Judea and Jerusalem
 and the coastal region of Tyre and Sidon
 came to hear him and to be healed of their diseases;
 and even those who were tormented by unclean spirits were cured.
Everyone in the crowd sought to touch him
 because power came forth from him and healed them all. ✛

WEDNESDAY, SEPTEMBER 13
St. John Chrysostom

† *Colossians 3:1-11*
You have died with Christ; put to death, then, the parts of you that are earthly.

Brothers and sisters:
If you were raised with Christ, seek what is above,
   where Christ is seated at the right hand of God.
Think of what is above, not of what is on earth.
For you have died, and your life is hidden with Christ in God.
When Christ your life appears,
   then you too will appear with him in glory.

Put to death, then, the parts of you that are earthly:
   immorality, impurity, passion, evil desire,
   and the greed that is idolatry.
Because of these the wrath of God is coming upon the disobedient.
By these you too once conducted yourselves, when you lived in that
      way.
But now you must put them all away:
   anger, fury, malice, slander,
   and obscene language out of your mouths.
Stop lying to one another,
   since you have taken off the old self with its practices
   and have put on the new self,
   which is being renewed, for knowledge,
   in the image of its creator.
Here there is not Greek and Jew,
   circumcision and uncircumcision,
   barbarian, Scythian, slave, free;
   but Christ is all and in all. ✛

   Psalm 145:2-3, 10-11, 12-13ab
R. (9) **The Lord is compassionate toward all his works.**
Every day will I bless you,
   and I will praise your name forever and ever.
Great is the LORD and highly to be praised;
   his greatness is unsearchable. **R.**
Let all your works give you thanks, O LORD,
   and let your faithful ones bless you.
Let them discourse of the glory of your Kingdom
   and speak of your might. **R.**
Making known to men your might
   and the glorious splendor of your Kingdom.

Your Kingdom is a Kingdom for all ages,
and your dominion endures through all generations. **R.**

Luke 6:23ab

R. Alleluia, alleluia.

Rejoice and leap for joy!
Your reward will be great in heaven. **R.**

✝ *Luke 6:20-26*

Blessed are you who are poor. Woe to you who are rich.

Raising his eyes toward his disciples Jesus said:

"Blessed are you who are poor,
for the Kingdom of God is yours.
Blessed are you who are now hungry,
for you will be satisfied.
Blessed are you who are now weeping,
for you will laugh.
Blessed are you when people hate you,
and when they exclude and insult you,
and denounce your name as evil
on account of the Son of Man.

"Rejoice and leap for joy on that day!
Behold, your reward will be great in heaven.
For their ancestors treated the prophets
in the same way.
But woe to you who are rich,
for you have received your consolation.
But woe to you who are filled now,
for you will be hungry.
Woe to you who laugh now,
for you will grieve and weep.
Woe to you when all speak well of you,
for their ancestors treated the false prophets in this way." ✝

THURSDAY, SEPTEMBER 14
THE EXALTATION OF THE HOLY CROSS

✝ *Numbers 21:4b-9*

*Whenever anyone who had been bitten by a serpent
looked at the bronze serpent, he lived.*

With their patience worn out by the journey,
the people complained against God and Moses,
"Why have you brought us up from Egypt to die in this desert,
where there is no food or water?

We are disgusted with this wretched food!"

In punishment the Lord sent among the people saraph serpents,
    which bit the people so that many of them died.
Then the people came to Moses and said,
    "We have sinned in complaining against the Lord and you.
Pray the Lord to take the serpents from us."
So Moses prayed for the people, and the Lord said to Moses,
    "Make a saraph and mount it on a pole,
    and if any who have been bitten look at it, they will live."
Moses accordingly made a bronze serpent and mounted it on a pole,
    and whenever anyone who had been bitten by a serpent
    looked at the bronze serpent, he lived. ✛

Psalm 78:1bc-2, 34-35, 36-37, 38
R. (see 7b) **Do not forget the works of the Lord!**
Hearken, my people, to my teaching;
    incline your ears to the words of my mouth.
I will open my mouth in a parable,
    I will utter mysteries from of old. **R.**
While he slew them they sought him
    and inquired after God again,
Remembering that God was their rock
    and the Most High God, their redeemer. **R.**
But they flattered him with their mouths
    and lied to him with their tongues,
Though their hearts were not steadfast toward him,
    nor were they faithful to his covenant. **R.**
But he, being merciful, forgave their sin
    and destroyed them not;
Often he turned back his anger
    and let none of his wrath be roused. **R.**

† Philippians 2:6-11
He humbled himself; because of this God greatly exalted him.

Brothers and sisters:
    Christ Jesus, though he was in the form of God,
        did not regard equality with God something to be grasped.
    Rather, he emptied himself,
    taking the form of a slave,
    coming in human likeness;
    and found human in appearance,
    he humbled himself,
    becoming obedient to death,
        even death on a cross.

Because of this, God greatly exalted him
and bestowed on him the name
that is above every name,
that at the name of Jesus
every knee should bend,
of those in heaven and on earth and under the earth,
and every tongue confess that
Jesus Christ is Lord,
to the glory of God the Father. ✛

R. Alleluia, alleluia.
We adore you, O Christ, and we bless you,
because by your Cross you have redeemed the world. **R.**

† *John 3:13-17*
So the Son of Man must be lifted up.

Jesus said to Nicodemus:
"No one has gone up to heaven
except the one who has come down from heaven, the Son of Man.
And just as Moses lifted up the serpent in the desert,
so must the Son of Man be lifted up,
so that everyone who believes in him may have eternal life."

For God so loved the world that he gave his only Son,
so that everyone who believes in him might not perish
but might have eternal life.
For God did not send his Son into the world to condemn the world,
but that the world might be saved through him. ✛

FRIDAY, SEPTEMBER 15
OUR LADY OF SORROWS

† *1 Timothy 1:1-2, 12-14*
I was once a blasphemer, but I have been mercifully treated.

Paul, an Apostle of Christ Jesus by command of God our savior
and of Christ Jesus our hope,
to Timothy, my true child in faith:
grace, mercy, and peace from God the Father
and Christ Jesus our Lord.

I am grateful to him who has strengthened me, Christ Jesus our
Lord,
because he considered me trustworthy
in appointing me to the ministry.
I was once a blasphemer and a persecutor and an arrogant man,
but I have been mercifully treated

because I acted out of ignorance in my unbelief.
Indeed, the grace of our Lord has been abundant,
   along with the faith and love that are in Christ Jesus. ✛

   Psalm 16:1b-2a and 5, 7-8, 11
R. (see 5) **You are my inheritance, O Lord.**
Keep me, O God, for in you I take refuge;
   I say to the LORD, "My Lord are you."
O LORD, my allotted portion and my cup,
   you it is who hold fast my lot. **R.**
I bless the LORD who counsels me;
   even in the night my heart exhorts me.
I set the LORD ever before me;
   with him at my right hand I shall not be disturbed. **R.**
You will show me the path to life,
   fullness of joys in your presence,
   the delights at your right hand forever. **R.**

The sequence Stabat Mater *may be sung optionally before the Alleluia.*

R. Alleluia, alleluia.
Blessed are you, O Virgin Mary;
without dying you won the martyr's crown
beneath the Cross of the Lord. **R.**

*✝ **John 19:25-27** (or Luke 2:33-35)*
How that loving mother was pierced with grief and anguish
when she saw the sufferings of her Son (Stabat Mater).

Standing by the cross of Jesus were his mother
   and his mother's sister, Mary the wife of Clopas,
   and Mary Magdalene.
When Jesus saw his mother and the disciple there whom he loved
   he said to his mother, "Woman, behold, your son."
Then he said to the disciple,
   "Behold, your mother."
And from that hour the disciple took her into his home. ✛

SATURDAY, SEPTEMBER 16
ST. POPE CORNELIUS AND ST. CYPRIAN

*✝ **1 Timothy 1:15-17***
Christ Jesus came into the world to save sinners.

Beloved:
This saying is trustworthy and deserves full acceptance:
   Christ Jesus came into the world to save sinners.
Of these I am the foremost.
But for that reason I was mercifully treated,

so that in me, as the foremost,
  Christ Jesus might display all his patience as an example
  for those who would come to believe in him for everlasting life.
To the king of ages, incorruptible, invisible, the only God,
  honor and glory forever and ever. Amen. ✝

Psalm 113:1b-2, 3-4, 5 and 6-7
R. (2) Blessed be the name of the Lord for ever.
Praise, you servants of the LORD,
  praise the name of the LORD.
Blessed be the name of the LORD
  both now and forever. **R.**
From the rising to the setting of the sun
  is the name of the LORD to be praised.
High above all nations is the LORD;
  above the heavens is his glory. **R.**
Who is like the LORD, our God,
  and looks upon the heavens and the earth below?
He raises up the lowly from the dust;
  from the dunghill he lifts up the poor. **R.**

John 14:23
R. Alleluia, alleluia.
Whoever loves me will keep my word,
and my Father will love him,
and we will come to him. **R.**

† *Luke 6:43-49*
Why do you call me, "Lord, Lord," but do not do what I command?

Jesus said to his disciples:
"A good tree does not bear rotten fruit,
  nor does a rotten tree bear good fruit.
For every tree is known by its own fruit.
For people do not pick figs from thornbushes,
  nor do they gather grapes from brambles.
A good person out of the store of goodness in his heart produces
    good,
  but an evil person out of a store of evil produces evil;
  for from the fullness of the heart the mouth speaks.

"Why do you call me, 'Lord, Lord,' but not do what I command?
I will show you what someone is like who comes to me,
  listens to my words, and acts on them.
That one is like a man building a house,
  who dug deeply and laid the foundation on rock;
  when the flood came, the river burst against that house

but could not shake it because it had been well built.
But the one who listens and does not act
   is like a person who built a house on the ground
   without a foundation.
When the river burst against it,
   it collapsed at once and was completely destroyed." ✛

SUNDAY, SEPTEMBER 17
TWENTY-FOURTH SUNDAY IN ORDINARY TIME

† *Sirach 27:30—28:7*
Forgive your neighbor's injustice; then when you pray,
your own sins will be forgiven.

Wrath and anger are hateful things,
   yet the sinner hugs them tight.
The vengeful will suffer the LORD's vengeance,
   for he remembers their sins in detail.
Forgive your neighbor's injustice;
   then when you pray, your own sins will be forgiven.
Could anyone nourish anger against another
   and expect healing from the LORD?
Could anyone refuse mercy to another like himself,
   can he seek pardon for his own sins?
If one who is but flesh cherishes wrath,
   who will forgive his sins?
Remember your last days, set enmity aside;
   remember death and decay, and cease from sin!
Think of the commandments, hate not your neighbor;
   remember the Most High's covenant, and overlook faults. ✛

   Psalm 103:1b-2, 3-4, 9-10, 11-12
R. (8) **The Lord is kind and merciful, slow to anger, and rich
   in compassion.**
Bless the LORD, O my soul;
   and all my being, bless his holy name.
Bless the LORD, O my soul,
and forget not all his benefits. **R.**
He pardons all your iniquities,
   heals all your ills.
He redeems your life from destruction,
   he crowns you with kindness and compassion. **R.**
He will not always chide,
   nor does he keep his wrath forever.
Not according to our sins does he deal with us,
   nor does he requite us according to our crimes. **R.**

For as the heavens are high above the earth,
  so surpassing is his kindness toward those who fear him.
As far as the east is from the west,
  so far has he put our transgressions from us. **R.**

† *Romans 14:7-9*
Whether we live or die, we are the Lord's.

Brothers and sisters:
None of us lives for oneself, and no one dies for oneself.
For if we live, we live for the Lord,
  and if we die, we die for the Lord;
  so then, whether we live or die, we are the Lord's.
For this is why Christ died and came to life,
  that he might be Lord of both the dead and the living. ✝

John 13:34
R. Alleluia, alleluia.
I give you a new commandment, says the Lord;
love one another as I have loved you. **R.**

† *Matthew 18:21-35*
I say to you, forgive not seven times, but seventy-seven times.

Peter approached Jesus and asked him,

"Lord, if my brother sins against me,
  how often must I forgive?
As many as seven times?"
Jesus answered, "I say to you, not seven times but seventy-seven
    times.
That is why the kingdom of heaven may be likened to a king
  who decided to settle accounts with his servants.
When he began the accounting,
  a debtor was brought before him who owed him a huge amount.
Since he had no way of paying it back,
  his master ordered him to be sold,
    along with his wife, his children, and all his property,
  in payment of the debt.
At that, the servant fell down, did him homage, and said,
  'Be patient with me, and I will pay you back in full.'
Moved with compassion the master of that servant
  let him go and forgave him the loan.
When that servant had left, he found one of his fellow servants
  who owed him a much smaller amount.
He seized him and started to choke him, demanding,
  'Pay back what you owe.'

Falling to his knees, his fellow servant begged him,
  'Be patient with me, and I will pay you back.'
But he refused.
Instead, he had the fellow servant put in prison
  until he paid back the debt.
Now when his fellow servants saw what had happened,
  they were deeply disturbed, and went to their master
  and reported the whole affair.
His master summoned him and said to him, 'You wicked servant!
I forgave you your entire debt because you begged me to.
Should you not have had pity on your fellow servant,
  as I had pity on you?'
Then in anger his master handed him over to the torturers
  until he should pay back the whole debt.
So will my heavenly Father do to you,
  unless each of you forgives your brother from your heart." ✛

MONDAY, SEPTEMBER 18
WEEKDAY

† *1 Timothy 2:1-8*
I ask that prayers be offered for everyone to God
who wills everyone to be saved.

Beloved:
First of all, I ask that supplications, prayers,
  petitions, and thanksgivings be offered for everyone,
  for kings and for all in authority,
  that we may lead a quiet and tranquil life
  in all devotion and dignity.
This is good and pleasing to God our savior,
  who wills everyone to be saved
  and to come to knowledge of the truth.

    For there is one God.
    There is also one mediator between God and men,
    the man Christ Jesus,
    who gave himself as ransom for all.

This was the testimony at the proper time.
For this I was appointed preacher and Apostle
  (I am speaking the truth, I am not lying),
  teacher of the Gentiles in faith and truth.

It is my wish, then, that in every place the men should pray,
  lifting up holy hands, without anger or argument. ✛

Psalm 28:2, 7, 8-9

R. (6) **Blessed be the Lord, for he has heard my prayer.**

Hear the sound of my pleading, when I cry to you,
    lifting up my hands toward your holy shrine. **R.**

The LORD is my strength and my shield.

In him my heart trusts, and I find help;
    then my heart exults, and with my song I give him thanks. **R.**

The LORD is the strength of his people,
    the saving refuge of his anointed.

Save your people, and bless your inheritance;
    feed them, and carry them forever! **R.**

John 3:16

R. Alleluia, alleluia.

God so loved the world that he gave his only-begotten Son,
so that everyone who believes in him might have eternal life. **R.**

† *Luke 7:1-10*

Not even in Israel have I found such faith.

When Jesus had finished all his words to the people,
    he entered Capernaum.

A centurion there had a slave who was ill and about to die,
    and he was valuable to him.

When he heard about Jesus, he sent elders of the Jews to him,
    asking him to come and save the life of his slave.

They approached Jesus and strongly urged him to come, saying,
    "He deserves to have you do this for him,
    for he loves our nation and he built the synagogue for us."

And Jesus went with them,
    but when he was only a short distance from the house,
    the centurion sent friends to tell him,
    "Lord, do not trouble yourself,
    for I am not worthy to have you enter under my roof.

Therefore, I did not consider myself worthy to come to you;
    but say the word and let my servant be healed.

For I too am a person subject to authority,
    with soldiers subject to me.

And I say to one, 'Go,' and he goes;
    and to another, 'Come here,' and he comes;
    and to my slave, 'Do this,' and he does it."

When Jesus heard this he was amazed at him
    and, turning, said to the crowd following him,
    "I tell you, not even in Israel have I found such faith."

When the messengers returned to the house,
    they found the slave in good health. ✛

TUESDAY, SEPTEMBER 19
WEEKDAY, ST. JANUARIUS

✝ *1 Timothy 3:1-13*
*The bishop must be irreproachable; similarly, deacons must hold fast
to the mystery of the faith with a clear conscience.*

Beloved, this saying is trustworthy:
  whoever aspires to the office of bishop desires a noble task.
Therefore, a bishop must be irreproachable,
  married only once, temperate, self-controlled,
  decent, hospitable, able to teach,
  not a drunkard, not aggressive, but gentle,
  not contentious, not a lover of money.
He must manage his own household well,
  keeping his children under control with perfect dignity;
  for if a man does not know how to manage his own household,
  how can he take care of the Church of God?
He should not be a recent convert,
  so that he may not become conceited
  and thus incur the Devil's punishment.
He must also have a good reputation among outsiders,
  so that he may not fall into disgrace, the Devil's trap.

Similarly, deacons must be dignified, not deceitful,
  not addicted to drink, not greedy for sordid gain,
  holding fast to the mystery of the faith with a clear conscience.
Moreover, they should be tested first;
  then, if there is nothing against them,
  let them serve as deacons.
Women, similarly, should be dignified, not slanderers,
  but temperate and faithful in everything.
Deacons may be married only once
  and must manage their children and their households well.
Thus those who serve well as deacons gain good standing
  and much confidence in their faith in Christ Jesus. ✛

Psalm 101:1b-2ab, 2cd-3ab, 5, 6
R. (2) **I will walk with blameless heart.**
Of mercy and judgment I will sing;
  to you, O LORD, I will sing praise.
I will persevere in the way of integrity;
  when will you come to me? **R.**
I will walk with blameless heart,
  within my house;
I will not set before my eyes
  any base thing. **R.**

Whoever slanders his neighbor in secret,
him will I destroy.
The man of haughty eyes and puffed-up heart
I will not endure. **R.**
My eyes are upon the faithful of the land,
that they may dwell with me.
He who walks in the way of integrity
shall be in my service. **R.**

Luke 7:16
R. Alleluia, alleluia.
A great prophet has arisen in our midst
and God has visited his people. **R.**

† *Luke 7:11-17*
Young man, I tell you, arise!

Jesus journeyed to a city called Nain,
and his disciples and a large crowd accompanied him.
As he drew near to the gate of the city,
a man who had died was being carried out,
the only son of his mother, and she was a widow.
A large crowd from the city was with her.
When the Lord saw her,
he was moved with pity for her and said to her,
"Do not weep."
He stepped forward and touched the coffin;
at this the bearers halted,
and he said, "Young man, I tell you, arise!"
The dead man sat up and began to speak,
and Jesus gave him to his mother.
Fear seized them all, and they glorified God, exclaiming,
"A great prophet has arisen in our midst,"
and "God has visited his people."
This report about him spread through the whole of Judea
and in all the surrounding region. ✢

WEDNESDAY, SEPTEMBER 20
St. Andrew Kim Tae-gŏn, St. Paul Chŏng Ha-sang and Companions

† *1 Timothy 3:14-16*
Undeniably great is the mystery of devotion.

Beloved:
I am writing you,
although I hope to visit you soon.
But if I should be delayed,
you should know how to behave in the household of God,

which is the Church of the living God,
   the pillar and foundation of truth.
Undeniably great is the mystery of devotion,

> Who was manifested in the flesh,
>   vindicated in the spirit,
>   seen by angels,
>   proclaimed to the Gentiles,
>   believed in throughout the world,
>   taken up in glory. ✛

Psalm 111:1-2, 3-4, 5-6
R. (2) How great are the works of the Lord!
I will give thanks to the Lord with all my heart
   in the company and assembly of the just.
Great are the works of the Lord,
   exquisite in all their delights. **R.**
Majesty and glory are his work,
   and his justice endures forever.
He has won renown for his wondrous deeds;
   gracious and merciful is the Lord. **R.**
He has given food to those who fear him;
   he will forever be mindful of his covenant.
He has made known to his people the power of his works,
   giving them the inheritance of the nations. **R.**

See John 6:63c, 68c
R. Alleluia, alleluia.
Your words, Lord, are Spirit and life,
you have the words of everlasting life. **R.**

†*Luke 7:31-35*
We played the flute for you, but you did not dance.
We sang a dirge, but you did not weep.

Jesus said to the crowds:
"To what shall I compare the people of this generation?
What are they like?
They are like children who sit in the marketplace and call to one
      another,

> 'We played the flute for you, but you did not dance.
>   We sang a dirge, but you did not weep.'

For John the Baptist came neither eating food nor drinking wine,
   and you said, 'He is possessed by a demon.'
The Son of Man came eating and drinking and you said,
   'Look, he is a glutton and a drunkard,

a friend of tax collectors and sinners.'
But wisdom is vindicated by all her children." ✢

THURSDAY, SEPTEMBER 21
St. Matthew

† *Ephesians 4:1-7, 11-13*
He gave some as Apostles, others as evangelists.

Brothers and sisters:
I, a prisoner for the Lord,
　urge you to live in a manner worthy of the call you have received,
　with all humility and gentleness, with patience,
　bearing with one another through love,
　striving to preserve the unity of the Spirit
　through the bond of peace:
　one Body and one Spirit,
　as you were also called to the one hope of your call;
　one Lord, one faith, one baptism;
　one God and Father of all,
　who is over all and through all and in all.

But grace was given to each of us
　according to the measure of Christ's gift.

And he gave some as Apostles, others as prophets,
　others as evangelists, others as pastors and teachers,
　to equip the holy ones for the work of ministry,
　for building up the Body of Christ,
　until we all attain to the unity of faith
　and knowledge of the Son of God, to mature manhood,
　to the extent of the full stature of Christ. ✢

　Psalm 19:2-3, 4-5ab
R. (5) **Their message goes out through all the earth.**
The heavens declare the glory of God;
　and the firmament proclaims his handiwork.
Day pours out the word to day,
　and night to night imparts knowledge. **R.**
Not a word nor a discourse
　whose voice is not heard;
Through all the earth their voice resounds,
　and to the ends of the world, their message. **R.**

See Te Deum
R. Alleluia, alleluia.
We praise you, O God,
we acclaim you as Lord;
the glorious company of Apostles praise you. **R.**

✝ *Matthew 9:9-13*
Follow me. And he got up and followed him.

As Jesus passed by,
  he saw a man named Matthew sitting at the customs post.
He said to him, "Follow me."
And he got up and followed him.
While he was at table in his house,
  many tax collectors and sinners came
  and sat with Jesus and his disciples.
The Pharisees saw this and said to his disciples,
  "Why does your teacher eat with tax collectors and sinners?"
He heard this and said,
  "Those who are well do not need a physician, but the sick do.
Go and learn the meaning of the words,
  I desire mercy, not sacrifice.
I did not come to call the righteous but sinners." ✛

FRIDAY, SEPTEMBER 22
Weekday

✝ *1 Timothy 6:2c-12*
But you, man of God, pursue righteousness.

Beloved:
Teach and urge these things.
Whoever teaches something different
  and does not agree with the sound words of our Lord Jesus Christ
  and the religious teaching
  is conceited, understanding nothing,
  and has a morbid disposition for arguments and verbal disputes.
From these come envy, rivalry, insults, evil suspicions,
  and mutual friction among people with corrupted minds,
  who are deprived of the truth,
  supposing religion to be a means of gain.
Indeed, religion with contentment is a great gain.
For we brought nothing into the world,
  just as we shall not be able to take anything out of it.
If we have food and clothing, we shall be content with that.
Those who want to be rich are falling into temptation and into a
  trap

and into many foolish and harmful desires,
which plunge them into ruin and destruction.
For the love of money is the root of all evils,
and some people in their desire for it have strayed from the faith
and have pierced themselves with many pains.

But you, man of God, avoid all this.
Instead, pursue righteousness, devotion,
faith, love, patience, and gentleness.
Compete well for the faith.
Lay hold of eternal life,
to which you were called when you made the noble confession
in the presence of many witnesses. ✛

Psalm 49:6-7, 8-10, 17-18, 19-20

R. Blessed the poor in spirit; the Kingdom of heaven is theirs!

Why should I fear in evil days
when my wicked ensnarers ring me round?
They trust in their wealth;
the abundance of their riches is their boast. **R.**
Yet in no way can a man redeem himself,
or pay his own ransom to God;
Too high is the price to redeem one's life; he would never have enough
to remain alive always and not see destruction. **R.**
Fear not when a man grows rich,
when the wealth of his house becomes great,
For when he dies, he shall take none of it;
his wealth shall not follow him down. **R.**
Though in his lifetime he counted himself blessed,
"They will praise you for doing well for yourself,"
He shall join the circle of his forebears
who shall never more see light. **R.**

See Matthew 11:25

R. Alleluia, alleluia.

Blessed are you, Father, Lord of heaven and earth;
you have revealed to little ones the mysteries of the Kingdom. **R.**

✝ Luke 8:1-3

*Accompanying them were some women,
who provided for them out of their resources.*

Jesus journeyed from one town and village to another,
preaching and proclaiming the good news of the Kingdom of God.
Accompanying him were the Twelve

and some women who had been cured of evil spirits and infirmities,
Mary, called Magdalene, from whom seven demons had gone out,
Joanna, the wife of Herod's steward Chuza,
Susanna, and many others
who provided for them out of their resources. ✛

SATURDAY, SEPTEMBER 23
St. Pius of Pietrelcina

† 1 Timothy 6:13-16
Keep the commandment without stain or reproach
until the appearance of our Lord Jesus Christ.

Beloved:
I charge you before God, who gives life to all things,
    and before Christ Jesus,
    who gave testimony under Pontius Pilate
    for the noble confession,
    to keep the commandment without stain or reproach
    until the appearance of our Lord Jesus Christ
    that the blessed and only ruler
    will make manifest at the proper time,
    the King of kings and Lord of lords,
    who alone has immortality, who dwells in unapproachable light,
    and whom no human being has seen or can see.
To him be honor and eternal power. Amen. ✛

Psalm 100:1b-2, 3, 4, 5
R. (2) **Come with joy into the presence of the Lord.**
Sing joyfully to the Lord all you lands;
    serve the Lord with gladness;
    come before him with joyful song. **R.**
Know that the Lord is God;
    he made us, his we are;
    his people, the flock he tends. **R.**
Enter his gates with thanksgiving,
    his courts with praise;
Give thanks to him; bless his name. **R.**
For he is good:
    the Lord, whose kindness endures forever,
    and his faithfulness, to all generations. **R.**

See Luke 8:15
R. Alleluia, alleluia.
Blessed are they who have kept the word with a generous heart
and yield a harvest through perseverance. **R.**

† *Luke 8:4-15*

*As for the seed that fell on rich soil, they are the ones who embrace
the word and bear much fruit through perseverance.*

When a large crowd gathered, with people from one town after
    another
  journeying to Jesus, he spoke in a parable.
"A sower went out to sow his seed.
And as he sowed, some seed fell on the path and was trampled,
  and the birds of the sky ate it up.
Some seed fell on rocky ground, and when it grew,
  it withered for lack of moisture.
Some seed fell among thorns,
  and the thorns grew with it and choked it.
And some seed fell on good soil, and when it grew,
  it produced fruit a hundredfold."
After saying this, he called out,
  "Whoever has ears to hear ought to hear."

Then his disciples asked him
  what the meaning of this parable might be.
He answered,
  "Knowledge of the mysteries of the Kingdom of God
  has been granted to you;
  but to the rest, they are made known through parables
  so that *they may look but not see, and hear but not understand.*

"This is the meaning of the parable.
The seed is the word of God.
Those on the path are the ones who have heard,
  but the Devil comes and takes away the word from their hearts
  that they may not believe and be saved.
Those on rocky ground are the ones who, when they hear,
  receive the word with joy, but they have no root;
  they believe only for a time and fall away in time of temptation.
As for the seed that fell among thorns,
  they are the ones who have heard, but as they go along,
  they are choked by the anxieties and riches and pleasures of life,
  and they fail to produce mature fruit.
But as for the seed that fell on rich soil,
  they are the ones who, when they have heard the word,
  embrace it with a generous and good heart,
  and bear fruit through perseverance." ✛

SUNDAY, SEPTEMBER 24
TWENTY-FIFTH SUNDAY IN ORDINARY TIME

† *Isaiah 55:6-9*
My thoughts are not your thoughts.

Seek the LORD while he may be found,
  call him while he is near.
Let the scoundrel forsake his way,
  and the wicked his thoughts;
let him turn to the LORD for mercy;
  to our God, who is generous in forgiving.
For my thoughts are not your thoughts,
  nor are your ways my ways, says the LORD.
As high as the heavens are above the earth,
  so high are my ways above your ways
  and my thoughts above your thoughts. ✛

Psalm 145:2-3, 8-9, 17-18

R. (18a) **The Lord is near to all who call upon him.**
Every day will I bless you,
  and I will praise your name forever and ever.
Great is the LORD and highly to be praised;
  his greatness is unsearchable. **R.**
The LORD is gracious and merciful,
  slow to anger and of great kindness.
The LORD is good to all
  and compassionate toward all his works. **R.**
The LORD is just in all his ways
  and holy in all his works.
The LORD is near to all who call upon him,
  to all who call upon him in truth. **R.**

† *Philippians 1:20c-24, 27a*
For me to live is Christ.

Brothers and sisters:
Christ will be magnified in my body, whether by life or by death.
For to me life is Christ, and death is gain.
If I go on living in the flesh,
  that means fruitful labor for me.
And I do not know which I shall choose.
I am caught between the two.
I long to depart this life and be with Christ,
  for that is far better.
Yet that I remain in the flesh
  is more necessary for your benefit.

Only, conduct yourselves in a way worthy of the gospel of Christ. ✛

See Acts 16:14b
R. Alleluia, alleluia.
Open our hearts, O Lord,
to listen to the words of your Son. **R.**

✝ *Matthew 20:1-16a*
Are you envious because I am generous?

Jesus told his disciples this parable:
  "The kingdom of heaven is like a landowner
  who went out at dawn to hire laborers for his vineyard.
After agreeing with them for the usual daily wage,
  he sent them into his vineyard.
Going out about nine o'clock,
  the landowner saw others standing idle in the marketplace,
  and he said to them, 'You too go into my vineyard,
  and I will give you what is just.'
So they went off.
And he went out again around noon,
  and around three o'clock, and did likewise.
Going out about five o'clock,
  the landowner found others standing around, and said to them,
  'Why do you stand here idle all day?'
They answered, 'Because no one has hired us.'
He said to them, 'You too go into my vineyard.'
When it was evening the owner of the vineyard said to his foreman,
  'Summon the laborers and give them their pay,
  beginning with the last and ending with the first.'
When those who had started about five o'clock came,
  each received the usual daily wage.
So when the first came, they thought that they would receive more,
  but each of them also got the usual wage.
And on receiving it they grumbled against the landowner, saying,
  'These last ones worked only one hour,
  and you have made them equal to us,
  who bore the day's burden and the heat.'
He said to one of them in reply,
  'My friend, I am not cheating you.
Did you not agree with me for the usual daily wage?
Take what is yours and go.
What if I wish to give this last one the same as you?
Or am I not free to do as I wish with my own money?
Are you envious because I am generous?'
Thus, the last will be first, and the first will be last." ✛

MONDAY, SEPTEMBER 25
Weekday

† *Ezra 1:1-6*

*Those who are any part of God's people, let them go up and
build the house of the Lord in Jerusalem.*

In the first year of Cyrus, king of Persia,
  in order to fulfill the word of the Lord spoken by Jeremiah,
  the Lord inspired King Cyrus of Persia
  to issue this proclamation throughout his kingdom,
  both by word of mouth and in writing:
"Thus says Cyrus, king of Persia:
'All the kingdoms of the earth
  the Lord, the God of heaven, has given to me,
  and he has also charged me to build him a house in Jerusalem,
  which is in Judah.
Therefore, whoever among you belongs to any part of his people,
  let him go up, and may his God be with him!
Let everyone who has survived, in whatever place he may have
      dwelt,
  be assisted by the people of that place
  with silver, gold, goods, and cattle,
  together with free-will offerings
  for the house of God in Jerusalem.'"

Then the family heads of Judah and Benjamin
  and the priests and Levites—
  everyone, that is, whom God had inspired to do so—
  prepared to go up to build the house of the Lord in Jerusalem.
All their neighbors gave them help in every way,
  with silver, gold, goods, and cattle,
  and with many precious gifts
  besides all their free-will offerings. ✚

Psalm 126:1b-2ab, 2cd-3, 4-5, 6

R. (3) **The Lord has done marvels for us.**
When the Lord brought back the captives of Zion,
  we were like men dreaming.
Then our mouth was filled with laughter,
  and our tongue with rejoicing. **R.**
Then they said among the nations,
  "The Lord has done great things for them."
The Lord has done great things for us;
  we are glad indeed. **R.**
Restore our fortunes, O Lord,
  like the torrents in the southern desert.

Those that sow in tears
  shall reap rejoicing. **R.**
Although they go forth weeping,
  carrying the seed to be sown,
They shall come back rejoicing,
  carrying their sheaves. **R.**

Matthew 5:16
R. Alleluia, alleluia.
Let your light shine before others,
that they may see your good deeds and glorify your heavenly Father. **R.**

† *Luke 8:16-18*
*A lamp is placed on a lampstand
so that those who enter may see the light.*

Jesus said to the crowd:
"No one who lights a lamp conceals it with a vessel
  or sets it under a bed;
  rather, he places it on a lampstand
  so that those who enter may see the light.
For there is nothing hidden that will not become visible,
  and nothing secret that will not be known and come to light.
Take care, then, how you hear.
To anyone who has, more will be given,
  and from the one who has not,
  even what he seems to have will be taken away." ✝

TUESDAY, SEPTEMBER 26
WEEKDAY, ST. COSMAS AND ST. DAMIAN

† *Ezra 6:7-8, 12b, 14-20*
They completed the temple of God, and ate the Passover.

King Darius issued an order to the officials
  of West-of-Euphrates:
  "Let the governor and the elders of the Jews
  continue the work on that house of God;
  they are to rebuild it on its former site.
I also issue this decree
  concerning your dealing with these elders of the Jews
  in the rebuilding of that house of God:
  From the royal revenue, the taxes of West-of-Euphrates,
  let these men be repaid for their expenses, in full and without delay.
I, Darius, have issued this decree;
  let it be carefully executed."

The elders of the Jews continued to make progress in the building,

supported by the message of the prophets,
Haggai and Zechariah, son of Iddo.
They finished the building according to the command
of the God of Israel
and the decrees of Cyrus and Darius
and of Artaxerxes, king of Persia.
They completed this house on the third day of the month Adar,
in the sixth year of the reign of King Darius.
The children of Israel–priests, Levites,
and the other returned exiles—
celebrated the dedication of this house of God with joy.
For the dedication of this house of God,
they offered one hundred bulls,
two hundred rams, and four hundred lambs,
together with twelve he-goats as a sin-offering for all Israel,
in keeping with the number of the tribes of Israel.
Finally, they set up the priests in their classes
and the Levites in their divisions
for the service of God in Jerusalem,
as is prescribed in the book of Moses.

The exiles kept the Passover on the fourteenth day of the first
month.
The Levites, every one of whom had purified himself for the occasion,
sacrificed the Passover for the rest of the exiles,
for their brethren the priests, and for themselves. ✛

Psalm 122:1-2, 3-4ab, 4cd-5
R. (1) **Let us go rejoicing to the house of the Lord.**
I rejoiced because they said to me,
"We will go up to the house of the LORD."
And now we have set foot
within your gates, O Jerusalem. **R.**
Jerusalem, built as a city
with compact unity.
To it the tribes go up,
the tribes of the LORD. **R.**
According to the decree for Israel,
to give thanks to the name of the LORD.
In it are set up judgment seats,
seats for the house of David. **R.**

Luke 11:28
R. Alleluia, alleluia.
Blessed are those who hear the word of God
and observe it. **R.**

†*Luke 8:19-21*
My mother and my brothers are those
who hear the word of God and act on it.

The mother of Jesus and his brothers came to him
   but were unable to join him because of the crowd.
He was told, "Your mother and your brothers are standing outside
   and they wish to see you."
He said to them in reply, "My mother and my brothers
   are those who hear the word of God and act on it." ✝

WEDNESDAY, SEPTEMBER 27
St. Vincent de Paul

†*Ezra 9:5-9*
In our servitude our God has not abandoned us.

At the time of the evening sacrifice, I, Ezra, rose in my wretchedness,
   and with cloak and mantle torn I fell on my knees,
   stretching out my hands to the LORD, my God.

I said: "My God, I am too ashamed and confounded to raise my face
      to you,
   O my God, for our wicked deeds are heaped up above our heads
   and our guilt reaches up to heaven.
From the time of our fathers even to this day
   great has been our guilt,
   and for our wicked deeds we have been delivered up,
   we and our kings and our priests,
   to the will of the kings of foreign lands,
   to the sword, to captivity, to pillage, and to disgrace,
   as is the case today.

"And now, but a short time ago, mercy came to us from the LORD, our
      God,
   who left us a remnant and gave us a stake in his holy place;
   thus our God has brightened our eyes
   and given us relief in our servitude.
For slaves we are, but in our servitude our God has not abandoned us;
   rather, he has turned the good will
   of the kings of Persia toward us.
Thus he has given us new life
   to raise again the house of our God and restore its ruins,
   and has granted us a fence in Judah and Jerusalem." ✝

Tobit 13:2, 3-4a, 4befghn, 7-8
R. (1b) Blessed be God, who lives for ever.
He scourges and then has mercy;

he casts down to the depths of the nether world,
and he brings up from the great abyss.
No one can escape his hand. **R.**
Praise him, you children of Israel, before the Gentiles,
for though he has scattered you among them,
he has shown you his greatness even there. **R.**
So now consider what he has done for you,
and praise him with full voice.
Bless the Lord of righteousness,
and exalt the King of ages. **R.**
In the land of my exile I praise him
and show his power and majesty to a sinful nation. **R.**
Bless the Lord, all you his chosen ones,
and may all of you praise his majesty.
Celebrate days of gladness, and give him praise. **R.**

Mark 1:15
R. Alleluia, alleluia.
The Kingdom of God is at hand;
repent and believe in the Gospel. **R.**

† *Luke 9:1-6*
He sent them to proclaim the Kingdom of God and to heal the sick.

Jesus summoned the Twelve and gave them power and authority
over all demons and to cure diseases,
and he sent them to proclaim the Kingdom of God
and to heal the sick.
He said to them, "Take nothing for the journey,
neither walking stick, nor sack, nor food, nor money,
and let no one take a second tunic.
Whatever house you enter, stay there and leave from there.
And as for those who do not welcome you,
when you leave that town,
shake the dust from your feet in testimony against them."
Then they set out and went from village to village
proclaiming the good news and curing diseases everywhere. ✛

THURSDAY, SEPTEMBER 28
WEEKDAY; ST. WENCESLAUS; ST. LAWRENCE RUIZ AND COMPANIONS

† *Haggai 1:1-8*
Build the house that I may take pleasure in it.

On the first day of the sixth month in the second year of King
Darius,
the word of the LORD came through the prophet Haggai
to the governor of Judah, Zerubbabel, son of Shealtiel,

and to the high priest Joshua, son of Jehozadak:

Thus says the LORD of hosts:
This people says:
"The time has not yet come to rebuild the house of the LORD."
(Then this word of the LORD came through Haggai, the prophet:)
Is it time for you to dwell in your own paneled houses,
while this house lies in ruins?

Now thus says the LORD of hosts:
Consider your ways!
You have sown much, but have brought in little;
you have eaten, but have not been satisfied;
You have drunk, but have not been exhilarated;
have clothed yourselves, but not been warmed;
And whoever earned wages
earned them for a bag with holes in it.

Thus says the LORD of hosts:
Consider your ways!
Go up into the hill country;
bring timber, and build the house
That I may take pleasure in it
and receive my glory, says the LORD. ✛

Psalm 149:1b-2, 3-4, 5-6a and 9b
R. (see 4a) **The Lord takes delight in his people.**
Sing to the LORD a new song
of praise in the assembly of the faithful.
Let Israel be glad in their maker,
let the children of Zion rejoice in their king. **R.**
Let them praise his name in the festive dance,
let them sing praise to him with timbrel and harp.
For the LORD loves his people,
and he adorns the lowly with victory. **R.**
Let the faithful exult in glory;
let them sing for joy upon their couches;
Let the high praises of God be in their throats.
This is the glory of all his faithful. Alleluia. **R.**

John 14:6
R. Alleluia, alleluia.
I am the way and the truth and the life, says the Lord;
no one comes to the Father except through me. **R.**

† *Luke 9:7-9*
John I beheaded. Who then is this about whom I hear such things?

Herod the tetrarch heard about all that was happening,
  and he was greatly perplexed because some were saying,
  "John has been raised from the dead";
  others were saying, "Elijah has appeared";
  still others, "One of the ancient prophets has arisen."
But Herod said, "John I beheaded.
Who then is this about whom I hear such things?"
And he kept trying to see him. ✛

FRIDAY, SEPTEMBER 29
St. Michael, St. Gabriel and St. Raphael

† *Daniel 7:9-10, 13-14 (or Revelation 12:7-12ab)*
Thousands upon thousands were ministering to him.

As I watched:

Thrones were set up
  and the Ancient One took his throne.
His clothing was bright as snow,
  and the hair on his head as white as wool;
His throne was flames of fire,
  with wheels of burning fire.
A surging stream of fire
  flowed out from where he sat;
Thousands upon thousands were ministering to him,
  and myriads upon myriads attended him.

The court was convened, and the books were opened.
As the visions during the night continued, I saw

One like a son of man coming,
  on the clouds of heaven;
When he reached the Ancient One
  and was presented before him,
He received dominion, glory, and kingship;
  nations and peoples of every language serve him.
His dominion is an everlasting dominion
  that shall not be taken away,
  his kingship shall not be destroyed. ✛

Psalm 138:1-2ab, 2cde-3, 4-5
R. (1) In the sight of the angels I will sing your praises, Lord.
I will give thanks to you, O Lord, with all my heart,
  for you have heard the words of my mouth;

in the presence of the angels I will sing your praise;
I will worship at your holy temple
   and give thanks to your name. **R.**
Because of your kindness and your truth;
   for you have made great above all things
   your name and your promise.
When I called, you answered me;
   you built up strength within me. **R.**
All the kings of the earth shall give thanks to you, O Lord,
   when they hear the words of your mouth;
And they shall sing of the ways of the Lord:
   "Great is the glory of the Lord." **R.**

   Psalm 103:21
R. Alleluia, alleluia.
Bless the Lord, all you angels,
you ministers, who do his will. **R.**

† *John 1:47-51*
You will see the sky opened and the angels of God
ascending and descending on the Son of Man.

Jesus saw Nathanael coming toward him and said of him,
   "Here is a true child of Israel.
There is no duplicity in him."
Nathanael said to him, "How do you know me?"
Jesus answered and said to him,
   "Before Philip called you, I saw you under the fig tree."
Nathanael answered him,
   "Rabbi, you are the Son of God; you are the King of Israel."
Jesus answered and said to him,
   "Do you believe
   because I told you that I saw you under the fig tree?
You will see greater things than this."
And he said to him, "Amen, amen, I say to you,
   you will see heaven opened
   and the angels of God ascending and descending on the Son of
   Man." ✛

SATURDAY, SEPTEMBER 30
St. Jerome

† *Zechariah 2:5-9, 14-15a*
See, I am coming to dwell among you.

I, Zechariah, raised my eyes and looked:
   there was a man with a measuring line in his hand.
I asked, "Where are you going?"

He answered, "To measure Jerusalem,
  to see how great is its width and how great its length."

Then the angel who spoke with me advanced,
  and another angel came out to meet him and said to him,
  "Run, tell this to that young man:
  People will live in Jerusalem as though in open country,
  because of the multitude of men and beasts in her midst.
But I will be for her an encircling wall of fire, says the LORD,
  and I will be the glory in her midst."

Sing and rejoice, O daughter Zion!
See, I am coming to dwell among you, says the LORD.
Many nations shall join themselves to the LORD on that day,
  and they shall be his people and he will dwell among you. ✛

Jeremiah 31:10, 11-12ab, 13

R. (see 10d) **The Lord will guard us as a shepherd guards his
  flock.**

Hear the word of the LORD, O nations,
  proclaim it on distant isles, and say:
He who scattered Israel, now gathers them together,
  he guards them as a shepherd guards his flock. **R.**
The LORD shall ransom Jacob,
  he shall redeem him from the hand of his conqueror.
Shouting, they shall mount the heights of Zion,
  they shall come streaming to the LORD's blessings. **R.**
Then the virgins shall make merry and dance,
  and young men and old as well.
I will turn their mourning into joy,
  I will console and gladden them after their sorrows. **R.**

See 2 Timothy 1:10

R. Alleluia, alleluia.

Our Savior Christ Jesus destroyed death
and brought life to light through the Gospel. **R.**

† *Luke 9:43b-45*
The Son of Man is to be handed over to men.
They were afraid to ask him about this saying.

While they were all amazed at his every deed,
  Jesus said to his disciples,
  "Pay attention to what I am telling you.
The Son of Man is to be handed over to men."
But they did not understand this saying;
  its meaning was hidden from them

so that they should not understand it,
and they were afraid to ask him about this saying. ✛

SUNDAY, OCTOBER 1
TWENTY-SIXTH SUNDAY IN ORDINARY TIME

†Ezekiel 18:25-28
By turning from wickedness, a wicked person shall preserve his life.

Thus says the LORD:
You say, "The LORD's way is not fair!"
Hear now, house of Israel:
  Is it my way that is unfair, or rather, are not your ways unfair?
When someone virtuous turns away from virtue to commit iniquity,
    and dies,
  it is because of the iniquity he committed that he must die.
But if he turns from the wickedness he has committed,
  he does what is right and just,
  he shall preserve his life;
  since he has turned away from all the sins that he has committed,
he shall surely live, he shall not die. ✛

Psalm 25:4-5, 6-7, 8-9
R. (6a) **Remember your mercies, O Lord.**
Your ways, O LORD, make known to me;
  teach me your paths,
guide me in your truth and teach me,
  for you are God my savior. **R.**
Remember that your compassion, O LORD,
  and your love are from of old.
The sins of my youth and my frailties remember not;
  in your kindness remember me,
  because of your goodness, O LORD. **R.**
Good and upright is the LORD;
  thus he shows sinners the way.
He guides the humble to justice,
  and teaches the humble his way. **R.**

†Philippians 2:1-11 *(or Philippians 2:1-5)*
Have in you the same attitude that is also in Christ Jesus.

Brothers and sisters:
If there is any encouragement in Christ,
  any solace in love,
  any participation in the Spirit,
  any compassion and mercy,
  complete my joy by being of the same mind, with the same love,

united in heart, thinking one thing.
Do nothing out of selfishness or out of vainglory;
  rather, humbly regard others as more important than yourselves,
  each looking out not for his own interests,
  but also for those of others.

Have in you the same attitude
  that is also in Christ Jesus,
    Who, though he was in the form of God,
      did not regard equality with God
      something to be grasped.
    Rather, he emptied himself,
      taking the form of a slave,
      coming in human likeness;
      and found human in appearance,
      he humbled himself,
      becoming obedient to the point of death,
      even death on a cross.
    Because of this, God greatly exalted him
      and bestowed on him the name
      which is above every name,
      that at the name of Jesus
      every knee should bend,
      of those in heaven and on earth and under the earth,
      and every tongue confess that
      Jesus Christ is Lord,
      to the glory of God the Father. ✛

John 10:27
R. Alleluia, alleluia.
My sheep hear my voice, says the Lord;
I know them, and they follow me. **R.**

† *Matthew 21:28-32*

He changed his mind and went. Tax collectors and prostitutes
are entering the kingdom of heaven before you.

Jesus said to the chief priests and elders of the people:
  "What is your opinion?
A man had two sons.
He came to the first and said,
  'Son, go out and work in the vineyard today.'
He said in reply, 'I will not,'
  but afterwards changed his mind and went.
The man came to the other son and gave the same order.
He said in reply, 'Yes, sir,' but did not go.

Which of the two did his father's will?"
They answered, "The first."
Jesus said to them, "Amen, I say to you,
    tax collectors and prostitutes
    are entering the kingdom of God before you.
When John came to you in the way of righteousness,
    you did not believe him;
    but tax collectors and prostitutes did.
Yet even when you saw that,
    you did not later change your minds and believe him." ✛

MONDAY, OCTOBER 2
THE HOLY GUARDIAN ANGELS

✝ Zechariah 8:1-8
I will rescue my people from the land of the rising sun,
and from the land of the setting sun.

This word of the LORD of hosts came:

Thus says the LORD of hosts:

I am intensely jealous for Zion,
        stirred to jealous wrath for her.
    Thus says the LORD:
I will return to Zion,
    and I will dwell within Jerusalem;
Jerusalem shall be called the faithful city,
    and the mountain of the LORD of hosts,
    the holy mountain.

Thus says the LORD of hosts: Old men and old women,
    each with staff in hand because of old age,
    shall again sit in the streets of Jerusalem.
The city shall be filled with boys and girls playing in its streets.
Thus says the LORD of hosts:
    Even if this should seem impossible
    in the eyes of the remnant of this people,
    shall it in those days be impossible in my eyes also,
    says the LORD of hosts?
Thus says the LORD of hosts:
    Lo, I will rescue my people from the land of the rising sun,
    and from the land of the setting sun.
I will bring them back to dwell within Jerusalem.
They shall be my people, and I will be their God,
    with faithfulness and justice. ✛

Psalm 102:16-18, 19-21, 29 and 22-23

R. (17) **The Lord will build up Zion again, and appear in all his glory.**

The nations shall revere your name, O LORD,
   and all the kings of the earth your glory,
When the LORD has rebuilt Zion
   and appeared in his glory;
When he has regarded the prayer of the destitute,
   and not despised their prayer. **R.**
Let this be written for the generation to come,
   and let his future creatures praise the LORD:
"The LORD looked down from his holy height,
   from heaven he beheld the earth,
To hear the groaning of the prisoners,
   to release those doomed to die." **R.**
The children of your servants shall abide,
   and their posterity shall continue in your presence.
That the name of the LORD may be declared in Zion;
   and his praise, in Jerusalem,
When the peoples gather together,
   and the kingdoms, to serve the LORD. **R.**

Psalm 103:21

R. Alleluia, alleluia.
Bless the LORD, all you angels,
you ministers, who do his will. **R.**

† *Matthew 18:1-5, 10*

Their angels in heaven always look upon the face of my heavenly Father.

The disciples approached Jesus and said,
   "Who is the greatest in the Kingdom of heaven?"
He called a child over, placed it in their midst, and said,
   "Amen, I say to you, unless you turn and become like children,
   you will not enter the Kingdom of heaven.
Whoever humbles himself like this child
   is the greatest in the Kingdom of heaven.
And whoever receives one child such as this in my name receives me.

"See that you do not despise one of these little ones,
   for I say to you that their angels in heaven
   always look upon the face of my heavenly Father." ✛

TUESDAY, OCTOBER 3
WEEKDAY

† *Zechariah 8:20-23*
Many peoples shall come to seek the LORD in Jerusalem.

Thus says the LORD of hosts:
There shall yet come peoples,
the inhabitants of many cities;
and the inhabitants of one city shall approach those of another,
and say, "Come! let us go to implore the favor of the LORD";
and, "I too will go to seek the LORD."
Many peoples and strong nations shall come
to seek the LORD of hosts in Jerusalem
and to implore the favor of the LORD.
Thus says the LORD of hosts:
In those days ten men of every nationality,
speaking different tongues, shall take hold,
yes, take hold of every Jew by the edge of his garment and say,

"Let us go with you, for we have heard that God is with you." ✛

Psalm 87:1b-3, 4-5, 6-7
R. (Zechariah 8:23) **God is with us.**
His foundation upon the holy mountains
the LORD loves:
The gates of Zion,
more than any dwelling of Jacob.
Glorious things are said of you,
O city of God! **R.**
I tell of Egypt and Babylon
among those that know the LORD;
Of Philistia, Tyre, Ethiopia:
"This man was born there."
And of Zion they shall say:
"One and all were born in her;
And he who has established her
is the Most High LORD." **R.**
They shall note, when the peoples are enrolled:
"This man was born there."
And all shall sing, in their festive dance:
"My home is within you." **R.**

Mark 10:45
R. Alleluia, alleluia.
The Son of Man came to serve
and to give his life as a ransom for many. **R.**

†*Luke 9:51-56*
He resolutely determined to journey to Jerusalem.

When the days for Jesus to be taken up were fulfilled,
   he resolutely determined to journey to Jerusalem,
   and he sent messengers ahead of him.
On the way they entered a Samaritan village
   to prepare for his reception there,
   but they would not welcome him
   because the destination of his journey was Jerusalem.
When the disciples James and John saw this they asked,
   "Lord, do you want us to call down fire from heaven
   to consume them?"
Jesus turned and rebuked them,
   and they journeyed to another village. ✛

WEDNESDAY, OCTOBER 4
St. Francis of Assisi

†*Nehemiah 2:1-8*
If it please the king, send me to the city of my ancestors and I will rebuild it.

In the month Nisan of the twentieth year of King Artaxerxes,
   when the wine was in my charge,
   I took some and offered it to the king.
As I had never before been sad in his presence,
   the king asked me, "Why do you look sad?
If you are not sick, you must be sad at heart."
Though I was seized with great fear, I answered the king:
   "May the king live forever!
How could I not look sad
   when the city where my ancestors are buried lies in ruins,
   and its gates have been eaten out by fire?"
The king asked me, "What is it, then, that you wish?"
I prayed to the God of heaven and then answered the king:
   "If it please the king,
   and if your servant is deserving of your favor,
   send me to Judah, to the city of my ancestors' graves,
   to rebuild it."
Then the king, and the queen seated beside him,
   asked me how long my journey would take
   and when I would return.
I set a date that was acceptable to him,
   and the king agreed that I might go.

I asked the king further: "If it please the king,
   let letters be given to me for the governors

of West-of-Euphrates,
that they may afford me safe-conduct until I arrive in Judah;
also a letter for Asaph, the keeper of the royal park,
that he may give me wood for timbering the gates
of the temple-citadel and for the city wall
and the house that I shall occupy."
The king granted my requests,
for the favoring hand of my God was upon me. ✛

Psalm 137:1-2, 3, 4-5, 6
R. (6ab) **Let my tongue be silenced if I ever forget you!**
By the streams of Babylon
we sat and wept
when we remembered Zion.
On the aspens of that land
we hung up our harps. **R.**
Though there our captors asked of us
the lyrics of our songs,
And our despoilers urged us to be joyous:
"Sing for us the songs of Zion!" **R.**
How could we sing a song of the LORD
in a foreign land?
If I forget you, Jerusalem,
may my right hand be forgotten! **R.**
May my tongue cleave to my palate
if I remember you not,
If I place not Jerusalem
ahead of my joy. **R.**

Philippians 3:8-9
R. Alleluia, alleluia.
I consider all things so much rubbish
that I may gain Christ and be found in him. **R.**

✝ *Luke 9:57-62*
I will follow you wherever you go.

As Jesus and his disciples were proceeding
on their journey, someone said to him,
"I will follow you wherever you go."
Jesus answered him,
"Foxes have dens and birds of the sky have nests,
but the Son of Man has nowhere to rest his head."
And to another he said, "Follow me."
But he replied, "Lord, let me go first and bury my father."
But he answered him, "Let the dead bury their dead.
But you, go and proclaim the Kingdom of God."

And another said, "I will follow you, Lord,
  but first let me say farewell to my family at home."
Jesus answered him, "No one who sets a hand to the plow
  and looks to what was left behind is fit for the Kingdom of God." ✛

THURSDAY, OCTOBER 5
WEEKDAY, ST. FAUSTINA KOWALSKA, BL. FRANCIS XAVIER SEELOS

† *Nehemiah 8:1-4a, 5-6, 7b-12*
Ezra opened the book of the law, blessed the LORD,
and all the people answered, Amen! Amen!

The whole people gathered as one in the open space before the
    Water Gate,
  and they called upon Ezra the scribe
  to bring forth the book of the law of Moses
  which the LORD prescribed for Israel.
On the first day of the seventh month, therefore,
  Ezra the priest brought the law before the assembly,
  which consisted of men, women,
  and those children old enough to understand.
Standing at one end of the open place that was before the Water
    Gate,
  he read out of the book from daybreak until midday,
  in the presence of the men, the women,
  and those children old enough to understand;
  and all the people listened attentively to the book of the law.
Ezra the scribe stood on a wooden platform
  that had been made for the occasion.
He opened the scroll
  so that all the people might see it
  (for he was standing higher up than any of the people);
  and, as he opened it, all the people rose.
Ezra blessed the LORD, the great God,
  and all the people, their hands raised high, answered,
  "Amen, amen!"
Then they bowed down and prostrated themselves before the LORD,
  their faces to the ground.
As the people remained in their places,
  Ezra read plainly from the book of the law of God,
  interpreting it so that all could understand what was read.
Then Nehemiah, that is, His Excellency, and Ezra the priest-scribe
  and the Levites who were instructing the people
  said to all the people:
  "Today is holy to the LORD your God.
Do not be sad, and do not weep"—

for all the people were weeping as they heard the words of the law.
He said further: "Go, eat rich foods and drink sweet drinks,
and allot portions to those who had nothing prepared;
for today is holy to our LORD.
Do not be saddened this day,
for rejoicing in the LORD must be your strength!"
And the Levites quieted all the people, saying,
"Hush, for today is holy, and you must not be saddened."
Then all the people went to eat and drink,
to distribute portions, and to celebrate with great joy,
for they understood the words that had been expounded to them. ✛

Psalm 19:8, 9, 10, 11
R. (9ab) **The precepts of the Lord give joy to the heart.**
The law of the LORD is perfect,
refreshing the soul;
The decree of the LORD is trustworthy,
giving wisdom to the simple. **R.**
The precepts of the LORD are right,
rejoicing the heart;
The command of the LORD is clear,
enlightening the eye. **R.**
The fear of the LORD is pure,
enduring forever;
The ordinances of the LORD are true,
all of them just. **R.**
They are more precious than gold,
than a heap of purest gold;
Sweeter also than syrup
or honey from the comb. **R.**

Mark 1:15
R. Alleluia, alleluia.
The Kingdom of God is at hand;
repent and believe in the Gospel. **R.**

✝ Luke 10:1-12
Your peace will rest on him.

Jesus appointed seventy-two other disciples
whom he sent ahead of him in pairs
to every town and place he intended to visit.
He said to them,
"The harvest is abundant but the laborers are few;
so ask the master of the harvest
to send out laborers for his harvest.
Go on your way;

behold, I am sending you like lambs among wolves.
Carry no money bag, no sack, no sandals;
    and greet no one along the way.
Into whatever house you enter, first say,
    'Peace to this household.'
If a peaceful person lives there,
    your peace will rest on him;
    but if not, it will return to you.
Stay in the same house and eat and drink what is offered to you,
    for the laborer deserves his payment.
Do not move about from one house to another.
Whatever town you enter and they welcome you,
    eat what is set before you,
    cure the sick in it and say to them,
    'The Kingdom of God is at hand for you.'
Whatever town you enter and they do not receive you,
    go out into the streets and say,
    'The dust of your town that clings to our feet,
    even that we shake off against you.'
Yet know this: the Kingdom of God is at hand.
I tell you,
    it will be more tolerable for Sodom on that day
        than for that town." ✟

FRIDAY, OCTOBER 6
WEEKDAY, ST. BRUNO, BL. MARIE ROSE DUROCHER

†*Baruch 1:15-22*
We have sinned in the LORD's sight and disobeyed him.

During the Babylonian captivity, the exiles prayed:
"Justice is with the Lord, our God;
    and we today are flushed with shame,
    we men of Judah and citizens of Jerusalem,
    that we, with our kings and rulers
    and priests and prophets, and with our ancestors,
    have sinned in the Lord's sight and disobeyed him.
We have neither heeded the voice of the Lord, our God,
    nor followed the precepts which the Lord set before us.
From the time the Lord led our ancestors out of the land of Egypt
    until the present day,
    we have been disobedient to the Lord, our God,
    and only too ready to disregard his voice.
And the evils and the curse that the Lord enjoined upon Moses, his
        servant,
    at the time he led our ancestors forth from the land of Egypt

to give us the land flowing with milk and honey,
cling to us even today.
For we did not heed the voice of the Lord, our God,
in all the words of the prophets whom he sent us,
but each one of us went off
after the devices of his own wicked heart,
served other gods,
and did evil in the sight of the Lord, our God." ✝

Psalm 79:1b-2, 3-5, 8, 9
R. (9) For the glory of your name, O Lord, deliver us.
O God, the nations have come into your inheritance;
they have defiled your holy temple,
they have laid Jerusalem in ruins.
They have given the corpses of your servants
as food to the birds of heaven,
the flesh of your faithful ones to the beasts of the earth. **R.**
They have poured out their blood like water
round about Jerusalem,
and there is no one to bury them.
We have become the reproach of our neighbors,
the scorn and derision of those around us.
O LORD, how long? Will you be angry forever?
Will your jealousy burn like fire? **R.**
Remember not against us the iniquities of the past;
may your compassion quickly come to us,
for we are brought very low. **R.**
Help us, O God our savior,
because of the glory of your name;
Deliver us and pardon our sins
for your name's sake. **R.**

Psalm 95:8
R. Alleluia, alleluia.
If today you hear his voice,
harden not your hearts. **R.**

✝ *Luke 10:13-16*
Whoever rejects me rejects the one who sent me.

Jesus said to them,
"Woe to you, Chorazin! Woe to you, Bethsaida!
For if the mighty deeds done in your midst
had been done in Tyre and Sidon,
they would long ago have repented,
sitting in sackcloth and ashes.
But it will be more tolerable for Tyre and Sidon

at the judgment than for you.
And as for you, Capernaum, 'Will you be exalted to heaven?
You will go down to the netherworld.'
Whoever listens to you listens to me.
Whoever rejects you rejects me.
And whoever rejects me rejects the one who sent me." ✛

SATURDAY, OCTOBER 7
OUR LADY OF THE ROSARY

†Baruch 4:5-12, 27-29
He who brought disaster upon you will bring you back enduring joy.

Fear not, my people!
  Remember, Israel,
You were sold to the nations
  not for your destruction;
It was because you angered God
  that you were handed over to your foes.
For you provoked your Maker
  with sacrifices to demons, to no-gods;
You forsook the Eternal God who nourished you,
  and you grieved Jerusalem who fostered you.
She indeed saw coming upon you
  the anger of God; and she said:

"Hear, you neighbors of Zion!
  God has brought great mourning upon me,
For I have seen the captivity
  that the Eternal God has brought
  upon my sons and daughters.
With joy I fostered them;
  but with mourning and lament I let them go.
Let no one gloat over me, a widow,
  bereft of many:
For the sins of my children I am left desolate,
  because they turned from the law of God.

"Fear not, my children; call out to God!
  He who brought this upon you will remember you.
As your hearts have been disposed to stray from God,
  turn now ten times the more to seek him;
For he who has brought disaster upon you
  will, in saving you, bring you back enduring joy." ✛

Psalm 69:33-35, 36-37

R. (34) **The Lord listens to the poor.**

"See, you lowly ones, and be glad;
   you who seek God, may your hearts revive!
For the LORD hears the poor,
   and his own who are in bonds he spurns not.
Let the heavens and the earth praise him,
   the seas and whatever moves in them!" **R.**
For God will save Zion
   and rebuild the cities of Judah.
They shall dwell in the land and own it,
   and the descendants of his servants shall inherit it,
   and those who love his name shall inhabit it. **R.**

See Matthew 11:25

R. Alleluia, alleluia.

Blessed are you, Father, Lord of heaven and earth;
you have revealed to little ones the mysteries of the Kingdom. **R.**

† *Luke 10:17-24*

Rejoice because your names are written in heaven.

The seventy-two disciples returned rejoicing and said to Jesus,
   "Lord, even the demons are subject to us because of your name."
Jesus said, "I have observed Satan fall like lightning from the sky.
Behold, I have given you the power
   'to tread upon serpents' and scorpions
   and upon the full force of the enemy
   and nothing will harm you.
Nevertheless, do not rejoice because the spirits are subject to you,
   but rejoice because your names are written in heaven."

At that very moment he rejoiced in the Holy Spirit and said,
   "I give you praise, Father, Lord of heaven and earth,
   for although you have hidden these things
   from the wise and the learned
   you have revealed them to the childlike.
Yes, Father, such has been your gracious will.
All things have been handed over to me by my Father.
No one knows who the Son is except the Father,
   and who the Father is except the Son
   and anyone to whom the Son wishes to reveal him."

Turning to the disciples in private he said,
   "Blessed are the eyes that see what you see.
For I say to you,
   many prophets and kings desired to see what you see,

but did not see it,
and to hear what you hear, but did not hear it." ✛

SUNDAY, OCTOBER 8
TWENTY-SEVENTH SUNDAY IN ORDINARY TIME

† Isaiah 5:1-7
The vineyard of the LORD of hosts is the house of Israel.

Let me now sing of my friend,
   my friend's song concerning his vineyard.
My friend had a vineyard
   on a fertile hillside;
he spaded it, cleared it of stones,
   and planted the choicest vines;
within it he built a watchtower,
   and hewed out a wine press.
Then he looked for the crop of grapes,
   but what it yielded was wild grapes.

Now, inhabitants of Jerusalem and people of Judah,
   judge between me and my vineyard:
What more was there to do for my vineyard
   that I had not done?
Why, when I looked for the crop of grapes,
   did it bring forth wild grapes?
Now, I will let you know
   what I mean to do with my vineyard:
take away its hedge, give it to grazing,
   break through its wall, let it be trampled!
Yes, I will make it a ruin:
   it shall not be pruned or hoed,
   but overgrown with thorns and briers;
I will command the clouds
   not to send rain upon it.
The vineyard of the LORD of hosts is the house of Israel,
   and the people of Judah are his cherished plant;
he looked for judgment, but see, bloodshed!
   for justice, but hark, the outcry! ✛

Psalm 80:9 and 12, 13-14, 15-16, 19-20
R. (Isaiah 5:7a) **The vineyard of the Lord is the house of Israel.**
A vine from Egypt you transplanted;
   you drove away the nations and planted it.
It put forth its foliage to the Sea,
   its shoots as far as the River. **R.**
Why have you broken down its walls,

so that every passer-by plucks its fruit,
the boar from the forest lays it waste,
 and the beasts of the field feed upon it? **R.**
Once again, O LORD of hosts,
 look down from heaven, and see;
take care of this vine,
 and protect what your right hand has planted,
 the son of man whom you yourself made strong. **R.**
Then we will no more withdraw from you;
 give us new life, and we will call upon your name.
O LORD, God of hosts, restore us;
 if your face shine upon us, then we shall be saved. **R.**

†Philippians 4:6-9
Do these things, and the God of peace will be with you.

Brothers and sisters:
Have no anxiety at all, but in everything,
 by prayer and petition, with thanksgiving,
 make your requests known to God.
Then the peace of God that surpasses all understanding
 will guard your hearts and minds in Christ Jesus.

Finally, brothers and sisters,
 whatever is true, whatever is honorable,
 whatever is just, whatever is pure,
 whatever is lovely, whatever is gracious,
 if there is any excellence
 and if there is anything worthy of praise,
 think about these things.
Keep on doing what you have learned and received
 and heard and seen in me.
Then the God of peace will be with you. ✛

 See John 15:16
R. Alleluia, alleluia.
I have chosen you from the world, says the Lord,
to go and bear fruit that will remain. **R.**

†Matthew 21:33-43
He will lease his vineyard to other tenants.

Jesus said to the chief priests and the elders of the people:
 "Hear another parable.
There was a landowner who planted a vineyard,
 put a hedge around it, dug a wine press in it, and built a tower.
Then he leased it to tenants and went on a journey.

When vintage time drew near,
he sent his servants to the tenants to obtain his produce.
But the tenants seized the servants and one they beat,
another they killed, and a third they stoned.
Again he sent other servants, more numerous than the first ones,
but they treated them in the same way.
Finally, he sent his son to them, thinking,
'They will respect my son.'
But when the tenants saw the son, they said to one another,
'This is the heir.
Come, let us kill him and acquire his inheritance.'
They seized him, threw him out of the vineyard, and killed him.
What will the owner of the vineyard do to those tenants when he
comes?"
They answered him,
"He will put those wretched men to a wretched death
and lease his vineyard to other tenants
who will give him the produce at the proper times."
Jesus said to them, "Did you never read in the Scriptures:
The stone that the builders rejected
has become the cornerstone;
by the Lord has this been done,
and it is wonderful in our eyes?
Therefore, I say to you,
the kingdom of God will be taken away from you
and given to a people that will produce its fruit." ✚

MONDAY, OCTOBER 9
WEEKDAY, ST. DENIS AND COMPANIONS, ST. JOHN LEONARDI

† *Jonah 1:1—2:2, 11*
But Jonah made ready to flee away from the LORD.

This is the word of the LORD that came to Jonah, son of Amittai:

"Set out for the great city of Nineveh, and preach against it;
their wickedness has come up before me."
But Jonah made ready to flee to Tarshish away from the LORD.
He went down to Joppa, found a ship going to Tarshish,
paid the fare, and went aboard to journey with them to Tarshish,
away from the LORD.

The LORD, however, hurled a violent wind upon the sea,
and in the furious tempest that arose
the ship was on the point of breaking up.
Then the mariners became frightened and each one cried to his god.

To lighten the ship for themselves, they threw its cargo into the sea.
Meanwhile, Jonah had gone down into the hold of the ship,
   and lay there fast asleep.
The captain came to him and said, "What are you doing asleep?
Rise up, call upon your God!
Perhaps God will be mindful of us so that we may not perish."

Then they said to one another, "Come, let us cast lots
   to find out on whose account we have met with this misfortune."
So they cast lots, and thus singled out Jonah.
"Tell us," they said, "what is your business?
Where do you come from?
What is your country, and to what people do you belong?"
Jonah answered them, "I am a Hebrew,
   I worship the LORD, the God of heaven,
   who made the sea and the dry land."

Now the men were seized with great fear and said to him,
   "How could you do such a thing!"—
They knew that he was fleeing from the LORD,
   because he had told them.—
They asked, "What shall we do with you,
   that the sea may quiet down for us?"
For the sea was growing more and more turbulent.
Jonah said to them, "Pick me up and throw me into the sea,
   that it may quiet down for you;
   since I know it is because of me
   that this violent storm has come upon you."

Still the men rowed hard to regain the land, but they could not,
   for the sea grew ever more turbulent.
Then they cried to the LORD: "We beseech you, O LORD,
   let us not perish for taking this man's life;
   do not charge us with shedding innocent blood,
   for you, LORD, have done as you saw fit."
Then they took Jonah and threw him into the sea,
   and the sea's raging abated.
Struck with great fear of the LORD,
   the men offered sacrifice and made vows to him.

But the LORD sent a large fish, that swallowed Jonah;
   and Jonah remained in the belly of the fish
   three days and three nights.
From the belly of the fish Jonah prayed
   to the LORD, his God.

Then the LORD commanded the fish to spew Jonah upon the shore. ✙

Jonah 2:3, 4, 5, 8

R. You will rescue my life from the pit, O Lord.
Out of my distress I called to the LORD,
　and he answered me;
From the midst of the nether world I cried for help,
　and you heard my voice. **R.**
For you cast me into the deep, into the heart of the sea,
　and the flood enveloped me;
All your breakers and your billows
　passed over me. **R.**
Then I said, "I am banished from your sight!
　yet would I again look upon your holy temple." **R.**
When my soul fainted within me,
　I remembered the LORD;
My prayer reached you
　in your holy temple. **R.**

John 13:34

R. Alleluia, alleluia.
I give you a new commandment:
love one another as I have loved you. **R.**

† *Luke 10:25-37*
Who is my neighbor?

There was a scholar of the law who stood up to test Jesus and said,
　"Teacher, what must I do to inherit eternal life?"
Jesus said to him, "What is written in the law?
How do you read it?"
He said in reply,
　"You shall love the Lord, your God,
　with all your heart,
　with all your being,
　with all your strength,
　and with all your mind,
　and your neighbor as yourself."
He replied to him, "You have answered correctly;
　do this and you will live."

But because he wished to justify himself, he said to Jesus,
　"And who is my neighbor?"
Jesus replied,
　"A man fell victim to robbers
　as he went down from Jerusalem to Jericho.
They stripped and beat him and went off leaving him half-dead.

A priest happened to be going down that road,
  but when he saw him, he passed by on the opposite side.
Likewise a Levite came to the place,
  and when he saw him, he passed by on the opposite side.
But a Samaritan traveler who came upon him
  was moved with compassion at the sight.
He approached the victim,
  poured oil and wine over his wounds and bandaged them.
Then he lifted him up on his own animal,
  took him to an inn, and cared for him.
The next day he took out two silver coins
    and gave them to the innkeeper with the instruction,
    'Take care of him.
If you spend more than what I have given you,
  I shall repay you on my way back.'
Which of these three, in your opinion,
  was neighbor to the robbers' victim?"
He answered, "The one who treated him with mercy."
Jesus said to him, "Go and do likewise." ✠

TUESDAY, OCTOBER 10
WEEKDAY

✝ *Jonah 3:1-10*
The Ninevites turned from their evil way and
God repented of the evil he had threatened.

The word of the LORD came to Jonah a second time:
"Set out for the great city of Nineveh,
  and announce to it the message that I will tell you."
So Jonah made ready and went to Nineveh,
  according to the LORD's bidding.
Now Nineveh was an enormously large city;
  it took three days to go through it.
Jonah began his journey through the city,
    and had gone but a single day's walk announcing,
    "Forty days more and Nineveh shall be destroyed,"
    when the people of Nineveh believed God;
    they proclaimed a fast and all of them, great and small,
    put on sackcloth.

When the news reached the king of Nineveh,
  he rose from his throne, laid aside his robe,
  covered himself with sackcloth, and sat in the ashes.
Then he had this proclaimed throughout Nineveh,
  by decree of the king and his nobles:

"Neither man nor beast, neither cattle nor sheep,
shall taste anything;
they shall not eat, nor shall they drink water.
Man and beast shall be covered with sackcloth
and call loudly to God;
every man shall turn from his evil way
and from the violence he has in hand.
Who knows, God may relent and forgive,
and withhold his blazing wrath,
so that we shall not perish."
When God saw by their actions how they turned from their evil way,
he repented of the evil that he had threatened to do to them;
he did not carry it out. ✛

Psalm 130:1b-2, 3-4ab, 7-8

R. (3) **If you, O Lord, mark iniquities, who can stand?**
Out of the depths I cry to you, O Lord;
Lord, hear my voice!
Let your ears be attentive
to my voice in supplication. **R.**
If you, O Lord, mark iniquities,
Lord, who can stand?
But with you is forgiveness,
that you may be revered. **R.**
Let Israel wait for the Lord,
For with the Lord is kindness
and with him is plenteous redemption;
And he will redeem Israel
from all their iniquities. **R.**

Luke 11:28

R. Alleluia, alleluia.
Blessed are those who hear the word of God
and observe it. **R.**

† *Luke 10:38-42*
Martha welcomed him into her house.
Mary has chosen the better part.

Jesus entered a village
where a woman whose name was Martha welcomed him.
She had a sister named Mary
who sat beside the Lord at his feet listening to him speak.
Martha, burdened with much serving, came to him and said,
"Lord, do you not care
that my sister has left me by myself to do the serving?
Tell her to help me."

The Lord said to her in reply,
  "Martha, Martha, you are anxious and worried about many
      things.
There is need of only one thing.
Mary has chosen the better part
  and it will not be taken from her." ✢

WEDNESDAY, OCTOBER 11
WEEKDAY, ST. POPE JOHN XXIII

† *Jonah 4:1-11*

You are concerned over a plant. And should I not
be concerned over Nineveh, the great city?

Jonah was greatly displeased
  and became angry that God did not carry out the evil
  he threatened against Nineveh.
He prayed, "I beseech you, LORD,
  is not this what I said while I was still in my own country?
This is why I fled at first to Tarshish.
I knew that you are a gracious and merciful God,
  slow to anger, rich in clemency, loath to punish.
And now, LORD, please take my life from me;
  for it is better for me to die than to live."
But the LORD asked, "Have you reason to be angry?"

Jonah then left the city for a place to the east of it,
  where he built himself a hut and waited under it in the shade,
  to see what would happen to the city.
And when the LORD God provided a gourd plant
  that grew up over Jonah's head,
  giving shade that relieved him of any discomfort,
  Jonah was very happy over the plant.
But the next morning at dawn
  God sent a worm that attacked the plant,
  so that it withered.
And when the sun arose, God sent a burning east wind;
  and the sun beat upon Jonah's head till he became faint.
Then Jonah asked for death, saying,
  "I would be better off dead than alive."

But God said to Jonah,
  "Have you reason to be angry over the plant?"
"I have reason to be angry," Jonah answered, "angry enough to die."
Then the LORD said,
  "You are concerned over the plant which cost you no labor
  and which you did not raise;

it came up in one night and in one night it perished.
And should I not be concerned over Nineveh, the great city,
in which there are more than a hundred and twenty thousand
persons
who cannot distinguish their right hand from their left,
not to mention the many cattle?" ✦

Psalm 86:3-4, 5-6, 9-10
R. (15) **Lord, you are merciful and gracious.**
Have mercy on me, O Lord,
for to you I call all the day.
Gladden the soul of your servant,
for to you, O Lord, I lift up my soul. **R.**
For you, O Lord, are good and forgiving,
abounding in kindness to all who call upon you.
Hearken, O LORD, to my prayer
and attend to the sound of my pleading. **R.**
All the nations you have made shall come
and worship you, O Lord,
and glorify your name.
For you are great, and you do wondrous deeds;
you alone are God. **R.**

Romans 8:15bc
R. Alleluia, alleluia.
You have received a spirit of adoption as sons
through which we cry: Abba! Father! **R.**

† Luke 11:1-4
Lord, teach us to pray.

Jesus was praying in a certain place, and when he had finished,
one of his disciples said to him,
"Lord, teach us to pray just as John taught his disciples."
He said to them, "When you pray, say:

Father, hallowed be your name,
your Kingdom come.
Give us each day our daily bread
and forgive us our sins
for we ourselves forgive everyone in debt to us,
and do not subject us to the final test." ✦

THURSDAY, OCTOBER 12
WEEKDAY

† *Malachi 3:13-20b*
The day is coming, blazing like an oven.

You have defied me in word, says the LORD,
  yet you ask, "What have we spoken against you?"
You have said, "It is vain to serve God,
  and what do we profit by keeping his command,
And going about in penitential dress
  in awe of the LORD of hosts?
Rather must we call the proud blessed;
  for indeed evildoers prosper,
  and even tempt God with impunity."
Then they who fear the LORD spoke with one another,
  and the LORD listened attentively;
And a record book was written before him
  of those who fear the LORD and trust in his name.
And they shall be mine, says the LORD of hosts,
  my own special possession, on the day I take action.
And I will have compassion on them,
  as a man has compassion on his son who serves him.
Then you will again see the distinction
  between the just and the wicked;
Between the one who serves God,
  and the one who does not serve him.
For lo, the day is coming, blazing like an oven,
  when all the proud and all evildoers will be stubble,
And the day that is coming will set them on fire,
  leaving them neither root nor branch,
  says the LORD of hosts.
But for you who fear my name, there will arise
  the sun of justice with its healing rays. ✛

Psalm 1:1-2, 3, 4 and 6
R. (Psalm 40:5a) **Blessed are they who hope in the Lord.**
Blessed the man who follows not
  the counsel of the wicked
Nor walks in the way of sinners,
  nor sits in the company of the insolent,
But delights in the law of the LORD
  and meditates on his law day and night. **R.**
He is like a tree
  planted near running water,

That yields its fruit in due season,
and whose leaves never fade.
Whatever he does, prospers. **R.**
Not so the wicked, not so;
they are like chaff which the wind drives away.
For the LORD watches over the way of the just,
but the way of the wicked vanishes. **R.**

See Acts 16:14b
R. Alleluia, alleluia.
Open our hearts, O Lord,
to listen to the words of your Son. **R.**

† *Luke 11:5-13*
Ask and you will receive.

Jesus said to his disciples:
"Suppose one of you has a friend
to whom he goes at midnight and says,
'Friend, lend me three loaves of bread,
for a friend of mine has arrived at my house from a journey
and I have nothing to offer him,'
and he says in reply from within,
'Do not bother me; the door has already been locked
and my children and I are already in bed.
I cannot get up to give you anything.'
I tell you, if he does not get up to give him the loaves
because of their friendship,
he will get up to give him whatever he needs
because of his persistence.

"And I tell you, ask and you will receive;
seek and you will find;
knock and the door will be opened to you.
For everyone who asks, receives;
and the one who seeks, finds;
and to the one who knocks, the door will be opened.
What father among you would hand his son a snake
when he asks for a fish?
Or hand him a scorpion when he asks for an egg?
If you then, who are wicked,
know how to give good gifts to your children,
how much more will the Father in heaven give the Holy Spirit
to those who ask him?" ✛

FRIDAY, OCTOBER 13
WEEKDAY

† *Joel 1:13-15; 2:1-2*
The day of the LORD is coming, a day of darkness and of gloom.

Gird yourselves and weep, O priests!
　wail, O ministers of the altar!
Come, spend the night in sackcloth,
　O ministers of my God!
The house of your God is deprived
　of offering and libation.
Proclaim a fast,
　call an assembly;
Gather the elders,
　all who dwell in the land,
Into the house of the LORD, your God,
　and cry to the LORD!

Alas, the day!
　for near is the day of the LORD,
　and it comes as ruin from the Almighty.

Blow the trumpet in Zion,
　sound the alarm on my holy mountain!
Let all who dwell in the land tremble,
　for the day of the LORD is coming;
Yes, it is near, a day of darkness and of gloom,
　a day of clouds and somberness!
Like dawn spreading over the mountains,
　a people numerous and mighty!
Their like has not been from of old,
　nor will it be after them,
　even to the years of distant generations. ✛

Psalm 9:2-3, 6 and 16, 8-9
R. (9) The Lord will judge the world with justice.
I will give thanks to you, O LORD, with all my heart;
　I will declare all your wondrous deeds.
I will be glad and exult in you;
　I will sing praise to your name, Most High. **R.**
You rebuked the nations and destroyed the wicked;
　their name you blotted out forever and ever.
The nations are sunk in the pit they have made;
　in the snare they set, their foot is caught. **R.**
But the LORD sits enthroned forever;
　he has set up his throne for judgment.

He judges the world with justice;
  he governs the peoples with equity. **R.**

  John 12:31b-32
R. Alleluia, alleluia.
The prince of this world will now be cast out,
and when I am lifted up from the earth
I will draw all to myself, says the Lord. **R.**

✝ *Luke 11:15-26*
If it is by the finger of God that I drive out demons,
then the Kingdom of God has come upon you.

When Jesus had driven out a demon, some of the crowd said:
"By the power of Beelzebul, the prince of demons,
  he drives out demons."
Others, to test him, asked him for a sign from heaven.
But he knew their thoughts and said to them,
  "Every kingdom divided against itself will be laid waste
  and house will fall against house.
And if Satan is divided against himself, how will his kingdom
    stand?
For you say that it is by Beelzebul that I drive out demons.
If I, then, drive out demons by Beelzebul,
  by whom do your own people drive them out?
Therefore they will be your judges.
But if it is by the finger of God that I drive out demons,
  then the Kingdom of God has come upon you.
When a strong man fully armed guards his palace,
  his possessions are safe.
But when one stronger than he attacks and overcomes him,
  he takes away the armor on which he relied
  and distributes the spoils.
Whoever is not with me is against me,
  and whoever does not gather with me scatters.

"When an unclean spirit goes out of someone,
  it roams through arid regions searching for rest
  but, finding none, it says,
  'I shall return to my home from which I came.'
But upon returning, it finds it swept clean and put in order.
Then it goes and brings back seven other spirits
  more wicked than itself who move in and dwell there,
  and the last condition of that man is worse than the first." ✛

SATURDAY, OCTOBER 14
WEEKDAY, ST. POPE CALLISTUS I, [BVM]

† *Joel 4:12-21*
Apply the sickle, for the harvest is ripe.

Thus says the LORD:
Let the nations bestir themselves and come up
  to the Valley of Jehoshaphat;
For there will I sit in judgment
  upon all the neighboring nations.

Apply the sickle,
  for the harvest is ripe;
Come and tread,
  for the wine press is full;
The vats overflow,
  for great is their malice.
Crowd upon crowd
  in the valley of decision;
For near is the day of the LORD
  in the valley of decision.
Sun and moon are darkened,
  and the stars withhold their brightness.
The LORD roars from Zion,
  and from Jerusalem raises his voice;
The heavens and the earth quake,
  but the LORD is a refuge to his people,
  a stronghold to the children of Israel.

Then shall you know that I, the LORD, am your God,
  dwelling on Zion, my holy mountain;
Jerusalem shall be holy,
  and strangers shall pass through her no more.
And then, on that day,
  the mountains shall drip new wine,
  and the hills shall flow with milk;
And the channels of Judah
  shall flow with water:
A fountain shall issue from the house of the LORD,
  to water the Valley of Shittim.
Egypt shall be a waste,
  and Edom a desert waste,
Because of violence done to the people of Judah,
  because they shed innocent blood in their land.
But Judah shall abide forever,

and Jerusalem for all generations.
I will avenge their blood,
  and not leave it unpunished.
The LORD dwells in Zion. ✛

Psalm 97:1-2, 5-6, 11-12

R. (12a) **Rejoice in the Lord, you just!**
The LORD is king; let the earth rejoice;
  let the many isles be glad.
Clouds and darkness are round about him,
  justice and judgment are the foundation of his throne. **R.**
The mountains melt like wax before the LORD,
  before the LORD of all the earth.
The heavens proclaim his justice,
  and all peoples see his glory. **R.**
Light dawns for the just;
  and gladness, for the upright of heart.
Be glad in the LORD, you just,
  and give thanks to his holy name. **R.**

Luke 11:28

R. Alleluia, alleluia.
Blessed are those who hear the word of God
and observe it. **R.**

† *Luke 11:27-28*
Blessed is the womb that carried you. Rather, blessed are
those who hear the word of God and observe it.

While Jesus was speaking,
  a woman from the crowd called out and said to him,
  "Blessed is the womb that carried you
  and the breasts at which you nursed."
He replied, "Rather, blessed are those
  who hear the word of God and observe it." ✛

SUNDAY, OCTOBER 15
TWENTY-EIGHTH SUNDAY IN ORDINARY TIME

† *Isaiah 25:6-10a*
The LORD will prepare a feast and wipe away the tears from every face.

On this mountain the LORD of hosts
  will provide for all peoples
a feast of rich food and choice wines,
  juicy, rich food and pure, choice wines.
On this mountain he will destroy
  the veil that veils all peoples,

the web that is woven over all nations;
  he will destroy death forever.
The Lord GOD will wipe away
  the tears from every face;
the reproach of his people he will remove
  from the whole earth; for the LORD has spoken.
  On that day it will be said:
"Behold our God, to whom we looked to save us!
  This is the LORD for whom we looked;
  let us rejoice and be glad that he has saved us!"
For the hand of the LORD will rest on this mountain. ✢

Psalm 23:1b-3a, 3b-4, 5, 6

R. (6cd) I shall live in the house of the Lord all the days of my life.

The LORD is my shepherd; I shall not want.
  In verdant pastures he gives me repose;
beside restful waters he leads me;
  he refreshes my soul. **R.**
He guides me in right paths
  for his name's sake.
Even though I walk in the dark valley
  I fear no evil; for you are at my side
with your rod and your staff
  that give me courage. **R.**
You spread the table before me
  in the sight of my foes;
you anoint my head with oil;
  my cup overflows. **R.**
Only goodness and kindness follow me
  all the days of my life;
and I shall dwell in the house of the LORD
  for years to come. **R.**

† *Philippians 4:12-14, 19-20*
I can do all things in him who strengthens me.

Brothers and sisters:
I know how to live in humble circumstances;
  I know also how to live with abundance.
In every circumstance and in all things
  I have learned the secret of being well fed and of going hungry,
  of living in abundance and of being in need.
I can do all things in him who strengthens me.
Still, it was kind of you to share in my distress.

My God will fully supply whatever you need,
  in accord with his glorious riches in Christ Jesus.
To our God and Father, glory forever and ever. Amen. ✛

    See Ephesians 1:17-18
R. Alleluia, alleluia.
May the Father of our Lord Jesus Christ
enlighten the eyes of our hearts,
so that we may know what is the hope
that belongs to our call. **R.**

            † *Matthew 22:1-14* (or Matthew 22:1-10)
              Invite to the wedding feast whomever you find.

Jesus again in reply spoke to the chief priests and elders of the
    people
  in parables, saying,
  "The kingdom of heaven may be likened to a king
  who gave a wedding feast for his son.
He dispatched his servants
  to summon the invited guests to the feast,
  but they refused to come.
A second time he sent other servants, saying,
  'Tell those invited: "Behold, I have prepared my banquet,
  my calves and fattened cattle are killed,
  and everything is ready; come to the feast."'
Some ignored the invitation and went away,
  one to his farm, another to his business.
The rest laid hold of his servants,
  mistreated them, and killed them.
The king was enraged and sent his troops,
  destroyed those murderers, and burned their city.
Then he said to his servants, 'The feast is ready,
  but those who were invited were not worthy to come.
Go out, therefore, into the main roads
  and invite to the feast whomever you find.'
The servants went out into the streets
  and gathered all they found, bad and good alike,
  and the hall was filled with guests.
But when the king came in to meet the guests,
  he saw a man there not dressed in a wedding garment.
The king said to him, 'My friend, how is it
  that you came in here without a wedding garment?'
But he was reduced to silence.
Then the king said to his attendants, 'Bind his hands and feet,
  and cast him into the darkness outside,

where there will be wailing and grinding of teeth.'
Many are invited, but few are chosen." ✛

MONDAY, OCTOBER 16
Weekday, St. Hedwig, St. Margaret Mary Alacoque

† *Romans 1:1-7*

Through Christ Jesus we have received the grace of apostleship,
to bring about the obedience of faith among the Gentiles.

Paul, a slave of Christ Jesus,
  called to be an Apostle and set apart for the Gospel of God,
  which he promised previously through his prophets in the holy
      Scriptures,
  the Gospel about his Son, descended from David according to the
      flesh,
  but established as Son of God in power
  according to the Spirit of holiness
  through resurrection from the dead, Jesus Christ our Lord.
Through him we have received the grace of apostleship,
  to bring about the obedience of faith,
  for the sake of his name, among all the Gentiles,
  among whom are you also, who are called to belong to Jesus Christ;
  to all the beloved of God in Rome, called to be holy.
Grace to you and peace from God our Father
  and the Lord Jesus Christ. ✛

Psalm 98:1bcde, 2-3ab, 3cd-4
R. (2a) **The Lord has made known his salvation.**
Sing to the LORD a new song,
  for he has done wondrous deeds;
His right hand has won victory for him,
  his holy arm. **R.**
The LORD has made his salvation known:
  in the sight of the nations he has revealed his justice.
He has remembered his kindness and his faithfulness
  toward the house of Israel. **R.**
All the ends of the earth have seen
  the salvation by our God.
Sing joyfully to the LORD, all you lands;
  break into song; sing praise. **R.**

Psalm 95:8
R. Alleluia, alleluia.
If today you hear his voice,
harden not your hearts. **R.**

† *Luke 11:29-32*

This generation seeks a sign, but no sign will be given it,
except the sign of Jonah.

While still more people gathered in the crowd, Jesus said to them,
"This generation is an evil generation;
  it seeks a sign, but no sign will be given it,
  except the sign of Jonah.
Just as Jonah became a sign to the Ninevites,
  so will the Son of Man be to this generation.
At the judgment
  the queen of the south will rise with the men of this generation
  and she will condemn them,
  because she came from the ends of the earth
  to hear the wisdom of Solomon,
  and there is something greater than Solomon here.
At the judgment the men of Nineveh will arise with this generation
  and condemn it,
  because at the preaching of Jonah they repented,
  and there is something greater than Jonah here." ✛

TUESDAY, OCTOBER 17
ST. IGNATIUS OF ANTIOCH

† *Romans 1:16-25*

Although they knew God they did not accord him glory as God.

Brothers and sisters:
I am not ashamed of the Gospel.
It is the power of God for the salvation of everyone who believes:
  for Jew first, and then Greek.
For in it is revealed the righteousness of God from faith to faith;
  as it is written, "The one who is righteous by faith will live."

The wrath of God is indeed being revealed from heaven
  against every impiety and wickedness
  of those who suppress the truth by their wickedness.
For what can be known about God is evident to them,
  because God made it evident to them.
Ever since the creation of the world,
  his invisible attributes of eternal power and divinity
  have been able to be understood and perceived in what he has
    made.
As a result, they have no excuse;
  for although they knew God
  they did not accord him glory as God or give him thanks.
Instead, they became vain in their reasoning,

and their senseless minds were darkened.
While claiming to be wise, they became fools
  and exchanged the glory of the immortal God
  for the likeness of an image of mortal man
  or of birds or of four-legged animals or of snakes.

Therefore, God handed them over to impurity
  through the lusts of their hearts
  for the mutual degradation of their bodies.
They exchanged the truth of God for a lie
  and revered and worshiped the creature rather than the creator,
  who is blessed forever. Amen. ✢

Psalm 19:2-3, 4-5ab

R. (2a) The heavens proclaim the glory of God.
The heavens declare the glory of God,
  and the firmament proclaims his handiwork.
Day pours out the word to day,
  and night to night imparts knowledge. **R.**
Not a word nor a discourse
  whose voice is not heard;
Through all the earth their voice resounds,
  and to the ends of the world, their message. **R.**

Hebrews 4:12

R. Alleluia, alleluia.
The word of God is living and effective,
able to discern reflections and thoughts of the heart. **R.**

† *Luke 11:37-41*
Give alms, and behold, everything will be clean for you.

After Jesus had spoken,
  a Pharisee invited him to dine at his home.
He entered and reclined at table to eat.
The Pharisee was amazed to see
  that he did not observe the prescribed washing before the meal.
The Lord said to him, "Oh you Pharisees!
Although you cleanse the outside of the cup and the dish,
  inside you are filled with plunder and evil.
You fools!
Did not the maker of the outside also make the inside?
But as to what is within, give alms,
  and behold, everything will be clean for you." ✢

WEDNESDAY, OCTOBER 18
St. Luke

† *2 Timothy 4:10-17b*
Luke is the only one with me.

Beloved:
Demas, enamored of the present world,
  deserted me and went to Thessalonica,
  Crescens to Galatia, and Titus to Dalmatia.
Luke is the only one with me.
Get Mark and bring him with you,
  for he is helpful to me in the ministry.
I have sent Tychicus to Ephesus.
When you come, bring the cloak I left with Carpus in Troas,
  the papyrus rolls, and especially the parchments.

Alexander the coppersmith did me a great deal of harm;
  the Lord will repay him according to his deeds.
You too be on guard against him,
  for he has strongly resisted our preaching.

At my first defense no one appeared on my behalf,
  but everyone deserted me.
May it not be held against them!
But the Lord stood by me and gave me strength,
  so that through me the proclamation might be completed
  and all the Gentiles might hear it. ✛

Psalm 145:10-11, 12-13, 17-18
R. (12) **Your friends make known, O Lord, the glorious
  splendor of your Kingdom.**
Let all your works give you thanks, O LORD,
  and let your faithful ones bless you.
Let them discourse of the glory of your Kingdom
  and speak of your might. **R.**
Making known to men your might
  and the glorious splendor of your Kingdom.
Your Kingdom is a Kingdom for all ages,
  and your dominion endures through all generations. **R.**
The LORD is just in all his ways
  and holy in all his works.
The LORD is near to all who call upon him,
  to all who call upon him in truth. **R.**

See *John 15:16*

R. Alleluia, alleluia.

I chose you from the world,
to go and bear fruit that will last, says the Lord. **R.**

† *Luke 10:1-9*
The harvest is abundant but the laborers are few.

The Lord Jesus appointed seventy-two disciples
  whom he sent ahead of him in pairs
  to every town and place he intended to visit.
He said to them,
  "The harvest is abundant but the laborers are few;
  so ask the master of the harvest
  to send out laborers for his harvest.
Go on your way;
  behold, I am sending you like lambs among wolves.
Carry no money bag, no sack, no sandals;
  and greet no one along the way.
Into whatever house you enter,
  first say, 'Peace to this household.'
If a peaceful person lives there,
  your peace will rest on him;
  but if not, it will return to you.
Stay in the same house and eat and drink what is offered to you,
  for the laborer deserves payment.
Do not move about from one house to another.
Whatever town you enter and they welcome you,
  eat what is set before you,
  cure the sick in it and say to them,
  'The Kingdom of God is at hand for you.'" ✠

THURSDAY, OCTOBER 19
St. John de Brébeuf, St. Isaac Jogues and Companions

† *Romans 3:21-30*
A person is justified by faith apart from works of the law.

Brothers and sisters:
Now the righteousness of God has been manifested apart from the
    law,
  though testified to by the law and the prophets,
  the righteousness of God through faith in Jesus Christ
  for all who believe.
For there is no distinction;
  all have sinned and are deprived of the glory of God.
They are justified freely by his grace

through the redemption in Christ Jesus,
whom God set forth as an expiation,
through faith, by his Blood, to prove his righteousness
because of the forgiveness of sins previously committed,
through the forbearance of God—
to prove his righteousness in the present time,
that he might be righteous
and justify the one who has faith in Jesus.

What occasion is there then for boasting? It is ruled out.
On what principle, that of works?
No, rather on the principle of faith.
For we consider that a person is justified by faith
 apart from works of the law.
Does God belong to Jews alone?
Does he not belong to Gentiles, too?
Yes, also to Gentiles, for God is one
 and will justify the circumcised on the basis of faith
 and the uncircumcised through faith. ✣

Psalm 130:1b-2, 3-4, 5-6ab

R. (7) **With the Lord there is mercy, and fullness of redemption.**
Out of the depths I cry to you, O LORD;
 LORD, hear my voice!
Let your ears be attentive
 to my voice in supplication. **R.**
If you, O LORD, mark iniquities,
 LORD, who can stand?
But with you is forgiveness,
 that you may be revered. **R.**
I trust in the LORD;
 my soul trusts in his word.
My soul waits for the LORD
 more than sentinels wait for the dawn. **R.**

John 14:6

R. Alleluia, alleluia.
I am the way and the truth and the life, says the Lord;
no one comes to the Father except through me. **R.**

† *Luke 11:47-54*

*The blood of the prophets is required, from the blood of Abel
to the blood of Zechariah.*

The Lord said:
"Woe to you who build the memorials of the prophets
 whom your fathers killed.

Consequently, you bear witness and give consent
  to the deeds of your ancestors,
  for they killed them and you do the building.
Therefore, the wisdom of God said,
  'I will send to them prophets and Apostles;
  some of them they will kill and persecute'
  in order that this generation might be charged
  with the blood of all the prophets
  shed since the foundation of the world,
  from the blood of Abel to the blood of Zechariah
  who died between the altar and the temple building.
Yes, I tell you, this generation will be charged with their blood!
Woe to you, scholars of the law!
You have taken away the key of knowledge.
You yourselves did not enter and you stopped those trying to enter."
When Jesus left, the scribes and Pharisees
  began to act with hostility toward him
  and to interrogate him about many things,
  for they were plotting to catch him at something he might say. ✛

FRIDAY, OCTOBER 20
WEEKDAY, ST. PAUL OF THE CROSS

† Romans 4:1-8
Abraham believed God, and it was credited to him as righteousness.

Brothers and sisters:
What can we say that Abraham found,
  our ancestor according to the flesh?
Indeed, if Abraham was justified on the basis of his works,
  he has reason to boast;
  but this was not so in the sight of God.
For what does the Scripture say?
Abraham believed God, and it was credited to him as righteousness.
A worker's wage is credited not as a gift, but as something due.
But when one does not work,
  yet believes in the one who justifies the ungodly,
  his faith is credited as righteousness.
So also David declares the blessedness of the person
  to whom God credits righteousness apart from works:

    Blessed are they whose iniquities are forgiven
      and whose sins are covered.
    Blessed is the man whose sin the Lord does not record. ✛

Psalm 32:1b-2, 5, 11

R. (see 7) **I turn to you, Lord, in time of trouble, and you fill me with the joy of salvation.**

Blessed is he whose fault is taken away,
   whose sin is covered.
Blessed the man to whom the LORD imputes not guilt,
   in whose spirit there is no guile. **R.**
Then I acknowledged my sin to you,
   my guilt I covered not.
I said, "I confess my faults to the LORD,"
   and you took away the guilt of my sin. **R.**
Be glad in the LORD and rejoice, you just;
   exult, all you upright of heart. **R.**

Psalm 33:22

R. Alleluia, alleluia.

May your kindness, O LORD, be upon us;
who have put our hope in you. **R.**

✝ Luke 12:1-7

Even the hairs of your head have all been counted.

At that time:
So many people were crowding together
   that they were trampling one another underfoot.
Jesus began to speak, first to his disciples,
   "Beware of the leaven—that is, the hypocrisy—of the Pharisees.

"There is nothing concealed that will not be revealed,
   nor secret that will not be known.
Therefore whatever you have said in the darkness
   will be heard in the light,
   and what you have whispered behind closed doors
   will be proclaimed on the housetops.
I tell you, my friends,
   do not be afraid of those who kill the body
   but after that can do no more.
I shall show you whom to fear.
Be afraid of the one who after killing
   has the power to cast into Gehenna;
   yes, I tell you, be afraid of that one.
Are not five sparrows sold for two small coins?
Yet not one of them has escaped the notice of God.
Even the hairs of your head have all been counted.
Do not be afraid.
You are worth more than many sparrows." ✛

SATURDAY, OCTOBER 21
WEEKDAY, *[BVM]*

† *Romans 4:13, 16-18*
Abraham believed, hoping against hope.

Brothers and sisters:
It was not through the law
   that the promise was made to Abraham and his descendants
   that he would inherit the world,
   but through the righteousness that comes from faith.
For this reason, it depends on faith,
   so that it may be a gift,
   and the promise may be guaranteed to all his descendants,
   not to those who only adhere to the law
   but to those who follow the faith of Abraham,
   who is the father of all of us, as it is written,
I have made you father of many nations.
He is our father in the sight of God,
   in whom he believed, who gives life to the dead
   and calls into being what does not exist.
He believed, hoping against hope,
   that he would become *the father of many nations,*
   according to what was said, *Thus shall your descendants be.* ✛

   Psalm 105:6-7, 8-9, 42-43
R. (8a) **The Lord remembers his covenant for ever.**
You descendants of Abraham, his servants,
   sons of Jacob, his chosen ones!
He, the LORD, is our God;
   throughout the earth his judgments prevail. **R.**
He remembers forever his covenant
   which he made binding for a thousand generations—
Which he entered into with Abraham
   and by his oath to Isaac. **R.**
For he remembered his holy word
   to his servant Abraham.
And he led forth his people with joy;
   with shouts of joy, his chosen ones. **R.**

   John 15:26b, 27a
R. Alleluia, alleluia.
The Spirit of truth will testify to me, says the Lord,
and you also will testify. **R.**

† Luke 12:8-12
The Holy Spirit will teach you at that moment what you should say.

Jesus said to his disciples:
"I tell you,
everyone who acknowledges me before others
the Son of Man will acknowledge before the angels of God.
But whoever denies me before others
will be denied before the angels of God.

"Everyone who speaks a word against the Son of Man will be forgiven,
but the one who blasphemes against the Holy Spirit
will not be forgiven.
When they take you before synagogues and before rulers and
authorities,
do not worry about how or what your defense will be
or about what you are to say.
For the Holy Spirit will teach you at that moment what you should
say." ✙

SUNDAY, OCTOBER 22
TWENTY-NINTH SUNDAY IN ORDINARY TIME

† Isaiah 45:1, 4-6
I have grasped the right hand of Cyrus to subdue the nations before him.

Thus says the LORD to his anointed, Cyrus,
whose right hand I grasp,
subduing nations before him,
and making kings run in his service,
opening doors before him
and leaving the gates unbarred:
For the sake of Jacob, my servant,
of Israel, my chosen one,
I have called you by your name,
giving you a title, though you knew me not.
I am the LORD and there is no other,
there is no God besides me.
It is I who arm you, though you know me not,
so that toward the rising and the setting of the sun
people may know that there is none besides me.
I am the LORD, there is no other. ✙

Psalm 96:1 and 3, 4-5, 7-8, 9-10ac
R. (7b) **Give the Lord glory and honor.**
Sing to the LORD a new song;
sing to the LORD, all you lands.

Tell his glory among the nations;
    among all peoples, his wondrous deeds. **R.**
For great is the LORD and highly to be praised;
    awesome is he, beyond all gods.
For all the gods of the nations are things of nought,
    but the LORD made the heavens. **R.**
Give to the LORD, you families of nations,
    give to the LORD glory and praise;
    give to the LORD the glory due his name!
Bring gifts, and enter his courts. **R.**
Worship the LORD, in holy attire;
    tremble before him, all the earth;
say among the nations: The LORD is king,
    he governs the peoples with equity. **R.**

† *1 Thessalonians 1:1-5b*
Calling to mind faith, love and hope.

Paul, Silvanus, and Timothy to the church of the Thessalonians
    in God the Father and the Lord Jesus Christ:
    grace to you and peace.
We give thanks to God always for all of you,
    remembering you in our prayers,
    unceasingly calling to mind your work of faith and labor of love
    and endurance in hope of our Lord Jesus Christ,
    before our God and Father,
    knowing, brothers and sisters loved by God,
    how you were chosen.
For our gospel did not come to you in word alone,
    but also in power and in the Holy Spirit and with much conviction. ✛

Philippians 2:15d, 16a
R. Alleluia, alleluia.
Shine like lights in the world
as you hold on to the word of life. **R.**

† *Matthew 22:15-21*
Repay to Caesar what belongs to Caesar and to God what belongs to God.

The Pharisees went off
    and plotted how they might entrap Jesus in speech.
They sent their disciples to him, with the Herodians, saying,
    "Teacher, we know that you are a truthful man
    and that you teach the way of God in accordance with the truth.
And you are not concerned with anyone's opinion,
    for you do not regard a person's status.
Tell us, then, what is your opinion:

Is it lawful to pay the census tax to Caesar or not?"
Knowing their malice, Jesus said,
    "Why are you testing me, you hypocrites?
Show me the coin that pays the census tax."
Then they handed him the Roman coin.
He said to them, "Whose image is this and whose inscription?"
They replied, "Caesar's."
At that he said to them,
    "Then repay to Caesar what belongs to Caesar
    and to God what belongs to God." ✛

MONDAY, OCTOBER 23
WEEKDAY, ST. JOHN OF CAPISTRANO

† *Romans 4:20-25*
It was written for us when it says that our faith in God will be counted.

Brothers and sisters:
Abraham did not doubt God's promise in unbelief;
    rather, he was empowered by faith and gave glory to God
    and was fully convinced that what God had promised
    he was also able to do.
That is why *it was credited to him as righteousness.*
But it was not for him alone that it was written
    that *it was credited to him;*
    it was also for us, to whom it will be credited,
    who believe in the one who raised Jesus our Lord from the dead,
    who was handed over for our transgressions
    and was raised for our justification. ✛

Luke 1:69-70, 71-72, 73-75
R. (see 68) **Blessed be the Lord, the God of Israel; he has come
    to his people.**
He has come to his people and set them free.
He has raised up for us a mighty savior,
    born of the house of his servant David. **R.**
Through his holy prophets he promised of old
    that he would save us from our enemies,
    from the hands of all who hate us.
He promised to show mercy to our fathers
    and to remember his holy covenant. **R.**
This was the oath he swore to our father Abraham:
    to set us free from the hands of our enemies,
    free to worship him without fear,
    holy and righteous in his sight all the days of our life. **R.**

Matthew 5:3
R. Alleluia, alleluia.
Blessed are the poor in spirit;
for theirs is the Kingdom of heaven. **R.**

† *Luke 12:13-21*
And the things you have prepared, to whom will they belong?

Someone in the crowd said to Jesus,
  "Teacher, tell my brother to share the inheritance with me."
He replied to him,
  "Friend, who appointed me as your judge and arbitrator?"
Then he said to the crowd,
  "Take care to guard against all greed,
  for though one may be rich,
  one's life does not consist of possessions."

Then he told them a parable.
"There was a rich man whose land produced a bountiful harvest.
He asked himself, 'What shall I do,
  for I do not have space to store my harvest?'
And he said, 'This is what I shall do:
  I shall tear down my barns and build larger ones.
There I shall store all my grain and other goods
  and I shall say to myself, "Now as for you,
  you have so many good things stored up for many years,
  rest, eat, drink, be merry!"'
But God said to him,
  'You fool, this night your life will be demanded of you;
  and the things you have prepared, to whom will they belong?'
Thus will it be for the one who stores up treasure for himself
  but is not rich in what matters to God." ✛

TUESDAY, OCTOBER 24
WEEKDAY, ST. ANTHONY MARY CLARET

† *Romans 5:12, 15b, 17-19, 20b-21*
If by the transgressions of one person death came to reign,
how much more will those who receive grace come to reign in life.

Brothers and sisters:
Through one man sin entered the world,
  and through sin, death,
  and thus death came to all men, inasmuch as all sinned.

If by that one person's transgression the many died,
  how much more did the grace of God
  and the gracious gift of the one man Jesus Christ

overflow for the many.
For if, by the transgression of the one,
    death came to reign through that one,
    how much more will those who receive the abundance of grace
    and the gift of justification
    come to reign in life through the one Jesus Christ.
In conclusion, just as through one transgression
    condemnation came upon all,
    so, through one righteous act
    acquittal and life came to all.
For just as through the disobedience of one man
    the many were made sinners,
    so, through the obedience of the one
    the many will be made righteous.
Where sin increased, grace overflowed all the more,
    so that, as sin reigned in death,
    grace also might reign through justification
    for eternal life through Jesus Christ our Lord. ✝

Psalm 40:7-8a, 8b-9, 10, 17
R. (8a and 9a) **Here I am, Lord; I come to do your will.**
Sacrifice or oblation you wished not,
    but ears open to obedience you gave me.
Burnt offerings or sin-offerings you sought not;
    then said I, "Behold I come." **R.**
"In the written scroll it is prescribed for me,
To do your will, O my God, is my delight,
    and your law is within my heart!" **R.**
I announced your justice in the vast assembly;
    I did not restrain my lips, as you, O Lord, know. **R.**
May all who seek you
    exult and be glad in you,
And may those who love your salvation
    say ever, "The Lord be glorified." **R.**

Luke 21:36
R. Alleluia, alleluia.
Be vigilant at all times and pray
that you may have the strength to stand before the Son of Man. **R.**

†*Luke 12:35-38*
Blessed are those servants whom the master finds vigilant on his arrival.

Jesus said to his disciples:
"Gird your loins and light your lamps
    and be like servants who await their master's return from a wedding,
    ready to open immediately when he comes and knocks.

Blessed are those servants
　whom the master finds vigilant on his arrival.
Amen, I say to you, he will gird himself,
　have them recline at table, and proceed to wait on them.
And should he come in the second or third watch
　and find them prepared in this way,
　blessed are those servants." ✢

WEDNESDAY, OCTOBER 25
Weekday

✝ Romans 6:12-18
Present yourselves to God as raised from the dead to life.

Brothers and sisters:
Sin must not reign over your mortal bodies
　so that you obey their desires.
And do not present the parts of your bodies to sin
　as weapons for wickedness,
　but present yourselves to God as raised from the dead to life
　and the parts of your bodies to God
　as weapons for righteousness.
For sin is not to have any power over you,
　since you are not under the law but under grace.

What then? Shall we sin because we are not under the law
　but under grace?
Of course not!
Do you not know that if you present yourselves
　to someone as obedient slaves,
　you are slaves of the one you obey,
　either of sin, which leads to death,
　or of obedience, which leads to righteousness?
But thanks be to God that, although you were once slaves of sin,
　you have become obedient from the heart
　to the pattern of teaching to which you were entrusted.
Freed from sin, you have become slaves of righteousness. ✢

　Psalm 124:1b-3, 4-6, 7-8
R. (8a) **Our help is in the name of the Lord.**
Had not the LORD been with us,
　let Israel say, had not the LORD been with us—
When men rose up against us,
　then would they have swallowed us alive;
When their fury was inflamed against us. **R.**
Then would the waters have overwhelmed us;
The torrent would have swept over us;

over us then would have swept the raging waters.
Blessed be the LORD, who did not leave us
 a prey to their teeth. **R.**
We were rescued like a bird
 from the fowlers' snare;
Broken was the snare,
 and we were freed.
Our help is in the name of the LORD,
 who made heaven and earth. **R.**

 Matthew 24:42a, 44
R. Alleluia, alleluia.
Stay awake!
For you do not know when the Son of Man will come. **R.**

† *Luke 12:39-48*
Much will be required of the person entrusted with much.

Jesus said to his disciples:
"Be sure of this:
 if the master of the house had known the hour
 when the thief was coming,
 he would not have let his house be broken into.
You also must be prepared,
 for at an hour you do not expect, the Son of Man will come."

Then Peter said,
 "Lord, is this parable meant for us or for everyone?"
And the Lord replied,
 "Who, then, is the faithful and prudent steward
 whom the master will put in charge of his servants
 to distribute the food allowance at the proper time?
Blessed is that servant whom his master on arrival finds doing so.
Truly, I say to you, he will put him
 in charge of all his property.
But if that servant says to himself,
 'My master is delayed in coming,'
 and begins to beat the menservants and the maidservants,
 to eat and drink and get drunk,
 then that servant's master will come
 on an unexpected day and at an unknown hour
 and will punish the servant severely
 and assign him a place with the unfaithful.
That servant who knew his master's will
 but did not make preparations nor act in accord with his will
 shall be beaten severely;

and the servant who was ignorant of his master's will
but acted in a way deserving of a severe beating
shall be beaten only lightly.
Much will be required of the person entrusted with much,
and still more will be demanded of the person entrusted with
more." ✝

THURSDAY, OCTOBER 26
WEEKDAY

✝ Romans 6:19-23
Now you have been freed from sin and have been become slaves of God.

Brothers and sisters:
I am speaking in human terms because of the weakness of your
nature.
For just as you presented the parts of your bodies as slaves to impurity
and to lawlessness for lawlessness,
so now present them as slaves to righteousness for sanctification.
For when you were slaves of sin, you were free from righteousness.
But what profit did you get then
from the things of which you are now ashamed?
For the end of those things is death.
But now that you have been freed from sin and have become slaves
of God,
the benefit that you have leads to sanctification,
and its end is eternal life.
For the wages of sin is death,
but the gift of God is eternal life in Christ Jesus our Lord. ✝

Psalm 1:1-2, 3, 4 and 6
R. (Psalm 40:5) **Blessed are they who hope in the Lord.**
Blessed the man who follows not
the counsel of the wicked
Nor walks in the way of sinners,
nor sits in the company of the insolent,
But delights in the law of the LORD
and meditates on his law day and night. **R.**
He is like a tree
planted near running water,
That yields its fruit in due season,
and whose leaves never fade.
Whatever he does, prospers. **R.**
Not so the wicked, not so;
they are like chaff which the wind drives away.
For the LORD watches over the way of the just,

but the way of the wicked vanishes. **R.**

Philippians 3:8-9
R. Alleluia, alleluia.
I consider all things so much rubbish
that I may gain Christ and be found in him. **R.**

✝ *Luke 12:49-53*
I have not come to establish peace but division.

Jesus said to his disciples:
"I have come to set the earth on fire,
   and how I wish it were already blazing!
There is a baptism with which I must be baptized,
   and how great is my anguish until it is accomplished!
Do you think that I have come to establish peace on the earth?
No, I tell you, but rather division.
From now on a household of five will be divided,
   three against two and two against three;
   a father will be divided against his son
   and a son against his father,
   a mother against her daughter
   and a daughter against her mother,
   a mother-in-law against her daughter-in-law
   and a daughter-in-law against her mother-in-law." ✛

FRIDAY, OCTOBER 27
WEEKDAY

✝ *Romans 7:18-25a*
Who will deliver me from this mortal body?

Brothers and sisters:
I know that good does not dwell in me, that is, in my flesh.
The willing is ready at hand, but doing the good is not.
For I do not do the good I want,
   but I do the evil I do not want.
Now if I do what I do not want, it is no longer I who do it,
   but sin that dwells in me.
So, then, I discover the principle
   that when I want to do right, evil is at hand.
For I take delight in the law of God, in my inner self,
   but I see in my members another principle
   at war with the law of my mind,
   taking me captive to the law of sin that dwells in my members.
Miserable one that I am!
Who will deliver me from this mortal body?
Thanks be to God through Jesus Christ our Lord. ✛

Psalm 119:66, 68, 76, 77, 93, 94

R. (68b) **Lord, teach me your statutes.**

Teach me wisdom and knowledge,
  for in your commands I trust. **R.**

You are good and bountiful;
  teach me your statutes. **R.**

Let your kindness comfort me
  according to your promise to your servants. **R.**

Let your compassion come to me that I may live,
  for your law is my delight. **R.**

Never will I forget your precepts,
  for through them you give me life. **R.**

I am yours; save me,
  for I have sought your precepts. **R.**

See Matthew 11:25

R. Alleluia, alleluia.

Blessed are you, Father, Lord of heaven and earth;
you have revealed to little ones the mysteries of the Kingdom. **R.**

† *Luke 12:54-59*

*You know how to interpret the appearance of the earth and sky;
why do you not know how to interpret the present time?*

Jesus said to the crowds,
  "When you see a cloud rising in the west
  you say immediately that it is going to rain—and so it does;
  and when you notice that the wind is blowing from the south
  you say that it is going to be hot—and so it is.
You hypocrites!
You know how to interpret the appearance of the earth and the sky;
  why do you not know how to interpret the present time?

"Why do you not judge for yourselves what is right?
If you are to go with your opponent before a magistrate,
  make an effort to settle the matter on the way;
  otherwise your opponent will turn you over to the judge,
  and the judge hand you over to the constable,
  and the constable throw you into prison.
I say to you, you will not be released
  until you have paid the last penny." **+**

SATURDAY, OCTOBER 28
St. Simon and St. Jude

† *Ephesians 2:19-22*
Built upon the foundation of the Apostles.

Brothers and sisters:
You are no longer strangers and sojourners,
  but you are fellow citizens with the holy ones
  and members of the household of God,
  built upon the foundation of the Apostles and prophets,
  with Christ Jesus himself as the capstone.
Through him the whole structure is held together
  and grows into a temple sacred in the Lord;
  in him you also are being built together
  into a dwelling place of God in the Spirit. ✛

Psalm 19:2-3, 4-5

R. (5a) **Their message goes out through all the earth.**
The heavens declare the glory of God,
  and the firmament proclaims his handiwork.
Day pours out the word to day,
  and night to night imparts knowledge. **R.**
Not a word nor a discourse
  whose voice is not heard;
Through all the earth their voice resounds,
  and to the ends of the world, their message. **R.**

See Te Deum

R. Alleluia, alleluia.
We praise you, O God,
we acclaim you as Lord;
the glorious company of Apostles praise you. **R.**

† *Luke 6:12-16*
From them Jesus chose Twelve, whom he also named Apostles.

Jesus went up to the mountain to pray,
  and he spent the night in prayer to God.
When day came, he called his disciples to himself,
  and from them he chose Twelve, whom he also named Apostles:
  Simon, whom he named Peter, and his brother Andrew,
  James, John, Philip, Bartholomew, Matthew,
  Thomas, James the son of Alphaeus,
  Simon who was called a Zealot,
  and Judas the son of James,
  and Judas Iscariot, who became a traitor. ✛

SUNDAY, OCTOBER 29
THIRTIETH SUNDAY IN ORDINARY TIME

† *Exodus 22:20-26*
If you wrong the widow and the orphan,
my wrath will flare up against you.

Thus says the LORD:
"You shall not molest or oppress an alien,
for you were once aliens yourselves in the land of Egypt.
You shall not wrong any widow or orphan.
If ever you wrong them and they cry out to me,
I will surely hear their cry.
My wrath will flare up, and I will kill you with the sword;
then your own wives will be widows, and your children orphans.

"If you lend money to one of your poor neighbors among my people,
you shall not act like an extortioner toward him
by demanding interest from him.
If you take your neighbor's cloak as a pledge,
you shall return it to him before sunset;
for this cloak of his is the only covering he has for his body.
What else has he to sleep in?
If he cries out to me, I will hear him; for I am compassionate." ✛

Psalm 18:2-3a, 3bc-4, 47 and 51ab
R. (2) **I love you, Lord, my strength.**
I love you, O LORD, my strength,
O LORD, my rock, my fortress, my deliverer. **R.**
My God, my rock of refuge,
my shield, the horn of my salvation, my stronghold!
Praised be the LORD, I exclaim,
and I am safe from my enemies. **R.**
The LORD lives and blessed be my rock!
Extolled be God my savior.
You who gave great victories to your king
and showed kindness to your anointed. **R.**

† *1 Thessalonians 1:5c-10*
You turned from idols to serve the living and true God
and to await his Son from heaven.

Brothers and sisters:
You know what sort of people we were among you for your sake.
And you became imitators of us and of the Lord,
receiving the word in great affliction, with joy from the Holy
Spirit,
so that you became a model for all the believers

in Macedonia and in Achaia.
For from you the word of the Lord has sounded forth
  not only in Macedonia and in Achaia,
  but in every place your faith in God has gone forth,
  so that we have no need to say anything.
For they themselves openly declare about us
  what sort of reception we had among you,
  and how you turned to God from idols
  to serve the living and true God
  and to await his Son from heaven,
  whom he raised from the dead,
  Jesus, who delivers us from the coming wrath. ✜

John 14:23

R. Alleluia, alleluia.
Whoever loves me will keep my word, says the Lord,
and my Father will love him and we will come to him. **R.**

† *Matthew 22:34-40*
You shall love the Lord your God and your neighbor as yourself.

When the Pharisees heard that Jesus had silenced the Sadducees,
  they gathered together, and one of them,
  a scholar of the law, tested him by asking,
  "Teacher, which commandment in the law is the greatest?"
He said to him,
  "You shall love the Lord, your God,
  with all your heart,
  with all your soul,
  and with all your mind.
This is the greatest and the first commandment.
The second is like it:
  You shall love your neighbor as yourself.
The whole law and the prophets depend on these two command-
    ments." ✜

MONDAY, OCTOBER 30
WEEKDAY

† *Romans 8:12-17*
You have received a spirit of adoption through which we cry, Abba, Father!

Brothers and sisters,
  we are not debtors to the flesh,
  to live according to the flesh.
For if you live according to the flesh, you will die,
  but if by the spirit you put to death the deeds of the body,
  you will live.

For those who are led by the Spirit of God are sons of God.
For you did not receive a spirit of slavery to fall back into fear,
    but you received a spirit of adoption,
    through which we cry, *"Abba,* Father!"
The Spirit himself bears witness with our spirit
    that we are children of God,
    and if children, then heirs,
    heirs of God and joint heirs with Christ,
    if only we suffer with him
    so that we may also be glorified with him. ✛

Psalm 68:2 and 4, 6-7ab, 20-21

R. (21a) **Our God is the God of salvation.**

God arises; his enemies are scattered,
    and those who hate him flee before him.
But the just rejoice and exult before God;
    they are glad and rejoice. **R.**
The father of orphans and the defender of widows
    is God in his holy dwelling.
God gives a home to the forsaken;
    he leads forth prisoners to prosperity. **R.**
Blessed day by day be the Lord,
    who bears our burdens; God, who is our salvation.
God is a saving God for us;
    the LORD, my Lord, controls the passageways of death. **R.**

John 17:17b, 17a

R. Alleluia, alleluia.

Your word, O Lord, is truth;
consecrate us in the truth. **R.**

† *Luke 13:10-17*

This daughter of Abraham, ought she not
to have been set free on the sabbath day?

Jesus was teaching in a synagogue on the sabbath.
And a woman was there who for eighteen years
    had been crippled by a spirit;
    she was bent over, completely incapable of standing erect.
When Jesus saw her, he called to her and said,
    "Woman, you are set free of your infirmity."
He laid his hands on her,
    and she at once stood up straight and glorified God.
But the leader of the synagogue,
    indignant that Jesus had cured on the sabbath,
    said to the crowd in reply,
    "There are six days when work should be done.

Come on those days to be cured, not on the sabbath day."
The Lord said to him in reply, "Hypocrites!
Does not each one of you on the sabbath
    untie his ox or his ass from the manger
    and lead it out for watering?
This daughter of Abraham,
    whom Satan has bound for eighteen years now,
    ought she not to have been set free on the sabbath day
    from this bondage?"
When he said this, all his adversaries were humiliated;
    and the whole crowd rejoiced at all the splendid deeds done by
        him. ✛

TUESDAY, OCTOBER 31
WEEKDAY

† *Romans 8:18-25*
Creation awaits with eager expectation the revelation of the children of God.

Brothers and sisters:
I consider that the sufferings of this present time are as nothing
    compared with the glory to be revealed for us.
For creation awaits with eager expectation
    the revelation of the children of God;
    for creation was made subject to futility,
    not of its own accord but because of the one who subjected it,
    in hope that creation itself
    would be set free from slavery to corruption
    and share in the glorious freedom of the children of God.
We know that all creation is groaning in labor pains even until now;
    and not only that, but we ourselves,
    who have the firstfruits of the Spirit,
    we also groan within ourselves
    as we wait for adoption, the redemption of our bodies.
For in hope we were saved.
Now hope that sees for itself is not hope.
For who hopes for what one sees?
But if we hope for what we do not see, we wait with endurance. ✛

Psalm 126:1b-2ab, 2cd-3, 4-5, 6
R. (3a) **The Lord has done marvels for us.**
When the LORD brought back the captives of Zion,
    we were like men dreaming.
Then our mouth was filled with laughter,
    and our tongue with rejoicing. **R.**
Then they said among the nations,

"The Lord has done great things for them."
The Lord has done great things for us;
  we are glad indeed. **R.**
Restore our fortunes, O Lord,
  like the torrents in the southern desert.
Those that sow in tears
  shall reap rejoicing. **R.**
Although they go forth weeping,
  carrying the seed to be sown,
They shall come back rejoicing,
  carrying their sheaves. **R.**

  See Matthew 11:25
R. Alleluia, alleluia.
Blessed are you, Father, Lord of heaven and earth;
you have revealed to little ones the mysteries of the Kingdom. **R.**

† *Luke 13:18-21*
When it was fully grown, it became a large bush.

Jesus said, "What is the Kingdom of God like?
To what can I compare it?
It is like a mustard seed that a man took and planted in the garden.
When it was fully grown, it became a large bush
  and 'the birds of the sky dwelt in its branches.'"

Again he said, "To what shall I compare the Kingdom of God?
It is like yeast that a woman took
  and mixed in with three measures of wheat flour
  until the whole batch of dough was leavened." ✝

WEDNESDAY, NOVEMBER 1
ALL SAINTS

† *Revelation 7:2-4, 9-14*
*I had a vision of a great multitude, which no one could count,
from every nation, race, people and tongue.*

I, John, saw another angel come up from the East,
  holding the seal of the living God.
He cried out in a loud voice to the four angels
  who were given power to damage the land and the sea,
  "Do not damage the land or the sea or the trees
  until we put the seal on the foreheads of the servants of our God."
I heard the number of those who had been marked with the seal,
  one hundred and forty-four thousand marked
  from every tribe of the children of Israel.

After this I had a vision of a great multitude,
  which no one could count,
  from every nation, race, people, and tongue.
They stood before the throne and before the Lamb,
  wearing white robes and holding palm branches in their hands.
They cried out in a loud voice:

"Salvation comes from our God, who is seated on the throne,
and from the Lamb."

All the angels stood around the throne
  and around the elders and the four living creatures.
They prostrated themselves before the throne,
  worshiped God, and exclaimed:

"Amen. Blessing and glory, wisdom and thanksgiving,
    honor, power, and might
    be to our God forever and ever. Amen."

Then one of the elders spoke up and said to me,
  "Who are these wearing white robes, and where did they come
      from?"
I said to him, "My lord, you are the one who knows."
He said to me,
  "These are the ones who have survived the time of great distress;
  they have washed their robes
  and made them white in the Blood of the Lamb." ✝

  Psalm 24:1bc-2, 3-4ab, 5-6

R. (see 6) **Lord, this is the people that longs to see your face.**
The Lord's are the earth and its fullness;
  the world and those who dwell in it.
For he founded it upon the seas
  and established it upon the rivers. **R.**
Who can ascend the mountain of the Lord?
  or who may stand in his holy place?
One whose hands are sinless, whose heart is clean,
  who desires not what is vain. **R.**
He shall receive a blessing from the Lord,
  a reward from God his savior.
Such is the race that seeks him,
  that seeks the face of the God of Jacob. **R.**

† *1 John 3:1-3*
We shall see God as he is.

Beloved:
See what love the Father has bestowed on us
   that we may be called the children of God.
Yet so we are.
The reason the world does not know us
   is that it did not know him.
Beloved, we are God's children now;
   what we shall be has not yet been revealed.
We do know that when it is revealed we shall be like him,
   for we shall see him as he is.
Everyone who has this hope based on him makes himself pure,
   as he is pure. ✢

Matthew 11:28
R. Alleluia, alleluia.
Come to me, all you who labor and are burdened,
and I will give you rest, says the Lord. **R.**

† *Matthew 5:1-12a*
Rejoice and be glad, for your reward will be great in heaven.

When Jesus saw the crowds, he went up the mountain,
   and after he had sat down, his disciples came to him.
He began to teach them, saying:

   "Blessed are the poor in spirit,
      for theirs is the Kingdom of heaven.
   Blessed are they who mourn,
      for they will be comforted.
   Blessed are the meek,
      for they will inherit the land.
   Blessed are they who hunger and thirst for righteousness,
      for they will be satisfied.
   Blessed are the merciful,
      for they will be shown mercy.
   Blessed are the clean of heart,
      for they will see God.
   Blessed are the peacemakers,
      for they will be called children of God.
   Blessed are they who are persecuted for the sake of righteousness,
      for theirs is the Kingdom of heaven.
   Blessed are you when they insult you and persecute you
      and utter every kind of evil against you falsely because of me.

Rejoice and be glad,
for your reward will be great in heaven." ✛

THURSDAY, NOVEMBER 2
THE COMMEMORATION OF ALL THE FAITHFUL DEPARTED (ALL SOULS' DAY)

(Other readings for All Souls include: Wisdom 4:7-14 • Isaiah 25:6ab, 7-9 •
Psalm 25:6 and 7b, 17-18, 20-21 • Psalm 27:1, 4, 7 and 8b and 9a, 13-14 • Romans 5:17-21 •
Romans 6:3-9 • Romans 8:14-23 • Romans 8:31b-35, 37-39 • Romans 14:7-9, 10c-12 •
1 Corinthians 15:20-28 • 1 Corinthians 15:51-57 • 2 Corinthians 4:14—5:1 •
2 Corinthians 5:1, 6-10 • Philippians 3:20-21 • 1 Thessalonians 4:13-18 •
2 Timothy 2:8-13 • Matthew 5:1-12a • Matthew 11:25-30 • Matthew 25:31-46 •
Luke 7:11-17 • Luke 23:44-46, 50, 52-53; 24:1-6a • Luke 24:13-16, 28-35 • John 5:24-29 •
John 6:51-58 • John 11:17-27 • John 11:32-45 • John 14:1-6, or use any readings from the
Lectionary for Mass, volume IV, the Masses for the Dead, numbers 1011–1016.)

† Wisdom 3:1-9
As sacrificial offerings he took them to himself.

The souls of the just are in the hand of God,
and no torment shall touch them.
They seemed, in the view of the foolish, to be dead;
and their passing away was thought an affliction
and their going forth from us, utter destruction.
But they are in peace.
For if before men, indeed, they be punished,
yet is their hope full of immortality;
chastised a little, they shall be greatly blessed,
because God tried them
and found them worthy of himself.
As gold in the furnace, he proved them,
and as sacrificial offerings he took them to himself.
In the time of their visitation they shall shine,
and shall dart about as sparks through stubble;
they shall judge nations and rule over peoples,
and the LORD shall be their King forever.
Those who trust in him shall understand truth,
and the faithful shall abide with him in love:
because grace and mercy are with his holy ones,
and his care is with his elect. ✛

Psalm 23:1b-3a, 3b-4, 5, 6
R. (1) **The Lord is my shepherd; there is nothing I shall want.**
or
(4ab) **Though I walk in the valley of darkness, I fear no evil,
for you are with me.**
The LORD is my shepherd; I shall not want.
In verdant pastures he gives me repose;

beside restful waters he leads me;
  he refreshes my soul. **R.**
He guides me in right paths
  for his name's sake.
Even though I walk in the dark valley
  I fear no evil; for you are at my side
with your rod and your staff
  that give me courage. **R.**
You spread the table before me
  in the sight of my foes;
You anoint my head with oil;
  my cup overflows. **R.**
Only goodness and kindness follow me
  all the days of my life;
and I shall dwell in the house of the Lord
  for years to come. **R.**

✝ ***Romans 5:5-11*** *(or Romans 6:3-9)*
Justified by his Blood, we will be saved through Christ from the wrath.

Brothers and sisters:
Hope does not disappoint,
  because the love of God has been poured out into our hearts
  through the Holy Spirit that has been given to us.
For Christ, while we were still helpless,
  died at the appointed time for the ungodly.
Indeed, only with difficulty does one die for a just person,
  though perhaps for a good person
  one might even find courage to die.
But God proves his love for us
  in that while we were still sinners Christ died for us.
How much more then, since we are now justified by his Blood,
  will we be saved through him from the wrath.
Indeed, if, while we were enemies,
  we were reconciled to God through the death of his Son,
  how much more, once reconciled,
  will we be saved by his life.
Not only that,
  but we also boast of God through our Lord Jesus Christ,
  through whom we have now received reconciliation. ✝

See John 6:40 (or see Lectionary no. 668 for more choices)

R. Alleluia, alleluia.
This is the will of my Father, says the Lord,
that everyone who sees the Son and believes in him
may have eternal life. **R.**

† John 6:37-40

*Everyone who believes in the Son will have eternal life
and I shall raise him up on the last day.*

Jesus said to the crowds:
"Everything that the Father gives me will come to me,
    and I will not reject anyone who comes to me,
    because I came down from heaven not to do my own will
    but the will of the one who sent me.
And this is the will of the one who sent me,
    that I should not lose anything of what he gave me,
    but that I should raise it on the last day.
For this is the will of my Father,
    that everyone who sees the Son and believes in him
    may have eternal life,
    and I shall raise him on the last day." ✣

FRIDAY, NOVEMBER 3
Weekday, St. Martin de Porres

† Romans 9:1-5

I could wish that I were accused for the sake of my own people.

Brothers and sisters:
I speak the truth in Christ, I do not lie;
    my conscience joins with the Holy Spirit in bearing me witness
    that I have great sorrow and constant anguish in my heart.
For I could wish that I myself were accursed and cut off from Christ
    for the sake of my own people,
    my kindred according to the flesh.
They are children of Israel;
    theirs the adoption, the glory, the covenants,
    the giving of the law, the worship, and the promises;
    theirs the patriarchs, and from them,
    according to the flesh, is the Christ,
    who is over all, God blessed forever. Amen. ✣

Psalm 147:12-13, 14-15, 19-20
R. Praise the Lord, Jerusalem.
Glorify the LORD, O Jerusalem;
    praise your God, O Zion.
For he has strengthened the bars of your gates;
    he has blessed your children within you. **R.**
He has granted peace in your borders;
    with the best of wheat he fills you.
He sends forth his command to the earth;
    swiftly runs his word! **R.**

He has proclaimed his word to Jacob,
  his statutes and his ordinances to Israel.
He has not done thus for any other nation;
  his ordinances he has not made known to them. Alleluia. **R.**

John 10:27
R. Alleluia, alleluia.
My sheep hear my voice, says the Lord;
I know them, and they follow me. **R.**

† *Luke 14:1-6*
Who among you, if your son or ox falls into a cistern,
would not immediately pull him out on the sabbath day?

On a sabbath Jesus went to dine
  at the home of one of the leading Pharisees,
  and the people there were observing him carefully.
In front of him there was a man suffering from dropsy.
Jesus spoke to the scholars of the law and Pharisees in reply, asking,
  "Is it lawful to cure on the sabbath or not?"
But they kept silent; so he took the man and,
  after he had healed him, dismissed him.
Then he said to them
  "Who among you, if your son or ox falls into a cistern,
  would not immediately pull him out on the sabbath day?"
But they were unable to answer his question. ✛

SATURDAY, NOVEMBER 4
St. Charles Borromeo

† *Romans 11:1-2a, 11-12, 25-29*
If their transgression is enrichment for the world,
how much more their full number.

Brothers and sisters:
I ask, then, has God rejected his people?
Of course not!
For I too am a child of Israel, a descendant of Abraham,
  of the tribe of Benjamin.
God has not rejected his people whom he foreknew.
Do you not know what the Scripture says about Elijah,
  how he pleads with God against Israel?

Hence I ask, did they stumble so as to fall?
Of course not!
But through their transgression
  salvation has come to the Gentiles,
  so as to make them jealous.

Now if their transgression is enrichment for the world,
    and if their diminished number is enrichment for the Gentiles,
    how much more their full number.

I do not want you to be unaware of this mystery, brothers and sisters,
    so that you will not become wise in your own estimation:
    a hardening has come upon Israel in part,
    until the full number of the Gentiles comes in,
    and thus all Israel will be saved, as it is written:

> *The deliverer will come out of Zion,*
>   *he will turn away godlessness from Jacob;*
> *and this is my covenant with them*
>   *when I take away their sins.*

In respect to the Gospel, they are enemies on your account;
    but in respect to election,
    they are beloved because of the patriarch.
For the gifts and the call of God are irrevocable. ✦

Psalm 94:12-13a, 14-15, 17-18
R. (14a) **The Lord will not abandon his people.**
Blessed the man whom you instruct, O LORD,
    whom by your law you teach,
Giving him rest from evil days. **R.**
For the LORD will not cast off his people,
    nor abandon his inheritance;
But judgment shall again be with justice,
    and all the upright of heart shall follow it. **R.**
Were not the LORD my help,
    my soul would soon dwell in the silent grave.
When I say, "My foot is slipping,"
    your mercy, O LORD, sustains me. **R.**

Matthew 11:29ab
R. Alleluia, alleluia.
Take my yoke upon you and learn from me,
for I am meek and humble of heart. **R.**

†*Luke 14:1, 7-11*
Everyone who exalts himself will be humbled,
but the one who humbles himself will be exalted.

On a sabbath Jesus went to dine
    at the home of one of the leading Pharisees,
    and the people there were observing him carefully.

He told a parable to those who had been invited,

noticing how they were choosing the places of honor at the table.
"When you are invited by someone to a wedding banquet,
do not recline at table in the place of honor.
A more distinguished guest than you may have been invited by him,
and the host who invited both of you may approach you and say,
'Give your place to this man,'
and then you would proceed with embarrassment
to take the lowest place.
Rather, when you are invited,
go and take the lowest place
so that when the host comes to you he may say,
'My friend, move up to a higher position.'
Then you will enjoy the esteem of your companions at the table.
For everyone who exalts himself will be humbled,
but the one who humbles himself will be exalted." ✛

SUNDAY, NOVEMBER 5
THIRTY-FIRST SUNDAY IN ORDINARY TIME

✝ Malachi 1:14b—2:2b, 8-10
You have turned aside from the way, and have caused
many to falter by your instruction.

A great King am I, says the LORD of hosts,
and my name will be feared among the nations.
And now, O priests, this commandment is for you:
If you do not listen,
if you do not lay it to heart,
to give glory to my name, says the LORD of hosts,
I will send a curse upon you
and of your blessing I will make a curse.
You have turned aside from the way,
and have caused many to falter by your instruction;
you have made void the covenant of Levi,
says the LORD of hosts.
I, therefore, have made you contemptible
and base before all the people,
since you do not keep my ways,
but show partiality in your decisions.
Have we not all the one father?
Has not the one God created us?
Why then do we break faith with one another,
violating the covenant of our fathers? ✛

Psalm 131:1, 2, 3

R. In you, Lord, I have found my peace.

O LORD, my heart is not proud,
  nor are my eyes haughty;
I busy not myself with great things,
  nor with things too sublime for me. **R.**
Nay rather, I have stilled and quieted
  my soul like a weaned child.
Like a weaned child on its mother's lap,
  so is my soul within me. **R.**
O Israel, hope in the LORD,
  both now and forever. **R.**

† *1 Thessalonians 2:7b-9, 13*
*We were determined to share with you not only the Gospel of God,
but our very selves as well.*

Brothers and sisters:
We were gentle among you, as a nursing mother cares for her children.
With such affection for you, we were determined to share with you
  not only the gospel of God, but our very selves as well,
  so dearly beloved had you become to us.
You recall, brothers and sisters, our toil and drudgery.
Working night and day in order not to burden any of you,
  we proclaimed to you the gospel of God.

And for this reason we too give thanks to God unceasingly,
  that, in receiving the word of God from hearing us,
  you received not a human word but, as it truly is, the word of God,
  which is now at work in you who believe. ✛

Matthew 23:9b, 10b

R. Alleluia, alleluia.

You have but one Father in heaven
and one master, the Christ. **R.**

† *Matthew 23:1-12*
They preach but they do not practice.

Jesus spoke to the crowds and to his disciples, saying,
  "The scribes and the Pharisees
  have taken their seat on the chair of Moses.
Therefore, do and observe all things whatsoever they tell you,
  but do not follow their example.
For they preach but they do not practice.
They tie up heavy burdens hard to carry
  and lay them on people's shoulders,
  but they will not lift a finger to move them.

All their works are performed to be seen.
They widen their phylacteries and lengthen their tassels.
They love places of honor at banquets, seats of honor in synagogues,
   greetings in marketplaces, and the salutation 'Rabbi.'
As for you, do not be called 'Rabbi.'
You have but one teacher, and you are all brothers.
Call no one on earth your father;
   you have but one Father in heaven.
Do not be called 'Master';
   you have but one master, the Christ.
The greatest among you must be your servant.
Whoever exalts himself will be humbled;
   but whoever humbles himself will be exalted." ✛

MONDAY, NOVEMBER 6
WEEKDAY

✝ *Romans 11:29-36*
God delivered all to disobedience,
that he might have mercy upon all.

Brothers and sisters:
The gifts and the call of God are irrevocable.

Just as you once disobeyed God
   but have now received mercy
   because of their disobedience,
   so they have now disobeyed in order that,
   by virtue of the mercy shown to you,
   they too may now receive mercy.
For God delivered all to disobedience,
   that he might have mercy upon all.

Oh, the depth of the riches and wisdom and knowledge of God!
How inscrutable are his judgments and how unsearchable his ways!

> *For who has known the mind of the Lord*
>   *or who has been his counselor?*
> *Or who has given him anything*
>   *that he may be repaid?*

For from him and through him and for him are all things.
To God be glory forever. Amen. ✛

   Psalm 69:30-31, 33-34, 36-37
R. (14c) **Lord, in your great love, answer me.**
But I am afflicted and in pain;
   let your saving help, O God, protect me.

I will praise the name of God in song,
   and I will glorify him with thanksgiving. **R.**
"See, you lowly ones, and be glad;
   you who seek God, may your hearts revive!
For the LORD hears the poor,
   and his own who are in bonds he spurns not." **R.**
For God will save Zion
   and rebuild the cities of Judah.
They shall dwell in the land and own it,
   and the descendants of his servants shall inherit it,
   and those who love his name shall inhabit it. **R.**

   John 8:31b-32
R. Alleluia, alleluia.
If you remain in my word, you will truly be my disciples,
and you will know the truth, says the Lord. **R.**

† *Luke 14:12-14*
Do not invite your friends, but those who are poor and crippled.

On a sabbath Jesus went to dine
   at the home of one of the leading Pharisees.
He said to the host who invited him,
   "When you hold a lunch or a dinner,
   do not invite your friends or your brothers or sisters
   or your relatives or your wealthy neighbors,
   in case they may invite you back and you have repayment.
Rather, when you hold a banquet,
   invite the poor, the crippled, the lame, the blind;
   blessed indeed will you be because of their inability to repay you.
For you will be repaid at the resurrection of the righteous." ✛

TUESDAY, NOVEMBER 7
WEEKDAY

† *Romans 12:5-16b*
We are individually parts of one another.

Brothers and sisters:
We, though many, are one Body in Christ
   and individually parts of one another.
Since we have gifts that differ according to the grace given to us,
   let us exercise them:
   if prophecy, in proportion to the faith;
   if ministry, in ministering;
   if one is a teacher, in teaching;
   if one exhorts, in exhortation;
   if one contributes, in generosity;

if one is over others, with diligence;
if one does acts of mercy, with cheerfulness.

Let love be sincere;
hate what is evil,
hold on to what is good;
love one another with mutual affection;
anticipate one another in showing honor.
Do not grow slack in zeal,
be fervent in spirit,
serve the Lord.
Rejoice in hope,
endure in affliction,
persevere in prayer.
Contribute to the needs of the holy ones,
exercise hospitality.
Bless those who persecute you,
bless and do not curse them.
Rejoice with those who rejoice,
weep with those who weep.
Have the same regard for one another;
do not be haughty but associate with the lowly. ✝

Psalm 131:1bcde, 2, 3
R. In you, O Lord, I have found my peace.
O LORD, my heart is not proud,
nor are my eyes haughty;
I busy not myself with great things,
nor with things too sublime for me. **R.**
Nay rather, I have stilled and quieted
my soul like a weaned child.
Like a weaned child on its mother's lap,
so is my soul within me. **R.**
O Israel, hope in the LORD,
both now and forever. **R.**

Matthew 11:28
R. Alleluia, alleluia.
Come to me, all you who labor and are burdened,
and I will give you rest, says the Lord. **R.**

✝ *Luke 14:15-24*
*Go out quickly into highways and hedgerows and
make people come in that my home may be filled.*

One of those at table with Jesus said to him,
"Blessed is the one who will dine in the Kingdom of God."

He replied to him,
"A man gave a great dinner to which he invited many.
When the time for the dinner came,
he dispatched his servant to say to those invited,
'Come, everything is now ready.'
But one by one, they all began to excuse themselves.
The first said to him,
'I have purchased a field and must go to examine it;
I ask you, consider me excused.'
And another said, 'I have purchased five yoke of oxen
and am on my way to evaluate them;
I ask you, consider me excused.'
And another said, 'I have just married a woman,
and therefore I cannot come.'
The servant went and reported this to his master.
Then the master of the house in a rage commanded his servant,
'Go out quickly into the streets and alleys of the town
and bring in here the poor and the crippled, the blind and the
lame.'
The servant reported, 'Sir, your orders have been carried out
and still there is room.'
The master then ordered the servant,
'Go out to the highways and hedgerows
and make people come in that my home may be filled.
For, I tell you, none of those men who were invited will taste my
dinner.'" ✝

WEDNESDAY, NOVEMBER 8
WEEKDAY

✝ *Romans 13:8-10*
Love is the fulfillment of the law.

Brothers and sisters:
Owe nothing to anyone, except to love one another;
for the one who loves another has fulfilled the law.
The commandments, *You shall not commit adultery;*
you shall not kill;
you shall not steal;
you shall not covet,
and whatever other commandment there may be,
are summed up in this saying, namely,
You shall love your neighbor as yourself.
Love does no evil to the neighbor;
hence, love is the fulfillment of the law. ✝

Psalm 112:1b-2, 4-5, 9

R. (5a) **Blessed the man who is gracious and lends to those in need.** *(or* **Alleluia.***)*

Blessed the man who fears the LORD,
  who greatly delights in his commands.
His posterity shall be mighty upon the earth;
  the upright generation shall be blessed. **R.**
He dawns through the darkness, a light for the upright;
  he is gracious and merciful and just.
Well for the man who is gracious and lends,
  who conducts his affairs with justice. **R.**
Lavishly he gives to the poor;
  his generosity shall endure forever;
  his horn shall be exalted in glory. **R.**

1 Peter 4:14

R. Alleluia, alleluia.

If you are insulted for the name of Christ, blessed are you,
for the Spirit of God rests upon you. **R.**

† *Luke 14:25-33*

*Everyone of you who does not renounce all
his possessions cannot be my disciple.*

Great crowds were traveling with Jesus,
  and he turned and addressed them,
  "If anyone comes to me without hating his father and mother,
  wife and children, brothers and sisters,
  and even his own life,
  he cannot be my disciple.
Whoever does not carry his own cross and come after me
  cannot be my disciple.
Which of you wishing to construct a tower
  does not first sit down and calculate the cost
  to see if there is enough for its completion?
Otherwise, after laying the foundation
  and finding himself unable to finish the work
  the onlookers should laugh at him and say,
  'This one began to build but did not have the resources to finish.'
Or what king marching into battle would not first sit down
  and decide whether with ten thousand troops
  he can successfully oppose another king
  advancing upon him with twenty thousand troops?
But if not, while he is still far away,
  he will send a delegation to ask for peace terms.
In the same way,

everyone of you who does not renounce all his possessions
cannot be my disciple." ✢

THURSDAY, NOVEMBER 9
THE DEDICATION OF THE LATERAN BASILICA

† *Ezekiel 47:1-2, 8-9, 12*

*I saw water flowing from the temple, and all who were touched by it were saved
(see Roman Missal, antiphon for the blessing and sprinkling of water during the
season of Easter).*

The angel brought me
back to the entrance of the temple,
and I saw water flowing out
from beneath the threshold of the temple toward the east,
for the façade of the temple was toward the east;
the water flowed down from the southern side of the temple,
south of the altar.
He led me outside by the north gate,
and around to the outer gate facing the east,
where I saw water trickling from the southern side.
He said to me,
"This water flows into the eastern district down upon the Arabah,
and empties into the sea, the salt waters, which it makes fresh.
Wherever the river flows,
every sort of living creature that can multiply shall live,
and there shall be abundant fish,
for wherever this water comes the sea shall be made fresh.
Along both banks of the river, fruit trees of every kind shall grow;
their leaves shall not fade, nor their fruit fail.
Every month they shall bear fresh fruit,
for they shall be watered by the flow from the sanctuary.
Their fruit shall serve for food, and their leaves for medicine." ✢

Psalm 46:2-3, 5-6, 8-9

R. (5) **The waters of the river gladden the city of God, the
holy dwelling of the Most High!**

God is our refuge and our strength,
an ever-present help in distress.
Therefore, we fear not, though the earth be shaken
and mountains plunge into the depths of the sea. **R.**
There is a stream whose runlets gladden the city of God,
the holy dwelling of the Most High.
God is in its midst; it shall not be disturbed;
God will help it at the break of dawn. **R.**
The LORD of hosts is with us;
our stronghold is the God of Jacob.

Come! behold the deeds of the LORD,
the astounding things he has wrought on earth. **R.**

† *1 Corinthians 3:9c-11, 16-17*
You are God's temple.

Brothers and sisters:
You are God's building.
According to the grace of God given to me,
like a wise master builder I laid a foundation,
and another is building upon it.
But each one must be careful how he builds upon it,
for no one can lay a foundation other than the one that is there,
namely, Jesus Christ.

Do you not know that you are the temple of God,
and that the Spirit of God dwells in you?
If anyone destroys God's temple,
God will destroy that person;
for the temple of God, which you are, is holy. ✛

2 Chronicles 7:16
R. Alleluia, alleluia.
I have chosen and consecrated this house, says the Lord,
that my name may be there forever. **R.**

† *John 2:13-22*
Jesus was speaking about the temple of his Body.

Since the Passover of the Jews was near,
Jesus went up to Jerusalem.
He found in the temple area those who sold oxen, sheep, and doves,
as well as the money-changers seated there.
He made a whip out of cords
and drove them all out of the temple area, with the sheep and
oxen,
and spilled the coins of the money-changers
and overturned their tables,
and to those who sold doves he said,
"Take these out of here,
and stop making my Father's house a marketplace."
His disciples recalled the words of Scripture,
Zeal for your house will consume me.
At this the Jews answered and said to him,
"What sign can you show us for doing this?"
Jesus answered and said to them,
"Destroy this temple and in three days I will raise it up."

The Jews said,
"This temple has been under construction for forty-six years,
and you will raise it up in three days?"
But he was speaking about the temple of his Body.
Therefore, when he was raised from the dead,
his disciples remembered that he had said this,
and they came to believe the Scripture
and the word Jesus had spoken. ✛

FRIDAY, NOVEMBER 10
St. Pope Leo the Great

† *Romans 15:14-21*
*A minister of Christ Jesus to the Gentiles, so that
the offering up of the Gentiles may be acceptable.*

I myself am convinced about you, my brothers and sisters,
that you yourselves are full of goodness,
filled with all knowledge, and able to admonish one another.
But I have written to you rather boldly in some respects to remind
you,
because of the grace given me by God
to be a minister of Christ Jesus to the Gentiles
in performing the priestly service of the Gospel of God,
so that the offering up of the Gentiles may be acceptable,
sanctified by the Holy Spirit.
In Christ Jesus, then, I have reason to boast in what pertains to God.
For I will not dare to speak of anything
except what Christ has accomplished through me
to lead the Gentiles to obedience by word and deed,
by the power of signs and wonders,
by the power of the Spirit of God,
so that from Jerusalem all the way around to Illyricum
I have finished preaching the Gospel of Christ.
Thus I aspire to proclaim the Gospel
not where Christ has already been named,
so that I do not build on another's foundation,
but as it is written:
*Those who have never been told of him shall see,
and those who have never heard of him shall understand.* ✛

Psalm 98:1bcde, 2-3ab, 3cd-4
R. (see 2b) **The Lord has revealed to the nations his saving
power.**
Sing to the LORD a new song,
for he has done wondrous deeds;

His right hand has won victory for him,
  his holy arm. **R.**
The LORD has made his salvation known:
  in the sight of the nations he has revealed his justice.
He has remembered his kindness and his faithfulness
  toward the house of Israel. **R.**
All the ends of the earth have seen
  the salvation by our God.
Sing joyfully to the LORD, all you lands;
  break into song; sing praise. **R.**

1 John 2:5
R. Alleluia, alleluia.
Whoever keeps the word of Christ,
the love of God is truly perfected in him. **R.**

† *Luke 16:1-8*
*For the children of this world are more prudent in dealing
with their own generation than are the children of light.*

Jesus said to his disciples, "A rich man had a steward
  who was reported to him for squandering his property.
He summoned him and said,
  'What is this I hear about you?
Prepare a full account of your stewardship,
  because you can no longer be my steward.'
The steward said to himself, 'What shall I do,
  now that my master is taking the position of steward away from
    me?
I am not strong enough to dig and I am ashamed to beg.
I know what I shall do so that,
  when I am removed from the stewardship,
  they may welcome me into their homes.'
He called in his master's debtors one by one.
To the first he said, 'How much do you owe my master?'
He replied, 'One hundred measures of olive oil.'
He said to him, 'Here is your promissory note.
Sit down and quickly write one for fifty.'
Then to another he said, 'And you, how much do you owe?'
He replied, 'One hundred measures of wheat.'
He said to him, 'Here is your promissory note;
  write one for eighty.'
And the master commended that dishonest steward for acting
    prudently.
For the children of this world

are more prudent in dealing with their own generation
than the children of light." ✛

SATURDAY, NOVEMBER 11
St. Martin of Tours

†*Romans 16:3-9, 16, 22-27*
Greet one another with a holy kiss.

Brothers and sisters:
Greet Prisca and Aquila, my co-workers in Christ Jesus,
   who risked their necks for my life,
   to whom not only I am grateful but also all the churches of the
      Gentiles;
   greet also the Church at their house.
Greet my beloved Epaenetus,
   who was the firstfruits in Asia for Christ.
Greet Mary, who has worked hard for you.
Greet Andronicus and Junia,
   my relatives and my fellow prisoners;
   they are prominent among the Apostles
   and they were in Christ before me.
Greet Ampliatus, my beloved in the Lord.
Greet Urbanus, our co-worker in Christ,
   and my beloved Stachys.
Greet one another with a holy kiss.
All the churches of Christ greet you.

I, Tertius, the writer of this letter, greet you in the Lord.
Gaius, who is host to me and to the whole Church, greets you.
Erastus, the city treasurer,
   and our brother Quartus greet you.

Now to him who can strengthen you,
   according to my Gospel and the proclamation of Jesus Christ,
   according to the revelation of the mystery kept secret for long ages
   but now manifested through the prophetic writings and,
   according to the command of the eternal God,
   made known to all nations to bring about the obedience of faith,
   to the only wise God, through Jesus Christ
   be glory forever and ever. Amen. ✛

   Psalm 145:2-3, 4-5, 10-11
R. (1b) **I will praise your name for ever, Lord.**
Every day will I bless you,
   and I will praise your name forever and ever.
Great is the LORD and highly to be praised;

his greatness is unsearchable. **R.**
Generation after generation praises your works
  and proclaims your might.
They speak of the splendor of your glorious majesty
  and tell of your wondrous works. **R.**
Let all your works give you thanks, O LORD,
  and let your faithful ones bless you.
Let them discourse of the glory of your Kingdom
  and speak of your might. **R.**

2 Corinthians 8:9
R. Alleluia, alleluia.
Jesus Christ became poor although he was rich,
so that by his poverty you might become rich. **R.**

† *Luke 16:9-15*
If, therefore, you are not trustworthy with dishonest wealth,
who will trust you with true wealth?

Jesus said to his disciples:
"I tell you, make friends for yourselves with dishonest wealth,
  so that when it fails, you will be welcomed into eternal dwellings.
The person who is trustworthy in very small matters
  is also trustworthy in great ones;
  and the person who is dishonest in very small matters
  is also dishonest in great ones.
If, therefore, you are not trustworthy with dishonest wealth,
  who will trust you with true wealth?
If you are not trustworthy with what belongs to another,
  who will give you what is yours?
No servant can serve two masters.
He will either hate one and love the other,
  or be devoted to one and despise the other.
You cannot serve God and mammon."

The Pharisees, who loved money,
  heard all these things and sneered at him.
And he said to them,
  "You justify yourselves in the sight of others,
  but God knows your hearts;
  for what is of human esteem is an abomination in the sight of
    God." †

SUNDAY, NOVEMBER 12
THIRTY-SECOND SUNDAY IN ORDINARY TIME
† *Wisdom 6:12-16*
Wisdom is found by those who seek her.

Resplendent and unfading is wisdom,
and she is readily perceived by those who love her,
and found by those who seek her.
She hastens to make herself known in anticipation of their desire;
whoever watches for her at dawn shall not be disappointed,
for he shall find her sitting by his gate.
For taking thought of wisdom is the perfection of prudence,
and whoever for her sake keeps vigil
shall quickly be free from care;
because she makes her own rounds, seeking those worthy of her,
and graciously appears to them in the ways,
and meets them with all solicitude. ✙

Psalm 63:2, 3-4, 5-6, 7-8
R. (2b) **My soul is thirsting for you, O Lord my God.**
O God, you are my God whom I seek;
for you my flesh pines and my soul thirsts
like the earth, parched, lifeless and without water. **R.**
Thus have I gazed toward you in the sanctuary
to see your power and your glory,
for your kindness is a greater good than life;
my lips shall glorify you. **R.**
Thus will I bless you while I live;
lifting up my hands, I will call upon your name.
As with the riches of a banquet shall my soul be satisfied,
and with exultant lips my mouth shall praise you. **R.**
I will remember you upon my couch,
and through the night-watches I will meditate on you:
you are my help,
and in the shadow of your wings I shout for joy. **R.**

† *1 Thessalonians 4:13-18 (or 1 Thessalonians 4:13-14)*
God, through Jesus, will bring with him those who have fallen asleep.

We do not want you to be unaware, brothers and sisters,
about those who have fallen asleep,
so that you may not grieve like the rest, who have no hope.
For if we believe that Jesus died and rose,
so too will God, through Jesus,
bring with him those who have fallen asleep.
Indeed, we tell you this, on the word of the Lord,

that we who are alive,
who are left until the coming of the Lord,
will surely not precede those who have fallen asleep.
For the Lord himself, with a word of command,
with the voice of an archangel and with the trumpet of God,
will come down from heaven,
and the dead in Christ will rise first.
Then we who are alive, who are left,
will be caught up together with them in the clouds
to meet the Lord in the air.
Thus we shall always be with the Lord.
Therefore, console one another with these words. ✝

Matthew 24:42a, 44
R. Alleluia, alleluia.
Stay awake and be ready!
For you do not know on what day your Lord will come. **R.**

✝ *Matthew 25:1-13*
Behold, the bridegroom! Come out to meet him!

Jesus told his disciples this parable:
"The kingdom of heaven will be like ten virgins
who took their lamps and went out to meet the bridegroom.
Five of them were foolish and five were wise.
The foolish ones, when taking their lamps,
brought no oil with them,
but the wise brought flasks of oil with their lamps.
Since the bridegroom was long delayed,
they all became drowsy and fell asleep.
At midnight, there was a cry,
'Behold, the bridegroom! Come out to meet him!'
Then all those virgins got up and trimmed their lamps.
The foolish ones said to the wise,
'Give us some of your oil,
for our lamps are going out.'
But the wise ones replied,
'No, for there may not be enough for us and you.
Go instead to the merchants and buy some for yourselves.'
While they went off to buy it,
the bridegroom came
and those who were ready went into the wedding feast with him.
Then the door was locked.
Afterwards the other virgins came and said,
'Lord, Lord, open the door for us!'

But he said in reply,
  'Amen, I say to you, I do not know you.'
Therefore, stay awake,
  for you know neither the day nor the hour." ✛

MONDAY, NOVEMBER 13
St. Frances Xavier Cabrini

† *Wisdom 1:1-7*
Wisdom is a kindly spirit, the Spirit of the Lord fills the world.

Love justice, you who judge the earth;
  think of the Lord in goodness,
  and seek him in integrity of heart;
Because he is found by those who test him not,
  and he manifests himself to those who do not disbelieve him.
For perverse counsels separate a man from God,
  and his power, put to the proof, rebukes the foolhardy;
Because into a soul that plots evil, wisdom enters not,
  nor dwells she in a body under debt of sin.
For the holy Spirit of discipline flees deceit
  and withdraws from senseless counsels;
  and when injustice occurs it is rebuked.
For wisdom is a kindly spirit,
  yet she acquits not the blasphemer of his guilty lips;
Because God is the witness of his inmost self
  and the sure observer of his heart
  and the listener to his tongue.
For the Spirit of the Lord fills the world,
  is all-embracing, and knows what man says. ✛

Psalm 139:1b-3, 4-6, 7-8, 9-10
R. (24b) **Guide me, Lord, along the everlasting way.**
O Lord, you have probed me and you know me;
  you know when I sit and when I stand;
  you understand my thoughts from afar.
My journeys and my rest you scrutinize,
  with all my ways you are familiar. **R.**
Even before a word is on my tongue,
  behold, O Lord, you know the whole of it.
Behind me and before, you hem me in
  and rest your hand upon me.
Such knowledge is too wonderful for me;
  too lofty for me to attain. **R.**
Where can I go from your spirit?
  From your presence where can I flee?

If I go up to the heavens, you are there;
   if I sink to the nether world, you are present there. **R.**
If I take the wings of the dawn,
   if I settle at the farthest limits of the sea,
Even there your hand shall guide me,
   and your right hand hold me fast. **R.**

Philippians 2:15d, 16a
R. Alleluia, alleluia.
Shine like lights in the world,
as you hold on to the word of life. **R.**

† *Luke 17:1-6*
If your brother wrongs you seven times in one day, and returns to you
seven times saying, "I am sorry," you should forgive him.

Jesus said to his disciples,
   "Things that cause sin will inevitably occur,
   but woe to the one through whom they occur.
It would be better for him if a millstone were put around his neck
   and he be thrown into the sea
   than for him to cause one of these little ones to sin.
Be on your guard!
If your brother sins, rebuke him;
   and if he repents, forgive him.
And if he wrongs you seven times in one day
   and returns to you seven times saying, 'I am sorry,'
   you should forgive him."

And the Apostles said to the Lord, "Increase our faith."
The Lord replied, "If you have faith the size of a mustard seed,
   you would say to this mulberry tree,
   'Be uprooted and planted in the sea,' and it would obey you." †

TUESDAY, NOVEMBER 14
WEEKDAY

† *Wisdom 2:23—3:9*
In the view of the foolish they seemed to be dead, but they are in peace.

God formed man to be imperishable;
   the image of his own nature he made them.
But by the envy of the Devil, death entered the world,
   and they who are in his possession experience it.

But the souls of the just are in the hand of God,
   and no torment shall touch them.
They seemed, in the view of the foolish, to be dead;

and their passing away was thought an affliction
and their going forth from us, utter destruction.
But they are in peace.
For if before men, indeed, they be punished,
   yet is their hope full of immortality;
Chastised a little, they shall be greatly blessed,
   because God tried them
   and found them worthy of himself.
As gold in the furnace, he proved them,
   and as sacrificial offerings he took them to himself.
In the time of their visitation they shall shine,
   and shall dart about as sparks through stubble;
They shall judge nations and rule over peoples,
   and the Lord shall be their King forever.
Those who trust in him shall understand truth,
   and the faithful shall abide with him in love:
Because grace and mercy are with his holy ones,
   and his care is with his elect. ✙

Psalm 34:2-3, 16-17, 18-19

R. (2a) **I will bless the Lord at all times.**
I will bless the LORD at all times;
   his praise shall be ever in my mouth.
Let my soul glory in the LORD;
   the lowly will hear me and be glad. **R.**
The LORD has eyes for the just,
   and ears for their cry.
The LORD confronts the evildoers,
   to destroy remembrance of them from the earth. **R.**
When the just cry out, the LORD hears them,
   and from all their distress he rescues them.
The LORD is close to the brokenhearted;
   and those who are crushed in spirit he saves. **R.**

John 14:23

R. Alleluia, alleluia.
Whoever loves me will keep my word,
and my Father will love him,
and we will come to him. **R.**

† *Luke 17:7-10*

We are unprofitable servants; we have done what we were obliged to do.

Jesus said to the Apostles:
"Who among you would say to your servant
   who has just come in from plowing or tending sheep in the field,

'Come here immediately and take your place at table'?
Would he not rather say to him,
'Prepare something for me to eat.
Put on your apron and wait on me while I eat and drink.
You may eat and drink when I am finished'?
Is he grateful to that servant because he did what was commanded?
So should it be with you.
When you have done all you have been commanded, say,
'We are unprofitable servants;
we have done what we were obliged to do.'" ✛

WEDNESDAY, NOVEMBER 15
WEEKDAY, ST. ALBERT THE GREAT

✝ Wisdom 6:1-11
Hear, kings, that you may learn wisdom.

Hear, O kings, and understand;
learn, you magistrates of the earth's expanse!
Hearken, you who are in power over the multitude
and lord it over throngs of peoples!
Because authority was given you by the Lord
and sovereignty by the Most High,
who shall probe your works and scrutinize your counsels.
Because, though you were ministers of his kingdom, you judged not rightly,
and did not keep the law,
nor walk according to the will of God,
Terribly and swiftly shall he come against you,
because judgment is stern for the exalted—
For the lowly may be pardoned out of mercy
but the mighty shall be mightily put to the test.
For the Lord of all shows no partiality,
nor does he fear greatness,
Because he himself made the great as well as the small,
and he provides for all alike;
but for those in power a rigorous scrutiny impends.
To you, therefore, O princes, are my words addressed
that you may learn wisdom and that you may not sin.
For those who keep the holy precepts hallowed shall be found holy,
and those learned in them will have ready a response.
Desire therefore my words;
long for them and you shall be instructed. ✛

Psalm 82:3-4, 6-7

R. (8a) **Rise up, O God, bring judgment to the earth.**

Defend the lowly and the fatherless;
　render justice to the afflicted and the destitute.
Rescue the lowly and the poor;
　from the hand of the wicked deliver them. **R.**
I said: "You are gods,
　all of you sons of the Most High;
yet like men you shall die,
　and fall like any prince." **R.**

1 Thessalonians 5:18

R. Alleluia, alleluia.

In all circumstances, give thanks,
for this is the will of God for you in Christ Jesus. **R.**

† *Luke 17:11-19*

Has none but this foreigner returned to give thanks to God?

As Jesus continued his journey to Jerusalem,
　he traveled through Samaria and Galilee.
As he was entering a village, ten lepers met him.
They stood at a distance from him and raised their voice, saying,
　"Jesus, Master! Have pity on us!"
And when he saw them, he said,
　"Go show yourselves to the priests."
As they were going they were cleansed.
And one of them, realizing he had been healed,
　returned, glorifying God in a loud voice;
　and he fell at the feet of Jesus and thanked him.
He was a Samaritan.
Jesus said in reply,
　"Ten were cleansed, were they not?
Where are the other nine?
Has none but this foreigner returned to give thanks to God?"
Then he said to him, "Stand up and go;
　your faith has saved you." ✛

THURSDAY, NOVEMBER 16
WEEKDAY, ST. MARGARET OF SCOTLAND, ST. GERTRUDE

† *Wisdom 7:22b—8:1*

For wisdom is the refulgence of eternal light,
the spotless mirror of the power of God.

In Wisdom is a spirit
　intelligent, holy, unique,
Manifold, subtle, agile,

clear, unstained, certain,
Not baneful, loving the good, keen,
  unhampered, beneficent, kindly,
Firm, secure, tranquil,
  all-powerful, all-seeing,
And pervading all spirits,
  though they be intelligent, pure and very subtle.
For Wisdom is mobile beyond all motion,
  and she penetrates and pervades all things by reason of her purity.
For she is an aura of the might of God
  and a pure effusion of the glory of the Almighty;
  therefore nought that is sullied enters into her.
For she is the refulgence of eternal light,
  the spotless mirror of the power of God,
  the image of his goodness.
And she, who is one, can do all things,
  and renews everything while herself perduring;
And passing into holy souls from age to age,
  she produces friends of God and prophets.
For there is nought God loves, be it not one who dwells with Wisdom.
For she is fairer than the sun
  and surpasses every constellation of the stars.
Compared to light, she takes precedence;
  for that, indeed, night supplants,
  but wickedness prevails not over Wisdom.

Indeed, she reaches from end to end mightily
  and governs all things well. ✛

Psalm 119:89, 90, 91, 130, 135, 175
R. (89a) Your word is for ever, O Lord.
Your word, O LORD, endures forever;
  it is firm as the heavens. **R.**
Through all generations your truth endures;
  you have established the earth, and it stands firm. **R.**
According to your ordinances they still stand firm:
  all things serve you. **R.**
The revelation of your words sheds light,
  giving understanding to the simple. **R.**
Let your countenance shine upon your servant,
  and teach me your statutes. **R.**
Let my soul live to praise you,
  and may your ordinances help me. **R.**

John 15:5
R. Alleluia, alleluia.
I am the vine, you are the branches, says the Lord:
whoever remains in me and I in him will bear much fruit. **R.**

† *Luke 17:20-25*
The Kingdom of God is among you.

Asked by the Pharisees when the Kingdom of God would come,
  Jesus said in reply,
"The coming of the Kingdom of God cannot be observed,
  and no one will announce, 'Look, here it is,' or, 'There it is.'
For behold, the Kingdom of God is among you."

Then he said to his disciples,
  "The days will come when you will long to see
  one of the days of the Son of Man, but you will not see it.
There will be those who will say to you,
  'Look, there he is,' or 'Look, here he is.'
Do not go off, do not run in pursuit.
For just as lightning flashes
  and lights up the sky from one side to the other,
  so will the Son of Man be in his day.
But first he must suffer greatly and be rejected by this generation." ✙

FRIDAY, NOVEMBER 17
St. Elizabeth of Hungary

† *Wisdom 13:1-9*
For if they so far succeeded in knowledge that they could speculate about the
world, how did they not more quickly find its Lord?

All men were by nature foolish who were in ignorance of God,
  and who from the good things seen did not succeed in knowing
    him who is,
  and from studying the works did not discern the artisan;
But either fire, or wind, or the swift air,
  or the circuit of the stars, or the mighty water,
  or the luminaries of heaven, the governors of the world, they
    considered gods.
Now if out of joy in their beauty they thought them gods,
  let them know how far more excellent is the Lord than these;
  for the original source of beauty fashioned them.
Or if they were struck by their might and energy,
  let them from these things realize how much more powerful is he
    who made them.
For from the greatness and the beauty of created things

their original author, by analogy, is seen.
But yet, for these the blame is less;
For they indeed have gone astray perhaps,
  though they seek God and wish to find him.
For they search busily among his works,
  but are distracted by what they see, because the things seen are fair.
But again, not even these are pardonable.
For if they so far succeeded in knowledge
  that they could speculate about the world,
  how did they not more quickly find its Lord? ✛

Psalm 19:2-3, 4-5ab

R. (2a) **The heavens proclaim the glory of God.**

The heavens declare the glory of God,
  and the firmament proclaims his handiwork.
Day pours out the word to day,
  and night to night imparts knowledge. **R.**
Not a word nor a discourse
  whose voice is not heard;
Through all the earth their voice resounds,
  and to the ends of the world, their message. **R.**

Luke 21:28

R. Alleluia, alleluia.

Stand erect and raise your heads
because your redemption is at hand. **R.**

† *Luke 17:26-37*
So it will be on the day the Son of Man is revealed.

Jesus said to his disciples:
"As it was in the days of Noah,
  so it will be in the days of the Son of Man;
  they were eating and drinking,
  marrying and giving in marriage up to the day
  that Noah entered the ark,
  and the flood came and destroyed them all.
Similarly, as it was in the days of Lot:
  they were eating, drinking, buying,
  selling, planting, building;
  on the day when Lot left Sodom,
  fire and brimstone rained from the sky to destroy them all.
So it will be on the day the Son of Man is revealed.
On that day, someone who is on the housetop
  and whose belongings are in the house
  must not go down to get them,
  and likewise one in the field

must not return to what was left behind.
Remember the wife of Lot.
Whoever seeks to preserve his life will lose it,
  but whoever loses it will save it.
I tell you, on that night there will be two people in one bed;
  one will be taken, the other left.
And there will be two women grinding meal together;
  one will be taken, the other left."
They said to him in reply, "Where, Lord?"
He said to them, "Where the body is,
  there also the vultures will gather." ✢

SATURDAY, NOVEMBER 18
WEEKDAY, THE DEDICATION OF THE BASILICAS OF ST. PETER AND ST. PAUL, ST. ROSE PHILIPPINE DUCHESNE, *[BVM]*
(For the memorial of the Dedication: Acts 28:11-16, 30-31 •
Psalm 98:1, 2-3ab, 3cd-4, 5-6 • Matthew 14:22–33 [679].)

† *Wisdom 18:14-16; 19:6-9*
Out of the Red Sea an unimpeded road appeared
and they bounded about like lambs.

When peaceful stillness compassed everything
  and the night in its swift course was half spent,
Your all-powerful word, from heaven's royal throne
  bounded, a fierce warrior, into the doomed land,
  bearing the sharp sword of your inexorable decree.
And as he alighted, he filled every place with death;
  he still reached to heaven, while he stood upon the earth.

For all creation, in its several kinds, was being made over anew,
  serving its natural laws,
  that your children might be preserved unharmed.
The cloud overshadowed their camp;
  and out of what had before been water, dry land was seen emerging:
Out of the Red Sea an unimpeded road,
  and a grassy plain out of the mighty flood.
Over this crossed the whole nation sheltered by your hand,
  after they beheld stupendous wonders.
For they ranged about like horses,
  and bounded about like lambs,
  praising you, O Lord! their deliverer. ✢

Psalm 105:2-3, 36-37, 42-43

R. (5a) **Remember the marvels the Lord has done!**
  (or **Alleluia.***)*

Sing to him, sing his praise,
  proclaim all his wondrous deeds.
Glory in his holy name;
  rejoice, O hearts that seek the LORD! **R.**
Then he struck every first-born throughout their land,
  the first fruits of all their manhood.
And he led them forth laden with silver and gold,
  with not a weakling among their tribes. **R.**
For he remembered his holy word
  to his servant Abraham.
And he led forth his people with joy;
  with shouts of joy, his chosen ones. **R.**

See 2 Thessalonians 2:14

R. Alleluia, alleluia.

God has called us through the Gospel,
to possess the glory of our Lord Jesus Christ. **R.**

† *Luke 18:1-8*

*Will not God then secure the rights of his chosen ones
who call out to him day and night?*

Jesus told his disciples a parable
  about the necessity for them to pray always without becoming
    weary.
He said, "There was a judge in a certain town
  who neither feared God nor respected any human being.
And a widow in that town used to come to him and say,
  'Render a just decision for me against my adversary.'
For a long time the judge was unwilling, but eventually he thought,
  'While it is true that I neither fear God nor respect any human
    being,
  because this widow keeps bothering me
  I shall deliver a just decision for her
  lest she finally come and strike me.'"
The Lord said, "Pay attention to what the dishonest judge says.
Will not God then secure the rights of his chosen ones
  who call out to him day and night?
Will he be slow to answer them?
I tell you, he will see to it that justice is done for them speedily.
But when the Son of Man comes, will he find faith on earth?" **✛**

SUNDAY, NOVEMBER 19
THIRTY-THIRD SUNDAY IN ORDINARY TIME

† *Proverbs 31:10-13, 19-20, 30-31*
She works with loving hands.

When one finds a worthy wife,
    her value is far beyond pearls.
Her husband, entrusting his heart to her,
    has an unfailing prize.
She brings him good, and not evil,
    all the days of her life.
She obtains wool and flax
    and works with loving hands.
She puts her hands to the distaff,
    and her fingers ply the spindle.
She reaches out her hands to the poor,
    and extends her arms to the needy.
Charm is deceptive and beauty fleeting;
    the woman who fears the LORD is to be praised.
Give her a reward for her labors,
    and let her works praise her at the city gates. ✛

Psalm 128:1-2, 3, 4-5
R. (see 1a) **Blessed are those who fear the Lord.**
Blessed are you who fear the LORD,
    who walk in his ways!
For you shall eat the fruit of your handiwork;
    blessed shall you be, and favored. **R.**
Your wife shall be like a fruitful vine
    in the recesses of your home;
your children like olive plants
    around your table. **R.**
Behold, thus is the man blessed
    who fears the LORD.
The LORD bless you from Zion:
    may you see the prosperity of Jerusalem
    all the days of your life. **R.**

† *1 Thessalonians 5:1-6*
Let the day of the Lord not overtake you like a thief.

Concerning times and seasons, brothers and sisters,
    you have no need for anything to be written to you.
For you yourselves know very well that the day of the Lord will come
    like a thief at night.
When people are saying, "Peace and security,"
    then sudden disaster comes upon them,

like labor pains upon a pregnant woman,
and they will not escape.

But you, brothers and sisters, are not in darkness,
for that day to overtake you like a thief.
For all of you are children of the light
and children of the day.
We are not of the night or of darkness.
Therefore, let us not sleep as the rest do,
but let us stay alert and sober. ✛

John 15:4a, 5b
R. Alleluia, alleluia.
Remain in me as I remain in you, says the Lord.
Whoever remains in me bears much fruit. **R.**

*†**Matthew 25:14-30** (or Matthew 25:14-15, 19-21)*
Since you were faithful in small matters, come, share your master's joy.

Jesus told his disciples this parable:
"A man going on a journey
called in his servants and entrusted his possessions to them.
To one he gave five talents; to another, two; to a third, one—
to each according to his ability.
Then he went away.
Immediately the one who received five talents went and traded with
them,
and made another five.
Likewise, the one who received two made another two.
But the man who received one went off and dug a hole in the ground
and buried his master's money.

"After a long time
the master of those servants came back
and settled accounts with them.
The one who had received five talents came forward
bringing the additional five.
He said, 'Master, you gave me five talents.
See, I have made five more.'
His master said to him, 'Well done, my good and faithful servant.
Since you were faithful in small matters,
I will give you great responsibilities.
Come, share your master's joy.'
Then the one who had received two talents also came forward and
said,
'Master, you gave me two talents.
See, I have made two more.'

His master said to him, 'Well done, my good and faithful servant.
Since you were faithful in small matters,
   I will give you great responsibilities.
Come, share your master's joy.'
Then the one who had received the one talent came forward and said,
   'Master, I knew you were a demanding person,
   harvesting where you did not plant
   and gathering where you did not scatter;
   so out of fear I went off and buried your talent in the ground.
Here it is back.'
His master said to him in reply, 'You wicked, lazy servant!
So you knew that I harvest where I did not plant
   and gather where I did not scatter?
Should you not then have put my money in the bank
   so that I could have got it back with interest on my return?
Now then! Take the talent from him and give it to the one with ten.
For to everyone who has,
   more will be given and he will grow rich;
   but from the one who has not,
   even what he has will be taken away.
And throw this useless servant into the darkness outside,
   where there will be wailing and grinding of teeth.'" ✛

MONDAY, NOVEMBER 20
Weekday

† *1 Maccabees 1:10-15, 41-43, 54-57, 62-63*
Terrible affliction was upon Israel.

[**F**rom the descendants of Alexander's officers]
   there sprang a sinful offshoot, Antiochus Epiphanes,
   son of King Antiochus, once a hostage at Rome.
He became king in the year one hundred and thirty-seven
   of the kingdom of the Greeks.

In those days there appeared in Israel
   men who were breakers of the law,
   and they seduced many people, saying:
   "Let us go and make an alliance with the Gentiles all around us;
   since we separated from them, many evils have come upon us."
The proposal was agreeable;
   some from among the people promptly went to the king,
   and he authorized them to introduce the way of living
   of the Gentiles.
Thereupon they built a gymnasium in Jerusalem
   according to the Gentile custom.

They covered over the mark of their circumcision
and abandoned the holy covenant;
they allied themselves with the Gentiles
and sold themselves to wrongdoing.

Then the king wrote to his whole kingdom that all should be one
people,
each abandoning his particular customs.
All the Gentiles conformed to the command of the king,
and many children of Israel were in favor of his religion;
they sacrificed to idols and profaned the sabbath.

On the fifteenth day of the month Chislev,
in the year one hundred and forty-five,
the king erected the horrible abomination
upon the altar of burnt offerings
and in the surrounding cities of Judah they built pagan altars.
They also burned incense at the doors of the houses and in the
streets.
Any scrolls of the law which they found they tore up and burnt.
Whoever was found with a scroll of the covenant,
and whoever observed the law,
was condemned to death by royal decree.
But many in Israel were determined
and resolved in their hearts not to eat anything unclean;
they preferred to die rather than to be defiled with unclean food
or to profane the holy covenant; and they did die.
Terrible affliction was upon Israel. ✛

Psalm 119:53, 61, 134, 150, 155, 158
R. (see 88) **Give me life, O Lord, and I will do your commands.**
Indignation seizes me because of the wicked
who forsake your law. **R**
Though the snares of the wicked are twined about me,
your law I have not forgotten. **R.**
Redeem me from the oppression of men,
that I may keep your precepts. **R.**
I am attacked by malicious persecutors
who are far from your law. **R.**
Far from sinners is salvation,
because they seek not your statutes. **R.**
I beheld the apostates with loathing,
because they kept not to your promise. **R.**

John 8:12
R. Alleluia, alleluia.
I am the light of the world, says the Lord;
whoever follows me will have the light of life. **R.**

† *Luke 18:35-43*

What do you want me to do for you? Lord, please let me see.

As Jesus approached Jericho
   a blind man was sitting by the roadside begging,
   and hearing a crowd going by, he inquired what was happening.
They told him,
   "Jesus of Nazareth is passing by."
He shouted, "Jesus, Son of David, have pity on me!"
The people walking in front rebuked him,
   telling him to be silent,
   but he kept calling out all the more,
   "Son of David, have pity on me!"
Then Jesus stopped and ordered that he be brought to him;
   and when he came near, Jesus asked him,
   "What do you want me to do for you?"
He replied, "Lord, please let me see."
Jesus told him, "Have sight; your faith has saved you."
He immediately received his sight
   and followed him, giving glory to God.
When they saw this, all the people gave praise to God. ✚

TUESDAY, NOVEMBER 21
THE PRESENTATION OF THE BLESSED VIRGIN MARY

† *2 Maccabees 6:18-31*

*I will leave to the young a noble example of how to die willingly
and generously for the revered and holy laws.*

Eleazar, one of the foremost scribes,
   a man of advanced age and noble appearance,
   was being forced to open his mouth to eat pork.
But preferring a glorious death to a life of defilement,
   he spat out the meat,
   and went forward of his own accord to the instrument of torture,
   as people ought to do who have the courage to reject the food
   which it is unlawful to taste even for love of life.
Those in charge of that unlawful ritual meal took the man aside
      privately,
   because of their long acquaintance with him,
   and urged him to bring meat of his own providing,
   such as he could legitimately eat,

and to pretend to be eating some of the meat of the sacrifice
prescribed by the king;
in this way he would escape the death penalty,
and be treated kindly because of their old friendship with him.
But Eleazar made up his mind in a noble manner,
worthy of his years, the dignity of his advanced age,
the merited distinction of his gray hair,
and of the admirable life he had lived from childhood;
and so he declared that above all
he would be loyal to the holy laws given by God.

He told them to send him at once
to the abode of the dead, explaining:
"At our age it would be unbecoming to make such a pretense;
many young people would think the ninety-year-old Eleazar
had gone over to an alien religion.
Should I thus pretend for the sake of a brief moment of life,
they would be led astray by me,
while I would bring shame and dishonor on my old age.
Even if, for the time being, I avoid the punishment of men,
I shall never, whether alive or dead,
escape the hands of the Almighty.
Therefore, by manfully giving up my life now,
I will prove myself worthy of my old age,
and I will leave to the young a noble example
of how to die willingly and generously
for the revered and holy laws."

Eleazar spoke thus,
and went immediately to the instrument of torture.
Those who shortly before had been kindly disposed,
now became hostile toward him because what he had said
seemed to them utter madness.
When he was about to die under the blows,
he groaned and said:
"The Lord in his holy knowledge knows full well that,
although I could have escaped death,
I am not only enduring terrible pain in my body from this scourging,
but also suffering it with joy in my soul
because of my devotion to him."
This is how he died,
leaving in his death a model of courage
and an unforgettable example of virtue
not only for the young but for the whole nation. ✝

Psalm 3:2-3, 4-5, 6-7

R. (6b) **The Lord upholds me.**

O LORD, how many are my adversaries!
  Many rise up against me!
Many are saying of me,
  "There is no salvation for him in God." **R.**
But you, O LORD, are my shield;
  my glory, you lift up my head!
When I call out to the LORD,
  he answers me from his holy mountain. **R.**
When I lie down in sleep,
  I wake again, for the LORD sustains me.
I fear not the myriads of people
  arrayed against me on every side. **R.**

1 John 4:10b

R. Alleluia, alleluia.

God loved us, and sent his Son
as expiation for our sins. **R.**

✝ *Luke 19:1-10*

The Son of Man has come to seek and to save what was lost.

At that time Jesus came to Jericho and intended to pass through
  the town.
Now a man there named Zacchaeus,
  who was a chief tax collector and also a wealthy man,
  was seeking to see who Jesus was;
  but he could not see him because of the crowd,
  for he was short in stature.
So he ran ahead and climbed a sycamore tree in order to see Jesus,
  who was about to pass that way.
When he reached the place, Jesus looked up and said,
  "Zacchaeus, come down quickly,
  for today I must stay at your house."
And he came down quickly and received him with joy.
When they saw this, they began to grumble, saying,
  "He has gone to stay at the house of a sinner."
But Zacchaeus stood there and said to the Lord,
  "Behold, half of my possessions, Lord, I shall give to the poor,
  and if I have extorted anything from anyone
  I shall repay it four times over."
And Jesus said to him,
  "Today salvation has come to this house
  because this man too is a descendant of Abraham.

For the Son of Man has come to seek
and to save what was lost." ✝

WEDNESDAY, NOVEMBER 22
St. Cecilia

✝ *2 Maccabees 7:1, 20-31*
The creator of the universe will give you back both breath and life.

It happened that seven brothers with their mother were arrested
and tortured with whips and scourges by the king,
to force them to eat pork in violation of God's law.

Most admirable and worthy of everlasting remembrance was the
mother,
who saw her seven sons perish in a single day,
yet bore it courageously because of her hope in the Lord.
Filled with a noble spirit that stirred her womanly heart with manly
courage,
she exhorted each of them
in the language of their ancestors with these words:
"I do not know how you came into existence in my womb;
it was not I who gave you the breath of life,
nor was it I who set in order
the elements of which each of you is composed.
Therefore, since it is the Creator of the universe
who shapes each man's beginning,
as he brings about the origin of everything,
he, in his mercy,
will give you back both breath and life,
because you now disregard yourselves for the sake of his law."

Antiochus, suspecting insult in her words,
thought he was being ridiculed.
As the youngest brother was still alive, the king appealed to him,
not with mere words, but with promises on oath,
to make him rich and happy if he would abandon his ancestral
customs:
he would make him his Friend
and entrust him with high office.
When the youth paid no attention to him at all,
the king appealed to the mother,
urging her to advise her boy to save his life.
After he had urged her for a long time,
she went through the motions of persuading her son.
In derision of the cruel tyrant,

she leaned over close to her son and said in their native language:
"Son, have pity on me, who carried you in my womb for nine
    months,
nursed you for three years, brought you up,
educated and supported you to your present age.
I beg you, child, to look at the heavens and the earth
    and see all that is in them;
    then you will know that God did not make them out of existing
        things;
    and in the same way the human race came into existence.
Do not be afraid of this executioner,
    but be worthy of your brothers and accept death,
    so that in the time of mercy I may receive you again with them."

She had scarcely finished speaking when the youth said:
    "What are you waiting for?
I will not obey the king's command.
I obey the command of the law given to our fathers through Moses.
But you, who have contrived every kind of affliction for the Hebrews,
    will not escape the hands of God." ✛

Psalm 17:1bcd, 5-6, 8 and 15

R. (15b) **Lord, when your glory appears, my joy will be full.**
Hear, O LORD, a just suit;
    attend to my outcry;
    hearken to my prayer from lips without deceit. **R.**
My steps have been steadfast in your paths,
    my feet have not faltered.
I call upon you, for you will answer me, O God;
    incline your ear to me; hear my word. **R.**
Keep me as the apple of your eye;
    hide me in the shadow of your wings.
But I in justice shall behold your face;
    on waking, I shall be content in your presence. **R.**

See John 15:16

R. Alleluia, alleluia.
I chose you from the world,
to go and bear fruit that will last, says the Lord. **R.**

† *Luke 19:11-28*
Why did you not put my money in a bank?

While people were listening to Jesus speak,
    he proceeded to tell a parable because he was near Jerusalem
    and they thought that the Kingdom of God
    would appear there immediately.

So he said,
   "A nobleman went off to a distant country
   to obtain the kingship for himself and then to return.
He called ten of his servants and gave them ten gold coins
   and told them, 'Engage in trade with these until I return.'
His fellow citizens, however, despised him
   and sent a delegation after him to announce,
'We do not want this man to be our king.'
But when he returned after obtaining the kingship,
   he had the servants called, to whom he had given the money,
   to learn what they had gained by trading.
The first came forward and said,
   'Sir, your gold coin has earned ten additional ones.'
He replied, 'Well done, good servant!
You have been faithful in this very small matter;
   take charge of ten cities.'
Then the second came and reported,
   'Your gold coin, sir, has earned five more.'
And to this servant too he said,
   'You, take charge of five cities.'
Then the other servant came and said,
   'Sir, here is your gold coin;
   I kept it stored away in a handkerchief,
   for I was afraid of you, because you are a demanding man;
   you take up what you did not lay down
   and you harvest what you did not plant.'
He said to him,
   'With your own words I shall condemn you,
   you wicked servant.
You knew I was a demanding man,
   taking up what I did not lay down
   and harvesting what I did not plant;
   why did you not put my money in a bank?
Then on my return I would have collected it with interest.'
And to those standing by he said,
   'Take the gold coin from him
   and give it to the servant who has ten.'
But they said to him,
   'Sir, he has ten gold coins.'
He replied, 'I tell you,
   to everyone who has, more will be given,
   but from the one who has not,
   even what he has will be taken away.

Now as for those enemies of mine who did not want me as their king,
    bring them here and slay them before me.'"

After he had said this,
    he proceeded on his journey up to Jerusalem. ✛

THURSDAY, NOVEMBER 23
Weekday, St. Pope Clement I, St. Columban, Bl. Miguel Agustín Pro, Thanksgiving Day, U.S.A.

For Thanksgiving Day, use any readings from the Mass "In Thanksgiving to God,"
Lectionary for Mass, volume IV, numbers 943-947.

† *1 Maccabees 2:15-29*
We will keep to the covenant of our ancestors.

The officers of the king in charge of enforcing the apostasy
    came to the city of Modein to organize the sacrifices.
Many of Israel joined them,
    but Mattathias and his sons gathered in a group apart.
Then the officers of the king addressed Mattathias:
    "You are a leader, an honorable and great man in this city,
    supported by sons and kin.
Come now, be the first to obey the king's command,
    as all the Gentiles and the men of Judah
    and those who are left in Jerusalem have done.
Then you and your sons shall be numbered among the King's
        Friends,
    and shall be enriched with silver and gold and many gifts."
But Mattathias answered in a loud voice:
    "Although all the Gentiles in the king's realm obey him,
    so that each forsakes the religion of his fathers
    and consents to the king's orders,
    yet I and my sons and my kin
    will keep to the covenant of our fathers.
God forbid that we should forsake the law and the commandments.
We will not obey the words of the king
    nor depart from our religion in the slightest degree."

As he finished saying these words,
    a certain Jew came forward in the sight of all
    to offer sacrifice on the altar in Modein
    according to the king's order.
When Mattathias saw him, he was filled with zeal;
    his heart was moved and his just fury was aroused;
    he sprang forward and killed him upon the altar.
At the same time, he also killed the messenger of the king

who was forcing them to sacrifice,
and he tore down the altar.
Thus he showed his zeal for the law,
just as Phinehas did with Zimri, son of Salu.

Then Mattathias went through the city shouting,
"Let everyone who is zealous for the law
and who stands by the covenant follow after me!"
Thereupon he fled to the mountains with his sons,
leaving behind in the city all their possessions.
Many who sought to live according to righteousness and religious
custom
went out into the desert to settle there. ✝

Psalm 50:1b-2, 5-6, 14-15
R. (23b) **To the upright I will show the saving power of God.**
God the LORD has spoken and summoned the earth,
from the rising of the sun to its setting.
From Zion, perfect in beauty,
God shines forth. **R.**
"Gather my faithful ones before me,
those who have made a covenant with me by sacrifice."
And the heavens proclaim his justice;
for God himself is the judge. **R.**
"Offer to God praise as your sacrifice
and fulfill your vows to the Most High;
Then call upon me in time of distress;
I will rescue you, and you shall glorify me." **R.**

Psalm 95:8
R. Alleluia, alleluia.
If today you hear his voice,
harden not your hearts. **R.**

✝ *Luke 19:41-44*
If you only knew what makes for peace.

As Jesus drew near Jerusalem,
he saw the city and wept over it, saying,
"If this day you only knew what makes for peace–
but now it is hidden from your eyes.
For the days are coming upon you
when your enemies will raise a palisade against you;
they will encircle you and hem you in on all sides.
They will smash you to the ground and your children within you,
and they will not leave one stone upon another within you
because you did not recognize the time of your visitation." ✝

FRIDAY, NOVEMBER 24
St. Andrew Dũng-Lac and Companions

† *1 Maccabees 4:36-37, 52-59*
*They celebrated the dedication of the altar
and joyfully offered burnt offerings.*

Judas and his brothers said,
  "Now that our enemies have been crushed,
  let us go up to purify the sanctuary and rededicate it."
So the whole army assembled, and went up to Mount Zion.

Early in the morning on the twenty-fifth day of the ninth month,
  that is, the month of Chislev,
  in the year one hundred and forty-eight,
  they arose and offered sacrifice according to the law
  on the new altar of burnt offerings that they had made.
On the anniversary of the day on which the Gentiles had defiled it,
  on that very day it was reconsecrated
  with songs, harps, flutes, and cymbals.
All the people prostrated themselves and adored and praised Heaven,
  who had given them success.

For eight days they celebrated the dedication of the altar
  and joyfully offered burnt offerings and sacrifices
  of deliverance and praise.
They ornamented the façade of the temple with gold crowns and
    shields;
  they repaired the gates and the priests' chambers
  and furnished them with doors.
There was great joy among the people
  now that the disgrace of the Gentiles was removed.
Then Judas and his brothers and the entire congregation of Israel
  decreed that the days of the dedication of the altar
  should be observed with joy and gladness
  on the anniversary every year for eight days,
  from the twenty-fifth day of the month Chislev. ✢

1 Chronicles 29:10bcd, 11abc, 11d-12a, 12bcd
R. (13b) **We praise your glorious name, O mighty God.**
"Blessed may you be, O LORD,
  God of Israel our father,
  from eternity to eternity." **R.**
"Yours, O LORD, are grandeur and power,
  majesty, splendor, and glory.
For all in heaven and on earth is yours." **R.**
"Yours, O LORD, is the sovereignty;

you are exalted as head over all.
Riches and honor are from you." **R.**
"You have dominion over all,
In your hand are power and might;
 it is yours to give grandeur and strength to all." **R.**

 John 10:27
R. Alleluia, alleluia.
My sheep hear my voice, says the Lord;
I know them, and they follow me. **R.**

✝ *Luke 19:45-48*
You have made it a den of thieves.

Jesus entered the temple area and proceeded to drive out
 those who were selling things, saying to them,
 "It is written, *My house shall be a house of prayer,*
 but you have made it a den of thieves."
And every day he was teaching in the temple area.
The chief priests, the scribes, and the leaders of the people, meanwhile,
 were seeking to put him to death,
 but they could find no way to accomplish their purpose
 because all the people were hanging on his words. ✝

SATURDAY, NOVEMBER 25
WEEKDAY, ST. CATHERINE OF ALEXANDRIA, *[BVM]*

✝ *1 Maccabees 6:1-13*
On account of the evils I did in Jerusalem, I am dying in bitter grief.

As King Antiochus was traversing the inland provinces,
 he heard that in Persia there was a city called Elymais,
 famous for its wealth in silver and gold,
 and that its temple was very rich,
 containing gold helmets, breastplates, and weapons
 left there by Alexander, son of Philip,
 king of Macedon, the first king of the Greeks.
He went therefore and tried to capture and pillage the city.
But he could not do so,
 because his plan became known to the people of the city
 who rose up in battle against him.
So he retreated and in great dismay withdrew from there
 to return to Babylon.

While he was in Persia, a messenger brought him news
 that the armies sent into the land of Judah had been put to flight;
 that Lysias had gone at first with a strong army
 and been driven back by the children of Israel;

that they had grown strong
by reason of the arms, men, and abundant possessions
taken from the armies they had destroyed;
that they had pulled down the Abomination
which he had built upon the altar in Jerusalem;
and that they had surrounded with high walls
both the sanctuary, as it had been before,
and his city of Beth-zur.

When the king heard this news,
   he was struck with fear and very much shaken.
Sick with grief because his designs had failed, he took to his bed.
There he remained many days, overwhelmed with sorrow,
   for he knew he was going to die.

So he called in all his Friends and said to them:
   "Sleep has departed from my eyes,
   for my heart is sinking with anxiety.
I said to myself: 'Into what tribulation have I come,
   and in what floods of sorrow am I now!
Yet I was kindly and beloved in my rule.'
But I now recall the evils I did in Jerusalem,
   when I carried away all the vessels of gold and silver
   that were in it, and for no cause
   gave orders that the inhabitants of Judah be destroyed.
I know that this is why these evils have overtaken me;
   and now I am dying, in bitter grief, in a foreign land." ✙

   Psalm 9:2-3, 4 and 6, 16 and 19
R. (see 16a) **I will rejoice in your salvation, O Lord.**
I will give thanks to you, O LORD, with all my heart;
   I will declare all your wondrous deeds.
I will be glad and exult in you;
   I will sing praise to your name, Most High. **R.**
Because my enemies are turned back,
   overthrown and destroyed before you.
You rebuked the nations and destroyed the wicked;
   their name you blotted out forever and ever. **R.**
The nations are sunk in the pit they have made;
   in the snare they set, their foot is caught.
For the needy shall not always be forgotten,
   nor shall the hope of the afflicted forever perish. **R.**

See 2 Timothy 1:10
R. Alleluia, alleluia.
Our Savior Jesus Christ has destroyed death
and brought life to light through the Gospel. **R.**

✝ Luke 20:27-40
He is not God of the dead, but of the living.

Some Sadducees, those who deny that there is a resurrection,
   came forward and put this question to Jesus, saying,
   "Teacher, Moses wrote for us,
If someone's brother dies leaving a wife but no child,
his brother must take the wife
and raise up descendants for his brother.
Now there were seven brothers;
   the first married a woman but died childless.
Then the second and the third married her,
   and likewise all the seven died childless.
Finally the woman also died.
Now at the resurrection whose wife will that woman be?
For all seven had been married to her."
Jesus said to them,
   "The children of this age marry and remarry;
   but those who are deemed worthy to attain to the coming age
   and to the resurrection of the dead
   neither marry nor are given in marriage.
They can no longer die,
   for they are like angels;
   and they are the children of God
   because they are the ones who will rise.
That the dead will rise
   even Moses made known in the passage about the bush,
   when he called 'Lord'
   the God of Abraham, the God of Isaac, and the God of Jacob;
   and he is not God of the dead, but of the living,
   for to him all are alive."
Some of the scribes said in reply,
   "Teacher, you have answered well."
And they no longer dared to ask him anything. ✝

SUNDAY, NOVEMBER 26
OUR LORD JESUS CHRIST, KING OF THE UNIVERSE

† *Ezekiel 34:11-12, 15-17*
As for you, my flock, I will judge between one sheep and another.

Thus says the Lord GOD:
 I myself will look after and tend my sheep.
As a shepherd tends his flock
 when he finds himself among his scattered sheep,
 so will I tend my sheep.
I will rescue them from every place where they were scattered
 when it was cloudy and dark.
I myself will pasture my sheep;
 I myself will give them rest, says the Lord GOD.
The lost I will seek out,
 the strayed I will bring back,
 the injured I will bind up,
 the sick I will heal,
 but the sleek and the strong I will destroy,
 shepherding them rightly.

As for you, my sheep, says the Lord GOD,
 I will judge between one sheep and another,
 between rams and goats. ✛

Psalm 23:1b-2a, 2b-3, 5-6
R. (1) **The Lord is my shepherd; there is nothing I shall want.**
The LORD is my shepherd; I shall not want.
 In verdant pastures he gives me repose. **R.**
Beside restful waters he leads me;
 he refreshes my soul.
He guides me in right paths
 for his name's sake. **R.**
You spread the table before me
 in the sight of my foes;
you anoint my head with oil;
 my cup overflows. **R.**
Only goodness and kindness follow me
 all the days of my life;
and I shall dwell in the house of the LORD
 for years to come. **R.**

† 1 Corinthians 15:20-26, 28

*Christ will hand over the kingdom to his God and Father
so that God may be all in all.*

Brothers and sisters:
Christ has been raised from the dead,
   the firstfruits of those who have fallen asleep.
For since death came through man,
   the resurrection of the dead came also through man.
For just as in Adam all die,
    so too in Christ shall all be brought to life,
    but each one in proper order:
    Christ the firstfruits;
    then, at his coming, those who belong to Christ;
    then comes the end,
    when he hands over the kingdom to his God and Father,
    when he has destroyed every sovereignty
    and every authority and power.
For he must reign until he has put all his enemies under his feet.
The last enemy to be destroyed is death.
When everything is subjected to him,
   then the Son himself will also be subjected
   to the one who subjected everything to him,
   so that God may be all in all. ✛

Mark 11:9, 10
R. Alleluia, alleluia.
Blessed is he who comes in the name of the Lord!
Blessed is the kingdom of our father David that is to come! **R.**

† Matthew 25:31-46

*The Son of Man will sit upon his glorious throne and
he will separate them one from another.*

Jesus said to his disciples:
   "When the Son of Man comes in his glory,
   and all the angels with him,
   he will sit upon his glorious throne,
   and all the nations will be assembled before him.
And he will separate them one from another,
   as a shepherd separates the sheep from the goats.
He will place the sheep on his right and the goats on his left.
Then the king will say to those on his right,
   'Come, you who are blessed by my Father.
Inherit the kingdom prepared for you from the foundation of the
    world.
For I was hungry and you gave me food,

I was thirsty and you gave me drink,
a stranger and you welcomed me,
naked and you clothed me,
ill and you cared for me,
in prison and you visited me.'
Then the righteous will answer him and say,
  'Lord, when did we see you hungry and feed you,
  or thirsty and give you drink?
When did we see you a stranger and welcome you,
  or naked and clothe you?
When did we see you ill or in prison, and visit you?'
And the king will say to them in reply,
  'Amen, I say to you, whatever you did
  for one of the least brothers of mine, you did for me.'
Then he will say to those on his left,
  'Depart from me, you accursed,
  into the eternal fire prepared for the devil and his angels.
For I was hungry and you gave me no food,
  I was thirsty and you gave me no drink,
  a stranger and you gave me no welcome,
  naked and you gave me no clothing,
  ill and in prison, and you did not care for me.'
Then they will answer and say,
  'Lord, when did we see you hungry or thirsty
  or a stranger or naked or ill or in prison,
  and not minister to your needs?'
He will answer them, 'Amen, I say to you,
  what you did not do for one of these least ones,
  you did not do for me.'
And these will go off to eternal punishment,
  but the righteous to eternal life." ✠

MONDAY, NOVEMBER 27
WEEKDAY (THIRTY-FOURTH OR LAST WEEK IN ORDINARY TIME)

†*Daniel 1:1-6, 8-20*
None were found equal to Daniel, Hananiah, Mishael, and Azariah.

In the third year of the reign of Jehoiakim, king of Judah,
  King Nebuchadnezzar of Babylon came
  and laid siege to Jerusalem.
The Lord handed over to him Jehoiakim, king of Judah,
  and some of the vessels of the temple of God;
  he carried them off to the land of Shinar,
  and placed the vessels in the temple treasury of his god.

The king told Ashpenaz, his chief chamberlain,
    to bring in some of the children of Israel of royal blood
    and of the nobility, young men without any defect,
    handsome, intelligent and wise,
    quick to learn, and prudent in judgment,
    such as could take their place in the king's palace;
    they were to be taught the language and literature of the Chaldeans;
    after three years' training they were to enter the king's service.
The king allotted them a daily portion of food and wine
    from the royal table.
Among these were men of Judah: Daniel, Hananiah,
    Mishael, and Azariah.

But Daniel was resolved not to defile himself
    with the king's food or wine;
    so he begged the chief chamberlain to spare him this defilement.
Though God had given Daniel the favor and sympathy
    of the chief chamberlain, he nevertheless said to Daniel,
    "I am afraid of my lord the king;
    it is he who allotted your food and drink.
If he sees that you look wretched
    by comparison with the other young men of your age,
    you will endanger my life with the king."
Then Daniel said to the steward whom the chief chamberlain
    had put in charge of Daniel, Hananiah,
    Mishael, and Azariah,
    "Please test your servants for ten days.
Give us vegetables to eat and water to drink.
Then see how we look in comparison with the other young men
    who eat from the royal table,
    and treat your servants according to what you see."
He acceded to this request, and tested them for ten days;
    after ten days they looked healthier and better fed
    than any of the young men who ate from the royal table.
So the steward continued to take away
    the food and wine they were to receive, and gave them vegetables.

To these four young men God gave knowledge and proficiency
    in all literature and science,
    and to Daniel the understanding of all visions and dreams.
At the end of the time the king had specified for their preparation,
    the chief chamberlain brought them before Nebuchadnezzar.
When the king had spoken with all of them,
    none was found equal to Daniel, Hananiah,
    Mishael, and Azariah;

and so they entered the king's service.
In any question of wisdom or prudence which the king put to them,
he found them ten times better
than all the magicians and enchanters in his kingdom. ✢

Daniel 3:52, 53, 54, 55, 56
R. (52b) **Glory and praise for ever!**
"Blessed are you, O Lord, the God of our fathers,
praiseworthy and exalted above all forever;
And blessed is your holy and glorious name,
praiseworthy and exalted above all for all ages." **R.**
"Blessed are you in the temple of your holy glory,
praiseworthy and glorious above all forever." **R.**
"Blessed are you on the throne of your Kingdom,
praiseworthy and exalted above all forever." **R.**
"Blessed are you who look into the depths
from your throne upon the cherubim,
praiseworthy and exalted above all forever." **R.**
"Blessed are you in the firmament of heaven,
praiseworthy and glorious forever." **R.**

Matthew 24:42a, 44
R. Alleluia, alleluia.
Stay awake!
For you do not know when the Son of Man will come. **R.**

† *Luke 21:1-4*
He noticed a poor widow putting in two small coins.

When Jesus looked up he saw some wealthy people
putting their offerings into the treasury
and he noticed a poor widow putting in two small coins.
He said, "I tell you truly,
this poor widow put in more than all the rest;
for those others have all made offerings from their surplus wealth,
but she, from her poverty, has offered her whole livelihood." ✢

TUESDAY, NOVEMBER 28
WEEKDAY

† *Daniel 2:31-45*
*The God of heaven will set up a kingdom that shall never be destroyed
and shall put an end to all these kingdoms.*

Daniel said to Nebuchadnezzar:
"In your vision, O king, you saw a statue,
very large and exceedingly bright,
terrifying in appearance as it stood before you.

The head of the statue was pure gold,
   its chest and arms were silver,
   its belly and thighs bronze, the legs iron,
   its feet partly iron and partly tile.
While you looked at the statue,
   a stone which was hewn from a mountain
   without a hand being put to it,
   struck its iron and tile feet, breaking them in pieces.
The iron, tile, bronze, silver, and gold all crumbled at once,
   fine as the chaff on the threshing floor in summer,
   and the wind blew them away without leaving a trace.
But the stone that struck the statue became a great mountain
   and filled the whole earth.

"This was the dream;
   the interpretation we shall also give in the king's presence.
You, O king, are the king of kings;
   to you the God of heaven
   has given dominion and strength, power and glory;
   men, wild beasts, and birds of the air, wherever they may dwell,
   he has handed over to you, making you ruler over them all;
   you are the head of gold.
Another kingdom shall take your place, inferior to yours,
   then a third kingdom, of bronze,
   which shall rule over the whole earth.
There shall be a fourth kingdom, strong as iron;
   it shall break in pieces and subdue all these others,
   just as iron breaks in pieces and crushes everything else.
The feet and toes you saw, partly of potter's tile and partly of iron,
   mean that it shall be a divided kingdom,
   but yet have some of the hardness of iron.
As you saw the iron mixed with clay tile,
   and the toes partly iron and partly tile,
   the kingdom shall be partly strong and partly fragile.
The iron mixed with clay tile
   means that they shall seal their alliances by intermarriage,
   but they shall not stay united, any more than iron mixes with clay.
In the lifetime of those kings
   the God of heaven will set up a kingdom
   that shall never be destroyed or delivered up to another people;
   rather, it shall break in pieces all these kingdoms
   and put an end to them, and it shall stand forever.
That is the meaning of the stone you saw hewn from the mountain
   without a hand being put to it,

which broke in pieces the tile, iron, bronze, silver, and gold.
The great God has revealed to the king what shall be in the future;
  this is exactly what you dreamed, and its meaning is sure." ✛

Daniel 3:57, 58, 59, 60, 61
R. (59b) **Give glory and eternal praise to him.**
"Bless the Lord, all you works of the Lord,
  praise and exalt him above all forever." **R.**
"Angels of the Lord, bless the Lord,
  praise and exalt him above all forever." **R.**
"You heavens, bless the Lord,
  praise and exalt him above all forever." **R.**
"All you waters above the heavens, bless the Lord,
  praise and exalt him above all forever." **R.**
"All you hosts of the Lord, bless the Lord;
  praise and exalt him above all forever." **R.**

Revelation 2:10c
R. Alleluia, alleluia.
Remain faithful until death,
and I will give you the crown of life. **R.**

† *Luke 21:5-11*
There will not be left a stone upon another stone.

While some people were speaking about
  how the temple was adorned with costly stones and votive offerings,
Jesus said, "All that you see here—
the days will come when there will not be left
a stone upon another stone that will not be thrown down."

Then they asked him,
  "Teacher, when will this happen?
And what sign will there be when all these things are about to
    happen?"
He answered,
"See that you not be deceived,
  for many will come in my name, saying,
  'I am he,' and 'The time has come.'
Do not follow them!
When you hear of wars and insurrections,
  do not be terrified; for such things must happen first,
  but it will not immediately be the end."
Then he said to them,
  "Nation will rise against nation, and kingdom against kingdom.
There will be powerful earthquakes, famines, and plagues

from place to place;
and awesome sights and mighty signs will come from the sky." ✛

WEDNESDAY, NOVEMBER 29
WEEKDAY

†*Daniel 5:1-6, 13-14, 16-17, 23-28*
The fingers of a human hand appeared, writing on the plaster of the wall.

King Belshazzar gave a great banquet for a thousand of his lords,
   with whom he drank.
Under the influence of the wine,
   he ordered the gold and silver vessels
   which Nebuchadnezzar, his father,
   had taken from the temple in Jerusalem,
   to be brought in so that the king, his lords,
   his wives and his entertainers might drink from them.
When the gold and silver vessels
   taken from the house of God in Jerusalem had been brought in,
   and while the king, his lords, his wives and his entertainers
   were drinking wine from them,
   they praised their gods of gold and silver,
   bronze and iron, wood and stone.

Suddenly, opposite the lampstand,
   the fingers of a human hand appeared,
   writing on the plaster of the wall in the king's palace.
When the king saw the wrist and hand that wrote, his face
      blanched;
   his thoughts terrified him, his hip joints shook,
   and his knees knocked.

Then Daniel was brought into the presence of the king.
The king asked him, "Are you the Daniel, the Jewish exile,
   whom my father, the king, brought from Judah?
I have heard that the Spirit of God is in you,
   that you possess brilliant knowledge and extraordinary wisdom.
I have heard that you can interpret dreams and solve difficulties;
   if you are able to read the writing and tell me what it means,
   you shall be clothed in purple,
   wear a gold collar about your neck,
   and be third in the government of the kingdom."

Daniel answered the king:
   "You may keep your gifts, or give your presents to someone else;
   but the writing I will read for you, O king,
   and tell you what it means.

You have rebelled against the Lord of heaven.
You had the vessels of his temple brought before you,
  so that you and your nobles, your wives and your entertainers,
  might drink wine from them;
  and you praised the gods of silver and gold,
  bronze and iron, wood and stone,
  that neither see nor hear nor have intelligence.
But the God in whose hand is your life breath
  and the whole course of your life, you did not glorify.
By him were the wrist and hand sent, and the writing set down.

"This is the writing that was inscribed:
  MENE, TEKEL, and PERES.
These words mean:
  MENE, God has numbered your kingdom and put an end to it;
  TEKEL, you have been weighed on the scales and found wanting;
  PERES, your kingdom has been divided and given to the Medes
    and Persians." ✢

Daniel 3:62, 63, 64, 65, 66, 67
R. (59b) **Give glory and eternal praise to him.**
"Sun and moon, bless the Lord;
  praise and exalt him above all forever." **R.**
"Stars of heaven, bless the Lord;
  praise and exalt him above all forever." **R.**
"Every shower and dew, bless the Lord;
  praise and exalt him above all forever." **R.**
"All you winds, bless the Lord;
  praise and exalt him above all forever." **R.**
"Fire and heat, bless the Lord;
  praise and exalt him above all forever." **R.**
"Cold and chill, bless the Lord;
  praise and exalt him above all forever." **R.**

Revelation 2:10c
R. Alleluia, alleluia.
Remain faithful until death,
and I will give you the crown of life. **R.**

† *Luke 21:12-19*
*You will be hated by all because of my name,
but not a hair on your head will be destroyed.*

Jesus said to the crowd:
"They will seize and persecute you,
  they will hand you over to the synagogues and to prisons,
  and they will have you led before kings and governors

because of my name.

It will lead to your giving testimony.

Remember, you are not to prepare your defense beforehand,
for I myself shall give you a wisdom in speaking
that all your adversaries will be powerless to resist or refute.

You will even be handed over by parents,
brothers, relatives, and friends,
and they will put some of you to death.

You will be hated by all because of my name,
but not a hair on your head will be destroyed.

By your perseverance you will secure your lives." ✝

THURSDAY, NOVEMBER 30
St. Andrew

✝ Romans 10:9-18
Thus faith comes from what is heard,
and what is heard comes through the word of Christ.

Brothers and sisters:

If you confess with your mouth that Jesus is Lord
and believe in your heart that God raised him from the dead,
you will be saved.

For one believes with the heart and so is justified,
and one confesses with the mouth and so is saved.

The Scripture says,
No one who believes in him will be put to shame.

There is no distinction between Jew and Greek;
the same Lord is Lord of all,
enriching all who call upon him.

For everyone who calls on the name of the Lord will be saved.

But how can they call on him in whom they have not believed?

And how can they believe in him of whom they have not heard?

And how can they hear without someone to preach?

And how can people preach unless they are sent?

As it is written,
How beautiful are the feet of those who bring the good news!

But not everyone has heeded the good news;
for Isaiah says, *Lord, who has believed what was heard from us?*

Thus faith comes from what is heard,
and what is heard comes through the word of Christ.

But I ask, did they not hear?

Certainly they did; for

Their voice has gone forth to all the earth,
and their words to the ends of the world. ✝

Psalm 19:8, 9, 10, 11

R. (10) **The judgments of the Lord are true, and all of them are just.**

or

(John 6:63) **Your words, Lord, are Spirit and life.**

The law of the LORD is perfect,
  refreshing the soul;
The decree of the LORD is trustworthy,
  giving wisdom to the simple. **R.**

The precepts of the LORD are right,
  rejoicing the heart;
The command of the LORD is clear,
  enlightening the eye. **R.**

The fear of the LORD is pure,
  enduring forever;
The ordinances of the LORD are true,
  all of them just. **R.**

They are more precious than gold,
  than a heap of purest gold;
Sweeter also than syrup
  or honey from the comb. **R.**

Matthew 4:19

R. Alleluia, alleluia.

Come after me, says the Lord,
and I will make you fishers of men. **R.**

✝ *Matthew 4:18-22*
Immediately they left their nets and followed him.

As Jesus was walking by the Sea of Galilee, he saw two brothers,
  Simon who is called Peter, and his brother Andrew,
  casting a net into the sea; they were fishermen.
He said to them,
  "Come after me, and I will make you fishers of men."
At once they left their nets and followed him.
He walked along from there and saw two other brothers,
  James, the son of Zebedee, and his brother John.
They were in a boat, with their father Zebedee, mending their nets.
He called them, and immediately they left their boat and their father
  and followed him. ✛

FRIDAY, DECEMBER 1
WEEKDAY

† *Daniel 7:2-14*

I saw one like a son of man coming, on the clouds of heaven.

In a vision I, Daniel, saw during the night,
the four winds of heaven stirred up the great sea,
from which emerged four immense beasts,
each different from the others.
The first was like a lion, but with eagle's wings.
While I watched, the wings were plucked;
it was raised from the ground to stand on two feet
like a man, and given a human mind.
The second was like a bear; it was raised up on one side,
and among the teeth in its mouth were three tusks.
It was given the order, "Up, devour much flesh."
After this I looked and saw another beast, like a leopard;
on its back were four wings like those of a bird,
and it had four heads.
To this beast dominion was given.
After this, in the visions of the night I saw the fourth beast,
different from all the others,
terrifying, horrible, and of extraordinary strength;
it had great iron teeth with which it devoured and crushed,
and what was left it trampled with its feet.
I was considering the ten horns it had,
when suddenly another, a little horn, sprang out of their midst,
and three of the previous horns were torn away to make room for it.
This horn had eyes like a man,
and a mouth that spoke arrogantly.
As I watched,

Thrones were set up
and the Ancient One took his throne.
His clothing was snow bright,
and the hair on his head as white as wool;
His throne was flames of fire,
with wheels of burning fire.
A surging stream of fire
flowed out from where he sat;
Thousands upon thousands were ministering to him,
and myriads upon myriads attended him.

The court was convened, and the books were opened.
I watched, then, from the first of the arrogant words

which the horn spoke, until the beast was slain
and its body thrown into the fire to be burnt up.
The other beasts, which also lost their dominion,
were granted a prolongation of life for a time and a season.
As the visions during the night continued, I saw

One like a son of man coming,
on the clouds of heaven;
When he reached the Ancient One
and was presented before him,
He received dominion, glory, and kingship;
nations and peoples of every language serve him.
His dominion is an everlasting dominion
that shall not be taken away,
his kingship shall not be destroyed. ✛

Daniel 3:75, 76, 77, 78, 79, 80, 81
R. Give glory and eternal praise to him!
"Mountains and hills, bless the Lord;
praise and exalt him above all forever." **R.**
"Everything growing from the earth, bless the Lord;
praise and exalt him above all forever." **R.**
"You springs, bless the Lord;
praise and exalt him above all forever." **R.**
"Seas and rivers, bless the Lord;
praise and exalt him above all forever." **R.**
"You dolphins and all water creatures, bless the Lord;
praise and exalt him above all forever." **R.**
"All you birds of the air, bless the Lord;
praise and exalt him above all forever." **R.**
"All you beasts, wild and tame, bless the Lord;
praise and exalt him above all forever." **R.**

Luke 21:28
R. Alleluia, alleluia.
Stand erect and raise your heads
because your redemption is at hand. **R.**

† *Luke 21:29-33*
*When you see these things happening,
know that the Kingdom of God is near.*

Jesus told his disciples a parable.
"Consider the fig tree and all the other trees.
When their buds burst open,
you see for yourselves and know that summer is now near;
in the same way, when you see these things happening,

know that the Kingdom of God is near.
Amen, I say to you, this generation will not pass away
  until all these things have taken place.
Heaven and earth will pass away,
  but my words will not pass away." ✝

SATURDAY, DECEMBER 2
WEEKDAY, *[BVM]*

✝ *Daniel 7:15-27*
Kingship and domain shall be given to the holy people of the Most High.

I, Daniel, found my spirit anguished within its covering of flesh,
  and I was terrified by the visions of my mind.
I approached one of those present
  and asked him what all this meant in truth;
  in answer, he made known to me the meaning of the things:
  "These four great beasts stand for four kingdoms
  which shall arise on the earth.
But the holy ones of the Most High shall receive the kingship,
  to possess it forever and ever."

But I wished to make certain about the fourth beast,
  so very terrible and different from the others,
  devouring and crushing with its iron teeth and bronze claws,
  and trampling with its feet what was left;
  about the ten horns on its head, and the other one that sprang up,
  before which three horns fell;
  about the horn with the eyes and the mouth that spoke arrogantly,
  which appeared greater than its fellows.
For, as I watched, that horn made war against the holy ones
  and was victorious until the Ancient One arrived;
  judgment was pronounced in favor of the holy ones of the Most High,
  and the time came when the holy ones possessed the kingdom.
He answered me thus:

  "The fourth beast shall be a fourth kingdom on earth
    different from all the others;
  It shall devour the whole earth,
    beat it down, and crush it.
  The ten horns shall be ten kings
    rising out of that kingdom;
    another shall rise up after them,
  Different from those before him,
    who shall lay low three kings.
  He shall speak against the Most High
    and oppress the holy ones of the Most High,

thinking to change the feast days and the law.
They shall be handed over to him
   for a year, two years, and a half-year.
But when the court is convened,
   and his power is taken away
   by final and absolute destruction,
Then the kingship and dominion and majesty
   of all the kingdoms under the heavens
   shall be given to the holy people of the Most High,
Whose Kingdom shall be everlasting:
   all dominions shall serve and obey him." ✚

Daniel 3:82, 83, 84, 85, 86, 87

R. Give glory and eternal praise to him.
"You sons of men, bless the Lord;
   praise and exalt him above all forever." **R.**
"O Israel, bless the Lord;
   praise and exalt him above all forever." **R.**
"Priests of the Lord, bless the Lord;
   praise and exalt him above all forever." **R.**
"Servants of the Lord, bless the Lord;
   praise and exalt him above all forever." **R.**
"Spirits and souls of the just, bless the Lord;
   praise and exalt him above all forever." **R.**
"Holy men of humble heart, bless the Lord;
   praise and exalt him above all forever." **R.**

Luke 21:36

R. Alleluia, alleluia.
Be vigilant at all times and pray
that you may have the strength to stand before the Son of Man. **R.**

Luke 21:34-36

*Be vigilant that you may have the strength to escape
the tribulations that are imminent.*

Jesus said to his disciples:
"Beware that your hearts do not become drowsy
   from carousing and drunkenness
   and the anxieties of daily life,
   and that day catch you by surprise like a trap.
For that day will assault everyone
   who lives on the face of the earth.
Be vigilant at all times
   and pray that you have the strength
   to escape the tribulations that are imminent
   and to stand before the Son of Man." ✚

READING GOD'S WORD

DAILY AND **SUNDAY** MASS READINGS

CHURCH YEAR B • 2024

Paper • $18.95 + shipping • Order Code RGW24
Payment in full must be included in your mail order.

Complete the form below and mail it, along with your check or money order, to LF Book Orders at the address below. Books may also be ordered with a credit card at:

For best shipping rates, mail or call
800-325-9414
to order

Great gift for family, friends, catechists, parish staff & YOU!

Please send _____ copies of RGW24 to:

_____

SEND TO

_____

PHONE (DAYTIME)

_____

P.O. BOX   (must include street address below)

_____

STREET ADDRESS

_____

CITY, STATE, ZIP   (Please Note: U.S. Customers Only)

PLEASE NOTE shipping and handling fees to a single address.	If your subtotal is:	
	$20.00 or less,	add $5.00
	$20.01-$40.00,	add $6.00
	$40.01-$70.00,	add $7.00
	$70.01 or more,	add 10%

SUBTOTAL _____

SHIPPING _____

Sales tax _____

States with applicable sales tax:
CA, CO, CT, IL, IN, MA, MN, MO, NC, NY, NJ, OH, PA, and TX

TOTAL _____
Prices subject to change.

LF Book Orders
1564 Fencorp Drive, Fenton, MO 63026-2942
1-800-325-9414 • 8 AM-5 PM (Central Time) Monday-Friday

RGWBC